Cricketers' Who's Who 2011

Foreword by
ALASTAIR COOK

Editor
MATT THACKER

Compiled by
ED DAVIS, JO HARMAN, SAM STOW & PHIL WALKER

Design
JOE PROVIS & ROB WHITEHOUSE

The
Cricketers'
Who's Who
2011

This edition first published in the UK by All Out Cricket Ltd

© All Out Cricket Ltd 2011
www.alloutcricket.co.uk

ISNB: 978-1-907803-53-6

Editor: *Matt Thacker*
Research and editorial: *Ed Davis, Jo Harman, Sam Stow, Phil Walker*
Design: *Joe Provis, Rob Whitehouse*
Images: *Getty Images unless stated*
Print: *Jellyfish Print Solutions*

Acknowledgements

The publishers would like to thank the county clubs, the Professional Cricketers' Association,
the players and journalists for their assistance in helping to put together this book.
Additional information has been gathered from cricinfo.com and cricketarchive.com.
Thanks also to Nick Teale, James May, William Chambers and Grace Robinson.

Thanks to the following for providing photographs:
James Boardman, Gordon Child, Joan Grundy, Andrew Hignell (Glamorgan Cricket
Archives), Donald MacLeod (www.donald-macleod.com), SW Pix, Nick Wood
(unshaken-photography), Roger Wootton, www.portraitcollective.com

CONTENTS

Openers

by Alastair Cook

Welcome to The Cricketers' Who's Who 2011. It is my privilege to write the foreword for this revamped edition and to introduce a new English season that promises so much.

It is a thrilling time for English cricket and an exciting period for the game itself. The final frontier of an Ashes win in Australia has just been achieved. I was immensely proud to be a part of that. For me personally the series couldn't have gone better and it is truly an honour to slot in behind the great Wally Hammond on the list of English runscorers in an Ashes series.

But there are many tough assignments to come. Sri Lanka and then India are here this summer. They can be guaranteed fervent support, and we can expect some seriously tough cricket. India are rightly ranked as the No.1 Test team in the world right now and beating them would be a considerable step forward for us.

When England beat Australia in 2005 we failed as a team to kick on. We had the chance to become the world's best Test team and we didn't take it. We are hugely determined to give ourselves the best chance this time around. That is the challenge: to become the best team on the planet, not just in Test cricket, but in all formats of the game. With Andrew Strauss and Andy Flower in charge and a team approaching its prime in terms of age and experience, we certainly won't be resting on our laurels.

The English game at domestic level appears in pretty rude health. The County Championship is now a tough and demanding standard of cricket that challenges the very best players to show their worth. Personally I love playing Championship cricket for Essex – there are no easy runs out there, I can tell you! The one-day competitions are closely fought and fantastically entertaining, and in FP t20 Finals Day we have a marquee event that does county cricket proud.

There is no getting away from the fact that it is a long and gruelling season for all of us. Those of us who play international cricket are fortunate to be given some opportunity by the management to recharge our batteries. But the challenge of maintaining the right performance-intensity also applies to county cricketers. We do play a lot and tiredness does play its part through a six-month season. As players we are aware of the strains a surfeit of cricket can have on our performances. The challenge going forward – at all levels of the professional game – is to protect that balance between the amount we play and the intensity of competition.

Finally, it's great to see the Who's Who going from strength to strength. It's an invaluable part of every cricket lover's kit bag – it's the English game's Bible. And you can be sure that the players value it just as highly as the fans. After all, where else do you think Swanny gets his material to use against his teammates?

Enjoy the summer…

Alastair Cook
Essex & England

EDITOR'S NOTES

Taking over an institution like the Cricketers' Who's Who is exciting and a real responsibility. Everyone involved in putting this year's edition together grew up with the Who's Who and recognises its value as a reference tool and part of cricket's heritage – it is undoubtedly one of the cricket-lover's indispensable travelling companions.

Over the last few years the book's usefulness has diminished in terms of providing accurate player comment so we have changed the format in 2011 before we take stock, and decide how to approach the publication in 2012. In talking to players over the last couple of months, we have found that many of them have had their Who's Who survey completed by others without their knowledge, and in some cases this has caused genuine distress. While not wishing to stamp out the players' sense of fun and mischief, we feel the Who's Who should be as accurate as possible so will endeavour to find a way of reintroducing player comment next year, while continuing to omit some entries we feel to be superfluous.

The major alteration from previous editions is the change from an entirely alphabetical listing to a county-by-county grouping. We canvassed widely on this point – aware of the dangers of root and branch reform of any longstanding institution – but ultimately felt that as a reference tool, it simply made more sense to have players grouped together under the team for which they play. There is a full index of players alphabetically listed at the back of the book should anyone feel they need to cling to old habits.

With the increasing importance of one-day cricket, we have added details on the squads for Scotland, the Netherlands and the Unicorns, one of the genuine success stories of last season. So every player in every 2011 squad should be accounted for, at least at the time of going to press at the end of March.

Unlike in years gone by, for ease of reading we have made sure that each player has one dedicated page allocated to them or, in the case of the chosen few, two pages. We have given more information and insight into those players in and around the England set-up, plus a few that we have picked out as especially noteworthy.

And we have also given details of the touring parties – or our educated guess at them at least – who will play England this summer. We have picked 30 players each from Sri Lanka and India so that when they appear this summer, you will not be completely in the dark as to who they are and what they do.

We have also attempted to allow more room for comment by codifying certain entries such as a player's role, his MVP ranking, and how many times they have scored 1,000 runs in a season or taken 50 wickets. You will find all of these entries in the bar after a player's name (see page 18 for more details).

We do not pretend to have all the answers and would appreciate any feedback you may have. Please drop me a line at *cwweditor@alloutcricket.co.uk* with any comments.

Matt Thacker
March 31, 2011

CHAMPIONSHIP CRICKET: BEST IN THE WORLD, NOT JUST BEST OF BRITISH

All Out Cricket's editor Andy Afford, a former Championship-winning cricketer, sings the praises of the four-day game in England.

Cricket – it certainly has its knockers. And domestic cricket has more knockers than most. But precisely why, I'm not entirely sure.

For instance, the County Championship has long-since been regarded as a sickly patient in need of a cure. And that's despite it still being regarded as the finishing school for cricketers, the place where trades are learned, skills honed. It has to be said, it is as much celebrated for adding lustre to other countries' players as to England's own, but as The Rolling Stones so famously said – 'you can't always get what you want'. Regardless of what you might need.

And it seems that some observers have always been searching for a cure, whether one is needed or not. The doom-mongers found themselves in their element throughout the '80s and '90s as the national side played the role of world cricket's fall-guy, with the weakness of the domestic game cited as a contributory, if not defining, factor in England's underachievement. And that somewhat jaundiced view has continued to this day, despite us enjoying the most successful period for English cricket in living memory and the domestic game exporting cricketers to all four corners of the cricketing world.

Over the years, the perceived cures have been endless. In the none-too-distant past, the pitches were believed to be too bowler-friendly and the ball regarded as equally swing-and-seam-tastic. At another time the rules were amended to prevent spinners landing the ball in the righthander's legstump rough at a time when the pitches and seam on the ball were as bare as Matt Prior's head. In came the calling of one-day wides in four-day cricket to 'stamp it out'. As if bowling the stuff wasn't hard enough in the first place?

Elsewhere, three days of play were deemed insufficient to produce Test cricketers capable of batting for long periods, especially if nestled lower in the order. Four-day cricket came in with a fanfare. Only for an increasing number of people to clamour for the declaration-heavy format of the three-dayer. And of course, matches weren't competitive enough – especially over the course of a whole season. And there were way too many of them in the first place. People, eh? There's no pleasin' 'em.

And it didn't stop there. As well as the format being all wrong, cricketers were even worse. They were generally regarded as being too friendly with each other. This mythical boys' club atmosphere has been blamed for the continued presence of a whole host of hangers-on – ageing journeymen blocking the progress, stealing the very oxygen, of younger, better and hungrier players. All of these perceived negative factors had many believe that the County Championship was breathing its last wheezy breaths, with no miracle cure in sight.

> The doom-mongers found themselves in their element throughout the '80s and '90s as the national side played the role of world cricket's fall-guy

But it isn't true, is it? Anyone watching any 'Champo' matches last summer will attest to a game in rude and vigorous health. And three of its unique playing conditions make it the best club competition in the world.

Firstly, the two-divisional nature of the competition functions brilliantly. So much so that despite multiple changes to the amount, style and frequency of one-day cricket played in the UK from 2012, two tiers in four-day cricket remains. It stands as is. And that's because it works. It maintains intensity throughout the season because as exciting as it is to play in a promotion campaign or a Championship challenge, the prospect of relegation is disproportionately worse. It lingers. Winters seem longer. Silence is the sound of a cricket club post 'drop'. Players feel it terribly. And the spectators want answers in the form of heads on pikes. Going down takes three years for a club to recover from, it's that bad an experience.

The second positive change has been the weighting of points in favour of rewarding positive cricket. Whereas in the past a solid season spent racking up draw after draw meant the retention of divisional status, it doesn't any more. With 16 points (previously 14) for a win and only three (previously four) for a draw, the risk of losing when going for a win is now suddenly worth it.

In 2009, Durham won the title with eight victories. The next highest win tally was four. In 2010, Nottinghamshire recorded the most victories (seven) and won the title, with three teams only a single win back. It has never been tighter at the top. And the benefits of stitching this 'he who dares' approach into the DNA of the sport was never more vividly illustrated than on the final day of last season when eventual second place finishers Somerset accepted an early draw against Durham only to watch Notts press on for the extra points they needed to win the title in the early evening at Old Trafford. The clubs eventually tied on points, meaning the title resides at Trent Bridge not Taunton due to – you might have guessed – Notts having won more games than the Cidermen. Perfect.

The final rule change has been the most significant in terms of making the cricket more exciting to watch. And it's an odd one. Last summer's 'red carding' of the heavy roller during County Championship cricket worked as the law-makers hoped it might.

 Silence is the sound of a cricket club post 'drop'. Players feel it terribly. And the spectators want answers in the form of heads on pikes.

From a spectator's point of view, I'm guessing that the perfect four-day match constitutes four crisp completed innings, each generating somewhere between 250 and 350 runs, culminating in a side either winning by a single wicket or losing by a handful of runs, the end coming soon after tea on the final day, leaving just enough time for a pint in the pub and a bit of a debrief on the way home.

And that was pretty much how things panned out last summer. The light roller tidied rather than flattened. The pace and bounce with which groundsmen lovingly infused their pitches at the start of a game more often than not remained throughout. It made for do-or-die cricket, season-defining sessions, matchwinning knocks and catches genuinely winning matches.

There were fewer draws than in any modern season past, and these pitches produced cricket that was great to watch and play in. Believe it or not but the County Championship is close to perfect. And always has been.

Now it works from every perspective. As a spectator experience, as a breeding ground and as an entity in itself. The domestic game is seeing superstars emerge in the form of players who have more than just cut their teeth on the format. In the shape of Graeme Swann, Tim Bresnan, Chris Tremlett and Jonathan Trott, England have players who have long trod the boards of the county game before stepping up and succeeding at the highest level. If it's good enough for them, it's good enough, full stop.

Andy Afford
Editor, All Out Cricket

YOUTH AND YOUNG MANHOOD

All Out Cricket's deputy editor Phil Walker on the realities of life for aspiring professional cricketers.

E very schoolkid who ever picked up a bat will at some stage have dreamt of making it. It's no more than a fleeting fancy for most of us, or perhaps if you're good, a distant possibility. But then there's this other group – the special ones. To the legions looking in, they are the gods. There's a catch though. Because a pile of realities are already emerging – job realities, mortgage realities, expectation pressures, targets – all bundled up into that overarching truth about how only the strongest survive. It's a tough school, professional cricket. Always has been. Only the most gifted, the brashest and toughest, graduate with distinction. For the others, tiptoeing that mile-high tightrope that stretches between success and failure, it can feel like a long way down.

The challenge for county cricket, then, is to inoculate its best young men from the mass of outside pressures that come with the modern game, and just let them play without fear. Clubs are more attuned than ever to the necessity of a support structure for young players, and they need to be, for it's a stark and sometimes debilitating transition from playing the game for love to performing it for money.

Robin Lett was Somerset's Second XI captain in 2010. It wasn't a job he particularly coveted – it's cricket's backhanded compliment – but after a handful of years on the professional staff and 12 first-class matches, the 23-year-old Millfield graduate was lumbered with steering "the stiffs".

"The thing with second team cricket," he says, "is that every time you walk out to bat you feel not only your employers breathing down your neck, but everything. It becomes a case of having to play for rent, and for food, and to keep a roof over your head. As well as playing for a career. It's like the weight of the world is on your shoulders. So your focus shifts from scoring runs just for the love of it, to trying to keep a contract going."

Faced with these circumstances, and sensing his chances slipping away, the self-expression that had marked Lett's game as a teenager, and which had led to a first-class debut at 19, simply "disappeared out of the window", escaping with that raw love of batting that had propelled him into the side in the first place. He adds that he's seen it time and time again with other young cricketers: "They come along and play a bit of second team cricket and you see all that expression of talent and fearlessness, and as soon as you throw them a contract it disappears. I know it did in my case." At the end of last year Lett was released from Somerset.

Essex's approachable head coach Paul Grayson would sympathise with Lett's story. Growing up in Yorkshire and coming through the ranks at Headingley, he understands how the pressures of expectation can sap and inhibit young cricketers. "Being an ex-player myself I know what they're feeling. I've been there myself when I was at Yorkshire. I had to go through it there. And that was a tough school. High expectations. Looking back at it, I couldn't get used to the expectations, so I know what these young lads are going through."

 It's a tough school, professional cricket. Always has been. Only the most gifted, the brashest and toughest, graduate with distinction.

But Grayson believes that county cricket's dressing rooms are more progressive and sensitive places than they used to be. "That Yorkshire dressing room containing the likes of Phil Carrick, David Bairstow, and Jim Love – tough characters. But I like to get away from that as a coach. We try and get our academy lads training with the first team so when they do come through they're not scared or intimidated."

Essex's inclusive, folksy approach has borne some rich fruit – Alastair Cook, Ravi Bopara, James Foster and Graham Napier are just some of their recent graduates, and more are lined up. A few miles away at a similar-sized club to Essex the trick is being repeated. Leicestershire have produced in Stuart Broad, Jimmy Taylor and Nathan Buck – and the brilliant 17-year-old Shiv Thakor – a clutch of English cricket's most promising youngsters. Phil Whitticase is the head coach and academy director at Grace Road, overseeing a system where academy players actively train and work with the professional squad, and is proud of how far his club, and the game itself, has progressed as a breeding ground. "The support that players get on and off the field now is fantastic," he says. "When I started playing we didn't even have a physio! The players are in 12 months of the year now working on their game. The flipside is that decisions are probably made quicker on players, but it has certainly moved on as a professional sport."

Yet the Grace Road story didn't always seem so rosy. It wasn't long ago that they were getting "slated" – Whitticase's word – for going down the line of Kolpak players, despite their presence hindering English youngsters. "At the time we probably didn't have enough young players ready to step up," he admits, highlighting the vexed issue that still bedevils certain county clubs: namely how to nurture young English players for the common good while at the same time fielding a bunch of names good enough to win cricket matches. But Leicestershire has now "gone through" that phase of employing non-English qualified players with EU passports, to enjoy the benefits of promoting homegrown players, both in terms of popularity and for their reputation as a haven for ambitious youngsters looking to learn their trade.

 The thing with second team cricket is that every time you walk out to bat you feel not only your employers breathing down your neck, but everything. It becomes a case of having to play for rent, and for food, and to keep a roof over your head.

The Kolpak issue isn't as divisive as it used to be. With ECB incentive payments now available to clubs fielding homegrown players, there are considerably fewer registered Kolpaks in 2011 compared to the high of 60 players in 2008. This reduction improves the chances for young English cricketers, makes a career as a cricketer more attractive, and makes county dressing rooms more harmonious places to work.

And now the ECB has placed a sturdy crashmat underneath that tightrope. The ECB Recreational XI – known as the Unicorns – is a masterstroke. Formed for the 2010 season to play in the CB40 competition to fill a hole created by Ireland's withdrawal, it's made up of players on the edges of the first-class game without full-time professional contracts. Last year 15 members of the 22-man squad were former county professionals.

"It's been great," says captain Keith Parsons, formerly of Somerset. "In this economic climate counties are tightening budgets and they have smaller staffs so Unicorns works in a couple of ways – partly for those who have tasted first-class cricket but been released and partly for youngsters on their way up. We had four lads last year in or around the Unicorns squad who got contracts – Wes Durston, Mike O'Shea, Ed Young and Rory Burns. It gives them a real taste of competitive cricket at that level."
Durston was last year's dream story. Released from Somerset in 2009 and without a club, he belted a bundle of runs for the Unicorns, including a whirlwind 68-ball 117 to reel in Sussex's 325 – the highest chase ever in 40-over history – and strolled away with a two-year contract with Derbyshire. "When I got the call about the Unicorns, I basically saw it as a 12-match trial. And if I did well, counties would take notice and hopefully I'd be able to get back in the game. That's exactly what happened. I couldn't have written it any better.

"It's a team environment. People have their own points to prove and they want to get back into the game. But while you're in that environment there's no way you can succeed if you're only playing for yourself. And because it's an amateur side rather than a county you can actually enjoy your cricket more."

Durston has another shot at the big time. But perhaps this year's story will involve the Unicorns' newest acquisition: Robin Lett. His harrowing 2010 now a fading memory, the lad is back in love with the game and can't wait for another crack. "After all," he says, "it's still a dream job at the end of the day."

Phil Walker
Deputy Editor, All Out Cricket

R – 1,000 or more first-class runs in an English season (the number next to 'R' denotes how many times the player has achieved this feat)

W – 50 or more first-class wickets in an English season (the number next to 'W' denotes how many times the player has achieved this feat)

MVP – Denotes a player's presence in the top 100 places of the 2010 Overall FTI MVP Points (the number next to 'MVP' denotes the player's specific placing)

---

* – Not out innings (e.g. 137*)
(s) – A competition has been shared between two or more winners
CB40 – Clydesdale Bank 40 (English domestic 40-over competition)
CC1 – County Championship Division One
CC2 – County Championship Division Two
FP t20 – Friends Provident t20 (English domestic 20-over competition)
ICC – International Cricket Council
LB – Legbreak bowler
LF – Left-arm fast bowler
LFM – Left-arm fast-medium bowler
LHB – Left-hand batsman
LM – Left-arm medium
LMF – Left-arm medium-fast bowler
MCCU – Marylebone Cricket Club University
OB – Offbreak bowler
ODI – One-Day International
RF – Right-arm fast bowler
RFM – Right-arm fast-medium bowler
RHB – Right-hand batsman
RM – Right-arm medium bowler
RMF – Right-arm medium-fast bowler
SLA – Slow left-arm orthodox
SLC – Slow left-arm Chinaman
T20 – Twenty20
T20I – Twenty20 International
WK – Wicketkeeper

Stats correct as of 31 March 2011

The
Counties

FORMED: 1870
HOME GROUND: County Ground, Derby
ONE-DAY NAME: Falcons
CAPTAIN: Luke Sutton
2010 RESULTS: CC2: 9/9; CB40: 4/7 in Group B; FP t20: 5/9 in North Group

HONOURS
County Championship: 1936; Gillette/NatWest/C&G/FP Trophy: 1981; Benson and Hedges Cup: 1993; Sunday League: 1990

THE LOWDOWN
Many people fancied Derbyshire to be in the shake-up for promotion to Division One in 2010, but they struggled in four-day cricket for much of the season, registering only three wins and finishing bottom of the pile. They made a better fist of it in one-day cricket, but they will be looking for an improved performance in 2011 under returning skipper Luke Sutton, who arrives back at the County Ground after a five-season stint with Lancashire. The departure of three senior players in Chris Rogers, Robin Peterson and Graham Wagg during the winter will place added pressure on the club's younger players, but the recruitment of Tony Palladino and Mark Turner will strengthen their seam attack and the likes of Jake Needham and Jonathan Clare look ready to accept greater responsibility. The club has also pulled off a major coup by signing two of international cricket's most promising young batsmen in Martin Guptill and Usman Khawaja as overseas players, a move that should mean that top-order runs are in abundant supply.

HEAD OF CRICKET: JOHN MORRIS
A former Derbyshire, Durham, Nottinghamshire and England middle-order batsman, Morris spent 11 seasons at the County Ground before moving to Durham in 1994. A stylish shotmaker who played in three Tests and eight ODIs, his role in the infamous Tiger Moth incident during England's tour of Australia in 1990/91 has gone down in cricketing folklore. He was appointed as the club's head of cricket in August 2007.

With thanks to: Mark Eklid, Derby Telegraph

Batting & Fielding

	Mat	Inns	NO	Runs	HS	Ave	SR	100	50	Ct	St
CJL Rogers	15	27	3	1285	200	53.54	64.25	4	5	19	-
CF Hughes	12	21	2	784	156	41.26	56.64	2	4	12	-
WL Madsen	16	29	1	940	179	33.57	44.04	4	2	11	-
PS Jones	12	18	4	427	86	30.50	70.81	0	1	4	-
GM Smith	16	27	1	721	165*	27.73	55.29	1	4	4	-
GT Park	11	19	2	431	124*	25.35	39.39	1	2	6	-
SJ Adshead	4	7	2	125	49	25.00	53.87	0	0	13	0
DJ Redfern	9	15	1	331	85	23.64	50.00	0	1	3	-
RJ Peterson	15	24	3	484	58	23.04	49.94	0	2	9	-
WJ Durston	6	11	0	240	69	21.81	53.21	0	1	9	-
TD Groenewald	13	19	9	216	35*	21.60	40.98	0	0	3	-
PM Borrington	7	13	1	246	79*	20.50	31.37	0	1	4	-
LJ Goddard	8	11	1	165	67	16.50	45.45	0	1	24	0
T Poynton	4	6	0	88	25	14.66	23.97	0	0	5	0
GG Wagg	4	7	0	82	37	11.71	73.87	0	0	1	-
JL Sadler	3	4	0	45	16	11.25	37.81	0	0	3	-
T Lungley	7	10	1	85	21	9.44	26.31	0	0	6	-
MHA Footitt	9	12	3	69	30	7.66	47.26	0	0	3	-
JL Clare	4	6	0	45	24	7.50	37.50	0	0	4	-
A Sheikh	1	2	0	6	6	3.00	21.42	0	0	1	-

Bowling

	Mat	Overs	Mdns	Runs	Wkts	BBI	BBM	Ave	Econ	SR	5w	10
GG Wagg	4	77.0	13	246	10	3/31	6/85	24.60	3.19	46.2	0	0
JL Clare	4	69.3	8	324	11	4/42	5/96	29.45	4.66	37.9	0	0
A Sheikh	1	25.0	1	152	5	3/78	5/152	30.40	6.08	30.0	0	0
RJ Peterson	15	553.3	129	1566	51	4/10	6/104	30.70	2.82	65.1	0	0
PS Jones	12	313.5	68	959	31	4/26	5/35	30.93	3.05	60.7	0	0
GM Smith	16	414.3	77	1368	42	5/54	6/93	32.57	3.30	59.2	1	0
T Lungley	7	165.0	25	630	19	3/39	4/104	33.15	3.81	52.1	0	0
TD Groenewald	13	413.5	105	1295	38	5/86	8/149	34.07	3.12	65.3	1	0
MHA Footitt	9	239.2	48	786	23	4/78	5/78	34.17	3.28	62.4	0	0
GT Park	11	83.3	9	327	9	2/20	3/51	36.33	3.91	55.6	0	0
T Poynton	4	8.0	0	96	2	2/96	2/96	48.00	12.00	24.0	0	0
WL Madsen	16	8.2	0	68	1	1/68	1/68	68.00	8.16	50.0	0	0
WJ Durston	6	16.0	0	76	1	1/9	1/29	76.00	4.75	96.0	0	0
CF Hughes	12	11.0	0	81	1	1/9	1/9	81.00	7.36	66.0	0	0
DJ Redfern	9	3.0	0	14	0	-	-	-	4.66	-	0	0
CJL Rogers	15	1.0	0	5	0	-	-	-	5.00	-	0	0

Derbyshire
FALCONS

Batting & Fielding

	Mat	Inns	NO	Runs	HS	Ave	SR	100	50	Ct	St
GG Wagg	5	5	3	137	48*	68.50	106.20	0	0	2	-
WL Madsen	10	10	2	404	71*	50.50	95.28	0	4	8	-
CJL Rogers	9	9	0	336	73	37.33	79.80	0	2	3	-
CF Hughes	12	12	0	422	72	35.16	86.47	0	5	5	-
JL Sadler	5	5	1	135	41	33.75	103.05	0	0	0	-
WJ Durston	8	8	2	189	72*	31.50	81.11	0	1	3	-
GT Park	9	8	2	153	43	25.50	81.81	0	0	3	-
DJ Redfern	4	4	0	86	37	21.50	76.10	0	0	30	-
RJ Peterson	8	6	0	124	51	20.66	91.17	0	1	3	-
PS Jones	4	2	0	37	22	18.50	154.16	0	0	0	-
GM Smith	11	11	0	191	46	17.36	72.07	0	0	2	-
TD Groenewald	9	6	3	45	13*	15.00	90.00	0	0	4	-
ID Hunter	1	1	0	14	14	14.00	82.35	0	0	0	-
JL Clare	5	5	1	50	21*	12.50	100.00	0	0	2	-
T Lungley	5	3	2	12	6*	12.00	133.33	0	0	2	-
LJ Goddard	7	5	1	36	24*	9.00	116.12	0	0	1	0
SJ Adshead	5	4	0	14	8	3.50	43.75	0	0	6	1
J Needham	7	4	0	10	5	2.50	38.46	0	0	0	-
MHA Footitt	8	2	1	1	1	1.00	25.00	0	0	0	-

Bowling

	Mat	Overs	Mdns	Runs	Wkts	BBI	Ave	Econ	SR	5w
GG Wagg	5	31.1	1	160	9	3/22	17.77	5.13	20.7	0
J Needham	7	49.0	0	225	9	3/36	25.00	4.59	32.6	0
MHA Footitt	8	49.0	1	273	10	3/20	27.30	5.57	29.4	0
T Lungley	5	37.0	3	214	7	3/41	30.57	5.78	31.7	0
TD Groenewald	9	63.0	4	345	10	2/42	34.50	5.47	37.8	0
PS Jones	4	26.0	0	142	4	3/27	35.50	5.46	39.0	0
RJ Peterson	8	52.5	0	260	7	3/38	37.14	4.92	45.2	0
GM Smith	11	60.0	1	344	7	2/34	49.14	5.73	51.4	0
WJ Durston	8	9.3	0	52	1	1/2	52.00	5.47	57.0	0
GT Park	9	29.5	0	199	1	1/17	199.00	6.67	179.0	0
JL Clare	5	12.0	0	72	0	-	-	6.00	-	0
CF Hughes	12	5.0	0	26	0	-	-	5.20	-	0
ID Hunter	1	5.0	0	25	0	-	-	5.00	-	0
JL Sadler	5	1.0	0	11	0	-	-	11.00	-	0

Derbyshire
FALCONS

	Mat	Inns	NO	Runs	HS	Ave	SR	100	50	Ct	St
WJ Durston	16	15	3	445	111	37.08	129.36	1	2	6	-
PS Jones	16	7	4	103	40	34.33	174.57	0	0	1	-
LJ Goddard	16	9	7	63	22*	31.50	134.04	0	0	5	1
JL Sadler	12	11	6	157	39	31.40	146.72	0	0	4	-
GT Park	15	9	1	241	66	30.12	101.68	0	2	4	-
LE Bosman	15	14	0	368	94	26.28	134.79	0	2	1	-
WL Madsen	5	4	1	59	29	19.66	113.46	0	0	0	-
RJ Peterson	16	15	2	252	35*	19.38	123.52	0	0	2	-
CF Hughes	12	10	0	164	65	16.40	103.79	0	1	3	-
GM Smith	15	14	0	225	38	16.07	105.14	0	0	11	-
JL Clare	6	5	1	53	18	13.25	135.89	0	0	5	-
CJL Rogers	3	3	1	18	13*	9.00	94.73	0	0	1	-
CK Langeveldt	12	2	1	9	5*	9.00	60.00	0	0	1	-
TD Groenewald	16	3	1	12	8	6.00	75.00	0	0	2	-

	Mat	Overs	Mdns	Runs	Wkts	BBI	Ave	Econ	SR	5w
WJ Durston	16	18.0	0	139	6	2/18	23.16	7.72	18.0	0
TD Groenewald	16	50.2	1	375	16	3/18	23.43	7.45	18.8	0
GM Smith	15	39.1	0	307	13	3/19	23.61	7.83	18.0	0
CK Langeveldt	12	42.0	0	309	13	3/36	23.76	7.35	19.3	0
GT Park	15	28.0	0	226	8	3/11	28.25	8.07	21.0	0
T Lungley	1	3.0	0	34	1	1/34	34.00	11.33	18.0	0
PS Jones	16	48.0	0	393	11	3/20	35.72	8.18	26.1	0
RJ Peterson	16	51.1	1	380	8	2/38	47.50	7.42	38.3	0

PAUL BORRINGTON

RHB RM

DERBYSHIRE

NAME: Paul Michael Borrington
BORN: May 24, 1988, Nottingham
HEIGHT: 5ft 10in
SQUAD Nº: 17
NICKNAME: Bozza
CAREER: First-class debut 2005; List A debut: 2009

AOC SAYS: An opening batsman by trade, Borrington is the son of former Derbyshire wicketkeeper Tony, who played for the club between 1970 and 1982. A graduate of Loughborough University, Borrington junior made his Championship debut as a 17-year-old in 2005 but made only fleeting appearances in the following two seasons while he completed his studies. However, 2008 proved a different story and saw him make 12 first-class appearances and notch his maiden century, an unbeaten 102 for Loughborough MCCU against Worcestershire. He followed this up with three appearances in 2009 but struggled for form in 2010, making just 246 runs from 13 innings. An organised, orthodox batsman who drives powerfully in the V, he will likely face added responsibility this season as the departure of Chris Rogers has opened up a slot at the top of the order.

LAST WORD: "This could be his season to kick on. He's highly rated by the club and times the ball nicely, but he needed to work on keeping the scoreboard ticking over to take some of the pressure off Madsen, his likely partner, and so has put in many hours with the coaching staff to refine his technique and expand his scoring range." *Mark Eklid*

Batting & Fielding

	Mat	Inns	NO	Runs	HS	Ave	SR	100	50	Ct	St
First-class	26	42	5	1109	105	29.97	36.85	2	5	16	0
List A	1	1	0	25	25	25.00	67.56	0	0	0	0

Bowling

	Mat	Balls	Runs	Wkts	BBI	BBM	Ave	Econ	SR	5w	10
First-class	26	6	5	0	-	-	-	5.00	-	0	0
List A	1	-	-	-	-	-	-	-	-	-	-

NAME: Jonathan Luke Clare
BORN: June 14, 1986, Burnley
HEIGHT: 6ft 3in
SQUAD Nº: 13
NICKNAME: JC, Sidewinder, Scream
CAREER: First-class debut: 2007; List A
debut: 2007; T20 debut: 2008

DERBYSHIRE

AOC SAYS: Clare burst onto the county scene in 2007, claiming his maiden five-wicket haul
on debut against Notts at Chesterfield, and his good form continued in 2008 as he scored
555 runs, including a brutal 129* against Northants. He also claimed 31 wickets at 28.09 in
the Championship, prompting the ECB to offer him a place on their fast bowling strength and
conditioning programme in Florida that winter. However, a succession of niggling injuries
have hampered his development over the last two seasons, although reports indicate that
he should be fit and firing for the start of this season. A former Lancashire academy player
who moved to Derbyshire in search of greater opportunities, Clare is an aggressive, athletic
seamer who elicits lively bounce and a punishing batsman unafraid to clear the infield.

LAST WORD: "He should be a big asset for the team this year, Graham Wagg's departure
means they'll need a strike bowler who can bat at No.8 and I think he's the man for the job.
He's a real talent." *Mark Eklid*

Batting & Fielding

	Mat	Inns	NO	Runs	HS	Ave	SR	100	50	Ct	St
First-class	24	32	5	655	129*	24.25	61.56	1	5	10	0
List A	24	19	2	193	34	11.35	94.60	0	0	7	0
Twenty20	12	8	2	63	18	10.50	116.66	0	0	6	0

Bowling

	Mat	Balls	Runs	Wkts	BBI	BBM	Ave	Econ	SR	5w	10
First-class	24	2973	1805	62	7/74	7/74	29.11	3.64	47.9	2	0
List A	24	787	736	15	3/39	3/39	49.06	5.61	52.4	0	0
Twenty20	12	53	72	2	2/20	2/20	36.00	8.15	26.5	0	0

WES DURSTON — RHB OB MVP90

DERBYSHIRE

NAME: Wesley John Durston
BORN: October 6, 1980, Taunton
HEIGHT: 5ft 10in
SQUAD Nº: 3
NICKNAME: Ace, Pringles
OTHER TEAMS: Somerset, Unicorns
CAREER: First-class debut: 2002; List A debut: 2000; T20 debut: 2003

AOC SAYS: A natural boundary-hitter as well as a tidy bowling option in limited-overs cricket, Durston – who has a four-year-old son called Joseph – made his county debut in 2000 and played a significant part in Somerset's 2005 Twenty20 Cup victory. But he fell out of favour over the next few seasons and was quietly released in 2009. He signed up to play for the Unicorns in 2010 and leapt into the headlines by making 117 off 68 deliveries to help his side chase down 326 against Sussex. Derbyshire promptly signed him for their Twenty20 campaign and he continued to impress, smashing a Derbyshire record of 111 off 59 deliveries against Notts to earn himself a full-time deal. He subsequently struggled for runs in the Championship but continued to score freely in limited-overs cricket.

LAST WORD: "The original FP t20 contract signed by Wes gave him an opportunity to prove himself. The way he performed in all facets of the game, as well as his attitude and professionalism both on and off the field, convinced us that he would be an excellent addition to our squad for all forms of cricket." *John Morris*

Batting & Fielding

	Mat	Inns	NO	Runs	HS	Ave	SR	100	50	Ct	St
First-class	40	68	12	1966	146*	35.10	55.07	1	14	43	0
List A	68	58	17	1342	117	32.73	-	1	8	19	0
Twenty20	54	45	10	831	111	23.74	122.56	1	3	20	0

Bowling

	Mat	Balls	Runs	Wkts	BBI	BBM	Ave	Econ	SR	5w	10
First-class	40	2253	1496	25	3/23	-	59.84	3.98	90.1	0	0
List A	68	1023	1027	24	3/44	3/44	42.79	6.02	42.6	0	0
Twenty20	54	322	477	23	3/25	3/25	20.73	8.88	14.0	0	0

NAME: Mark Harold Alan Footitt
BORN: November 25, 1985, Nottingham
HEIGHT: 6ft 2in
SQUAD Nº: 4
NICKNAME: Foots
OTHER TEAMS: Nottinghamshire
CAREER: First-class debut: 2005; List A
debut: 2002; T20 debut: 2005

DERBYSHIRE

AOC SAYS: A former England under 19 international, Footitt is a cricketing rarity: a left-arm seamer capable of clocking in at over 90mph. He started out at Nottinghamshire and claimed 4-45 on his first-class debut in 2005, but a string of injuries restricted him to just 10 first-class appearances during his time at Trent Bridge and he was released at the end of the 2009 season. Derbyshire picked him up on an initial one-year contract, and his form in 2010, which saw him claim 23 first-class wickets at 34.17, prompted the club to offer him a two-year extension during the winter. Still raw and occasionally wayward, he has been working hard with Derbyshire bowling coach Steffan Jones to iron out his action and will be looking to build on his encouraging performances last season.

LAST WORD: "In Mark Footitt we have a bowler capable of genuine pace, who took promising strides forward in 2010. He is aiming to continue that development over the next two years and become a frontline first-class bowler." *John Morris*

Batting & Fielding

	Mat	Inns	NO	Runs	HS	Ave	SR	100	50	Ct	St
First-class	18	19	8	118	30	10.72	48.96	0	0	4	0
List A	9	2	1	1	1	1.00	25.00	0	0	0	0
Twenty20	1	-	-	-	-	-	-	-	-	0	0

Bowling

	Mat	Balls	Runs	Wkts	BBI	BBM	Ave	Econ	SR	5w	10
First-class	18	2367	1515	46	5/45	-	32.93	3.84	51.4	2	0
List A	9	312	291	10	3/20	3/20	29.10	5.59	31.2	0	0
Twenty20	1	12	34	0	-	-	-	17.00	-	0	0

G

TIM GROENEWALD RHB RFM MVP73

DERBYSHIRE

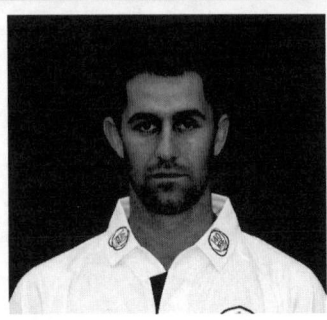

NAME: Timothy Duncan Groenewald
BORN: January 10, 1984, Pietermaritzburg, South Africa
HEIGHT: 6ft 2in
SQUAD Nº: 12
NICKNAME: TG
OTHER TEAMS: KwaZulu-Natal Inland, Warwickshire
CAREER: First-class debut: 2006; List A debut: 2006; T20 debut: 2006

AOC SAYS: Allrounder Groenewald joined Derbyshire from Warwickshire for the 2009 season having grown frustrated at a lack of Championship opportunities at Edgbaston. A natural swing bowler who can keep it tight as well as a counter-attacking lower-order batsman, the 27-year-old South African qualifies as a Kolpak player thanks to his English mother and has proven a reliable wicket-taker for the club in all forms of the game. A willing workhorse who bowled more than 521 overs in all forms of cricket last summer, his ability to move the ball both ways in the air has seen him become the Falcons' first-choice new-ball bowler, and given the youthful nature of the rest of the Derbyshire's seam attack he will likely be one of the first bowlers his skipper turns to when he needs a breakthrough this season.

LAST WORD: "He's been a terrific signing for the club and is as reliable as the day is long. A really good character who leads the attack manfully." *Mark Eklid*

Batting & Fielding

	Mat	Inns	NO	Runs	HS	Ave	SR	100	50	Ct	St
First-class	39	51	14	778	78	21.02	48.62	0	3	16	0
List A	46	33	8	330	36	13.20	97.34	0	0	10	0
Twenty20	46	19	9	247	41	24.70	127.31	0	0	12	0

Bowling

	Mat	Balls	Runs	Wkts	BBI	BBM	Ave	Econ	SR	5w	10
First-class	39	6172	3345	98	6/50	8/149	34.13	3.25	62.9	4	0
List A	46	1591	1483	41	3/25	3/25	36.17	5.59	38.8	0	0
Twenty20	46	759	1020	39	3/18	3/18	26.15	8.06	19.4	0	0

28

OVERSEAS PLAYER

NAME: Martin James Guptill
BORN: September 30, 1986, Auckland
SQUAD Nº: 31
OTHER TEAMS: New Zealand, Auckland
CAREER: Test debut: 2009; ODI debut: 2009;
T20I debut: 2009; First-class debut: 2006;
List A debut: 2006; T20 debut: 2006

DERBYSHIRE

AOC SAYS: One of two overseas players signed by the Falcons this season, Guptill is a top-order batsman who is capable of adapting his approach for all forms of the game. He made his domestic bow for Auckland in a limited-overs game against Canterbury in 2006, and although he didn't initially set the world alight in first-class cricket he built a reputation as a player with an excellent temperament. His breakthrough season was 2007/08, which saw him amass 596 runs at 59.60 in limited-overs cricket, and he followed that up with 548 limited-over runs at 45.66 and his maiden first-class hundred in 2008/09. This was enough for the New Zealand selectors to call him up to the ODI squad to face West Indies, and he celebrated with an excellent unbeaten 122 at Auckland. He's been a steady performer for his country ever since and notched his maiden Test century, a resolute 189 against Bangladesh at Hamilton in 2010, although he has otherwise displayed a frustrating tendency to fail to convert useful starts into big scores. Also a capable offspinner unafraid to give the ball some air, the 24-year-old right-hander is scheduled to join the club for the start of their FP t20 campaign and will remain with the team for the rest of the season. Calm and composed at the crease, he possesses a vicious pull shot and is a superb fielder in all positions despite having only two toes on one of his feet following a forklift accident that occurred when he was 13.

INSIDE TRACK: "The signing of Guptill and Khawaja has got a lot of people quite excited, not just at the club but around the game. It has created a buzz that will hopefully give the club a real lift. From what I've seen he looks a fine player who has the technique to handle the conditions at Derby; he won't be perturbed if the ball swings or seams about a bit because he's seen it before playing in New Zealand. I don't think they'll push him up to open in the Championship, I think he'll slot in at No.3, but he might get that job in the FP t20 because he's done well there in international cricket." *Mark Eklid*

MARTIN GUPTILL

DERBYSHIRE

Batting & Fielding

	Mat	Inns	NO	Runs	HS	Ave	SR	100	50	Ct	St
Tests	15	28	1	944	189	34.96	44.73	1	6	11	0
ODIs	52	50	6	1572	122*	35.72	79.75	1	11	19	0
T20Is	23	21	2	439	54	23.10	116.13	0	1	9	0
First-class	39	68	3	2038	189	31.35	42.77	2	12	27	0
List A	84	80	8	2688	156	37.33	79.47	5	15	38	0
Twenty20	46	42	4	1016	97*	26.73	126.05	0	4	27	0

Bowling

	Mat	Balls	Runs	Wkts	BBI	BBM	Ave	Econ	SR	5w	10
Tests	15	194	136	3	3/37	3/37	45.33	4.20	64.6	0	0
ODIs	52	65	53	2	2/7	2/7	26.50	4.89	32.5	0	0
T20Is	23	6	11	0	-	-	-	11.00	-	0	0
First-class	39	314	216	4	3/37	3/37	54.00	4.12	78.5	0	0
List A	84	65	53	2	2/7	2/7	26.50	4.89	32.5	0	0
Twenty20	46	6	11	0	-	-	-	11.00	-	0	0

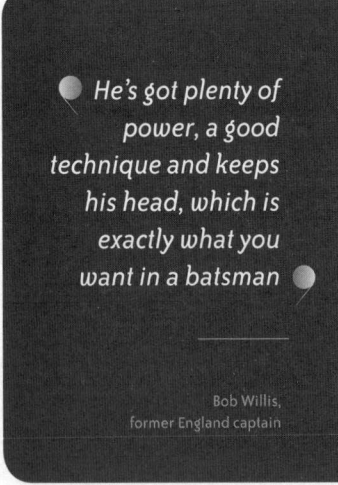

● *He's got plenty of power, a good technique and keeps his head, which is exactly what you want in a batsman* ●

Bob Willis,
former England captain

NAME: Matthew Higginbottom
BORN: October 20, 1990, Stockport
SQUAD Nº: 20
CAREER: Yet to make first-team debut

DERBYSHIRE

AOC SAYS: A brisk right-arm seamer, Higginbottom is a student at Leeds Metropolitan University and has a handful of appearances for Bradford/Leeds MCCU under his belt, several of which were made during a winter tour to South Africa early last season. The first cricketer from the High Peak borough of Derbyshire for almost 20 years to earn a contract with the club, he is a product of the Derbyshire academy and turned out several times for the Second XI in 2010, although he has yet to make a significant impact at that level. He plays club cricket for Chesterfield in the Derbyshire Premier League and last summer took 37 wickets at an impressive average of just 17.65.

LAST WORD: "Matthew has done really well. He's a medium-quick bowler, and we hope to get him a bit quicker over time, but he's got a decent stature and a good line and length. We think a lot of him." *Karl Krikken, Derbyshire academy director*

EXTRAS

Guptill's score of 122 not out is the highest debut score in New Zealand ODI history, and second highest debut score ever in ODIs. He also became the first New Zealander to carry his bat through a completed ODI innings.

ALEX HUGHES

RHB RM

DERBYSHIRE

NAME: Alex Lloyd Hughes
BORN: September 29, 1991, Wordsley
SQUAD Nº: 18
CAREER: Yet to make first-team debut

AOC SAYS: Hughes is a product of the Derbyshire academy and has been granted a summer contract by the club for the 2011 season. He has represented Staffordshire in the Minor Counties Championship and plays his club cricket for Wombourne CC. A top-order batsman who scored 223 runs at 37.16 – including two half-centuries and a top-score of 85* – in the Second XI Championship last season, he learnt his cricket at the Staffordshire academy and is one of five cricketers from that institution, the others being Worcestershire's Dave Wheeldon, Jack Manuel and Joe Leach and Nottinghamshire's Scott Elstone, to hold a county contract this summer.

LAST WORD: "Alex performed well in our Second XI and academy games last summer and we are delighted that he has made the transition to the professional staff." *Karl Krikken Derbyshire academy director*

EXTRAS

Derbyshire announced a £187,037 loss for 2010. The club said a change to ECB's performance-related payments and the impact of the football World Cup last summer were big factors in the outcome.

NAME: Chesney Francis Hughes
BORN: January 20, 1991, Anguilla
SQUAD Nº: 22
OTHER TEAMS: Anguilla, Leeward Islands
CAREER: First-class debut: 2010; List A
debut: 2007; T20 debut: 2006

AOC SAYS: Recommended to Derbyshire's head of cricket John Morris by former Hampshire stalwart Cardigan Connor, Hughes is a hugely exciting talent: a powerful batsman who can destroy attacks but who also seems to possess the application to knuckle down when conditions are tricky. A product of the Leewards Islands youth set-up, he has represented West Indies at under 19 level but does not count as an overseas player as he holds a British passport. He impressed many people by battling his way to a dogged 41 against a strong Middlesex attack on his Championship debut, but it was undeniably his two performances against Gloucestershire that underlined his great potential: the first his maiden first-class hundred made in only his third first-class match when Derbyshire had slumped to 50-3, and the second a brilliant 96* made on a vicious Bristol track in a game where no other batsman made 50.

LAST WORD: "When he first set eyes on him, John Morris said he was the best 18-year-old he'd ever seen. He was the find of the season for me. He could end up batting anywhere in the order, maybe even opening in four-day as well as well as one-day cricket." *Mark Eklid*

Batting & Fielding

	Mat	Inns	NO	Runs	HS	Ave	SR	100	50	Ct	St
First-class	12	21	2	784	156	41.26	56.64	2	4	12	0
List A	25	24	1	612	81	26.60	-	0	6	7	0
Twenty20	17	15	0	242	65	16.13	104.76	0	2	5	0

Bowling

	Mat	Balls	Runs	Wkts	BBI	BBM	Ave	Econ	SR	5w	10
First-class	12	66	81	1	1/9	1/9	81.00	7.36	66.0	0	0
List A	25	246	215	2	1/17	1/17	107.50	5.24	123.0	0	0
Twenty20	17	24	36	1	1/17	1/17	36.00	9.00	24.0	0	0

STEFFAN JONES

RHB RFM W2

NAME: Philip Steffan Jones
BORN: February 9, 1974, Llanelly, Wales
HEIGHT: 6ft 1in
SQUAD Nº: 11
NICKNAME: Jona
OTHER TEAMS: Kent, Northamptonshire, Somerset
CAREER: First-class debut: 1997; List A debut: 1994; T20 debut: 2003; County cap: 2001 (Somerset)

AOC SAYS: A player of immense experience, Jones will combine bowling duties with his role as coach at the County Ground this season. A broad shouldered, muscular seamer and a dangerous hitter down the order, Jones made his first-class debut for Cambridge University in 1997, taking 9-148 in the Varsity match, before spending seven years with Somerset. Something of a cricketing nomad, he moved to Northants for the 2004 season before relocating to Derbyshire in 2006, where he enjoyed his most successful season, claiming 59 Championship wickets. He left Derbyshire to return to Somerset the following year but was loaned out to first Kent and then Derbyshire in search of regular cricket. At the end of 2009, he was offered a two-year contract that combined playing and coaching duties, an offer he happily accepted.

LAST WORD: "Steffan is looking to fill in where needed this season and he's a great character. He loves his role as a coach and says he is still fit enough to do a job as a bowler for a couple of year yet." *Mark Eklid*

Batting & Fielding

	Mat	Inns	NO	Runs	HS	Ave	SR	100	50	Ct	St
First-class	146	175	43	2655	114	20.11	-	2	8	33	0
List A	184	98	45	676	42	12.75	-	0	0	31	0
Twenty20	42	19	10	165	40	18.33	117.85	0	0	6	0

Bowling

	Mat	Balls	Runs	Wkts	BBI	BBM	Ave	Econ	SR	5w	10
First-class	146	24164	14122	384	6/25	-	36.77	3.50	62.9	10	1
List A	184	8271	7256	245	6/56	6/56	29.61	5.26	33.7	3	0
Twenty20	42	820	1169	38	3/20	3/20	30.76	8.55	21.5	0	0

OVERSEAS PLAYER

NAME: Usman Tariq Khawaja
BORN: December 18, 1986, Islamabad
HEIGHT: 5ft 9in
SQUAD Nº: TBC
NICKNAME: Usie
OTHER TEAMS: Australia, New South Wales
CAREER: Test debut: 2011; First-class debut: 2008; List A debut: 2008; T20 debut: 2010

AOC SAYS: A charismatic strokeplayer with good poise, temperament and technique, top-order batsman Khawaja will be Derbyshire's overseas player for the first half of the 2011 campaign. He was born in Pakistan but moved to Australia as a youngster and made history when he became the first Muslim to don the Baggy Green when he made his debut in the 2010/11 Ashes Test at Sydney. Playing in place of injured captain Ricky Ponting, Khawaja batted at No.3 and impressed with some well-timed shots and a willingness to graft, though he only made 37 and 21 in his two innings. The left-handed batsman earned his Australia call on the back of three impressive seasons in state cricket with New South Wales. He was named State Player of the Year for the 2010/11 season, during which he averaged 48.85, having notched up 698 runs at an average of 63.45 the previous season. Last summer he was due to follow in the footsteps of his New South Wales teammate Michael Clarke by playing in the Lancashire League, but his stint with Ramsbottom CC was cancelled when he was selected to attend the Cricket Australia Centre of Excellence. By reputation a calm, unflustered character who eschews alcohol (a characteristic that according to his state skipper Simon Katich makes him extremely popular with his teammates when it's time to head home after a night out), he'll be available to play for Derbyshire from the start of the season until the end of the FP t20 and will doubtless be hoping to follow in the footsteps of the many other Aussie batsmen who have sharpened their game playing county cricket.

INSIDE TRACK: "Usman is an extremely talented batsman whose prolific record in Sheffield Shield Cricket has fired him into the thoughts of the Australian selectors. Although he made his debut in the final Test of the Ashes series, Usman has been part of the Australia set-up for several months and was part of the touring squad that visited the County Ground last season. Successful stints in county cricket have played an integral part in the development of many successful Australian cricketers and I'm sure Usman will benefit hugely from this experience. He has scored runs consistently for New South Wales and is also proving to be a very entertaining player to watch." *John Morris*

DERBYSHIRE

Batting & Fielding

	Mat	Inns	NO	Runs	HS	Ave	SR	100	50	Ct	St
Tests	1	2	0	58	37	29.00	34.52	0	0	0	0
First-class	29	48	4	2141	214	48.65	52.14	6	10	15	0
List A	9	9	0	277	121	30.77	75.89	1	1	3	0
Twenty20	7	6	0	119	65	19.83	127.95	0	1	1	0

Bowling

	Mat	Balls	Runs	Wkts	BBI	BBM	Ave	Econ	SR	5w	10
Tests	1	-	-	-	-	-	-	-	-	-	-
First-class	29	66	45	1	1/21	1/21	45.00	4.09	66.0	0	0
List A	9	-	-	-	-	-	-	-	-	-	-
Twenty20	7	-	-	-	-	-	-	-	-	-	-

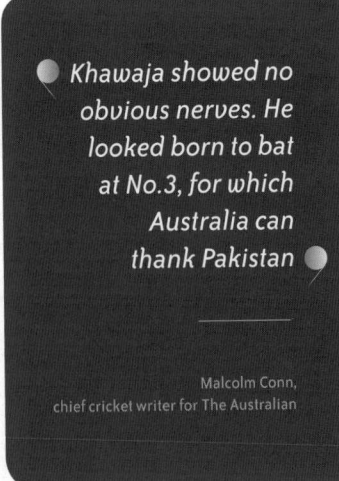

Khawaja showed no obvious nerves. He looked born to bat at No.3, for which Australia can thank Pakistan

Malcolm Conn,
chief cricket writer for The Australian

NAME: Thomas Craig Knight
BORN: June 28, 1993, Sheffield
SQUAD №: 27
CAREER: Yet to make first-team debut

DERBYSHIRE

AOC SAYS: A highly-rated left-arm spinner who attends Eckington School, Knight played four Second XI Championship games for Derbyshire last season – claiming seven wickets at 32.42, with his best figures of 3-41 coming against Glamorgan at Pontarddulais Park – and was a prolific wicket-taker for the club's under 17 side. A regular captain of the club's academy side, he was named as part of the Derbyshire squad that jetted out to the Caribbean for warm-up matches against Yorkshire, Hampshire, Warwickshire and Esssex and will likely look to spend the season developing his game in the Second XI.

LAST WORD: "He's got a few people talking around the club but shouldn't feature too much this season – Needham's their first-choice spinner." *Mark Eklid*

EXTRAS

Khawaja is a qualified pilot, completing a Bachelors degree in Aviation from the University of New South Wales before he made his Test debut – he got his pilot licence before his driving licence.

MATT LINEKER — LHB SLA

DERBYSHIRE

NAME: Matthew Steven Lineker
BORN: January 22, 1985, Derby
SQUAD Nº: 15
CAREER: Yet to make first-team debut

AOC SAYS: A dominant force in the Derbyshire Premier League for several seasons now, Lineker has signed a summer contract with the club after five years of being touted as a potential county cricketer. A stylish, strokemaking opening batsman from Alfreton, he has won the league's Player of the Season award for the last three summers but has always been wary of committing himself to cricket full-time. However, a change in his circumstances – coupled with the realisation he would always wonder how good he could have been if he did not test himself at the professional level –prompted a rethink and John Morris, himself a former Derbyshire league cricketer, was quick to offer him a deal. Lineker has spent the winter playing club cricket in Australia and will be keen to make up for lost time should he get the nod this season.

LAST WORD: "If I hadn't done this, there might always have been a nagging doubt in my mind. Could I do it? Am I good enough? I got to thinking that I didn't want to be kicking myself in 20 years' time and wonder if I might have been." *Matt Lineker*

EXTRAS

Derbyshire reached the final of the Barbados County Cup Twenty20 before the season started, with Jonathan Clare's unbeaten 57 not enough to thwart Warwickshire.

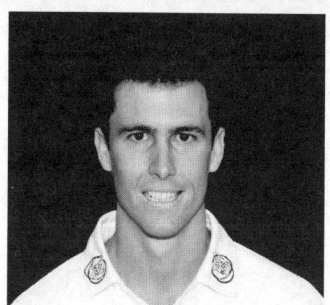

NAME: Wayne Lee Madsen
BORN: January 2, 1984, Durban
SQUAD Nº: 77
OTHER TEAMS: Derbyshire, Dolphins, KwaZulu-Natal
CAREER: First-class debut: 2004; List A debut: 2004; T20 debut: 2010

DERBYSHIRE

AOC SAYS: A methodical opening batsman who has an envious talent for converting half-centuries into big hundreds, Madsen joined Derbyshire in 2009 after several seasons turning out for KwaZulu-Natal in his native South Africa and plying his trade in the Lancashire leagues during the English summer. He was an instant success, marking his Championship debut with a patient 170* against Gloucestershire at Cheltenham, and went on to form an excellent understanding with fellow opener Chris Rogers. He was rewarded with a two-year deal and finished the season with 809 first-class runs at 57.78. Success was slightly harder to come by in 2010, although he did notch a first-class career-best of 179 whilst putting on a club-record opening partnership of 273 with Rogers. However, with Rogers having moved to Middlesex during the winter, extra responsibility will fall on his shoulders this year.

LAST WORD: "Wayne Madsen has brought great professionalism and an exemplary attitude to the squad as well as maintaining the happy habit of scoring centuries." *John Morris*

Batting & Fielding

	Mat	Inns	NO	Runs	HS	Ave	SR	100	50	Ct	St
First-class	49	86	7	3057	179	38.69	48.30	8	14	52	0
List A	24	23	5	627	71*	34.83	81.11	0	5	22	0
Twenty20	5	4	1	59	29	19.66	113.46	0	0	0	0

Bowling

	Mat	Balls	Runs	Wkts	BBI	BBM	Ave	Econ	SR	5w	10
First-class	49	686	372	7	3/45	-	53.14	3.25	98.0	0	0
List A	24	102	74	5	2/18	2/18	14.80	4.35	20.4	0	0
Twenty20	5	-	-	-	-	-	-	-	-	-	-

JAKE NEEDHAM

RHB OB

DERBYSHIRE

NAME: Jake Needham
BORN: September 30, 1986, Portsmouth
HEIGHT: 6ft 1in
SQUAD Nº: 24
CAREER: First-class debut: 2005: List A
debut: 2005; T20 debut: 2007

AOC SAYS: This summer could well be the making of Needham, who will start the year as the Falcons' first-choice spinner in all formats. An intelligent bowler who flights the ball well, he has represented England at under 19 level and signed his first professional deal with the club in 2006. The presence of Robin Peterson meant that his opportunities were limited to seven appearances in the CB40 competition last year, where he impressed on his way to picking up nine wickets at 25, but he was one of the club's standout performers in second XI cricket last, claiming 13 wickets at 20.69 in the Championship and averaging 30.60 with the bat.

LAST WORD: "This year's his chance. He was in the shadow of Peterson last year and it will be interesting to see how he copes with being attacked by good players, but he's an intelligent lad and should be able to adapt. The club is really desperate to make sure Greg Smith isn't over-bowled like he was last year, so they need Needham to step up." *Mark Eklid*

Batting & Fielding

	Mat	Inns	NO	Runs	HS	Ave	SR	100	50	Ct	St
First-class	19	31	12	384	48	20.21	37.72	0	0	10	0
List A	41	28	11	223	42	13.11	72.40	0	0	13	0
Twenty20	14	5	3	16	7*	8.00	66.66	0	0	4	0

Bowling

	Mat	Balls	Runs	Wkts	BBI	BBM	Ave	Econ	SR	5w	10
First-class	19	2263	1268	35	6/49	-	36.22	3.36	64.6	1	0
List A	41	1365	1176	26	3/36	3/36	45.23	5.16	52.5	0	0
Twenty20	14	159	212	8	4/21	4/21	26.50	8.00	19.8	0	0

NAME: Antonio Paul Palladino
BORN: June 29, 1983, London
HEIGHT: 6ft
SQUAD Nº: 28
NICKNAME: Dino, Italian Stallion
OTHER TEAMS: Essex, Mountaineers, Namibia
CAREER: First-class debut: 2003; List A debut: 2002; T20 debut: 2005

DERBYSHIRE

AOC SAYS: A busy, attacking seamer, Palladino made his first appearance for the Essex Second XI in 2000 and, having turned out for Cambridge MCCU over the preceding three seasons, he made his full county debut in 2003 against the touring Zimbabweans. In his second Championship match he claimed career-best figures of 6-41 against Kent, but further first-team opportunities proved difficult to come by and a dislocated shoulder picked up in 2006 pushed him further down the Chelmsford pecking order. He continued to toil away in the Second XI and in the first team whenever circumstances allowed, and even had a spell playing for Namibia in domestic cricket matches in South Africa during 2009/10, but at the end of last season it became clear he would need to move to further his career, an opportunity that John Morris was happy to offer him.

LAST WORD: "The move to Derbyshire is a fresh start for my career and I will be looking to cement more of a first-team spot in the team. My opportunities in the first team at Essex were sporadic so more first-team cricket is important for me." *Tony Palladino*

Batting & Fielding

	Mat	Inns	NO	Runs	HS	Ave	SR	100	50	Ct	St
First-class	52	66	18	620	66	12.91	41.27	0	2	24	0
List A	35	19	3	125	31	7.81	70.62	0	0	4	0
Twenty20	16	5	3	21	8*	10.50	87.50	0	0	2	0

Bowling

	Mat	Balls	Runs	Wkts	BBI	BBM	Ave	Econ	SR	5w	10
First-class	52	7225	3994	117	6/41	-	34.13	3.31	61.7	2	0
List A	35	1308	1193	33	3/32	3/32	36.15	5.47	39.6	0	0
Twenty20	16	287	347	22	4/21	4/21	15.77	7.25	13.0	0	0

P

GARRY PARK

RHB RMF WK R1

DERBYSHIRE

NAME: Garry Terence Park
BORN: April 19, 1983, Empangeni, South Africa
SQUAD Nº: 9
OTHER TEAMS: Durham
CAREER: First-class debut: 2003; List A debut: 2005; T20 debut: 2007

AOC SAYS: Park started life as a wicketkeeper but since joining Derbyshire he's shelved the gloves and now plays as a nuggety middle-order batsman who can bowl very effective medium-pacers. He moved to the Falcons from Durham in 2008 in search of greater opportunities, and in his first summer at the County Ground passed 1,000 first-class runs for the first time in his career. He was unable to carry that good form through into 2010 and struggled badly at times, although his 124* made down at Worcester reminded everyone how effective he can be. A resourceful batsman who rotates the strike well and one of best fielders in county cricket, Park will be keen to put that season behind him and push on in 2011.

LAST WORD: "After a great debut season, Park struggled for most of last year. I think he maybe tried to become something that he's not; he's one of those guys who digs in and grinds you down. In his first year it felt like he'd score a century in singles if he could, but last season he maybe got a bit too adventurous." *Mark Eklid*

Batting & Fielding

	Mat	Inns	NO	Runs	HS	Ave	SR	100	50	Ct	St
First-class	45	76	10	2335	178*	35.37	46.69	4	14	41	0
List A	38	33	7	648	64	24.92	64.86	0	1	12	0
Twenty20	34	23	3	485	66	24.25	102.32	0	3	7	0

Bowling

	Mat	Balls	Runs	Wkts	BBI	BBM	Ave	Econ	SR	5w	10
First-class	45	1434	958	18	3/25	3/25	53.22	4.00	79.6	0	0
List A	38	556	542	7	2/40	2/40	77.42	5.84	79.4	0	0
Twenty20	34	336	428	19	3/11	3/11	22.52	7.64	17.6	0	0

NAME: Thomas Poynton
BORN: November 25, 1989, Burton-on-Trent,
SQUAD Nº: 23
CAREER: First-class debut: 2007; List A
debut: 2007; T20 debut: 2007

DERBYSHIRE

AOC SAYS: Another former England under 19 international, Poynton will serve as Luke Sutton's understudy this season and will likely play much of his cricket in the county's Second XI. Having come through the club's academy, Poynton was thrust into the first team last season when Lee Goddard lost form, but an unfortunate finger injury put him out of action after only a handful of games and the experienced former Gloucestershire keeper Steve Adshead was drafted in as a short-term stand-in. Reputedly an excellent keeper whose game is characterised by slick glovework and a willingness to stand up to all but the quickest bowlers, Poynton opens the batting successfully for Lullington Park CC in the Derbyshire Premier League but will be keen to improve on his batting performances at second XI level last season – he averaged 12.90 in the Championship.

LAST WORD: "Having Luke Sutton at the club should be good for Poynton; he'll help massively with his development. He strikes you as an intelligent lad who's thoughtful about his game, and he's very highly-rated as a gloveman." *Mark Eklid*

Batting & Fielding

	Mat	Inns	NO	Runs	HS	Ave	SR	100	50	Ct	St
First-class	7	11	0	105	25	9.54	22.92	0	0	12	2
List A	6	3	1	52	24	26.00	104.00	0	0	5	1
Twenty20	2	1	0	3	3	3.00	37.50	0	0	0	2

Bowling

	Mat	Balls	Runs	Wkts	BBI	BBM	Ave	Econ	SR	5w	10
First-class	7	48	96	2	2/96	2/96	48.00	12.00	24.0	0	0
List A	6	-	-	-	-	-	-	-	-	-	-
Twenty20	2	-	-	-	-	-	-	-	-	-	-

DAN REDFERN

LHB OB

NAME: Daniel James Redfern
BORN: April 18, 1990, Shrewsbury
SQUAD Nº: 19
CAREER: First-class debut: 2007; List A debut: 2006; T20 debut: 2008

AOC SAYS: Promising young batsman Redfern was a Championship regular for Derbyshire in 2009 and made a further nine first-class appearances last season, averaging 23.64; a disappointing return for one so talented and one he will be keen to improve upon. He has played two youth Test matches and a string of one-day games for the England under 19 side, and to date has scored eight first-class half-centuries with a best score of 95 that came against Northants in 2009; a summer in which he scored 668 runs at an average of 30.36. A very capable offspinner who has made a habit of breaking difficult partnerships as well as a very safe pair of hands in the field, he will be one of several young batsmen looking to cement a spot in the Falcons' middle-order.

LAST WORD: "He's a very capable player but needs a good year after he underperformed last season. If he can sharpen up his concentration and make sure he cashes in when he gets a start, he should start delivering the scores the club have been hoping for." *Mark Eklid*

Batting & Fielding

	Mat	Inns	NO	Runs	HS	Ave	SR	100	50	Ct	St
First-class	32	51	4	1338	95	28.46	51.12	0	8	17	0
List A	27	24	1	496	57*	21.56	73.26	0	2	5	0
Twenty20	1	1	0	9	9	9.00	81.81	0	0	0	0

Bowling

	Mat	Balls	Runs	Wkts	BBI	BBM	Ave	Econ	SR	5w	10
First-class	32	432	255	5	1/7	2/15	51.00	3.54	86.4	0	0
List A	27	226	188	5	2/10	2/10	37.60	4.99	45.2	0	0
Twenty20	1	-	-	-	-	-	-	-	-	-	-

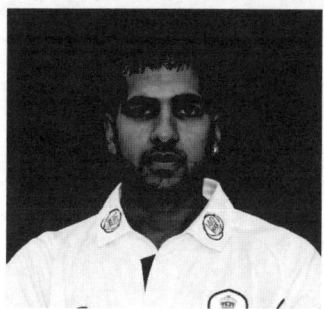

NAME: Atif Sheikh
BORN: February 18, 1991, Nottingham
SQUAD Nº: 99
CAREER: First class debut: 2010

DERBYSHIRE

AOC SAYS: A decidedly rapid left-arm seam bowler who entered the local headlines in
July 2010 when he roughed up the Australian batting line-up during a warm-up match
at the County Ground, dismissing Test openers Shane Watson and Simon Katich on
his way to figures of 2-58 from 15 impressive overs. Earlier that season Sheikh – who
plays club cricket for Attenborough in the Nottinghamshire Premier League – had
celebrated his county debut by claiming match-figures of 5-152 against Gloucestershire
in the Championship, with Gladiators captain Alex Gidman and former New Zealand
international Hamish Marshall among his victims. With two T20Is and a Test at under 19
level already under his belt, it looks likely he will continue his development in the Second
XI for much of the season but will be pushing hard for further first-team opportunities.

LAST WORD: "He's decidedly nippy and really troubled the Aussies during that two-day
match. He doesn't always know where it's going, but he's a good prospect. He's a flat
skiddy bowler who seams it a little bit but pace is definitely his major weapon." *Mark Eklid*

Batting & Fielding

	Mat	Inns	NO	Runs	HS	Ave	SR	100	50	Ct	St
First-class	1	2	0	6	6	3.00	21.42	0	0	1	0

Bowling

	Mat	Balls	Runs	Wkts	BBI	BBM	Ave	Econ	SR	5w	10
First-class	1	150	152	5	3/78	5/152	30.40	6.08	30.0	0	0

HAMZA SIDDIQUE

DERBYSHIRE

NAME: Hamza Ghani Siddique
BORN: January 19, 1991, Stoke-on-Trent
SQUAD Nº: 14
CAREER: Yet to make first-team debut

AOC SAYS: A top-order batsman by trade, Siddique broke the record for the highest innings ever made by a student at Repton School when he amassed 207 not out against Wolverhampton Grammar in 2008, a record that had previously stood for 94 years. A heavy runscorer at academy level who captained the Repton First XI to the National Twenty20 Championship in 2008, he plays for Moddershall in the North Staffordshire and South Cheshire Premier League and scored 328 Second XI Championship runs at an average of 27.33 last season, with a best of 101* that came against Worcestershire at Belper Meadows. However, he met with less success in the Second XI trophy, averaging just 8.60 across five innings. A former student of Denstone College, Siddique has played club cricket in Melbourne and marked his Second XI debut in 2009 by making a composed 47* against Warwickshire.

LAST WORD: "We've been impressed by the strides Hamza has made and we are excited about what he can achieve." *John Morris*

EXTRAS

"I don't look around and think in terms of what we've not got, I think we've got plenty and if we don't do well in all three forms of the game, I will see that as a major disappointment. What happened last year with Derbyshire is in the past. I don't give it that much thought." Luke Sutton

NAME: Benjamin Thomas Slater
BORN: August 26, 1991, Chesterfield
SQUAD №: 26
CAREER: Yet to make first-team debut

DERBYSHIRE

AOC SAYS: A heavy runscorer for Chesterfield CC in the Derbyshire Premier League, the same club that Falcons stalwart and current physio James Pipe plays for, Slater is an opening batsman who has come through the Derbyshire age groups and been awarded a summer contract for the 2011 season. He was one of the success stories of the club's Second XI last season, scoring 392 runs across 12 Championship innings at an average of 32.66 with four half-centuries and a top score of 86. He is currently studying for a Sports Business Management degree at Leeds Metropolitan University and turned out for Leeds/ Bradford MCCU, with whom he toured South Africa in 2009/10.

LAST WORD: "Slater is an exciting talent but we don't want to put pressure on him too early." *Karl Krikken, Derbyshire academy director*

EXTRAS

Derbyshire will receive a £300,000 ECB grant in 2011. Don Amott, the Derbyshire chairman, said: "The club have been developing their county home ground in the last few years and the cash from the ECB will go towards continuing that work. This ECB grant is a timely boost and rich reward for the hard work and vision it took from all concerned to bring the improvements to the ground to fruition."

GREG SMITH

NAME: Gregory Marc Smith
BORN: April 20, 1983, Johannesburg
HEIGHT: 6ft 2in
SQUAD Nº: 83
NICKNAME: Smithy
OTHER TEAMS: Griqualand West, Mountaineers
CAREER: First-class debut: 2003; List A debut: 2003; T20 debut: 2007; County cap: 2009

AOC SAYS: An adaptable allrounder and a key member of the Derbyshire squad, Smith came through the ranks at Griqualand West and played for South Africa under 19s during the 2002 World Cup. A dangerous middle-order strokemaker and a brilliant fielder at point, he is a resourceful seamer who often surprises the batsman with his pace off the pitch and an improving offspinner capable of giving the ball a big rip, and with Robin Peterson having left the club it is this latter skill that could come to the fore this season. Smith joined Derbyshire in 2004 as a Kolpak player and skippered the side for part of last season after Chris Rogers stood down from the role. He has spent the winter playing for the Mountaineers franchise in Zimbabwe, averaging 44.16 in first-class cricket with a top-score of 118.

LAST WORD: "He was overworked as a bowler last year and towards the end of the season it really started affecting his game. They need to make sure they don't do that again this season." *Mark Eklid*

Batting & Fielding

	Mat	Inns	NO	Runs	HS	Ave	SR	100	50	Ct	St
First-class	75	128	10	3573	165*	30.27	54.08	4	24	22	0
List A	66	66	5	1479	88	24.24	84.80	0	6	25	0
Twenty20	48	46	2	973	100*	22.11	113.93	1	4	19	0

Bowling

	Mat	Balls	Runs	Wkts	BBI	BBM	Ave	Econ	SR	5w	10
First-class	75	7779	4238	120	5/54	-	35.31	3.26	64.8	2	0
List A	66	1801	1703	52	4/53	4/53	32.75	5.67	34.6	0	0
Twenty20	48	502	663	27	5/27	5/27	24.55	7.92	18.5	1	0

NAME: Luke David Sutton
BORN: October 4, 1976, Keynsham
HEIGHT: 5ft 11in
SQUAD Nº: 10
NICKNAME: Sutts
OTHER TEAMS: Lancashire, Somerset
CAREER: First-class debut: 1997; List A
debut: 1998; T20 debut: 2003; County cap:
2002 (Derbyshire), 2007 (Lancashire)

DERBYSHIRE

AOC SAYS: One of the most popular characters on the county circuit, Sutton has returned
to Derbyshire as captain after five seasons at Old Trafford. Swift and assured behind the
stumps, he is an organised, orthodox batsman who can be relied upon to steady the innings
when required. He began his career at Somerset but moved to Derbyshire in 2000 in search
of regular cricket and established himself as a firm favourite at the County Ground. He
inherited the captaincy in trying circumstances in 2004, after Dominic Cork resigned and his
earmarked replacement Michael Di Venuto was forced to miss the season through injury.
Sutton did an admirable job for two seasons before moving on to Lancashire in 2006, where
he instantly looked at home as he made 666 first-class runs at 51.23, including a career-best
151* against Yorkshire, the highest first-class score by a Red Rose wicketkeeper.

LAST WORD: "He's a natural leader. He's signed a two-year deal and is talking about
seeing out his career at Derbyshire. He's hugely popular at the club and looks a really good
appointment – he'll be a big influence on the pitch and in the dressing room." *Mark Eklid*

Batting & Fielding

	Mat	Inns	NO	Runs	HS	Ave	SR	100	50	Ct	St
First-class	160	254	39	6780	151*	31.53	-	11	19	408	22
List A	159	132	28	2055	83	19.75	-	0	6	176	24
Twenty20	16	14	4	306	61*	30.60	111.27	0	1	9	7

Bowling

	Mat	Balls	Runs	Wkts	BBI	BBM	Ave	Econ	SR	5w	10
First-class	160	-	-	-	-	-	-	-	-	-	-
List A	159	-	-	-	-	-	-	-	-	-	-
Twenty20	16	-	-	-	-	-	-	-	-	-	-

MARK TURNER

RHB RMF

DERBYSHIRE

NAME: Mark Leif Turner
BORN: October 23, 1984, Sunderland
HEIGHT: 5ft 11in
SQUAD Nº: 6
NICKNAME: Tina
OTHER TEAMS: Somerset
CAREER: First-class debut: 2005; List A
debut: 2007; T20 debut: 2005

AOC SAYS: A lively, aggressive strike bowler who possesses a sharp bouncer, Turner began his career at Durham bowling alongside England internationals Steve Harmison, Liam Plunkett and Graham Onions, so unsurprisingly he found first-team opportunities difficult to come by. A former England under 19 international who was included in the ECB's 2008 Fast Bowling Programme, he moved to Somerset in 2006 in search of regular cricket and became a fixture in their one-day side, specialising in breaking tricky partnerships with a mixture of yorkers and slower balls, although he proved expensive on occasion. However, his Championship appearances proved few and far between and at the end of last season he signed a two-year deal with Derbyshire in the hope of more regular four-day cricket.

LAST WORD: "The fact that he has been prepared to make this move in search of first-team cricket demonstrates that Mark is an ambitious cricketer who is striving to better himself. That is just the kind of player we want to bring to Derbyshire." *John Morris*

Batting & Fielding

	Mat	Inns	NO	Runs	HS	Ave	SR	100	50	Ct	St
First-class	9	8	2	89	57	14.83	65.92	0	1	3	0
List A	22	9	5	49	15*	12.25	64.47	0	0	5	0
Twenty20	33	10	4	25	11*	4.16	69.44	0	0	6	0

Bowling

	Mat	Balls	Runs	Wkts	BBI	BBM	Ave	Econ	SR	5w	10
First-class	9	1323	853	17	4/30	-	50.17	3.86	77.8	0	0
List A	22	802	820	31	4/36	4/36	26.45	6.13	25.8	0	0
Twenty20	33	564	837	30	3/25	3/25	27.90	8.90	18.8	0	0

NAME: Ross Andrew Whiteley
BORN: September 13, 1988, Sheffield
SQUAD Nº: 44
CAREER: First-class debut: 2008; List A
debut: 2008

DERBYSHIRE

AOC SAYS: A big-hitting allrounder who loves to smash the ball back down the ground,
Whiteley made his county debut against Glamorgan in a Pro40 game during the 2008
season and has been a consistent performer in the club's Second XI for some time now.
He made the local press last year when he smashed a remarkable 204 not out off just 117
balls for Chesterfield against Alfreton, a knock that included 18 sixes as well as 18 fours. It
was the fourth highest score ever made in the Derbyshire Premier League and an excellent
indication of how dangerous a player he can be. Also a handy seamer who can tie up
an end, he is the younger brother of Adam who played several Second XI matches for
Derbyshire between 2003 and 2007.

LAST WORD: "He's very destructive on his day and could be a good impact batter down
the order in Twenty20 and the CB40. He's making a serious effort to turn a summer contract
into a full-time deal, although he needs to work on his bowling if he's going to be a genuine
all-round option" *Mark Eklid*

Batting & Fielding

	Mat	Inns	NO	Runs	HS	Ave	SR	100	50	Ct	St
First-class	1	2	0	45	27	22.50	39.82	0	0	0	0
List A	4	3	0	41	24	13.66	87.23	0	0	2	0

Bowling

	Mat	Balls	Runs	Wkts	BBI	BBM	Ave	Econ	SR	5w	10
First-class	1	66	38	0	-	-	-	3.45	-	0	0
List A	4	24	28	0	-	-	-	7.00	-	0	0

FORMED: 1882
HOME GROUND: Emirates Durham International Cricket Ground
ONE-DAY NAME: Dynamos
CAPTAIN: Phil Mustard (Championship)/Dale Benkenstein (Limited-overs)
2010 RESULTS: CC1: 5/9; CB40: 5/7 in Group C; FP t20: 8/9 in North Group

HONOURS
County Championship: (2) 2008, 2009; Gillette/NatWest/C&G/FP Trophy: 2007

THE LOWDOWN
Last season was largely a tale of frustration for Durham. Having successfully defended their Championship title in 2009 they were heavily fancied to repeat this achievement in 2010, but a swathe of injuries to their seam attack robbed them of their bowling potency and they struggled to force results in four-day cricket. Coupled with the loss of form of skipper Will Smith – one of their leading batsmen in previous seasons but so short of runs at the start of the year that he handed over the captaincy to Phil Mustard – and some erratic displays in one-day cricket, 2010 will go down as a season to forget at Chester-le-Street. However, with the likes of Steve Harmison, Graham Onions and Callum Thorp all returning to fitness, the continued development of the likes of youngsters Scott Borthwick and Ben Harmison, and the news that Paul Collingwood will be available for at least a portion of the season following his retirement from Test cricket, 2011 could well be a very different story.

DIRECTOR OF CRICKET: GEOFF COOK
An opening batsman for Northants, Durham, Eastern Province and England, Cook holds the honour of being Durham's first county captain. Following his retirement from the game he took charge of the club's youth academy, and in 2007 he was promoted and placed in charge of the first team. He subsequently guided the club to victory in the Friends Provident Trophy, their first silverware, in 2007 and successive Championships in 2008 and 2009.

With thanks to: Geoff Cook; Tim Wellock, Durham correspondent, Northern Echo; Luke Edwards, chief sports writer, The Journal

	Mat	Inns	NO	Runs	HS	Ave	SR	100	50	Ct	St
MJ Di Venuto	17	28	3	1223	131	48.92	58.99	4	7	30	-
BA Stokes	14	21	3	798	161*	44.33	67.62	2	3	8	-
P Mustard	17	26	6	815	120	40.75	56.59	2	5	43	2
KJ Coetzer	8	15	2	526	172	40.46	46.26	1	3	3	-
GJ Muchall	10	15	1	520	140*	37.14	48.10	2	1	3	-
ID Blackwell	16	26	2	833	86	34.70	66.80	0	8	2	-
MD Stoneman	11	17	1	525	118	32.81	51.21	1	4	5	-
DM Benkenstein	17	28	1	840	114	31.11	47.53	1	5	14	-
BW Harmison	6	10	0	286	96	28.60	37.23	0	2	0	-
CD Thorp	6	8	2	143	79*	23.83	66.20	0	1	3	-
SG Borthwick	12	17	3	315	68	22.50	50.64	0	2	9	-
WR Smith	6	10	0	195	57	19.50	37.00	0	1	3	-
ME Claydon	13	16	4	185	38*	15.41	54.73	0	0	2	-
LE Plunkett	14	17	0	238	51	14.00	46.66	0	1	8	-
PD Collingwood	1	1	0	12	12	12.00	70.58	0	0	0	-
M Davies	6	5	2	32	27	10.66	29.62	0	0	0	-
C Rushworth	9	14	2	127	28	10.58	56.19	0	0	1	-
GR Breese	2	3	0	27	14	9.00	45.76	0	0	1	-
SJ Harmison	10	12	6	36	11*	6.00	29.75	0	0	2	-
RMR Brathwaite	1	2	1	2	2	2.00	20.00	0	0	0	-
MJ Richardson	1	1	0	2	2	2.00	28.57	0	0	0	0
L Evans	1	1	1	4	4*	-	50.00	0	0	0	-

Batting & Fielding

	Mat	Overs	Mdn	Runs	Wkts	BBI	BBM	Ave	Econ	SR	5w	10
PD Collingwood	1	7.0	3	11	1	1/11	1/11	11.00	1.57	42.0	0	0
SJ Harmison	10	265.4	55	895	34	7/29	9/74	26.32	3.36	46.8	1	0
ID Blackwell	16	488.3	139	1291	47	5/78	9/180	27.46	2.64	62.3	2	0
CD Thorp	6	158.3	46	452	16	4/54	4/77	28.25	2.85	59.4	0	0
BW Harmison	6	86.4	10	402	14	4/70	6/98	28.71	4.63	37.1	0	0
RMR Brathwaite	1	30.1	2	118	4	3/93	4/118	29.50	3.91	45.2	0	0
SG Borthwick	12	173.4	20	702	23	4/27	8/84	30.52	4.04	45.3	0	0
ME Claydon	13	303.1	53	1140	35	3/17	5/111	32.57	3.76	51.9	0	0
DM Benkenstein	17	81.0	43	143	4	2/17	2/17	35.75	1.76	121.5	0	0
C Rushworth	9	214.4	43	821	21	4/90	5/159	39.09	3.82	61.3	0	0
LE Plunkett	14	384.4	57	1386	35	4/107	6/193	39.60	3.60	65.9	0	0
BA Stokes	14	75.3	7	365	6	2/32	3/47	60.83	4.83	75.5	0	0
M Davies	6	131.0	47	282	2	2/10	2/10	141.00	2.15	393.0	0	0
GR Breese	2	3.0	1	5	0	-	-	-	1.66	-	0	0
KJ Coetzer	8	7.0	0	33	0	-	-	-	4.71	-	0	0
L Evans	1	2.0	0	11	0	-	-	-	5.50	-	0	0
GJ Muchall	10	1.0	0	2	0	-	-	-	2.00	-	0	0
WR Smith	6	4.0	0	27	0	-	-	-	6.75	-	0	0

Bowling

DURHAM DYNAMOS

Batting & Fielding

	Mat	Inns	NO	Runs	HS	Ave	SR	100	50	Ct	St
KJ Coetzer	2	2	1	43	35	43.00	75.43	0	0	1	-
GJ Muchall	11	11	2	318	77	35.33	76.25	0	1	9	-
MJ Di Venuto	4	4	0	134	63	33.50	105.51	0	1	3	-
BW Harmison	11	11	1	323	52	32.30	70.67	0	1	3	-
WR Smith	5	5	2	88	50*	29.33	101.14	0	1	0	-
P Mustard	11	11	0	304	90	27.63	84.44	0	3	9	6
GR Breese	11	8	1	171	42	24.42	104.26	0	0	6	-
DM Benkenstein	5	5	0	110	34	22.00	83.33	0	0	3	-
BA Stokes	10	10	1	182	39	20.22	86.25	0	0	3	-
ID Blackwell	10	10	0	196	35	19.60	94.68	0	0	0	-
MD Stoneman	4	4	0	73	25	18.25	89.02	0	0	2	-
SG Borthwick	4	4	3	16	10*	16.00	48.48	0	0	0	-
ME Claydon	6	5	3	20	9*	10.00	105.26	0	0	0	-
SJ Harmison	3	1	0	8	8	8.00	100.00	0	0	1	-
C Rushworth	9	4	2	15	7*	7.50	78.94	0	0	2	-
LE Plunkett	8	6	2	29	12*	7.25	85.29	0	0	2	-
N Killeen	2	1	0	6	6	6.00	54.54	0	0	0	-
L Evans	2	1	1	1	1*	-	33.33	0	0	1	-

Bowling

	Mat	Overs	Mdns	Runs	Wkts	BBI	Ave	Econ	SR	5w
WRS Gidman	2	10.4	0	54	6	4/36	9.00	5.06	10.6	0
DM Benkenstein	5	6.0	0	27	3	3/27	9.00	4.50	12.0	0
BA Stokes	10	8.0	0	43	3	2/22	14.33	5.37	16.0	0
C Rushworth	9	52.0	7	226	15	3/6	15.06	4.34	20.8	0
N Killeen	2	12.0	1	67	3	3/24	22.33	5.58	24.0	0
ID Blackwell	10	56.2	1	275	10	3/22	27.50	4.88	33.8	0
ME Claydon	6	36.5	2	189	6	3/51	31.50	5.13	36.8	0
SJ Harmison	3	13.0	0	63	2	2/17	31.50	4.84	39.0	0
GR Breese	11	60.4	0	327	9	2/13	36.33	5.39	40.4	0
LE Plunkett	8	30.5	0	192	5	2/46	38.40	6.22	37.0	0
BW Harmison	11	42.0	3	252	6	2/13	42.00	6.00	42.0	0
L Evans	2	10.0	0	61	1	1/28	61.00	6.10	60.0	0
SG Borthwick	4	12.0	0	66	1	1/40	66.00	5.50	72.0	0
M Davies	1	8.0	1	51	0	-	-	6.37	-	0
GJ Muchall	11	1.0	0	7	0	-	-	7.00	-	0

DURHAM DYNAMOS

	Mat	Inns	NO	Runs	HS	Ave	SR	100	50	Ct	St
LRPL Taylor	11	9	1	315	80*	39.37	173.07	0	2	4	-
JA Morkel	15	11	3	272	48	34.00	128.90	0	0	1	-
MD Stoneman	3	3	0	85	46	28.33	100.00	0	0	1	-
LE Plunkett	13	7	3	102	31	25.50	141.66	0	0	2	-
DM Benkenstein	15	13	3	249	57*	24.90	125.75	0	1	2	-
P Mustard	15	13	1	284	70*	23.66	124.56	0	2	11	3
ID Blackwell	12	10	0	198	79	19.80	125.31	0	1	2	-
BW Harmison	11	6	3	51	24	17.00	175.86	0	0	2	-
BA Stokes	15	12	1	180	44	16.36	108.43	0	0	4	-
GR Breese	15	8	3	75	30*	15.00	97.40	0	0	9	-
WR Smith	10	5	1	41	19	10.25	100.00	0	0	2	-
GJ Muchall	4	3	0	30	16	10.00	90.90	0	0	1	-
SJ Harmison	12	2	1	0	0*	0.00	0.00	0	0	0	-
ME Claydon	8	1	1	0	0*	-	-	0	0	1	-

	Mat	Overs	Mdns	Runs	Wkts	BBI	Ave	Econ	SR	5w
PD Collingwood	2	6.2	0	34	4	4/13	8.50	5.36	9.5	0
SJ Harmison	12	33.0	0	283	14	5/41	20.21	8.57	14.1	1
GR Breese	15	35.5	1	242	11	3/14	22.00	6.75	19.5	0
ID Blackwell	12	29.0	0	213	8	2/14	26.62	7.34	21.7	0
BW Harmison	11	27.0	0	228	8	2/22	28.50	8.44	20.2	0
BA Stokes	15	5.0	0	37	1	1/23	37.00	7.40	30.0	0
LE Plunkett	13	32.0	0	291	7	2/18	41.57	9.09	27.4	0
JA Morkel	15	33.2	0	297	7	2/25	42.42	8.91	28.5	0
DM Benkenstein	15	5.0	0	48	1	1/9	48.00	9.60	30.0	0
ME Claydon	8	23.0	0	209	4	1/17	52.25	9.08	34.5	0
N Killeen	2	6.0	0	54	1	1/35	54.00	9.00	36.0	0
SG Borthwick	2	0.2	0	3	0	-	-	9.00	-	0
WR Smith	10	11.5	0	93	0	-	-	7.85	-	0

DALE BENKENSTEIN   RHB RM MVP95 R4

DURHAM

NAME: Dale Martin Benkenstein
BORN: June 9, 1974, Harare
HEIGHT: 5ft 10in
SQUAD Nº: 44
OTHER TEAMS: South Africa, Delhi Giants, Dolphins, KwaZulu-Natal, Natal
CAREER: ODI debut: 1998; First-class debut: 1993; List A debut: 1992; T20 debut: 2004

AOC SAYS: A quiet, undemonstrative institution of county cricket. The man who masterminded the Durham revolution, dragging a struggling side up by its bootlaces, firstly making it tough to beat, then tough to repel, and finally turning Durham into the most feared team in the land. Benkenstein's crowning glory arrived in 2008 when he became the man who lifted the County Championship trophy for the first time in Durham's history. Job done, he promptly passed on the captaincy, but after two years scoring useful runs as a foot soldier in 2009 and 2010, he returns to lead the one-day side in 2011. In a garlanded career that includes 23 ODIs for South Africa he has won nine trophies as a captain, both for Durham and for Natal in South Africa. Universally respected throughout the club, he is likely to stay on in a coaching capacity at Durham when he finally retires.

LAST WORD: "Hugely instrumental in our turnaround. He took over a team that had just avoided relegation, led by example and the team followed." *Geoff Cook*

Batting & Fielding

	Mat	Inns	NO	Runs	HS	Ave	SR	100	50	Ct	St
ODIs	23	20	3	305	69	17.94	65.87	0	1	3	0
First-class	226	343	38	13741	259	45.05	-	34	72	153	0
List A	279	252	58	6826	107*	35.18	-	1	42	104	0
Twenty20	74	70	14	1428	57*	25.50	126.25	0	4	25	0

Bowling

	Mat	Balls	Runs	Wkts	BBI	BBM	Ave	Econ	SR	5w	10
ODIs	23	65	44	4	3/5	3/5	11.00	4.06	16.2	0	0
First-class	226	7037	3375	97	4/16	-	34.79	2.87	72.5	0	0
List A	279	3071	2572	86	4/16	4/16	29.90	5.02	35.7	0	0
Twenty20	74	366	455	16	3/10	3/10	28.43	7.45	22.8	0	0

NAME: Ian David Blackwell
BORN: June 10, 1978, Chesterfield
HEIGHT: 6ft 2in
SQUAD Nº: 37
NICKNAME: Black Dog, Donk, Ying, Goatage
OTHER TEAMS: England, Central Districts, Derbyshire, Somerset
CAREER: Test debut: 2006; ODI debut: 2002; First-class debut: 1997; List A debut: 1997; T20 debut: 2003; County cap: 2001 (Somerset)

DURHAM

AOC SAYS: One of county cricket's characters, Blackwell has been brilliant for Durham since moving up from Somerset for the 2009 season, bringing flair and unpredictability to their middle-order, and street-smart nous to their spin-bowling department. Good enough in terms of talent to play both Test and ODI cricket, but his hefty frame and love of the good things in life didn't exactly correspond to the England set-up's strict fitness requirements. His county career is littered with outstanding individual feats: he became the first batsman in Championship history to score two hundreds in the same match from No.7 in the order; he hit a 134-ball double century versus Derbyshire at Taunton in 2003, the fastest by an Englishman in terms of balls faced, and has 12 five-wicket hauls in his 181 first-class matches.

LAST WORD: "You tend to find that when he's playing well Durham are playing well."
Luke Edwards

Batting & Fielding

	Mat	Inns	NO	Runs	HS	Ave	SR	100	50	Ct	St
Tests	1	1	0	4	4	4.00	25.00	0	0	0	0
ODIs	34	29	2	403	82	14.92	86.66	0	1	8	0
First-class	181	271	21	9936	247*	39.74	-	23	55	61	0
List A	241	222	18	5533	134*	27.12	-	3	33	60	0
Twenty20	61	56	7	988	82	20.16	132.97	0	4	14	0

Bowling

	Mat	Balls	Runs	Wkts	BBI	BBM	Ave	Econ	SR	5w	10
Tests	1	114	71	0	-	-	-	3.73	-	0	0
ODIs	34	1230	877	24	3/26	3/26	36.54	4.27	51.2	0	0
First-class	181	27354	12431	333	7/85	-	37.33	2.72	82.1	12	0
List A	241	8393	6697	194	5/26	5/26	34.52	4.78	43.2	1	0
Twenty20	61	1111	1293	46	4/26	4/26	28.10	6.98	24.1	0	0

SCOTT BORTHWICK

DURHAM

NAME: Scott George Borthwick
BORN: April 19, 1990, Sunderland
SQUAD Nº: 16
CAREER: First-class debut: 2009; List A debut: 2009; T20 debut: 2008

AOC SAYS: Durham are cautiously excited about their feisty legspinning allrounder. A multi-faceted cricketer whose versatility sees him adept at all formats, he is a genuine 50-50 allrounder, able to bat in the top three in Championship cricket – as he did for large parts of last season – and bowl the final overs of a Twenty20 match. He has been out in Adelaide for the winter on an ECB scholarship, fine-tuning his skills in readiness for what could be a breakthrough season. Durham are aware he has yet to carve out a place in this team, but even considering the incredible challenges standing in the way of young legspinners in county cricket, they are quietly confident that Borthwick, another local lad, has the tools to get the job done.

LAST WORD: "When you look at the characteristics that a young guy needs to make it, irrespective of whether he's a legspin bowler or a batsman, the psychological and physical characteristics, Borthwick carries a few of those with him." *Geoff Cook*

Batting & Fielding

	Mat	Inns	NO	Runs	HS	Ave	SR	100	50	Ct	St
First-class	13	18	4	341	68	24.35	50.14	0	2	9	0
List A	10	6	5	21	10*	21.00	46.66	0	0	4	0
Twenty20	5	-	-	-	-	-	-	-	-	2	0

Bowling

	Mat	Balls	Runs	Wkts	BBI	BBM	Ave	Econ	SR	5w	10
First-class	13	1204	797	26	4/27	8/84	30.65	3.97	46.3	0	0
List A	10	192	244	5	2/11	2/11	48.80	7.62	38.4	0	0
Twenty20	5	38	58	3	3/23	3/23	19.33	9.15	12.6	0	0

NAME: Ruel Marlon Ricardo Brathwaite
BORN: September 6, 1985, Barbados
SQUAD Nº: 8
CAREER: First-class debut: 2006; List A
debut: 2007; T20 debut: 2010

DURHAM

AOC SAYS: With the acquisition of Bajan seamer Brathwaite, Durham have taken a punt on a largely untested talent. But a cursory glance at his fiery performances last year on trial with the Chester-le-Street club would suggest a canny bit of business. At 25 he is older than many other quicks lurking on the outskirts of county cricket, but the flipside is that without too many miles on the clock, he will be sharp and fresh. Barbados-born, he has played for various representative sides ranging from Loughborough MCCU, to the MCC, to the Surrey Second XI. After doing the rounds, Durham have snapped him up. They will be hoping he can complement the other top-class seamers on the staff.

LAST WORD: "He has a lot of raw talent and impressed the club on trial last season. He's one for the future and could learn from the other bowlers in the group." *Luke Edwards*

Batting & Fielding

	Mat	Inns	NO	Runs	HS	Ave	SR	100	50	Ct	St
First-class	13	14	4	144	76*	14.40	57.14	0	1	0	0
List A	1	-	-	-	-	-	-	-	-	0	0
Twenty20	1	1	0	0	0	0.00	0.00	0	0	0	0

Bowling

	Mat	Balls	Runs	Wkts	BBI	BBM	Ave	Econ	SR	5w	10
First-class	13	2163	1294	30	5/54	8/130	43.13	3.58	72.1	1	0
List A	1	18	19	1	1/19	1/19	19.00	6.33	18.0	0	0
Twenty20	1	18	33	1	1/33	1/33	33.00	11.00	18.0	0	0

DURHAM

GARETH BREESE

RHB OB

NAME: Gareth Rohan Breese
BORN: January 9, 1976, Montego Bay, Jamaica
HEIGHT: 5ft 8in
SQUAD Nº: 70
NICKNAME: Briggy
OTHER TEAMS: West Indies, Jamaica
CAREER: Test debut: 2002; First-class debut: 1995; List A debut: 1996; T20 debut: 2004

AOC SAYS: A popular presence at Durham since joining the club in 2004, West Indian Breese has served the club well whenever called upon. An offspinning allrounder who has carved out a very good career both in England and for Jamaica, his game is probably best suited to the cut and thrust of one-day cricket, although his most famous feat in a Durham shirt will always be the triumphant century (121*) he made against Kent to clinch the club's inaugural County Championship. He only played two Championship matches last season but was a regular fixture in the one-day team, and 2011 will see more of the same. He played a single Test for the West Indies in 2002, without much success, before decamping to England for good.

LAST WORD: "Although he's approaching the end of his time as a county cricketer, his experience will means he's still going to be an important member of the one-day attack."
Tim Wellock

Batting & Fielding

	Mat	Inns	NO	Runs	HS	Ave	SR	100	50	Ct	St
Tests	1	2	0	5	5	2.50	19.23	0	0	1	0
First-class	116	185	20	4359	165*	26.41	-	4	27	96	0
List A	149	114	28	1740	68*	20.23	-	0	3	61	0
Twenty20	61	40	9	358	37	11.54	110.83	0	0	26	0

Bowling

	Mat	Balls	Runs	Wkts	BBI	BBM	Ave	Econ	SR	5w	10
Tests	1	188	135	2	2/108	2/135	67.50	4.30	94.0	0	0
First-class	116	18093	8369	280	7/60	-	29.88	2.77	64.6	12	3
List A	149	5704	4414	155	5/41	5/41	28.47	4.64	36.8	2	0
Twenty20	61	1032	1156	54	4/14	4/14	21.40	6.72	19.1	0	0

NAME: Mitchell Eric Claydon
BORN: November 25, 1982, Fairfield, Australia
HEIGHT: 6ft 4in
SQUAD Nº: 25
NICKNAME: Lips
OTHER TEAMS: Canterbury, Yorkshire
CAREER: First-class debut: 2005; List A
debut: 2006; T20 debut: 2006

DURHAM

AOC SAYS: A strapping Australian hulk of a man who booms in for Durham whenever called upon and is often very effective with the new ball. Along with Liam Plunkett he was Durham's second-highest Championship wicket-taker last term, capping a breakthrough season for the New South Welshman after three years in the ranks at Durham. In the off-season he played for Canterbury in New Zealand's Plunket Shield, taking six cheap wickets in his first match. A huge rugby fan and a keen surfer, Claydon is the beach bum in Geordieland.

LAST WORD: "He's a steadily improving player, a happy-go-lucky sort of person who brings a bit of humour to the dressing room. He is a big, strong lad who bowls quite quickly but his problem is he's inconsistent. If he can find that consistency he'll probably play a bit more often but again only if there are others missing; he wouldn't be a part of the first-choice attack." *Tim Wellock*

Batting & Fielding

	Mat	Inns	NO	Runs	HS	Ave	SR	100	50	Ct	St
First-class	32	34	6	404	40	14.42	56.74	0	0	5	0
List A	33	16	3	99	19	7.61	91.66	0	0	1	0
Twenty20	28	9	6	40	12*	13.33	125.00	0	0	7	0

Bowling

	Mat	Balls	Runs	Wkts	BBI	BBM	Ave	Econ	SR	5w	10
First-class	32	4268	2548	76	4/90	-	33.52	3.58	56.1	0	0
List A	33	1476	1173	40	4/39	4/39	29.32	4.76	36.9	0	0
Twenty20	28	565	751	27	5/26	5/26	27.81	7.97	20.9	1	0

KYLE COETZER

RHB RM

DURHAM

NAME: Kyle James Coetzer
BORN: April 14, 1984, Aberdeen
HEIGHT: 5ft 11in
SQUAD Nº: 30
NICKNAME: Costa, Meerkat
OTHER TEAMS: Scotland, Western Province
CAREER: ODI debut: 2008; T20I debut: 2008;
First-class debut: 2004; List A debut: 2003;
T20 debut: 2007

AOC SAYS: An adaptable top-order batsman and a brilliant fielder, Coetzer started last summer in fine form, smashing 224 runs in the traditional season opener against MCC, but he couldn't quite carry that form into the rest of the season and eventually lost his place to upcoming opener Mark Stoneman. A Scotland international who produced arguably the catch of the 2009 ICC World Twenty20, a spectacular one-handed grab at long-on to dismiss Mark Boucher, Coetzer is a key part of the Saltires' team and has on occasion been given dispensation to appear for them in the CB40 when Durham haven't required his services.

LAST WORD: "He'll get a game if he's in form. He did well at the start of the season and then faded so Stoneman came in and Coetzer didn't get another chance. He'll have to score runs in the Second XI to merit a place in the first team, but as we saw last year the opening partnership isn't nailed down; there's a good chance he'll get it back. He's quite an ambitious lad and he'll be determined to get his spot back this summer." *Tim Wellock*

Batting & Fielding

	Mat	Inns	NO	Runs	HS	Ave	SR	100	50	Ct	St
ODIs	5	5	0	132	51	26.40	75.86	0	1	3	0
T20Is	9	9	1	234	48*	29.25	104.00	0	0	2	0
First-class	43	76	9	2259	172	33.71	48.79	5	7	26	0
List A	58	56	7	1479	127	30.18	74.92	1	9	22	0
Twenty20	23	22	2	469	64	23.45	104.92	0	1	5	0

Bowling

	Mat	Balls	Runs	Wkts	BBI	BBM	Ave	Econ	SR	5w	10
ODIs	5	12	23	0	-	-	-	11.50	-	0	0
T20Is	9	48	47	5	3/25	3/25	9.40	5.87	9.6	0	0
First-class	43	162	83	2	2/16	2/16	41.50	3.07	81.0	0	0
List A	58	96	96	0	-	-	-	6.00	-	0	0
Twenty20	23	78	85	6	3/25	3/25	14.16	6.53	13.0	0	0

NAME: Paul David Collingwood
BORN: May 26, 1976, Shotley Bridge
HEIGHT: 5ft 11in
SQUAD Nº: 5
NICKNAME: Colly
MAJOR TEAMS: England, Delhi Daredevils
CAREER: Test debut: 2003; ODI debut: 2001;
T20I debut: 2005; First-class debut: 1996;
List A debut: 1995; T20 debut: 2005

DURHAM

AOC SAYS: Collingwood has called time on a Test career that has encompassed three Ashes victories, finishing with a better average than Michael Atherton and more centuries than Ted Dexter; not bad for a player constantly having to battle the perception he was playing above himself. Having undergone an operation on his knee following England's defeat in the World Cup, he will miss the early part of the season, although as he was already scheduled to be away playing for Rajasthan Royals in the IPL, Durham will not be too inconvenienced. A consummate team-man, Collingwood is most famous for his ability to play defiant rearguard innings, such as his 245-ball epic at Cardiff in 2009 that kept England level in the series, but that is to do a disservice to a man who has consistently shown he can adapt his game to suit any situation. England's most-capped one-day player marked his first-class debut for Durham in 1996 by taking a wicket with his first delivery, and he became a key part of the side over the following seasons, eventually earning himself a call-up to the England one-day side in 2001. He didn't enjoy the greatest of starts, but he won the respect of coach Duncan Fletcher and gradually began to look the part at international level. A Test debut against Sri Lanka followed in 2003, and then two years later he produced the finest all-round performance by an Englishman in ODIs, hitting 112* and claming 6-31 against Bangladesh. Later that summer he was memorably called up for the final Test of the epic 2005 Ashes series, and while his innings of 10 would later attract derision from Shane Warne, everyone who saw that game knew its true value. From then on he grew into an international batsman of real stature, making a double-hundred during England's gut-wrenching defeat at Adelaide in 2006, scoring runs in all conditions and against all opponents, and in 2009 becoming the first captain to lead England to an international trophy by skippering them to victory in the ICC World Twenty20 in the Caribbean. If he can return to his best following surgery and an exhausting winter, Durham's middle-order will look very potent indeed.

INSIDE TRACK: "He wants to play as much as he can for Durham but we won't see him until the Twenty20 starts. We'll be monitoring his enthusiasm and accepting how he feels about things but at this stage he's talking very positively." *Geoff Cook*

PAUL COLLINGWOOD

DURHAM

Batting & Fielding											
	Mat	Inns	NO	Runs	HS	Ave	SR	100	50	Ct	St
Tests	68	115	10	4259	206	40.56	46.44	10	20	96	0
ODIs	197	181	37	5092	120*	35.36	76.98	5	26	108	0
T20Is	35	33	2	583	79	18.80	127.01	0	3	14	0
First-class	197	337	27	11310	206	36.48	-	24	58	228	0
List A	367	345	61	9583	120*	33.74	-	8	54	185	0
Twenty20	54	49	5	877	79	19.93	124.57	0	6	18	0

Bowling										
	Mat	Balls	Runs	Wkts	BBI	BBM	Ave	Econ	SR	5w	10
Tests	68	1905	1018	17	3/23	3/35	59.88	3.20	112.0	0	0
ODIs	197	5186	4294	111	6/31	6/31	38.68	4.96	46.7	1	0
T20Is	35	222	329	16	4/22	4/22	20.56	8.89	13.8	0	0
First-class	197	10024	5067	128	5/52	-	39.58	3.03	78.3	1	0
List A	367	9732	7850	226	6/31	6/31	34.73	4.83	43.0	1	0
Twenty20	54	463	579	36	5/14	5/14	16.08	7.50	12.8	1	0

When all else fails, it's time to send for Brigadier Block

Nasser Hussain,
former England captain

NAME: Mark Anthony Davies
BORN: October 4, 1980, Stockton-on-Tees
HEIGHT: 6ft 3in
SQUAD Nº: 4
NICKNAME: Davo
OTHER TEAMS: Nottinghamshire
CAREER: First-class debut: 2002; List A debut: 1998; T20 debut: 2003

DURHAM

AOC SAYS: A talented swing bowler, Davies has been hampered by injuries throughout his career. He managed just six first-class appearances last summer, but when he is able to play regular cricket, Durham reap the rewards. Going into the 2011 season he had 253 first-class wickets to his name at an average of 22.63 each. His best first-class form came in 2004 and 2005, when he collected 50 wickets at 18.76 and 49 at 16.53 in those respective seasons. In August 2008 he destroyed Hampshire, taking a career-best 8-24, one of 12 career five-wicket hauls.

LAST WORD: "It was a difficult year for him last year with injuries but when he's fit he's probably as good as anyone at swinging the ball. He was on the fringes of the England squad but had an awful summer with injuries. If they keep him fit he moves it around a bit and as part of an attack he's crucial." *Luke Edwards*

Batting & Fielding

	Mat	Inns	NO	Runs	HS	Ave	SR	100	50	Ct	St
First-class	83	107	41	733	62	11.10	33.01	0	1	17	0
List A	73	36	14	166	31*	7.54	-	0	0	10	0
Twenty20	9	4	3	11	6	11.00	78.57	0	0	2	0

Bowling

	Mat	Balls	Runs	Wkts	BBI	BBM	Ave	Econ	SR	5w	10
First-class	83	12540	5726	253	8/24	-	22.63	2.73	49.5	12	2
List A	73	2982	2087	68	4/13	4/13	30.69	4.19	43.8	0	0
Twenty20	9	204	241	8	2/14	2/14	30.12	7.08	25.5	0	0

MICHAEL DI VENUTO

LHB RM R10

NAME: Michael James di Venuto
BORN: December 12, 1973, Hobart, Tasmania
HEIGHT: 5ft 11in
SQUAD Nº: 23
NICKNAME: Diva
CAREER: ODI debut: 1996; First-class debut: 1991; List A debut: 1992; T20 debut: 2003; County cap: 1999 (Sussex), 2000 (Derbyshire)

AOC SAYS: In four seasons at Durham, Di Venuto has scored 5,321 runs at an average of 59.12, a phenomenal record that is testament to one of county cricket's outstanding performers. The Australian plays for Durham as a non-overseas player due to his Italian passport but he'd be a coup for any county whatever his status. A quality batsman in all forms of the game, he averages 30.07 in one-day cricket for Durham but didn't play T20 cricket last summer. He played nine times in ODIs for Australia in 1997.

LAST WORD: "He's a desperately keen cricketer. To our benefit he goes back to Tasmania and he doesn't play any cricket – instead hoping to coach the Tasmanian players – so last year he came back really hungry and he's making the same noises this year. He's got a fantastic record for us and it's just a testament to his hunger for the game." *Geoff Cook*

Batting & Fielding

	Mat	Inns	NO	Runs	HS	Ave	SR	100	50	Ct	St
ODIs	9	9	0	241	89	26.77	85.76	0	2	1	0
First-class	315	556	41	23974	254*	46.55	-	57	141	379	0
List A	299	293	18	9082	173*	33.02	-	15	46	123	0
Twenty20	46	44	4	951	95*	23.77	126.12	0	7	10	0

Bowling

	Mat	Balls	Runs	Wkts	BBI	BBM	Ave	Econ	SR	5w	10
ODIs	9	-	-	-	-	-	-	-	-	-	-
First-class	315	807	484	5	1/0	-	96.80	3.59	161.4	0	0
List A	299	200	181	5	1/10	1/10	36.20	5.43	40.0	0	0
Twenty20	46	78	88	5	3/19	3/19	17.60	6.76	15.6	0	0

NAME: Ben William Harmison
BORN: January 9, 1986, Ashington
HEIGHT: 6ft 5in
SQUAD №: 14
NICKNAME: Harmy
CAREER: First-class debut: 2006; List A debut: 2005; T20 debut: 2006

DURHAM

AOC SAYS: A valuable one-day player for Durham, the taller, younger brother of Stephen is a middle-order left-hand bat. A former England under 19 international, he hit his maiden first-class century against Warwickshire in 2007 but has never been able to nail down a regular place in Durham's Championship side. Last season saw him play six times in four-day cricket, the high point coming when he fell four runs short of a century against Essex in September. He's also proved a useful bowler at times in the Championship and claimed 14 wickets last summer, while his career best came in 2008 when he recorded figures of 4-27 against Surrey. He averaged 31.10 in the CB40 last summer but struggled in the FP t20, averaging just 17.

LAST WORD: "He's a quiet presence, but he's got talent and it's just about getting him to perform and find consistency." *Luke Edwards*

Batting & Fielding

	Mat	Inns	NO	Runs	HS	Ave	SR	100	50	Ct	St
First-class	37	62	5	1488	110	26.10	44.44	3	7	23	0
List A	47	43	4	950	67	24.35	71.64	0	3	17	0
Twenty20	30	17	7	117	24	11.70	107.33	0	0	9	0

Bowling

	Mat	Balls	Runs	Wkts	BBI	BBM	Ave	Econ	SR	5w	10
First-class	37	1557	1144	33	4/27	6/98	34.66	4.40	47.1	0	0
List A	47	859	840	24	3/43	3/43	35.00	5.86	35.7	0	0
Twenty20	30	348	471	23	3/20	3/20	20.47	8.12	15.1	0	0

STEPHEN HARMISON · RHB RF W6

DURHAM

NAME: Stephen James Harmison
BORN: October 23, 1978, Ashington
HEIGHT: 6ft 4in
SQUAD Nº: 10
NICKNAME: Harmy
OTHER TEAMS: England
CAREER: Test debut: 2002; ODI debut: 2002;
T20I debut: 2005; First-class debut: 1996;
List A debut: 1998; T20 debut: 2005

AOC SAYS: It was back in 2004 in Jamaica when Harmison announced himself as one of the world's best bowlers, delivering a frightening spell that ripped through the West Indies line-up and handed him figures of 7-12. Since losing his place in the national team following the Ashes victory of 2009, the towering quickie remains a destructive force for Durham. He took 53 first-class wickets in the summer of 2007, 65 the following summer and 63 at 23.85 in 2009, this form earning him one final recall to the England team. Injury, which has affected Harmy throughout the years, meant he only managed nine first-class appearances last summer but he still managed to take 30 wickets.

LAST WORD: "He is one of the great English seamers and I think history will judge him a lot more kindly than people do now. He loves Durham but had a really difficult season last year when he was never really fit. He'll have benefited from a winter of fitness work and if Harmison's fit I think Durham will win the title; if he's fit and firing he's guaranteed to take you 50 wickets." *Luke Edwards*

Batting & Fielding

	Mat	Inns	NO	Runs	HS	Ave	SR	100	50	Ct	St
Tests	63	86	23	743	49*	11.79	57.19	0	0	7	0
ODIs	58	25	14	91	18*	8.27	64.53	0	0	10	0
T20Is	2	-	-	-	-	-	-	-	-	1	0
First-class	199	258	74	1812	49*	9.84	-	0	0	29	0
List A	143	67	34	267	25*	8.09	-	0	0	23	0
Twenty20	28	6	1	11	6	2.20	84.61	0	0	3	0

Bowling

	Mat	Balls	Runs	Wkts	BBI	BBM	Ave	Econ	SR	5w	10
Tests	63	13375	7192	226	7/12	11/76	31.82	3.22	59.1	8	1
ODIs	58	2899	2481	76	5/33	5/33	32.64	5.13	38.1	1	0
T20Is	2	39	42	1	1/13	1/13	42.00	6.46	39.0	0	0
First-class	199	38078	19927	713	7/12	-	27.94	3.13	53.4	27	1
List A	143	6838	5658	184	5/33	5/33	30.75	4.96	37.1	1	0
Twenty20	28	505	668	29	5/41	5/41	23.03	7.93	17.4	1	0

OVERSEAS PLAYER

NAME: David Andrew Miller
BORN: June 10, 1989, Pietermaritzburg
SQUAD Nº: 12
OTHER TEAMS: South Africa, Dolphins
CAREER: ODI debut: 2010; First-class debut:
2008; List A debut: 2008; T20 debut: 2010

DURHAM

AOC SAYS: At the age of just 21, Miller already has an impressive track record and could be an excellent coup for Durham, who have signed the South African on a summer contract to play as an overseas player exclusively in this season's FP t20. An explosive middle-order batsman, Miller has already played in 13 ODIs and six Twenty20 matches for South Africa. He is a powerful striker of the ball and a great innings finisher, and made his first-class debut for Dolphins at the age of just 17. He earned his first international call-up in May 2010 following a successful stint with South Africa A and was unlucky to miss out on the 2011 World Cup squad.

LAST WORD: "We really benefited from having the extra power in the batting unit last season with Ross Taylor and Albie Morkel, so we're pleased to be able to add David to our current line-up to strengthen the middle-order. He played alongside our T20 captain Dale Benkenstein in South Africa and Dale was really impressed by his talent." *Geoff Cook*

Batting & Fielding											
	Mat	Inns	NO	Runs	HS	Ave	SR	100	50	Ct	St
ODIs	13	10	3	186	51	26.57	120.77	0	1	4	0
T20Is	6	6	3	123	36*	41.00	133.69	0	0	1	0
First-class	26	41	4	993	108*	26.83	55.19	1	5	21	0
List A	52	45	10	1323	115*	37.80	105.41	1	8	18	0
Twenty20	20	20	7	436	90*	33.53	129.37	0	2	5	0

Bowling										
	Mat	Balls	Runs	Wkts	BBI	BBM	Ave	Econ	SR	5w	10
ODIs	13	-	-	-	-	-	-	-	-	-	-
T20Is	6	-	-	-	-	-	-	-	-	-	-
First-class	26	26	23	0	-	-	-	5.30	-	0	0
List A	52	-	-	-	-	-	-	-	-	-	-
Twenty20	20	18	31	0	-	-	-	10.33	-	0	0

GORDON MUCHALL RHB RM

DURHAM

NAME: Gordon James Muchall
BORN: November 2, 1982, Newcastle upon Tyne
HEIGHT: 6ft
SQUAD Nº: 24
NICKNAME: Much
CAREER: First-class debut: 2002; List A debut: 2002; T20 debut: 2003

AOC SAYS: Top-order batsman Muchall made his Durham debut in 2002 and has scored 10 first-class centuries for the county since. He was part of the first intake of England's academy, which went to Australia in 2002 and was given a chance at the end of May when out-of-form Will Smith resigned the captaincy and returned to second XI cricket in search of form. Muchall took his opportunity and averaged 37.14 in first-class cricket for the season; his best knock an unbeaten 140 against Hampshire. He also averaged 38.75 in the CB40 but only featured four times in the FP t20, his top score being 16. Athletic and powerful, he is one of several players vying for a spot in the Dynamos middle-order.

LAST WORD: "He came into the side about halfway through last season. He showed some character, got two hundreds and has done well enough to get a starting place this year."
Geoff Cook

Batting & Fielding

	Mat	Inns	NO	Runs	HS	Ave	SR	100	50	Ct	St
First-class	115	200	10	5576	219	29.34	53.43	10	26	77	0
List A	97	88	14	2153	101*	29.09	-	1	10	37	0
Twenty20	40	34	8	706	64*	27.15	107.29	0	2	16	0

Bowling

	Mat	Balls	Runs	Wkts	BBI	BBM	Ave	Econ	SR	5w	10
First-class	115	896	617	15	3/26	-	41.13	4.13	59.7	0	0
List A	97	168	144	1	1/15	1/15	144.00	5.14	168.0	0	0
Twenty20	40	12	8	1	1/8	1/8	8.00	4.00	12.0	0	0

NAME: Philip Mustard
BORN: October 8, 1982, Sunderland
HEIGHT: 5ft 11in
SQUAD Nº: 19
NICKNAME: Colonel
OTHER TEAMS: England
CAREER: ODI debut: 2007; T20I debut:
2008; First-class debut: 2002; List A debut:
2000; T20 debut: 2003

DURHAM

AOC SAYS: Durham's four-day captain Phil Mustard took the reins from Will Smith early last season. His aggressive, no-fear style of batting was unaffected by the added responsibility, and the wicketkeeper finished the Championship campaign with an average of 39.05. An equally impressive gloveman, Mustard will still hold ambitions of returning to the England side, having toured with the Three Lions in the winter of 2007/08 and kept wicket during one-day tournaments against Sri Lanka and New Zealand. Described by Shane Warne as 'the best one-day wicketkeeper in England', Mustard is a talented all-round sportsman and was a youth footballer on the books of Manchester United and Middlesbrough.

LAST WORD: "I've got nothing but admiration for the way he's controlled his fitness levels, he's hardly missed a game in the four or five years he's been involved in the first team. Being captain is very much about having the respect of the team he's dealing with and in that regard Phillip commands the respect of the other guys." *Geoff Cook*

Batting & Fielding

	Mat	Inns	NO	Runs	HS	Ave	SR	100	50	Ct	St
ODIs	10	10	0	233	83	23.30	92.46	0	1	9	2
T20Is	2	2	0	60	40	30.00	162.16	0	0	0	0
First-class	118	182	20	4771	130	29.45	63.96	4	27	389	15
List A	128	114	6	3135	108	29.02	-	2	22	129	31
Twenty20	67	65	3	1431	70*	23.08	127.65	0	8	30	17

Bowling

	Mat	Balls	Runs	Wkts	BBI	BBM	Ave	Econ	SR	5w	10
ODIs	10	-	-	-	-	-	-	-	-	-	-
T20Is	2	-	-	-	-	-	-	-	-	-	-
First-class	118	-	-	-	-	-	-	-	-	-	-
List A	128	-	-	-	-	-	-	-	-	-	-
Twenty20	67	-	-	-	-	-	-	-	-	-	-

GRAHAM ONIONS

RHB RFM W2

DURHAM

NAME: Graham Onions
BORN: September 9, 1982, Gateshead
HEIGHT: 6ft 2in
SQUAD Nº: 9
NICKNAME: Wills, Bunny
OTHER TEAMS: England
CAREER: Test debut: 2009; ODI debut: 2009;
First-class debut: 2004; List A debut: 2003;
T20 debut: 2004

AOC SAYS: A huge success story in the England's Ashes victory of 2009 and a player of genuine international class, Onions was dealt a cruel blow when a serious back injury ruled him out for the entirety of last season. The right-arm quick took 5-38 on Test debut against West Indies, and later that summer he claimed 10 wickets in three matches during the 2009 Ashes series, including 4-58 at Edgbaston in a spell that ripped through the Australian top-order. Expected to return to fitness early this summer, Onions will be a star in Durham's frightening attack if he can return to the form that saw him take an incredible 69 first-class wickets at 19.95 in 2009.

LAST WORD: "Eighteen months ago he was named one of the Wisden Cricketers of the Year, but he hasn't really bowled since. We just hope that he can regain some of that form; to do that well so quickly and not to be able to kick on on must have been very hard for him. He's kept his spirits up very well but he's got the green light now." *Geoff Cook*

Batting & Fielding

	Mat	Inns	NO	Runs	HS	Ave	SR	100	50	Ct	St
Tests	8	10	7	30	17*	10.00	30.92	0	0	0	0
ODIs	4	1	0	1	1	1.00	50.00	0	0	1	0
First-class	71	93	32	758	41	12.42	51.88	0	0	17	0
List A	53	21	5	107	19	6.68	71.81	0	0	8	0
Twenty20	19	8	3	54	31	10.80	112.50	0	0	4	0

Bowling

	Mat	Balls	Runs	Wkts	BBI	BBM	Ave	Econ	SR	5w	10
Tests	8	1429	869	28	5/38	7/102	31.03	3.64	51.0	1	0
ODIs	4	204	185	4	2/58	2/58	46.25	5.44	51.0	0	0
First-class	71	11558	6923	230	8/101	-	30.10	3.59	50.2	9	0
List A	53	2203	1918	60	3/39	3/39	31.96	5.22	36.7	0	0
Twenty20	19	408	437	15	3/25	3/25	29.13	6.42	27.2	0	0

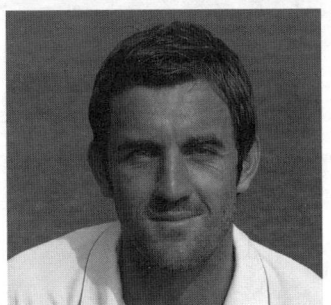

NAME: Liam Edward Plunkett
BORN: April 6, 1985, Middlesbrough
HEIGHT: 6ft 3in
SQUAD №: 20
NICKNAME: Pudsy
MAJOR TEAMS: England, Dolphins
CAREER: Test debut: 2005; ODI debut: 2005;
T20I debut: 2006; First-class debut: 2003;
List A debut: 2003; T20 debut: 2003

DURHAM

AOC SAYS: A tall, athletic bowler who – when his rhythm is right – gets the ball to swing late,
Plunkett is also a powerful lower-order batsman. He was called up to the England squad that
toured Pakistan in 2005/06 and, although he remained inconsistent, showed glimpses that
he could thrive at that level. However, a series of tweaks to his bowling action compounded
his erratic tendencies, and, although he played a big part in England's CB series victory in
2007 and travelled to the World Cup in the same year, he slipped down the pecking order.
Nevertheless, he remains a strong performer and still has a chance of adding considerably to
his international career. If he can marry his bowling performance of 2009 with his batting of
last season, Durham and England will have a fomidable allrounder at their disposal.

LAST WORD: "He's a very talented boy. He had a really good 2009 but was infuriatingly
inconsistent last season. I don't think all the tinkering with his action has served him well."
Luke Edwards

Batting & Fielding

	Mat	Inns	NO	Runs	HS	Ave	SR	100	50	Ct	St
Tests	9	13	2	126	44*	11.45	39.62	0	0	3	0
ODIs	29	25	10	315	56	21.00	83.33	0	1	7	0
T20Is	1	-	-	-	-	-	-	-	-	0	0
First-class	102	139	25	2373	94*	20.81	-	0	10	63	0
List A	111	76	27	927	72	18.91	90.26	0	2	24	0
Twenty20	38	21	11	175	31	17.50	119.86	0	0	10	0

Bowling

	Mat	Balls	Runs	Wkts	BBI	BBM	Ave	Econ	SR	5w	10
Tests	9	1538	916	23	3/17	6/60	39.82	3.57	66.8	0	0
ODIs	29	1363	1321	39	3/24	3/24	33.87	5.81	34.9	0	0
T20Is	1	24	37	1	1/37	1/37	37.00	9.25	24.0	0	0
First-class	102	16061	9695	310	6/63	-	31.27	3.62	51.8	8	1
List A	111	4692	4208	132	4/15	4/15	31.87	5.38	35.5	0	0
Twenty20	38	680	880	29	3/16	3/16	30.34	7.76	23.4	0	0

MICHAEL RICHARDSON   RHB WK

DURHAM

NAME: Michael John Richardson
BORN: October 4, 1986, Port Elizabeth
HEIGHT: 5ft 10in
SQUAD Nº: 18
NICKNAME: Richie
CAREER: First-class debut: 2010

AOC SAYS: Durham's second-choice wicketkeeper, Richardson has played just once since signing as a professional for the county ahead of last season, a rain-affected clash against Durham MCCU that saw Richardson run out for two in his only innings. With first-choice keeper Mustard maintaining both form and fitness last summer, Richardson was a regular in the Second XI and was outstanding with the bat. He averaged 70.25 in the Second XI Championship and lost his wicket just once in six innings in the Second XI Trophy.

LAST WORD: "Michael has been here for a long time as a youngster. He was educated here and was on the Lord's groundstaff before he joined us as a professional last year." *Geoff Cook*

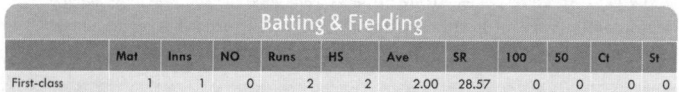

Batting & Fielding

	Mat	Inns	NO	Runs	HS	Ave	SR	100	50	Ct	St
First-class	1	1	0	2	2	2.00	28.57	0	0	0	0

Bowling

	Mat	Balls	Runs	Wkts	BBI	BBM	Ave	Econ	SR	5w	10
First-class	1	-	-	-	-	-	-	-	-	-	-

NAME: Christopher Rushworth
BORN: July 11, 1986, Sunderland
HEIGHT: 6ft 2in
SQUAD №: 22
NICKNAME: Rushy
CAREER: First-class debut: 2010; List A
debut: 2004

DURHAM

AOC SAYS: Released by Durham in 2008, seamer Rushworth impressed playing club cricket for Sunderland the following summer and was re-signed by Durham for the 2010 season. Injuries to key bowlers enabled Rushworth to play nine first-class matches last summer. He took 21 wickets at 39.09, including a four-wicket haul in the second innings against Essex at Chelmsford, as well as 13 wickets at 18.53 in three Second XI Championship fixtures. Rushworth spent the winter playing grade cricket in Australia for Claremont-Nedlands.

LAST WORD: "He had a solid season last year but was a bit up and down, a bit inconsistent. Geoff Cook certainly likes him and sees him as a long-term replacement for someone like Callum Thorp. And he's a local lad too." *Luke Edwards*

Batting & Fielding

	Mat	Inns	NO	Runs	HS	Ave	SR	100	50	Ct	St
First-class	9	14	2	127	28	10.58	56.19	0	0	1	0
List A	10	5	3	16	7*	8.00	69.56	0	0	2	0

Bowling

	Mat	Balls	Runs	Wkts	BBI	BBM	Ave	Econ	SR	5w	10
First-class	9	1288	821	21	4/90	5/159	39.09	3.82	61.3	0	0
List A	10	354	262	15	3/6	3/6	17.46	4.44	23.6	0	0

WILL SMITH

DURHAM

NAME: William Rew Smith
BORN: September 28, 1982, Luton
HEIGHT: 5ft 10in
SQUAD Nº: 2
NICKNAME: Posh Kid
OTHER TEAMS: Nottinghamshire
CAREER: First-class debut: 2002; List A
debut: 2002; T20 debut: 2003

AOC SAYS: After a poor start last season, Smith handed the Durham captaincy to Phil Mustard in May and spent the remainder of the summer trying to rediscover his form in the Second XI. He played 16 times across the Second XI Championship and Trophy, averaging 32 in both competitions. He had been handed the captaincy at the end of the 2008 season, his most profitable summer in the County Championship, having scored three centuries (including 201 not out against Surrey) and averaged 51.38 in first-class cricket to help Durham claim their first Championship title.

LAST WORD: "He was obviously disappointed [with his start to last season] but he agreed he had to go away and try and get some runs on the board. Justifying your place is always tricky as captain but now he looks pretty fresh to me. He has a very good approach, very optimistic, and he'll be pushing hard." *Geoff Cook*

Batting & Fielding

	Mat	Inns	NO	Runs	HS	Ave	SR	100	50	Ct	St
First-class	76	122	8	3628	201*	31.82	44.35	8	12	36	0
List A	70	65	5	1527	103	25.45	69.69	1	11	24	0
Twenty20	55	44	9	624	55	17.82	116.20	0	3	32	0

Bowling

	Mat	Balls	Runs	Wkts	BBI	BBM	Ave	Econ	SR	5w	10
First-class	76	729	552	8	3/34	-	69.00	4.54	91.1	0	0
List A	70	53	51	2	1/6	1/6	25.50	5.77	26.5	0	0
Twenty20	55	95	132	1	1/31	1/31	132.00	8.33	95.0	0	0

BEN STOKES

LHB RM

NAME: Ben Andrew Stokes
BORN: June 4, 1991, Christchurch, New Zealand
HEIGHT: 6ft 2in
SQUAD Nº: 38
CAREER: First-class debut: 2010; List A debut: 2009; T20 debut: 2010

AOC SAYS: A hard-hitting allrounder, Stokes emerged from Durham's youth ranks last season and became a regular in all forms of the game. Batting in the middle-order, he marked his first-class debut with a first-innings 53 against the MCC in Abu Dhabi and went on to average 46.25 in the County Championship. Most memorably, he scored centuries in consecutive matches, the youngest player in the history of county cricket to do so, registering 106 against Notts and smashing a magnificent 161 at Canterbury. Having featured in three one-day games in 2009 he played nine times in last year's CB40 and was rewarded for his fine Championship form with a place on the England Lions touring party to West Indies over the winter. Many good judges expect Stokes to be pushing for full England honours in the near future.

LAST WORD: "He's a very talented lad, a very good timer of the ball who can hit it a long way; he's very much a modern-day batsman. His bowling is a little bit raw, he needs some more overs under his belt to get some experience but it's got potential." *Geoff Cook*

Batting & Fielding

	Mat	Inns	NO	Runs	HS	Ave	SR	100	50	Ct	St
First-class	16	23	3	818	161*	40.90	-	2	3	9	0
List A	13	13	2	204	39	18.54	81.27	0	0	4	0
Twenty20	15	12	1	180	44	16.36	108.43	0	0	4	0

Bowling

	Mat	Balls	Runs	Wkts	BBI	BBM	Ave	Econ	SR	5w	10
First-class	16	495	404	7	2/32	3/47	57.71	4.89	70.7	0	0
List A	13	84	79	5	2/22	2/22	15.80	5.64	16.8	0	0
Twenty20	15	30	37	1	1/23	1/23	37.00	7.40	30.0	0	0

MARK STONEMAN

LHB RM

DURHAM

NAME: Mark Daniel Stoneman
BORN: June 26, 1987, Newcastle upon Tyne
HEIGHT: 5ft 11in
SQUAD Nº: 26
NICKNAME: Rocky, Doug
CAREER: First-class debut: 2007; List A debut: 2008; T20 debut: 2010

AOC SAYS: Still just 23, Stoneman is a talented batsman who has been a regular in Durham's Championship top-order since making his debut against Sussex in July 2007. His maiden first-class century came against the same county later that season but he had to wait until May 2010 for his next ton, a knock of 118 against Durham University. Stoneman rarely plays one-day cricket but has steadily improved his Championship batting average in each of the last three seasons. A former England under 19 player, Durham expect him to be a fixture at the top of the order for many years to come.

LAST WORD: "They call him the Di Venuto clone because he picks up all these little nuances of Di Venuto's game. The challenge for him is to get the big scores but he's certainly a very talented batsman. He gets 30s and 40s and then gets himself out, so it's frustrating because he is a very talented player." *Tim Wellock*

Batting & Fielding

	Mat	Inns	NO	Runs	HS	Ave	SR	100	50	Ct	St
First-class	45	75	3	1789	118	24.84	45.15	2	9	28	0
List A	5	5	0	94	25	18.80	94.94	0	0	2	0
Twenty20	3	3	0	85	46	28.33	100.00	0	0	1	0

Bowling

	Mat	Balls	Runs	Wkts	BBI	BBM	Ave	Econ	SR	5w	10
First-class	45	-	-	-	-	-	-	-	-	-	-
List A	5	-	-	-	-	-	-	-	-	-	-
Twenty20	3	-	-	-	-	-	-	-	-	-	-

NAME: Callum David Thorp
BORN: January 11, 1975, Mount Lawley,
Perth, Australia
HEIGHT: 6ft 3in
SQUAD Nº: 36
OTHER TEAMS: Western Australia
CAREER: First-class debut: 2003; List A
debut: 2003; T20 debut: 2005

DURHAM

AOC SAYS: An Australian with an English passport, injury restricted Thorp to just five first-class appearances last summer. However, when he was fit he continued to be a pivotal part of the Durham attack, as he demonstrated with a haul of 4-54 in the first innings of a home Championship fixture against Warwickshire in June. In 2009 he took 34 first-class wickets at 24.88, having claimed 50 first-class victims at a 19.62 apiece the previous summer. When fit Thorp is a fixture in Durham's Championship side but rarely plays in one-day and Twenty20 matches. Now 36, the veteran seamer has also played for Western Australia in his homeland.

LAST WORD: "He's the unsung hero of the Durham attack and he's a really useful lower-order batsman too. He was really badly missed last year when he wasn't fit. He doesn't get the limelight but takes a lot of wickets." *Luke Edwards*

Batting & Fielding

	Mat	Inns	NO	Runs	HS	Ave	SR	100	50	Ct	St
First-class	56	74	9	976	79*	15.01	56.02	0	3	33	0
List A	38	25	8	286	52	16.82	97.61	0	1	7	0
Twenty20	9	6	0	63	13	10.50	114.54	0	0	1	0

Bowling

	Mat	Balls	Runs	Wkts	BBI	BBM	Ave	Econ	SR	5w	10
First-class	56	8417	4168	159	7/88	-	26.21	2.97	52.9	7	1
List A	38	1765	1286	47	6/17	6/17	27.36	4.37	37.5	1	0
Twenty20	9	162	266	3	2/32	2/32	88.66	9.85	54.0	0	0

FORMED: 1876
HOME GROUND: The Ford County Ground, Chelmsford
ONE-DAY NAME: Eagles
CAPTAIN: James Foster
2010 RESULTS: CC1: 9/9; CB40: Semi-finalists; FP t20: Semi-finalists

HONOURS

County Championship: (6) 1979, 1983, 1984, 1986, 1991, 1992; Gillette/NatWest/C&G/ FP Trophy: (3) 1985, 1997, 2008; Benson and Hedges Cup: (2) 1979, 1998; Pro40/National League/CB40: (2) 2005, 2006; Sunday League: (3) 1981, 1984, 1985

THE LOWDOWN

Last season was an ultimately frustrating one for Essex, who saw a good start to their Championship campaign fall away after a series of injuries exposed a lack of depth in the squad. They were eventually relegated after just one season in the top flight, which compounded the disappointment of reaching the semi-final of both one-day competitions without making either final. But they still have an excellent collection of homegrown cricketers to call upon, a respected and popular captain in James Foster, a top coach, and the sort of passionate, vociferous support to carry the club back near the summit of the domestic game. Questions will be asked about the spin-bowling department following Danish Kaneria's departure. Much will be expected of the left-armer Tim Phillips, but Kaneria's are big boots to fill. Essex will look more to the pace bowlers this term, with the emerging Maurice Chambers on the verge of big things.

HEAD COACH: PAUL GRAYSON

Grayson is a progressive coach with sound, modern methods to dealing with today's players. Approachable, reasonable, quietly authoritative, his coaching style leans on his experiences as a Yorkshire player, and latterly as a canny left-arm spinning allrounder with the county he now coaches.

With thanks to: Paul Grayson; Paul Hiscock, freelance journalist and Essex CCC expert

Batting & Fielding

	Mat	Inns	NO	Runs	HS	Ave	SR	100	50	Ct	St
RS Bopara	8	15	2	550	142	42.30	56.06	2	3	4	-
GW Flower	3	5	2	123	46	41.00	41.69	0	0	3	-
AJ Wheater	1	2	1	41	22	41.00	51.25	0	0	7	0
AN Cook	7	12	0	474	102	39.50	54.10	1	3	6	-
MJ Walker	12	24	2	838	105	38.09	42.97	1	4	8	-
RN ten Doeschate	11	19	2	577	85	33.94	63.47	0	5	9	-
JS Foster	16	27	1	839	169	32.26	45.94	1	4	48	5
JC Mickleburgh	16	30	0	852	174	28.40	41.74	1	3	11	-
T Westley	9	18	1	440	132	25.88	44.67	1	2	1	-
BA Godleman	12	22	0	569	106	25.86	49.30	1	2	12	-
JK Maunders	7	12	0	307	126	25.58	55.51	1	1	6	-
ML Pettini	15	27	3	599	96	24.95	39.17	0	2	7	-
BE McGain	2	4	2	46	24	23.00	32.16	0	0	0	-
TJ Phillips	10	16	3	240	46*	18.46	40.13	0	0	8	-
DD Masters	14	22	1	356	50	16.95	61.06	0	1	8	-
AP Palladino	5	9	1	130	66	16.25	63.72	0	1	1	-
CJC Wright	11	17	5	161	28*	13.41	44.84	0	0	2	-
GR Napier	4	6	1	67	35	13.40	37.01	0	0	1	-
A Carter	3	5	1	45	16*	11.25	77.58	0	0	2	-
CS Martin	1	2	1	11	11	11.00	73.33	0	0	0	-
MA Comber	2	3	0	19	19	6.33	27.53	0	0	1	-
M Osborne	2	3	2	5	5	5.00	19.23	0	0	0	-
MA Chambers	11	16	5	53	14	4.81	26.23	0	0	5	-
Danish Kaneria	6	9	1	28	9	3.50	68.29	0	0	1	-

Bowling

	Mat	Overs	Mdns	Runs	Wkts	BBI	BBM	Ave	Econ	SR	5w	10
DD Masters	14	487.0	138	1223	53	5/43	8/96	23.07	2.51	55.1	1	0
MA Comber	2	22.2	2	94	4	2/34	3/78	23.50	4.20	33.5	0	0
MJ Walker	12	18.0	2	71	3	3/35	3/35	23.66	3.94	36.0	0	0
MA Chambers	11	269.3	51	909	38	6/68	10/123	23.92	3.37	42.5	2	1
A Carter	3	100.5	15	311	13	5/40	7/121	23.92	3.08	46.5	1	0
RS Bopara	8	25.0	2	99	4	2/33	4/82	24.75	3.96	37.5	0	0
M Osborne	2	36.0	5	151	6	3/35	5/95	25.16	4.19	36.0	0	0
BE McGain	2	64.3	4	260	10	5/151	5/90	26.00	4.03	38.7	1	0
RN ten Doeschate	11	191.3	16	716	27	5/13	6/59	26.51	3.73	42.5	1	0
AP Palladino	5	142.0	30	499	18	4/57	6/166	27.72	3.51	47.3	0	0
T Westley	9	68.0	10	174	6	2/68	2/55	29.00	2.55	68.0	0	0
GW Flower	3	9.0	0	32	1	1/19	1/32	32.00	3.55	54.0	0	0
Danish Kaneria	6	226.4	45	753	23	4/51	6/93	32.73	3.32	59.1	0	0
AN Cook	7	8.0	1	36	1	1/33	1/33	36.00	4.50	48.0	0	0
CJC Wright	11	301.5	55	1156	31	5/70	6/118	37.29	3.82	58.4	1	0
TJ Phillips	10	246.2	45	752	20	4/94	7/121	37.60	3.05	73.9	0	0
CS Martin	1	25.0	10	84	1	1/84	1/84	84.00	3.36	150.0	0	0
GR Napier	4	95.0	18	280	3	1/47	2/129	93.33	2.94	190.0	0	0
JC Mickleburgh	16	1.1	0	11	0	-	-	-	9.42	-	0	0

LIST A AVERAGES 2010

Batting & Fielding

	Mat	Inns	NO	Runs	HS	Ave	SR	100	50	Ct	St
RS Bopara	6	6	2	308	88*	77.00	95.35	0	2	1	-
GW Flower	12	11	3	527	116	65.87	95.64	2	2	6	-
AJ Wheater	7	3	1	96	55*	48.00	123.07	0	1	1	-
RN ten Doeschate	10	10	4	272	109*	45.33	134.65	1	1	1	-
MJ Walker	9	7	1	232	71	38.66	93.92	0	1	2	-
AN Cook	6	6	1	167	101*	33.40	83.08	1	0	3	-
ML Pettini	12	12	0	342	82	28.50	87.91	0	3	8	-
JS Foster	12	8	2	154	58	25.66	114.92	0	1	10	4
JC Mickleburgh	4	4	0	84	46	21.00	81.55	0	0	2	-
BA Godleman	3	3	0	21	16	7.00	38.18	0	0	0	-
DD Masters	11	4	1	18	16	6.00	72.00	0	0	1	-
GR Napier	3	2	0	8	6	4.00	133.33	0	0	1	-
T Westley	2	1	0	4	4	4.00	44.44	0	0	0	-
AP Palladino	7	3	1	4	2	2.00	36.36	0	0	2	-
TJ Phillips	6	3	1	3	3*	1.50	50.00	0	0	2	-
CJC Wright	11	4	2	3	3*	1.50	42.85	0	0	0	-
Danish Kaneria	6	2	1	1	1*	1.00	33.33	0	0	1	-
CS Martin	2	1	0	0	0	0.00	0.00	0	0	1	-
MA Comber	1	1	1	52	52*	-	104.00	0	1	0	-

Bowling

	Mat	Overs	Mdns	Runs	Wkts	BBI	Ave	Econ	SR	5w
RS Bopara	6	8.0	0	31	2	2/31	15.50	3.87	24.0	0
A Carter	1	8.0	0	31	2	2/31	15.50	3.87	24.0	0
GR Napier	3	24.0	1	143	7	3/54	20.42	5.95	20.5	0
DD Masters	11	85.0	2	392	15	4/41	26.13	4.61	34.0	0
CJC Wright	11	72.5	2	442	13	3/43	34.00	6.06	33.6	0
TJ Phillips	6	35.3	0	209	6	4/37	34.83	5.88	35.5	0
RN ten Doeschate	10	59.0	0	391	10	2/30	39.10	6.62	35.4	0
Danish Kaneria	6	41.0	0	213	5	2/41	42.60	5.19	49.2	0
GW Flower	12	44.0	0	255	5	2/31	51.00	5.79	52.8	0
T Westley	2	11.0	0	59	1	1/34	59.00	5.36	66.0	0
CS Martin	2	13.0	2	82	1	1/24	82.00	6.30	78.0	0
AP Palladino	7	41.0	1	255	2	1/21	127.50	6.21	123.0	0
BE McGain	1	7.0	0	46	0	-	-	6.57	-	0

www.essexcricket.org.uk / tel: 01245 252420

	Mat	Inns	NO	Runs	HS	Ave	SR	100	50	Ct	St
RN ten Doeschate	6	6	1	296	102	59.20	177.24	1	1	2	-
AN Cook	11	11	1	388	73	38.80	132.42	0	3	5	-
SB Styris	15	13	2	392	106*	35.63	161.98	1	1	2	-
RS Bopara	16	16	2	473	105*	33.78	128.88	1	2	5	-
ML Pettini	13	13	1	333	81	27.75	126.61	0	4	5	-
MJ Walker	19	18	3	380	74*	25.33	120.63	0	2	2	-
JC Mickleburgh	10	5	2	76	32	25.33	89.41	0	0	7	-
TJ Phillips	16	9	4	98	57*	19.60	118.07	0	1	8	-
JS Foster	19	16	6	194	54*	19.40	143.70	0	1	5	9
GW Flower	19	15	5	185	54	18.50	120.91	0	1	5	-
JK Maunders	5	4	1	49	25*	16.33	104.25	0	0	3	-
GR Napier	1	1	0	12	12	12.00	109.09	0	0	0	-
Danish Kaneria	12	4	1	24	9*	8.00	150.00	0	0	0	-
DD Masters	16	6	4	11	10*	5.50	78.57	0	0	2	-
DJ Bravo	1	1	0	5	5	5.00	62.50	0	0	0	-
MA Comber	1	1	0	5	5	5.00	100.00	0	0	0	-
CJC Wright	19	3	2	2	1*	2.00	100.00	0	0	2	-
AP Palladino	1	1	0	1	1	1.00	25.00	0	0	1	-
MA Chambers	6	1	1	9	9*	-	90.00	0	0	1	-

	Mat	Overs	Mdns	Runs	Wkts	BBI	Ave	Econ	SR	5w
Danish Kaneria	12	45.3	1	337	18	3/32	18.72	7.40	15.1	0
GR Napier	1	3.4	0	40	2	2/40	20.00	10.90	11.0	0
RS Bopara	16	54.0	0	397	16	3/13	24.81	7.35	20.2	0
RN ten Doeschate	6	11.0	0	75	3	1/16	25.00	6.81	22.0	0
CJC Wright	19	70.0	0	641	21	4/25	30.52	9.15	20.0	0
SB Styris	15	49.0	0	408	13	2/28	31.38	8.32	22.6	0
MA Chambers	6	21.0	0	208	6	2/29	34.66	9.90	21.0	0
DD Masters	16	53.1	0	418	12	2/18	34.83	7.86	26.5	0
TJ Phillips	16	38.0	0	321	9	1/7	35.66	8.44	25.3	0
DJ Bravo	1	4.0	0	46	1	1/46	46.00	11.50	24.0	0
GW Flower	19	13.0	0	106	2	1/16	53.00	8.15	39.0	0
A Carter	2	7.0	0	69	0	-	-	9.85	-	0
AP Palladino	1	3.0	0	29	0	-	-	9.66	-	0

RAVI BOPARA

RHB RM R1 MVP31

ESSEX

NAME: Ravinder Singh Bopara
BORN: May 4, 1985, Forest Gate
HEIGHT: 5ft 10in
SQUAD Nº: 25
NICKNAME: Puppy
OTHER TEAMS: England, Dolphins, Kings XI Punjab
CAREER: Test debut: 2007; ODI debut: 2008; T20I debut: 2008; First-class debut: 2002; List A debut: 2002; T20 debut: 2003; County cap: 2005

AOC SAYS: Essex were handed a huge boost in December 2010 with the news that Bopara had signed a two-year contract extension. The gifted strokeplayer is a graduate of Essex's academy and has scored over 10,000 runs for his county in all forms of the game since making his debut in 2002. Bopara has already represented England in all formats, enjoying some success without yet nailing a permanent place in any side. Three explosive centuries against the West Indies in early 2009 got him the prime position at No.3 for that summer's Ashes series, but he struggled in his four Tests, with a highest score of 35, before eventually making way for the final Test to be replaced at first drop by Ian Bell. He is yet to return to the Test side, although he did feature in England's 2011 World Cup squad – his second World Cup – making a composed 60 against South Africa in his first appearance of the tournament. Domestically, Bopara has been nothing short of inspirational. He enjoyed a record-breaking summer in 2008, the highlight being his 201 not out in the Friends Provident Trophy quarter-final against Leicestershire – the highest one-day score ever by an Essex player and one of only 10 'doubles' in one-day cricket history. That knock helped him secure the Young Cricketer of the Year award. Although predominantly a batsman, Bopara has taken 76 one-day wickets for the Eagles at an average of 27.06, figures that alerted the cash-rich franchises of the IPL. Bopara was snapped up by Kings XI Punjab in 2009 on a two-year contract, but he will not be appearing this year. Still very much on England's radar, a sparkling start to the season with Essex would certainly help push his international claims, and with the Test retirement of Paul Collingwood, there is a place up for grabs. Bopara will be eyeing it.

INSIDE TRACK: "We expect him to be available for our first Championship game this season and he will bowl alongside three other pace bowlers. He is a Test player who still has the ability to play at the highest level. He doesn't need to put himself under great pressure. He knows there is an opportunity there and what he has to get right first is playing well for Essex. If he does that then the England selectors will see it and he will get his chance." *Paul Grayson*

Batting & Fielding

	Mat	Inns	NO	Runs	HS	Ave	SR	100	50	Ct	St
Tests	10	15	0	502	143	33.46	53.63	3	0	5	0
ODIs	59	55	11	1281	60	29.11	72.61	0	5	19	0
T20Is	11	10	0	191	55	19.10	100.52	0	1	4	0
First-class	106	177	22	6535	229	42.16	53.78	17	26	70	0
List A	176	167	34	5049	201*	37.96	-	0	6	29	52	0
Twenty20	91	81	9	1807	105*	25.09	117.71	1	10	29	0

Bowling

	Mat	Balls	Runs	Wkts	BBI	BBM	Ave	Econ	SR	5w	10
Tests	10	296	199	1	1/39	1/39	199.00	4.03	296.0	0	0
ODIs	59	491	394	12	4/38	4/38	32.83	4.81	40.9	0	0
T20Is	11	-	-	-	-	-	-	-	-	-	-
First-class	106	7252	4757	109	5/75	-	43.64	3.93	66.5	1	0
List A	176	3613	3275	124	5/63	5/63	26.41	5.43	29.1	1	0
Twenty20	91	1108	1431	60	3/13	3/13	23.85	7.74	18.4	0	0

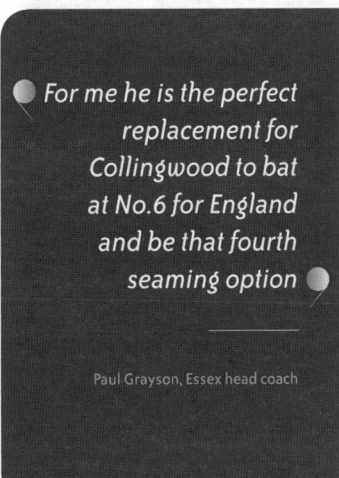

For me he is the perfect replacement for Collingwood to bat at No.6 for England and be that fourth seaming option

Paul Grayson, Essex head coach

MAURICE CHAMBERS

RHB RFM

ESSEX

NAME: Maurice Anthony Chambers
BORN: September 14, 1987, Port Antonio, Jamaica
HEIGHT: 6ft 3in
SQUAD Nº: 29
NICKNAME: Mozza
CAREER: First-class debut: 2005; List A debut: 2008; T20 debut: 2008

AOC SAYS: Fast bowler Chambers made his debut for Essex in 2005 after coming through their academy and catching the eye with his raw pace and natural athleticism. Jamaica-born, Chambers was granted British citizenship in 2007 after previously appearing for England under 19s under special dispensation granted by the ECB. Despite missing large chunks of the season with various niggles, the quick man still took 32 Championship wickets last season including a career best 6-68 against Northants, helping him towards his first 10-wicket match haul. A recent call-up to the England Lions squad can only help his progress; if Essex can keep him on the field, they have a diamond here.

LAST WORD: "His biggest qualities are his repeatability and his disciplines with the ball. He bowls a good line and good length and he has pace. He is a big lad and he bowls at the top of off stump, but he is a young boy and he's still learning the game." *Paul Grayson*

Batting & Fielding

	Mat	Inns	NO	Runs	HS	Ave	SR	100	50	Ct	St
First-class	24	32	16	87	14	5.43	-	0	0	7	0
List A	3	1	1	1	1*	-	100.00	0	0	1	0
Twenty20	18	8	5	28	10*	9.33	96.55	0	0	6	0

Bowling

	Mat	Balls	Runs	Wkts	BBI	BBM	Ave	Econ	SR	5w	10
First-class	24	3229	1943	64	6/68	-	30.35	3.61	50.4	2	1
List A	3	90	93	3	1/26	1/26	31.00	6.20	30.0	0	0
Twenty20	18	312	461	17	3/31	3/31	27.11	8.86	18.3	0	0

NAME: Michael Andrew Comber
BORN: October 26, 1989, Colchester
HEIGHT: 6ft 3in
SQUAD Nº: 35
CAREER: First-class debut: 2010; List A
debut: 2010; T20 debut: 2010

ESSEX

AOC SAYS: Comber graduated from Essex's academy in 2009, and although injuries initially limited his first-team opportunities, the tall allrounder put in a number of composed displays for the Essex Second XI. Comber was offered a full professional deal last year and responded well in his limited opportunities, making his debut against the touring Bangladeshis and scoring an excellent 52 on his List A debut against Northamptonshire, taking his team to victory. The 21-year-old was given his Championship debut in the final match of the season against Durham.

LAST WORD: "He's a driven character who is hungry to succeed, a batting allrounder who hits the ball extremely hard. He did well last year and we are hoping he'll kick on this season." *Paul Grayson*

Batting & Fielding

	Mat	Inns	NO	Runs	HS	Ave	SR	100	50	Ct	St
First-class	2	3	0	19	19	6.33	27.53	0	0	1	0
List A	1	1	1	52	52*	-	104.00	0	1	0	0
Twenty20	1	1	0	5	5	5.00	100.00	0	0	0	0

Bowling

	Mat	Balls	Runs	Wkts	BBI	BBM	Ave	Econ	SR	5w	10
First-class	2	134	94	4	2/34	3/78	23.50	4.20	33.5	0	0
List A	1	-	-	-	-	-	-	-	-	-	-
Twenty20	1	-	-	-	-	-	-	-	-	-	-

ALASTAIR COOK

ESSEX

NAME: Alastair Nathan Cook
BORN: December 25, 1984, Gloucester
HEIGHT: 6ft 2in
SQUAD Nº: 26
NICKNAME: Cooky, Chef, Woody
OTHER TEAMS: England
CAREER: Test debut: 2006; ODI debut: 2006;
T20I debut: 2007; First-class debut: 2003;
List A debut: 2003; T20 debut: 2005; County
cap: 2005

AOC SAYS: Man-of-the-moment Cook is another gem off the Essex production line and is currently one of Test cricket's hottest properties. He made his first-class debut for the club in 2003, has represented his county at all age levels, and has been breaking records since he was a schoolboy. A former England under 19 captain, it was no surprise to see him making his England Test debut after only two full seasons of county cricket; that Cook began with scores of 60 and 104 in Nagpur was no surprise either. He maintained his development with a century against Australia in Perth during the ill-fated 2006/07 Ashes tour, to become the first Englishman to score four Test tons before turning 22. A year later, on tour to New Zealand, he became the youngest Englishman in history to pass the 2,000 Test-run mark. Cook made his captaincy bow against Bangladesh in the spring of 2010 and has been touted as a permanent replacement for Andrew Strauss once the current skipper steps down from his post. A poor series against Pakistan last summer raised questions about his technique, but he proved his critics wrong in spectacular fashion in Australia last winter, claiming the Man of the Series award as England retained the Ashes. 'Woody' amassed 766 runs at an average of 127.66, with three centuries, including a mammoth unbeaten 235 at Brisbane. Essex are unlikely to see much of Cook this season, although it is a significant consolation for the club to have nurtured a player of such calibre and propelled him to the summit of the world game.

INSIDE TRACK: "Cook had a particularly outstanding Ashes series in Australia. He is a very strong young man and he has displayed that strength in a number of ways throughout his career. He has overcome most of the challenges that have been put in front of him, which is testament to his strength of character and, considering that people were calling for his head not so long ago, it is an outstanding riposte, although that's not why he did so well in Australia. It was because of the pride he has in his own performance and because he is very proud to play for England. I am very happy for him personally, and we are all thankful that he made those contributions to the team for us." *Andy Flower, England head coach*

Batting & Fielding

	Mat	Inns	NO	Runs	HS	Ave	SR	100	50	Ct	St
Tests	65	115	7	5130	235*	47.50	49.01	16	24	57	0
ODIs	26	26	0	858	102	33.00	71.38	1	5	10	0
T20Is	4	4	0	61	26	15.25	112.96	0	0	1	0
First-class	142	252	21	10722	235*	46.41	53.42	30	55	135	0
List A	75	74	6	2486	125	36.55	76.91	5	14	33	0
Twenty20	28	27	2	834	100*	33.36	129.90	1	5	9	0

Bowling

	Mat	Balls	Runs	Wkts	BBI	BBM	Ave	Econ	SR	5w	10
Tests	65	6	1	0	-	-	-	1.00	-	0	0
ODIs	26	-	-	-	-	-	-	-	-	-	-
T20Is	4	-	-	-	-	-	-	-	-	-	-
First-class	142	270	205	6	3/13	-	34.16	4.55	45.0	0	0
List A	75	18	10	0	-	-	-	3.33	-	0	0
Twenty20	28	-	-	-	-	-	-	-	-	-	-

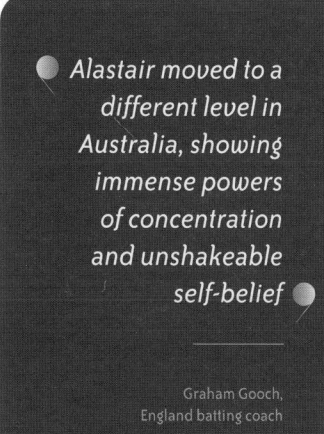

Alastair moved to a different level in Australia, showing immense powers of concentration and unshakeable self-belief

Graham Gooch,
England batting coach

ESSEX

NAME: James Savin Foster
BORN: April 15, 1980, Whipps Cross
HEIGHT: 6ft
SQUAD Nº: 7
NICKNAME: Fozzy, Chief
OTHER TEAMS: England
CAREER: Test debut: 2001; ODI debut: 2001;
T20I debut: 2009; First-class debut: 2000;
List A debut: 2000; T20 debut: 2003; County
cap: 2001

AOC SAYS: Born-and-bred Essex boy Foster is set to embark on his twelfth first-class season for his home county. An unflashy, consistently top-notch wicketkeeper and a considered thinker on the game, Foster was the obvious man to take over when Mark Pettini handed over captaincy duties midway through last year. It was a tough induction for Foster, assuming control of a young team struggling in the top-tier of the Championship and with a long injury list, and though he couldn't keep Essex up or lift a one-day trophy despite two semi-final appearances, his calm and considered approach drew many plaudits, and he is a resoundingly popular choice to take the reins full-time in 2011. Foster enjoyed a whirlwind start to his career. Aged 22 and with just two seasons as Essex's first-choice stumper behind him he was called into the England squad for the 2001/02 tour of India. By stumping Sachin Tendulkar and scrapping hard with the bat, he did well enough to secure a touring berth for the following winter's Ashes tour. A tough experience for many of the squad resulted in subsequent changes in personnel, and Foster, due to perceived shortcomings in his batting, was sent back to the shires. He has not played for England's Test or ODI side since, although he did receive a call-up to England's World Twenty20 squad in 2009. These days he is a much-improved batsman with a first-class double century to his name and 14 tons in all, a reliable middle-order man in four-day cricket and a wildly inventive improviser in the shorter forms. He has power too, launching the legspinner Scott Borthwick for five sixes in a row when Essex faced Durham in 2009. This season looms large for Foster as he juggles a number of key duties – fortunately he has the class to pouch everything that comes his way.

INSIDE TRACK: "He's an outstanding wicketkeeper-batsman. I don't know if it will be tough for him being captain and wicketkeeper. The only person I know who has done that for a long time is Alec Stewart. During the middle of last season our ex-captain Mark Pettini was struggling with form and confidence and he felt it was the right moment to step aside and I was convinced Fozzy was the right man to take up the role. He has had a busy year, he has just got married and it's his Benefit Year so he's got a lot on his plate, but he's aware that he will be well supported by all the staff here at the club." *Paul Grayson*

Batting & Fielding

	Mat	Inns	NO	Runs	HS	Ave	SR	100	50	Ct	St
Tests	7	12	3	226	48	25.11	34.55	0	0	17	1
ODIs	11	6	3	41	13	13.66	57.74	0	0	13	7
T20Is	5	5	2	37	14*	12.33	115.62	0	0	3	3
First-class	174	263	30	8213	212	35.24	-	14	41	484	44
List A	163	123	34	2411	83*	27.08	-	0	11	193	53
Twenty20	77	64	17	969	62*	20.61	137.64	0	4	30	30

Bowling

	Mat	Balls	Runs	Wkts	BBI	BBM	Ave	Econ	SR	5w	10
Tests	7	-	-	-	-	-	-	-	-	-	-
ODIs	11	-	-	-	-	-	-	-	-	-	-
T20Is	5	-	-	-	-	-	-	-	-	-	-
First-class	174	84	128	1	1/122	1/122	128.00	9.14	84.0	0	0
List A	163	-	-	-	-	-	-	-	-	-	-
Twenty20	77	-	-	-	-	-	-	-	-	-	-

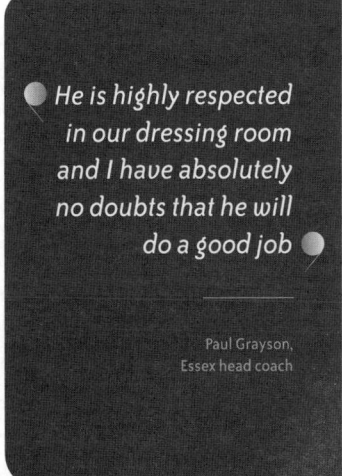

He is highly respected in our dressing room and I have absolutely no doubts that he will do a good job

Paul Grayson,
Essex head coach

BILLY GODLEMAN

LHB LB

ESSEX

NAME: Billy Ashley Godleman
BORN: February 11, 1989, Camden
HEIGHT: 6ft 3in
SQUAD Nº: 34
OTHER TEAMS: Middlesex
CAREER: First-class debut: 2005; List A debut: 2007; T20 debut: 2006

AOC SAYS: Godleman, a combative left-handed opening batsman, held his first professional county contract at the age of 17, having made his debut for first club Middlesex a year earlier. Another member of the Essex clan who has England under 19s honours under his belt, the Londoner scored nearly 800 runs for Middlesex in 2008 but found first-team opportunities limited the following season and joined Essex initially on loan in 2009 before signing a three-year deal. The 22-year-old had a patchy first full season at Chelmsford, the highlight being a classy century against Somerset. But he has age on his side, and the sort of feisty temperament that Essex supporters appreciate; there are plenty of runs stored inside this son of a Camden cabbie.

LAST WORD: "People expected him to be the next Mark Ramprakash when he came through at an early age at Middlesex but he lost his way a little bit. We are hoping to get Billy back on track this season." *Paul Grayson*

Batting & Fielding

	Mat	Inns	NO	Runs	HS	Ave	SR	100	50	Ct	St
First-class	48	81	3	2376	113*	30.46	41.11	3	12	42	0
List A	17	17	1	342	82	21.37	70.80	0	1	4	0
Twenty20	24	23	0	419	69	18.21	107.43	0	3	11	0

Bowling

	Mat	Balls	Runs	Wkts	BBI	BBM	Ave	Econ	SR	5w	10
First-class	48	30	35	0	-	-	-	7.00	-	0	0
List A	17	-	-	-	-	-	-	-	-	-	-
Twenty20	24	-	-	-	-	-	-	-	-	-	-

NAME: David Daniel Masters
BORN: April 22, 1978, Chatham
HEIGHT: 6ft 4in
SQUAD Nº: 9
NICKNAME: Hod, Race Horse, Hoddy
OTHER TEAMS: Kent, Leicestershire
CAREER: First-class debut: 2000; List A debut: 2000; T20 debut: 2003; County cap: 2007 (Leicestershire), 2008 (Essex)

ESSEX

AOC SAYS: Right-arm seamer Masters is Essex's 'Mr Reliable'. A tireless paceman in all forms of the game who can be lethal with the white ball in the early overs, the 32-year-old has matured into his role over the years, finishing last season as the Eagles' leading wicket-taker. With 53 first-class wickets at an average of 23.07, he established himself as Essex's most dynamic seam-bowling option. Tall and rangy, his height is his main weapon, allied to a deadly late-seaming away-swinger. Hitting just back of a length, he is miserly with it – an economy rate of 2.5 an over in first-class cricket last year is exceptional. Formerly at Kent and Leicestershire, Masters has been at Essex since 2007.

LAST WORD: "A tremendous workhorse. He gets through his overs. He's a proven performer and they've done well to hold on to him because he'll be a big performer for them in 2011 in all forms of the game." *Paul Hiscock*

Batting & Fielding

	Mat	Inns	NO	Runs	HS	Ave	SR	100	50	Ct	St
First-class	132	165	27	2039	119	14.77	-	1	5	45	0
List A	131	65	27	467	39	12.28	-	0	0	14	0
Twenty20	70	24	10	77	14	5.50	70.00	0	0	17	0

Bowling

	Mat	Balls	Runs	Wkts	BBI	BBM	Ave	Econ	SR	5w	10
First-class	132	23560	10892	376	6/24	-	28.96	2.77	62.6	12	0
List A	131	5463	4062	126	5/17	5/17	32.23	4.46	43.3	2	0
Twenty20	70	1326	1663	57	3/7	3/7	29.17	7.52	23.2	0	0

JAIK MICKLEBURGH

RHB RM

ESSEX

NAME: Jaik Charles Mickleburgh
BORN: March 30, 1990, Norwich
SQUAD Nº: 32
CAREER: First-class debut: 2008; List A
debut: 2010; T20 debut: 2010

AOC SAYS: Academy graduate Mickleburgh is another stylish young batsman to fall off the Essex production line. After being awarded a full-time contract in 2008, the right-hander has progressed nicely since marking his debut with a half-century against Leicestershire. He was duly rewarded with an England under 19 call-up in 2009, and although his county campaign was halted by injury that year, Mickleburgh was still named in the England Performance Programme squad for the winter of 2009/10. Propelled into the 2010 summer, he delivered his maiden first-class century, a brilliant 174 against Durham, and enjoyed his best season to date, missing only one match and scoring 852 runs, the most by an Essex player.

LAST WORD: "He's a quick learner and very motivated with a good knowledge for the game. He did well last year and got a big hundred at Durham. He'll be a far better player this year and his average will rise." *Paul Grayson*

Batting & Fielding

	Mat	Inns	NO	Runs	HS	Ave	SR	100	50	Ct	St
First-class	25	46	0	1287	174	27.97	44.00	1	7	17	0
List A	4	4	0	84	46	21.00	81.55	0	0	2	0
Twenty20	10	5	2	76	32	25.33	89.41	0	0	7	0

Bowling

	Mat	Balls	Runs	Wkts	BBI	BBM	Ave	Econ	SR	5w	10
First-class	25	78	50	0	-	-	-	3.84	-	0	0
List A	4	-	-	-	-	-	-	-	-	-	-
Twenty20	10	-	-	-	-	-	-	-	-	-	-

NAME: Graham Richard Napier
BORN: January 6, 1980, Colchester
HEIGHT: 5ft 10in
SQUAD Nº: 17
NICKNAME: George
OTHER TEAMS: Central Districts, Mumbai Indians, Wellington
CAREER: First-class debut: 1997; List A debut: 1997; T20 debut: 2003; County cap: 2003

ESSEX

AOC SAYS: On his day, this canny seam-bowling allrounder has the potential to hit a cricket ball as far as any other man in the game, as he proved in 2008 when he struck a world-record 16 sixes in a Twenty20 match against Sussex at Chelmsford. That stupendous innings of 152 from 58 balls, caught live on TV, propelled his name across the cricket world. It led to Napier securing an IPL contract with the Mumbai Indians, and a call-up to the 15-man England squad for the 2009 World Twenty20. However, he didn't actually appear in that tournament, and he remains uncapped at the highest level despite being part of the squad that won the 1998 Under 19 World Cup. After a consistent 2009 with the ball, he was struck down by a back injury that ruled him out of the vast majority of last season. A local lad, Napier has been at Essex since he was 10 years old.

LAST WORD: "Essex were hit badly by the loss of Napier last season. He'd be a big player for any side but got injured halfway through the season and didn't play again. It's a big year for him." *Paul Hiscock*

Batting & Fielding

	Mat	Inns	NO	Runs	HS	Ave	SR	100	50	Ct	St
First-class	103	142	30	3350	125	29.91	-	3	20	39	0
List A	196	151	19	2370	79	17.95	-	0	12	41	0
Twenty20	67	49	7	697	152*	16.59	148.61	1	0	20	0

Bowling

	Mat	Balls	Runs	Wkts	BBI	BBM	Ave	Econ	SR	5w	10
First-class	103	13257	8134	210	6/103	-	38.73	3.68	63.1	3	0
List A	196	6600	5593	225	6/29	6/29	24.85	5.08	29.3	1	0
Twenty20	67	1419	1720	90	4/10	4/10	19.11	7.27	15.7	0	0

MAX OSBORNE

RHB RMF

ESSEX

NAME: Max Osborne
BORN: November 21, 1990, Orsett
HEIGHT: 6ft 3in
SQUAD Nº: 36
CAREER: First-class debut: 2010

AOC SAYS: Right-arm fast bowler Osborne was handed an Essex debut against Bangladesh last season and went on to make his Championship bow against Durham in the final match of the season. He was spotted by county coaches during the pre-season nets in 2009 and offered a place with the academy squad, excelling to be given a two-year professional contract last season. Osborne is a useful squad member who will continue to learn his game in the Second XI in 2011.

LAST WORD: "He's a local lad who has progressed through league cricket playing for Brentwood. If he wants to break into the first team he will have to make an impression for the Second XI. You need lads like this coming through." *Paul Grayson*

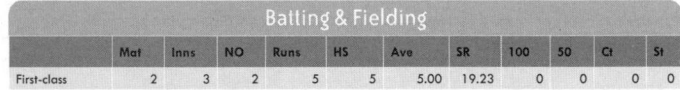

Batting & Fielding

	Mat	Inns	NO	Runs	HS	Ave	SR	100	50	Ct	St
First-class	2	3	2	5	5	5.00	19.23	0	0	0	0

Bowling

	Mat	Balls	Runs	Wkts	BBI	BBM	Ave	Econ	SR	5w	10
First-class	2	216	151	6	3/35	5/95	25.16	4.19	36.0	0	0

NAME: Mark Lewis Pettini
BORN: August 7, 1983, Brighton
HEIGHT: 5ft 11in
SQUAD Nº: 24
NICKNAME: Swampy
CAREER: First-class debut: 2001; List A debut: 2001; T20 debut: 2003; County cap: 2006

ESSEX

AOC SAYS: Pettini began 2010 as Essex captain, and despite his popularity in the dressing room, his struggles for form in the first-class game resulted in a transfer of power to James Foster midway through the campaign. After taking a short break from the game the former England under 19 batsman returned to the squad to bring his accustomed flair and power to their one-day side. An aggressive player, Pettini excels in the short form and received a provisional call-up to England's Twenty20 World Cup squad in 2007. In his first full season as captain, Pettini led Essex to two one-day titles and promotion to the County Championship's top tier in 2009. After the trauma of 2010's captaincy-handover, Pettini will be approaching this season with renewed vigour.

LAST WORD: "He's as good an opener as anyone around in one-day cricket but last year as soon as it was a red ball it seemed to faze him." *Paul Hiscock*

Batting & Fielding

	Mat	Inns	NO	Runs	HS	Ave	SR	100	50	Ct	St
First-class	93	158	20	4663	208*	33.78	47.90	5	26	67	0
List A	112	103	6	2529	144	26.07	86.22	4	17	42	0
Twenty20	62	59	5	1444	87	26.74	130.09	0	10	22	0

Bowling

	Mat	Balls	Runs	Wkts	BBI	BBM	Ave	Econ	SR	5w	10
First-class	93	113	191	0	-	-	-	10.14	-	0	0
List A	112	-	-	-	-	-	-	-	-	-	-
Twenty20	62	-	-	-	-	-	-	-	-	-	-

TIM PHILLIPS

LHB SLA

ESSEX

NAME: Timothy James Phillips
BORN: March 13, 1981, Cambridge
HEIGHT: 6ft 1in
SQUAD Nº: 23
NICKNAME: Pips
CAREER: First-class debut: 1999; List A debut: 1999; T20 debut: 2006; County cap: 2006

AOC SAYS: Left-armer Phillips will be Essex's senior spinner this summer after the Chelmsford club decided not to re-sign Pakistan international Danish Kaneria. Injury has disrupted much of his Essex career since he made his debut in 1999. A cruciate ligament injury ruled him out of the entire 2003 campaign and it wasn't until 2006 that he finally became a first-team regular, leading the wicket-taking charts for the Eagles that year. If Phillips is given suitable pitches to bowl on he could be a useful asset for Essex this year, but the pressure is now on to improve on just one five-wicket haul in a first-class career spanning over a decade. He is also a useful lower-order batsman, with four first-class fifties to his name.

LAST WORD: "He's been on the fringes of the squad for the last few years because of injury. It's time for us to say to him: 'You are our main spinner, now show us what you can do'. He's talented and it's up to him to deliver." *Paul Grayson*

Batting & Fielding

	Mat	Inns	NO	Runs	HS	Ave	SR	100	50	Ct	St
First-class	61	85	11	1436	89	19.40	-	0	4	40	0
List A	48	28	11	263	41	15.47	-	0	0	15	0
Twenty20	33	17	6	163	57*	14.81	114.78	0	1	15	0

Bowling

	Mat	Balls	Runs	Wkts	BBI	BBM	Ave	Econ	SR	5w	10
First-class	61	8393	5046	110	5/41	-	45.87	3.60	76.3	1	0
List A	48	1439	1215	52	5/34	5/34	23.36	5.06	27.6	2	0
Twenty20	33	423	557	16	2/11	2/11	34.81	7.90	26.4	0	0

NAME: Owais Alam Shah
BORN: October 22, 1978, Karachi
HEIGHT: 6ft 1in
SQUAD Nº: 3
NICKNAME: Ace
OTHER TEAMS: England, Cape Cobras,
Delhi Daredevils, Kolkata Knight Riders,
Middlesex, Wellington
CAREER: Test debut: 2006; ODI debut: 2001;
T20I debut: 2007; First-class debut: 1996;
List A debut: 1995; T20 debut: 2003; County
cap: 2000 (Middlesex)

ESSEX

AOC SAYS: The former England international was recruited on a three-year deal after being released by Middlesex at the end of last season. Pakistan-born but raised in north London, Shah has 15 years of county experience under his belt, scoring over 14,000 first-class runs. Shah could prove pivotal for Essex as they aim to bounce back from last season's Championship relegation. Elegant, stylish and impudent, his technique owes more than a touch to the Asian stylists of his birth, and he cites Mohammad Azharuddin as an early influence. Some feel he was harshly discarded by England after just two Tests and a series of ODIs in which he was often England's most expansive and threatening batsman. Essex have secured the coveted signature, knowing that if fit, Shah is a stick-on for 1,000 runs.

LAST WORD: "Shah is a vastly experienced player with a terrific record. I think he will fit into our Essex philosophy pretty easily." *Paul Grayson*

Batting & Fielding

	Mat	Inns	NO	Runs	HS	Ave	SR	100	50	Ct	St
Tests	6	10	0	269	88	26.90	41.90	0	2	2	0
ODIs	71	66	6	1834	107*	30.56	78.67	1	12	21	0
T20Is	17	15	1	347	55*	24.78	122.18	0	1	5	0
First-class	225	382	34	14703	203	42.25	-	40	72	171	0
List A	331	313	39	9623	134	35.12	-	13	62	112	0
Twenty20	96	92	20	2414	80	33.52	129.29	0	13	36	0

Bowling

	Mat	Balls	Runs	Wkts	BBI	BBM	Ave	Econ	SR	5w	10
Tests	6	30	31	0	-	-	-	6.20	-	0	0
ODIs	71	193	184	7	3/15	3/15	26.28	5.72	27.5	0	0
T20Is	17	-	-	-	-	-	-	-	-	-	-
First-class	225	2237	1489	26	3/33	-	57.26	3.99	86.0	0	0
List A	331	912	896	27	4/11	4/11	33.18	5.89	33.7	0	0
Twenty20	96	45	64	4	2/26	2/26	16.00	8.53	11.2	0	0

SCOTT STYRIS

RHB RM

OVERSEAS PLAYER

NAME: Scott Bernard Styris
BORN: July 10, 1975, Brisbane
HEIGHT: 5ft 10in
SQUAD Nº: 56
NICKNAME: Miley, The Rus
OTHER TEAMS: New Zealand, Auckland, Deccan Chargers, Durham, Middlesex, Northern Districts
CAREER: Test debut: 2002; ODI debut: 1999; T20I debut: 2005; First-class debut: 1994; List A debut: 1994; T20 debut: 2005; County cap: 2006 (Middlesex)

AOC SAYS: Essex moved quickly during pre-season to secure the services of New Zealand's hefty batting allrounder for the 2011 FP t20. A hit at Chelmsford last year, Styris put in a number of impressive displays in the group stages of last year's tournament before receiving a New Zealand call-up which made him unable to play in the knockout stages. With more than 4,500 runs and over 150 wickets in ODIs and international Twenty20 cricket combined – not to mention five Test centuries – Styris will provide huge experience for Essex as they aim to appear at Twenty20 Finals Day for the second successive year. 'The Rus' will feel he has unfinished business after missing the big day last year and he adds to the list of explosive hitters in the Essex line-up.

LAST WORD: "He proved to be a matchwinner in his own right and a shrewd choice particularly following the injuries to Napier and ten Doeschate." *Paul Hiscock*

Batting & Fielding

	Mat	Inns	NO	Runs	HS	Ave	SR	100	50	Ct	St
Tests	29	48	4	1586	170	36.04	51.34	5	6	23	0
ODIs	188	161	23	4483	141	32.48	79.41	4	28	73	0
T20Is	31	29	2	578	66	21.40	119.66	0	1	8	0
First-class	128	213	20	6048	212*	31.33	-	10	30	102	0
List A	332	292	48	8196	141	33.59	-	6	55	128	0
Twenty20	109	103	10	2256	106*	24.25	129.72	1	9	27	0

Bowling

	Mat	Balls	Runs	Wkts	BBI	BBM	Ave	Econ	SR	5w	10
Tests	29	1960	1015	20	3/28	3/44	50.75	3.10	98.0	0	0
ODIs	188	6114	4839	137	6/25	6/25	35.32	4.74	44.6	1	0
T20Is	31	309	349	18	3/5	3/5	19.38	6.77	17.1	0	0
First-class	128	12826	6446	204	6/32	-	31.59	3.01	62.8	9	1
List A	332	11946	9154	296	6/25	6/25	30.92	4.59	40.3	1	0
Twenty20	109	1736	2182	81	3/5	3/5	26.93	7.54	21.4	0	0

NAME: Ryan Neil ten Doeschate
BORN: June 30, 1980, Port Elizabeth
HEIGHT: 5ft 11in
SQUAD Nº: 27
NICKNAME: Tendo
OTHER TEAMS: Netherlands, Canterbury, Mashonaland Eagles, Tasmania, Western Province
CAREER: ODI debut: 2006; T20I debut: 2008; First-class debut: 2003; List A debut: 2003; T20 debut: 2003; County cap: 2006

ESSEX

AOC SAYS: Ryan ten Doeschate is today one of county cricket's prime draw cards. An explosive batsman with huge Popeye forearms (and a pull shot to rival the very best), a nagging, inventive medium-pacer with the knack of snaring big wickets at crucial moments and a brilliant fielder anywhere in the outfield, this Dutch-South African-Essex boy is pure box office. Initially seen as a bowler who could bat – he finished as Essex's top first-class wicket-taker in 2008 – ten Doeschate has grown to become one of county cricket's most feared batsmen. He has starred for the Netherlands on several occasions, with two memorable appearances against England. He was the key man in the World Twenty20 victory at Lord's in 2009, and scored a superb century when the teams met in the 2011 World Cup. He was the ICC Associate Player of the Year in 2008.

LAST WORD: "He is a top-class person to work with and his work ethic is exceptional."
Paul Grayson

Batting & Fielding

	Mat	Inns	NO	Runs	HS	Ave	SR	100	50	Ct	St
ODIs	33	32	9	1541	119	67.00	87.70	5	9	13	0
T20Is	9	9	4	214	56	42.80	128.91	0	1	3	0
First-class	81	118	15	4950	259*	48.05	-	16	17	44	0
List A	131	107	32	3529	134*	47.05	-	6	20	41	0
Twenty20	86	76	18	1555	102	26.81	130.12	1	3	26	0

Bowling

	Mat	Balls	Runs	Wkts	BBI	BBM	Ave	Econ	SR	5w	10
ODIs	33	1580	1327	55	4/31	4/31	24.12	5.03	28.7	0	0
T20Is	9	204	241	12	3/23	3/23	20.08	7.08	17.0	0	0
First-class	81	7916	5258	158	6/20	-	33.27	3.98	50.1	7	0
List A	131	3890	3583	131	5/50	5/50	27.35	5.52	29.6	1	0
Twenty20	86	881	1149	52	4/24	4/24	22.09	7.82	16.9	0	0

MATT WALKER — LHB RM R4 MVP86

ESSEX

NAME: Matthew Jonathan Walker
BORN: January 2, 1974, Gravesend
HEIGHT: 5ft 6in
SQUAD Nº: 22
NICKNAME: Walks
OTHER TEAMS: Kent
CAREER: First-class debut: 1993; List A
debut: 1994; T20 debut: 2003; County cap:
2000 (Kent), 2010 (Essex)

AOC SAYS: Essex's senior professional signed a contract extension with the Eagles last year after enjoying another fine season. The outgoing 37-year-old enjoyed a long career with Kent after making his debut in 1992 but was released in 2008 and Essex duly snapped up the classy left-hander. Walker reached 1,000 Championship runs in three different seasons for Kent, collecting a clutch of records along the way – 275* is still the highest individual score made by a Kent player at Canterbury – and he continued to plunder runs for Essex throughout 2009 and 2010. The diminutive strokemaker – a film buff and music junkie – was awarded his county cap by Essex last season and will be looking to defy his age to enjoy another run-filled season. He is also an exceptional fielder, although not quite as sharp across the ground as he once was…

LAST WORD: "Matt is a terrific character to have around the place and is as enthusiastic as ever." *Paul Grayson*

Batting & Fielding

	Mat	Inns	NO	Runs	HS	Ave	SR	100	50	Ct	St
First-class	212	356	37	11610	275*	36.39	-	28	47	142	0
List A	280	253	38	6153	117	28.61	-	3	36	74	0
Twenty20	69	65	10	1302	74*	23.67	117.72	0	4	6	0

Bowling

	Mat	Balls	Runs	Wkts	BBI	BBM	Ave	Econ	SR	5w	10
First-class	212	2004	1214	25	3/35	-	48.56	3.63	80.1	0	0
List A	280	904	759	30	4/24	4/24	25.30	5.03	30.1	0	0
Twenty20	69	-	-	-	-	-	-	-	-	-	-

NAME: Thomas Westley
BORN: March 13, 1989, Cambridge
HEIGHT: 6ft 2in
SQUAD Nº: 21
NICKNAME: Spongebob, Pup
CAREER: First-class debut: 2007; List A debut: 2006, T20 debut: 2010

ESSEX

AOC SAYS: Westley is yet another richly talented young Essex hopeful who has progressed through the club's academy into the first team. A tall, elegant middle-order strokemaker in the classical vein, he already has two first-class hundreds to his name. The former England under 19 international made nine Championship appearances last summer, combining his cricket with his studies at Durham University, where he was Durham MCCU's captain. Westley learnt his game under the tutelage of Graham Gooch, made his Second XI debut as a 15-year-old, and is also an improving offspinner.

LAST WORD: "His offspin will provide back-up to our main spinner Tim Phillips. He has a good knowledge of the game but was affected by his commitments to university last year – being up at Durham meant we didn't see as much of him as we would have liked."
Paul Grayson

Batting & Fielding

	Mat	Inns	NO	Runs	HS	Ave	SR	100	50	Ct	St
First-class	35	61	9	1517	132	29.17	46.95	2	7	15	0
List A	6	4	0	41	36	10.25	71.92	0	0	0	0
Twenty20	1	-	-	-	-	-	-	-	-	0	0

Bowling

	Mat	Balls	Runs	Wkts	BBI	BBM	Ave	Econ	SR	5w	10
First-class	35	825	415	14	4/55	4/55	29.64	3.01	58.9	0	0
List A	6	66	59	1	1/34	1/34	59.00	5.36	66.0	0	0
Twenty20	1	-	-	-	-	-	-	-	-	-	-

ADAM WHEATER

RHB WK

ESSEX

NAME: Adam Jack Wheater
BORN: February 13, 1990, Whipps Cross
HEIGHT: 5ft 6in
SQUAD Nº: 31
NICKNAME: Wheates
CAREER: First-class debut: 2008; List A debut: 2010; T20 debut: 2009

AOC SAYS: Wheater is a hugely impressive young wicketkeeper who has been limited to just a few first-team opportunities due to the presence of James Foster, but has a big future ahead of him. He came to prominence last season when in partnership with another young gun in Michael Comber, the pair saw Essex home in a CB40 fixture against Northants. Playing just as a batsman, his unbeaten 52 that day in a tight run-chase gave a glimpse of his talent. The 21-year-old has proved to be a secure deputy for Foster, and although he says he is happy to wait in the wings for the upcoming season, Essex will be acutely aware that a player of such promise won't be waiting around forever. Wheater was called up for the England under 19s tour of South Africa in 2008/09 and is certainly one to watch.

LAST WORD: "I think he's ahead of a number of the other young wicketkeepers on the circuit but he won't want to stagnate. It's an interesting dilemma but with the loan system in place it may be that he has to spend some time elsewhere." *Paul Hiscock*

Batting & Fielding

	Mat	Inns	NO	Runs	HS	Ave	SR	100	50	Ct	St
First-class	17	22	4	865	126	48.05	63.04	1	6	37	0
List A	13	7	1	202	69	33.66	103.58	0	2	3	0
Twenty20	9	7	1	52	14	8.66	73.23	0	0	5	3

Bowling

	Mat	Balls	Runs	Wkts	BBI	BBM	Ave	Econ	SR	5w	10
First-class	17	-	-	-	-	-	-	-	-	-	-
List A	13	-	-	-	-	-	-	-	-	-	-
Twenty20	9	-	-	-	-	-	-	-	-	-	-

NAME: Christopher Julian Clement Wright
BORN: July 14, 1985, Chipping Norton
HEIGHT: 6ft 3in
SQUAD Nº: 14
NICKNAME: The Baron
OTHER TEAMS: Middlesex, Tamil Union
Cricket and Athletic Club
CAREER: First-class debut: 2004; List A
debut: 2004; T20 debut: 2004

ESSEX

AOC SAYS: A lively seamer who has improved gradually with each season in county cricket, Wright struggled to get a game at his former club Middlesex but after signing for Essex in 2007 after a short stint playing winter cricket in Sri Lanka, he has thrived. He took 31 Championship wickets last season to follow 40 scalps in 2009, as well as proving his worth in the one-day game. The 25-year-old continues to develop as a county player and has found an extra yard of pace since joining Essex.

LAST WORD: "An integral member of the side since his move from Middlesex. One of those players who has thrived with opportunity and has often taken on the role in the limited-overs game of 'death' bowler with positive effect." *Paul Hiscock*

Batting & Fielding

	Mat	Inns	NO	Runs	HS	Ave	SR	100	50	Ct	St
First-class	54	70	18	916	76	17.61	52.07	0	3	13	0
List A	59	25	10	121	23	8.06	76.58	0	0	10	0
Twenty20	31	7	6	15	6*	15.00	136.36	0	0	4	0

Bowling

	Mat	Balls	Runs	Wkts	BBI	BBM	Ave	Econ	SR	5w	10
First-class	54	8097	5110	123	6/22	-	41.54	3.78	65.8	2	0
List A	59	2273	2118	51	3/3	3/3	41.52	5.59	44.5	0	0
Twenty20	31	650	947	31	4/24	4/24	30.54	8.74	20.9	0	0

GlamorganCricket
Criced**Morgannwg**

FORMED: 1888
HOME GROUND: SWALEC Stadium, Cardiff
ONE-DAY NAME: Dragons
CAPTAIN: Alviro Petersen
2010 RESULTS: CC2: 3/9; CB40: 7/7 in Group A; FP t20: 8/9 in South Group

HONOURS

County Championship: (3) 1948, 1969, 1997; Pro40/National League/CB40: (2) 2002, 2004; Sunday League: 1993

THE LOWDOWN

After an acrimonious season in 2010, Glamorgan's embattled supporters will be praying that a new captain/coach partnership can somehow improve the club's fortunes. Last term saw the departures of captain Jamie Dalrymple and head of cricket Matthew Maynard after the club failed, by just five points, to achieve promotion in the County Championship. The break-up was messy, and supporters are still reeling from the loss of Maynard – a Glamorgan institution – his son Tom, who is a hugely promising batsman in his own right, and Dalrymple himself. The club has moved to install the South African opening batsman Alviro Petersen as their new captain, and he will be expected to work with new coach Matthew Mott to bring about a degree of unity after the factionalism of last season. It's a big job, but with players like Jim Allenby, James Harris and Mark Wallace on the staff, they will at least have proven, quality cricketers to call upon.

HEAD COACH: MATTHEW MOTT

Of the many new faces at Glamorgan this term, the appointment of the Australian Matthew Mott, hotfooting it straight from the New South Wales job, is perhaps the most interesting of all. Mott served as NSW coach for four years and for three years previous as assistant to Trevor Bayliss, and brings huge experience and a winning mentality to a club that will need every ounce of his leadership qualities to thrive once again.

With thanks to: Mark Wallace, Glamorgan wicketkeeper; Gareth Griffiths, sports reporter, Media Wales

Batting & Fielding

	Mat	Inns	NO	Runs	HS	Ave	SR	100	50	Ct	St
NA James	1	2	1	75	60*	75.00	42.61	0	1	0	-
DO Brown	1	2	0	114	99	57.00	62.98	0	1	1	-
MJ Cosgrove	15	26	2	1187	142	49.45	85.95	5	4	10	-
J Allenby	16	25	4	933	105	44.42	59.69	1	10	16	-
GP Rees	17	30	4	918	106*	35.30	49.16	2	5	6	-
BJ Wright	17	27	1	847	172	32.57	63.92	2	4	7	-
TL Maynard	11	18	0	495	98	27.50	71.53	0	4	11	-
MA Wallace	16	24	1	626	113	27.21	58.94	1	4	43	4
JWM Dalrymple	15	22	0	554	105	25.18	45.18	1	2	19	-
MJ Powell	7	12	1	275	55	25.00	44.57	0	1	1	-
RDB Croft	9	14	3	244	63	22.18	56.87	0	2	0	-
AJ Shantry	1	1	0	22	22	22.00	27.50	0	0	0	-
DA Cosker	16	24	10	268	49*	19.14	33.62	0	0	7	-
JAR Harris	13	19	2	257	49	15.11	37.79	0	0	2	-
DS Harrison	12	18	0	253	35	14.05	79.81	0	0	2	-
WT Owen	3	4	1	38	38	12.66	79.16	0	0	0	-
CP Ashling	3	5	2	37	20	12.33	42.04	0	0	0	-
WD Bragg	3	6	0	56	44	9.33	32.74	0	0	3	1
HT Waters	11	13	4	67	16	7.44	19.19	0	0	1	-

Bowling

	Mat	Overs	Mdn	Runs	Wkts	BBI	BBM	Ave	Econ	SR	5w	10
JAR Harris	13	443.4	115	1293	63	5/56	8/114	20.52	2.91	42.2	2	0
J Allenby	16	330.1	82	885	41	5/59	5/41	21.58	2.68	48.3	1	0
DA Cosker	16	432.0	101	1128	51	5/93	7/127	22.11	2.61	50.8	1	0
RDB Croft	9	323.3	67	805	26	4/20	5/62	30.96	2.48	74.6	0	0
DS Harrison	12	323.3	44	1156	37	7/45	8/88	31.24	3.57	52.4	2	0
CP Ashling	3	55.1	5	200	6	3/18	3/22	33.33	3.62	55.1	0	0
HT Waters	11	297.4	79	898	26	4/39	5/93	34.53	3.01	68.6	0	0
JWM Dalrymple	15	127.0	13	391	11	4/71	4/71	35.54	3.07	69.2	0	0
AJ Shantry	1	14.0	4	41	1	1/21	1/41	41.00	2.92	84.0	0	0
MJ Cosgrove	15	35.0	5	140	3	1/12	1/13	46.66	4.00	70.0	0	0
WT Owen	3	54.0	8	232	3	3/65	3/93	77.33	4.29	108.0	0	0
NA James	1	1.0	0	1	0	-	-	-	1.00	-	0	0
TL Maynard	11	3.0	0	20	0	-	-	-	6.66	-	0	0
GP Rees	17	1.0	0	3	0	-	-	-	3.00	-	0	0
MA Wallace	16	1.0	0	3	0	-	-	-	3.00	-	0	0
BJ Wright	17	2.0	0	7	0	-	-	-	3.50	-	0	0

Batting & Fielding

	Mat	Inns	NO	Runs	HS	Ave	SR	100	50	Ct	St
MJ Cosgrove	10	8	0	397	88	49.62	120.30	0	5	4	-
RDB Croft	3	3	1	74	53*	37.00	101.36	0	1	0	-
TL Maynard	11	10	1	285	103*	31.66	102.51	1	1	5	-
BJ Wright	11	10	2	217	79	27.12	78.33	0	1	2	-
DA Cosker	11	7	5	51	22*	25.50	113.33	0	0	2	-
JWM Dalrymple	7	7	1	142	54*	23.66	80.22	0	1	5	-
J Allenby	8	8	0	182	61	22.75	81.25	0	1	1	-
GP Rees	5	4	1	66	51*	22.00	81.48	0	1	1	-
MA Wallace	11	7	0	140	38	20.00	78.21	0	0	4	2
DO Brown	10	9	1	139	31*	17.37	83.23	0	0	3	-
NA James	2	1	0	15	15	15.00	50.00	0	0	1	-
WD Bragg	6	5	0	52	28	10.40	69.33	0	0	1	-
DS Harrison	4	3	0	31	12	10.33	83.78	0	0	0	-
WT Owen	8	6	1	35	12	7.00	83.33	0	0	1	-
AJ Jones	1	1	0	5	5	5.00	55.55	0	0	0	-
CP Ashling	5	4	3	4	3*	4.00	23.52	0	0	0	-
JAR Harris	3	1	0	1	1	1.00	12.50	0	0	1	-

Bowling

	Mat	Overs	Mdns	Runs	Wkts	BBI	Ave	Econ	SR	5w
NA James	2	3.0	0	19	2	2/19	9.50	6.33	9.0	0
WT Owen	8	49.0	1	320	13	5/49	24.61	6.53	22.6	1
JAR Harris	3	21.0	0	141	4	2/41	35.25	6.71	31.5	0
DA Cosker	11	73.0	2	415	11	4/33	37.72	5.68	39.8	0
MJ Cosgrove	10	16.0	0	120	3	2/21	40.00	7.50	32.0	0
JWM Dalrymple	7	27.0	0	163	3	2/55	54.33	6.03	54.0	0
HT Waters	5	26.0	0	187	3	1/30	62.33	7.19	52.0	0
J Allenby	8	47.0	1	263	3	2/28	87.66	5.59	94.0	0
DS Harrison	4	29.4	1	265	3	3/54	88.33	8.93	59.3	0
RDB Croft	3	24.0	1	132	1	1/31	132.00	5.50	144.0	0
DO Brown	10	38.0	0	283	2	1/31	141.50	7.44	114.0	0
CP Ashling	5	25.4	1	197	1	1/39	197.00	7.67	154.0	0
WD Bragg	6	1.0	0	15	0	-	-	15.00	-	0
AJ Jones	1	8.0	0	74	0	-	-	9.25	-	0
TL Maynard	11	2.0	0	32	0	-	-	16.00	-	0

GLAMORGAN
DRAGONS

	Mat	Inns	NO	Runs	HS	Ave	SR	100	50	Ct	St
MJ Cosgrove	16	16	0	562	89	35.12	132.23	0	4	2	-
TL Maynard	16	16	3	380	78*	29.23	150.19	0	3	5	-
JWM Dalrymple	16	15	3	281	46*	23.41	100.35	0	0	4	-
J Allenby	15	15	1	317	54	22.64	105.66	0	2	4	-
GP Rees	15	15	5	183	35	18.30	104.57	0	0	5	-
BJ Wright	7	6	1	83	27	16.60	115.27	0	0	1	-
MA Wallace	16	13	5	130	42*	16.25	120.37	0	0	8	6
WD Bragg	1	1	0	15	15	15.00	68.18	0	0	0	-
RDB Croft	16	6	3	37	22*	12.33	78.72	0	0	3	-
JAR Harris	10	5	2	37	18	12.33	123.33	0	0	0	-
DO Brown	12	7	1	66	21	11.00	104.76	0	0	4	-
DS Harrison	2	1	0	8	8	8.00	53.33	0	0	0	-
WT Owen	4	1	0	8	8	8.00	114.28	0	0	0	-
SW Tait	10	2	1	6	5	6.00	100.00	0	0	1	-
DA Cosker	12	4	2	8	6	4.00	53.33	0	0	3	-
CP Ashling	4	2	0	6	6	3.00	66.66	0	0	0	-
HT Waters	4	2	2	11	11*	-	84.61	0	0	0	-

Batting & Fielding

	Mat	Overs	Mdns	Runs	Wkts	BBI	Ave	Econ	SR	5w
RDB Croft	16	57.5	0	343	22	3/19	15.59	5.93	15.7	0
DS Harrison	2	5.0	0	61	2	2/45	30.50	12.20	15.0	0
JWM Dalrymple	16	32.0	0	246	8	3/25	30.75	7.68	24.0	0
DA Cosker	12	37.0	0	278	9	2/23	30.88	7.51	24.6	0
MJ Cosgrove	16	7.0	0	71	2	1/6	35.50	10.14	21.0	0
CP Ashling	4	11.0	0	118	3	2/39	39.33	10.72	22.0	0
HT Waters	4	14.1	0	118	3	3/30	39.33	8.32	28.3	0
JAR Harris	10	30.0	0	285	7	2/23	40.71	9.50	25.7	0
SW Tait	10	36.0	1	285	7	2/28	40.71	7.91	30.8	0
J Allenby	15	45.1	0	368	9	3/23	40.88	8.14	30.1	0
DO Brown	12	13.0	0	143	2	2/30	71.50	11.00	39.0	0
WT Owen	4	9.0	0	104	0	-	-	11.55	-	0

Bowling

GLAMORGAN

NAME: James Allenby
BORN: September 12, 1982,
Western Australia
HEIGHT: 6ft
SQUAD Nº: 6
OTHER TEAMS: Leicestershire, Western
Australia
CAREER: First-class debut: 2006; List A
debut: 2003; T20 debut: 2005; County cap:
2010 (Glamorgan)

AOC SAYS: Allenby was a key man for Glamorgan last summer as the Welsh side narrowly missed out on promotion in the County Championship. He averaged 44.42 with the bat and took 41 wickets at 21.58 apiece, enjoying his most profitable season to date with both bat and ball. Australia-born but England qualified, he previously played for Leicestershire before moving to Cardiff on loan in 2009 and then signed a three-year contract with the Dragons last summer. Allenby is a hard-hitting strokemaker who is given free rein to hit out at the top of the order in limited-overs cricket and a canny medium-pacer.

LAST WORD: "Allenby was integral in the Championship last year. He's very steady and could bat higher than No.6 but that's his preferred position. He's very elegant and a very good player through the covers. He's also very skilful medium-pace bowler" *Gareth Griffiths*

Batting & Fielding

	Mat	Inns	NO	Runs	HS	Ave	SR	100	50	Ct	St
First-class	63	96	15	3175	138*	39.19	56.71	4	25	60	0
List A	59	54	7	1189	91*	25.29	82.74	0	6	18	0
Twenty20	55	51	9	1146	110	27.28	119.74	1	8	20	0

Bowling

	Mat	Balls	Runs	Wkts	BBI	BBM	Ave	Econ	SR	5w	10
First-class	63	6059	2777	99	5/59	6/196	28.05	2.74	61.2	2	0
List A	59	1768	1524	49	5/43	5/43	31.10	5.17	36.0	1	0
Twenty20	55	748	986	37	5/21	5/21	26.64	7.90	20.2	2	0

NAME: Chris Paul Ashling
BORN: November 26, 1988, Manchester
SQUAD Nº: 32
CAREER: First-class debut: 2009; List A
debut: 2009; T20 debut: 2009

GLAMORGAN

AOC SAYS: A former England youth international, Ashling played for Lancashire's Second XI before joining Glamorgan in 2007, where he also played second-string cricket before making his first-class and List A debuts in 2009. To date he has played four first-class matches for Glamorgan, eight List A fixtures and four T20 matches. He took 21 Second XI Championship wickets last summer at an impressive average of 15.81. He'll be looking to force his way into Glamorgan's first team this summer and will be hoping for more appearances in all forms of the game.

LAST WORD: "Chris has done a lot of work with our bowling coach Steve Watkin and he is one of a few young bowlers vying for one first-team spot really." *Mark Wallace*

Batting & Fielding

	Mat	Inns	NO	Runs	HS	Ave	SR	100	50	Ct	St
First-class	4	6	2	49	20	12.25	38.58	0	0	0	0
List A	8	6	4	11	6*	5.50	33.33	0	0	0	0
Twenty20	4	2	0	6	6	3.00	66.66	0	0	0	0

Bowling

	Mat	Balls	Runs	Wkts	BBI	BBM	Ave	Econ	SR	5w	10
First-class	4	499	316	9	3/18	3/22	35.11	3.79	55.4	0	0
List A	8	274	304	5	2/33	2/33	60.80	6.65	54.8	0	0
Twenty20	4	66	118	3	2/39	2/39	39.33	10.72	22.0	0	0

WILL BRAGG

LHB WK

NAME: William David Bragg
BORN: October 24, 1986, Newport, Wales
SQUAD Nº: 22
CAREER: First-class debut: 2007; List A debut: 2005; T20 debut: 2010

AOC SAYS: Bragg made his Glamorgan debut in 2007 and acts as understudy to first-choice wicketkeeper Mark Wallace. However, he has made a number of appearances as a batsman only and in 2009 played nine Championship matches, averaging 30.58. His highest score to date came against Gloucestershire when he was pushed up to open and, going forward, Glamorgan see him as a potential top-order batsman with a technique suited to blunting the new ball. He made 78 batting at No.3 in a Pro40 defeat to Leicestershire during the same summer. Throughout his time at Glamorgan he has continued to represent Wales in the Minor Counties Championship.

LAST WORD: "He might start the season batting at No.3, but he didn't get many chances last year. There are a few guys going for one or two batting positions in the side and No.3 is a problem position. I can see Bragg filling that slot." *Gareth Griffiths*

Batting & Fielding

	Mat	Inns	NO	Runs	HS	Ave	SR	100	50	Ct	St
First-class	14	22	0	474	92	21.54	47.02	0	2	7	1
List A	13	12	1	283	78	25.72	70.92	0	1	2	0
Twenty20	1	1	0	15	15	15.00	68.18	0	0	0	0

Bowling

	Mat	Balls	Runs	Wkts	BBI	BBM	Ave	Econ	SR	5w	10
First-class	14	30	23	0	-	-	-	4.60	-	0	0
List A	13	6	15	0	-	-	-	15.00	-	0	0
Twenty20	1	-	-	-	-	-	-	-	-	-	-

NAME: David Owen Brown
BORN: December 8, 1982, Burnley
HEIGHT: 6ft
SQUAD Nº: 12
OTHER TEAMS: Gloucestershire
CAREER: First-class debut: 2003; List A
debut: 2006; T20 debut: 2006

GLAMORGAN

AOC SAYS: Former Gloucestershire man Brown joined Glamorgan for the 2010 season and scored 99 against West Indies A in his only first-class match for the Welsh county. He was a more permanent fixture in their one-day side, however, appearing on 10 occasions in the CB40 and making 12 appearances in the FP t20. He didn't have a great season for the first team but then no one excelled in one-day cricket throughout the club. His average of 32.55 in nine innings in the Second XI Championship included 109 against Lancashire. Brown is one of many peripheral players hoping that 2011 could be the year it all clicks.

LAST WORD: "He did really well for the Second XI and produces the odd performance in one-day cricket. A right-arm medium-pace bowler, he looks to hit the ball from the lower-order." *Gareth Griffiths*

Batting & Fielding

	Mat	Inns	NO	Runs	HS	Ave	SR	100	50	Ct	St
First-class	24	41	4	1089	99	29.43	52.18	0	8	13	0
List A	38	31	7	500	63*	20.83	77.16	0	1	13	0
Twenty20	30	22	2	329	56	16.45	117.92	0	1	10	0

Bowling

	Mat	Balls	Runs	Wkts	BBI	BBM	Ave	Econ	SR	5w	10
First-class	24	1755	1251	28	5/38	-	44.67	4.27	62.6	1	0
List A	38	732	804	14	3/29	3/29	57.42	6.59	52.2	0	0
Twenty20	30	138	214	6	2/30	2/30	35.66	9.30	23.0	0	0

CHRIS COOKE

RHB WK

GLAMORGAN

NAME: Christopher Barry Cooke
BORN: May 30, 1986, Johannesburg
SQUAD Nº: 24
OTHER TEAMS: Western Province
CAREER: First-class debut: 2009; List A debut: 2009

AOC SAYS: Wicketkeeper-batsman Cooke was rewarded for his Second XI form last September with a two-year contract. Across the Second XI Championship and Trophy competitions he notched over 500 runs and received some excellent reviews for his glovework. The South Africa-born 25-year-old has previously played for Western Province in his homeland, playing six first-class matches and averaging 37.72 in 14 one-dayers. Helped by the presence of fellow countryman Petersen at the helm, Cooke will be hoping to push Mark Wallace for a place in the Glamorgan one-day side this summer but sources close to the club believe he has the power and technique to break through as a specialist batsman.

LAST WORD: "He played for the Second XI last year and can hit the ball long and hard, giving him one-day potential." *Gareth Griffiths*

Batting & Fielding

	Mat	Inns	NO	Runs	HS	Ave	SR	100	50	Ct	St
First-class	6	11	1	186	44*	18.60	36.97	0	0	12	1
List A	14	14	3	415	109*	37.72	98.10	1	1	9	2

Bowling

	Mat	Balls	Runs	Wkts	BBI	BBM	Ave	Econ	SR	5w	10
First-class	6	-	-	-	-	-	-	-	-	-	-
List A	14	-	-	-	-	-	-	-	-	-	-

MARK COSGROVE

OVERSEAS PLAYER

GLAMORGAN

NAME: Mark James Cosgrove
BORN: June 14, 1984, Adelaide
HEIGHT: 5ft 9in
SQUAD Nº: 4
NICKNAME: Cozzie
OTHER TEAMS: Australia, South Australia, Tasmania
CAREER: ODI debut: 2006; First-class debut: 2003; List A debut: 2003; T20 debut: 2006; County cap: 2006

AOC SAYS: This talented left-hander returns to Glamorgan as their second overseas player for the FP t20 this summer after three previous seasons with the Welsh county. The bulky Australian scored 1,187 first-class runs for Glamorgan last summer at an average just under 50, and was the country's third-highest runscorer in Twenty20 cricket, notching 562 runs. He continued his outstanding 2010 form with Tasmania over the winter and will be a huge asset to Glamorgan in this summer's FP t20. While a perceived lack of physical conditioning has so far held him back from adding to his three ODI appearances for Australia, he has not given up hope of wearing the Baggy Green, and few doubt he has the technique and skill to score Test match runs if given the chance.

LAST WORD: "He hits the ball as clean as anyone I have ever seen." *Darren Lehmann, former Australian batsman*

Batting & Fielding

	Mat	Inns	NO	Runs	HS	Ave	SR	100	50	Ct	St
ODIs	3	3	0	112	74	37.33	96.55	0	1	0	0
First-class	101	178	14	7255	233	44.23	66.30	21	40	74	0
List A	107	104	4	3497	121	34.97	90.17	4	27	29	0
Twenty20	48	46	3	1113	89	25.88	119.29	0	6	9	0

Bowling

	Mat	Balls	Runs	Wkts	BBI	BBM	Ave	Econ	SR	5w	10
ODIs	3	30	13	1	1/1	1/1	13.00	2.60	30.0	0	0
First-class	101	2628	1493	35	3/3	-	42.65	3.40	75.0	0	0
List A	107	905	964	17	2/21	2/21	56.70	6.39	53.2	0	0
Twenty20	48	153	260	6	2/11	2/11	43.33	10.19	25.5	0	0

DEAN COSKER · RHB SLA W1 MVP72

NAME: Dean Andrew Cosker
BORN: January 7, 1978, Weymouth
HEIGHT: 5ft 11in
SQUAD Nº: 23
NICKNAME: Lurks
CAREER: First-class debut: 1996; List A
debut: 1996; T20 debut: 2003; County cap:
2000

AOC SAYS: Cosker is an experienced and vastly underrated spinner who enjoyed his most successful campaign for Glamorgan last summer, collecting 51 first-class wickets at an average of 22.11. This season he will celebrate 15 years since making his County Championship debut and last autumn he signed a contract extension which will see him continue at the SWALEC until the end of 2013. An ever-present in the Glamorgan side, Cosker is often their matchwinner and will be crucial if the Welsh side are to earn County Championship promotion this summer.

LAST WORD: "Dean is underrated; he's been in Robert Croft's shadow for quite a while. Last year he came on really well and got 50 wickets. That's a really positive thing for us to have two spinnrs, especially when conditions suit." *Mark Wallace*

Batting & Fielding

	Mat	Inns	NO	Runs	HS	Ave	SR	100	50	Ct	St
First-class	178	232	71	2174	52	13.50	-	0	1	110	0
List A	201	106	47	646	50*	10.94	-	0	1	78	0
Twenty20	62	21	16	67	16*	13.40	79.76	0	0	19	0

Bowling

	Mat	Balls	Runs	Wkts	BBI	BBM	Ave	Econ	SR	5w	10
First-class	178	33117	15890	445	6/91	-	35.70	2.87	74.4	7	1
List A	201	8539	6822	205	5/54	5/54	33.27	4.79	41.6	1	0
Twenty20	62	1086	1459	49	3/18	3/18	29.77	8.06	22.1	0	0

NAME: Robert Damien Bale Croft
BORN: May 25, 1970, Swansea
HEIGHT: 5ft 11in
SQUAD Nº: 10
NICKNAME: Crofty
OTHER TEAMS: England
CAREER: Test debut: 1996; ODI debut: 1996;
First-class debut: 1989; List A debut: 1989;
T20 debut: 2003;

GLAMORGAN

AOC SAYS: A true legend of the valleys, Croft the evergreen schemer signed a two-year player/coach contract at the end of last season. The deal sustains his association with Glamorgan well into his fourth decade of professional cricket. Since he made his debut in 1989, no bowler has taken more County Championship wickets than Croft. As a testament to his skill and tenacity, the former England offspinner reached the golden milestone of 1,000 wickets and 10,000 first-class runs for Glamorgan in 2010. He also recorded his first ever first-class hat-trick en route to a win against Gloucestershire in August. His international career had its moments. If his five-wicket haul at Christchurch against New Zealand in 1997 remains his most telling Test performance with the ball, arguably his most famous stand in an England shirt came against South Africa at Old Trafford in 1998, when he held up the visitors throughout a heart-stopping final session, eventually steering his team, and last man Angus Fraser, to safety. England escaped, nine down, and went on to win the series. That rearguard innings may be his most famous, but it was unrepresentative of a naturally expansive, daredevil batsman, who for many years opened in one-day cricket for Glamorgan and has a 69-ball 119 against Surrey to his name, one of four one-day tons. Typically, he is buzzing about the new season, positive that he can still cut it at the top level and have an impact on Glamorgan's fortunes. With Dean Cosker a top-quality spinner in his own right, Croft's workload will be managed this campaign, but when Cardiff presents him with a turning pitch he will be the first in line to exploit it. If Croft is likely to spend more time coaching than playing when the four-day games are taking place, he is going to play another key role in the FP t20. In last summer's competition he claimed 22 wickets at an average of 15.59 – the only Glamorgan player to reach double figures. The legend lives on.

INSIDE TRACK: "Both on and off the field he's seen a lot and experienced a lot, he's been successful no matter where he's been – Test cricket, ODI cricket, domestic cricket – and he's got a phenomenal record. It's great to speak to him and I know for the younger lads – the spinners, the seamers and the batters – you can't get experience like that anywhere else." *Jim Allenby, Glamorgan teammate*

GLAMORGAN

Batting & Fielding

	Mat	Inns	NO	Runs	HS	Ave	SR	100	50	Ct	St
Tests	21	34	8	421	37*	16.19	36.29	0	0	10	0
ODIs	50	36	12	345	32	14.37	66.47	0	0	11	0
First-class	391	576	103	12609	143	26.65	-	8	54	175	0
List A	402	337	61	6474	143	23.45	-	4	32	94	0
Twenty20	67	44	11	670	62*	20.30	125.46	0	4	21	0

Bowling

	Mat	Balls	Runs	Wkts	BBI	BBM	Ave	Econ	SR	5w	10
Tests	21	4619	1825	49	5/95	7/143	37.24	2.37	94.2	1	0
ODIs	50	2466	1743	45	3/51	3/51	38.73	4.24	54.8	0	0
First-class	391	86536	39995	1133	8/66	-	35.30	2.77	76.3	49	9
List A	402	18349	13270	409	6/20	6/20	32.44	4.33	44.8	1	0
Twenty20	67	1371	1647	68	3/12	3/12	24.22	7.20	20.1	0	0

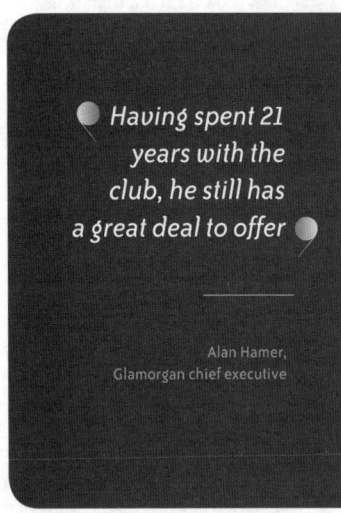

Having spent 21 years with the club, he still has a great deal to offer

Alan Hamer,
Glamorgan chief executive

NAME: John Charles Glover
BORN: August 29, 1989, Cardiff
HEIGHT: 6ft 3in
SQUAD Nº: 36
CAREER: First-class debut: 2008

GLAMORGAN

AOC SAYS: A Durham University graduate, Glover will play for Glamorgan on a development contract after some successful performances in the Second XI last summer. The right-arm swing bowler played four Second XI Championship matches, taking nine wickets including 4-37 against Derbyshire. In the Trophy competition he played five times and returned figures of 3-27 against Warwickshire. As a member of the Durham University team, Glover took 15 wickets at an average of 14.40 in the MCC Universities Championship last summer.

LAST WORD: "Glover has an interesting background. He's a Welsh lad who did very well for Durham MCCU and he arrived with us through that. He was quite impressive during our pre-season in South Africa." *Mark Wallace*

Batting & Fielding

	Mat	Inns	NO	Runs	HS	Ave	SR	100	50	Ct	St
First-class	8	10	2	41	14	5.12	18.98	0	0	1	0

Bowling

	Mat	Balls	Runs	Wkts	BBI	BBM	Ave	Econ	SR	5w	10
First-class	8	1024	601	15	5/38	5/56	40.06	3.52	68.2	1	0

JAMES HARRIS

GLAMORGAN

NAME: James Alexander Russell Harris
BORN: May 16, 1990, Swansea
HEIGHT: 6ft
SQUAD Nº: 9
NICKNAME: Rolf, Bones
CAREER: First-class debut: 2007; List A debut: 2007; T20 debut: 2008

AOC SAYS: One of the most exciting young players to come out of Glamorgan in recent years, seam bowler Harris has been turning heads for some time now. At 14 he became the youngest person to appear for Glamorgan's Second XI, he signed his first contract at 15 and then became the youngest man to take a seven-wicket haul in the County Championship when he was just 17, ripping through Gloucestershire's top-order in just his second first-class match. Last summer he claimed 63 Championship wickets at 21.52, earning himself a place on the England Lions tour to West Indies at the start of this year. It seems only a matter of time before this impressive young cricketer receives a full international call-up. His forceful lower-order batting is another useful string to his bow.

LAST WORD: "He's a very bright prospect and he'll have a very long career." *Matthew Maynard, former Glamorgan director of cricket*

Batting & Fielding

	Mat	Inns	NO	Runs	HS	Ave	SR	100	50	Ct	St
First-class	48	66	12	1064	87*	19.70	-	0	4	10	0
List A	21	14	1	98	21	7.53	56.64	0	0	5	0
Twenty20	19	10	4	66	18	11.00	117.85	0	0	2	0

Bowling

	Mat	Balls	Runs	Wkts	BBI	BBM	Ave	Econ	SR	5w	10
First-class	48	8563	4455	164	7/66	12/118	27.16	3.12	52.2	4	1
List A	21	887	770	27	4/48	4/48	28.51	5.20	32.8	0	0
Twenty20	19	336	479	17	4/23	4/23	28.17	8.55	19.7	0	0

NAME: David Stuart Harrison
BORN: July 30, 1981, Newport, Wales
HEIGHT: 6ft 4in
SQUAD Nº: 20
NICKNAME: Desmond, Haz
CAREER: First-class debut: 1999; List A debut: 2000; T20 debut: 2003; County cap: 2006

GLAMORGAN

AOC SAYS: A Glamorgan wicket-taker for over a decade, Harrison took a career best 7-45 against Worcestershire last summer, but though once considered a potential international bowler, he hasn't built on the success he enjoyed early in his career. In large part that has been due to injuries but when fit he is still a hugely important member of the Glamorgan attack in first-class cricket, even if one-day opportunities have become limited. A hip injury meant Harrison – the son of former Glamorgan seamer Stuart – missed the Welsh county's pre-season tour to South Africa and this ongoing problem means he's unlikely to be fit in time for the start of the Championship campaign.

LAST WORD: "When he gets on the park, Haz is our most experienced seamer and he's the guy the others look up to. On wickets that suit his style, he can get a lot of bounce and swing it." *Mark Wallace*

Batting & Fielding

	Mat	Inns	NO	Runs	HS	Ave	SR	100	50	Ct	St
First-class	102	141	18	2017	88	16.39	-	0	7	30	0
List A	85	55	19	454	37*	12.61	-	0	0	9	0
Twenty20	27	8	2	20		3.33	54.05	0	0	4	0

Bowling

	Mat	Balls	Runs	Wkts	BBI	BBM	Ave	Econ	SR	5w	10
First-class	102	16005	9276	257	7/45	-	36.09	3.47	62.2	8	0
List A	85	3583	3015	98	5/26	5/26	30.76	5.04	36.5	2	0
Twenty20	27	471	707	21	2/17	2/17	33.66	9.00	22.4	0	0

NICK JAMES

LHB SLA

GLAMORGAN

NAME: Nicholas Alexander James
BORN: September 17, 1986, Sandwell
HEIGHT: 5ft 10in
SQUAD Nº: 11
NICKNAME: Jaymo
OTHER TEAMS: Warwickshire
CAREER: First-class debut: 2008; List A
debut: 2006; T20 debut: 2007

AOC SAYS: One of the leading lights of Glamorgan's Second XI last summer, James appears ready to break through into the first team this season. The left-handed batsman made consistent runs in the Second XI Championship, as well as taking 18 wickets with his tweakers. His good work behind the scenes resulted in a brace of CB40 appearances, as well as an unbeaten 60 in his only first-class match, against West Indies A. James joined Glamorgan ahead of the 2009 season after making 12 appearances for Warwickshire in various forms of the game. The allrounder bowls tidy left-arm spin and will be looking to break into the Dragons' limited-overs side this season.

LAST WORD: "Nick had a very good season for the Second XI last year but when he got his chance in the first team he broke his finger. He could break into the senior team in the upcoming campaign." *Mark Wallace*

Batting & Fielding

	Mat	Inns	NO	Runs	HS	Ave	SR	100	50	Ct	St
First-class	2	3	1	109	60*	54.50	46.58	0	1	1	0
List A	13	9	2	127	30	18.14	86.39	0	0	3	0
Twenty20	2	2	1	13	12*	13.00	144.44	0	0	2	0

Bowling

	Mat	Balls	Runs	Wkts	BBI	BBM	Ave	Econ	SR	5w	10
First-class	2	24	7	1	1/6	1/6	7.00	1.75	24.0	0	0
List A	13	264	195	9	2/19	2/19	21.66	4.43	29.3	0	0
Twenty20	2	-	-	-	-	-	-	-	-	-	-

NAME: Alexander John Jones
BORN: November 10, 1988, Bridgend
SQUAD Nº: 27
CAREER: List A debut: 2010

GLAMORGAN

AOC SAYS: A left-arm seamer who has come through Glamorgan's academy system, Jones is another young bowler on a development contract at the SWALEC Stadium. He made his Dragons debut in a CB40 match against Somerset in September 2010 but failed to take a wicket. A Second XI regular since 2007, Jones will be looking for a first-team chance in one-day cricket this summer but will probably have to be patient and continue taking wickets in the Seconds. One of several tyro quicks in Glamorgan's squad hoping for a break in 2011.

LAST WORD: "Alex has been in Australia all winter and hopefully that experience will push him on this season. A lot of players go to Australia and come back much better cricketers and a bit more mature, and hopefully that will prove the case." *Mark Wallace*

Batting & Fielding

	Mat	Inns	NO	Runs	HS	Ave	SR	100	50	Ct	St
List A	1	1	0	5	5	5.00	55.55	0	0	0	0

Bowling

	Mat	Balls	Runs	Wkts	BBI	BBM	Ave	Econ	SR	5w	10
List A	1	48	74	0	-	-	-	9.25	-	0	0

ANEURIN NORMAN

RHB RM

GLAMORGAN

NAME: Aneurin John Norman
BORN: March 22, 1991, Cardiff
HEIGHT: 6ft 1in
SQUAD Nº: 37
NICKNAME: Noddy, Mr Bean
CAREER: Yet to make first-team debut

AOC SAYS: A young, untried bowling allrounder, Norman could be in line for a Glamorgan first-team debut this summer. An ever-present in the Second XI Championship last summer, Norman took 14 wickets with his nagging medium-pace swingers but would have been disappointed with his batting average of 13.79. He played 10 Minor Counties matches for Wales last summer, top-scoring with 71 against Wiltshire and taking 4-12 against Dorset. Norman was named Glamorgan's Academy Player of the Year in 2009 and awarded a development contract the following season.

LAST WORD: "A handy bowling allrounder who is developing his game. He's got plenty of potential." *Matthew Maynard, former Glamorgan director of cricket*

EXTRAS

New head coach Matthew Mott guided New South Wales to the Pura Cup in his first season in charge in 2007-08, followed by a Big Bash triumph in 2008-09. He then became known on the world stage when he steered New South Wales to the inaugural Champions League Twenty20 title in India in October 2009, when they defeated Trinidad and Tobago in the final.

NAME: Michael Paul O'Shea
BORN: September 4, 1987, Barry
HEIGHT: 5th 11in
SQUAD №: 13
NICKNAME: Rik
CAREER: First-class debut: 2005; List A
debut: 2005; T20 debut: 2009

GLAMORGAN

AOC SAYS: Having been released by Glamorgan at the end of the 2009 season, O'Shea
rejoins the Welsh county for the 2011 campaign. During his time away from the SWALEC
Stadium, O'Shea played in the CB40 for the Unicorns, averaging 50 with the bat. His best
score came against Worcestershire when he smashed 90 off 62 balls, an innings which
included five sixes. A right-hand bat, O'Shea can also bowl offspin. In his previous spell
with Glamorgan he played six first-class matches, averaging 15.22 with the bat. The former
England under 19 international could fill the breach left by Tom Maynard's departure.

LAST WORD: "We are delighted that Mike has rejoined Glamorgan. He is a talented
cricketer who, since leaving the club in 2009, has continued to impress with the Unicorns."
Colin Metson, Glamorgan managing director of cricket

Batting & Fielding

	Mat	Inns	NO	Runs	HS	Ave	SR	100	50	Ct	St
First-class	6	9	0	137	50	15.22	45.06	0	1	1	0
List A	17	16	1	504	90	33.60	88.11	0	3	5	0
Twenty20	2	1	0	5	5	5.00	45.45	0	0	1	0

Bowling

	Mat	Balls	Runs	Wkts	BBI	BBM	Ave	Econ	SR	5w	10
First-class	6	-	-	-	-	-	-	-	-	-	-
List A	17	314	334	5	2/37	2/37	66.80	6.38	62.8	0	0
Twenty20	2	-	-	-	-	-	-	-	-	-	-

WILL OWEN   RHB RFM

NAME: William Thomas Owen
BORN: September 2, 1988, St Asaph
HEIGHT: 6ft
SQUAD Nº: 34
NICKNAME: Swillo
CAREER: First-class debut: 2007; List A
debut: 2010; T20 debut: 2010

AOC SAYS: Seamer Owen struggled to make an impact when handed an opportunity in the County Championship last summer. He failed to take a wicket in his two appearances but did claim 3-65 against West Indies A. He fared better in the CB40, taking 13 wickets at 24.61 in the eight matches he played, earning himself a professional contract. Owen's pace is his strongest asset and he claimed 14 victims in four Second XI Championship matches last summer. He'll be hoping to impress again in the CB40 this year and will also be looking for more chances in first-class cricket.

LAST WORD: "With Owen it's a case of whether he can get the ball in the right place. He didn't do very well in Championship cricket last year but at almost 90mph, he's potentially the quickest bowler at the club." *Gareth Griffiths*

Batting & Fielding

	Mat	Inns	NO	Runs	HS	Ave	SR	100	50	Ct	St
First-class	4	4	1	38	38	12.66	79.16	0	0	0	0
List A	8	6	1	35	12	7.00	83.33	0	0	1	0
Twenty20	4	1	0	8	8	8.00	114.28	0	0	0	0

Bowling

	Mat	Balls	Runs	Wkts	BBI	BBM	Ave	Econ	SR	5w	10
First-class	4	372	269	3	3/65	3/93	89.66	4.33	124.0	0	0
List A	8	294	320	13	5/49	5/49	24.61	6.53	22.6	1	0
Twenty20	4	54	104	0	-	-	-	11.55	-	0	0

OVERSEAS PLAYER

GLAMORGAN

NAME: Alviro Nathan Petersen
BORN: November 25, 1980, Port Elizabeth
SQUAD Nº: 73
OTHER TEAMS: South Africa, Lions, North West, Northerns, Titans
CAREER: Test debut: 2010; ODI debut: 2006; T20I debut: 2010; First-class debut: 2001; List A debut: 2001; T20 debut: 2004

AOC SAYS: The controversial arrival as captain of Petersen sparked a winter of discontent at Glamorgan but the South African will be looking to ensure it's his cricket that gets people talking this summer. The opening batsman has been a regular in the South Africa Test side since making his debut in February 2010 and averages 33.64 for the Proteas. His debut, against India, was marked by an even hundred at Kolkata; in the process becoming only the third South African to hit a Test century in his first match. It was rich reward for a combative, consistent and stylish top-order strokemaker whose elegance through the covers evokes one of the finest South African batsmen of recent years, Daryll Cullinan. Signed on a one-year contract with a brief to help bring through the club's next long-term leader, Petersen's first foray into county cricket looks like being a tough assignment, but at least he has experience of the role, as captain of the South African side Highveld Lions. He will open the batting with Gareth Rees, and his first requirement will be to score sufficient runs to cover for the loss of Mark Cosgrove, the Australian overseas star who has been re-signed only for the FP t20 competition.

INSIDE TRACK: "We are an ambitious club and share our supporters' desire to bring success back to the club. In particular, Glamorgan's record in one-day cricket over the past few years has been very poor and the appointment of Alviro as our captain forms a crucial part of the club's strategy to improve our playing fortunes over the coming seasons. As well as being a high quality international player, he is also an outstanding leader and we look forward to working with him as we strive for improvements in our performances." *Alan Hamer, Glamorgan chief executive*

Batting & Fielding

	Mat	Inns	NO	Runs	HS	Ave	SR	100	50	Ct	St
Tests	9	17	0	572	100	33.64	52.86	1	3	5	0
ODIs	14	12	1	377	80	34.27	83.40	0	4	2	0
T20Is	2	2	0	14	8	7.00	73.68	0	0	1	0
First-class	108	194	10	6915	152	37.58	-	19	31	86	0
List A	121	116	7	3465	124	31.78	-	5	22	41	0
Twenty20	45	41	7	1075	84*	31.61	125.87	0	11	24	0

Bowling

	Mat	Balls	Runs	Wkts	BBI	BBM	Ave	Econ	SR	5w	10
Tests	9	72	36	1	1/2	1/2	36.00	3.00	72.0	0	0
ODIs	14	6	7	0	-	-	-	7.00	-	0	0
T20Is	2	-	-	-	-	-	-	-	-	-	-
First-class	108	462	259	6	2/7	-	43.16	3.36	77.0	0	0
List A	121	161	140	3	1/13	1/13	46.66	5.21	53.6	0	0
Twenty20	45	24	44	0	-	-	-	11.00	-	0	0

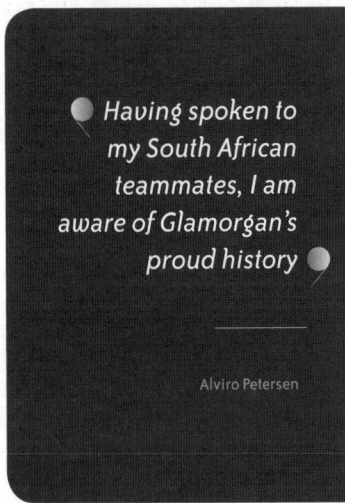

Having spoken to my South African teammates, I am aware of Glamorgan's proud history

Alviro Petersen

NAME: Michael John Powell
BORN: February 3, 1977, Abergavenny
HEIGHT: 6ft 1in
SQUAD N°: 14
NICKNAME: Powelly
CAREER: First-class debut: 1997; List A
debut: 1997; T20 debut: 2003; County cap:
2000

GLAMORGAN

AOC SAYS: Powell's sidelining last season, when he was dropped after a fruitless first half
to the season, divided the club's members straight down the middle. A highest score of
55 in seven first-class matches was a poor return, but Powell has been one of the most
popular Glamorgan cricketers of recent years, and his overall record, with over 15,000
runs in all competitions for his only club, stands up extremely well. This season marks his
Benefit Year, and at 34, in the final year of his current contract, Powell will be desperate to
roll back the years. Famed for his epic 299 against Gloucestershire at Cheltenham in 2006,
Powell spent some time in intensive care when forced to undergo a serious operation to
remove a rib in 2007.

LAST WORD: "He's Welsh through and through, and he'll be needed because the club want
to keep hold of their identity and there aren't as many Welsh lads in the dressing room this
year." *Gareth Griffiths*

Batting & Fielding

	Mat	Inns	NO	Runs	HS	Ave	SR	100	50	Ct	St
First-class	201	337	31	11813	299	38.60	-	25	59	123	0
List A	204	193	20	4665	114*	26.96	-	1	25	79	0
Twenty20	44	41	4	844	68*	22.81	116.41	0	5	16	0

Bowling

	Mat	Balls	Runs	Wkts	BBI	BBM	Ave	Econ	SR	5w	10
First-class	201	164	132	2	2/39	-	66.00	4.82	82.0	0	0
List A	204	24	26	1	1/26	1/26	26.00	6.50	24.0	0	0
Twenty20	44	-	-	-	-	-	-	-	-	-	-

MIKE REED

RHB RFM

GLAMORGAN

NAME: Michael Thomas Reed
BORN: September 10, 1988, Leicester
HEIGHT: 6ft 7in
SQUAD Nº: 35
NICKNAME: Frank
CAREER: Yet to make first-team debut

AOC SAYS: One of a clutch of players on a development contract after graduating through the academy system, Reed is a towering seam bowler who relies on his height to extract alarming bounce. Glamorgan hoped he would come through last season but injuries put paid to that, and he approaches the second year of his contract hoping to break through into the first team. A Cardiff University boy, where he has been studying Mathematics, Glamorgan's supporters will be impatient to see what this beanpole quick is capable of achieving at the top level.

LAST WORD: "Mike is still at university but he could potentially feature in the first team when he's available. He's a big seamer who gets a lot of bounce." *Mark Wallace*

EXTRAS

"I have had a fantastic seven years at Cricket New South Wales and will miss the place and the people immensely, but the challenge at Glamorgan is something that really excites me on a number of different levels, The opportunity to experience a different culture and broaden my cricketing horizons, as well as provide my family with an opportunity to see another part of the world, is something that I very much look forward to." Head coach Matthew Mott

NAME: Gareth Peter Rees
BORN: April 8, 1985, Swansea
HEIGHT: 6ft 1in
SQUAD Nº: 28
NICKNAME: Gums
CAREER: First-class debut: 2006; List A
debut: 2004; T20 debut: 2009; County cap:
2009

GLAMORGAN

AOC SAYS: A studious left-handed opening batsman, Rees struggled for form last term after breaking the 1,000 runs barrier in 2009 and topping Glamorgan's averages in 2008, but he will resume at the top of the order hoping to build on a promising first-class record of 10 hundreds in 63 matches. Less successful in one-day cricket, Rees' approach to scoring runs is not immediately suited to the shorter formats, although he does boast a one-day century. A multi-talented individual, he chose cricket over rugby despite representing Wales at youth level and Llanelli under 21s, and as one of county cricket's more cerebral figures, he graduated from Bath University with a First in Physics and Mathematics. In the County Championship he will open with the new skipper Alviro Petersen.

LAST WORD: "Gareth had a rough time last year, but he is a potential 1,000 runs-a-season man." *Gareth Griffiths*

Batting & Fielding

	Mat	Inns	NO	Runs	HS	Ave	SR	100	50	Ct	St
First-class	63	106	8	3580	154	36.53	48.37	10	18	50	0
List A	21	20	2	556	123*	30.88	-	1	4	4	0
Twenty20	18	18	5	198	35	15.23	101.02	0	0	7	0

Bowling

	Mat	Balls	Runs	Wkts	BBI	BBM	Ave	Econ	SR	5w	10
First-class	63	6	3	0	-	-	-	3.00	-	0	0
List A	21	-	-	-	-	-	-	-	-	-	-
Twenty20	18	-	-	-	-	-	-	-	-	-	-

ADAM SHANTRY · LHB LMF

NAME: Adam John Shantry
BORN: November 13, 1982, Bristol
HEIGHT: 6ft 3in
SQUAD Nº: 5
NICKNAME: Shants
OTHER TEAMS: Northamptonshire, Warwickshire
CAREER: First-class debut: 2003; List A debut: 2003; T20 debut: 2004

AOC SAYS: A left-arm swing bowler with the priceless ability to arc the ball back into the right-hander, county cricket's elder Shantry (his younger brother Jack is at Worcestershire) has endured an injury-ravaged time since joining Glamorgan from Warwickshire for the 2008 season. He missed the whole of last year after undergoing operations on both knees for chronic tendonitis, but has wintered in Australia and reports are that he his fit and bowling well. Glamorgan will need his wicket-taking ability, and a few lower-order runs – he has a first-class century against Leicestershire to his credit – won't go amiss either.

LAST WORD: "He hasn't played much due to injury, but when he has, he's done very well for Glamorgan." *Gareth Griffiths*

Batting & Fielding

	Mat	Inns	NO	Runs	HS	Ave	SR	100	50	Ct	St
First-class	29	37	12	444	100	17.76	39.15	1	0	6	0
List A	12	6	3	48	19*	16.00	-	0	0	6	0
Twenty20	1	-	-	-	-	-	-	-	-	-	-

Bowling

	Mat	Balls	Runs	Wkts	BBI	BBM	Ave	Econ	SR	5w	10
First-class	29	3684	1923	81	5/49	-	23.74	3.13	45.4	4	1
List A	12	408	325	13	5/37	5/37	25.00	4.77	31.3	1	0
Twenty20	1	12	31	0	-	-	-	15.50	-	0	0

NAME: Graham Grant Wagg
BORN: April 28, 1983, Rugby
HEIGHT: 6ft
SQUAD №: 8
NICKNAME: Waggy
OTHER TEAMS: Derbyshire, Warwickshire
CAREER: First-class debut: 2002; List A
debut: 2000; T20 debut: 2003; County cap:
2007 (Derbyshire)

GLAMORGAN

AOC SAYS: Wagg is a fine acquisition for Glamorgan. Signed on a three-year deal from
Derbyshire at the end of last season, he will spearhead the county's challenge to finally
break into the top tier of the County Championship. A left-arm swing bowler who certainly
knows the right end of a bat, he has claimed 216 first-class wickets and eight five-wicket
hauls in a career that began at Warwickshire. He served a 15-month ban in 2004 after
admitting taking cocaine, but put his troubles behind him to become a trusted county-
level seamer and useful lower-order bat, with a first-class century against Northants to
his name. That 2009 match at Northampton also saw him take 10 wickets. An ebullient,
outgoing character, Wagg will bring energy and buzz to a dressing room still reeling from
the winter's boardroom shenanigans.

LAST WORD: "He was out with injury last season but he seems fit and he's a good all-round
cricketer that Glamorgan have done well to capture." *Gareth Griffiths*

Batting & Fielding

	Mat	Inns	NO	Runs	HS	Ave	SR	100	50	Ct	St
First-class	68	94	11	2024	108	24.38	65.71	1	10	23	0
List A	76	61	9	901	48*	17.32	-	0	0	21	0
Twenty20	45	38	8	455	62	15.16	127.09	0	1	13	0

Bowling

	Mat	Balls	Runs	Wkts	BBI	BBM	Ave	Econ	SR	5w	10
First-class	68	11609	7026	216	6/35	-	32.52	3.63	53.7	8	1
List A	76	2886	2632	86	4/35	4/35	30.60	5.47	33.5	0	0
Twenty20	45	724	989	34	3/23	3/23	29.08	8.19	21.2	0	0

MARK WALLACE   LHB WK

GLAMORGAN

NAME: Mark Alexander Wallace
BORN: November 19, 1981, Abergavenny
HEIGHT: 5ft 9in
SQUAD Nº: 18
NICKNAME: Gromit
CAREER: First-class debut: 1999; List A debut: 1999; T20 debut: 2003; County cap: 2003

AOC SAYS: A Welshman through and through, Wallace became the club's youngest ever wicketkeeper in Championship cricket when he made his debut in 1999, aged 17 years and 287 days. He has served the club with distinction ever since. An expert gloveman acknowledged to be one of the best keepers standing up to the stumps in the county game, international honours have eluded him despite consistent runs in first-class cricket and more centuries (nine) than any other keeper in Glamorgan's history. A left-handed touch player, his one-day stats with the bat may have held him back from higher honours. Wallace is the favourite to be Alviro Petersen's official vice-captain this season, having served as deputy under Jamie Dalrymple. A qualified journalist with a degree in Professional Sports Writing and Broadcasting from Staffordshire University, in the off-season Wallace reports on sporting events throughout Wales.

LAST WORD: "Mark is a well-respected senior player who has a wealth of experience as vice-captain." *Colin Metson, Glamorgan managing director of cricket*

Batting & Fielding

	Mat	Inns	NO	Runs	HS	Ave	SR	100	50	Ct	St
First-class	167	265	17	6848	139	27.61	-	9	32	418	37
List A	153	120	26	1829	85	19.45	-	0	3	142	38
Twenty20	67	55	17	717	42*	18.86	133.27	0	0	26	18

Bowling

	Mat	Balls	Runs	Wkts	BBI	BBM	Ave	Econ	SR	5w	10
First-class	167	6	3	0	-	-	-	3.00	-	0	0
List A	153	-	-	-	-	-	-	-	-	-	-
Twenty20	67	-	-	-	-	-	-	-	-	-	-

NAME: Stewart Jonathan Walters
BORN: June 25, 1983, Mornington, Australia
HEIGHT: 6ft 1in
SQUAD Nº: 26
NICKNAME: Forrest
OTHER TEAMS: Surrey
CAREER: First-class debut: 2006; List A
2005; T20 debut: 2006

GLAMORGAN

AOC SAYS: Australia-born Walters began his county career at Surrey, working his way through the ranks and establishing a reputation for hard work and dedication. That work ethic was rewarded in 2009 when Surrey appointed him as their interim captain, despite his relative inexperience at first-class level. He didn't disgrace himself in the job, but without the weight of runs behind him, he was never a realistic candidate for the job on a full-time basis. And it is this lack of top-level runs – only two centuries in 34 matches over four seasons – that makes Glamorgan's acquisition something of a gamble. A prolific scorer in grade cricket in Australia, he has the shots and the attitude to succeed, but aged 27, it needs to happen now.

LAST WORD: "He comes highly recommended from a number of strong sources. He will strengthen the batting in both formats of the game and add to both the fielding unit and professionalism at the club." *Colin Metson, Glamorgan managing director of cricket*

Batting & Fielding

	Mat	Inns	NO	Runs	HS	Ave	SR	100	50	Ct	St
First-class	34	54	1	1336	188	25.20	49.04	2	4	38	0
List A	45	42	7	1000	91	28.57	84.96	0	6	16	0
Twenty20	33	26	9	376	53*	22.11	110.91	0	1	21	0

Bowling

	Mat	Balls	Runs	Wkts	BBI	BBM	Ave	Econ	SR	5w	10
First-class	34	426	239	3	1/4	1/9	79.66	3.36	142.0	0	0
List A	45	165	179	3	1/12	1/12	59.66	6.50	55.0	0	0
Twenty20	33	18	26	1	1/9	1/9	26.00	8.66	18.0	0	0

GLAMORGAN

NAME: Huw Thomas Waters
BORN: September 26, 1986, Cardiff
HEIGHT: 6ft 2in
SQUAD Nº: 17
CAREER: First-class debut: 2005; List A debut: 2005; T20 debut: 2010

AOC SAYS: Plenty of fanfare accompanied the emergence of this tall, lithe and rapid seamer when he made his debut in 2005. Armed with a classical, side-on action and able to extract good bounce from his considerable frame, good judges envisioned a new Simon Jones, and there was much excited talk of Waters moving up from the ranks of the England under 19s to the senior squad before too long. Subsequent injuries and bouts of indifferent form have quietened the buzz around this Cardiff lad, and it is now five years since his maiden, and so far only first-class five-fer, but Glamorgan have high hopes for him this season. The raw materials are all there; 2011 looms large for Waters.

LAST WORD: "Huw is one of those that lads that whenever he has played, he's impressed. If he can get a good run in the side, he will only get better and better. He's an old-fashioned seamer and should get a lot of games this year." *Mark Wallace*

Batting & Fielding											
	Mat	Inns	NO	Runs	HS	Ave	SR	100	50	Ct	St
First-class	34	50	22	212	34	7.57	15.64	0	0	7	0
List A	20	8	3	24	8	4.80	42.10	0	0	3	0
Twenty20	4	2	2	11	11*	-	84.61	0	0	0	0

Bowling											
	Mat	Balls	Runs	Wkts	BBI	BBM	Ave	Econ	SR	5w	10
First-class	34	4318	2377	65	5/86	-	36.56	3.30	66.4	1	0
List A	20	780	809	14	3/47	3/47	57.78	6.22	55.7	0	0
Twenty20	4	85	118	3	3/30	3/30	39.33	8.32	28.3	0	0

BEN WRIGHT

RHB RM

NAME: Ben James Wright
BORN: December 5, 1987, Preston
HEIGHT: 5ft 9in
SQUAD Nº: 29
NICKNAME: Bej
CAREER: First-class debut: 2006; List A
debut: 2006; T20 debut: 2007

GLAMORGAN

AOC SAYS: One of a clutch of young batsmen at the club, Wright was quietly impressive last year in the middle-order, making 847 first-class runs and smashing a career-best 172 against Gloucestershire's strong bowling unit. His season tailed off somewhat towards the end, but as a young player still attuning himself to the rigours of a gruelling county season, Glamorgan will be hoping that this former England under 19 player can maintain his consistency throughout this time around. A former Wales under 16 rugby starlet, Wright is a natural sportsman, as evidenced by his brilliant fielding. He became Glamorgan's second youngest first-class centurion and following the departure of Tom Maynard, Wright is the club's biggest homegrown batting hope.

LAST WORD: "A stylish young player who is strong through the offside, he will want to push on to 1,000 runs this year." *Gareth Griffiths*

Batting & Fielding

	Mat	Inns	NO	Runs	HS	Ave	SR	100	50	Ct	St
First-class	38	60	3	1527	172	26.78	49.21	3	7	25	0
List A	49	46	6	966	79	24.15	70.30	0	5	11	0
Twenty20	26	24	9	394	55*	26.26	111.61	0	1	8	0

Bowling

	Mat	Balls	Runs	Wkts	BBI	BBM	Ave	Econ	SR	5w	10
First-class	38	192	137	2	1/14	1/14	68.50	4.28	96.0	0	0
List A	49	132	126	1	1/19	1/19	126.00	5.72	132.0	0	0
Twenty20	26	24	22	1	1/16	1/16	22.00	5.50	24.0	0	0

FORMED: 1871
HOME GROUND: County Ground, Bristol
ONE-DAY NAME: Gladiators
CAPTAIN: Alex Gidman
2010 RESULTS: CC2: 5/9; CB40: 3/7 in Group B; FP t20: 9/9 in South Group

HONOURS

Gillette/NatWest/C&G/FP Trophy: (5); 1973, 1999, 2000, 2003, 2004; Benson and Hedges Cup: (3) 1977, 1999, 2000; Pro40/National League/CB40: 2000

THE LOWDOWN

With the glory years of one-day dominance now a fading memory, Gloucestershire's supporters have spent much of the last decade wondering where the good times went. A tough, run-less season last year deflated the Bristol club, who saw their genuine pre-season hopes of promotion in the Championship fizzle out as established players and young hopefuls alike suffered from a collective crisis of batting form. And with the Gladiators also struggling to hold it together in one-day cricket, all in all 2010 was a season best forgotten. This year sees an intriguing overseas appointment in Kiwi batsman Kane Williamson, a multi-faceted cricketer who will bring zest and energy to a youthful-looking team. On the negative side of the ledger, Gloucestershire's seam-bowling department has been weakened with the departures of Steve Kirby and Gemaal Hussain, opening the door to the likes of Ian Saxelby, David Payne and ex-soldier David Wade to share the load carried so impressively by stalwart Jon Lewis.

HEAD COACH: JOHN BRACEWELL

A huge, legendary presence at Bristol, first as a player and then as the schemer behind the club's one-day heyday at the turn of the century, Bracewell returned to the saddle in 2009 following an uneven, unfulfilled spell in charge of his native New Zealand. His avuncular, arm-round-the-shoulders approach was tested last season; this is a big year for both club and coach.

With thanks to: Richard Latham, Bristol & West News Agency Ltd

	Mat	Inns	NO	Runs	HS	Ave	SR	100	50	Ct	St
WTS Porterfield	7	14	0	531	175	37.92	70.14	2	1	6	-
HJH Marshall	15	27	2	884	89*	35.36	59.56	0	7	15	-
JEC Franklin	16	29	3	862	108	33.15	47.72	1	4	7	-
CG Taylor	15	27	2	803	89	32.12	58.18	0	6	11	-
CDJ Dent	16	31	3	725	98	25.89	50.62	0	4	24	-
APR Gidman	16	29	0	679	99	23.41	50.97	0	3	16	-
Kadeer Ali	6	12	1	240	74	21.81	43.39	0	2	5	-
EGC Young	2	3	0	58	38	19.33	33.52	0	0	3	-
SD Snell	10	19	1	322	71	17.88	63.88	0	2	18	0
J Lewis	16	28	2	419	50	16.11	68.01	0	1	7	-
JN Batty	15	30	2	450	61	16.07	36.79	0	1	53	3
V Banerjee	7	14	3	108	35	9.81	22.22	0	0	1	-
GM Hussain	15	26	10	153	28*	9.56	25.88	0	0	1	-
SP Kirby	10	17	5	100	22*	8.33	31.94	0	0	2	-
JMR Taylor	2	4	0	11	6	2.75	20.75	0	0	2	-
AJ Ireland	8	12	2	21	11	2.10	20.19	0	0	0	-

Batting & Fielding

	Mat	Overs	Mdn	Runs	Wkts	BBI	BBM	Ave	Econ	SR	5w	10
JMR Taylor	2	5.0	2	13	1	1/8	1/13	13.00	2.60	30.0	0	0
AJ Ireland	8	222.5	33	784	36	5/25	7/106	21.77	3.51	37.1	2	0
GM Hussain	15	417.4	86	1497	67	5/36	9/98	22.34	3.58	37.4	2	0
APR Gidman	16	53.0	7	203	9	2/10	3/44	22.55	3.83	35.3	0	0
J Lewis	16	419.3	103	1222	54	4/25	6/74	22.62	2.91	46.6	0	0
JEC Franklin	16	334.2	69	1083	46	7/14	8/81	23.54	3.23	43.6	1	0
SP Kirby	10	261.4	59	835	29	4/50	7/86	28.79	3.19	54.1	0	0
V Banerjee	7	222.0	28	793	23	5/74	6/100	34.47	3.57	57.9	2	0
CG Taylor	15	52.2	5	172	3	1/19	1/19	57.33	3.28	104.6	0	0
EGC Young	2	38.0	1	154	1	1/75	1/125	154.00	4.05	228.0	0	0
CDJ Dent	16	11.0	0	43	0	-	-	-	3.90	-	0	0
HJH Marshall	15	61.0	19	153	0	-	-	-	2.50	-	0	0
WTS Porterfield	7	5.0	0	49	0	-	-	-	9.80	-	0	0

Bowling

LIST A AVERAGES 2010

GLADIATORS

Batting & Fielding

	Mat	Inns	NO	Runs	HS	Ave	SR	100	50	Ct	St
JEC Franklin	12	12	5	511	133*	73.00	91.74	2	2	3	-
CG Taylor	12	11	2	385	105	42.77	108.75	1	2	5	-
APR Gidman	12	12	1	452	104*	41.09	87.42	1	2	7	-
SD Snell	12	9	2	267	95	38.14	118.66	0	2	13	1
HJH Marshall	12	10	0	333	85	33.30	103.41	0	2	5	-
RKJ Dawson	8	4	3	32	17*	32.00	123.07	0	0	6	-
WTS Porterfield	11	11	0	303	65	27.54	93.80	0	2	7	-
DA Payne	6	3	2	21	13	21.00	72.41	0	0	1	-
JN Batty	4	4	0	65	54	16.25	59.63	0	1	4	1
J Lewis	10	6	2	51	22*	12.75	137.83	0	0	2	-
EGC Young	6	3	0	34	25	11.33	87.17	0	0	2	-
CDJ Dent	5	3	0	13	8	4.33	76.47	0	0	0	-
SP Kirby	11	3	0	12	9	4.00	75.00	0	0	2	-
AJ Ireland	8	4	1	8	3	2.66	66.66	0	0	0	-
Kadeer Ali	1	1	1	7	7*	-	140.00	0	0	0	-
V Banerjee	2	1	1	1	1*	-	100.00	0	0	1	-

Bowling

	Mat	Overs	Mdns	Runs	Wkts	BBI	Ave	Econ	SR	5w
DA Payne	6	36.5	2	179	16	7/29	11.18	4.85	13.8	1
V Banerjee	2	13.0	0	51	4	2/20	12.75	3.92	19.5	0
CDJ Dent	5	2.0	0	17	1	1/17	17.00	8.50	12.0	0
J Lewis	10	67.0	4	350	16	3/3	21.87	5.22	25.1	0
SP Kirby	11	73.0	5	400	17	3/41	23.52	5.47	25.7	0
RKJ Dawson	8	48.3	1	271	10	3/41	27.10	5.58	29.1	0
AJ Ireland	8	47.0	0	357	12	3/36	29.75	7.59	23.5	0
CG Taylor	12	21.0	0	123	4	2/15	30.75	5.85	31.5	0
EGC Young	6	30.0	0	148	3	2/42	49.33	4.93	60.0	0
APR Gidman	12	39.0	0	223	4	2/23	55.75	5.71	58.5	0
JEC Franklin	12	52.0	3	263	3	1/9	87.66	5.05	104.0	0
HJH Marshall	12	2.0	0	15	0	-	-	7.50	-	0

GLADIATORS

	Mat	Inns	NO	Runs	HS	Ave	SR	100	50	Ct	St
JEC Franklin	15	15	3	470	90	39.16	130.19	0	2	3	-
HJH Marshall	13	12	2	283	52*	28.30	125.22	0	1	7	-
WTS Porterfield	13	13	1	331	65	27.58	151.83	0	2	7	-
CDJ Dent	7	6	0	162	63	27.00	122.72	0	1	0	-
APR Gidman	12	11	2	204	42	22.66	117.24	0	0	1	-
CG Taylor	15	13	0	257	67	19.76	146.02	0	1	1	-
SD Snell	15	12	3	166	50	18.44	143.10	0	1	8	3
AJ Redmond	8	8	0	132	33	16.50	121.10	0	0	4	-
IG Butler	4	3	0	47	28	15.66	180.76	0	0	0	-
Kadeer Ali	10	8	3	75	24*	15.00	93.75	0	0	3	-
RKJ Dawson	8	5	1	38	24*	9.50	88.37	0	0	2	-
J Lewis	13	10	0	78	26	7.80	102.63	0	0	1	-
V Banerjee	9	3	2	4	2	4.00	57.14	0	0	3	-
SP Kirby	10	6	2	10	3*	2.50	38.46	0	0	3	-
GM Hussain	4	2	0	5	3	2.50	41.66	0	0	1	-
AJ Ireland	13	4	1	5	2	1.66	38.46	0	0	4	-
JN Batty	4	3	3	19	8*	-	126.66	0	0	1	2
DA Payne	3	1	1	1	1*	-	100.00	0	0	0	-

	Mat	Overs	Mdns	Runs	Wkts	BBI	Ave	Econ	SR	5w
DA Payne	3	11.0	0	81	6	3/25	13.50	7.36	11.0	0
SP Kirby	10	34.5	0	269	13	3/17	20.69	7.72	16.0	0
RKJ Dawson	8	26.0	0	217	10	2/20	21.70	8.34	15.6	0
IG Butler	4	13.5	0	122	5	3/8	24.40	8.81	16.6	0
Kadeer Ali	10	6.0	0	78	3	2/28	26.00	13.00	12.0	0
AJ Ireland	13	39.3	0	389	12	3/35	32.41	9.84	19.7	0
V Banerjee	9	32.0	0	262	7	2/30	37.42	8.18	27.4	0
JEC Franklin	15	36.0	0	318	8	2/33	39.75	8.83	27.0	0
AJ Redmond	8	17.5	0	184	4	2/38	46.00	10.31	26.7	0
J Lewis	13	45.0	0	372	8	2/26	46.50	8.26	33.7	0
GM Hussain	4	13.0	0	147	2	1/41	73.50	11.30	39.0	0
APR Gidman	12	8.4	0	76	1	1/17	76.00	8.76	52.0	0
HJH Marshall	13	1.0	0	14	0	-	-	14.00	-	0
CG Taylor	15	2.0	0	15	0	-	-	7.50	-	0

VIKRAM BANERJEE

LHB SLA

NAME: Vikram Banerjee
BORN: March 20, 1984, Bradford
HEIGHT: 6ft
SQUAD Nº: 20
NICKNAME: Banners
CAREER: First-class debut: 2004; List A
debut: 2009; T20 debut: 2009

AOC SAYS: Banerjee is yet to cement a regular place in Gloucestershire's Championship side despite arriving on the scene in 2006 and picking up the Denis Compton Award, handed out to the most promising youngster at each of the 18 professional counties. A left-arm spinner, Banerjee moved to Bristol after coming up through the ranks at Warwickshire, where he never made a senior appearance. He spun Gloucestershire to success against Surrey at The Oval last season with a career-best 5-74, and Banerjee will be hoping to become a Championship regular this summer, establishing himself as the team's premier spinner while continuing to develop in Gloucestershire's one-day side.

LAST WORD: "He's been in the England Performance squad before so he's highly-rated and he's a good lad who works hard; there's every chance he will come through."
Richard Latham

Batting & Fielding

	Mat	Inns	NO	Runs	HS	Ave	SR	100	50	Ct	St
First-class	40	62	20	386	35	9.19	23.47	0	0	9	0
List A	12	7	4	12	6	4.00	54.54	0	0	5	0
Twenty20	15	5	4	9	5*	9.00	90.00	0	0	5	0

Bowling

	Mat	Balls	Runs	Wkts	BBI	BBM	Ave	Econ	SR	5w	10
First-class	40	7311	4184	93	5/74	-	44.98	3.43	78.6	2	0
List A	12	570	437	18	3/47	3/47	24.27	4.60	31.6	0	0
Twenty20	15	330	437	13	2/30	2/30	33.61	7.94	25.3	0	0

GLOUCESTERSHIRE

NAME: Jonathan Neil Batty
BORN: April 18, 1974, Chesterfield
HEIGHT: 5ft 10in
SQUAD Nº: 1
NICKNAME: JB
OTHER TEAMS: Surrey
CAREER: First-class debut: 1994; List A debut: 1994; T20 debut: 2003; County cap: 2001 (Surrey)

AOC SAYS: After 12 fruitful years with Surrey, Batty joined Gloucestershire ahead of the 2010 campaign and took a career-best 53 catches in his first season at Bristol. He has consistently been one of the best wicketkeeper-batsmen on the county scene over the last decade but despite his excellent glovework in 2010, Batty struggled with the bat during his first season away from The Oval, averaging just 16.07. Members at Bristol will be hoping Batty can recapture his batting form this summer, especially as he's on the cusp of the 10,000 first-class runs milestone. He has claimed over 600 victims during his first-class career and holds a joint world-record after taking eight catches in a single innings against Kent in 2004. A one-time Surrey captain to boot, Batty is one of county cricket's great survivors.

LAST WORD: "Jonathan is a really resilient character and as good a professional as you will find on the county circuit. He is excellent in the dressing room and his attitude is spot-on. A player like that can always turn the tide of a spell of poor form and I'm very confident he will have a good year in 2011." *Jack Russell, former Gloucestershire wicketkeeper*

Batting & Fielding

	Mat	Inns	NO	Runs	HS	Ave	SR	100	50	Ct	St
First-class	206	324	36	9238	168*	32.07	-	20	39	553	67
List A	185	152	26	2808	158*	22.28	-	1	14	195	34
Twenty20	55	47	18	612	59	21.10	111.88	0	2	32	20

Bowling

	Mat	Balls	Runs	Wkts	BBI	BBM	Ave	Econ	SR	5w	10
First-class	206	78	61	1	1/21	-	61.00	4.69	78.0	0	0
List A	185	-	-	-	-	-	-	-	-	-	-
Twenty20	55	-	-	-	-	-	-	-	-	-	-

IAN COCKBAIN

NAME: Ian Andrew Cockbain
BORN: February 17, 1987, Liverpool
HEIGHT: 6ft
SQUAD Nº: 28
CAREER: Yet to make first-team debut

AOC SAYS: A graduate of the MCC Young Cricketers programme, Cockbain signed a two-year deal with Gloucestershire in December 2010. A top-order batsman, Cockbain was recommended to Gloucestershire by the club's former captain and current MCC head coach Mark Alleyne. Cockbain scored 749 second XI runs at an average of 44.20 in 2010 and, as an excellent fielder, was selected by England as 12th man in each of their fixtures at Lord's last summer. Before joining the MCC programme Ian was on the books at Lancashire, the county his father Ian Snr played for between 1979 and 1983.

LAST WORD: "We are delighted to have signed Ian as an opening batsman from the MCC Young Cricketers. He comes highly recommended by Mark Alleyne and we are confident that Ian's cricket will kick on in the professional environment." *John Bracewell*

EXTRAS

Gloucestershire announced a £216,000 loss for 2010, the second successive year the club has recorded a loss. Tony Elgood, Gloucestershire treasurer said: "Looking to the longer term, our ground development plans seek to ensure that we maximise the income from the use of the ground throughout the whole year. If we can significantly increase this source of income, we can not only trade more profitably but will also be in a position to make greater investments in the playing squad."

NAME: Richard George Coughtrie
BORN: September 1, 1988, North Shields
HEIGHT: 5ft 9in
SQUAD Nº: 12
CAREER: First-class debut: 2009

GLOUCESTERSHIRE

AOC SAYS: Gloucestershire's back-up wicketkeeper will begin the season behind Jon Batty in the pecking order but after cutting short his time at Oxford Brookes University to become a full-time player at Gloucestershire when he signed a two-year contract with the county in November 2010, he is clearly a man in a hurry. He played Second XI cricket for Gloucestershire last summer, making important runs without hitting a century, and he will be looking to build on that start in 2011. He also has first-class experience playing for Oxford MCCU.

LAST WORD: "Richard possesses a wonderful mixture of natural talent and strong dedication. His hard work over the last couple of years has been rewarded and knowing Richard he will now push his game forward to try and establish himself on the first-class stage." *Jack Russell, former Gloucestershire wicketkeeper*

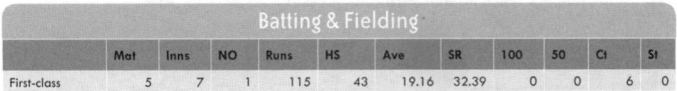

Batting & Fielding

	Mat	Inns	NO	Runs	HS	Ave	SR	100	50	Ct	St
First-class	5	7	1	115	43	19.16	32.39	0	0	6	0

Bowling

	Mat	Balls	Runs	Wkts	BBI	BBM	Ave	Econ	SR	5w	10
First-class	5	-	-	-	-	-	-	-	-	-	-

RICHARD DAWSON

RHB OB

GLOUCESTERSHIRE

NAME: Richard Kevin James Dawson
BORN: August 4, 1980, Doncaster
HEIGHT: 6ft 4in
SQUAD Nº: 31
NICKNAME: Billy Dog, Sauce
OTHER TEAMS: Northamptonshire, Yorkshire
CAREER: Test debut: 2001; First-class debut: 2000; List A debut: 1999; T20 debut: 2004; County cap: 2004 (Yorkshire)

AOC SAYS: One of county cricket's most recognisable and popular characters, the former Yorkshire and England spinner signed for Gloucestershire in the summer of 2008 after a season at Northants. The zenith of Dawson's sprawling career probably came in 2002 when he was selected as part of England's Ashes squad, in recognition of some sterling work on his first senior tour the previous winter in India. He was part of a triumphant team at Sydney in the final Test, but that was his last appearance in an England shirt. Dawson joined the coaching staff at Gloucestershire last winter as a spin bowling coach and while he will still be available to play for the county, his principle role will be as a coach. Smart and articulate, Dawson is also a qualified journalist.

LAST WORD: "With the club's emphasis on producing young cricketers and having seen his coaching close-up during academy sessions, Richard is a great acquisition to the coaching staff. His experience and knowledge will be extremely valuable to our developing players." *Jack Russell, former Gloucestershire wicketkeeper*

Batting & Fielding

	Mat	Inns	NO	Runs	HS	Ave	SR	100	50	Ct	St
Tests	7	13	3	114	19*	11.40	31.40	0	0	3	0
First-class	103	153	17	2927	87	21.52	-	0	12	63	0
List A	127	78	18	626	41	10.43	-	0	0	45	0
Twenty20	41	22	5	178	27*	10.47	111.94	0	0	13	0

Bowling

	Mat	Balls	Runs	Wkts	BBI	BBM	Ave	Econ	SR	5w	10
Tests	7	1116	677	11	4/134	4/134	61.54	3.63	101.4	0	0
First-class	103	15467	8770	199	6/82	-	44.07	3.40	77.7	5	0
List A	127	4766	3918	128	4/13	4/13	30.60	4.93	37.2	0	0
Twenty20	41	809	1045	39	3/24	3/24	26.79	7.75	20.7	0	0

NAME: Christopher David James Dent
BORN: January 20, 1991, Bristol
HEIGHT: 5ft 9in
SQUAD Nº: 15
NICKNAME: Denty
CAREER: First-class debut: 2010; List A
debut: 2009; T20 debut: 2010

GLOUCESTERSHIRE

AOC SAYS: A product of Gloucestershire's academy, Dent is a left-handed batsman who bowls left-arm spin and occasionally keeps wicket. Although his chances were limited last year, he helped Gloucestershire beat Derbyshire last season with an explosive 98 from 85 deliveries, giving a glimpse of his power and potential. Dent, who represented England at the Under 19 World Cup in 2010, will be hoping to secure a regular slot in the Championship side while also making strides in the one-day game.

LAST WORD: "Dent had a good season in 2010 and was used in some tough situations. You would always see him come in when they were in trouble. He showed a good temperament, he's a very hard-working lad and a bloke who hates losing his wicket."
Richard Latham

Batting & Fielding

	Mat	Inns	NO	Runs	HS	Ave	SR	100	50	Ct	St
First-class	16	31	3	725	98	25.89	50.62	0	4	24	0
List A	6	3	0	13	8	4.33	76.47	0	0	2	0
Twenty20	7	6	0	162	63	27.00	122.72	0	1	0	0

Bowling

	Mat	Balls	Runs	Wkts	BBI	BBM	Ave	Econ	SR	5w	10
First-class	16	66	43	0	-	-	-	3.90	-	0	0
List A	6	12	17	1	1/17	1/17	17.00	8.50	12.0	0	0
Twenty20	7	-	-	-	-	-	-	-	-	-	-

JAMES FULLER

RHB RF

GLOUCESTERSHIRE

NAME: James Kerr Fuller
BORN: January 24, 1990, Cape Town
SQUAD Nº: 26
OTHER TEAMS: Otago
CAREER: First-class debut: 2010

AOC SAYS: Gloucestershire have high hopes for pace bowler Fuller, who signed a three-year deal with the county in August 2010 and has joined up full-time with the squad ahead of the 2011 season. The South Africa-born paceman plays for Otago in New Zealand but holds a British passport so does not need to be registered as an overseas player. Fuller is also a useful batter and scored an unbeaten 62 for Otago in the domestic New Zealand under 23 competition in January 2011. Fuller has also played for New Zealand's under 19s, and his presence at Bristol continues the club's rich partnership with New Zealand cricket.

LAST WORD: "Fuller is rated very highly in New Zealand. Gloucestershire have very high hopes of him but he is an unknown quantity." *Richard Latham*

Batting & Fielding

	Mat	Inns	NO	Runs	HS	Ave	SR	100	50	Ct	St
First-class	2	3	0	31	24	10.33	46.96	0	0	1	0

Bowling

	Mat	Balls	Runs	Wkts	BBI	BBM	Ave	Econ	SR	5w	10
First-class	2	342	231	2	1/33	1/113	115.50	4.05	171.0	0	0

GLOUCESTERSHIRE

NAME: Alexander Peter Richard Gidman
BORN: June 22, 1981, High Wycombe
HEIGHT: 6ft 2in
SQUAD Nº: 5
NICKNAME: Giddo
OTHER TEAMS: Otago
CAREER: First-class debut: 2002; List A
debut: 2001; T20 debut: 2003

AOC SAYS: It was no surprise when Gloucestershire's captain and heartbeat began 2011 by signing a contract extension that will keep him at Bristol until 2013. The elder of Gloucester's two Gidman brothers, Alex is a middle-order batsman and a nagging medium-pacer who can be unhittable on Bristol's slow, low one-day pitches. As one of the more experienced players in a fairly youthful side, the Gladiators will be looking to Gidman to drive the kids on in his third season as skipper. After taking over from Jon Lewis in 2009, Gidman amassed 1,028 Championship runs at an average of 44.69, but he struggled last summer, averaging 23.41 in a middle-order bereft of runs. He fell one run short of a century against Leicestershire, and tellingly this was his best contribution. However, he did smash an unbeaten century in the CB40 against Netherlands, his fourth limited-overs hundred. With the ball he has taken 49 one-day wickets for the Gladiators, and 88 first-class wickets, with a career-best of 4-47 against Glamorgan. A player who emerged during Gloucestershire's period of one-day dominance, Gidman helped his team win back-to-back C&G Trophies in 2003 and 2004. In the first of those two finals, both against Worcestershire, Gidman took 2-12 off seven overs before hitting the winning runs as the Gladiators successfully chased down a target of 150. Gidman was once touted as a potential England star but, despite a number of appearances for England A, he has never played for the full side in any form of the game. Although uncapped, he is unquestionably one of county cricket's most consistent performers. The closest he came to an England berth was a call-up to the provisional squad for the 2004 ICC Champions Trophy.

INSIDE TRACK: "Alex is so passionate about Gloucestershire. He is a good and knowledgeable captain who needs some of the senior players around him to stand up and share responsibility so he can concentrate more on his batting. I have no doubt that he is the right man to take the team forward at a time when financial cutbacks are inevitable and not making the job easy." *John Bracewell*

ALEX GIDMAN

Batting & Fielding											
	Mat	Inns	NO	Runs	HS	Ave	SR	100	50	Ct	St
First-class	130	227	20	7348	176	35.49	56.57	15	40	80	0
List A	154	145	15	3420	116	26.30	-	4	17	49	0
Twenty20	58	51	9	884	64	21.04	114.80	0	3	12	0

Bowling											
	Mat	Balls	Runs	Wkts	BBI	BBM	Ave	Econ	SR	5w	10
First-class	130	6857	4251	97	4/47	-	43.82	3.71	70.6	0	0
List A	154	2992	2593	61	5/42	5/42	42.50	5.19	49.0	1	0
Twenty20	58	256	347	8	2/24	2/24	43.37	8.13	32.0	0	0

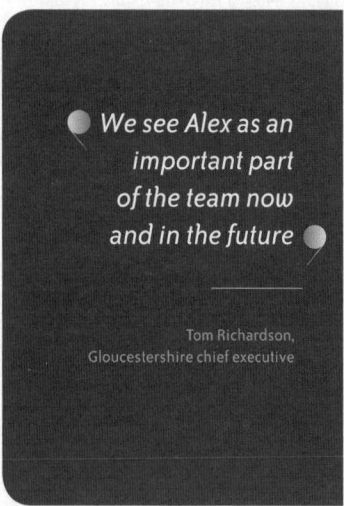

We see Alex as an important part of the team now and in the future

Tom Richardson,
Gloucestershire chief executive

NAME: William Robert Simon Gidman
BORN: February 14, 1985, High Wycombe
HEIGHT: 6ft 2in
SQUAD Nº: 23
NICKNAME: Gidders, Giddo
OTHER TEAMS: Durham
CAREER: First-class debut: 2007; List A debut: 2003

AOC SAYS: Gidman was on Gloucestershire's books before joining Durham in 2006 after finding his chances restricted to a single one-day appearance. Yet to play in the County Championship, he is returning to Gloucestershire on a two-year contract to play under his older brother Alex. A right-arm seamer who bats left-handed, Gidman will be hoping that his versatility – long considered a bowling allrounder, he has opened the batting in Second XI cricket for Durham – will enable him to break through into the first team in all forms of the game.

LAST WORD: "Will and Alex have very rarely played in the same team, even as kids. At Durham he was mainly a bowler who could bat but he's coming to Gloucestershire looking to get a top-six batting place." *Richard Latham*

Batting & Fielding

	Mat	Inns	NO	Runs	HS	Ave	SR	100	50	Ct	St
First-class	1	2	0	8	8	4.00	27.58	0	0	0	0
List A	18	10	2	105	21	13.12	-	0	0	6	0

Bowling

	Mat	Balls	Runs	Wkts	BBI	BBM	Ave	Econ	SR	5w	10
First-class	1	138	86	4	3/37	4/86	21.50	3.73	34.5	0	0
List A	18	562	423	19	4/36	4/36	22.26	4.51	29.5	0	0

JON LEWIS

GLOUCESTERSHIRE

NAME: Jonathan Lewis
BORN: August 26, 1975, Aylesbury
HEIGHT: 6ft 3in
SQUAD Nº: 18
NICKNAME: Lewy
OTHER TEAMS: England
CAREER: Test debut: 2006; ODI debut: 2005;
T20I debut: 2005; First-class debut: 1995;
List A debut: 1995; T20 debut: 2003; County
cap: 1998

AOC SAYS: A consistent first-class wicket-taker for well over a decade now, Lewis spent three seasons as Gloucestershire captain before stepping down from the role at the end of the 2008 campaign. As the county's most senior bowler, this one-club man will be relied upon as much as ever as Gloucestershire look to blood new talent. His solitary England Test cap came against Sri Lanka in 2006 but he has represented his country 13 times in one-day cricket, and whilst he probably lacked the penetration to thrive at international level, his accuracy and ability to shape the new ball are invaluable for his county. His finest moment in an England shirt came in a feisty T20I against Australia at The Rose Bowl in 2005, when he dismissed Symonds, Clarke and Ponting en route to figures of 4-24.

LAST WORD: "I made a discovery recently. I got a cameraman to take some footage of me because I am trying to disguise my inswinger better. Watching the film, I discovered some cues that a batsman might pick up. You never stop learning about your own game." *Jon Lewis*

Batting & Fielding

	Mat	Inns	NO	Runs	HS	Ave	SR	100	50	Ct	St
Tests	1	2	0	27	20	13.50	60.00	0	0	0	0
ODIs	13	8	2	50	17	8.33	79.36	0	0	0	0
T20Is	2	2	1	1	1	1.00	25.00	0	0	1	0
First-class	212	302	61	3666	62	15.21	-	0	9	53	0
List A	209	122	44	873	54	11.19	-	0	1	39	0
Twenty20	48	31	7	325	43	13.54	127.45	0	0	8	0

Bowling

	Mat	Balls	Runs	Wkts	BBI	BBM	Ave	Econ	SR	5w	10
Tests	1	246	122	3	3/68	3/122	40.66	2.97	82.0	0	0
ODIs	13	716	500	18	4/36	4/36	27.77	4.18	39.7	0	0
T20Is	2	42	55	4	4/24	4/24	13.75	7.85	10.5	0	0
First-class	212	38197	19102	733	8/95	-	26.06	3.00	52.1	33	5
List A	209	9628	7287	277	5/19	5/19	26.30	4.54	34.7	2	0
Twenty20	48	1014	1401	49	4/24	4/24	28.59	8.28	20.6	0	0

RHB RM R1 MVP84

NAME: Hamish John Hamilton Marshall
BORN: February 15, 1979, Auckland
SQUAD Nº: 9
NICKNAME: Marshy
OTHER TEAMS: New Zealand, Royal Bengal Tigers
CAREER: Test debut: 2000; ODI debut: 2003; T20I debut: 2005; First-class debut: 1999; List A debut: 1998; T20 debut: 2005

GLOUCESTERSHIRE

AOC SAYS: Signed initially as an overseas player, Marshall has been at Gloucestershire since 2006 and is now ensconced as one of Gloucestershire's naturalised Kiwis. He has represented New Zealand in 13 Test matches, making a brace of hundreds, including a maiden ton against Australia, and 66 one-day internationals but surprised everyone when he refused a contract with his country for the 2007/08 season in order to extend his time in county cricket as a non-overseas player, which he was able to do by that stage via an Irish passport. He has previously stated his intention to resume his international career with Ireland, and became eligible to do so in April 2011.

LAST WORD: "I'm happy with my technique, but there is a mental issue to sort out. Last season I was getting too relaxed and comfortable after reaching 30 or 40 and I needed to respect the opposition and the conditions more." *Hamish Marshall*

Batting & Fielding

	Mat	Inns	NO	Runs	HS	Ave	SR	100	50	Ct	St
Tests	13	19	2	652	160	38.35	47.31	2	2	1	0
ODIs	66	62	9	1454	101*	27.43	73.06	1	12	18	0
T20Is	3	3	0	12	8	4.00	85.71	0	0	1	0
First-class	155	263	18	8884	170	36.26	-	18	46	87	0
List A	239	227	24	5770	122	28.42	-	6	38	90	0
Twenty20	49	48	3	1080	100	24.00	136.53	1	3	26	0

Bowling

	Mat	Balls	Runs	Wkts	BBI	BBM	Ave	Econ	SR	5w	10
Tests	13	6	4	0	-	-	-	4.00	-	0	0
ODIs	66	-	-	-	-	-	-	-	-	-	-
T20Is	3	-	-	-	-	-	-	-	-	-	-
First-class	155	2874	1483	30	4/24	-	49.43	3.09	95.8	0	0
List A	239	248	258	4	2/21	2/21	64.50	6.24	62.0	0	0
Twenty20	49	6	14	0	-	-	-	14.00	-	0	0

MUTTIAH MURALITHARAN RHB OB W3

GLOUCESTERSHIRE

OVERSEAS PLAYER

NAME: Muttiah Muralitharan
BORN: April 17, 1972, Kandy
HEIGHT: 5ft 7in
SQUAD Nº: 800
OTHER TEAMS: Sri Lanka, Chennai Super Kings, Kandurata, Kent, Kochi, Lancashire, Tamil Union Cricket and Athletic Club
CAREER: Test debut: 1992; ODI debut: 1993; T20I debut: 2006; First-class debut: 1990; List A debut:1992; T20 debut: 2005; County cap: 1999 (Lancashire), 2003 (Kent)

AOC SAYS: The only cricketer to have taken 800 Test wickets, the magical Muttiah Muralitharan is one of the all-time greats. He has claimed 1,374 victims in first-class cricket at an average of 19.64, maintained his humour and humility in the face of demoralising questions about the legitimacy of his bowling action, and given cricket many great memories. A World Cup winner and a holder of multiple world records, he will join his third county, Gloucestershire, to play exclusively in Twenty20 cricket in 2011 and 2012. Murali retired from all forms of international cricket at the end of the 2011 World Cup and will play in the IPL for new franchise Kochi before linking up with Gloucestershire.

LAST WORD: "This is an exciting and once-in-a-lifetime opportunity to work and play with one of the greatest cricketers in the history of the game." *John Bracewell*

Batting & Fielding

	Mat	Inns	NO	Runs	HS	Ave	SR	100	50	Ct	St
Tests	133	164	56	1261	67	11.67	70.28	0	1	72	0
ODIs	349	162	63	674	33*	6.80	77.56	0	0	130	0
T20Is	12	2	0	1	1	0.50	20.00	0	0	1	0
First-class	232	276	83	2192	67	11.35	-	0	1	123	0
List A	449	204	76	938	33*	7.32	-	0	0	158	0
Twenty20	73	15	3	38	11	3.16	80.85	0	0	21	0

Bowling

	Mat	Balls	Runs	Wkts	BBI	BBM	Ave	Econ	SR	5w	10
Tests	133	44039	18180	800	9/51	16/220	22.72	2.47	55.0	67	22
ODIs	349	18763	12287	534	7/30	7/30	23.00	3.92	35.1	10	0
T20Is	12	282	297	13	3/29	3/29	22.84	6.31	21.6	0	0
First-class	232	66933	26997	1374	9/51	-	19.64	2.42	48.7	119	34
List A	449	23524	15110	673	7/30	7/30	22.45	3.84	35.2	12	0
Twenty20	73	1686	1732	95	4/16	4/16	18.23	6.16	17.7	0	0

LIAM NORWELL

RHB RM

NAME: Liam Connor Norwell
BORN: December 27, 1991, Bournemouth
SQUAD Nº: 24
CAREER: Yet to make first team debut

AOC SAYS: A Gloucestershire academy graduate, Norwell delayed going to university to concentrate on his cricketing career. A strapping pace bowler who can swing the ball away from the right-hander, Norwell was selected in the ECB's Elite Player Development squad last summer and travelled to Australia as part of the England Performance Programme over the winter. He represented Cornwall as a youth player and played eight times for the Gloucestershire Second XI in 2010, claiming 11 wickets in five matches.

LAST WORD: "Our specialist coaching and physical development department will spend valuable time with Liam over the next two years which will allow him to put his attributes into practice." *John Bracewell*

EXTRAS

"Whenever I have watched and observed Murali he has always shown an infectious love for the game of cricket. I can't wait to meet and to play with him. From the players' point of view, it will be a great experience and I am sure we will learn a huge amount from him. This has given us a huge boost going into the 2011 season." John Bracewell

DAVID PAYNE

LHB LFM

GLOUCESTERSHIRE

NAME: David Alan Payne
BORN: February 15, 1991, Poole
SQUAD Nº: 14
NICKNAME: Pepperami
CAREER: List A debut: 2009; T20 debut: 2010

AOC SAYS: Payne made his mark at Gloucestershire last summer with some excellent one-day performances, including taking a club record 7-29 in the CB40 match against Essex. In nine matches he claimed 22 wickets at an average of 11.50 and was a permanent fixture in the England under 19 squad throughout 2010. He signed a new three-year deal with Gloucestershire at the end of last season and is likely to feature prominently in all forms of the game this summer. One to watch.

LAST WORD: "David is already one of our outstanding one-day bowlers and he will be introduced into more four-day cricket next season. But the amount of one-day cricket he has played has already enabled him to develop a good slower ball and deceptive changes of pace. Perhaps his best quality is that he is game-smart, which is terrific in a young player."
John Bracewell

Batting & Fielding

	Mat	Inns	NO	Runs	HS	Ave	SR	100	50	Ct	St
List A	9	5	4	25	13	25.00	69.44	0	0	2	0
Twenty20	3	1	1	1	1*	-	100.00	0	0	0	0

Bowling

	Mat	Balls	Runs	Wkts	BBI	BBM	Ave	Econ	SR	5w	10
List A	9	299	253	22	7/29	7/29	11.50	5.07	13.5	1	0
Twenty20	3	66	81	6	3/25	3/25	13.50	7.36	11.0	0	0

IAN SAXELBY

RHB RMF

NAME: Ian David Saxelby
BORN: May 22, 1989, Nottingham
SQUAD Nº: 21
NICKNAME: Sax
CAREER: First-class debut: 2008; List A debut: 2009; T20 debut: 2009

GLOUCESTERSHIRE

AOC SAYS: Gloucestershire will be hoping to have Saxelby fit this summer after he missed the entire 2010 campaign due to twice dislocating his bowling shoulder. A burly seamer, he took 20 first-class wickets in nine matches in 2009, showing sufficient promise as an economical line-and-length merchant, and has been a part of both the England under 19 squad and the England Performance Squad. On his Championship debut in 2008 he helped save the match for Gloucestershire, sharing a final-wicket stand with Ant Ireland which lasted over an hour.

LAST WORD: "He was out for the whole of last season with a bad shoulder injury and he has been building up gradually for the start of the season. If he's fit it will be a big boost for Gloucestershire. There will be some question marks over him but they could do with him being fit." *Richard Latham*

Batting & Fielding

	Mat	Inns	NO	Runs	HS	Ave	SR	100	50	Ct	St
First-class	12	16	4	188	60*	15.66	44.13	0	1	6	0
List A	6	5	2	25	7*	8.33	59.52	0	0	0	0
Twenty20	5	3	1	4	2	2.00	40.00	0	0	0	0

Bowling

	Mat	Balls	Runs	Wkts	BBI	BBM	Ave	Econ	SR	5w	10
First-class	12	1394	838	22	3/31	4/94	38.09	3.60	63.3	0	0
List A	6	182	171	8	4/31	4/31	21.37	5.63	22.7	0	0
Twenty20	5	111	166	5	2/32	2/32	33.20	8.97	22.2	0	0

CHRIS TAYLOR

GLOUCESTERSHIRE

NAME: Christopher Glyn Taylor
BORN: September 27, 1976, Bristol
HEIGHT: 5ft 8in
SQUAD №: 8
NICKNAME: Tales
CAREER: First-class debut: 2000; List A debut: 1999; T20 debut: 2003; County cap: 2001

AOC SAYS: Widely regarded as a world-class fieldsman, Taylor coaches fielding for Gloucestershire as well as working within the England set-up, on the England Performance Programme and with England Lions. But although his athletic work at backward point marks him out as a superstar in his field, his busy, combative batting has provided ballast to Gloucestershire in all formats for well over a decade now. He marked his Gloucestershire debut with a century against Middlesex at Lord's in 2000, captained the side in 2004 and 2005 and has twice racked up over 1,000 first-class runs in a summer. Last season he averaged just 32.12 with the bat in the County Championship, which by his normally excellent standards was a poor return, but he fared better in one-day cricket, hitting a century against Northamptonshire and finishing with a List A average of 47.37. As well as being an exceptional fielder, Taylor occasionally bowls offspin.

LAST WORD: "We have spoken a lot about the senior batsmen taking more responsibility and allowing the less experienced ones to flourish around us. As a senior player myself, I am very much aware of the role I need to play." *Chris Taylor*

Batting & Fielding

	Mat	Inns	NO	Runs	HS	Ave	SR	100	50	Ct	St
First-class	144	250	18	7944	196	34.24	-	17	37	96	0
List A	169	152	22	3383	105	26.02	-	1	20	70	1
Twenty20	65	59	10	1180	83	24.08	137.36	0	5	21	0

Bowling

	Mat	Balls	Runs	Wkts	BBI	BBM	Ave	Econ	SR	5w	10
First-class	144	2497	1452	27	4/52	-	53.77	3.48	92.4	0	0
List A	169	700	613	16	2/5	2/5	38.31	5.25	43.7	0	0
Twenty20	65	36	60	1	1/22	1/22	60.00	10.00	36.0	0	0

NAME: Jack Martin Robert Taylor
BORN: November 12, 1991, Banbury
SQUAD Nº: 10
CAREER: First-class debut: 2010

GLOUCESTERSHIRE

AOC SAYS: A former England under 19 starlet, Taylor made his first-class debut for Gloucestershire in August 2010 and took his first wicket in his following match against Surrey. After signing a development contract in 2009, his full-time professional contract at Bristol came into effect last October once he had completed his studies. A pugnacious batting allrounder who bowls offspin, Taylor has been involved in the England Development Squad and his younger brother Matthew is currently a part of the Gloucestershire academy. After getting a taste of First XI cricket at the end of last season, Taylor will be keen to stake a claim for a regular place in the team this summer.

LAST WORD: "Jack has worked very hard to get his foot in the door. He has huge potential and I am sure we will see very good things from this gifted young cricketer." *Owen Dawkins, Gloucestershire academy director*

Batting & Fielding

	Mat	Inns	NO	Runs	HS	Ave	SR	100	50	Ct	St
First-class	2	4	0	11	6	2.75	20.75	0	0	2	0

Bowling

	Mat	Balls	Runs	Wkts	BBI	BBM	Ave	Econ	SR	5w	10
First-class	2	30	13	1	1/8	1/13	13.00	2.60	30.0	0	0

DAVID WADE

RHB RFM

GLOUCESTERSHIRE

NAME: David Neil Wade
BORN: September 27, 1983, Chichester
SQUAD Nº: 27
CAREER: Yet to make first-team debut

AOC SAYS: Wade's is an intriguing story. Aged 27, he is a latecomer to the professional game having left his job as a lance corporal with the Royal Signals Corps to join Gloucestershire. During his time as a soldier he represented the army against a number of counties and was due to return for a second tour of duty in Afghanistan when he was offered a contract at Bristol. A tall pace bowler, Wade was on Hampshire's books as a youngster and took four wickets in a Second XI match for Gloucestershire at the end of last season, alerting the Bristol club to his potential.

LAST WORD: "David was discovered through our scouting programme. He trialled with us early last year and impressed us with his pace, bounce and outswing. With his proven discipline and obvious courage through the armed forces, he has shown throughout the winter months a dedication to training and coaching." *John Bracewell*

EXTRAS

"We have long had a really good association with New Zealand from the time John Bracewell has spent coaching the national team, and with Craig Spearman, Hamish Marshall, Ian Butler and of course James Franklin having played for Gloucestershire. We have a very good relationship with the cricket association and their chief executive, Justin Vaughan, another former Gloucestershire player, and we want to continue to foster this." Tom Richardson, Gloucestershire chief executive

OVERSEAS PLAYER

GLOUCESTERSHIRE

NAME: Kane Stuart Williamson
BORN: August 8, 1990, Tauranga
SQUAD Nº: 87
OTHER TEAMS: New Zealand, Northern Districts
CAREER: Test debut; 2010; ODI debut: 2010; First-class debut: 2007; List A debut: 2007; T20 debut: 2009

AOC SAYS: Gloucestershire's latest Kiwi recruit is the club's overseas player for 2010. But Gloucester fans concerns at the 21-year-old's inexperience should be assuaged by the maturity Williamson has shown so far in his short career. Thrown into the cauldron of a Test match in India last winter, he scored a century on his debut, and prior to joining Gloucestershire he had notched up 1,727 first-class runs at an average of 43.17. After captaining his country at the 2008 Under 19 World Cup, he continued to impress his countrymen by scoring more runs in New Zealand's domestic one-day competition in 2009/10 than any other player. He made his international breakthrough last winter and up until the World Cup had played in five Test matches, attracting plaudits for that brilliant 131 against India – the second highest Test-match score by a New Zealander making his debut. But prior to his Test debut his Kiwi career spluttered through an up-and-down ODI series against Bangladesh, when he was out for a duck in each of his first two ODI appearances. But he returned for the fourth match of the series, demonstrating his mental strength to graft a maiden ODI century. He was a member of New Zealand's World Cup squad and is a part-time offspinner with two Test wickets to his name. Recruited for all formats and for the whole season, he'll be looking to become a pivotal member of Gloucestershire's batting line-up this summer. If the young Kiwi continues to progress his career in the same manner as he has shown so far, John Bracewell may well have made one of the most astute signings of the summer.

INSIDE TRACK: " I am aware of his work ethic and personal drive to not just be a good international cricketer but a great one. He is a player from the Mike Hussey mould; driven to succeed through hard work and dedication and will be a great example not only to our younger players but also to some of our more senior batsmen."
John Bracewell

KANE WILLIAMSON

Batting & Fielding											
	Mat	Inns	NO	Runs	HS	Ave	SR	100	50	Ct	St
Tests	5	9	0	299	131	33.22	42.83	1	2	1	0
ODIs	15	14	2	352	108	29.33	68.48	1	0	3	0
First-class	25	42	2	1727	192	43.17	53.33	5	8	25	0
List A	39	36	9	1343	108*	49.74	75.02	4	7	16	0
Twenty20	10	10	1	100	30	11.11	84.74	0	0	6	0

Bowling											
	Mat	Balls	Runs	Wkts	BBI	BBM	Ave	Econ	SR	5w	10
Tests	5	240	176	2	1/45	1/45	88.00	4.40	120.0	0	0
ODIs	15	156	133	1	1/2	1/2	133.00	5.11	156.0	0	0
First-class	25	2530	1458	32	5/75	5/59	45.56	3.45	79.0	1	0
List A	39	1003	784	19	5/51	5/51	41.26	4.68	52.7	1	0
Twenty20	10	114	161	1	1/21	1/21	161.00	8.47	114.0	0	0

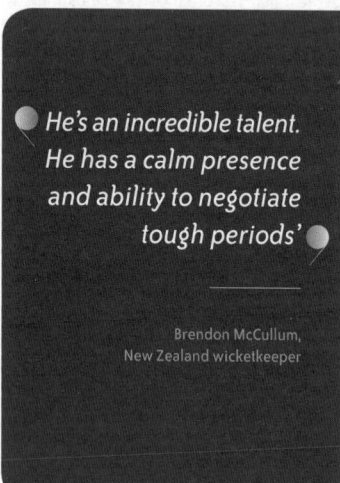

He's an incredible talent. He has a calm presence and ability to negotiate tough periods'

Brendon McCullum,
New Zealand wicketkeeper

NAME: Edward George Christopher Young
BORN: May 21, 1989, Chertsey
HEIGHT: 6ft
SQUAD Nº: 30
OTHER TEAMS: Unicorns
CAREER: First-class debut: 2009; List A debut: 2010

GLOUCESTERSHIRE

AOC SAYS: A slow left-arm spinning allrounder, Young signed a two-year development contract with Gloucestershire in August 2010 and played in two County Championship and six CB40 games for the Gladiators at the end of the season, having already represented Unicorns. Young attended Oxford Brookes University and played for Oxford MCCU. He was also a member of the MCC Universities combined team, competing in Second XI Championship matches.

LAST WORD: "A professional contract was what I had been working towards for a long time so it was good to get a reward for all my hard work at university. Now that has been signed I am looking forward to the next stage of my career." *Ed Young*

Batting & Fielding

	Mat	Inns	NO	Runs	HS	Ave	SR	100	50	Ct	St
First-class	7	9	1	265	79	33.12	49.71	0	2	6	0
List A	8	5	0	47	25	9.40	75.80	0	0	2	0

Bowling

	Mat	Balls	Runs	Wkts	BBI	BBM	Ave	Econ	SR	5w	10
First-class	7	588	379	3	2/74	2/129	126.33	3.86	196.0	0	0
List A	8	220	206	3	2/42	2/42	68.66	5.61	73.3	0	0

FORMED: 1863
HOME GROUND: The Rose Bowl
ONE-DAY NAME: Royals
CAPTAIN: Dominic Cork
2010 RESULTS: CC1: 7/9; CB40: 4/7 in Group C; FP t20: Champions

HAMPSHIRE
CRICKET

HONOURS
County Championship: (2) 1961, 1973; Gillette/NatWest/C&G/FP Trophy: (2) 1991, 2005; Benson and Hedges Cup: (2) 1988, 1992; Sunday League: (3) 1975, 1978, 1986; Twenty20 Cup: 2010

THE LOWDOWN
Hampshire have the potential to be a serious force this year. In past seasons the Royals have perhaps been short of one quality batsman, but the signing of South African strokemaker Johann Myburgh should solve that, and with the addition of Friedel de Wet to their pace attack they look formidable across all departments. Giles White's side began sluggishly last season, losing their first eight matches, and they have undergone a rigorous pre-season schedule, including taking part in the Caribbean Twenty20, to avoid a repeat in 2011. Hampshire harbour strong hopes of winning their first County Championship title for 38 years and with a powerful batting line-up and well-balanced bowling attack, they look capable of challenging for silverware on all fronts.

FIRST TEAM MANAGER: GILES WHITE
White began his cricketing career for Devon and was on the staff at Somerset before he joined Hampshire in 1994. A graduate of Loughborough University and a top-order batsman, White scored 6,048 first-class runs for the county before retiring in 2002. He subsequently joined the coaching staff and was promoted to the role of first team manager after Paul Terry stood down in 2008.

With thanks to: Giles White; Kevan James, sports editor, BBC Radio Solent

	Mat	Inns	NO	Runs	HS	Ave	SR	100	50	Ct	St
MJ Lumb	5	7	0	381	158	54.42	51.34	1	1	4	-
MA Carberry	16	28	1	1385	164	51.29	52.38	6	4	9	-
JHK Adams	16	29	1	1351	196	48.25	43.58	3	8	16	-
ND McKenzie	15	25	5	942	141*	47.10	47.24	3	4	21	-
SM Ervine	17	27	4	976	237*	42.43	69.41	1	5	7	-
JM Vince	16	27	4	891	180	38.73	62.17	1	4	11	-
N Pothas	9	15	0	531	87	35.40	48.71	0	4	33	0
DT Christian	1	2	0	64	36	32.00	54.23	0	0	0	-
LA Dawson	8	13	1	348	86	29.00	45.91	0	3	4	-
DG Cork	13	17	3	380	55	27.14	62.19	0	2	8	-
CC Benham	7	13	0	278	45	21.38	38.99	0	0	11	-
HMRKB Herath	4	6	3	59	17*	19.66	54.62	0	0	1	-
CP Wood	3	4	0	68	35	17.00	61.26	0	0	0	-
PJ Hughes	3	6	0	85	38	14.16	48.02	0	0	0	-
JA Tomlinson	15	21	5	198	42	12.37	31.13	0	0	3	-
AM Bates	8	11	3	92	31	11.50	40.35	0	0	28	0
DA Griffiths	5	9	6	34	9*	11.33	20.48	0	0	1	-
DJ Balcombe	8	6	1	56	30	11.20	56.56	0	0	2	-
DR Briggs	13	14	3	116	28	10.54	38.28	0	0	2	-
Kabir Ali	4	8	0	64	18	8.00	37.20	0	0	2	-
SP Jones	1	2	2	0	0*	-	0.00	0	0	0	-

Batting & Fielding

	Mat	Overs	Mdn	Runs	Wkts	BBI	BBM	Ave	Econ	SR	5w	10
H Riazuddin	1	13.0	6	29	2	1/0	2/29	14.50	2.23	39.0	0	0
SP Jones	1	22.0	5	60	4	4/60	4/60	15.00	2.72	33.0	0	0
CP Wood	3	71.1	17	240	13	5/54	7/84	18.46	3.37	32.8	1	0
DG Cork	13	407.2	102	1042	45	5/50	7/66	23.15	2.55	54.3	2	0
Kabir Ali	4	137.2	27	488	19	5/33	6/104	25.68	3.55	43.3	2	0
MA Carberry	16	42.0	11	110	4	1/0	1/0	27.50	2.61	63.0	0	0
DJ Balcombe	8	246.1	52	812	27	3/69	5/117	30.07	3.29	54.7	0	0
DA Griffiths	5	152.0	18	646	19	5/85	7/160	34.00	4.25	48.0	1	0
JA Tomlinson	15	559.1	149	1624	46	7/85	7/85	35.30	2.90	72.9	2	0
DR Briggs	13	377.2	59	1294	34	4/93	5/116	38.05	3.42	66.5	0	0
HMRKB Herath	4	175.3	42	463	10	4/98	4/98	46.30	2.63	105.3	0	0
ND McKenzie	15	32.0	3	95	2	2/30	2/30	47.50	2.96	96.0	0	0
SM Ervine	17	362.5	77	1073	20	4/31	5/78	53.65	2.95	108.8	0	0
DT Christian	1	22.1	1	115	2	2/115	2/115	57.50	5.18	66.5	0	0
LA Dawson	8	33.0	5	107	1	1/61	1/61	107.00	3.24	198.0	0	0
JHK Adams	16	2.0	1	5	0	-	-	-	2.50	-	0	0
JM Vince	16	5.2	1	24	0	-	-	-	4.50	-	0	0

Bowling

HAMPSHIRE
ROYALS

Batting & Fielding

	Mat	Inns	NO	Runs	HS	Ave	SR	100	50	Ct	St
JHK Adams	11	11	1	496	131	49.60	95.56	1	4	3	-
ND McKenzie	11	11	3	319	62*	39.87	79.75	0	2	3	-
SM Ervine	10	10	0	359	96	35.90	113.96	0	2	2	-
MA Carberry	12	11	1	346	103	34.60	113.81	1	1	4	-
MJ Lumb	4	4	0	130	75	32.50	86.09	0	2	3	-
JM Vince	11	11	0	263	62	23.90	88.25	0	1	5	-
LA Dawson	10	9	2	162	47*	23.14	104.51	0	0	5	-
DG Cork	11	9	4	101	28	20.20	124.69	0	0	2	-
PJ Hughes	2	2	0	33	32	16.50	63.46	0	0	1	-
N Pothas	6	6	0	96	40	16.00	81.35	0	0	7	1
JA Tomlinson	5	2	1	16	14	16.00	80.00	0	0	0	-
H Riazuddin	5	4	1	40	23*	13.33	95.23	0	0	2	-
DR Briggs	7	3	2	13	10*	13.00	92.85	0	0	4	-
BAC Howell	2	2	0	17	12	8.50	48.57	0	0	0	-
HMRKB Herath	5	2	1	6	6*	6.00	85.71	0	0	3	-
AM Bates	6	3	1	3	2*	1.50	21.42	0	0	5	2
CP Wood	10	6	2	5	3	1.25	29.41	0	0	3	-
DT Christian	1	1	1	4	4*	-	40.00	0	0	1	-
Kabir Ali	1	1	1	1	1*	-	33.33	0	0	2	-

Bowling

	Mat	Overs	Mdns	Runs	Wkts	BBI	Ave	Econ	SR	5w
CP Wood	10	71.1	4	368	18	4/33	20.44	5.17	23.7	0
JA Tomlinson	5	33.4	1	195	9	3/33	21.66	5.79	22.4	0
BAC Howell	2	11.0	0	55	2	1/23	27.50	5.00	33.0	0
SM Ervine	10	68.2	1	419	14	4/39	29.92	6.13	29.2	0
HMRKB Herath	5	31.0	1	170	5	2/28	34.00	5.48	37.2	0
DG Cork	11	69.0	0	445	13	3/30	34.23	6.44	31.8	0
Kabir Ali	1	5.0	0	39	1	1/39	39.00	7.80	30.0	0
SP Jones	1	8.0	0	41	1	1/41	41.00	5.12	48.0	0
DT Christian	1	8.0	0	46	1	1/46	46.00	5.75	48.0	0
DA Griffiths	1	8.0	1	56	1	1/56	56.00	7.00	48.0	0
H Riazuddin	5	34.0	0	190	3	1/20	63.33	5.58	68.0	0
DR Briggs	7	54.0	0	262	4	1/26	65.50	4.85	81.0	0
LA Dawson	10	36.0	1	198	3	1/29	66.00	5.50	72.0	0
MA Carberry	12	8.0	0	69	1	1/24	69.00	8.62	48.0	0

HAMPSHIRE
ROYALS

	Mat	Inns	NO	Runs	HS	Ave	SR	100	50	Ct	St
ND McKenzie	17	17	6	440	73	40.00	123.94	0	5	7	-
JHK Adams	19	19	2	668	101*	39.29	132.27	2	2	6	-
SM Ervine	19	19	6	470	74*	36.15	146.41	0	3	4	-
JM Vince	14	14	1	353	77	27.15	144.08	0	2	10	-
N Pothas	15	11	4	165	59	23.57	120.43	0	1	8	1
MA Carberry	12	11	1	205	41	20.50	107.89	0	0	6	-
Abdul Razzaq	10	10	1	183	44	20.33	127.97	0	0	1	-
KP Pietersen	1	1	0	15	15	15.00	150.00	0	0	0	-
CC Benham	3	3	1	26	16*	13.00	76.47	0	0	1	-
CP Wood	19	6	2	41	18	10.25	105.12	0	0	7	-
DT Christian	12	8	4	33	10*	8.25	91.66	0	0	7	-
DG Cork	19	9	2	56	15	8.00	140.00	0	0	4	-
MJ Lumb	10	10	0	76	21	7.60	93.82	0	0	3	-
LA Dawson	9	5	0	29	19	5.80	90.62	0	0	3	-
DR Briggs	19	5	3	9	9	4.50	75.00	0	0	4	-
SP Jones	6	1	1	1	1*	-	50.00	0	0	0	-
AM Bates	4	-	-	-	-	-	-	-	-	3	0

	Mat	Overs	Mdns	Runs	Wkts	BBI	Ave	Econ	SR	5w
DR Briggs	19	67.0	0	445	31	3/5	14.35	6.64	12.9	0
AD Mascarenhas	1	3.0	0	21	1	1/21	21.00	7.00	18.0	0
SM Ervine	19	44.0	1	386	16	4/12	24.12	8.77	16.5	0
SP Jones	6	23.0	0	195	8	3/20	24.37	8.47	17.2	0
CP Wood	19	65.1	1	551	20	3/27	27.55	8.45	19.5	0
DG Cork	19	68.5	0	455	15	2/9	30.33	6.61	27.5	0
DT Christian	12	36.2	1	284	9	2/37	31.55	7.81	24.2	0
Abdul Razzaq	10	31.2	0	245	7	2/16	35.00	7.81	26.8	0
MA Carberry	12	1.0	0	3	0	-	-	3.00	-	0
LA Dawson	9	13.4	0	106	0	-	-	7.75	-	0
KP Pietersen	1	1.0	0	14	0	-	-	14.00	-	0
AM Bates	4	-	-	-	-	-	-	-	-	-

JIMMY ADAMS

HAMPSHIRE

NAME: James Henry Kenneth Adams
BORN: September 23, 1980, Winchester
HEIGHT: 6ft 1in
SQUAD Nº: 4
NICKNAME: Bison
OTHER TEAMS: Auckland
CAREER: First-class debut: 2002; List A debut: 2002; T20 debut: 2005; County Cap: 2006

AOC SAYS: A former England under 19 international, Adams is a lynchpin of the Royals' top-order, equally happy anchoring a four-day innings or blazing away against the white ball. An outstanding season in 2010 – which saw him score 2,441 runs across all competitions – earned him a stint with England Lions over the winter as well as a slot opening for Auckland in New Zealand's domestic T20 competition. A fine fielder who was initially pigeonholed as a Championship specialist until the introduction of an exaggerated trigger movement brought added fluency to his one-day game, Adams studied at Loughborough University prior to taking up cricket full-time and is reportedly a devoted fan of thrash metal.

LAST WORD: "Jimmy's a hugely popular figure at the club. He's mentally very strong and works hard at his game. He speaks well about the game and should be a key member of our side this season." *Giles White*

Batting & Fielding

	Mat	Inns	NO	Runs	HS	Ave	SR	100	50	Ct	St
First-class	110	196	16	6823	262*	37.90	-	11	38	96	0
List A	47	44	3	1554	131	37.90	83.05	1	12	19	0
Twenty20	59	51	8	1241	101*	28.86	124.34	2	4	14	0

Bowling

	Mat	Balls	Runs	Wkts	BBI	BBM	Ave	Econ	SR	5w	10
First-class	110	961	662	11	2/16	-	60.18	4.13	87.3	0	0
List A	47	79	105	1	1/34	1/34	105.00	7.97	79.0	0	0
Twenty20	59	36	60	0	-	-	-	10.00	-	0	0

NAME: Kabir Ali
BORN: November 24, 1980, Moseley
HEIGHT: 6ft
SQUAD Nº: 33
NICKNAME: Kabby, Taxi
OTHER TEAMS: England, Rajasthan,
Worcestershire
CAREER: Test debut: 2003; ODI debut: 2003;
First-class debut: 1999; List A debut: 2000;
T20 debut: 2004

HAMPSHIRE

AOC SAYS: One of the most dangerous seamers on the domestic circuit for several years, and a handy lower-order batsman to boot, Kabir can consider himself unlucky not to have played more cricket for his country. Having joined the club from Worcestershire in the winter, he started 2010 in fine form – claiming 19 wickets at 26 – before a serious knee injury curtailed his season. By all accounts his recovery has gone well but the club are keen to manage his workload in 2011, an understandable approach as a fit Kabir is a dangerous proposition for any county batting line-up. Capable of producing conventional and reverse-swing from a slingy, low-slung action, Kabir generates good pace, possesses a fine yorker and has an outstanding strike-rate in all forms of the game.

LAST WORD: "My guess is Hampshire will be happy to get half a season out of him once he's returned to full fitness. Early indications are he's come through a hard winter's training in excellent shape, so the signs are encouraging." *Kevan James*

Batting & Fielding

	Mat	Inns	NO	Runs	HS	Ave	SR	100	50	Ct	St
Tests	1	2	0	10	9	5.00	35.71	0	0	0	0
ODIs	14	9	3	93	39*	15.50	86.11	0	0	1	0
First-class	117	164	23	2383	84*	16.90	-	0	7	32	0
List A	157	98	26	1092	92	15.16	-	0	3	27	0
Twenty20	27	20	4	264	49	16.50	136.08	0	0	8	0

Bowling

	Mat	Balls	Runs	Wkts	BBI	BBM	Ave	Econ	SR	5w	10
Tests	1	216	136	5	3/80	5/136	27.20	3.77	43.2	0	0
ODIs	14	673	682	20	4/45	4/45	34.10	6.08	33.6	0	0
First-class	117	20052	12008	448	8/50	-	26.80	3.59	44.7	23	4
List A	157	6683	5752	227	5/36	5/36	25.33	5.16	29.4	2	0
Twenty20	27	555	738	33	4/44	4/44	22.36	7.97	16.8	0	0

DAVID BALCOMBE

RHB RFM

HAMPSHIRE

NAME: David John Balcombe
BORN: December 24, 1984, London
HEIGHT: 6ft 4in
SQUAD Nº: 84
NICKNAME: Balcs, Polar Bear
CAREER: First-class debut: 2005; List A debut: 2007; T20 debut: 2006

AOC SAYS: A tall, bustling seamer who hits the deck hard, Balcombe was handed a run in the Hampshire first team in 2010 following injuries to Kabir Ali and David Griffiths, and he responded by claiming 27 wickets at 30 in Championship cricket before a fractured back put paid to his summer. A graduate of Durham University, for whom he made his first-class debut against Durham back in 2005, Balcombe has undergone an intense rehabilitation process in the winter and should be fit for the early stages of the new season. A muscular figure who bowls a heavy ball, Balcombe complements the other, skiddier seamers in the Royals' squad and can also serve as a dangerous hitter down the order.

LAST WORD: "When he gets his rhythm going, David is one of those bowlers who gets good players out – he's got it in him to produce those magic deliveries. We've got high hopes for him, it's just a question of making sure he gets enough games." *Giles White*

Batting & Fielding

	Mat	Inns	NO	Runs	HS	Ave	SR	100	50	Ct	St
First-class	29	36	7	422	73	14.55	46.42	0	1	8	0
List A	9	3	0	4	2	1.33	28.57	0	0	3	0
Twenty20	1	1	0	3	3	3.00	60.00	0	0	0	0

Bowling

	Mat	Balls	Runs	Wkts	BBI	BBM	Ave	Econ	SR	5w	10
First-class	29	4558	2832	72	5/112	-	39.33	3.72	63.3	1	0
List A	9	384	378	10	2/39	2/39	37.80	5.90	38.4	0	0
Twenty20	1	12	15	0	-	-	-	7.50	-	0	0

MICHAEL BATES

RHB WK

NAME: Alexander Michael Bates
BORN: October 10, 1990, Portsmouth
HEIGHT: 5ft 9in
SQUAD Nº: 16
NICKNAME: Batesy
CAREER: First-class debut: 2010; List A
debut: 2010; T20 debut: 2010

HAMPSHIRE

AOC SAYS: Part of the England under 19 side that competed in the 2009/10 World Cup, Bates is a product of Hampshire's academy and took the gloves for much of last season after injury curtailed Nic Pothas' campaign. A fine gloveman who showed a liking for the big stage on 2010 FP t20 Finals Day – where his slick work behind the stumps played a big part in Hampshire's success – he has a reputation as a busy, well-organised batsman who sweeps especially well, although he struggled for runs at times in the Championship and will likely have to bide his time this season following Pothas' return to fitness. However, Bates remains highly-rated at The Rose Bowl and will doubtless receive further opportunities in the future.

LAST WORD: "His glovework is really good, he's agile and makes it look easy, which is the sign of a great keeper. Pothas is 37 and won't keep going forever; if Bates can up his batting just a little then he'll be an ideal candidate to take the gloves once he goes." *Kevan James*

	Mat	Inns	NO	Runs	HS	Ave	SR	100	50	Ct	St
First-class	8	11	3	92	31	11.50	40.35	0	0	28	0
List A	6	3	1	3	2*	1.50	21.42	0	0	5	2
Twenty20	10	2	1	15	10	15.00	100.00	0	0	6	1

Batting & Fielding

	Mat	Balls	Runs	Wkts	BBI	BBM	Ave	Econ	SR	5w	10
First-class	8	-	-	-	-	-	-	-	-	-	-
List A	6	-	-	-	-	-	-	-	-	-	-
Twenty20	10	-	-	-	-	-	-	-	-	-	-

Bowling

DANNY BRIGGS

RHB SLA MVP63

NAME: Danny Richard Briggs
BORN: April 30, 1991, Newport, Isle of Wight
HEIGHT: 6ft 3in
SQUAD Nº: 19
NICKNAME: Briggsy
CAREER: First-class debut: 2009; List A debut: 2009; T20 debut: 2010

AOC SAYS: Briggs shot into the limelight with a series of miserly spells during Hampshire's 2010 FP t20 campaign. Tall, accurate and blessed with a deceptive change of pace, his greatest attribute is an ice-cold temperament; he rarely seems to get flustered whatever the state of the game. Picked for the England Performance Programme that headed out to Australia this winter, Briggs topped the bowling averages and followed this up with several impressive performances for England Lions out in the West Indies. The possibility of him bowling in tandem with Imran Tahir (or Shahid Afridi in Twenty20 cricket) should have Hampshire fans very excited this season.

LAST WORD: "He's a very composed character. It's interesting talking to him as he bowls in the nets; he has a very wise head on his shoulders. He's been working on spinning the ball that bit harder, but his biggest test will be how he responds when things don't go so well for him." *Giles White*

Batting & Fielding

	Mat	Inns	NO	Runs	HS	Ave	SR	100	50	Ct	St
First-class	22	23	5	219	38*	12.16	-	0	0	7	0
List A	11	4	2	17	10*	8.50	94.44	0	0	5	0
Twenty20	25	5	3	9	9	4.50	75.00	0	0	4	0

Bowling

	Mat	Balls	Runs	Wkts	BBI	BBM	Ave	Econ	SR	5w	10
First-class	22	4136	2212	75	6/45	9/96	29.49	3.20	55.1	2	0
List A	11	522	418	6	2/36	2/36	69.66	4.80	87.0	0	0
Twenty20	25	528	570	36	3/5	3/5	15.83	6.47	14.6	0	0

NAME: Michael Alexander Carberry
BORN: 29 September 1980, Croydon
HEIGHT: 5ft 11in
SQUAD Nº: 15
NICKNAME: Carbs
OTHER TEAMS: England, Kent, Surrey
CAREER: Test debut: 2010; First-class debut: 2001; List A debut: 1999; T20 debut: 2003; County cap: 2006 (Hampshire)

HAMPSHIRE

AOC SAYS: A cultured left-hander and a superlative fielder, Carberry has become an integral part of the Hampshire set-up since joining from Kent in 2006. An outstanding batsman at youth level, Carberry has established a successful opening partnership with Jimmy Adams and his tally of 1,251 first-class runs in 2009 earned him a Test debut against Bangladesh that winter. He followed this up by amassing 1,385 runs in 2010 but was prevented from taking a spot on the England Performance Programme in Australia when he developed a blood clot in his lungs – the condition has been successfully treated but means he is unable to take long haul flights. England's loss may well be Hampshire's gain though; Carberry, as well as being a keen DJ in his spare time, is a formidable player at county level.

LAST WORD: "He's a strong character who absolutely loves batting – he would bat all day if he could and regularly wears out my arm asking for throwdowns! His partnership with Jimmy Adams is one of our key strengths." *Giles White*

Batting & Fielding

	Mat	Inns	NO	Runs	HS	Ave	SR	100	50	Ct	St
Tests	1	2	0	64	34	32.00	45.71	0	0	1	0
First-class	112	198	18	7832	204	43.51	52.10	23	36	50	0
List A	118	111	11	2901	121*	29.01	-	2	21	46	0
Twenty20	66	61	9	1441	90	27.71	114.54	0	10	30	0

Bowling

	Mat	Balls	Runs	Wkts	BBI	BBM	Ave	Econ	SR	5w	10
Tests	1	-	-	-	-	-	-	-	-	-	-
First-class	112	1201	873	13	2/85		67.15	4.36	92.3	0	0
List A	118	174	170	4	2/11	2/11	42.50	5.86	43.5	0	0
Twenty20	66	18	19	1	1/16	1/16	19.00	6.33	18.0	0	0

DOMINIC CORK

HAMPSHIRE

NAME: Dominic Gerald Cork
BORN: August 7, 1971, Newcastle-under-Lyme
HEIGHT: 6ft 2in
SQUAD Nº: 12
NICKNAME: Corky
OTHER TEAMS: England, Derbyshire, Lancashire
CAREER: Test debut: 1995; ODI debut: 1992; First-class debut: 1990; List A debut: 1991; T20 debut: 2003; County cap: 1993 (Derbyshire), 2004 (Lancashire), 2009 (Hampshire)

AOC SAYS: Newly installed as Hampshire's official captain for the 2011 season, having filled the role for much of 2010 after injury ended Dimitri Mascarenhas' season prematurely, Cork brings a wealth of experience and enthusiasm to the role. A natural swing bowler and uninhibited strokemaker, Cork began his career at Derbyshire and claimed 57 first-class wickets in his first full season, earning him a call-up to the England A tour to the West Indies that winter, and made his bow for the national side in an ODI against Pakistan at Old Trafford the following summer. Several seasons of consistent performances at county and ODI level followed before an electric start to the 1995 season earned him a call-up for the second Test against West Indies at Lord's, an opportunity that Cork seized with both hands when he recorded figures of 7-43 – the best figures for an Englishman on Test debut – in the second innings. Two games later, he became the first Englishman in 38 years to claim a Test hat-trick and went on to enjoy a successful tour of South Africa. However, a succession of injuries and an unhappy tenure as captain of Derbyshire resulted in a gradual loss of form, and, although there were highlights along the way, such as his matchwinning innings against West Indies at Lord's in 2000, he fell out of favour with the England selectors in 2002. A subsequent move to Lancashire in 2003 reinvigorated his career, and he played a crucial role in getting the club promoted to Division One in 2005 and put in a Herculean effort on the last day of 2007 season to bring Lancashire agonisingly close to securing their first Championship title since 1950. He was surprisingly let go at the end of the 2008 season but was quickly snapped up by Hampshire and his all-action approach has brought him 72 first-class wickets at 25.12 and 670 runs at 24.81 for the club and helped him play a starring role in Hampshire's dramatic FP t20 victory last season, where he produced figures of 2-24 from his four overs and forced Somerset's dangerman Kieron Pollard to retire hurt.

INSIDE TRACK: "We signed Dominic first and foremost because we felt he would turn in some good performances for us, but he's also brought that enthusiasm and confidence he has to the squad and it has helped the group. He leads from the front and felt like the natural successor to Dimi." *Giles White*

Batting & Fielding

	Mat	Inns	NO	Runs	HS	Ave	SR	100	50	Ct	St
Tests	37	56	8	864	59	18.00	41.30	0	3	18	0
ODIs	32	21	3	180	31*	10.00	66.42	0	0	6	0
First-class	311	450	60	9797	200*	25.12	-	8	53	231	0
List A	307	234	39	4157	93	21.31	-	0	19	112	0
Twenty20	65	44	12	401	28	12.53	120.05	0	0	12	0

Bowling

	Mat	Balls	Runs	Wkts	BBI	BBM	Ave	Econ	SR	5w	10
Tests	37	7678	3906	131	7/43	9/162	29.81	3.05	58.6	5	0
ODIs	32	1772	1368	41	3/27	3/27	33.36	4.63	43.2	0	0
First-class	311	52643	25637	967	9/43		26.51	2.92	54.4	35	5
List A	307	14465	10406	380	6/21	6/21	27.38	4.31	38.0	4	0
Twenty20	65	1187	1390	56	4/16	4/16	24.82	7.02	21.1	0	0

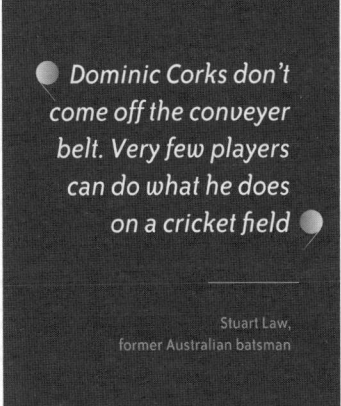

Dominic Corks don't come off the conveyer belt. Very few players can do what he does on a cricket field

Stuart Law,
former Australian batsman

HAMPSHIRE

NAME: Liam Andrew Dawson
BORN: March 1, 1990, Swindon
HEIGHT: 5ft 8in
SQUAD Nº: 8
NICKNAME: Daws, Lemmy
CAREER: First-class debut: 2007; List A
debut: 2007; T20 debut: 2008

AOC SAYS: A talented allrounder who initially caught the eye for his restrictive left-arm spin, Dawson was highlighted by former Hampshire skipper Shane Warne as a player with the potential to bat in the top-order, and in recent seasons it is his batting that has emerged as his strongest suit, partially because the emergence of Danny Briggs and the presence of Imran Tahir have limited his bowling opportunities. A former England under 19 captain who notched his maiden first-class hundred on the last day of the 2008 season – an innings that scuppered Notts' Championship ambitions – Dawson recently signed a two-year deal that will keep him at the club until 2012.

LAST WORD: "Liam batted well for us towards the end of last season. With his bowling it's a question of getting him on at the right time; it's often the case with youngsters that they don't get enough of a chance to use their second string, but we've got a plan for him and we're confident he'll develop nicely this year." *Giles White*

Batting & Fielding

	Mat	Inns	NO	Runs	HS	Ave	SR	100	50	Ct	St
First-class	29	44	6	1112	100*	29.26	48.53	1	7	17	0
List A	38	32	7	632	69*	25.28	93.76	0	2	21	0
Twenty20	31	21	5	144	23	9.00	95.36	0	0	17	0

Bowling

	Mat	Balls	Runs	Wkts	BBI	BBM	Ave	Econ	SR	5w	10
First-class	29	1123	741	17	2/3	3/109	43.58	3.95	66.0	0	0
List A	38	1041	928	27	4/45	4/45	34.37	5.34	38.5	0	0
Twenty20	31	262	355	8	3/25	3/25	44.37	8.12	32.7	0	0

NAME: Friedel de Wet
BORN: June 26, 1980, Durban
HEIGHT: 6ft 1in
SQUAD №: 30
OTHER TEAMS: South Africa, Lions, North West, Northerns
CAREER: Test debut: 2009; First-class debut: 2002; List A debut: 2001; T20 debut: 2005

HAMPSHIRE

AOC SAYS: The 30-year-old had been a consistent performer on the South African domestic circuit for several years before he was called up to face England in the 2009 Test at Centurion, and it almost proved a masterstroke as a pumped-up de Wet nearly bowled South Africa to a dramatic victory. A stress fracture picked up during the following match put him out of the series and he subsequently fell out of contention as South Africa looked towards youth, but he remained a high-class operator for the Highveld Lions. Snapped up by the Royals on a one-year Kolpak deal, de Wet will bring pace, aggression and an unerring ability to hit the seam to Hampshire's attack.

LAST WORD: "I think he's going to be a really good signing for them, he brings a bit of extra thrust to the attack and looks like a genuine wicket-taker. His signing should mean Hampshire have real depth in their seam attack." *Kevan James*

Batting & Fielding

	Mat	Inns	NO	Runs	HS	Ave	SR	100	50	Ct	St
Tests	2	2	0	20	20	10.00	28.16	0	0	1	0
First-class	52	71	15	931	56	16.62	42.35	0	1	22	0
List A	65	28	16	287	56*	23.91	86.70	0	1	12	0
Twenty20	16	7	4	43	17	14.33	82.69	0	0	5	0

Bowling

	Mat	Balls	Runs	Wkts	BBI	BBM	Ave	Econ	SR	5w	10
Tests	2	426	186	6	4/55	5/127	31.00	2.61	71.0	0	0
First-class	52	10401	4904	206	7/61		23.80	2.82	50.4	10	2
List A	65	2853	2291	73	5/59	5/59	31.38	4.81	39.0	1	0
Twenty20	16	322	439	17	2/18	2/18	25.82	8.18	18.9	0	0

SEAN ERVINE

LHB RM MVP7

HAMPSHIRE

NAME: Sean Michael Ervine
BORN: December 6, 1982, Harare
HEIGHT: 6ft 2in
SQUAD Nº: 7
NICKNAME: Siuc, Slug
MAJOR TEAMS: Zimbabwe, Midlands, Southern Rocks, Western Australia
CAREER: Test debut: 2003; ODI debut: 2001; First-class debut: 2001; List A: 2001; T20 debut: 2005; County cap: 2005

AOC SAYS: Hampshire received a welcome boost this winter when Ervine elected to pull out of the Zimbabwe World Cup squad, a party that contained his younger brother Craig, in order to be able to continue his county career as a Kolpak player. After a promising start to his international career, Ervine was one of several players who turned his back on the Zimbabwe regime and – after a brief stint in Australia – has become a key part of the Royals' line-up thanks to his aggressive strokeplay, tidy seamers and excellent fielding. Last season was arguably his best yet as he amassed 976 runs, including a majestic 237* against Somerset, and claimed 20 wickets in the Championship.

LAST WORD: "He's a very popular figure at the club; just an honest, confident guy who goes about his business. He's a real asset to the club; he makes balancing the side much easier. He's always right up there in the PCA's MVP rankings." *Giles White*

Batting & Fielding

	Mat	Inns	NO	Runs	HS	Ave	SR	100	50	Ct	St
Tests	5	8	0	261	86	32.62	55.41	0	3	7	0
ODIs	42	34	7	698	100	25.85	85.53	1	2	5	0
First-class	117	185	19	5863	237*	35.31	-	11	30	96	0
List A	169	151	24	4035	167*	31.77	-	6	17	46	0
Twenty20	76	72	15	1374	74*	24.10	135.50	0	6	28	0

Bowling

	Mat	Balls	Runs	Wkts	BBI	BBM	Ave	Econ	SR	5w	10
Tests	5	570	388	9	4/146	4/146	43.11	4.08	63.3	0	0
ODIs	42	1649	1561	41	3/29	3/29	38.07	5.67	40.2	0	0
First-class	117	13145	7838	181	6/82	-	43.30	3.57	72.6	5	0
List A	169	5995	5577	166	5/50	5/50	33.59	5.58	36.1	2	0
Twenty20	76	812	1193	48	4/12	4/12	24.85	8.81	16.9	0	0

NAME: David Andrew Griffiths
BORN: September 10, 1985, Newport, Isle of Wight
HEIGHT: 6ft 1in
SQUAD Nº: 18
NICKNAME: Griff
CAREER: First-class debut: 2006; List A debut: 2008; T20 debut: 2007

HAMPSHIRE

AOC SAYS: Generating genuine pace from an explosive, slingy action, Griffiths caught the eye of the Sky punditry team on the back of a couple of hostile spells in televised 40-over matches during 2009. He started the 2010 season in fine form and claimed 19 Championship wickets before picking up an injury that meant he struggled to reach full fitness for the rest of the summer. With a natural talent for getting the ball to reverse, Griffiths often clocks in at around the 90mph mark and should be pushing hard for first-team opportunities this season.

LAST WORD: "Griff bowls a great wicket-to-wicket line and is seriously quick when he's going well. We need to get him fit because he's a great asset. He's a quiet, relaxed sort of character off the pitch, but he can be fiery with the ball in hand, although he tends to let the ball do the talking." *Giles White*

Batting & Fielding

	Mat	Inns	NO	Runs	HS	Ave	SR	100	50	Ct	St
First-class	22	32	14	141	31*	7.83	24.82	0	0	2	0
List A	5	1	1	3	3*	-	21.42	0	0	2	0
Twenty20	3	1	1	4	4*	-	36.36	0	0	0	0

Bowling

	Mat	Balls	Runs	Wkts	BBI	BBM	Ave	Econ	SR	5w	10
First-class	22	3503	2303	65	5/85	7/160	35.43	3.94	53.8	1	0
List A	5	222	227	6	4/29	4/29	37.83	6.13	37.0	0	0
Twenty20	3	42	55	3	3/13	3/13	18.33	7.85	14.0	0	0

BENNY HOWELL RHB RM

NAME: Benny Alexander Cameron Howell
BORN: October 5, 1988, Bordeaux
HEIGHT: 6ft 2in
SQUAD Nº: 13
CAREER: List A debut: 2010; T20 debut: 2011

HAMPSHIRE

AOC SAYS: A dynamic batsman who bowls useful medium-pace, Howells made his first-team debut in the CB40 last season before impressing many observers with his performances during the Caribbean T20 competition this winter, weighing in with useful cameos down the order, picking up the odd wicket and enacting several brilliant run-outs. Lightning fast across the outfield and widely regarded as one of the best fielders at the club, Howell will most likely come into consideration for a slot in the shorter forms of the game.

LAST WORD: "He strikes the ball very well, he's probably one of the better strikers of a cricket ball at the club, and he's worked hard on his bowling. He could be useful option on certain types of wicket. With the squad as it is, he's probably looking at one-day cricket as his way of forcing himself into the first team." *Giles White*

Batting & Fielding

	Mat	Inns	NO	Runs	HS	Ave	SR	100	50	Ct	St
List A	2	2	0	17	12	8.50	48.57	0	0	0	0
Twenty20	6	4	4	80	29*	-	131.14	0	0	2	0

Bowling

	Mat	Balls	Runs	Wkts	BBI	BBM	Ave	Econ	SR	5w	10
List A	2	66	55	2	1/23	1/23	27.50	5.00	33.0	0	0
Twenty20	6	41	56	3	2/14	2/14	18.66	8.19	13.6	0	0

OVERSEAS PLAYER

NAME: Mohammad Imran Tahir
BORN: March 27, 1979, Lahore, Punjab
SQUAD №: 42
OTHER TEAMS: Dolphins, Easterns, Lahore, Middlesex, Redco Pakistan Ltd, Sui Gas Corporation of Pakistan, Titans, Warwickshire, Water and Power Development Authority, Yorkshire
CAREER: ODI debut: 2011; First-class debut: 1996; List A debut: 1998; T20 debut: 2006; County cap: 2009 (Hampshire)

HAMPSHIRE

AOC SAYS: An attacking legspinner who possesses all the variations, in particular a big-spinning and well-disguised googly, Tahir is a recently naturalised South African and tipped by many pundits as the bowler who will turn the Proteas into the dominant force in all forms of the game. Having begun his career with Lahore City, Tahir represented an array of teams in his native Pakistan before venturing to England to play three games for Middlesex under the captaincy of Andrew Strauss in 2003. He continued to be a force in Pakistan cricket and earned a call-up to the Pakistan A side to face Sri Lanka in 2005, but the presence of Danish Kaneria kept him from the national side and he eventually resolved to try his luck in South Africa, a country he first travelled to in 1998 as a member of Pakistan's under 19 side and the home of his wife. He enjoyed considerable success with the Titans and also continued to try his luck in England, eventually signing for Hampshire as their overseas player for the 2008 season, claiming 44 wickets at 16.68 and following this up with 52 wickets in the 2009 season. His good form continued in South Africa as well, despite a switch to the Dolphins after the Titans curiously dropped him despite being one of the country's leading bowlers, and he began to be seriously talked about as a potential South African international. He was selected in the squad to face England in January 2010 but had to be withdrawn when it emerged he was not yet fully eligible, a mistake that caused considerable embarrassment to CSA, but he finally qualified in January 2011 and went on to be one of South Africa's outstanding performers during the recent World Cup. A lively, enthusiastic character who spent last summer effectively on loan at Warwickshire, for whom he claimed 98 wickets in all competitions and played a major part in the club's CB40 success, Tahir's aggressive approach and lusty late-order hitting has made him a firm favourite with The Rose Bowl crowd.

INSIDE TRACK: "He's one of very few spinners around who you can just throw the ball to and know he'll get you wickets on most pitches. It's rare to come across a wristspinner with his accuracy, and I think how Hampshire use him and Danny Briggs, who has been taking first-class wickets all winter for the Lions, is the key talking point of the squad. It could well be to Hampshire's advantage to produce turning pitches at The Rose Bowl because there won't be many sides with a better spin attack out there." *Kevan James*

IMRAN TAHIR

Batting & Fielding

	Mat	Inns	NO	Runs	HS	Ave	SR	100	50	Ct	St
ODIs	5	2	2	1	1*	-	50.00	0	0	2	0
First-class	128	161	34	1845	77*	14.52	-	0	3	60	0
List A	101	33	11	305	41*	13.86	-	0	0	22	0
Twenty20	37	11	4	47	13	6.71	127.02	0	0	9	0

Bowling

	Mat	Balls	Runs	Wkts	BBI	BBM	Ave	Econ	SR	5w	10
ODIs	5	237	150	14	4/38	4/38	10.71	3.79	16.9	0	0
First-class	128	25265	13642	547	8/76	-	24.93	3.23	46.1	41	9
List A	101	4435	3334	154	5/27	5/27	21.64	4.51	28.7	3	0
Twenty20	37	822	868	40	3/13	3/13	21.70	6.33	20.5	0	0

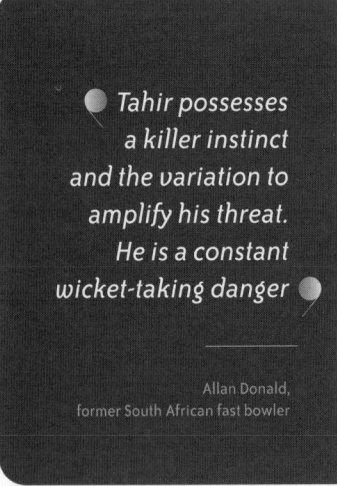

Tahir possesses a killer instinct and the variation to amplify his threat. He is a constant wicket-taking danger

Allan Donald,
former South African fast bowler

NAME: Simon Philip Jones
BORN: December 25, 1978, Swansea
HEIGHT: 6ft 3in
SQUAD Nº: 10
NICKNAME: Horse
OTHER TEAMS: England, Glamorgan,
Worcestershire
CAREER: Test debut: 2002; ODI debut:
2004; First-class debut: 1998; List A debut:
1999; T20 debut: 2008; County cap: 2002
(Glamorgan)

HAMPSHIRE

AOC SAYS: It's eminently possible that if injury hadn't played such a huge part in his career, Jones would be talked about as one of England's finest modern bowlers. Having signed him from financially stricken Worcestershire in 2009, Hampshire elected not to risk him in any form of cricket that season but gave him a couple of run-outs during the back end of 2010. The signs are that he will play a larger role this year, especially after he turned in a series of brilliant performances during the Caribbean T20, claiming 12 wickets at an average of 10.25. If he gets back to anywhere near his 2005 pomp, when he combined brilliant reverse-swing with genuine pace, Hampshire will be delighted.

LAST WORD: "I think they'll look to get half a season in the Championship out of Simon this year. Some of the spells he bowled out in the Caribbean were incredible and he looks as fit as anyone, but they'll play it as sensibly as they can." *Kevan James*

Batting & Fielding

	Mat	Inns	NO	Runs	HS	Ave	SR	100	50	Ct	St
Tests	18	18	5	205	44	15.76	51.89	0	0	4	0
ODIs	8	1	0	1	1	1.00	50.00	0	0	0	0
First-class	89	110	37	899	46	12.31	-	0	0	17	0
List A	35	13	8	76	26	15.20	-	0	0	2	0
Twenty20	16	5	3	26	11*	13.00	144.44	0	0	0	0

Bowling

	Mat	Balls	Runs	Wkts	BBI	BBM	Ave	Econ	SR	5w	10
Tests	18	2821	1666	59	6/53	7/110	28.23	3.54	47.8	3	0
ODIs	8	348	275	7	2/43	2/43	39.28	4.74	49.7	0	0
First-class	89	13131	8007	264	6/45	-	30.32	3.65	49.7	15	1
List A	35	1502	1280	32	5/32	5/32	40.00	5.11	46.9	1	0
Twenty20	16	362	468	22	4/10	4/10	21.27	7.75	16.4	0	0

MICHAEL LUMB

HAMPSHIRE

NAME: Michael John Lumb
BORN: February 12, 1980, Johannesburg
HEIGHT: 6ft
SQUAD Nº: 6
NICKNAME: Joe
OTHER TEAMS: England, Deccan Chargers, Queensland, Rajasthan Royals, Yorkshire
CAREER: T20I debut: 2010; First-class debut: 2000; List A debut: 2001; T20 debut: 2003; County cap: 2003 (Yorkshire), 2008 (Hampshire)

AOC SAYS: One of relatively few English players to have picked up an IPL contract this year – an $85,000 deal with the Deccan Chargers – Lumb will consequently miss the start of the domestic season. An instrumental figure in England's 2010 ICC World Twenty20 success, Lumb, the son of former Yorkshire opener Richard, struggled to translate that success into runs during last season's FP t20, although he finished the season strongly in the Championship and enjoyed a successful stint with Queensland in Australia's domestic T20 competition over the winter. Expect him to be charged with getting the innings off to a flier in the shorter forms of the game via an array of muscular drives, pulls and slog sweeps.

LAST WORD: "Michael's a fine striker of a cricket ball and that skill comes to the fore in one-day cricket. We'll look forward to welcoming him back after his time with the IPL, he's one of those guys who can score quickly." *Giles White*

Batting & Fielding

	Mat	Inns	NO	Runs	HS	Ave	SR	100	50	Ct	St
T20Is	7	7	0	137	33	19.57	141.23	0	0	3	0
First-class	134	224	15	7266	219	34.76	-	12	45	92	0
List A	164	158	11	4752	110	32.32	84.18	3	37	56	0
Twenty20	92	92	5	1962	124*	22.55	143.00	1	11	31	0

Bowling

	Mat	Balls	Runs	Wkts	BBI	BBM	Ave	Econ	SR	5w	10
T20Is	7	-	-	-	-	-	-	-	-	-	-
First-class	134	318	242	6	2/10	-	40.33	4.56	53.0	0	0
List A	164	12	28	0	-	-	-	14.00	-	0	0
Twenty20	92	36	65	3	3/32	3/32	21.66	10.83	12.0	0	0

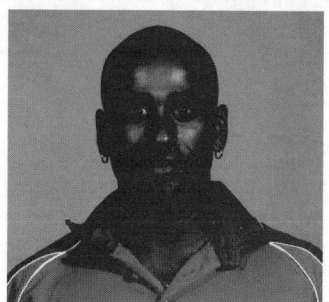

NAME: Adrian Dimitri Mascarenhas
BORN: October 30, 1977, Chiswick
HEIGHT: 6ft 1in
SQUAD Nº: 17
NICKNAME: Dimi
OTHER TEAMS: England, Otago, Rajasthan Royals
CAREER: ODI debut: 2007; T20I debut: 2007; First-class debut: 1996; List A debut: 1996; T20 debut: 2003; County cap: 1998

HAMPSHIRE

AOC SAYS: A hard-hitting allrounder who bowls miserly medium-pace, Mascarenhas picked up a serious Achilles injury while playing for the Rajasthan Royals in last season's IPL which put paid to his season and looks likely to keep him out of action for the early part of the summer. As a result, Mascarenhas has handed over the captaincy reins to Dominic Cork and will concentrate on his rehabilitation, with the start of the FP t20 foremost in his thoughts as it is in this form of the game that Mascarenhas' ability to clear the ropes and vary his pace with the ball most comes to the fore.

LAST WORD: "Dimi's a big character at the club. He's getting better, but slowly so we're not trying to rush him. We'd love him for the Twenty20 because he has such an impact on the game. He brings great balance and experience to the side." Giles White

Batting & Fielding

	Mat	Inns	NO	Runs	HS	Ave	SR	100	50	Ct	St
ODIs	20	13	2	245	52	22.27	95.33	0	1	4	0
T20Is	14	13	5	123	31	15.37	123.00	0	0	7	0
First-class	181	271	30	6185	131	25.66	-	8	22	72	0
List A	244	205	43	4107	79	25.35	-	0	27	62	0
Twenty20	66	63	19	960	57*	21.81	124.67	0	3	20	0

Bowling

	Mat	Balls	Runs	Wkts	BBI	BBM	Ave	Econ	SR	5w	10
ODIs	20	822	634	13	3/23	3/23	48.76	4.62	63.2	0	0
T20Is	14	252	309	12	3/18	3/18	25.75	7.35	21.0	0	0
First-class	181	26181	11818	418	6/25	-	28.27	2.70	62.6	16	0
List A	244	10389	7376	281	5/27	5/27	26.24	4.25	36.9	1	0
Twenty20	66	1327	1587	81	5/14	5/14	19.59	7.17	16.3	1	0

NEIL McKENZIE

RHB RM MVP65

HAMPSHIRE

NAME: Neil Douglas McKenzie
BORN: November 24, 1975, Johannesburg
HEIGHT: 6ft
SQUAD №: 27
OTHER TEAMS: South Africa, Durham,
Gauteng, Lions, Northerns, Transvaal
CAREER: Test debut: 2000; ODI debut:
2000; T20I debut: 2006; First-class: 1995;
List A debut: 1995; T20 debut: 2004

AOC SAYS: McKenzie signed for Hampshire on a Kolpak deal for the 2010 season and went on to amass 1,878 runs in all competitions, earning himself the Man of the Match award for his composed 44* in the FP t20 final in the process. Regarded as a dasher in his early career, McKenzie broke into the South African side as an opener but was shunted down into the middle-order before losing his spot in 2004. He battled back to earn a recall as an opener in 2008, making several obdurate centuries in the process, before South Africa turned their attentions to younger prospects. Renowned as one of the more superstitious cricketers currently playing, McKenzie is a compact, methodical presence at the crease as well as a brilliant slip fielder.

LAST WORD: "He's been a great figure to have in the dressing room, even if he lights the place up sometimes when he hasn't done so well! He's got a great cricket brain and gets everyone going. I think his superstitions have calmed down a bit as well!" *Giles White*

Batting & Fielding

	Mat	Inns	NO	Runs	HS	Ave	SR	100	50	Ct	St
Tests	58	94	7	3253	226	37.39	42.00	5	16	54	0
ODIs	64	55	10	1688	131*	37.51	69.40	2	10	21	0
T20Is	2	1	1	7	7*	-	87.50	0	0	0	0
First-class	216	364	43	14334	226	44.65	-	38	70	194	0
List A	237	215	31	6600	131*	35.86	-	8	46	71	0
Twenty20	60	58	16	1400	85*	33.33	122.27	0	10	23	0

Bowling

	Mat	Balls	Runs	Wkts	BBI	BBM	Ave	Econ	SR	5w	10
Tests	58	90	68	0	-	-	-	4.53	-	0	0
ODIs	64	46	27	0	-	-	-	3.52	-	0	0
T20Is	2	-	-	-	-	-	-	-	-	-	-
First-class	216	900	478	10	2/13		47.80	3.18	90.0	0	0
List A	237	255	248	4	2/19	2/19	62.00	5.83	63.7	0	0
Twenty20	60	24	34	1	1/4	1/4	34.00	8.50	24.0	0	0

NAME: Johannes Gerhardus Myburgh
BORN: October 22, 1980, Pretoria
HEIGHT: 6ft
SQUAD Nº: 98
NICKNAME: Mybs
OTHER TEAMS: Auckland, Canterbury, Northerns, Titans
CAREER: First-class debut: 1997; List A debut: 2000; T20 debut: 2005

AOC SAYS: Myburgh was a schoolboy prodigy in South Africa, breaking Graeme Pollock's record for being the youngest scorer of a double century in South African first-class cricket when he smashed 203 as a 17-year-old for Northerns B against Easterns in 1998. He subsequently quit South Africa to play domestic cricket in New Zealand with considerable success before relocating to The Rose Bowl for the 2011 season. Arguably Hampshire's outstanding player in this winter's Caribbean T20, scoring 223 runs at 44.60 and contributing several overs of thrifty offspin, Myburgh's a powerful all-round strokemaker who many are tipping to have a big season in 2011.

LAST WORD: "I think he'll be a real force this year. He played shots all round the ground during the Caribbean competition and gets through his overs before the opposition know what's going on. He seems a pretty quiet, considered kind of guy too." *Kevan James*

Batting & Fielding

	Mat	Inns	NO	Runs	HS	Ave	SR	100	50	Ct	St
First-class	73	132	18	5180	203	45.43	-	13	30	50	0
List A	90	85	9	2239	112	29.46	-	1	13	19	0
Twenty20	36	33	6	798	88	29.55	115.65	0	4	10	0

Bowling

	Mat	Balls	Runs	Wkts	BBI	BBM	Ave	Econ	SR	5w	10
First-class	73	2610	1326	30	4/56	-	44.20	3.04	87.0	0	0
List A	90	1612	1354	23	2/22	2/22	58.86	5.03	70.0	0	0
Twenty20	36	319	402	10	3/16	3/16	40.20	7.56	31.9	0	0

NIC POTHAS

RHB WK

NAME: Nic Pothas
BORN: November 18, 1973, Johannesburg
HEIGHT: 6ft 1in
SQUAD Nº: 9
NICKNAME: The Greek, Skeg
OTHER TEAMS: South Africa, Delhi Giants, Gauteng, Transvaal
CAREER: ODI debut: 2000; First-class debut: 1993; List A debut: 1993; T20 debut: 2003; County cap: 2003

AOC SAYS: Pothas has been a remarkable servant to Hampshire since joining the club in 2002, and his longevity has been rewarded as the club have named him as their beneficiary this year. Qualified as a Kolpak player thanks to his Greek heritage, the 37-year-old keeper missed most of last season after developing a cartilage defect in his right knee but he should be fit to play a full role in 2011. An outstanding batsman who averages 45.86 in first-class cricket for the county, Pothas' vast experience, safe hands behind the stumps and relish for the big occasion makes him a key element in the Royals' plans.

LAST WORD: "A guy who bats as well as he does and keeps wicket is worth his weight in gold to any cricket team. The signs are good that he'll be fully fit for the season and we're looking forward to having him back." *Giles White*

Batting & Fielding

	Mat	Inns	NO	Runs	HS	Ave	SR	100	50	Ct	St
ODIs	3	1	0	24	24	24.00	58.53	0	0	4	1
First-class	210	325	59	11135	165	41.86	-	24	58	594	45
List A	235	198	70	4552	114*	35.56	-	3	24	211	53
Twenty20	68	50	20	653	59	21.76	107.93	0	3	26	11

Bowling

	Mat	Balls	Runs	Wkts	BBI	BBM	Ave	Econ	SR	5w	10
ODIs	3	-	-	-	-	-	-	-	-	-	-
First-class	210	120	63	1	1/16	1/16	63.00	3.15	120.0	0	0
List A	235	-	-	-	-	-	-	-	-	-	-
Twenty20	68	-	-	-	-	-	-	-	-	-	-

HAMZA RIAZUDDIN RHB RMF

NAME: Hamza Riazuddin
BORN: December 19, 1989, Hendon,
SQUAD Nº: 38
CAREER: First-class debut: 2008; List A
debut: 2008; T20 debut: 2008

AOC SAYS: Yet another Hampshire youngster who has won England honours at under 19 level, Riazuddin is a bustling seamer who made his First XI debut in the run-up to his A-levels and claimed Durham's Ian Blackwell as his maiden Championship wicket. Another player who performed well out in the Caribbean this winter, claiming 12 wickets at an average of 10.08 from six matches, he bowls with an energetic action, possesses a deceptive slower ball and is a good enough batsman to have notched hundreds at second XI level.

LAST WORD: "He's a nice all-round package, he showed in the West Indies what a good one-day bowler he is, he fields well and his batting is improving. He's still a work in progress and is probably at the moment more of an asset in the shorter formats, but he's progressing well." *Giles White*

Batting & Fielding

	Mat	Inns	NO	Runs	HS	Ave	SR	100	50	Ct	St
First-class	3	2	0	7	4	3.50	22.58	0	0	0	0
List A	17	6	3	42	23*	14.00	95.45	0	0	5	0
Twenty20	17	6	3	24	13*	8.00	88.88	0	0	2	0

Bowling

	Mat	Balls	Runs	Wkts	BBI	BBM	Ave	Econ	SR	5w	10
First-class	3	384	200	5	1/0	2/29	40.00	3.12	76.8	0	0
List A	17	738	592	11	2/47	2/47	53.81	4.81	67.0	0	0
Twenty20	17	348	417	21	4/15	4/15	19.85	7.18	16.5	0	0

SHAHID AFRIDI

HAMPSHIRE

OVERSEAS PLAYER

NAME: Sahibzada Mohammad Shahid Khan Afridi
BORN: March 1, 1980, Khyber Agency
SQUAD Nº: TBC
NICKNAME: Boom Boom
OTHER TEAMS: Pakistan, Deccan Chargers, Griqualand West, Habib Bank Limited, Karachi, Leicestershire, South Australia
CAREER: Test debut: 1998; ODI debut: 1996; T20I debut: 2006; First-class debut: 1995; List A debut: 1995; T20 debut: 2004

AOC SAYS: One of the most recognisable and charismatic players on the planet, Afridi, if available, provides Hampshire's T20 side with considerable firepower. Ever since he first burst onto the scene as a precocious 16-year-old and smashed the fastest century in ODI history (a mere 102 runs off 37 deliveries) in only his second match, the cricket world has been in awe of the allrounder's ability and desire to clear the rope, but it is now arguably his bowling – a vicious mix of leggies, topspinners and absurdly fast quicker balls – that is his foremost asset. A player who has been no stranger to controversy over the course of his career, his stint as captain of Pakistan's limited-overs sides has seemingly matured him, although it's not changed his desire to smash every ball he faces out of the ground.

LAST WORD: "He's a matchwinner with bat and ball, he's got a good cricket brain and he will add a bit of an intimidation factor to our side. With him, Briggs and Tahir all potentially available, we should be a side that's pretty difficult to score off during the middle overs." *Giles White*

Batting & Fielding

	Mat	Inns	NO	Runs	HS	Ave	SR	100	50	Ct	St
Tests	27	48	1	1716	156	36.51	86.97	5	8	10	0
ODIs	320	300	18	6667	124	23.64	113.88	6	31	106	0
T20Is	42	40	3	671	54*	18.13	144.61	0	3	12	0
First-class	111	183	4	5631	164	31.45	-	12	30	75	0
List A	411	388	21	9317	124	25.38	-	8	50	129	0
Twenty20	81	74	5	1274	54*	18.46	159.84	0	3	24	0

Bowling

	Mat	Balls	Runs	Wkts	BBI	BBM	Ave	Econ	SR	5w	10
Tests	27	3194	1709	48	5/52	5/43	35.60	3.21	66.5	1	0
ODIs	320	13805	10613	313	6/38	6/38	33.90	4.61	44.1	5	0
T20Is	42	953	975	53	4/11	4/11	18.39	6.13	17.9	0	0
First-class	111	13493	7023	258	6/101	-	27.22	3.12	52.2	8	0
List A	411	17900	13771	417	6/38	6/38	33.02	4.61	42.9	7	0
Twenty20	81	1760	1865	98	4/11	4/11	19.03	6.35	17.9	0	0

NAME: James Andrew Tomlinson
BORN: June 12, 1982, Winchester
HEIGHT: 6ft 2in
SQUAD Nº: 21
NICKNAME: Thommo
CAREER: First-class debut: 2002; List A debut: 2000; T20 debut: 2006; County cap: 2008

HAMPSHIRE

AOC SAYS: One of the best left-arm seamers in the country, Tomlinson's haul of 68 wickets at 24.76 made him the Championship's leading wicket-taker in 2008. While he hasn't quite hit those heights since, he's been a reliable source of wickets for the club over the last two seasons, as well as a willing and obstinate nightwatchman when called upon. A graduate of Cardiff University, Tomlinson is a natural swing bowler who operates at around the 80mph mark and would bowl all day if he were allowed to. Primarily a Championship bowler, he'll face stiff competition for the new ball as Hampshire's seam bowling stocks look especially strong this season.

LAST WORD: "Thommo's a fine four-day bowler and one of those guys who will run in all day for you. He wears his heart on his sleeve and would run through a brick wall for the team if he had to. He's one of those characters who you need around a cricket club and we're very lucky to have him." *Giles White*

Batting & Fielding

	Mat	Inns	NO	Runs	HS	Ave	SR	100	50	Ct	St
First-class	65	85	35	530	42	10.60	31.08	0	0	16	0
List A	27	14	5	34	14	3.77	-	0	0	3	0
Twenty20	2	1	0	5	5	5.00	125.00	0	0	0	0

Bowling

	Mat	Balls	Runs	Wkts	BBI	BBM	Ave	Econ	SR	5w	10
First-class	65	11374	6735	190	8/46	-	35.44	3.55	59.8	8	1
List A	27	1089	910	29	4/47	4/47	31.37	5.01	37.5	0	0
Twenty20	2	42	48	1	1/20	1/20	48.00	6.85	42.0	0	0

JAMES VINCE

HAMPSHIRE

NAME: James Michael Vince
BORN: March 14, 1991, Cuckfield
SQUAD Nº: 14
CAREER: First-class debut: 2009; List A debut: 2009; T20 debut: 2010

AOC SAYS: A young batsman who former England coach Duncan Fletcher has likened to Michael Vaughan, Vince has become a feature of the Hampshire top-order since making his first-team debut back in 2009 and it's easy to see what prompted Fletcher to make the comparison: the same natural timing, the same ease against pace and the same vicious pull stroke are all present and correct. One of England's star acts during the Under 19 World Cup in 2009/10, Vince served notice of his talent last season by compiling a brilliant 180 off just 205 deliveries against a strong Yorkshire attack at Scarborough, and Hampshire will be keen for him to deliver more of the same this year.

LAST WORD: "He's a very natural striker of a cricket ball who has an edge to him; he's competitive and hates getting out. He's a fine fielder and would practise all day if we let him. His other great strength is he's willing to listen to older and wiser heads around him." *Giles White*

Batting & Fielding

	Mat	Inns	NO	Runs	HS	Ave	SR	100	50	Ct	St
First-class	25	40	5	1192	180	34.05	58.57	1	5	14	0
List A	17	17	1	520	93	32.50	93.86	0	3	6	0
Twenty20	20	19	1	428	77	23.77	130.88	0	2	20	0

Bowling

	Mat	Balls	Runs	Wkts	BBI	BBM	Ave	Econ	SR	5w	10
First-class	25	92	61	0	-	-	-	3.97	-	0	0
List A	17	-	-	-	-	-	-	-	-	-	-
Twenty20	20	-	-	-	-	-	-	-	-	-	-

NAME: Christopher Philip Wood
BORN: June 27, 1990, Basingstoke,
HEIGHT: 6ft 3in
SQUAD Nº: 25
CAREER: First-class debut: 2010; List A
debut: 2010; T20 debut: 2010

HAMPSHIRE

AOC SAYS: An allrounder who took the new ball for much of Hampshire's FP t20 campaign last season, Wood uses his height to extract lively bounce off the pitch and was the club's leading wicket-taker in the Second XI Championship last season, claiming 19 wickets at an average of 19.94 with best figures of 9-48. Also a reliable fielder who's regularly shifted to key positions whenever the slog is on, Wood has had some success with the bat in second XI and youth level cricket but has yet to have much opportunity to show his talents for the first team.

LAST WORD: "He's a three-dimensional cricketer in that he bats, bowls and fields, and in Twenty20 it's a huge boost to have bowlers who you don't have to hide in the field. We're hoping to develop him into an allrounder who can do a job for us in all forms of the game, but he's still a work in progress like all the academy lads." *Giles White*

Batting & Fielding

	Mat	Inns	NO	Runs	HS	Ave	SR	100	50	Ct	St
First-class	3	4	0	68	35	17.00	61.26	0	0	0	0
List A	10	6	2	5	3	1.25	29.41	0	0	3	0
Twenty20	25	9	3	47	18	7.83	94.00	0	0	12	0

Bowling

	Mat	Balls	Runs	Wkts	BBI	BBM	Ave	Econ	SR	5w	10
First-class	3	427	240	13	5/54	7/84	18.46	3.37	32.8	1	0
List A	10	427	368	18	4/33	4/33	20.44	5.17	23.7	0	0
Twenty20	25	492	696	25	3/27	3/27	27.84	8.48	19.6	0	0

TEAM PROFILE

FORMED: 1806
HOME GROUND: The St Lawrence Ground, Canterbury
ONE-DAY NAME: Spitfires
CAPTAIN: Rob Key
2010 RESULTS: CC1: 8/9; CB40: 2/7 in Group C; FP t20: 7/9 in South Group

HONOURS

County Champions: (7) 1906, 1909, 1910, 1913, 1970, 1977(s) 1978; Gillette/NatWest/C&G/FP Trophy: (2) 1967, 1974; Benson and Hedges Cup: (3) 1973, 1976, 1978; Pro40/National League/CB40: 2001; Sunday League: (4) 1972, 1973, 1976, 1995; Twenty20 Cup: 2007

THE LOWDOWN

The coming season looks likely to mark the start of a period of consolidation for Kent, who were relegated from Division One of the Championship last season and have considerable financial concerns centred around the long-delayed redevelopment of their beautiful home ground. However, the club appears to have dealt with this adversity with aplomb, tightening their belts where necessary and looking to promote players from within their own youth set-up, and it could be argued that a spell in Division Two honing their talent could be extremely beneficial to the development of players like Sam Northeast, Matt Coles and Alex Blake. The Spitfires have also retained a core of proven senior players – although the likes of Rob Key and Joe Denly will be keen to improve on their 2010 showings – who should serve as good role models to their emerging youngsters, and if they remain injury free they will be a handful for any side.

COACH: PAUL FABRACE

A wicketkeeper who turned out for both Kent and Middlesex during his career, Farbrace retired from playing in 1995 and had spells at the helm of both the England under 19 side and England Women. He was in charge of the Kent academy for a period before he was appointed assistant coach of Sri Lanka under Trevor Bayliss in 2007. He was subsequently appointed first team coach at Kent in 2009.

With thanks to: Paul Fabrace; Glenn Pearson, sports editor, Kent Newsgroup

www.kentcricket.co.uk / tel: 01227 456 886

	Mat	Inns	NO	Runs	HS	Ave	SR	100	50	Ct	St
JE Goodman	1	2	1	59	59	59.00	44.02	0	1	0	-
M van Jaarsveld	17	29	2	1188	110*	44.00	56.49	3	6	36	-
DI Stevens	15	26	3	979	197	42.56	64.07	4	2	6	-
GO Jones	17	31	0	1003	178	32.35	57.97	3	2	49	6
RWT Key	16	28	2	814	261	31.30	59.67	2	1	1	-
MAK Lawson	1	1	0	31	31	31.00	91.17	0	0	0	-
RH Joseph	2	3	2	30	18*	30.00	34.88	0	0	0	-
JC Tredwell	12	20	2	489	115	27.16	45.13	1	1	21	-
JL Denly	18	33	0	848	106	25.69	53.63	1	5	10	-
SA Northeast	17	30	0	719	71	23.96	47.02	0	4	6	-
Azhar Mahmood	8	14	0	317	64	22.64	64.69	0	2	1	-
AJ Blake	9	17	1	359	105*	22.43	63.31	1	0	5	-
MT Coles	14	23	6	378	51	22.23	64.72	0	1	4	-
PG Dixey	1	1	0	22	22	22.00	57.89	0	0	0	3
CD Piesley	1	2	0	43	43	21.50	61.42	0	0	0	-
HMCM Bandara	6	10	3	105	29	15.00	47.51	0	0	5	-
JB Hockley	6	11	1	141	82	14.10	47.00	0	1	6	0
SJ Cook	15	24	7	205	26*	12.05	57.10	0	0	2	-
PD Edwards	2	3	1	20	13	10.00	27.77	0	0	0	-
RS Ferley	1	2	0	20	19	10.00	39.21	0	0	0	-
A Khan	12	18	5	115	24	8.84	45.09	0	0	5	-
M Ntini	5	8	3	25	13	5.00	38.46	0	0	0	-
JD Nel	3	2	0	6	4	3.00	13.63	0	0	2	-

	Mat	Overs	Mdns	Runs	Wkts	BBI	BBM	Ave	Econ	SR	5w	10
JE Goodman	1	6.0	0	16	1	1/16	1/16	16.00	2.66	36.0	0	0
JD Nel	3	54.0	12	190	10	6/62	9/119	19.00	3.51	32.4	1	0
M Ntini	5	164.0	44	474	24	6/51	10/104	19.75	2.89	41.0	2	1
RWT Key	16	15.2	3	45	2	2/31	2/31	22.50	2.93	46.0	0	0
AJ Blake	9	19.0	2	69	3	2/9	2/9	23.00	3.63	38.0	0	0
MAK Lawson	1	34.0	2	164	6	4/93	6/164	27.33	4.82	34.0	0	0
DI Stevens	15	280.1	74	768	28	4/38	7/101	27.42	2.74	60.0	0	0
Azhar Mahmood	8	279.3	55	847	30	5/62	7/116	28.23	3.03	55.9	2	0
JC Tredwell	12	377.0	71	1151	38	7/22	8/22	30.28	3.05	59.5	2	0
SJ Cook	15	331.3	68	1132	37	4/62	7/141	30.59	3.41	53.7	0	0
A Khan	12	372.2	82	1258	38	5/43	7/72	33.10	3.37	58.7	1	0
MT Coles	14	280.0	42	1040	27	4/55	5/102	38.51	3.71	62.2	0	0
HMCM Bandara	6	210.4	32	745	18	4/42	8/141	41.38	3.53	70.2	0	0
PD Edwards	2	34.0	10	145	3	2/60	2/68	48.33	4.26	68.0	0	0
M van Jaarsveld	17	123.0	17	332	5	2/50	2/33	66.40	2.69	147.6	0	0
RS Ferley	1	26.0	2	142	2	1/54	2/142	71.00	5.46	78.0	0	0
JL Denly	18	53.0	2	215	3	2/100	2/138	71.66	4.05	106.0	0	0
JB Hockley	6	43.0	5	175	2	1/8	1/8	87.50	4.06	129.0	0	0
RH Joseph	2	52.0	9	185	2	2/112	2/112	92.50	3.55	156.0	0	0
GO Jones	17	1.0	0	8	0	-	-	-	8.00	-	0	0
SA Northeast	17	6.0	3	8	0	-	-	-	1.33	-	0	0

Batting & Fielding

Bowling

Batting & Fielding

	Mat	Inns	NO	Runs	HS	Ave	SR	100	50	Ct	St
AJ Blake	8	4	3	128	81*	128.00	126.73	0	1	1	-
M van Jaarsveld	11	11	4	388	104*	55.42	101.04	1	4	6	-
RS Ferley	2	1	0	52	52	52.00	78.78	0	1	0	-
JL Denly	11	11	1	467	102*	46.70	79.42	1	2	3	-
RWT Key	10	10	1	352	87	39.11	94.87	0	2	1	-
Azhar Mahmood	7	5	2	109	44	36.33	126.74	0	0	1	-
DI Stevens	11	9	3	212	55	35.33	99.06	0	1	2	-
PB Muchall	1	1	0	22	22	22.00	57.89	0	0	0	-
GO Jones	11	8	1	133	40	19.00	85.80	0	0	3	8
JC Tredwell	8	2	0	21	11	10.50	77.77	0	0	4	-
SJ Cook	9	2	1	10	9	10.00	83.33	0	0	0	-
SA Northeast	4	2	0	15	9	7.50	62.50	0	0	3	-
AJ Ball	1	1	0	5	5	5.00	71.42	0	0	0	-
HMCM Bandara	5	1	0	5	5	5.00	62.50	0	0	0	-
MT Coles	6	1	0	1	1	1.00	33.33	0	0	1	-
JB Hockley	2	1	1	9	9*	-	81.81	0	0	0	-
A Khan	6	1	1	5	5*	-	62.50	0	0	3	-
M Ntini	4	1	1	3	3*	-	75.00	0	0	0	-
JD Nel	4	1	1	2	2*	-	66.66	0	0	1	-

Bowling

	Mat	Overs	Mdns	Runs	Wkts	BBI	Ave	Econ	SR	5w
MT Coles	6	25.0	2	150	14	4/47	10.71	6.00	10.7	0
HMCM Bandara	5	33.0	1	143	13	5/35	11.00	4.33	15.2	1
M van Jaarsveld	11	13.4	0	65	5	3/23	13.00	4.75	16.4	0
AJ Ball	1	5.0	1	16	1	1/16	16.00	3.20	30.0	0
JC Tredwell	8	55.0	3	207	11	4/20	18.81	3.76	30.0	0
SJ Cook	9	51.0	2	251	10	3/39	25.10	4.92	30.6	0
M Ntini	4	23.0	2	96	3	1/28	32.00	4.17	46.0	0
PB Muchall	1	4.0	0	34	1	1/34	34.00	8.50	24.0	0
Azhar Mahmood	7	41.0	1	223	6	2/7	37.16	5.43	41.0	0
A Khan	6	29.0	1	151	4	3/32	37.75	5.20	43.5	0
JD Nel	4	18.5	0	137	3	1/20	45.66	7.27	37.6	0
DI Stevens	11	39.0	3	199	3	1/15	66.33	5.10	78.0	0
RS Ferley	2	9.0	0	47	0	-	-	5.22	-	0
JB Hockley	2	3.0	0	29	0	-	-	9.66	-	0

www.kentcricket.co.uk / tel: 01227 456 886

Batting & Fielding

	Mat	Inns	NO	Runs	HS	Ave	SR	100	50	Ct	St
DI Stevens	14	13	4	369	52*	41.00	149.39	0	2	5	-
JL Denly	12	12	0	382	65	31.83	115.75	0	1	6	-
M van Jaarsveld	16	16	1	421	82	28.06	128.35	0	4	5	-
RWT Key	12	12	1	277	98*	25.18	137.81	0	1	4	-
SA Northeast	4	4	2	48	21	24.00	102.12	0	0	1	-
SJ Cook	16	6	5	19	8*	19.00	90.47	0	0	5	-
GO Jones	16	15	1	240	54	17.14	118.22	0	1	8	2
Azhar Mahmood	16	15	3	194	34	16.16	109.60	0	0	2	-
AJ Blake	15	12	2	122	33	12.20	127.08	0	0	9	-
JC Tredwell	10	7	1	47	25	7.83	87.03	0	0	5	-
MT Coles	14	9	1	60	16*	7.50	122.44	0	0	5	-
JB Hockley	6	6	0	39	18	6.50	97.50	0	0	3	-
HMCM Bandara	16	7	1	38	10	6.33	86.36	0	0	5	-
A Khan	4	3	2	6	2*	6.00	85.71	0	0	3	-
SA Shaw	4	2	2	4	3*	-	133.33	0	0	2	-

Bowling

	Mat	Overs	Mdns	Runs	Wkts	BBI	Ave	Econ	SR	5w
SJ Cook	16	57.0	1	413	21	3/13	19.66	7.24	16.2	0
MT Coles	14	37.2	0	324	15	3/30	21.60	8.67	14.9	0
HMCM Bandara	16	48.0	0	384	17	3/14	22.58	8.00	16.9	0
DI Stevens	14	39.0	1	287	12	3/17	23.91	7.35	19.5	0
JC Tredwell	10	31.0	0	268	11	3/13	24.36	8.64	16.9	0
M van Jaarsveld	16	12.0	0	75	3	3/25	25.00	6.25	24.0	0
A Khan	4	10.2	0	104	4	2/27	26.00	10.06	15.5	0
Azhar Mahmood	16	57.0	2	394	15	2/18	26.26	6.91	22.8	0
JB Hockley	6	4.5	0	32	1	1/9	32.00	6.62	29.0	0
SA Shaw	4	10.0	0	84	2	1/10	42.00	8.40	30.0	0
RH Joseph	1	2.0	0	25	0	-	-	12.50	-	0

AZHAR MAHMOOD RHB RFM MVP66

KENT

NAME: Azhar Mahmood Sagar
BORN: February 28, 1975, Rawalpindi
HEIGHT: 5ft 11in
SQUAD Nº: 11
NICKNAME: Aju
OTHER TEAMS: Pakistan, Islamabad Cricket Association, Kent, Lahore Badshahs, Pakistan International Airlines, Rawalpindi, Surrey, United Bank Limited
CAREER: Test debut: 1997; ODI debut: 1996; First-class debut: 1994; List A debut: 1994; T20 debut: 2003; County cap: 2004 (Surrey), 2008 (Kent)

AOC SAYS: It speaks volumes of Pakistan's depth of talent and their penchant for inconsistent selection that Mahmood never became a mainstay on the international scene, especially as he began his Test career by notching three centuries in his first eight Tests. An enthusiastic allrounder who has claimed 72 wickets at 22.68 in first-class cricket since joining Kent from Surrey in 2007, the 36-year-old is a punishing batsman who excels at raising the tempo of an innings with an array of lofted drives and murderous pulls as well as a skilful swing bowler. The Spitfires have used him sparingly in Championship cricket, saving him for limited-overs matches where his all-round skills come to the fore, but expect him to play a bigger role this year as Kent look to find the right mix of youth and experience.

LAST WORD: "He bowled brilliantly for us last year. He doesn't always get the rewards he deserves but he's brilliant at building pressure at one end so that the guy down the other end can pick up wickets." *Paul Farbrace*

Batting & Fielding

	Mat	Inns	NO	Runs	HS	Ave	SR	100	50	Ct	St
Tests	21	34	4	900	136	30.00	50.79	3	1	14	0
ODIs	143	110	26	1521	67	18.10	76.50	0	3	37	0
First-class	168	259	29	7133	204*	31.01	-	9	37	132	0
List A	291	233	47	3946	101*	21.21	-	2	15	86	0
Twenty20	81	70	20	1243	65*	24.86	143.20	0	3	12	0

Bowling

	Mat	Balls	Runs	Wkts	BBI	BBM	Ave	Econ	SR	5w	10
Tests	21	3015	1402	39	4/50	5/95	35.94	2.79	77.3	0	0
ODIs	143	6242	4813	123	6/18	6/18	39.13	4.62	50.7	3	0
First-class	168	28411	14720	586	8/61	-	25.11	3.10	48.4	26	3
List A	291	12836	9919	310	6/18	6/18	31.99	4.63	41.4	5	0
Twenty20	81	1658	2004	91	4/20	4/20	22.02	7.25	18.2	0	0

ADAM BALL

RHB LFM

NAME: Adam James Ball
BORN: March 1, 1993, Greenwich
HEIGHT: 6ft 2in
SQUAD Nº: 24
NICKNAME: Bally
CAREER: List A debut: 2010

KENT

AOC SAYS: A talented all-round sportsman who has played youth level football for Arsenal, Ball is a fast, lively seamer and a sufficiently good batsman to be earmarked as a potential allrounder by the Kent coaching staff. A member of the England team that competed in the Under 19 World Cup in New Zealand in 2010/11, the 18-year-old was called up to the side again for the recent winter tour to Sri Lanka alongside fellow Spitfire Daniel Bell-Drummond and featured in two youth Tests and five youth ODIs. Named as Young Player of the Year in the Kent League in 2009, he made his first-team debut against Durham at Chester-le-Street in September last year. Handed the new ball, he removed opposing skipper Phil Mustard with just his fifth delivery and went on to bowl five economical overs as Kent romped to a 31-run win.

LAST WORD: "Adam coped really well on his debut. I'm sure he was nervous but he certainly didn't show it. He's got a good temperament and hopefully he'll develop further this year." *Paul Farbrace*

Batting & Fielding

	Mat	Inns	NO	Runs	HS	Ave	SR	100	50	Ct	St
List A	1	1	0	5	5	5.00	71.42	0	0	0	0

Bowling

	Mat	Balls	Runs	Wkts	BBI	BBM	Ave	Econ	SR	5w	10
List A	1	30	16	1	1/16	1/16	16.00	3.20	30.0	0	0

DANIEL BELL-DRUMMOND   RHB RM

KENT

NAME: Daniel James Bell-Drummond
BORN: August 4, 1993, Lewisham
HEIGHT: 6ft
NICKNAME: DBD, Deebs
CAREER: Yet to make first-team debut

AOC SAYS: One of several former academy players on the Kent staff, Bell-Drummond is an opening batsman and an improving seamer who spent some of the winter touring Sri Lanka with the England under 19 team, scoring 102 runs at 34 in the two youth Tests in testing conditions. A pupil of Millfield School, a notorious breeding ground for first-class cricketers, he idolises Brian Lara and has a reputation as a batsman who is comfortable batting time and digging in for the long haul.

LAST WORD: "We don't want to put too much pressure on him, but we see a lot of potential so it's just a case of working hard with him to make sure he develops as he should. He's got all the shots, is a good striker of the ball and is just a good old-fashioned batter – he loves spending time at the crease. He's probably more suited to Championship cricket at the minute, but he's learning how to adapt his game." *Paul Farbrace*

EXTRAS

Kent have begun the redevelopment of the St Lawrence Ground, which will include retractable floodlights, a two-storey dressing room building and new member facilities. Chief executive Jamie Clifford says: "It's been a long haul getting to this point, but it's tremendous to know now that this project is going to happen. There is now the opportunity to really invest in our infrastructure and make sure the asset we have here is really as good as it can be."

NAME: Samuel William Billings
BORN: June 15, 1991, Pembury
HEIGHT: 5ft 11in
NICKNAME: Bilbo, Doug
CAREER: Yet to make first-team debut

KENT

AOC SAYS: Following the release of Paul Dixey, Geraint Jones' long-standing number two, from the club due to financial issues, Billings will fill in as the Spitfires' reserve keeper this season. A former academy player who has represented England at under 16, 17 and 19 level, Billings played six Second XI Championship matches, scoring 209 runs at 29.85 with a top-score of 56*, and four Trophy games in which he scored 181 runs at 45.25 with a top-score of 73 made while opening the batting against Sussex at Hove.

LAST WORD: "Sam's been in our system for a long time and is a highly competent keeper whose batting has come on no end in the last season or so. He's one of those energetic keeper-batsmen, although he's still got some way to go to put pressure on Geraint Jones for a place. He knows that and will keep working hard on his game this year." *Paul Farbrace*

EXTRAS

"I believe in Twenty20 cricket – not because I dislike Championship cricket, quite the opposite. If the right balance can be achieved, it simply offers the best chance of ensuring the long term survival of all forms of cricket." Jamie Clifford

ALEX BLAKE
LHB RMF

KENT

NAME: Alexander James Blake
BORN: January 25, 1989, Farnborough, Kent
HEIGHT: 6ft 1in
SQUAD Nº: 18
NICKNAME: Blakey
CAREER: First-class debut: 2008; List A debut: 2007; T20 debut: 2010

AOC SAYS: Blake ended the 2010 season in excellent fashion by notching his maiden first-class century against Yorkshire at Headingley, a masterful 105* that came off just 143 deliveries and contained 18 boundaries. A student at Leeds Met University, the 22-year-old allrounder has represented England at under 19 level and played some enterprising one-day knocks for the Spitfires last season – including a matchwinning 81* off 56 balls against Scotland at Canterbury. An aggressive, hard-hitting batsman and an improving bowler who has worked hard on his accuracy and variations over the winter, he'll likely play a significant role for Kent this season.

LAST WORD: "Alex's knock up at Headingley was exceptional, his batting has really improved and he plays pace really well. We want him to bring on his bowling so that we could use him as a third or fourth seamer, but he's in contention for a place in the top-order this year in all forms but especially one-day cricket." *Paul Farbrace*

Batting & Fielding

	Mat	Inns	NO	Runs	HS	Ave	SR	100	50	Ct	St
First-class	14	22	1	484	105*	23.04	59.75	1	0	6	0
List A	18	12	5	285	81*	40.71	105.55	0	2	7	0
Twenty20	15	12	2	122	33	12.20	127.08	0	0	9	0

Bowling

	Mat	Balls	Runs	Wkts	BBI	BBM	Ave	Econ	SR	5w	10
First-class	14	162	101	3	2/9	2/9	33.66	3.74	54.0	0	0
List A	18	72	61	1	1/25	1/25	61.00	5.08	72.0	0	0
Twenty20	15	-	-	-	-	-	-	-	-	-	-

NAME: Matthew Thomas Coles
BORN: May 26, 1990, Maidstone
HEIGHT: 6ft 3in
SQUAD Nº: 26
NICKNAME: Colesy
CAREER: First-class debut: 2009; List A
debut: 2009; T20 debut: 2010

KENT

AOC SAYS: One of the success stories of Kent's 2010 season, Coles is a hostile, muscular seamer who extracts lift off the pitch, a powerful striker of a cricket ball and an enthusiastic fielder. Kent's injury troubles last season meant a great deal of responsibility was thrust upon his shoulders last season, and he responded with 56 wickets in all competitions and a handful of blistering cameos with the bat. Having spent the off-season playing league cricket in Australia, he has reportedly put on an extra yard of pace and, with Amjad Khan having moved to Sussex, it is likely he will form a key part of the Spitfires attack this season.

LAST WORD: "He's highly-rated by the club. The fact that they've given him a three-year contract when they have the financial worries that they do is a sign of how much potential they think he's got. I expect him to take the new ball, but watch out for his batting; if he gets his eye in he'll hit the ball out of the ground." *Glenn Pearson*

Batting & Fielding

	Mat	Inns	NO	Runs	HS	Ave	SR	100	50	Ct	St
First-class	16	25	6	408	51	21.47	64.05	0	1	4	0
List A	10	3	0	11	5	3.66	57.89	0	0	1	0
Twenty20	14	9	1	60	16*	7.50	122.44	0	0	5	0

Bowling

	Mat	Balls	Runs	Wkts	BBI	BBM	Ave	Econ	SR	5w	10
First-class	16	1786	1170	29	4/55	5/102	40.34	3.93	61.5	0	0
List A	10	252	277	18	4/47	4/47	15.38	6.59	14.0	0	0
Twenty20	14	224	324	15	3/30	3/30	21.60	8.67	14.9	0	0

SIMON COOK
RHB RFM MVP59

KENT

NAME: Simon James Cook
BORN: January 15, 1977, Oxford
HEIGHT: 6ft 4in
SQUAD Nº: 7
NICKNAME: Chef
OTHER TEAMS: Middlesex
CAREER: First-class debut: 1999; List A
debut: 1997; T20 debut: 2003; County cap:
2003 (Middlesex), 2007 (Kent)

AOC SAYS: Certain phrases always seem to crop up when Cook's name is mentioned:
reliable, honest and unsung hero being just a few of them. A tall, naggingly accurate seamer
who started out with Middlesex before moving to Canterbury for the 2005 season, Cook was
an instrumental figure in the Spitfires' successful Twenty20 Cup campaign in 2007, claiming
17 wickets at an average of 16.17 and a miserly economy rate of 6.90. A dogged lower-order
batsman who strives to sell his wicket dearly, Cook provides his skipper with control; he
rarely gets hit out of the attack and varies his pace intelligently. Kent will be hoping that the
34-year-old will recreate his steady form in 2010, which saw him take 37 first-class wickets
at 30.59, his third most successful season in the county game.

LAST WORD: "Simon is just one of those guys you need at a club. Rob Key can throw the
ball to him in any conditions and know he will attack the game and do a job. He's very
good with our younger bowlers too; he passes on his knowledge but doesn't ram it down
their throats." *Glenn Pearson*

Batting & Fielding

	Mat	Inns	NO	Runs	HS	Ave	SR	100	50	Ct	St
First-class	132	170	29	2312	93*	16.39	-	0	6	33	0
List A	179	107	33	1244	67*	16.81	-	0	2	28	0
Twenty20	67	21	13	134	25*	16.75	119.64	0	0	14	0

Bowling

	Mat	Balls	Runs	Wkts	BBI	BBM	Ave	Econ	SR	5w	10
First-class	132	20094	10526	330	8/63	-	31.89	3.14	60.8	12	0
List A	179	7873	6195	224	6/37	6/37	27.65	4.72	35.1	2	0
Twenty20	67	1429	1761	81	3/13	3/13	21.74	7.39	17.6	0	0

NAME: Joseph Liam Denly
BORN: March 16, 1986, Canterbury
HEIGHT: 6ft
SQUAD Nº: 6
NICKNAME: Joey, No Pants
OTHER TEAMS: England
CAREER: ODI debut: 2009; T20I debut: 2009; First-class debut: 2004; List A debut: 2004; T20 debut: 2004; County cap: 2008

KENT

AOC SAYS: A flamboyant opening batsman who reminds many observers of Australian legend Michael Slater, Denly uses his feet to both the spinners and the pace bowlers, drives sweetly and plays the pull shot especially well, but struggled for form for much of Kent's 2010 campaign and 848 runs from 33 innings at 25.69 was a poor return for one so talented. Having played for Kent at every age level, the 25-year-old made his first-class debut against Oxford University in 2004 before going on to hit three half-centuries in consecutive youth Tests while touring India with the England under 19 team. The following season he struck his maiden first-class hundred against Cambridge University and went on to consolidate his place in the Spitfires' batting order; especially in one-day cricket where his high strike-rate marked him out as a natural. He was part of the Kent side that romped to victory in the 2007 Twenty20 Cup, carried his bat for 115* out of a total of only 199 against Hampshire at Canterbury in the Championship and marked his call-up to the England Lions side by making 83 off 90 balls against India. His good form continued into 2009 as he averaged 51.85 in the Friends Provident Trophy, and on the back of that he was called up to the full England ODI side. He celebrated his debut at the highest level by scoring 67 against Ireland, but he struggled in the following matches against Australia (although he certainly wasn't alone in that), failed to set the world alight on the subsequent tour of South Africa and was eased out of the England side, a move that may have damaged his confidence judging by his returns for Kent in 2010. However, he remains an enormous talent and a season spent rediscovering his touch in Division Two could be just what the doctor ordered.

INSIDE TRACK: "Joe has huge potential. I think people forget just how young he is because he has been around for a while now, but he's still learning his game. He didn't have the best time in the Championship last year, but he's working hard on setting it right because he desperately wants to get back to playing international cricket. The danger will come if he tries to tinker with his natural game too much, we want to encourage him to get back to doing what he does best which is taking the attack to the bowlers." *Paul Farbrace*

JOE DENLY

KENT

Batting & Fielding											
	Mat	Inns	NO	Runs	HS	Ave	SR	100	50	Ct	St
ODIs	9	9	0	268	67	29.77	65.52	0	2	5	0
T20Is	5	5	0	20	14	4.00	68.96	0	0	1	0
First-class	70	121	5	3906	149	33.67	58.42	10	19	33	0
List A	77	75	7	2296	115	33.76	72.17	4	11	24	0
Twenty20	60	57	3	1341	91	24.83	112.97	0	7	23	0

Bowling										
	Mat	Balls	Runs	Wkts	BBI	BBM	Ave	Econ	SR	5w	10
ODIs	9	-	-	-	-	-	-	-	-	-	-
T20Is	5	6	9	1	1/9	1/9	9.00	9.00	6.0	0	0
First-class	70	1195	662	13	2/13	3/60	50.92	3.32	91.9	0	0
List A	77	30	35	1	1/20	1/20	35.00	7.00	30.0	0	0
Twenty20	60	18	32	1	1/9	1/9	32.00	10.66	18.0	0	0

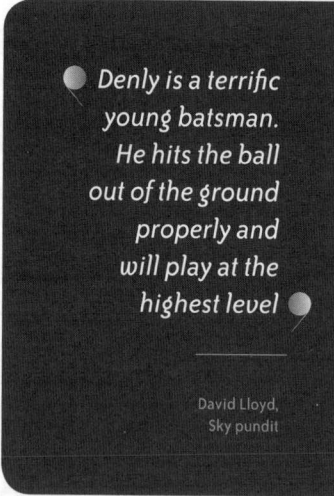

Denly is a terrific young batsman. He hits the ball out of the ground properly and will play at the highest level

David Lloyd,
Sky pundit

NAME: James Elliott Goodman
BORN: November 19, 1990, Farnborough, Kent
HEIGHT: 5ft 10in
SQUAD Nº: 19
NICKNAME: Goody
CAREER: First-class debut: 2010; List A
debut: 2007

KENT

AOC SAYS: A top-order batsman and yet another product of Kent's prolific academy,
Goodman made his first-class debut against the Pakistan touring side in 2010. Against an
attack containing Umar Gul, Mohammad Amir and Wahab Riaz, he impressed observers
by making a composed 59 off 127 deliveries. A former England under 16 captain, Goodman
was part of the squad that took part in the Under 19 World Cup in 2008, the same squad
that contained England internationals Steve Finn and Chris Woakes, and has been a
consistent runscorer for the Kent Second XI as well as an occasional source of wickets via
his developing seamers.

LAST WORD: "He's highly thought of around the club and looks to have something about
him whenever I've seen him play. I think he'll get a go this season in a fair few games,
possibly in the CB40 towards the back end of the season." *Glenn Pearson*

Batting & Fielding

	Mat	Inns	NO	Runs	HS	Ave	SR	100	50	Ct	St
First-class	1	2	1	59	59	59.00	44.02	0	1	0	0
List A	3	2	1	38	26*	38.00	102.70	0	0	2	0

Bowling

	Mat	Balls	Runs	Wkts	BBI	BBM	Ave	Econ	SR	5w	10
First-class	1	36	16	1	1/16	1/16	16.00	2.66	36.0	0	0
List A	3	-	-	-	-	-	-	-	-	-	-

GERAINT JONES

RHB RM WK R2 MVP54

NAME: Geraint Owen Jones
BORN: July 14, 1976, Kundiawa, Papua New Guinea
HEIGHT: 5ft 10in
SQUAD Nº: 9
NICKNAME: Jonesy, Joner
OTHER TEAMS: England
CAREER: Test debut: 2004; ODI debut: 2004; T20I debut: 2005; First-class debut: 2001; List A debut: 2001; T20 debut: 2003; County cap: 2003

AOC SAYS: England's wicketkeeper during their 2005 Ashes triumph, Jones has arguably produced the best cricket of his career over the last two seasons; he's passed 1,000 first-class runs on each occasion, a milestone he had never previously reached. A counter-attacking batsman who loves to cut and pull, his glovework – the subject of endless debate during his England days – has never been better; he's claimed 90 catches and nine stumpings in first-class cricket over the same period. Hailed as a consummate team man by his teammates, he has batted in a variety of positions for Kent in recent years but a stint at No.3 in 2009 – the last time the Spitfires were in Division Two – saw him rack up 1,345 runs, a haul that could well seem him restored up the order for this campaign.

LAST WORD: "Jonesy's so passionate about Kent cricket, he's been a great servant to the club. He's fiercely competitive and never lets us down. His willingness to move about the order and help our youngsters along shows you what type of character he is." *Paul Farbrace*

Batting & Fielding

	Mat	Inns	NO	Runs	HS	Ave	SR	100	50	Ct	St
Tests	34	53	4	1172	100	23.91	54.13	1	6	128	5
ODIs	49	41	8	815	80	24.69	78.21	0	4	68	4
T20Is	2	2	1	33	19	33.00	132.00	0	0	2	0
First-class	143	218	20	6699	178	33.83	-	15	32	431	31
List A	160	135	23	2702	86	24.12	79.61	0	11	174	35
Twenty20	61	51	10	681	56	16.60	115.61	0	2	33	15

Bowling

	Mat	Balls	Runs	Wkts	BBI	BBM	Ave	Econ	SR	5w	10
Tests	34	-	-	-	-	-	-	-	-	-	-
ODIs	49	-	-	-	-	-	-	-	-	-	-
T20Is	2	-	-	-	-	-	-	-	-	-	-
First-class	143	24	26	0	-	-	-	6.50	-	0	0
List A	160	-	-	-	-	-	-	-	-	-	-
Twenty20	61	-	-	-	-	-	-	-	-	-	-

NAME: Robert Hartman Joseph
BORN: January 20, 1982, Antigua
HEIGHT: 6ft 1in
SQUAD Nº: 8
NICKNAME: RJ, Bluey
OTHER TEAMS: Leeward Islands
CAREER: First-class debut: 2000; List A
debut: 2004; T20 debut: 2008

KENT

AOC SAYS: A bowler of genuine pace, Joseph is nursing his way back to full fitness
following a serious shoulder injury picked up in 2009. He played just three matches for
the county in 2010, including a friendly against the touring Pakistan team, but signs are
promising that he will play a full part this season, although the Kent backroom staff are
understandably cautious about pushing him too hard, too soon. Joseph joined the county
in 2004 after serving his residency qualification period and instantly turned heads with
his raw pace, but it wasn't until 2008 that he clearly demonstrated his potential; he claimed
55 Championship wickets at 26.05 to earn himself an England Lions call-up for the tour to
India. A wicket-to-wicket bowler who possesses a skiddy, dangerous bouncer, a fully fit
Joseph is a dangerous prospect in Division Two.

LAST WORD: "Bowling-wise he looks in pretty good shape. There's a big battle for him to get
back on the field, it can be quite a mental battle to come back after missing so much cricket,
but we'll take it slow and hopefully he can get among the wickets this year." *Paul Farbrace*

Batting & Fielding

	Mat	Inns	NO	Runs	HS	Ave	SR	100	50	Ct	St
First-class	46	59	22	414	36*	11.18	-	0	0	9	0
List A	33	14	12	43	15	21.50	61.42	0	0	4	0
Twenty20	9	1	1	1	1*	-	100.00	0	0	3	0

Bowling

	Mat	Balls	Runs	Wkts	BBI	BBM	Ave	Econ	SR	5w	10
First-class	46	6982	4258	130	6/32	-	32.75	3.65	53.7	5	0
List A	33	1307	1114	39	5/13	5/13	28.56	5.11	33.5	1	0
Twenty20	9	168	213	10	2/14	2/14	21.30	7.60	16.8	0	0

ROB KEY

RHB OB R5 MVP97

KENT

NAME: Robert William Trevor Key
BORN: 12 May 1979, East Dulwich
HEIGHT: 6ft 1in
SQUAD Nº: 4
NICKNAME: Keysy
OTHER TEAMS: England
CAREER: Test debut: 2002; ODI debut: 2003;
T20I debut: 2009; First-class debut: 1998;
List A debut: 1998; T20 debut: 2004; County
cap: 2001

AOC SAYS: By his usual standards, Key did not have a great season in 2010; his haul of 814 first-class runs was bolstered by his innings of 261 against Durham and without it his figures would have made for pretty unhappy reading. A classy yet pugnacious top-order batsman and an astute, streetwise captain, Key is probably unlucky not to have played more international cricket, as anyone who saw his magnificent 221 against West Indies at Lord's in 2004 will attest, but England's loss has been Kent's gain; he's been a reliable source of runs for them across all formats ever since his breakthrough season in 2001. One of the best liked figures on the county circuit, he's also a regular Sky pundit and has reportedly been working hard in the nets to ensure he returns to his runscoring best in 2011.

LAST WORD: "I think he's as good a domestic captain as there is out there. He's a Kent man through and through and the lads all want to get behind him and fight for him, which is the mark of a good leader." *Paul Farbrace*

Batting & Fielding

	Mat	Inns	NO	Runs	HS	Ave	SR	100	50	Ct	St
Tests	15	26	1	775	221	31.00	47.28	1	3	11	0
ODIs	5	5	0	54	19	10.80	40.00	0	0	0	0
T20Is	1	1	1	10	10*	-	125.00	0	0	1	0
First-class	226	390	28	15039	270*	41.54	-	43	56	128	0
List A	194	187	13	5467	120*	31.41	-	5	34	40	0
Twenty20	58	58	9	1390	98*	28.36	126.59	0	8	15	0

Bowling

	Mat	Balls	Runs	Wkts	BBI	BBM	Ave	Econ	SR	5w	10
Tests	15	-	-	-	-	-	-	-	-	-	-
ODIs	5	-	-	-	-	-	-	-	-	-	-
T20Is	1	-	-	-	-	-	-	-	-	-	-
First-class	226	388	198	3	2/31	2/31	66.00	3.06	129.3	0	0
List A	194	-	-	-	-	-	-	-	-	-	-
Twenty20	58	-	-	-	-	-	-	-	-	-	-

NAME: Johann Dewald Nel
BORN: June 6, 1980, Klerksdorp, South
Africa
HEIGHT: 6ft
SQUAD Nº: 21
NICKNAME: Nella
OTHER TEAMS: Scotland, Worcestershire
CAREER: ODI debut: 2006; T20I debut:
2007; First-class debut: 2004; List A debut:
2004; T20 debut: 2007

KENT

AOC SAYS: A brisk, line and length seamer who prides himself on his accuracy, Nel was
signed on a two-year contract by Kent at the start of 2010 after impressing on a pre-
season trial. Having moved to the UK from South Africa as a teenager, Nel has become a
significant part of the Saltires' attack and was one of only six players contracted full-time
with Scotland. However, when the opportunity for him to play regular county cricket
again – having previously played for Worcestershire in 2007 – came about he elected
to take the opportunity, but sadly a back injury prevented him from playing until late in
the season, although he made up for lost time by claiming match-figures of 9-119 against
Yorkshire at Headingley.

LAST WORD: "He's a great credit to Scottish cricket. He bowled brilliantly at Headingley
and should have had 11 wickets in the game. We're just sorry we didn't see more of him
last year but that shouldn't be the case this season." *Paul Farbrace*

Batting & Fielding

	Mat	Inns	NO	Runs	HS	Ave	SR	100	50	Ct	St
ODIs	19	10	8	31	11*	15.50	57.40	0	0	3	0
T20Is	10	5	2	34	13*	11.33	136.00	0	0	1	0
First-class	18	23	10	154	36	11.84	32.97	0	0	6	0
List A	84	49	28	202	36*	9.61	52.74	0	0	15	0
Twenty20	15	5	2	34	13*	11.33	136.00	0	0	1	0

Bowling

	Mat	Balls	Runs	Wkts	BBI	BBM	Ave	Econ	SR	5w	10
ODIs	19	730	649	14	4/25	4/25	46.35	5.33	52.1	0	0
T20Is	10	186	169	12	3/10	3/10	14.08	5.45	15.5	0	0
First-class	18	2424	1374	51	6/62	-	26.94	3.40	47.5	2	0
List A	84	3398	2969	83	4/25	4/25	35.77	5.24	40.9	0	0
Twenty20	15	289	278	17	3/10	3/10	16.35	5.77	17.0	0	0

SAM NORTHEAST — RHB OB

KENT

NAME: Sam Alexander Northeast
BORN: October 16, 1989, Ashford, Kent
HEIGHT: 5ft 11in
SQUAD Nº: 17
NICKNAME: Bam, North, Knighty, Chumley
CAREER: First-class debut: 2007; List A debut: 2007; T20 debut: 2010

AOC SAYS: A schoolboy prodigy who, as a 13-year-old, scored 19 hundreds in a single term, Northeast has long been talked about as an exciting talent, although he suffered from a case of second season syndrome in 2010 and will want to improve on a tally of 719 Championship runs at 23.96. A talented all-round sportsman and a national schools rackets champion, he is a flexible batsman able to bat anywhere in the top-order, although it looks likely that he will be given the chance to open the innings in the Championship this year. A former England under 19 international and Bunbury scholar, he attended Harrow School prior to signing a contract with Kent and made his maiden first-class hundred at Bristol against Gloucestershire in 2009.

LAST WORD: "I think he was a little bit taken aback by the mental side of the game last season and maybe struggled a bit outside off stump, but I reckon he'll have a big year in 2011. He's got fantastic hand-eye coordination and just needs the confidence of an early score." *Glenn Pearson*

Batting & Fielding

	Mat	Inns	NO	Runs	HS	Ave	SR	100	50	Ct	St
First-class	29	51	2	1391	128*	28.38	49.30	1	7	16	0
List A	11	8	0	159	69	19.87	76.07	0	1	4	0
Twenty20	4	4	2	48	21	24.00	102.12	0	0	1	0

Bowling

	Mat	Balls	Runs	Wkts	BBI	BBM	Ave	Econ	SR	5w	10
First-class	29	42	10	0	-	-	-	1.42	-	0	0
List A	11	-	-	-	-	-	-	-	-	-	-
Twenty20	4	-	-	-	-	-	-	-	-	-	-

NAME: Adam Edward N Riley
BORN: March 23, 1992, Sidcup, Kent
HEIGHT: 6ft 2in
NICKNAME: Riles, Rilo, Mad Dog, Ron Weasley
CAREER: Yet to make first-team debut

KENT

AOC SAYS: A tall, feisty offspinner who came on leaps and bounds while playing for the Second XI last season, Riley will provide spin bowling back-up to James Tredwell this season. His tally of 18 wickets at 27.72 made him Kent's leading wicket-taker in the Second XI Championship, and he followed this up with seven wickets in the Second XI Trophy, impressing with his control and competitive spirit. He represents Bexley in the Kent Premier League, is a resilient lower-order batsman often saddled with nightwatchman duties, catches well at slip and rates Shane Warne as his favourite sports personality.

LAST WORD: "He's mentally very strong and has shown the ability to cope well under pressure. John Emburey has had a close look at him and said that he thinks Riley can be a real top-drawer bowler, and Embers knows his offspin." *Paul Farbrace*

EXTRAS

"The landscape of cricket is changing massively and the thing I love about Kent is that the club doesn't merely want to exist, they want to evolve and move forward. Things like this redevelopment plan are crucial to that." Rob Key

CHRIS PIESLEY   LHB OB

KENT

NAME: Christopher Damien Piesley
BORN: March 12, 1992, Chatham
HEIGHT: 5ft 10in
CAREER: First-class debut: 2010

AOC SAYS: A left-handed top-order batsman who marked his first-team debut by making 43 in the second innings of a friendly against Pakistan in 2010, Piesley is another former academy player who will ideally play a lot of second XI cricket under the guidance of Kent's high performance director Simon Willis this season and continue his development there. Possessing a solid, orthodox technique, he was educated at Fulston Manor School in Sittingbourne and is by all accounts very useful in the field.

LAST WORD: "His innings against a very good Pakistan attack showed guts and character, but he's a work in progress and we'll only have a full idea of what he's capable of once he has got more cricket under his belt." *Paul Farbrace*

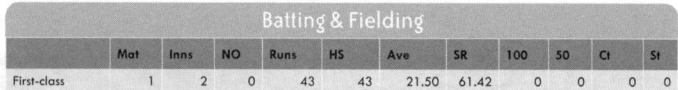

Batting & Fielding

	Mat	Inns	NO	Runs	HS	Ave	SR	100	50	Ct	St
First-class	1	2	0	43	43	21.50	61.42	0	0	0	0

Bowling

	Mat	Balls	Runs	Wkts	BBI	BBM	Ave	Econ	SR	5w	10
First-class	1	-	-	-	-	-	-	-	-	-	-

NAME: Stuart Ashley Shaw
BORN: April 15, 1991, Crewe
HEIGHT: 5ft 11in
SQUAD Nº: 22
NICKNAME: Ash
CAREER: T20 debut: 2010

KENT

AOC SAYS: A skiddy, aggressive left-arm swing bowler who possesses a handy slower ball, Shaw was spotted playing club cricket in Melbourne and invited to Kent for a trial ahead of the 2010 season, during which he impressed with his commitment and ability to swing the ball. A forceful, confident character on the pitch who plays for Nantwich in the Cheshire Premier League, he was quickly offered a contract and played four Twenty20 matches last term, catching the eye with economical spells against Glamorgan and Gloucestershire, before a case of shin splints put him out of action. Nevertheless, he had made an enough of an impression to be offered a two-year deal over the winter, and will be looking forward, if fit, to further outings this season.

LAST WORD: "Ashley's a really gutsy cricketer and has a lot of potential. He's quite raw but he's skiddy, can swing the ball both ways and has shown plenty of bottle when he's been given an opportunity." *Paul Farbrace*

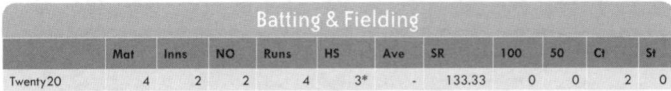

Batting & Fielding

	Mat	Inns	NO	Runs	HS	Ave	SR	100	50	Ct	St
Twenty20	4	2	2	4	3*	-	133.33	0	0	2	0

Bowling

	Mat	Balls	Runs	Wkts	BBI	BBM	Ave	Econ	SR	5w	10
Twenty20	4	60	84	2	1/10	1/10	42.00	8.40	30.0	0	0

DARREN STEVENS

KENT

NAME: Darren Ian Stevens
BORN: April 30, 1976, Leicester
HEIGHT: 5ft 11in
SQUAD Nº: 3
NICKNAME: Stevo, Dazzer
OTHER TEAMS: Leicestershire, Midwest Rhinos, Otago
CAREER: First-class debut: 1997; List A: 1997; T20 debut: 2003; County cap: 2002 (Leicestershire), 2005 (Kent)

AOC SAYS: Stevens started last season in tremendous form, amassing more than 700 Championship runs by early June, but injuries to the likes of Robbie Joseph meant he was increasingly burdened with bowling duties and his form with the bat suffered. Nevertheless, he can be rightly proud when he looks back on his achievements in 2010, which saw him rack up 979 runs – including a brilliant 197 against eventual champions Notts – and 28 wickets in first-class cricket to go alongside 451 runs in the CB40 and 369 runs in the FP t20, returns that earned him a contract as Otago's overseas player in New Zealand's domestic Twenty20 competition this winter. A blistering strokemaker gifted with enormous power, a canny medium-pacer and an excellent fielder, Stevens is a crucial player for Kent in all forms but especially in limited-overs cricket where his ability to clear the ropes comes to the fore.

LAST WORD: "Over the last couple of years Stevo has been as good a one-day player as there is in the country. People tend not to go and get a cup of tea when he's batting." *Paul Farbrace*

Batting & Fielding

	Mat	Inns	NO	Runs	HS	Ave	SR	100	50	Ct	St
First-class	170	276	20	8836	208	34.51	-	21	42	128	0
List A	224	210	24	5640	133	30.32	-	4	37	84	0
Twenty20	91	84	19	1848	77	28.43	132.28	0	8	27	0

Bowling

	Mat	Balls	Runs	Wkts	BBI	BBM	Ave	Econ	SR	5w	10
First-class	170	6786	3407	94	4/36	-	36.24	3.01	72.1	0	0
List A	224	2399	1995	56	5/32	5/32	35.62	4.98	42.8	1	0
Twenty20	91	792	999	42	4/14	4/14	23.78	7.56	18.8	0	0

NAME: James Cullum Tredwell
BORN: February 27, 1982, Ashford, Kent
HEIGHT: 6ft
SQUAD Nº: 15
NICKNAME: Tredders, Tredman, Pingu, Chad, Jimmy T
OTHER TEAMS: England
CAREER: Test debut: 2010; ODI debut: 2010; First-class debut: 2001; List A debut: 2000; Twenty20 debut: 2003; County cap: 2007

KENT

AOC SAYS: Tredwell's matchwinning performance in England's crunch match against West Indies in the 2011 World Cup – coming as it did after months of carrying the drinks during a hectic winter – confirmed to the world what everyone at Kent, and his county captain Rob Key in particular, had been saying for years, namely that the 29-year-old offspinner is a bowler who can more than hold his own on the international stage. While not the biggest turner of the ball, Tredwell more than makes up for it with his probing accuracy, cunning flight and steady temperament – to say nothing of his resourceful batting and excellent fielding – and while the continued excellence of Graeme Swann means that he will have to content himself with only occasional appearances for his country, he remains a key component of the Spitfires attack in all forms of the game. A former England under 19 captain, Tredwell broke into the Kent side in 2001 but his all-round talents initially saw him labelled as a one-day specialist. However, his increasing assurance with the ball eventually saw him recognised as Kent's first-choice spinner in all forms of the game and in 2009 he enjoyed his best season in county cricket, taking 69 wickets in the Championship at an average of 26.63. Already a regular with the various academy and lions sides, he received his first call-up to the England ODI squad in 2008 and made his debut against Bangladesh at Dhaka in March 2010. His Test debut swiftly followed, and he did himself no harm by claiming match-figures of 6-181 as England recorded an easy victory. However, his finest moment in an England shirt to date was to follow almost a year later when he was selected for England's do-or-die World Cup match and returned figures of 4-48 to bowl Andrew Strauss' side to a crucial victory.

INSIDE TRACK: "He's our Mr Dependable. He's got a very good cricket brain and has made the spinner's position his own here at Kent through the consistency of his performances. He's a great fielder too, which is an element of his game that often gets overlooked. We think there is more to come from him as well, particularly with his batting – he's good enough to move up the order and score consistent runs for us. He's working hard at that area of his game." *Paul Fabrace*

JAMES TREDWELL

KENT

Batting & Fielding

	Mat	Inns	NO	Runs	HS	Ave	SR	100	50	Ct	St
Tests	1	1	0	37	37	37.00	58.73	0	0	1	0
ODIs	5	3	1	27	16	13.50	52.94	0	0	0	0
First-class	101	145	19	3005	123*	23.84	42.83	3	13	106	0
List A	153	106	36	1269	88	18.12	-	0	4	63	0
Twenty20	76	35	8	299	34	11.07	106.02	0	0	26	0

Bowling

	Mat	Balls	Runs	Wkts	BBI	BBM	Ave	Econ	SR	5w	10
Tests	1	390	181	6	4/82	6/181	30.16	2.78	65.0	0	0
ODIs	5	222	200	4	4/48	4/48	50.00	5.40	55.5	0	0
First-class	101	18033	9534	267	8/66	-	35.70	3.17	67.5	9	3
List A	153	6162	4853	144	6/27	6/27	33.70	4.72	42.7	1	0
Twenty20	76	1380	1660	69	4/21	4/21	24.05	7.21	20.0	0	0

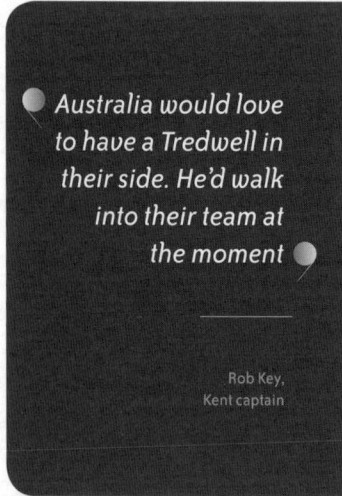

Australia would love to have a Tredwell in their side. He'd walk into their team at the moment

Rob Key,
Kent captain

KENT

NAME: Martin van Jaarsveld
BORN: June 18, 1974, Klerksdorp, South Africa
HEIGHT: 6ft 2in
SQUAD №: 41
NICKNAME: Jarre, VJ
OTHER TEAMS: South Africa,
Northamptonshire, Northern Transvaal,
Northerns, Titans
CAREER: Test debut: 2002; ODI debut: 2002;
First-class debut: 1994; List A debut: 1996;
T20 debut: 2004; County cap: 2005 (Kent)

AOC SAYS: An upright, methodical batsman who possesses near inexhaustible patience, as well as a more than useful part-time offspinner, van Jaarsveld has never failed to top 1,000 first-class runs in his time at the club and was so successful in 2008 – amassing 1,150 Championship runs and 907 limited-overs runs over the course of the season – that he was named as PCA Player of the Year. Kent's financial difficulties almost saw him move to Old Trafford in the close season, but Lancashire's own money worries eventually scuppered the deal, much to the delight of the Canterbury faithful. Registered as a Kolpak player having retired from international cricket in 2005, he will be heavily fancied to continue his prolific scoring in Division Two this season.

LAST WORD: "Jarre sets incredibly high standards, he prepares and practises as well as anyone I've seen in world cricket and his dedication is a brilliant example to our younger players. He's very generous with his time too. We're delighted that he has stayed and hopefully we will see him score plenty more runs for us in the future." *Peter Farbrace*

Batting & Fielding

	Mat	Inns	NO	Runs	HS	Ave	SR	100	50	Ct	St
Tests	9	15	2	397	73	30.53	47.54	0	3	11	0
ODIs	11	7	1	124	45	20.66	73.37	0	0	4	0
First-class	239	402	36	16775	262*	45.83	-	51	81	364	0
List A	261	243	41	8361	132*	41.39	-	15	52	149	0
Twenty20	96	87	11	1994	82	26.23	131.61	0	15	57	0

Bowling

	Mat	Balls	Runs	Wkts	BBI	BBM	Ave	Econ	SR	5w	10
Tests	9	42	28	0	-	-	-	4.00	-	0	0
ODIs	11	31	18	2	1/0	1/0	9.00	3.48	15.5	0	0
First-class	239	3678	1848	47	5/33	-	39.31	3.01	78.2	1	0
List A	261	1483	1304	36	3/13	3/13	36.22	5.27	41.1	0	0
Twenty20	96	150	191	7	3/25	3/25	27.28	7.64	21.4	0	0

FORMED: 1864
HOME GROUND: Old Trafford
ONE-DAY NAME: Lightning
CAPTAIN: Glen Chapple
2010 RESULTS: CC1: 4/9; CB40: 4/7 in Group A; FP t20: Quarter-finalists

Lancashire County Cricket Club

HONOURS

County Championship: (8) 1897, 1904, 1926, 1927, 1928, 1930, 1934, 1950(s); Gillette/NatWest/C&G/FP Trophy: (7) 1970, 1971, 1972, 1975, 1990, 1996, 1998; Benson and Hedges Cup: (4) 1984, 1990, 1995, 1996; Pro40/National League/CB40: 1999; Sunday League: (4) 1969, 1970, 1989, 1998

THE LOWDOWN

The club's recent financial struggles – which have hopefully come to an end now the local authorities have given their permission for the Old Trafford redevelopment to continue – have forced them to keep a relatively small playing staff, but the players they do have are either proven veterans such as captain Glen Chapple, established players now entering their prime such as Tom Smith or Steven Croft or youngsters of great promise such as Simon Kerrigan and Steve Parry. No side will be taking them lightly in any form of the game, and expect them to push hard in both the Championship and the FP t20, where their array of allrounders and canny spinners will come to the fore.

HEAD COACH: PETER MOORES

Moores played 231 first-class games for Sussex before he took over as coach and led the club to their first Championship title. He was appointed as England coach in 2007 but his tenure ended in unhappy circumstances when both he and then skipper Kevin Pietersen were dismissed in 2009. Moores had little time to feel sorry for himself, however, as he secured the job of Lancashire coach a month later.

With thanks to: Glen Chapple, Lancashire captain; Graham Hardcastle, www.lccc.co.uk and The Northern Echo;

	Mat	Inns	NO	Runs	HS	Ave	SR	100	50	Ct	St
S Chanderpaul	8	14	1	698	120	53.69	50.00	2	5	2	-
AG Prince	7	13	2	450	115	40.90	54.41	1	4	7	-
SJ Croft	16	26	3	883	93	38.39	52.12	0	8	13	-
KW Hogg	9	13	4	301	88	33.44	54.13	0	2	3	-
SI Mahmood	15	20	2	564	72	31.33	82.45	0	5	2	-
MJ Chilton	16	29	4	750	69	30.00	37.07	0	4	6	-
GD Cross	7	11	1	290	100*	29.00	58.23	1	1	12	0
LD Sutton	13	21	2	530	118	27.89	38.40	2	0	37	5
TC Smith	14	25	3	576	128	26.18	49.48	2	2	14	-
G Chapple	14	22	6	403	54*	25.18	54.38	0	2	4	-
SC Moore	9	17	0	426	61	25.05	51.76	0	2	6	-
PJ Horton	16	30	2	634	123	22.64	46.17	1	3	19	-
LA Procter	2	3	0	64	32	21.33	38.55	0	0	0	-
SM Katich	1	2	0	40	32	20.00	36.36	0	0	1	-
G Keedy	7	9	2	89	34	12.71	34.90	0	0	0	-
DBL Powell	4	4	1	29	16*	9.66	61.70	0	0	0	-
JM Anderson	4	5	1	35	25*	8.75	29.91	0	0	0	-
KR Brown	2	3	0	25	21	8.33	40.32	0	0	0	-
SC Kerrigan	13	15	5	45	16*	4.50	16.85	0	0	3	-

Batting & Fielding

	Mat	Overs	Mdns	Runs	Wkts	BBI	BBM	Ave	Econ	SR	5w	10
G Chapple	14	372.4	89	1027	52	5/27	9/96	19.75	2.75	43.0	2	0
JM Anderson	4	130.5	39	345	16	6/44	9/97	21.56	2.63	49.0	1	0
G Keedy	7	246.5	43	688	31	7/68	10/128	22.19	2.78	47.7	2	0
TC Smith	14	279.5	58	913	32	6/94	9/134	28.53	3.26	52.4	1	0
SC Kerrigan	13	319.0	66	967	30	6/74	7/87	32.23	3.03	63.8	3	0
KW Hogg	9	202.2	48	650	20	4/53	6/103	32.50	3.21	60.7	0	0
SI Mahmood	15	348.0	54	1263	33	5/55	7/76	38.27	3.62	63.2	1	0
LA Procter	2	7.3	0	47	1	1/26	1/39	47.00	6.26	45.0	0	0
DBL Powell	4	99.0	16	343	7	2/45	4/133	49.00	3.46	84.8	0	0
SJ Croft	16	14.0	2	51	1	1/17	1/17	51.00	3.64	84.0	0	0

Bowling

Batting & Fielding

	Mat	Inns	NO	Runs	HS	Ave	SR	100	50	Ct	St
LA Procter	6	4	1	165	97	55.00	94.82	0	2	2	-
AG Prince	6	5	1	207	102*	51.75	97.18	1	0	1	-
SJ Croft	13	12	3	436	93*	48.44	95.61	0	4	5	-
SC Moore	8	8	1	337	118	48.14	105.97	2	1	2	-
KR Brown	7	7	1	286	65*	47.66	81.01	0	3	2	-
PJ Horton	13	12	2	383	78*	38.30	81.48	0	4	5	-
J Clark	1	1	0	32	32	32.00	80.00	0	0	0	-
LD Sutton	10	7	2	144	47	28.80	73.46	0	0	8	3
KW Hogg	11	7	3	100	36*	25.00	95.23	0	0	2	-
TC Smith	8	8	0	175	61	21.87	82.54	0	1	2	-
GD Cross	7	5	0	108	30	21.60	100.93	0	0	3	2
MJ Chilton	8	6	0	124	68	20.66	99.20	0	1	4	-
G Chapple	3	1	0	13	13	13.00	43.33	0	0	0	-
SD Parry	12	7	2	58	26	11.60	89.23	0	0	2	-
SI Mahmood	6	2	0	23	16	11.50	143.75	0	0	0	-
DBL Powell	10	5	2	32	11*	10.66	82.05	0	0	5	-
G Keedy	7	3	1	12	11	6.00	70.58	0	0	2	-
SP Cheetham	2	1	0	4	4	4.00	80.00	0	0	0	-
OJ Newby	1	1	0	0	0	0.00	0.00	0	0	0	-
JM Anderson	1	1	1	2	2*	-	50.00	0	0	1	-
GS Montgomery	3	1	1	0	0*	-	0	0	0	1	-

Bowling

	Mat	Overs	Mdns	Runs	Wkts	BBI	Ave	Econ	SR	5w
MJ Chilton	8	4.0	0	19	1	1/19	19.00	4.75	24.0	0
G Keedy	7	53.0	0	257	12	4/41	21.41	4.84	26.5	0
LA Procter	6	38.0	0	203	9	3/29	22.55	5.34	25.3	0
SI Mahmood	6	46.0	2	255	11	4/40	23.18	5.54	25.0	0
TC Smith	8	55.0	0	339	13	3/49	26.07	6.16	25.3	0
KW Hogg	11	71.2	3	423	14	2/27	30.21	5.92	30.5	0
DBL Powell	10	59.4	3	333	9	4/49	37.00	5.58	39.7	0
SP Cheetham	2	10.0	0	77	2	1/38	38.50	7.70	30.0	0
SD Parry	12	87.5	0	471	11	2/18	42.81	5.36	47.9	0
OJ Newby	1	8.0	0	45	1	1/45	45.00	5.62	48.0	0
SJ Croft	13	25.0	0	176	3	1/17	58.66	7.04	50.0	0
GS Montgomery	3	17.0	0	127	1	1/61	127.00	7.47	102.0	0
JM Anderson	1	8.0	1	38	0	-	-	4.75	-	0
G Chapple	3	22.0	1	136	0	-	-	6.18	-	0

www.lccc.co.uk / tel: 0161 874 3333

	Mat	Inns	NO	Runs	HS	Ave	SR	100	50	Ct	St
TC Smith	17	17	2	543	92*	36.20	119.60	0	3	9	-
SM Katich	9	8	1	185	41*	26.42	117.83	0	0	5	-
SJ Croft	17	16	1	394	88	26.26	127.92	0	2	13	-
SC Moore	17	16	3	331	83*	25.46	152.53	0	3	9	-
PJ Horton	17	16	3	270	44	20.76	106.29	0	0	5	-
GD Cross	17	12	3	184	65*	20.44	138.34	0	1	7	2
NL McCullum	13	11	2	155	32*	17.22	124.00	0	0	5	-
SI Mahmood	15	6	1	84	34	16.80	190.90	0	0	9	-
MJ Chilton	11	10	5	82	34	16.40	110.81	0	0	4	-
G Chapple	14	7	2	77	28*	15.40	126.22	0	0	2	-
SD Parry	17	5	4	13	7	13.00	108.33	0	0	1	-
SC Kerrigan	12	1	1	4	4*	-	200.00	0	0	6	-
KW Hogg	1	1	1	2	2*	-	100.00	0	0	0	-
JM Anderson	2	1	1	0	0*	-	-	0	0	2	-

Batting & Fielding

	Mat	Overs	Mdns	Runs	Wkts	BBI	Ave	Econ	SR	5w
SJ Croft	17	8.5	0	70	5	3/18	14.00	7.92	10.6	0
SD Parry	17	60.0	0	427	26	4/28	16.42	7.11	13.8	0
SI Mahmood	15	53.0	0	430	23	4/21	18.69	8.11	13.8	0
TC Smith	17	41.4	0	306	13	3/12	23.53	7.34	19.2	0
SC Kerrigan	12	40.0	0	264	11	3/17	24.00	6.60	21.8	0
G Keedy	4	12.1	0	105	4	2/27	26.25	8.63	18.2	0
NL McCullum	13	50.0	0	325	11	3/31	29.54	6.50	27.2	0
G Chapple	14	45.5	0	397	13	3/36	30.53	8.66	21.1	0
JM Anderson	2	8.0	0	77	2	2/38	38.50	9.62	24.0	0
KW Hogg	1	2.0	0	17	0	-	-	8.50	-	0
SM Katich	9	2.0	0	14	0	-	-	7.00	-	0
DBL Powell	4	9.0	0	87	0	-	-	9.66	-	0

Bowling

ANDREA AGATHAGELOU

LANCASHIRE

NAME: Andrea Peter Agathagelou
BORN: November 16, 1989, Rustenberg
HEIGHT: 6ft 3in
SQUAD №: 11
OTHER TEAMS: Lions, North West
CAREER: First-class debut: 2008; List A debut: 2008

AOC SAYS: One of the standout players for the club's Second XI in 2010 and a prolific runscorer in Lancashire league cricket, Agathagelou has been awarded a full-time deal for 2011 and will provide keeping back-up to Gareth Cross. Qualified as a Kolpak player thanks to his Cypriot passport, he has enjoyed plenty of success at first-class level in his native South Africa; he followed up his haul of 1,076 first-class runs from 13 games in 2009/10 with 578 runs from nine matches in 2010/11. Primarily a top-order batsman, the 21-year-old is also a more than useful leggie who claimed nine wickets at 7.88 in the Second XI Championship last term in addition to being a fine gloveman.

LAST WORD: "I think he's going to come in and straight away challenge for first-team cricket. He captained the Second XI at times last year, looks a real talent and has been going along nicely in first-class cricket in South Africa, albeit at a level just below the franchise sides." *Graham Hardcastle*

Batting & Fielding

	Mat	Inns	NO	Runs	HS	Ave	SR	100	50	Ct	St
First-class	26	51	2	1813	158	37.00	53.99	4	11	37	0
List A	23	22	2	654	94	32.70	78.13	0	5	9	1

Bowling

	Mat	Balls	Runs	Wkts	BBI	BBM	Ave	Econ	SR	5w	10
First-class	26	441	299	6	2/62	3/66	49.83	4.06	73.5	0	0
List A	23	30	35	0	-	-	-	7.00	-	0	0

NAME: James Michael Anderson
BORN: July 30, 1982, Burnley
HEIGHT: 6ft 2in
SQUAD Nº: 9
NICKNAME: Jimmy
OTHER TEAMS: England, Auckland
CAREER: Test debut: 2003; ODI debut: 2002; T20I debut: 2007; First-class debut: 2002; List A debut: 2000; T20 debut: 2004; County cap: 2003

LANCASHIRE

AOC SAYS: England's spearhead during the 2010/11 Ashes, Anderson is one of the most complete bowlers in the international game. He burst onto the scene in 2002, claiming 50 first-class wickets to book a slot on the England National Academy tour to Australia, and following a swathe of injuries to the first team he was called up to make his ODI debut at Melbourne. In the following game he produced a spell of 1-12 from 10 overs at Adelaide, and in the summer of 2003 became the youngest player in Lancashire history to take a first-class hat-trick, just one week before he marked his Test debut with a five-wicket haul. He was subsequently picked in England's 2003 World Cup squad, but could do little to galvanise a campaign that was hindered by the squad's decision to boycott matches played in Zimbabwe, and – despite a one-day hat-trick against South Africa in 2004 – his international career stuttered following a stress fracture to his back and some ill-fated technical tweaks to his action. Undeterred, Anderson went back to Lancashire, returned to his natural action and emerged a better bowler, reclaiming his place for the Test series against India in 2007 and graduating to England's attack leader against West Indies in 2009. An increasingly versatile bowler, Anderson is at his best with a new ball – he is one of very few bowlers in the world who can swing the ball either way with no change to his action – but his increasing mastery of reverse-swing has made him a threat in all conditions. Also an exceptional fielder, Anderson is a dogged lower-order batsman and famously took part in a defiant last-wicket stand with Monty Panesar in the first Test of the 2009 Ashes, although his exploits in Australia this winter have now eclipsed even that performance.

INSIDE TRACK: When the ball is swinging there is no better bowler in world cricket than Jimmy. He is truly awesome. The great swing bowlers of the past, like Sir Ian Botham, would send outswingers to right-handers as their stock deliveries and then throw in, say, one inswinger an over to keep them guessing. Where Anderson is different is that he keeps mixing it up with no discernible change of action, so a typical over could contain three of each. And he swings the ball late, too, which makes batting against him such a challenge. It is a real skill." *Nasser Hussain, former England captain*

JAMES ANDERSON

LANCASHIRE

Batting & Fielding

	Mat	Inns	NO	Runs	HS	Ave	SR	100	50	Ct	St
Tests	57	76	31	524	34	11.64	35.38	0	0	25	0
ODIs	142	60	32	187	20*	6.67	41.28	0	0	38	0
T20Is	19	4	3	1	1*	1.00	50.00	0	0	3	0
First-class	118	138	54	818	37*	9.73	-	0	0	50	0
List A	193	81	49	280	20*	8.75	-	0	0	47	0
Twenty20	39	8	6	22	16	11.00	95.65	0	0	8	0

Bowling

	Mat	Balls	Runs	Wkts	BBI	BBM	Ave	Econ	SR	5w	10
Tests	57	12056	6595	212	7/43	11/71	31.10	3.28	56.8	10	1
ODIs	142	7062	5949	190	5/23	5/23	31.31	5.05	37.1	1	0
T20Is	19	422	552	18	3/23	3/23	30.66	7.84	23.4	0	0
First-class	118	22363	12137	439	7/43	-	27.64	3.25	50.9	22	3
List A	193	9382	7656	262	5/23	5/23	29.22	4.89	35.8	1	0
Twenty20	39	831	1136	35	3/23	3/23	32.45	8.20	23.7	0	0

He has improved his game so much he's either No.1 or No.2. Obviously Steyn is a class bowler. It's neck and neck for those two as the best fast bowlers in the world

David Saker,
England bowling coach

NAME: Karl Robert Brown
BORN: May 17, 1988, Bolton
HEIGHT: 5ft 10in
SQUAD Nº: 14
NICKNAME: Brownie, Charlie
CAREER: First-class debut: 2006; List A
debut: 2007

LANCASHIRE

AOC SAYS: Brown joined the Lancashire squad in 2006 from the club's scholarship and academy programmes and enjoyed a breakthrough season in one-day cricket during 2010, scoring 286 runs in seven innings at 47.66, including a top-score of 65* off 70 balls against the Unicorns. A free-flowing opening batsman who loves to take the aerial route, Brown represented England at under 19 level and made a century against an Indian attack that included current internationals Ishant Sharma and Piyush Chawla in 2007. A prolific runscorer at second XI level, Brown has played grade cricket in Australia and looks likely to enjoy an extended run in the first team this season.

LAST WORD: "He's a talented one-day cricketer, he hits the ball as sweetly as you like and his natural game is to score quickly. He'll want to build on his performances from last year and make the step up to playing four-day cricket, which he's got a great chance of doing if he can just improve his consistency that little bit." *Glen Chapple*

Batting & Fielding

	Mat	Inns	NO	Runs	HS	Ave	SR	100	50	Ct	St
First-class	9	15	1	181	40	12.92	42.09	0	0	7	0
List A	12	12	1	358	65*	32.54	78.85	0	3	3	0

Bowling

	Mat	Balls	Runs	Wkts	BBI	BBM	Ave	Econ	SR	5w	10
First-class	9	66	44	2	2/30	2/37	22.00	4.00	33.0	0	0
List A	12	-	-	-	-	-	-	-	-	-	-

GLEN CHAPPLE

RHB RMF W5 MVP35

LANCASHIRE

NAME: Glen Chapple
BORN: January 23, 1974, Skipton
HEIGHT: 6ft 1in
SQUAD Nº: 3
NICKNAME: Boris, Chappie
OTHER TEAMS: England
CAREER: ODI debut: 2006; First-class debut: 1992; List A debut: 1993; T20 debut: 2003; County cap: 1994

AOC SAYS: A mere 55 runs is all that separates Chapple from becoming only the fifth player in Lancashire's history to achieve the double of 7,000 runs and 700 wickets in first-class cricket. An adaptable swing and seam bowler who rarely gives the batsman anything to hit, he has led the club's attack with distinction for umpteen seasons but never more so than during the 1996 NatWest final when he took 6-18 to help skittle Essex for an incredible 57. Also a resourceful, hard-hitting batsman good enough to register six first-class centuries, Chapple was appointed club captain in 2009 and appears to be flourishing under the responsibility – he averages 21.97 with the ball and 28.32 with bat since taking on the role.

LAST WORD: "Chapple has just been exceptional over the last two seasons, he carries the attack in a lot of ways, bowling over after over and getting good players out. It feels like he might actually be getting better – he still has pace when he needs it but his skills, his cutters and so on, look really sharp at the minute." *Graham Hardcastle*

Batting & Fielding

	Mat	Inns	NO	Runs	HS	Ave	SR	100	50	Ct	St
ODIs	1	1	0	14	14	14.00	200.00	0	0	0	0
First-class	252	346	65	7104	155	25.28	-	6	33	83	0
List A	269	154	41	2000	81*	17.69	-	0	9	60	0
Twenty20	50	28	9	280	55*	14.73	110.67	0	1	14	0

Bowling

	Mat	Balls	Runs	Wkts	BBI	BBM	Ave	Econ	SR	5w	10
ODIs	1	24	14	0	-	-	-	3.50	-	0	0
First-class	252	42769	21124	780	7/53	-	27.08	2.96	54.8	31	2
List A	269	11583	8716	299	6/18	6/18	29.15	4.51	38.7	4	0
Twenty20	50	935	1197	50	3/36	3/36	23.94	7.68	18.7	0	0

NAME: Steven Philip Cheetham
BORN: September 5, 1987, Oldham
HEIGHT: 6ft 5in
SQUAD Nº: 18
NICKNAME: Cheets
OTHER TEAMS: Surrey
CAREER: First-class debut: 2007; List A debut: 2008

AOC SAYS: A tall, athletic seamer with an unconventional action, Cheetham had to spend most of the last two seasons battling his way back to full fitness after a bone spur on his ankle forced him to undergo surgery in 2009. Capable of consistently breaking the 85mph barrier, the 23-year-old is a product of the club's academy and plays for Heywood CC in the Central Lancashire League. A successful season of second XI cricket – which saw him claim 21 Championship wickets at 24.14 – and a month spent on loan at Surrey in 2010 indicate that he has returned to something approaching his best so expect him to push hard for first-team opportunities this summer.

LAST WORD: "Cheets' return is almost like having a completely new player for this season, he's had so many injury problems he's just keen to get out there and show us what he can do. He's a thinking bowler; he's very meticulous in his planning and preparation." *Glen Chapple*

Batting & Fielding

	Mat	Inns	NO	Runs	HS	Ave	SR	100	50	Ct	St
First-class	2	1	1	0	0*	-	0.00	0	0	1	0
List A	10	5	3	20	13*	10.00	43.47	0	0	1	0

Bowling

	Mat	Balls	Runs	Wkts	BBI	BBM	Ave	Econ	SR	5w	10
First-class	2	240	198	3	2/71	2/71	66.00	4.95	80.0	0	0
List A	10	378	399	14	4/32	4/32	28.50	6.33	27.0	0	0

MARK CHILTON

LANCASHIRE

NAME: Mark James Chilton
BORN: October 2, 1976, Sheffield
HEIGHT: 6ft 2in
SQUAD Nº: 21
NICKNAME: Chilly, Jimmy Chill, Rodney
CAREER: First-class debut: 1997; List A debut: 1997; T20 debut: 2003; County cap: 2002

AOC SAYS: An enduring presence in the Lancashire batting order for more than a decade, Chilton is an adaptable batsman capable of slotting in anywhere in the top six as well as a useful medium-pacer when a long standing back complaint allows him to bowl. Once considered to be a four-day specialist, Chilton has enjoyed a second coming as a one-day player since Peter Moores took charge of the club and averages 37.18 in List A cricket across the last two seasons. A former student of Manchester Grammar, the same school that educated Red Rose greats Mike Atherton and John Crawley, Chilton captained Lancashire for three seasons from 2005 but stood down in 2007 to concentrate on his batting after he steered the club to Twenty20 Finals Day and came agonisingly close to ending the club's barren run in the County Championship. As a mark of his dedication, the club has nominated 2011 as his Benefit Year.

LAST WORD: "Chilly's a great character to have around the club, he'll bat anywhere and do whatever is required. I know he wasn't overly happy with his results last year and is looking to score big this season. He'll be an important player for us this year." *Glen Chapple*

Batting & Fielding

	Mat	Inns	NO	Runs	HS	Ave	SR	100	50	Ct	St
First-class	182	297	27	8909	131	32.99	-	20	36	132	0
List A	184	171	24	4480	115	30.47	-	5	21	57	0
Twenty20	52	38	15	376	38	16.34	93.53	0	0	20	0

Bowling

	Mat	Balls	Runs	Wkts	BBI	BBM	Ave	Econ	SR	5w	10
First-class	182	1343	667	12	2/3	-	55.58	2.97	111.9	0	0
List A	184	1106	1011	42	5/26	5/26	24.07	5.48	26.3	1	0
Twenty20	52	-	-	-	-	-	-	-	-	-	-

NAME: Steven John Croft
BORN: October 11, 1984, Blackpool
HEIGHT: 5ft 11in
SQUAD Nº: 15
NICKNAME: Crofty
OTHER TEAMS: Auckland
CAREER: First-class debut: 2005; List A debut: 2002; T20 debut: 2006

AOC SAYS: Croft started the 2010 season in terrific form, registering a half-century in his first six innings across all competitions, and ended the campaign as the club's leading runscorer in the Championship with a tally of 883 runs at 38.39. An attacking, powerful batsman who often produces his best in pressure situations and has caught the eye of the Sky punditry team on several occasions, Croft is also a lively seamer who possesses a useful bouncer. The first Lancashire academy graduate to be awarded a professional contract by the club, he has appeared as an overseas player for Auckland Aces and represented England in the 2010 Hong Kong Sixes tournament, a format ideally suited to a player who can clear the ropes with ease and has a penchant for pulling off the spectacular in the field.

LAST WORD: "I like the look of Steven Croft. He gives the ball a whack, bowls his overs and fields brilliantly, and best of all he seems to love the big occasion." *Nasser Hussain, former England captain*

Batting & Fielding

	Mat	Inns	NO	Runs	HS	Ave	SR	100	50	Ct	St
First-class	59	90	9	2509	122	30.97	50.32	1	17	48	0
List A	76	67	15	1663	93*	31.98	-	0	11	27	0
Twenty20	58	53	8	1174	88	26.08	118.82	0	5	31	0

Bowling

	Mat	Balls	Runs	Wkts	BBI	BBM	Ave	Econ	SR	5w	10
First-class	59	2149	1375	31	4/51	4/100	44.35	3.83	69.3	0	0
List A	76	1392	1241	39	4/24	4/24	31.82	5.34	35.6	0	0
Twenty20	58	423	580	22	3/6	3/6	26.36	8.22	19.2	0	0

GARETH CROSS

RHB RM WK

LANCASHIRE

NAME: Gareth David Cross
BORN: June 20, 1984, Bury
HEIGHT: 5ft 9in
SQUAD Nº: 7
NICKNAME: Crossy
CAREER: First-class debut: 2005; List A
debut: 2002; T20 debut: 2006

AOC SAYS: This season could be an important one in Cross' career. With the departure of Luke Sutton to Derbyshire, Cross will start the season as Lancashire's first-choice keeper and many pundits suspect it could be the making of him. A stylish gloveman and a punishing middle-order batsman who once scored 24 runs off a single Mushtaq Ahmed over in the Championship, Cross is also a handy medium-pacer and recorded figures of 2-26 in a Friends Provident Trophy match in 2008. While he didn't enjoy the most fruitful of seasons last term, he did find the time to register his maiden first-class century, against Hampshire at The Rose Bowl.

LAST WORD: "Mal Loye once told me that Cross will play for England, he's got that much talent, but the things is you don't get to play for your country playing for Lancashire's Second XI. He's a dangerous batsman who can turn a game in a flash and my tip for the club's breakthrough player this season." *Graham Hardcastle*

Batting & Fielding

	Mat	Inns	NO	Runs	HS	Ave	SR	100	50	Ct	St
First-class	15	24	2	599	100*	27.22	67.68	1	4	39	8
List A	42	34	3	599	76	19.32	-	0	1	24	11
Twenty20	51	37	9	497	65*	17.75	133.60	0	2	32	12

Bowling

	Mat	Balls	Runs	Wkts	BBI	BBM	Ave	Econ	SR	5w	10
First-class	15	-	-	-	-	-	-	-	-	-	-
List A	42	36	26	2	2/26	2/26	13.00	4.33	18.0	0	0
Twenty20	51	-	-	-	-	-	-	-	-	-	-

NAME: Kyle William Hogg
BORN: July 2, 1983, Birmingham
HEIGHT: 6ft 4in
SQUAD №: 22
NICKNAME: Hoggy
MAJOR TEAMS: Nottinghamshire, Otago, Worcestershire
CAREER: First-class debut: 2001; List A debut: 2001; T20 debut: 2003

LANCASHIRE

AOC SAYS: The grandson of legendary West Indian spinner Sonny Ramadhin, who played for Lancashire in the mid 60s, Hogg is a seamer who is particularly adept at varying his pace as well as a feisty lower-order batsman. He first broke through into the Lancashire side as a teenager back in 2001 and in his second season claimed 26 wickets at 19.19 in List A cricket to prompt talk of a possible call-up to the England one-day side. Since then a succession of injuries have hampered his development, but he has remained an important member of Lancashire's one-day team and has looked an increasingly assured member of the Championship side over the last two seasons, not least when he made a career-best 88 in the Roses match at Old Trafford in 2010.

LAST WORD: "He's a skilful bowler who's very accurate and a destructive batter. It feels like he's been around forever because he started out so young, but we feel he's only getting better and is ready to deliver his best season yet." *Glen Chapple*

Batting & Fielding

	Mat	Inns	NO	Runs	HS	Ave	SR	100	50	Ct	St
First-class	64	78	11	1649	88	24.61	58.30	0	11	16	0
List A	126	78	21	935	66*	16.40	69.10	0	1	22	0
Twenty20	22	16	3	211	44	16.23	140.66	0	0	3	0

Bowling

	Mat	Balls	Runs	Wkts	BBI	BBM	Ave	Econ	SR	5w	10
First-class	64	8466	4406	124	5/48	-	35.53	3.12	68.2	1	0
List A	126	4788	3785	127	4/20	4/20	29.80	4.74	37.7	0	0
Twenty20	22	283	405	12	2/10	2/10	33.75	8.58	23.5	0	0

LANCASHIRE

PAUL HORTON   RHB RM R2 MVP89

NAME: Paul James Horton
BORN: September 20, 1982, Sydney
HEIGHT: 5ft 10in
SQUAD Nº: 20
NICKNAME: Horts
OTHER TEAMS: Matabeleland Tuskers
CAREER: First-class debut: 2003; List A debut: 2003; T20 debut: 2005; County cap: 2007

AOC SAYS: An Australia-born top-order batsman who can graft or score quickly as the situation requires, Horton's career took off in 2007 with a first-class haul of 1,116 runs and a top-score of 152. He followed this up with a further 1,087 runs in 2008, although he has yet to quite hit those heights in England since and will be mildly disappointed with his tally of 634 Championship runs last season. Especially strong off his legs, Horton has spent this winter turning out for Matabeleland Tuskers in Zimbabwe and has enjoyed considerable success; he scored 773 first-class runs in just nine matches including his maiden double-century, a brilliant 209 against Southern Rocks. Also a fantastic fielder and a useful part-time wicketkeeper, Horton will be one of Lancashire's key batsmen this season.

LAST WORD: "Paul's very much one of our senior batsmen now. He's pretty adaptable, he can be very fluent but he can also knuckle down if he needs to. I think his time in Zimbabwe will really help him push on; he'll have a lot of confidence after playing so well out there." *Glen Chapple*

Batting & Fielding

	Mat	Inns	NO	Runs	HS	Ave	SR	100	50	Ct	St
First-class	84	140	12	5092	209	39.78	50.17	12	25	74	1
List A	60	55	4	1463	111*	28.68	-	2	7	20	0
Twenty20	37	35	5	634	71	21.13	111.61	0	2	14	0

Bowling

	Mat	Balls	Runs	Wkts	BBI	BBM	Ave	Econ	SR	5w	10
First-class	84	18	16	0	-	-	-	5.33	-	0	0
List A	60	-	-	-	-	-	-	-	-	-	-
Twenty20	37	-	-	-	-	-	-	-	-	-	-

NAME: Gary Keedy
BORN: November 27, 1974, Wakefield
HEIGHT: 5ft 11in
SQUAD Nº: 23
NICKNAME: Keeds
OTHER TEAMS: Yorkshire
CAREER: First-class debut: 1994; List A debut: 1995; T20 debut: 2004; County cap: 2000 (Lancashire)

LANCASHIRE

AOC SAYS: Consistently one of the best spinners in county cricket, Keedy joined Lancashire in 1994 having turned out once for his native Yorkshire. A deceptive bowler who favours using flight and guile to deceive the batsman, he reportedly came close to winning a spot on the tours to Bangladesh and Pakistan in 2003 and 2005 respectively, but ultimately it looks like he will have to content himself with a career spent excelling in first-class cricket, although he did deliver a glimpse of what might have been when he took 3-70 against Australia for England Lions in 2009. Having missed the early part of last season due to a broken collarbone, the 36-year-old made up for lost time by claming 31 wickets at 22.19 in the Championship in the final seven matches of the season.

LAST WORD: "Keeds is one of those bowlers who is unafraid to give the ball a bit of air, and when he's bowling at his best he's got great control. He's been brilliant for us over the years and has been working hard with our other young spinners to pass on what he knows, although he's not done playing quite yet!" Glen Chapple

Batting & Fielding

	Mat	Inns	NO	Runs	HS	Ave	SR	100	50	Ct	St
First-class	195	221	106	1304	64	11.33	-	0	2	46	0
List A	75	26	11	141	33	9.40	-	0	0	11	0
Twenty20	47	7	4	19	9*	6.33	118.75	0	0	4	0

Bowling

	Mat	Balls	Runs	Wkts	BBI	BBM	Ave	Econ	SR	5w	10
First-class	195	39562	18578	587	7/68	-	31.64	2.81	67.3	29	6
List A	75	3088	2383	90	5/30	5/30	26.47	4.63	34.3	1	0
Twenty20	47	910	995	43	4/15	4/15	23.13	6.56	21.1	0	0

SIMON KERRIGAN

RHB SLA

LANCASHIRE

NAME: Simon Christopher Kerrigan
BORN: May 10, 1989, Preston
HEIGHT: 5ft 9in
SQUAD Nº: 10
CAREER: First-class debut: 2010; T20 debut: 2010

AOC SAYS: Named as the club's Young Player of the Season last term, Kerrigan shouldered the responsibility of being Lancashire's first-choice spinner in the Championship for much of 2010 following the injury-enforced absence of Gary Keedy, and his tally of 30 wickets at 32.23 – to go with 11 Twenty20 scalps – ensured that his senior partner was not as missed as many feared he would be. Originally a medium-pacer, Kerrigan converted to spin in his mid-teens and has met with considerable success for his club side Ormskirk and the Lancashire Second XI. Willing and able to get plenty of revs on his deliveries, Kerrigan is a big spinner of the ball who specialises in getting his deliveries 'up and down' sharply and marked his Championship debut with a five-wicket haul against Warwickshire.

LAST WORD: "An outstanding prospect with a massive future in the game. He has the ability to overtake Monty Panesar as the country's number one left-arm spinner." *Mal Loye, former Lancashire teammate*

Batting & Fielding

	Mat	Inns	NO	Runs	HS	Ave	SR	100	50	Ct	St
First-class	13	15	5	45	16*	4.50	16.85	0	0	3	0
Twenty20	12	1	1	4	4*	-	200.00	0	0	6	0

Bowling

	Mat	Balls	Runs	Wkts	BBI	BBM	Ave	Econ	SR	5w	10
First-class	13	1914	967	30	6/74	7/87	32.23	3.03	63.8	3	0
Twenty20	12	240	264	11	3/17	3/17	24.00	6.60	21.8	0	0

OVERSEAS PLAYER

NAME: Mohamed Farveez Maharoof
BORN: September 7, 1984, Colombo
HEIGHT: 6ft 4in
SQUAD Nº: 5
MAJOR TEAMS: Sri Lanka, Delhi Daredevils, Wayamba
CAREER: Test debut: 2004; ODI debut: 2004; T20I debut: 2006; First-class debut: 2002; List A debut: 2003; T20 debut: 2004

AOC SAYS: A bowling allrounder who was tipped for big things from an early age, Maharoof hasn't quite managed to consistently deliver the performances his talent suggests he is capable of, although time remains very much on his side. An upright, busy seamer and elegant batsman, Maharoof was a sensation at schoolboy level, with a top-score of 243 and best figures of 8-20, and captained Sri Lanka's under 19 side before he was fast-tracked into the national side in 2004. Injuries, a loss of form and the emergence of Angelo Mathews and Thisara Perera eventually saw him jettisoned from the side, although he did claim an ODI hat-trick against India in 2010 and a strong season in county cricket could well see him reclaim his place on the international stage.

LAST WORD: "Farveez has a track record of getting important runs and picking up vital wickets. He's available to us for the full season and will be a competitive addition to our squad." *Peter Moores*

Batting & Fielding

	Mat	Inns	NO	Runs	HS	Ave	SR	100	50	Ct	St
Tests	20	31	4	538	72	19.92	40.00	0	3	6	0
ODIs	94	64	15	984	69*	20.08	85.19	0	2	20	0
T20Is	7	4	1	23	13*	7.66	85.18	0	0	2	0
First-class	55	80	7	1758	118	24.08	49.77	3	6	33	0
List A	158	118	25	2077	70*	22.33	78.22	0	7	36	0
Twenty20	45	30	11	293	39	15.42	114.90	0	0	13	0

Bowling

	Mat	Balls	Runs	Wkts	BBI	BBM	Ave	Econ	SR	5w	10
Tests	20	2628	1458	24	4/52	5/122	60.75	3.32	109.5	0	0
ODIs	94	3932	3133	121	6/14	6/14	25.89	4.78	32.4	2	0
T20Is	7	144	173	7	2/18	2/18	24.71	7.20	20.5	0	0
First-class	55	6174	3336	103	7/73	-	32.38	3.24	59.9	1	0
List A	158	6534	5239	186	6/14	6/14	28.16	4.81	35.1	2	0
Twenty20	45	912	1125	45	3/21	3/21	25.00	7.40	20.2	0	0

SAJ MAHMOOD

RHB RFM MVP25

NAME: Sajid Iqbal Mahmood
BORN: December 21, 1981, Bolton
HEIGHT: 6ft 4in
SQUAD Nº: 19
NICKNAME: Saj, King
OTHER TEAMS: England, Western Australia
CAREER: Test debut: 2006; ODI debut: 2004;
T20I debut: 2006; First-class debut: 2002;
List A debut: 2002; T20 debut: 2003; County
cap: 2007

AOC SAYS: A player possessing immense physical gifts, Mahmood – the cousin of boxing champion Amir Khan – has long been considered as someone with the ability to succeed at international level. A tall, genuinely fast bowler who can utilise either conventional or reverse-swing, an accomplished athlete in the field and a fearsome striker of a cricket ball, he was initially signed by Lancashire on a scholarship deal in 2002 on the back of some searingly quick spells in the Bolton leagues, and was soon singled out by the ECB's former academy coach Rodney Marsh as a player who should be fast-tracked into the national side. A succession of injuries to England's senior bowlers meant that it was only a matter of time before he got his wish, and Mahmood – after a less than ideal ODI debut against New Zealand at Bristol – has often offered glimpses of what he could achieve, never more so than during his ferocious three-wicket burst on debut at Lord's against Sri Lanka in 2006 and his return of 4-22 against Pakistan at Headingley later that summer. But consistency at the highest level has eluded him and he has gradually fallen away from the international side, although the chairman of England selectors Geoff Miller has indicated Mahmood remains a player they regularly keeps tabs on. The 29-year-old, who famously worked as a shelf stacker prior to joining the Lancashire staff, enjoyed mixed fortunes in 2010, claiming 33 first-class wickets at 38.27 but smashing 564 runs at an average of 31.33, including a top-score of 72 against Warwickshire. He also proved a revelation in the FP t20, claiming 23 wickets at 18.69 and scoring 84 runs, including a blistering 34 in Lancashire's unfortunate defeat to Essex in the quarter-final, a return that prompted Western Australia to recruit him as an overseas pro for the 2010/11 Big Bash. If he can ally his new-found potency with the bat with the discipline he displays when bowling at his best, there is no reason Mahmood shouldn't once again challenge for higher honours.

INSIDE TRACK: "Saj is going through a really positive process, a bit like the one Ryan Sidebottom went through – he played early, got an opportunity, saw what was going on and went back to county cricket to hone his skills. I have watched him in the nets and he is bowling well and just has to keep progressing. He is a young man getting ready for his next England chance." *Peter Moores*

Batting & Fielding

	Mat	Inns	NO	Runs	HS	Ave	SR	100	50	Ct	St
Tests	8	11	1	81	34	8.10	50.31	0	0	0	0
ODIs	26	15	4	85	22*	7.72	84.15	0	0	1	0
T20Is	4	2	2	1	1*	-	50.00	0	0	1	0
First-class	96	122	18	1698	94	16.32	67.89	0	8	22	0
List A	137	72	21	435	29	8.52	-	0	0	18	0
Twenty20	57	22	6	138	34	8.62	148.38	0	0	15	0

Bowling

	Mat	Balls	Runs	Wkts	BBI	BBM	Ave	Econ	SR	5w	10
Tests	8	1130	762	20	4/22	6/130	38.10	4.04	56.5	0	0
ODIs	26	1197	1169	30	4/50	4/50	38.96	5.85	39.9	0	0
T20Is	4	84	155	3	1/31	1/31	51.66	11.07	28.0	0	0
First-class	96	14231	8754	264	6/30	-	33.15	3.69	53.9	7	1
List A	137	6017	5192	192	5/16	5/16	27.04	5.17	31.3	1	0
Twenty20	57	1187	1579	64	4/21	4/21	24.67	7.98	18.5	0	0

I have had time to reflect upon what I need to improve on. I think my game has moved forward mentally, physically and tactically

Sajid Mahmood

STEPHEN MOORE

RHB RM R3

LANCASHIRE

NAME: Stephen Colin Moore
BORN: November 4, 1980, Johannesburg
HEIGHT: 6ft 1in
SQUAD Nº: 6
NICKNAME: Mandy
OTHER TEAMS: Worcestershire
CAREER: First-class debut: 2003; List A debut: 2003; T20 debut: 2003

AOC SAYS: A prolific runscorer for Worcestershire before he joined Lancashire, Moore is a resourceful opening batsman who has represented England Lions and long been touted as a player who could make the step up to international cricket. Born in South Africa to English parents, Moore moved to England when he turned 18 and was snapped up by Lancashire ahead of the 2010 season. A keen musician who plays both the guitar and the saxophone, Moore notched two superb one-day hundreds in 40-over cricket last year, including one against his former employers at New Road, but struggled for form in the Championship before a dislocated shoulder picked up in the Twenty20 quarter-final against Essex brought an early end to his season. A dedicated athlete, Moore has reportedly attacked his rehabilitation with gusto and is keen to make up for lost time in 2011.

LAST WORD: "Stephen was really unlucky last year, he got injured just when he looked like he was entering his best form. He's very driven and puts everything into his fitness training and his cricket." *Glen Chapple*

Batting & Fielding

	Mat	Inns	NO	Runs	HS	Ave	SR	100	50	Ct	St
First-class	113	206	16	7371	246	38.79	57.75	15	36	56	0
List A	103	99	10	2536	118	28.49	69.23	4	13	28	0
Twenty20	63	57	8	1231	83*	25.12	128.09	0	6	21	0

Bowling

	Mat	Balls	Runs	Wkts	BBI	BBM	Ave	Econ	SR	5w	10
First-class	113	342	321	5	1/13	-	64.20	5.63	68.4	0	0
List A	103	41	53	1	1/1	1/1	53.00	7.75	41.0	0	0
Twenty20	63	-	-	-	-	-	-	-	-	-	-

NAME: Oliver James Newby
BORN: August 26, 1984, Blackburn
HEIGHT: 6ft 5in
SQUAD Nº: 8
NICKNAME: Newbz
OTHER TEAMS: Gloucestershire, Nottinghamshire
CAREER: First-class debut: 2003; List A debut: 2003; T20 debut: 2003

LANCASHIRE

AOC SAYS: A bowler blessed with genuine pace, Newby has had to contend with more than his fair share of injuries but remains one of relatively few bowlers on the county circuit who can trouble even the best batsmen with his speed. Tall, wiry and possessing a quick, dynamic action, Newby is another product of Lancashire's prolific academy and has spent time on loan at both Gloucestershire and Notts during his career. Last season looked set to be a big year for the right-arm paceman as he had finished 2009 strongly on his way to claiming a career-best haul of 25 Championship wickets, but he picked up an anterior cruciate ligament injury in training at the start of last summer and consequently missed the entire season. Now fully returned to fitness, he will be striving to remind Lancashire's supporters what they missed last year.

LAST WORD: "He's just desperate to get out there and play some cricket. It's like having a new player in the squad because we didn't have him at all last year, which was a real shame because he's a good, aggressive seamer who will get top-order wickets."
Glen Chapple

Batting & Fielding

	Mat	Inns	NO	Runs	HS	Ave	SR	100	50	Ct	St
First-class	43	37	8	238	38*	8.20	38.69	0	0	8	0
List A	18	13	7	36	12*	6.00	60.00	0	0	3	0
Twenty20	10	4	2	14	6*	7.00	87.50	0	0	3	0

Bowling

	Mat	Balls	Runs	Wkts	BBI	BBM	Ave	Econ	SR	5w	10
First-class	43	5509	3505	105	5/69	-	33.38	3.81	52.4	1	0
List A	18	692	677	16	4/41	4/41	42.31	5.86	43.2	0	0
Twenty20	10	162	216	6	2/34	2/34	36.00	8.00	27.0	0	0

STEPHEN PARRY

RHB SLA

NAME: Stephen David Parry
BORN: January 12, 1986, Manchester
HEIGHT: 6ft
SQUAD Nº: 4
NICKNAME: Pazza
CAREER: First-class debut: 2007; List A
debut: 2009; T20 debut: 2009

AOC SAYS: Parry marked his county debut by taking five wickets against Durham University, but since then has primarily been used as a one-day bowler by Lancashire, a role he has played with considerable success. Likened to a young Daniel Vettori by Lancashire coach Peter Moores, Parry possesses a deceptive change of pace, an excellent slower ball and seems to relish the challenge posed by batsmen looking to attack him. Also a dynamic fielder and a doughty lower-order batsman, Parry regularly spends his winter in Australia playing grade cricket and has already had a taste of the highest level when he was called up to the England Lions team that played India A in a limited-overs match in 2010 – a match where Parry looked right at home as he claimed figures of 3-48 from his 10 overs.

LAST WORD: "He won't thank me for saying it because he wants to show what he can do in all forms of the game, but Pazza suits the one-day game superbly well. He's got all the tricks you need to build scoreboard pressure." *Glen Chapple*

Batting & Fielding

	Mat	Inns	NO	Runs	HS	Ave	SR	100	50	Ct	St
First-class	3	2	0	3	2	1.50	10.34	0	0	1	0
List A	22	11	2	102	31	11.33	71.32	0	0	2	0
Twenty20	26	6	4	17	7	8.50	100.00	0	0	3	0

Bowling

	Mat	Balls	Runs	Wkts	BBI	BBM	Ave	Econ	SR	5w	10
First-class	3	523	256	9	5/23	5/46	28.44	2.93	58.1	1	0
List A	22	983	771	27	3/48	3/48	28.55	4.70	36.4	0	0
Twenty20	26	558	650	36	4/28	4/28	18.05	6.98	15.5	0	0

LUKE PROCTER

LHB RM

NAME: Luke Anthony Procter
BORN: June 24, 1988, Oldham
HEIGHT: 5ft 11in
SQUAD Nº: 2
CAREER: First-class debut: 2010; List A
debut: 2010

AOC SAYS: Procter broke into Lancashire's injury-ravaged side last season and instantly looked right at home in the middle-order while scoring a lively unbeaten 64 off just 59 deliveries against Worcestershire at Liverpool, although his most prominent performance arguably came in a friendly against West Indies A, a match in which he top-scored with 97 from the top of the order. Also a canny one-day bowler who gives the appearance of bowling off the wrong foot and surprises people with his pace off the pitch, he has become something of an institution at his club side Royston, who he has played for in Central Lancashire League since 2005 and now plays for as a professional.

LAST WORD: "He made a big impression when he came in last year and is a talented batter who manipulates the ball very well – he's tough to stop scoring and can drive bowlers nuts. He's also pretty decent in the field and a more than useful bowler." *Glen Chapple*

Batting & Fielding

	Mat	Inns	NO	Runs	HS	Ave	SR	100	50	Ct	St
First-class	2	3	0	64	32	21.33	38.55	0	0	0	0
List A	7	5	1	167	97	41.75	87.89	0	2	2	0

Bowling

	Mat	Balls	Runs	Wkts	BBI	BBM	Ave	Econ	SR	5w	10
First-class	2	45	47	1	1/26	1/39	47.00	6.26	45.0	0	0
List A	7	228	203	9	3/29	3/29	22.55	5.34	25.3	0	0

TOM SMITH

NAME: Thomas Christopher Smith
BORN: December 26, 1985, Liverpool
HEIGHT: 6ft 3in
SQUAD Nº: 24
NICKNAME: Smudger
OTHER TEAMS: Leicestershire
CAREER: First-class debut: 2005; List A debut: 2005; T20 debut: 2006; County cap: 2010 (Lancashire)

AOC SAYS: One of the best allrounders in English cricket at present, Smith is being widely touted as a player with an international future. Initially considered by the media to be a bowling allrounder who could hold a bat, he has developed into a genuine top six batsman in the Championship, a dangerous, expansive opener in one-day cricket and an exceptional slip fielder. A former England under 19 international who started out playing for Chorley CC in the Lancashire leagues and has played grade cricket for St Kilda in Australia, the same side that Shane Warne used to turn out for, he caught the eye during his first full season in county cricket back in 2006, regularly slanting his lively seamers into the right-hander and developing a reputation as a bowler who was never safe to leave on his way to a tally of 35 wickets at 30.65. Such was his success that he was picked for the England A tour of Bangladesh that winter, but he suffered from a case of second season syndrome in 2007, playing only six games in the Championship and making a limited contribution with bat and ball. His struggles continued in 2008, so much so that he was loaned out to Leicestershire in order to try and get some confidence back into his game. It was a move that proved a masterstroke; Smith regained his touch with the ball and weighed in with several useful contributions with the bat, and from there he's scarcely looked back. The following season he notched his maiden first-class century against Durham University and claimed 15 wickets in the Pro40, but 2010 saw him take his game to new heights by notching 1,294 runs and 58 wickets in all competitions and being named as the club's One-Day Player of the Year. A hernia operation ensured he missed out on a slot on the England Performance Programme that travelled to Australia this winter, but another season of similar success could well see him brought into the England fold before too long.

INSIDE TRACK: "Smith was exceptional in most forms of cricket last year, he's improved himself as a cricketer dramatically. He opened for the team in all forms of the game, but I think he's probably best suited to No.6 in the Championship. However, there is no question that he won't keep going up top in one-day cricket. He's also a much-improved bowler. I don't think he'll ever be the type who blasts out the other team's top-order but he's very useful; swings it if conditions suit, bowls a heavy ball and will bowl all day." *Graham Hardcastle*

Batting & Fielding

	Mat	Inns	NO	Runs	HS	Ave	SR	100	50	Ct	St
First-class	56	78	16	1626	128	26.22	44.71	3	5	50	0
List A	45	35	7	742	87*	26.50	77.94	0	6	12	0
Twenty20	38	32	8	765	92*	31.87	111.19	0	4	18	0

Bowling

	Mat	Balls	Runs	Wkts	BBI	BBM	Ave	Econ	SR	5w	10
First-class	56	7588	3792	116	6/46	-	32.68	2.99	65.4	2	0
List A	45	1772	1467	57	3/8	3/8	25.73	4.96	31.0	0	0
Twenty20	38	578	690	28	3/12	3/12	24.64	7.16	20.6	0	0

🔵 *He's got a sound technique, sweeps well and hits the ball hard, catches everything, bowls well and is as fit as anyone on the staff* 🔵

Glen Chapple,
Lancashire captain

FORMED: 1879
HOME GROUND: County Ground, Grace Road
ONE-DAY NAME: Foxes
CAPTAIN: Matthew Hoggard
2010 RESULTS: CC2: 4/9; FP t20: 7/9 in North Group; CB40: 6/7 in Group C

TEAM PROFILE

LEICESTERSHIRE
COUNTY CRICKET CLUB

HONOURS
County Championship: (3) 1975, 1996, 1998; Benson and Hedges Cup: (3) 1972, 1975, 1985; Sunday League: (2) 1974, 1977; Twenty20 Cup: (2) 2004, 2006

THE LOWDOWN
Leicestershire bounced back from finishing bottom of the pile in the Championship in 2009 to narrowly miss out on promotion last season. Matthew Hoggard and Nathan Buck led a strong seam attack that was well supported by spin duo Claude Henderson and Jigar Naik, while promising young batsman James Taylor once again impressed as the mainstay of the top six. Leicestershire attracted a lot of criticism for fielding so many Kolpak players in past seasons but things have turned full circle at Grace Road with a crop of local youngsters progressing through the ranks and making their mark in the first team. Promotion to Division One in the Championship remains a clear priority but the Foxes will look to improve their form in limited-overs cricket after losing twice to the Scottish Saltires in the CB40 and failing to win a home match in the FP t20.

HEAD COACH: PHIL WHITTICASE
The former Leicestershire wicketkeeper spent 11 seasons at Grace Road as a player and was put in charge of first-team affairs in November after Tim Boon left the county to become head coach of England's Development Programme. Whitticase will also continue to oversee the development and progress of the young players at the county as academy director.

With thanks to: Phil Whitticase; Paul Jones, Leicester Mercury

www.leicestershireccc.co.uk / tel: 0871 282 1879

	Mat	Inns	NO	Runs	HS	Ave	SR	100	50	Ct	St
GP Smith	5	10	4	509	158*	84.83	55.68	2	3	6	-
JGE Benning	1	2	1	55	29	55.00	122.22	0	0	1	-
J du Toit	13	20	1	899	154	47.31	61.07	2	6	16	-
JWA Taylor	17	28	4	1083	206*	45.12	48.43	3	4	15	-
AB McDonald	6	11	1	442	176*	44.20	69.82	2	1	2	-
WI Jefferson	11	20	1	722	135	38.00	63.50	2	4	14	-
WA White	9	13	2	394	101*	35.81	51.16	1	1	4	-
PA Nixon	16	27	1	915	106	35.19	43.22	1	7	4	-
JKH Naik	8	12	3	301	72	33.44	37.95	0	1	5	-
TJ New	17	27	4	746	91	32.43	55.75	0	6	46	1
MAG Boyce	15	27	3	761	90	31.70	42.27	0	6	19	-
JJ Cobb	5	10	2	153	55*	19.12	43.34	0	1	3	-
MN Malik	8	9	3	88	35*	14.66	38.26	0	0	0	-
CW Henderson	16	21	1	265	33	13.25	49.34	0	0	6	-
AJ Harris	4	7	4	27	20*	9.00	26.21	0	0	2	-
NL Buck	15	20	5	93	26	6.20	20.89	0	0	4	-
MJ Hoggard	15	17	6	31	6	2.81	14.76	0	0	5	-
HF Gurney	5	4	1	6	4	2.00	31.57	0	0	0	-

Batting & Fielding

	Mat	Overs	Mdns	Runs	Wkts	BBI	BBM	Ave	Econ	SR	5w	10
PA Nixon	16	2.1	1	7	1	1/7	1/7	7.00	3.23	13.0	0	0
JKH Naik	8	205.0	40	619	35	7/96	8/133	17.68	3.01	35.1	1	0
JGE Benning	1	19.0	2	59	3	2/38	3/59	19.66	3.10	38.0	0	0
CW Henderson	16	489.3	136	1179	56	6/21	8/68	21.05	2.40	52.4	3	0
MJ Hoggard	15	416.4	105	1222	50	6/63	7/117	24.44	2.93	50.0	3	0
AB McDonald	6	103.0	21	320	12	5/40	7/94	26.66	3.10	51.5	1	0
NL Buck	15	381.5	88	1340	49	4/44	7/79	27.34	3.50	46.7	0	0
MN Malik	8	193.2	45	599	21	4/32	5/69	28.52	3.09	55.2	0	0
HF Gurney	5	96.0	22	332	10	3/82	3/82	33.20	3.45	57.6	0	0
AJ Harris	4	96.4	23	385	9	3/43	3/92	42.77	3.98	64.4	0	0
SJ Cliff	1	21.0	6	54	1	1/29	1/54	54.00	2.57	126.0	0	0
WA White	9	134.2	20	531	8	4/58	4/93	66.37	3.95	100.7	0	0
MAG Boyce	15	1.0	0	2	0	-	-	-	2.00	-	0	0
JJ Cobb	5	8.0	2	38	0	-	-	-	4.75	-	0	0
J du Toit	13	2.0	0	20	0	-	-	-	10.00	-	0	0
JWA Taylor	17	4.0	0	15	0	-	-	-	3.75	-	0	0

Bowling

Batting & Fielding

	Mat	Inns	NO	Runs	HS	Ave	SR	100	50	Ct	St
JWA Taylor	12	12	3	407	103*	45.22	89.64	1	3	3	-
PA Nixon	5	5	1	166	40	41.50	88.29	0	0	2	-
WI Jefferson	3	3	0	123	55	41.00	119.41	0	1	2	-
J du Toit	12	12	0	485	141	40.41	89.64	1	3	6	-
JGE Benning	7	7	0	228	62	32.57	106.04	0	1	2	-
MAG Boyce	8	6	0	176	60	29.33	79.27	0	1	3	-
TJ New	10	8	2	173	47*	28.83	94.02	0	0	11	3
WA White	7	7	2	126	36	25.20	105.00	0	0	0	-
MJ Hoggard	10	3	2	21	17*	21.00	75.00	0	0	2	-
AB McDonald	5	5	0	90	46	18.00	95.74	0	0	4	-
JJ Cobb	7	7	1	105	43*	17.50	100.96	0	0	3	-
GP Smith	7	7	1	67	26	11.16	62.61	0	0	3	-
CW Henderson	6	5	3	17	12*	8.50	73.91	0	0	1	-
JKH Naik	8	7	3	26	8*	6.50	65.00	0	0	2	-
JI Pope	2	2	0	13	9	6.50	144.44	0	0	1	0
HF Gurney	6	2	0	7	7	3.50	46.66	0	0	0	-
D Masters	2	1	0	2	2	2.00	25.00	0	0	0	-
ACF Wyatt	2	1	0	1	1	1.00	33.33	0	0	0	-
MN Malik	4	1	1	8	8*	-	114.28	0	0	0	-
NL Buck	5	1	1	5	5*	-	100.00	0	0	0	-
SJ Cliff	3	1	1	0	0*	-	0.00	0	0	0	-

Bowling

	Mat	Overs	Mdns	Runs	Wkts	BBI	Ave	Econ	SR	5w
SJ Cliff	3	19.0	2	71	4	3/27	17.75	3.73	28.5	0
CW Henderson	6	42.0	2	219	12	4/25	18.25	5.21	21.0	0
JWA Taylor	12	11.0	0	98	5	4/61	19.60	8.90	13.2	0
HF Gurney	6	41.0	6	183	9	5/24	20.33	4.46	27.3	1
MN Malik	4	26.5	1	154	7	4/40	22.00	5.73	23.0	0
WA White	7	25.0	0	189	8	6/29	23.62	7.56	18.7	1
JGE Benning	7	41.0	0	204	8	2/29	25.50	4.97	30.7	0
NL Buck	5	36.4	4	204	7	2/16	29.14	5.56	31.4	0
MJ Hoggard	10	67.0	0	364	11	3/43	33.09	5.43	36.5	0
AJ Harris	1	8.0	0	53	1	1/53	53.00	6.62	48.0	0
JJ Cobb	7	21.0	0	107	2	1/25	53.50	5.09	63.0	0
JKH Naik	8	51.1	2	279	5	1/35	55.80	5.45	61.4	0
ACF Wyatt	2	8.2	0	61	1	1/24	61.00	7.32	50.0	0
AB McDonald	5	28.0	0	192	3	1/40	64.00	6.85	56.0	0
D Masters	2	9.0	0	73	1	1/46	73.00	8.11	54.0	0

Batting & Fielding

	Mat	Inns	NO	Runs	HS	Ave	SR	100	50	Ct	St
AB McDonald	3	3	1	174	67	87.00	134.88	0	2	1	-
JWA Taylor	14	14	3	407	62*	37.00	136.12	0	4	5	-
BJ Hodge	15	15	0	431	103	28.73	124.20	1	2	5	-
MJ Hoggard	15	3	2	27	12*	27.00	168.75	0	0	1	-
WI Jefferson	13	13	0	289	83	22.23	138.94	0	3	4	-
JGE Benning	14	14	5	193	45	21.44	104.32	0	0	5	-
J du Toit	14	14	0	273	69	19.50	119.21	0	1	12	-
PA Nixon	15	14	3	214	44*	19.45	127.38	0	0	7	6
CW Henderson	15	9	5	77	32	19.25	154.00	0	0	3	-
WA White	8	8	2	84	26	14.00	102.43	0	0	4	-
JJ Cobb	8	5	1	31	15	7.75	103.33	0	0	3	-
MN Malik	14	3	1	6	3	3.00	66.66	0	0	1	-
JKH Naik	1	1	0	1	1	1.00	50.00	0	0	0	-
MAG Boyce	1	1	1	15	15*	-	187.50	0	0	0	-
HF Gurney	5	1	1	5	5*	-	166.66	0	0	0	-
NL Buck	9	1	1	3	3*	-	100.00	0	0	2	-
SJ Cliff	1	1	1	1	1*	-	100.00	0	0	0	-

Bowling

	Mat	Overs	Mdns	Runs	Wkts	BBI	Ave	Econ	SR	5w
AB McDonald	3	10.0	0	80	7	5/13	11.42	8.00	8.5	1
BJ Hodge	15	25.0	0	187	10	3/26	18.70	7.48	15.0	0
NL Buck	9	30.0	0	251	10	3/20	25.10	8.36	18.0	0
MJ Hoggard	15	54.5	0	465	18	3/19	25.83	8.48	18.2	0
SJ Cliff	1	3.0	0	28	1	1/28	28.00	9.33	18.0	0
CW Henderson	15	57.0	0	396	14	3/33	28.28	6.94	24.4	0
MN Malik	14	46.1	1	371	13	4/25	28.53	8.03	21.3	0
JGE Benning	14	18.3	0	155	5	1/10	31.00	8.37	22.2	0
JJ Cobb	8	9.0	0	101	2	2/16	50.50	11.22	27.0	0
HF Gurney	5	14.0	1	137	2	1/15	68.50	9.78	42.0	0
WA White	8	10.1	0	124	1	1/42	124.00	12.19	61.0	0
JKH Naik	1	3.0	0	27	0	-	-	9.00	-	0
JWA Taylor	14	2.0	0	16	0	-	-	8.00	-	0

MATT BOYCE   LHB RM

NAME: Matthew Andrew Golding Boyce
BORN: August 13, 1985, Cheltenham
HEIGHT: 5ft 10in
SQUAD №: 11
NICKNAME: Boycey, Ferret
CAREER: First-class debut: 2006; List A
debut: 2007; T20 debut: 2008

AOC SAYS: Boyce is a tenacious opening batsman who has been a regular for
Leicestershire for the past three seasons. Educated at Oakham School, where he opened
the batting with Stuart Broad and played scrum-half behind England rugby union star
Tom Croft, the left-hander scored his maiden first-class ton against Warwickshire in 2008
in just his fifth match. He has failed to register a Championship century since, despite
passing fifty on 15 occasions. His patient, accumulative style has seen his opportunities
restricted in limited-overs cricket but he is set to partner Will Jefferson at the top of the
order in Championship cricket.

LAST WORD: "The main problem with Matthew has been his failure to go on and reach
three figures but he is a gritty opener who cuts and drives strongly." Paul Jones

Batting & Fielding

	Mat	Inns	NO	Runs	HS	Ave	SR	100	50	Ct	St
First-class	49	85	6	2188	106	27.69	40.60	1	15	26	0
List A	32	28	3	720	80	28.80	79.38	0	4	7	0
Twenty20	17	13	2	243	34	22.09	107.04	0	0	3	0

Bowling

	Mat	Balls	Runs	Wkts	BBI	BBM	Ave	Econ	SR	5w	10
First-class	49	42	63	0	-	-	-	9.00	-	0	0
List A	32	-	-	-	-	-	-	-	-	-	-
Twenty20	17	-	-	-	-	-	-	-	-	-	-

NAME: Nathan Liam Buck
BORN: April 26, 1991, Leicester
HEIGHT: 6ft 2in
SQUAD Nº: 17
NICKNAME: Bucky, Rogers
CAREER: First-class debut: 2009, List A debut: 2009; T20 debut: 2009

LEICESTERSHIRE

AOC SAYS: Buck is a promising paceman with a burgeoning reputation after a breakthrough season in 2010. Having played a handful of matches in 2009, the former England under 19 seamer was entrusted with the new ball last season and revelled in the role alongside his evergreen skipper Matthew Hoggard. A tall bowler who possesses good natural pace and is capable of moving the ball both ways, Buck returned career-best figures of 4-44 against Derbyshire and took another three wickets in the second innings to lead Leicestershire to a 203-run victory in just his sixth first-class match before impressing against Worcestershire at Grace Road with a six-wicket match haul. He fell one shy of a 50-wicket Championship haul for the season and was rewarded with an England Lions call-up for the tour of the Caribbean after Steven Finn joined the senior squad in Australia. Buck has been on England's radar for some time, having worked with former England bowling coach Ottis Gibson as a 15-year-old. Before turning 17, Buck had trained with England A, played for England under 16s and England under 17s and picked up league and cup winners medals for his club Loughborough Town. In 2008 he spent two weeks developing his craft at the Dennis Lillee Foundation in Chennai.

INSIDE TRACK: "Sharing the new ball with Hoggard has been a dream come true for Nathan. To go straight into the first team and open the bowling with a man of his experience was an amazing opportunity. I think at the start of the season he was a bit daunted but they started travelling together and Oggie took him under his wing and obviously shared a few secrets with him. Nathan was generally operating around the 82 or 83mph mark last season and the feedback we've had from his winter at the National Cricket Performance Centre in Loughborough is that he's filled out physically and he can probably gain an extra yard of pace. He received just reward for his hard work with an England Lions call-up for the tour of the Caribbean. I haven't been at all surprised by how quickly he has adapted to first-class cricket. He's very level-headed, he relishes a challenge and he's got all the necessary skills." *Phil Whitticase*

NATHAN BUCK

Batting & Fielding

	Mat	Inns	NO	Runs	HS	Ave	SR	100	50	Ct	St
First-class	23	27	9	141	26	7.83	-	0	0	6	0
List A	9	2	1	26	21	26.00	113.04	0	0	1	0
Twenty20	9	1	1	3	3*	-	100.00	0	0	2	0

Bowling

	Mat	Balls	Runs	Wkts	BBI	BBM	Ave	Econ	SR	5w	10
First-class	23	3303	1860	57	4/44	7/79	32.63	3.37	57.9	0	0
List A	9	370	355	11	2/16	2/16	32.27	5.75	33.6	0	0
Twenty20	9	180	251	10	3/20	3/20	25.10	8.36	18.0	0	0

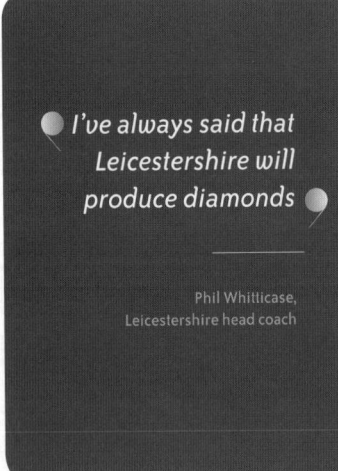

I've always said that Leicestershire will produce diamonds

Phil Whitticase,
Leicestershire head coach

NAME: Joshua James Cobb
BORN: August 17, 1990, Leicester
HEIGHT: 6ft 1in
SQUAD №: 5
NICKNAME: Cobby
CAREER: First-class debut: 2007; List A
debut: 2008; T20 debut: 2008

LEICESTERSHIRE

AOC SAYS: Cobb became Leicestershire's youngest-ever centurion when he made
an unbeaten 148 against Middlesex at Lord's at the age of 18. A silky middle-
order batsman, the Oakham School educated right-hander is the son of former
Leicestershire batsman Russell, who now works at the club as high performance
coach. After his breakthrough season in 2008, Cobb has struggled for runs in the past
two campaigns and only registered one half-century in all competitions in 2010. He
subsequently lost his place and must now fight his way back into the first team with a
weight of runs in Second XI cricket.

LAST WORD: "Josh is a very talented batsman and probably has more flair than James
Taylor but technically he's not as tight and that proved his down downfall last season."
Paul Jones

Batting & Fielding

	Mat	Inns	NO	Runs	HS	Ave	SR	100	50	Ct	St
First-class	28	48	5	1105	148*	25.69	42.45	1	7	12	0
List A	17	15	2	222	43*	17.07	82.83	0	0	5	0
Twenty20	9	6	2	33	15	8.25	103.12	0	0	3	0

Bowling

	Mat	Balls	Runs	Wkts	BBI	BBM	Ave	Econ	SR	5w	10
First-class	28	336	243	5	2/11	2/11	48.60	4.33	67.2	0	0
List A	17	132	119	3	1/12	1/12	39.66	5.40	44.0	0	0
Twenty20	9	54	101	2	2/16	2/16	50.50	11.22	27.0	0	0

JACQUES DU TOIT

RHB RMF MVP85

LEICESTERSHIRE

NAME: Jacques Du Toit
BORN: January 2, 1980, Port Elizabeth
SQUAD Nº: 8
OTHER TEAMS: Colombo Cricket Club,
Easterns
CAREER: First-class debut: 1999; List A
debut: 2004; T20 debut: 2008

AOC SAYS: Since leaving his native South Africa and joining Leicestershire in 2008, du Toit has become an integral member of the side across all formats. He was initially used primarily as a limited-overs specialist but was promoted to fill the problematic position at No.3 in Championship cricket last season and was subsequently named the Supporters' Player of the Year after an impressive campaign. He is used as an opener in one-day cricket, where his hard-hitting style makes him an ideal candidate to make use of powerplays. Du Toit signed a new contract in November that will keep him at Grace Road until at least the end of the 2012 season.

LAST WORD: "Jacques is an aggressive but elegant batsman. He was promoted to bat at No.3 in Championship cricket in the second half of last season and handled it pretty well."
Paul Jones

Batting & Fielding

	Mat	Inns	NO	Runs	HS	Ave	SR	100	50	Ct	St
First-class	29	44	3	1600	154	39.02	-	4	9	24	0
List A	36	34	2	888	144	27.75	88.62	2	3	15	0
Twenty20	31	30	3	480	69	17.77	124.03	0	1	22	0

Bowling

	Mat	Balls	Runs	Wkts	BBI	BBM	Ave	Econ	SR	5w	10
First-class	29	474	355	5	3/31	-	71.00	4.49	94.8	0	0
List A	36	66	66	2	2/30	2/30	33.00	6.00	33.0	0	0
Twenty20	31	32	41	2	2/15	2/15	20.50	7.68	16.0	0	0

NAME: Harry Frederick Gurney
BORN: October 25, 1986, Nottingham
HEIGHT: 6ft 2in
SQUAD Nº: 5
NICKNAME: Sicknote, Contract, Chicken Legs
CAREER: First-class debut: 2007; List A debut: 2009; T20 debut: 2009

LEICESTERSHIRE

AOC SAYS: Gurney is a left-arm seamer who possesses genuine pace and the ability to move the ball both ways but his career has so far been disrupted by injury problems and a lack of consistency. A career-best haul of 5-24 in the CB40 against Hampshire last season demonstrated his potential but he has found regular first-team cricket hard to come by due to the impressive battery of seamers at Grace Road. After missing most of the 2007 season with an ankle injury Gurney was released by the club but was subsequently awarded a new contract ahead of the 2009 season after impressing the coaching staff.

LAST WORD: "Gurney has got some pace about him and has the potential to be a real handful but he needs to work on his accuracy if he is to progress." *Paul Jones*

Batting & Fielding

	Mat	Inns	NO	Runs	HS	Ave	SR	100	50	Ct	St
First-class	16	17	8	61	24*	6.77	30.96	0	0	2	0
List A	16	3	0	7	7	2.33	41.17	0	0	0	0
Twenty20	14	1	1	5	5*	-	166.66	0	0	2	0

Bowling

	Mat	Balls	Runs	Wkts	BBI	BBM	Ave	Econ	SR	5w	10
First-class	16	2165	1334	28	5/82	5/82	47.64	3.69	77.3	1	0
List A	16	591	510	12	5/24	5/24	42.50	5.17	49.2	1	0
Twenty20	14	246	321	10	3/21	3/21	32.10	7.82	24.6	0	0

CLAUDE HENDERSON

RHB SLA W1 MVP36

NAME: Claude William Henderson
BORN: June 14, 1972, Worcester, South Africa
HEIGHT: 6ft 2in
SQUAD Nº: 15
NICKNAME: Hendy, Hendo
OTHER TEAMS: South Africa, Boland, Cape Cobras, Lions, Western Province
CAREER: Test debut: 2001; ODI debut: 2001; First-class debut: 1990; List A debut: 1991; T20 debut: 2004; County cap: 2004

AOC SAYS: The veteran South African spinner has been awarded a Benefit this season after a hugely impressive 2010 that saw him named Players' Player of the Year. Henderson finished as the club's Championship leading wicket-taker and he was a model of consistency in limited-overs cricket with his canny left-arm twirlers. He is also a valuable asset off the field where he has helped the development of fellow Foxes spinner Jigar Naik. Now a British resident, Henderson was perhaps unfortunate not to have featured on more than a handful of occasions for his country but South Africa's loss has been Leicestershire's gain and Henderson enters his eighth season at Grace Road looking as strong as ever.

LAST WORD: "Over a number of years he has been one of the best spin bowlers in the country. Last year he bowled as well as ever and his Benefit is well deserved." *Tim Boon, former Leicestershire senior coach*

Batting & Fielding

	Mat	Inns	NO	Runs	HS	Ave	SR	100	50	Ct	St
Tests	7	7	0	65	30	9.28	32.17	0	0	2	0
ODIs	4	-	-	-	-	-	-	-	-	0	0
First-class	244	330	70	4847	81	18.64	-	0	15	82	0
List A	245	138	66	1110	45	15.41	-	0	0	55	0
Twenty20	76	31	11	161	32	8.05	108.05	0	0	19	0

Bowling

	Mat	Balls	Runs	Wkts	BBI	BBM	Ave	Econ	SR	5w	10
Tests	7	1962	928	22	4/116	7/176	42.18	2.83	89.1	0	0
ODIs	4	217	132	7	4/17	4/17	18.85	3.64	31.0	0	0
First-class	244	58694	24996	816	7/57	-	30.63	2.55	71.9	32	2
List A	245	10849	7799	308	6/29	6/29	25.32	4.31	35.2	2	0
Twenty20	76	1474	1709	70	3/23	3/23	24.41	6.95	21.0	0	0

NAME: Matthew James Hoggard
BORN: December 31, 1976, Leeds
HEIGHT: 6ft 2in
SQUAD Nº: 77
NICKNAME: Oggie, Hoggy
OTHER TEAMS: England, Free State, Yorkshire
CAREER: Test debut: 2000; ODI debut: 2001; First-class debut: 1996; List A debut 1998; T20 debut: 2004; County cap: 2000 (Yorkshire)

LEICESTERSHIRE

AOC SAYS: Hoggard sits sixth on England's list of all-time leading Test wicket-takers after a celebrated international career. The bustling swing bowler claimed 248 wickets in a Test career spanning eight years and was an integral member of the side that reclaimed the Ashes in 2005 after an 18-year wait. A tireless workhorse who never shirks a challenge, Hoggard produced a series of devastating spells for his country. The peak of his international career was a second-innings haul of 7-61 against South Africa at The Wanderers in 2005 to bowl his side to a memorable victory. He produced two other seven-wicket hauls in an England shirt – taking 7-63 against New Zealand in the victory at Christchurch in 2002 and 7-109 at Adelaide during the ill-fated 2006/07 Ashes tour. He was unceremoniously dropped from the side after the first Test defeat to New Zealand at Hamilton in 2008 to bring an abrupt end to his England career. After 14 years of faithful service and 331 first-class wickets, Hoggard left Yorkshire in acrimonious circumstances at the end of 2009 season and rejected a move to Sussex to take over the captaincy at Grace Road. The pace may have dropped but his trademark shape away from the right-hander remains and he has formed a lethal new ball partnership with young tyro Nathan Buck. He took his 700th first-class wicket last season and rolled back the years with a season-best haul of 6-63 against Middlesex at Lord's. He also impressed in his new role as skipper – galvanising a crop of young players and instilling a strong team spirit despite unrest in the boardroom.

INSIDE TRACK: "Matthew has done really well since taking over the captaincy. To have somebody of his stature in the game helping our younger players has proved invaluable. A team of youngsters can get swamped by the opposition but Matthew and another couple of the older lads have added great experience, as well as ability. He tends to captain in two ways. He leads by example and if individuals aren't performing he will take them aside for a quiet word and speak to them privately. But he'll blow up occasionally if he thinks the team attitude isn't right and he will speak to them as a collective." *Phil Whitticase*

MATTHEW HOGGARD

Batting & Fielding											
	Mat	Inns	NO	Runs	HS	Ave	SR	100	50	Ct	St
Tests	67	92	27	473	38	7.27	22.63	0	0	24	0
ODIs	26	6	2	17	7	4.25	56.66	0	0	5	0
First-class	210	263	77	1684	89*	9.05	-	0	4	60	0
List A	140	43	24	88	17*	4.63	-	0	0	16	0
Twenty20	30	5	3	46	18	23.00	158.62	0	0	5	0

Bowling											
	Mat	Balls	Runs	Wkts	BBI	BBM	Ave	Econ	SR	5w	10
Tests	67	13909	7564	248	7/61	12/205	30.50	3.26	56.0	7	1
ODIs	26	1306	1152	32	5/49	5/49	36.00	5.29	40.8	1	0
First-class	210	38061	19510	718	7/49	-	27.17	3.07	53.0	25	1
List A	140	6529	4899	190	5/28	5/28	25.78	4.50	34.3	4	0
Twenty20	30	653	937	31	3/19	3/19	30.22	8.60	21.0	0	0

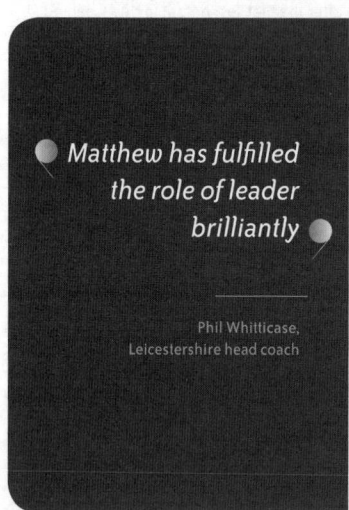

Matthew has fulfilled the role of leader brilliantly

Phil Whitticase,
Leicestershire head coach

NAME: William Ingleby Jefferson
BORN: October 25, 1979, Derby
HEIGHT: 6ft 10in
SQUAD Nº: 1
NICKNAME: Santa, Lemar, Jeffer
OTHER TEAMS: Essex, Nottinghamshire
CAREER: First-class debut: 2000; List A
debut: 2000; T20 debut: 2003; County cap:
2002 (Essex)

LEICESTERSHIRE

AOC SAYS: The giant right-handed opener joined Leicestershire at the end of the 2009 season and enjoyed a solid start to life at Grace Road, despite suffering from a debilitating Achilles injury for the majority of the campaign. Jefferson – the son of former Surrey seamer Richard – was touted as a future England batsman during his time with Essex after a stunning 2004 season that saw him amass 1,555 first-class runs. But an alarming slump followed and the Durham University graduate left Chelmsford for Nottinghamshire in 2006. Still the runs failed to flow and Jefferson departed Trent Bridge in a bid to resurrect his career.

LAST WORD: "Will is quite a sponge for taking in information and he's prepared to listen to a lot of people. He maybe suffered a bit of paralysis by analysis and it was a case of going back to basics with his batting." *Phil Whitticase*

Batting & Fielding

	Mat	Inns	NO	Runs	HS	Ave	SR	100	50	Ct	St
First-class	102	179	13	6014	222	36.22	-	14	24	102	0
List A	96	94	6	3092	132	35.13	-	4	18	43	0
Twenty20	48	47	4	922	83	21.44	124.93	0	5	16	0

Bowling

	Mat	Balls	Runs	Wkts	BBI	BBM	Ave	Econ	SR	5w	10
First-class	102	120	60	1	1/16	-	60.00	3.00	120.0	0	0
List A	96	24	9	2	2/9	2/9	4.50	2.25	12.0	0	0
Twenty20	48	-	-	-	-	-	-	-	-	-	-

WILL JONES

RHB LB

NAME: William Stephen Jones
BORN: March 29, 1990, Perth, Australia
SQUAD Nº: 25
CAREER: Yet to make first-team debut

AOC SAYS: Jones is a talented opening batsman who signed a summer contract with Leicestershire at the end of last season. He earned a trial at Grace Road after impressing for Hertfordshire in the Minor Counties Championship and demonstrated his potential by averaging 53 in the Second XI Trophy. He furthered his cricketing education over the winter by spending time at the Global Cricket Academy in Pune, India with fellow Foxes opener Greg Smith. Jones, who is currently studying at Cardiff University and is part of the successful Cardiff MCCU, lists Mike Atherton and Andrew Strauss among his most admired cricketers.

LAST WORD: "Jones is a top-order batsman who is currently on the fringes of the side and is likely feature in Second XI cricket this season." *Paul Jones*

EXTRAS

Leicestershire announced a loss of £404,862 for the year to September 30. The county was beset with problems last summer, with the resignations of chief executive David Smith, senior coach Tim Boon and chairman Neil Davidson. "The results are bad but we have known for some time that costs have not been controlled and income from membership and Twenty20 was way down on budget," said chief executive Mike Siddall. "The club needs rebuilding from the bottom and although we have a tough job on our hands it is far from an impossible task."

NADEEM MALIK

RHB RMF

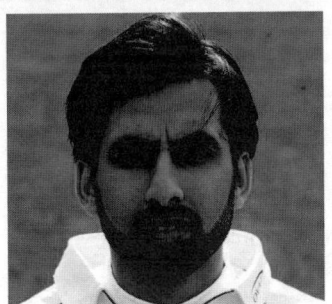

NAME: Muhammad Nadeem Malik
BORN: October 6, 1982, Nottingham
HEIGHT: 6ft 5in
SQUAD Nº: 21
NICKNAME: Nad, Busta, Nigel, Gerz
OTHER TEAMS: Nottinghamshire, Worcestershire
CAREER: First-class debut: 2001; List A debut: 2000; T20 debut: 2004

LEICESTERSHIRE

AOC SAYS: Malik is a tall seam bowler whose main assets are his bounce and ability to move the ball away from the right-hander. He emerged on the scene as a fiery paceman but has reduced his pace in search of greater consistency in recent years. After beginning his career with Nottinghamshire, Malik moved to Worcestershire in 2004 but struggled to make an impression. Leicestershire snapped him up on a one-year deal in 2008 and he made an immediate impact by taking eight wickets on debut against Middlesex. A series of injuries forced Malik to miss the entire 2009 season but he returned last year to become a key member of the attack and was rewarded with a new one-year contract.

LAST WORD: "Nadeem bounced back from an injury-blighted 2009 season to secure a place in a strong seam attack in 2010 and will be looking to reproduce that kind of form this season." *Paul Jones*

Batting & Fielding

	Mat	Inns	NO	Runs	HS	Ave	SR	100	50	Ct	St
First-class	74	96	33	646	41	10.25	40.04	0	0	10	0
List A	73	29	19	105	11	10.50	-	0	0	10	0
Twenty20	38	9	4	12	3*	2.40	50.00	0	0	3	0

Bowling

	Mat	Balls	Runs	Wkts	BBI	BBM	Ave	Econ	SR	5w	10
First-class	74	11730	7066	200	6/46	-	35.33	3.61	58.6	7	0
List A	73	2872	2525	73	4/40	4/40	34.58	5.27	39.3	0	0
Twenty20	38	751	1021	41	4/16	4/16	24.90	8.15	18.3	0	0

ANDREW MCDONALD RHB RMF

LEICESTERSHIRE

OVERSEAS PLAYER

NAME: Andrew Barry McDonald
BORN: June 5, 1981, Wodonga, Australia
HEIGHT: 6ft 4in
SQUAD Nº: 4
NICKNAME: Ronnie
OTHER TEAMS: Australia, Delhi Daredevils, Victoria
CAREER: Test debut: 2009; First-class debut: 2002; List A debut: 2002; T20 debut: 2006

AOC SAYS: The Australian allrounder is Leicestershire's overseas player and will arrive at Grace Road after the completion of his IPL stint with Delhi Daredevils. Injury and a call-up to captain Australia A restricted McDonald to six Championship appearances last season but he still made a significant impact with a career-best 176 not out in a county record fourth-wicket stand of 360 with James Taylor against Middlesex. The hard-hitting batsman and metronomic medium-pacer won a surprise Test call-up to face South Africa in 2009 but has since fallen down the pecking order, despite continuing to perform impressively with bat and ball in the Pura Cup for his state side Victoria.

LAST WORD: "Andrew has been a very consistent performer for Victoria for several seasons. He is capable of batting in the top six and adds flexibility and versatility to a bowling attack."
Andrew Hilditch, Australia chairman of selectors

Batting & Fielding

	Mat	Inns	NO	Runs	HS	Ave	SR	100	50	Ct	St
Tests	4	6	1	107	68	21.40	49.30	0	1	2	0
First-class	75	120	27	3688	176*	39.65	59.15	9	19	57	0
List A	83	72	22	1555	67	31.10	80.48	0	8	33	0
Twenty20	46	40	15	749	67	29.96	125.25	0	2	13	0

Bowling

	Mat	Balls	Runs	Wkts	BBI	BBM	Ave	Econ	SR	5w	10
Tests	4	732	300	9	3/25	3/72	33.33	2.45	81.3	0	0
First-class	75	10475	4873	170	6/34	-	28.66	2.79	61.6	4	0
List A	83	3260	2775	69	4/50	4/50	40.21	5.10	47.2	0	0
Twenty20	46	800	1025	50	5/13	5/13	20.50	7.68	16.0	1	0

JIGAR NAIK

RHB OB

NAME: Jigar Kumar Hakumatrai Naik
BORN: August 10, 1984, Leicester
HEIGHT: 6ft 2in
SQUAD Nº: 22
NICKNAME: Jigs, Jiggy, Jigsy
OTHER TEAMS: Colombo Cricket Club
CAREER: First-class debut: 2006; List A
debut: 2002; T20 debut: 2008

LEICESTERSHIRE

AOC SAYS: Naik is a promising offspinner who made great strides in 2010 to finish top of the county's first-class bowling averages. He was restricted to eight Championship matches – with Leicestershire often relying on Claude Henderson to fulfil the spin duties – but impressed when called upon and returned career-best figures of 7-96 to bowl his side to an innings victory over Surrey. A tall man who turns the ball sharply, Naik is also a handy lower-order batsman with a first-class century to his name. His spin partnership with Henderson will prove a major asset for Leicestershire as the pitches dry out over the season.

LAST WORD: "Naik is learning his trade under the guidance of the experienced Claude Henderson. He showed himself to be a matchwinner last year and will provide a real threat on turning surfaces." *Paul Jones*

Batting & Fielding

	Mat	Inns	NO	Runs	HS	Ave	SR	100	50	Ct	St
First-class	24	32	9	620	109*	26.95	39.01	1	1	12	0
List A	21	15	6	85	18	9.44	-	0	0	3	0
Twenty20	12	5	3	14	7*	7.00	100.00	0	0	2	0

Bowling

	Mat	Balls	Runs	Wkts	BBI	BBM	Ave	Econ	SR	5w	10
First-class	24	2843	1618	52	7/96	8/133	31.11	3.41	54.6	1	0
List A	21	809	694	19	3/21	3/21	36.52	5.14	42.5	0	0
Twenty20	12	180	230	4	2/22	2/22	57.50	7.66	45.0	0	0

TOM NEW

LHB RM WK

LEICESTERSHIRE

NAME: Thomas James New
BORN: January 18, 1985, Sutton-In-Ashfield
HEIGHT: 5ft 9in
SQUAD Nº: 18
NICKNAME: Newy
OTHER TEAMS: Derbyshire
CAREER: First-class debut: 2004; List A
debut: 2001; T20 debut: 2008; County cap:
2009 (Leicestershire)

AOC SAYS: Having acted as an able deputy to Paul Nixon for several seasons, New took over wicketkeeping duties midway through the 2009 season and has performed admirably in the role. The keeper-batsman is among the longest serving players at Grace Road and is considered a reliable pair of hands behind the stumps. He featured regularly as a specialist batter before Nixon relinquished the gloves and the left-hander has opened the batting in one-day cricket in the past. However, he has found his route into the Foxes' T20 side blocked by Nixon, who continues to keep wicket in that format.

LAST WORD: "The feeling appears to be that Tom isn't a T20 player but I don't necessarily go along with it. He is quite capable of taking advantage of the powerplays at the top of the order." *Paul Jones*

Batting & Fielding

	Mat	Inns	NO	Runs	HS	Ave	SR	100	50	Ct	St
First-class	85	141	18	3926	125	31.91	50.13	2	29	140	7
List A	54	48	6	1114	68	26.52	-	0	4	26	7
Twenty20	1	1	0	18	18	18.00	94.73	0	0	1	1

Bowling

	Mat	Balls	Runs	Wkts	BBI	BBM	Ave	Econ	SR	5w	10
First-class	85	229	211	5	2/18	2/18	42.20	5.52	45.8	0	0
List A	54	-	-	-	-	-	-	-	-	-	-
Twenty20	1	-	-	-	-	-	-	-	-	-	-

NAME: Paul Andrew Nixon
BORN: October 21, 1970, Carlisle
HEIGHT: 6ft
SQUAD Nº: 3
NICKNAME: Badger, Nico
OTHER TEAMS: England, Delhi Giants, Kent,
CAREER: ODI debut: 2007; T20I debut:
2007; First-class debut: 1989; List A debut:
1989; T20 debut: 2003; County cap: 1994
(Leicestershire), 2000 (Kent)

LEICESTERSHIRE

AOC SAYS: Nixon has been a Leicestershire stalwart for the best part of 20 years. The charismatic wicketkeeper won two Championship titles in his first spell with the county and returned to Grace Road in 2003 after three seasons with Kent. At the age of 36, Nixon received the international call-up he thought would never come and went on to play in the 2007 World Cup. His age counted against him and he was discarded despite some strong performances but he has continued to stack up the runs for his county. He handed over the gloves to Tom New in Championship and one-day cricket but remains the Foxes' T20 stumper and a key player in all formats with his wristy middle-order batting.

LAST WORD: "Nico is still very much a key member of the batting line-up. He can move the score along when needed or play the anchor role in the middle-order." *Paul Jones*

Batting & Fielding

	Mat	Inns	NO	Runs	HS	Ave	SR	100	50	Ct	St
ODIs	19	18	4	297	49	21.21	85.59	0	0	20	3
T20Is	1	1	1	31	31*	-	140.90	0	0	0	1
First-class	351	526	111	14401	173*	34.70	-	21	72	889	67
List A	406	349	72	7300	101	26.35	-	1	33	419	99
Twenty20	75	70	14	1309	65	23.37	118.89	0	4	40	19

Bowling

	Mat	Balls	Runs	Wkts	BBI	BBM	Ave	Econ	SR	5w	10
ODIs	19	-	-	-	-	-	-	-	-	-	-
T20Is	1	-	-	-	-	-	-	-	-	-	-
First-class	351	125	157	1	1/7	1/7	157.00	7.53	125.0	0	0
List A	406	3	1	0	-	-	-	2.00	-	0	0
Twenty20	75	-	-	-	-	-	-	-	-	-	-

GREG SMITH

RHB SLA

LEICESTERSHIRE

NAME: Gregory Paul Smith
BORN: November 16, 1988, Leicester
SQUAD №: 14
CAREER: First-class debut: 2008; List A debut: 2008

AOC SAYS: Smith is a former England under 19 opening batsman of great promise who is currently studying at Durham University. There are high hopes for the right-hander at Grace Road after a stunning 2010, in which he scored three first-class centuries to average 93.14 in seven first-class appearances. He struck his first ton for the county in the Championship home encounter with Gloucestershire, hitting an unbeaten 158 in a 329-run victory, and followed it up with his second century in as many matches against Northamptonshire. His university studies will restrict his availability but he should be available from the beginning of June to put pressure on Will Jefferson and Matt Boyce.

LAST WORD: "Greg had a fantastic season in 2010 and took his chance really well. He'll provide competition for places at the top of the order after he has finished his university exams." *Phil Whitticase*

Batting & Fielding

	Mat	Inns	NO	Runs	HS	Ave	SR	100	50	Ct	St
First-class	20	36	6	1098	158*	36.60	46.29	3	5	11	0
List A	10	10	1	139	58	15.44	64.65	0	1	3	0

Bowling

	Mat	Balls	Runs	Wkts	BBI	BBM	Ave	Econ	SR	5w	10
First-class	20	30	64	1	1/64	1/64	64.00	12.80	30.0	0	0
List A	10	-	-	-	-	-	-	-	-	-	-

NAME: James William Arthur Taylor
BORN: January 6, 1990, Nottingham
HEIGHT: 5ft 7in
SQUAD Nº: 9
NICKNAME: Jimmy, Titch
CAREER: First-class debut: 2008; List A debut: 2008; T20 debut: 2008; County cap: 2009

LEICESTERSHIRE

AOC SAYS: Taylor is considered to be among the best young batsmen in the country, having excelled for the past two seasons with Leicestershire and England Lions. The right-hand middle-order batsman was named PCA Young Player of the Year in 2009 after a prolific first full season in first-class cricket in which he became the youngest ever double centurion for the county, making an unbeaten 207 against Surrey at The Oval. The former England under 19 star was duly rewarded with selection for the England Performance Programme tour to South Africa that winter. While Taylor did not reach quite the same heights last season he still topped 1,000 Championship runs and scored his second double ton in a county record fourth-wicket partnership of 360 with Andrew McDonald against Middlesex at Grace Road. His record is equally as strong in limited-overs cricket, where he acts as an accumulator and has shown himself to have the skill and maturity to carry his side over the finishing line. Taylor attracted rave reviews this winter from Graham Thorpe during England Lions' tour of the Caribbean and further demonstrated his ability to play long innings with a mammoth 186 against Barbados. Taylor will now have his sights set firmly on the role in England's middle-order vacated by Paul Collingwood.

INSIDE TRACK: "James is mentally very strong and understands his game extremely well. He's got an unbelievable desire to score runs when he's out in the middle and absolutely hates getting out. I had a chat with Graham Thorpe, who has been working with James in the Caribbean, and he was keen to put his skill levels under a bit more pressure and take a look at him at the top of the order. To be honest I see him as a No.3 or No.4 but he has shown he is adaptable and that will stand him in good stead. As you would expect from a small lad, he's strong square of the wicket but he's also very strong down the ground. He's always looking for scoring opportunities and scores his runs all round the wicket. In one-day cricket James is very much an accumulator when he first goes in, rather than someone who hits straight from the off in the powerplays. Because of his determination and how much he values his wicket I think he could play Test cricket before he plays ODIs." *Phil Whitticase*

JAMES TAYLOR

LEICESTERSHIRE

Batting & Fielding

	Mat	Inns	NO	Runs	HS	Ave	SR	100	50	Ct	St
First-class	46	74	12	2932	207*	47.29	-		7	13	35	0
List A	36	33	8	1150	103*	46.00	80.81	2	7	5	0
Twenty20	27	26	6	644	62*	32.20	118.16	0	4	7	0

Bowling

	Mat	Balls	Runs	Wkts	BBI	BBM	Ave	Econ	SR	5w	10
First-class	46	216	160	0	-	-	-	4.44	-	0	0
List A	36	138	170	5	4/61	4/61	34.00	7.39	27.6	0	0
Twenty20	27	74	100	2	1/10	1/10	50.00	8.10	37.0	0	0

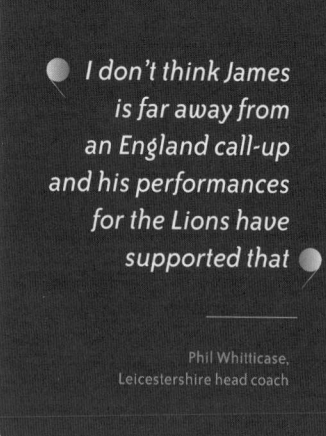

I don't think James is far away from an England call-up and his performances for the Lions have supported that

Phil Whitticase,
Leicestershire head coach

NAME: Shivsinh Jaysinh Thakor
BORN: October 22, 1993, Leicester
SQUAD Nº: 57
CAREER: Yet to make first-team debut

LEICESTERSHIRE

AOC SAYS: Thakor is an allrounder with bags of potential who has already represented England under 19 at the age of 17. He is one of a crop of local cricketers who have worked their way up through the ranks at Grace Road and is considered to be among the best the county have produced in recent times. He became the youngest centurion for Leicestershire in age-group cricket after reaching three figures for the under 9s against Surrey. At this early stage of his career he is predominantly a batsman and that is his most likely route into the first team but his accurate seam bowling makes him an exciting all-round prospect.

LAST WORD: "Leicestershire have extremely high hopes for Shiv. He agreed a three-year deal at the end of last season which shows just how highly they think of him" *Paul Jones*

EXTRAS

"I am very optimistic for the future. Sponsors, including main club sponsor The Oval Group, are backing the club and sales of attractively priced membership packages have been good. We finished last season on a very positive note and skipper Matthew Hoggard and the team are really looking forward to the new season." Mike Siddall, Leicestershire chief executive

WAYNE WHITE

RHB RMF

NAME: Wayne Andrew White
BORN: September 22, 1985, Derby
HEIGHT: 6ft 2in
SQUAD Nº: 35
NICKNAME: Chalky
OTHER TEAMS: Derbyshire
CAREER: First-class debut: 2005; List A debut: 2006; T20 debut: 2009

AOC SAYS: White is a burly allrounder who arrived at Grace Road from Derbyshire in 2009. A bustling seamer and hard-hitting lower-order batsman, he acted as Leicestershire's fourth seamer last season and is likely to be competing with offspinner Jigar Naik for the fifth bowling slot in Championship cricket. A promising goalkeeper in his youth, the former Derby County trainee chose cricket over football but struggled with injury in the early stages of his career and made only fleeting appearances for Derbyshire. He started the last campaign strongly with a haul of 4-48 against Northamptonshire before hitting his maiden first-class ton against his former county but injury struck again as a broken finger disrupted his season.

LAST WORD: "White is a talented young seamer who offers lots with both bat and ball. He will get better and better." *Tim Boon, former Leicestershire senior coach*

Batting & Fielding

	Mat	Inns	NO	Runs	HS	Ave	SR	100	50	Ct	St
First-class	32	48	7	880	101*	21.46	46.56	1	2	14	0
List A	36	28	11	345	46*	20.29	98.01	0	0	8	0
Twenty20	18	14	3	117	26	10.63	102.63	0	0	12	0

Bowling

	Mat	Balls	Runs	Wkts	BBI	BBM	Ave	Econ	SR	5w	10
First-class	32	3736	2583	58	5/87	-	44.53	4.14	64.4	1	0
List A	36	1144	1193	31	6/29	6/29	38.48	6.25	36.9	1	0
Twenty20	18	249	367	11	3/27	3/27	33.36	8.84	22.6	0	0

NAME: Alexander Charles Frederick Wyatt
BORN: July 23, 1990, Roehampton
HEIGHT: 6ft 7in
SQUAD Nº: 16
NICKNAME: Waz, Goober, Dave
CAREER: First-class debut: 2009; List A debut: 2009; T20 debut: 2009

AOC SAYS: Wyatt is giant right-arm seamer who relies on bounce and movement rather than pace to create problems for batsmen. He impressed during a handful of appearances in 2009, including a three-wicket haul against West Indies in just his second first-class appearance before returning figures of 3-14 on his T20 debut against Durham. However, his season was curtailed by a back problem that continued to hamper him throughout the 2010 campaign and reduced him to two CB40 appearances. The former student of Oakham School is now back to full fitness but faces a battle to leapfrog Nadeem Malik and Wayne White to claim a place in Leicestershire's seam attack.

LAST WORD: "Injuries have held Wyatt back so far but he swings the ball and is exceptionally tall, which means he gets a lot of bounce and troubles batsmen." *Paul Jones*

Batting & Fielding

	Mat	Inns	NO	Runs	HS	Ave	SR	100	50	Ct	St
First-class	3	3	1	4	3	2.00	40.00	0	0	1	0
List A	4	1	0	1	1	1.00	33.33	0	0	1	0
Twenty20	2	-	-	-	-	-	-	-	-	1	0

Bowling

	Mat	Balls	Runs	Wkts	BBI	BBM	Ave	Econ	SR	5w	10
First-class	3	366	159	7	3/42	3/42	22.71	2.60	52.2	0	0
List A	4	116	123	3	1/24	1/24	41.00	6.36	38.6	0	0
Twenty20	2	42	36	3	3/14	3/14	12.00	5.14	14.0	0	0

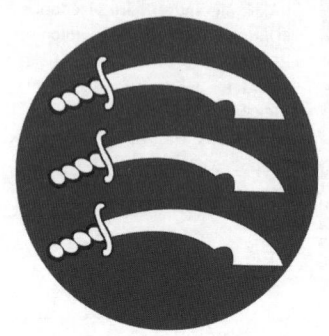

FORMED: 1864
HOME GROUND: Lord's
ONE-DAY NAME: Panthers
CAPTAIN: Neil Dexter
2010 RESULTS: CC2: 8/9; CB40 6/7 in
Group B; FP t20: 8/9 in South Group

HONOURS

County Championship: (12) 1903, 1920, 1921, 1947, 1949(s), 1976, 1977(s), 1980, 1982, 1985, 1990, 1993; Gillette/NatWest/C&G/FP Trophy: (4) 1977, 1980, 1984, 1988; Benson and Hedges Cup Winners: (2) 1983, 1986 ; Sunday League: 1992; Twenty20 Cup: 2008

THE LOWDOWN

Middlesex are desperate to return to county cricket's top table after four seasons languishing in the second tier of the Championship. They opened their 2010 Championship campaign with four successive defeats to effectively end their promotion challenge before it had begun but showed signs of improvement after Neil Dexter took over the captaincy midway through the season. Hampered by a consistent failure to post big first-innings totals they have signed Australian opener Chris Rogers in an attempt to remedy the situation, while Corey Collymore and Anthony Ireland have been recruited to boost the seam attack. There is also plenty of room for improvement in limited-overs cricket, but promotion in the Championship is the firm priority.

MANAGING DIRECTOR OF CRICKET: ANGUS FRASER

The former England seamer took charge of the county he served as a player throughout his 18-year first-class career in 2009 after working as cricket correspondent for The Independent. Fraser took 177 Test wickets in an international career spanning nine years and twice collected eight-wicket hauls against West Indies in 1994 and 1998.

With thanks to: Angus Fraser; Jon Batham, freelance reporter for Trinity Mirror South

	Mat	Inns	NO	Runs	HS	Ave	SR	100	50	Ct	St
EJG Morgan	1	2	1	116	58*	116.00	52.25	0	2	0	-
DM Housego	2	4	1	144	102*	48.00	62.33	1	0	1	-
NJ Dexter	12	21	2	907	118	47.73	60.38	2	5	10	-
SW Poynter	1	1	0	42	42	42.00	54.54	0	0	3	0
DJ Malan	16	29	3	1001	115	38.50	53.75	3	5	19	-
OA Shah	13	23	1	804	156	36.54	50.15	2	3	10	-
GK Berg	15	26	5	761	125	36.23	69.30	1	3	7	-
SA Newman	15	27	0	945	126	35.00	61.56	2	6	8	-
SD Robson	8	15	0	513	204	34.20	52.99	1	2	8	-
JH Davey	4	7	0	220	72	31.42	42.06	0	3	3	-
AJ Strauss	8	15	0	460	92	30.66	49.62	0	3	16	-
JA Simpson	16	27	2	657	101*	26.28	44.96	1	2	42	2
AB London	4	7	1	137	77	22.83	36.43	0	1	3	-
TJ Murtagh	15	23	10	241	50*	18.53	50.10	0	1	4	-
TMJ Smith	4	7	1	110	33	18.33	33.23	0	0	3	-
KS Toor	1	1	0	15	15	15.00	34.09	0	0	0	-
SD Udal	13	19	1	216	55	12.00	49.20	0	1	6	-
TS Roland-Jones	8	12	1	124	26	11.27	53.91	0	0	3	-
D Evans	4	5	2	23	19*	7.66	31.08	0	0	1	-
IE O'Brien	7	9	1	39	14*	4.87	31.20	0	0	1	-
ST Finn	7	11	3	34	18	4.25	18.88	0	0	1	-
PT Collins	10	13	4	36	13	4.00	40.00	0	0	0	-
AM Rossington	1	1	0	1	1	1.00	6.25	0	0	1	-
RH Patel	1	1	1	19	19*	-	45.23	0	0	0	-
TRG Hampton	1	1	1	1	1*	-	25.00	0	0	0	-

Batting & Fielding

	Mat	Overs	Mdns	Runs	Wkts	BBI	BBM	Ave	Econ	SR	5w	10
AB London	4	8.0	3	15	1	1/15	1/15	15.00	1.87	48.0	0	0
TS Roland-Jones	8	230.2	34	745	38	5/41	9/134	19.60	3.23	36.3	2	0
ST Finn	7	261.1	54	844	36	9/37	14/106	23.44	3.23	43.5	2	1
RH Patel	1	47.0	8	134	5	3/52	5/134	26.80	2.85	56.4	0	0
IE O'Brien	7	205.1	36	628	23	7/48	8/105	27.30	3.06	53.5	1	0
PT Collins	10	284.4	51	999	36	4/46	6/131	27.75	3.50	47.4	0	0
NJ Dexter	12	120.0	25	378	13	3/50	4/71	29.07	3.15	55.3	0	0
OA Shah	13	43.5	5	133	4	1/16	2/69	33.25	3.03	65.7	0	0
SD Udal	13	284.3	38	917	27	5/128	7/98	33.96	3.22	63.2	1	0
D Evans	4	102.3	19	397	11	5/87	5/150	36.09	3.87	55.9	1	0
GK Berg	15	235.0	32	877	24	4/72	7/131	36.54	3.73	58.7	0	0
TJ Murtagh	15	459.2	127	1405	38	5/52	8/123	36.97	3.05	72.5	2	0
TRG Hampton	1	14.0	3	42	1	1/15	1/42	42.00	3.00	84.0	0	0
JH Davey	4	27.0	2	107	2	2/41	2/65	53.50	3.96	81.0	0	0
DJ Malan	16	74.1	2	339	6	2/51	2/79	56.50	4.57	74.1	0	0
KS Toor	1	25.0	2	84	1	1/36	1/84	84.00	3.36	150.0	0	0
TMJ Smith	4	72.0	12	262	2	1/30	1/75	131.00	3.63	216.0	0	0
SD Robson	8	2.0	0	17	0	-	-	-	8.50	-	0	0

Bowling

Batting & Fielding

	Mat	Inns	NO	Runs	HS	Ave	SR	100	50	Ct	St
OA Shah	12	12	2	490	111	49.00	77.40	1	4	6	-
AC Gilchrist	1	1	0	38	38	38.00	88.37	0	0	0	0
SA Newman	12	12	1	412	122	37.45	99.03	1	3	4	-
NJ Dexter	12	10	2	295	56*	36.87	87.53	0	1	3	-
GK Berg	12	12	3	322	53	35.77	96.69	0	1	5	-
JA Simpson	12	9	1	219	82	27.37	77.65	0	1	8	3
DJ Malan	13	13	1	265	42	22.08	66.91	0	0	5	-
AJ Strauss	4	4	0	67	26	16.75	95.71	0	0	0	-
TS Roland-Jones	8	6	2	56	23*	14.00	88.88	0	0	3	-
JH Davey	3	3	1	28	15	14.00	38.88	0	0	1	-
SD Udal	10	7	1	82	33*	13.66	113.88	0	0	3	-
TE Scollay	6	6	0	78	32	13.00	86.66	0	0	2	-
PT Collins	7	3	2	13	6*	13.00	118.18	0	0	3	-
TMJ Smith	8	3	0	31	18	10.33	57.40	0	0	2	-
TJ Murtagh	11	7	3	41	20	10.25	73.21	0	0	1	-
JG Thompson	1	1	0	8	8	8.00	72.72	0	0	0	-
DA Warner	1	1	0	5	5	5.00	100.00	0	0	0	-
D Evans	1	1	0	0	0	0.00	0.00	0	0	0	-
REM Williams	5	1	1	2	2*	-	28.57	0	0	0	-

Bowling

	Mat	Overs	Mdns	Runs	Wkts	BBI	Ave	Econ	SR	5w
IE O'Brien	1	6.4	1	41	4	4/41	10.25	6.15	10.0	0
D Evans	1	10.0	1	51	3	3/51	17.00	5.10	20.0	0
ST Finn	2	16.0	1	71	4	2/31	17.75	4.43	24.0	0
PT Collins	7	45.4	1	244	13	4/25	18.76	5.34	21.0	0
TE Scollay	6	4.0	0	21	1	1/21	21.00	5.25	24.0	0
TJ Murtagh	11	85.2	4	474	17	3/35	27.88	5.55	30.1	0
TMJ Smith	8	48.0	0	253	8	3/26	31.62	5.27	36.0	0
TS Roland-Jones	8	61.0	3	362	11	3/55	32.90	5.93	33.2	0
SD Udal	10	57.0	0	315	6	2/18	52.50	5.52	57.0	0
GK Berg	12	25.0	1	121	2	1/13	60.50	4.84	75.0	0
OA Shah	12	9.0	0	63	1	1/28	63.00	7.00	54.0	0
REM Williams	5	24.5	0	199	2	2/60	99.50	8.01	74.5	0
NJ Dexter	12	65.0	0	336	2	1/31	168.00	5.16	195.0	0
JH Davey	3	3.0	0	24	0	-	-	8.00	-	0
DJ Malan	13	10.0	0	61	0	-	-	6.10	-	0
RH Patel	1	5.0	0	38	0	-	-	7.60	-	0
JG Thompson	1	3.0	0	20	0	-	-	6.66	-	0

	Mat	Inns	NO	Runs	HS	Ave	SR	100	50	Ct	St
EJG Morgan	4	4	2	148	79*	74.00	189.74	0	1	1	-
BJM Scott	9	5	3	89	43*	44.50	127.14	0	0	4	2
OA Shah	16	15	3	421	80	35.08	110.20	0	1	8	-
DJ Malan	16	16	5	364	86	33.09	130.00	0	1	2	-
AC Gilchrist	7	7	0	212	106	30.28	153.62	1	1	4	5
NJ Dexter	16	16	3	349	62*	26.84	114.05	0	1	6	-
GK Berg	14	10	4	160	41	26.66	170.21	0	0	7	-
JG Thompson	2	2	0	46	32	23.00	143.75	0	0	0	-
DA Warner	13	13	0	268	43	20.61	126.41	0	0	4	-
SA Newman	10	9	0	183	48	20.33	104.57	0	0	4	-
TMJ Smith	14	6	4	22	9*	11.00	84.61	0	0	4	-
T Henderson	9	6	0	44	17	7.33	115.78	0	0	0	-
JH Davey	2	2	1	7	7*	7.00	87.50	0	0	2	-
TJ Murtagh	15	2	0	6	6	3.00	75.00	0	0	5	-
PR Stirling	1	1	0	2	2	2.00	66.66	0	0	0	-
SD Udal	8	4	2	3	3	1.50	60.00	0	0	2	-
PT Collins	16	2	1	1	1*	1.00	25.00	0	0	2	-
IE O'Brien	1	1	1	1	1*	-	50.00	0	0	0	-

	Mat	Overs	Mdns	Runs	Wkts	BBI	Ave	Econ	SR	5w
JG Thompson	2	1.0	0	8	1	1/8	8.00	8.00	6.0	0
OA Shah	16	5.0	0	43	3	2/26	14.33	8.60	10.0	0
TMJ Smith	14	39.5	0	311	18	5/24	17.27	7.80	13.2	1
NJ Dexter	16	45.5	0	317	14	2/8	22.64	6.91	19.6	0
TJ Murtagh	15	48.2	2	393	16	3/24	24.56	8.13	18.1	0
PT Collins	16	54.0	0	422	16	3/27	26.37	7.81	20.2	0
T Henderson	9	35.0	0	258	9	3/25	28.66	7.37	23.3	0
SD Udal	8	21.0	0	146	5	3/24	29.20	6.95	25.2	0
GK Berg	14	37.0	0	292	6	2/45	48.66	7.89	37.0	0
JH Davey	2	5.0	0	48	0	-	-	9.60	-	0
ST Finn	1	2.0	0	30	0	-	-	15.00	-	0
DJ Malan	16	6.0	0	63	0	-	-	10.50	-	0
IE O'Brien	1	2.2	0	27	0	-	-	11.57	-	0
REM Williams	2	4.0	0	55	0	-	-	13.75	-	0

GARETH BERG

RHB RMF MVP64

NAME: Gareth Kyle Berg
BORN: January 18, 1981, Cape Town
HEIGHT: 6ft
SQUAD Nº: 8
NICKNAME: Bergy, Ice, Ford
OTHER TEAMS: Western Province
CAREER: First-class debut: 2008; List A debut: 2008; T20 debut: 2009; County cap: 2010

AOC SAYS: Berg was a latecomer to first-class cricket, making his Middlesex debut as a 27-year-old after a spell playing for Northamptonshire Second XI. The South Africa-born allrounder moved to England after playing a handful of one-day matches for Western Province B and has gone on to become a pivotal member of the Middlesex side across all formats since joining the county in 2007. A brisk seamer and versatile middle-order batsman, Berg enjoyed his most successful season with the bat in 2010, scoring his maiden first-class ton against Derbyshire. A back injury hampered his bowling, however, and he was forced to play as a specialist batsman in the latter half of the campaign.

LAST WORD: "Berg plays a key role, batting at No.6 and bowling useful overs. It is vital for Middlesex that he is fully fit and able to bowl." *Jon Batham*

Batting & Fielding

	Mat	Inns	NO	Runs	HS	Ave	SR	100	50	Ct	St
First-class	31	54	7	1547	125	32.91	67.82	1	10	17	0
List A	33	28	5	550	65	23.91	88.28	0	2	9	0
Twenty20	21	17	7	297	41	29.70	151.53	0	0	8	0

Bowling

	Mat	Balls	Runs	Wkts	BBI	BBM	Ave	Econ	SR	5w	10
First-class	31	3217	1934	52	5/55	7/131	37.19	3.60	61.8	2	0
List A	33	774	704	24	4/50	4/50	29.33	5.45	32.2	0	0
Twenty20	21	327	443	9	2/31	2/31	49.22	8.12	36.3	0	0

NAME: Steven Paul Crook
BORN: May 28, 1983, Adelaide
HEIGHT: 5ft 11in
SQUAD Nº: 25
NICKNAME: Crooky, Crookster
OTHER TEAMS: Lancashire,
Northamptonshire
CAREER: First-class debut: 2003; List A
debut: 2003; T20 debut: 2004

MIDDLESEX

AOC SAYS: Middlesex recruited Crook over the winter and he will initially act as cover for allrounder Gareth Berg in Championship cricket. A skiddy seamer and aggressive lower-order batsman, Crook was a member of Australia's under 19 squad in the 2001/02 World Cup and attended the Australian Institute of Sport cricket academy. He holds a British passport through his English parents and signed for Lancashire in 2001, but after struggling for regular first-team cricket he moved to Northamptonshire in 2006 following a successful loan spell at Wantage Road. For a time Crook was a regular in the Steelbacks' one-day and T20 sides but he slipped out of the reckoning and signed a one-year deal with Middlesex in February following his release by Northants.

LAST WORD: "Steven has worked exceptionally hard during the sessions he has attended and made a positive impression on the coaches." *Angus Fraser*

Batting & Fielding

	Mat	Inns	NO	Runs	HS	Ave	SR	100	50	Ct	St
First-class	35	47	7	1261	97	31.52	70.40	0	9	12	0
List A	30	20	2	281	72	15.61	92.13	0	1	6	0
Twenty20	33	18	3	186	27	12.40	118.47	0	0	6	0

Bowling

	Mat	Balls	Runs	Wkts	BBI	BBM	Ave	Econ	SR	5w	10
First-class	35	4303	2842	59	5/71	-	48.16	3.96	72.9	1	0
List A	30	1050	1059	21	4/20	4/20	50.42	6.05	50.0	0	0
Twenty20	33	228	352	9	2/24	2/24	39.11	9.26	25.3	0	0

COREY COLLYMORE

MIDDLESEX

NAME: Corey Dalanelo Collymore
BORN: 21 December, 1977, Boscobelle, Barbados
HEIGHT: 6ft
SQUAD Nº: 32
NICKNAME: Screw, CC
OTHER TEAMS: West Indies, Barbados, Sussex, Warwickshire
CAREER: Test debut: 1999; ODI debut: 1999; First-class debut: 1999; List A debut: 1999; T20 debut: 2006

AOC SAYS: Middlesex pulled off a coup by signing veteran Kolpak seamer Collymore over the winter from Sussex as a like-for-like replacement for the outgoing Iain O'Brien. The former West Indies paceman is ideally suited to English conditions, where his metronomic accuracy and ability to move the ball away from the right-hander make him a formidable opponent, and he proved age is no barrier last season by collecting the highest wicket tally of his career with 57 Championship wickets. Described by Brian Lara as a "thinking man's bowler", Collymore was a valuable servant to West Indian cricket at a difficult time and twice collected seven-wicket hauls at Jamaica, against Sri Lanka in 2003 and again in 2005 against Pakistan.

LAST WORD: "Collymore is proud and hard working and we expect his input to be extremely valuable at Middlesex." *Angus Fraser*

Batting & Fielding

	Mat	Inns	NO	Runs	HS	Ave	SR	100	50	Ct	St
Tests	30	52	27	197	16*	7.88	30.68	0	0	6	0
ODIs	84	35	17	104	13*	5.77	39.84	0	0	12	0
First-class	134	187	85	819	23	8.02	-	0	0	45	0
List A	131	50	25	151	13*	6.04	-	0	0	20	0
Twenty20	6	2	1	5	4	5.00	45.45	0	0	4	0

Bowling

	Mat	Balls	Runs	Wkts	BBI	BBM	Ave	Econ	SR	5w	10
Tests	30	6337	3004	93	7/57	11/134	32.30	2.84	68.1	4	1
ODIs	84	4074	2924	83	5/51	5/51	35.22	4.30	49.0	1	0
First-class	134	22970	10717	406	7/57	-	26.39	2.79	56.5	12	2
List A	131	6139	4374	139	5/27	5/27	31.46	4.27	44.1	2	0
Twenty20	6	95	133	3	1/21	1/21	44.33	8.40	31.6	0	0

NAME: Joshua Henry Davey
BORN: August 3, 1990, Aberdeen
SQUAD Nº: 24
OTHER TEAMS: Scotland
CAREER: ODI debut: 2010; First-class debut:
2010; List A debut: 2010; T20 debut: 2010

MIDDLESEX

AOC SAYS: Davey is a promising allrounder who has already represented Scotland in ODIs.
He demonstrated his potential with the ball by returning the best ever bowling figures for
Scotland in ODI cricket with a haul of 5-9 against Afghanistan but he is predominantly a
batsman. After making 72 on his first-class debut against Oxford University last season,
Davey made his Championship bow against Gloucestershire on a difficult Bristol track
and again impressed with a half-century to earn the praise of batting coach Mark O'Neill.
With Eoin Morgan likely to be away on international duty and Owais Shah moving to Essex,
Davey will hope to make a middle-order spot his own this season and he can expect to be
given fair opportunity in the one-day side.

LAST WORD: "Davey is on the fringes of the first-team and I expect him to feature in more
one-day than four-day cricket this season." *Jon Batham*

Batting & Fielding

	Mat	Inns	NO	Runs	HS	Ave	SR	100	50	Ct	St
ODIs	4	4	0	46	24	11.50	45.09	0	0	2	0
First-class	4	7	0	220	72	31.42	42.06	0	3	3	0
List A	7	7	1	74	24	12.33	42.52	0	0	3	0
Twenty20	2	2	1	7	7*	7.00	87.50	0	0	2	0

Bowling

	Mat	Balls	Runs	Wkts	BBI	BBM	Ave	Econ	SR	5w	10
ODIs	4	122	94	6	5/9	5/9	15.66	4.62	20.3	1	0
First-class	4	162	107	2	2/41	2/65	53.50	3.96	81.0	0	0
List A	7	140	118	6	5/9	5/9	19.66	5.05	23.3	1	0
Twenty20	2	30	48	0	-	-	-	9.60	-	0	0

NAME: Neil John Dexter
BORN: August 21, 1984, Johannesburg
HEIGHT: 6ft
SQUAD Nº: 4
NICKNAME: Ted, Dex, Sexy Dexy
OTHER TEAMS: Essex, Kent
CAREER: First-class debut: 2005; List A
debut: 2005; T20 debut: 2006; County cap:
2010 (Middlesex)

AOC SAYS: Dexter became the third youngest captain in Middlesex's history midway through last season following Shaun Udal's resignation, and the batting allrounder rose to the challenge. He impressed with the bat and showed himself to be a strong leader, despite the county's disappointing campaign. He joined Kent as a Kolpak player in 2005 and made an immediate impact with an unbeaten 79 on debut against Nottinghamshire. Dexter continued to show glimpses of his talent as an aggressive middle-order batsman and steady seamer but became frustrated with a lack of opportunities and rejected a three-year contract to sign for Middlesex in 2008. He was initially blighted by a back problem but has not looked back since making a career-best 146 against his former county in 2009.

LAST WORD: "Dexter is very well respected in the dressing room for a relatively young player and he led the side well after taking over the captaincy." *Jon Batham*

Batting & Fielding

	Mat	Inns	NO	Runs	HS	Ave	SR	100	50	Ct	St
First-class	51	81	12	2955	146	42.82	54.76	7	15	44	0
List A	52	45	8	1250	135*	33.78	80.85	2	5	12	0
Twenty20	53	47	6	870	73	21.21	111.68	0	2	22	0

Bowling

	Mat	Balls	Runs	Wkts	BBI	BBM	Ave	Econ	SR	5w	10
First-class	51	2064	1167	28	3/50		41.67	3.39	73.7	0	0
List A	52	1120	968	19	3/17	3/17	50.94	5.18	58.9	0	0
Twenty20	53	419	555	19	3/27	3/27	29.21	7.94	22.0	0	0

NAME: Steven Thomas Finn
BORN: April 4, 1989, Watford
HEIGHT: 6ft 7in
SQUAD Nº: 9
NICKNAME: Finny, Lurch, Streak
OTHER TEAMS: England
CAREER: Test debut: 2010; ODI debut: 2011;
First-class debut: 2005; List A debut: 2007;
T20 debut: 2008; County cap: 2009

MIDDLESEX

AOC SAYS: Finn was named the ICC's Emerging Player of the Year in 2010 after a meteoric rise that saw him progress from a hot prospect to an Ashes winner in the space of nine months. The beanpole paceman had been earmarked as an England bowler since he made his county debut as a 16-year-old, becoming Middlesex's youngest debutant since Fred Titmus in 1949. After steady progression, Finn enjoyed a breakthrough year in 2009 when he picked up 53 first-class wickets and was subsequently picked to tour UAE with England Lions. A series of injuries to England's bowlers during the tour of Bangladesh saw Finn parachuted in as cover and after making an impression on Andy Flower he was handed a shock Test debut in Chittagong. After opening the 2010 county season with a career-best haul of 9-37 against Worcestershire he retained his England place for the return series against Bangladesh and took nine wickets on his home debut at Lord's to scoop the Man of the Match award. He secured his place in the Ashes squad with a fine series against Pakistan and began well Down Under, taking 6-125 on a docile track in the first Test at Brisbane. He continued to take wickets but was replaced by Tim Bresnan for the final two Tests after tiring and proving expensive. Despite that setback, his natural pace and bounce make him England's brightest fast bowling prospect.

INSIDE TRACK: "I think Steven had mixed emotions after the Ashes. He was delighted to have played in an Ashes winning side, taken 14 wickets and had an impact on the series but disappointed he didn't bowl as well has he can do and to miss out on the last two Test matches. But if you'd asked him a year ago if he'd take an England central contract, 46 Test wickets and be part of an Ashes winning side, he would have bitten your arm off. He is hard on himself but it's a good trait to never be satisfied. It didn't surprise me that Chris Tremlett went past him in Australia because he's been around a little bit longer and has greater consistency. The challenge for Steven is to get to where Tremlett is now in a year or 18 months and produce his best on a slightly more consistent basis." *Angus Fraser*

STEVEN FINN

MIDDLESEX

Batting & Fielding

	Mat	Inns	NO	Runs	HS	Ave	SR	100	50	Ct	St
Tests	11	12	9	16	9*	5.33	16.66	0	0	3	0
ODIs	3	2	0	35	35	17.50	129.62	0	0	1	0
First-class	51	65	23	248	26*	5.90	26.52	0	0	13	0
List A	35	11	2	70	35	7.77	67.96	0	0	5	0
Twenty20	16	3	2	14	8	14.00	93.33	0	0	4	0

Bowling

	Mat	Balls	Runs	Wkts	BBI	BBM	Ave	Econ	SR	5w	10
Tests	11	1828	1207	46	6/125	9/187	26.23	3.96	39.7	3	0
ODIs	3	180	169	3	2/51	2/51	56.33	5.63	60.0	0	0
First-class	51	8571	5226	181	9/37	-	28.87	3.65	47.3	6	1
List A	35	1470	1281	40	3/23	3/23	32.02	5.22	36.7	0	0
Twenty20	16	308	431	15	3/22	3/22	28.73	8.39	20.5	0	0

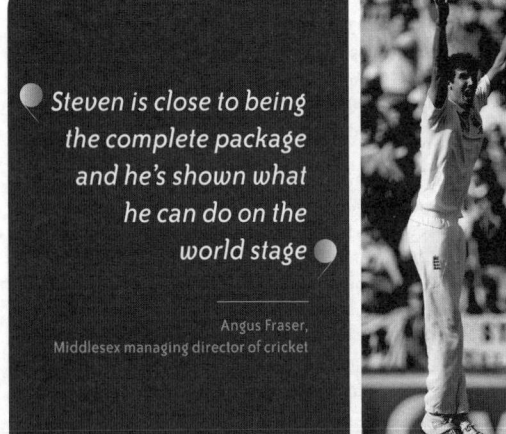

Steven is close to being the complete package and he's shown what he can do on the world stage

Angus Fraser,
Middlesex managing director of cricket

NAME: Daniel Mark Housego
BORN: October 12, 1988, Windsor
HEIGHT: 5ft 9in
SQUAD Nº: 3
NICKNAME: Harry Housego, Housey, The Estate Agent
CAREER: First-class debut: 2008; T20 debut: 2008

MIDDLESEX

AOC SAYS: Housego is a middle-order batsman who is held in high regard at Lord's. A talented all-round sportsman, he was under 12 national champion at 200m and a trainee footballer for Oxford United but chose to pursue a career in cricket. After being named Middlesex's Youth Player of the Year in 2005 he boosted his reputation with an unbeaten 170 for Berkshire in the Minor Counties Championship and stacked up the runs in second XI cricket. He is yet to grasp the handful of opportunities he has been given in Championship cricket but registered his maiden first-class ton last season against Oxford University. 2011 promises to be a definitive season for Housego after he admitted during the winter that he may have to leave Middlesex if he fails to secure a first-team place.

LAST WORD: "Housego is a technically sound, classical batsman who Middlesex have been expecting to blossom for a year or two. This year could be his time to do so." *Jon Batham*

Batting & Fielding

	Mat	Inns	NO	Runs	HS	Ave	SR	100	50	Ct	St
First-class	7	14	1	296	102*	22.76	50.59	1	0	3	0
Twenty20	5	4	0	37	18	9.25	88.09	0	0	0	0

Bowling

	Mat	Balls	Runs	Wkts	BBI	BBM	Ave	Econ	SR	5w	10
First-class	7	7	17	0	-	-	-	14.57	-	0	0
Twenty20	5	-	-	-	-	-	-	-	-	-	-

MIDDLESEX

NAME: Anthony John Ireland
BORN: August 30, 1984, Masvingo, Zimbabwe
SQUAD №: 88
OTHER TEAMS: Zimbabwe,
Gloucestershire, Midlands, Southern Rocks
CAREER: ODI debut: 2005; T20I debut:
2006; First-class debut: 2003; List A debut:
2004; T20 debut: 2006; County cap: 2007
(Gloucestershire)

AOC SAYS: The former Zimbabwe seamer brought an end to a four-year spell with
Gloucestershire to boost Middlesex's pace attack ahead of the 2011 campaign. A tall bowler
who troubles batsmen with his bounce, Ireland had the best season of his career in 2010,
profiting from a juicy Bristol track to take 36 first-class wickets at a miserly average. He
first came to England in 2004 to play club cricket after the player rebellion in Zimbabwe
but returned to represent his country in the 2007 World Cup. He quit international cricket
immediately after the tournament to join Gloucestershire as a Kolpak player.

LAST WORD: "I am delighted Anthony has chosen to join Middlesex where he will add
strength, variety and quality to our fast bowling resources. I have always been impressed
by Anthony, not just as a cricketer but as a person too." *Angus Fraser*

Batting & Fielding

	Mat	Inns	NO	Runs	HS	Ave	SR	100	50	Ct	St
ODIs	26	13	5	30	8*	3.75	29.70	0	0	2	0
T20Is	1	1	1	2	2*	-	66.66	0	0	0	0
First-class	36	53	16	135	16*	3.64	22.53	0	0	10	0
List A	65	31	15	90	17	5.62	39.13	0	0	9	0
Twenty20	31	10	4	32	8*	5.33	61.53	0	0	9	0

Bowling

	Mat	Balls	Runs	Wkts	BBI	BBM	Ave	Econ	SR	5w	10
ODIs	26	1326	1115	38	3/41	3/41	29.34	5.04	34.8	0	0
T20Is	1	18	33	1	1/33	1/33	33.00	11.00	18.0	0	0
First-class	36	5313	3271	113	7/36	-	28.94	3.69	47.0	4	1
List A	65	2805	2519	88	4/16	4/16	28.62	5.38	31.8	0	0
Twenty20	31	569	845	35	3/10	3/10	24.14	8.91	16.2	0	0

NAME: Adam Brian London
BORN: October 12, 1988, Ashford, Middlesex
SQUAD Nº: 19
CAREER: First-class debut: 2009; List A
debut: 2009

MIDDLESEX

AOC SAYS: London is a tenacious middle-order batsman who made a half-century on his first-class debut against Gloucestershire at Lord's in 2009. He followed that up by making 65 on the final day of the season to help Middlesex to a draw against Derbyshire and avoid the Championship wooden spoon for the first time in their history, despite batting with a broken finger for the entirety of his innings. The left-hander only featured in two Championship fixtures last season but enjoyed a solid season in the Second XI. He sustained a serious knee injury at the end of the campaign that required surgery but after a successful operation London is among the contenders to fill the batting spot vacated by Owais Shah.

LAST WORD: "Adam is a determined cricketer, a gritty batsman and an absolutely brilliant fielder." *Jon Batham*

Batting & Fielding

	Mat	Inns	NO	Runs	HS	Ave	SR	100	50	Ct	St
First-class	8	15	2	327	77	25.15	38.51	0	3	4	0
List A	2	-	-	-	-	-	-	-	-	0	0

Bowling

	Mat	Balls	Runs	Wkts	BBI	BBM	Ave	Econ	SR	5w	10
First-class	8	96	54	1	1/15	1/15	54.00	3.37	96.0	0	0
List A	2	6	5	0	-	-	-	5.00	-	0	0

MIDDLESEX

NAME: Dawid Johannes Malan
BORN: September 3, 1987, Roehampton
HEIGHT: 6ft
SQUAD №: 29
NICKNAME: AC
OTHER TEAMS: Boland
CAREER: First-class debut: 2006; List A
debut: 2006; T20 debut: 2006; County
cap: 2010

AOC SAYS: Malan is a mercurial strokemaker who has been Middlesex's leading
runscorer for the past two seasons. In 2010 he topped 1,000 Championship runs in
a season for the first time and is regarded as a prodigious talent with international
prospects. Like most left-handers, he is very strong square of the wicket but a
classical technique allows him to play straight down the ground with ease. Malan is of
South African parentage and made his first-class debut for Boland before signing for
Middlesex in 2006. His father Dawid played a handful of games for Western Province,
while his younger brother Charl has played first-class cricket for Loughborough
University and the MCC. After finishing as leading runscorer in second XI cricket
in 2007, the following season he struck an unbeaten 132 on Championship debut
against Northamptonshire and a week later made a breathtaking 103 off 51 balls in
the Twenty20 quarter-final victory over Lancashire at The Oval. He was subsequently
named in England's Performance Programme squad. A problem in the early stages
of his career had been his failure to convert starts into three figure scores but
he developed his game last season, hitting three first-class tons in all, including
matchwinning efforts against Surrey and Sussex. Malan signed a new contract in
November that will keep him at Lord's until at least the end of the 2014 season and he
is set to be the bedrock of their batting in the pivotal No.4 slot.

INSIDE TRACK: "I am thrilled Dawid has chosen to commit his long-term future to
Middlesex. He is a young man with a huge amount of potential. He works incredibly
hard and has the ability to achieve great things in the game. For the past two seasons
Dawid has been the club's most consistent batsman, which was a pretty good effort
for a 22-year-old. He wins games of cricket, as he showed last year against Sussex
at Hove, Surrey at Lord's and Glamorgan in Cardiff when he played the innings that
sealed Middlesex Championship victories. When in top form he is a delight to watch.
In the past two seasons he has made steady progress and I expect his batting to
develop further over the coming years as he works things out." *Angus Fraser*

Batting & Fielding

	Mat	Inns	NO	Runs	HS	Ave	SR	100	50	Ct	St
First-class	47	84	8	2770	132*	36.44	50.00	4	19	45	0
List A	42	42	4	742	60	19.52	69.08	0	2	13	0
Twenty20	43	41	13	916	103	32.71	118.96	1	2	8	0

Bowling

	Mat	Balls	Runs	Wkts	BBI	BBM	Ave	Econ	SR	5w	10
First-class	47	1678	1152	24	4/20	4/88	48.00	4.11	69.9	0	0
List A	42	413	405	10	2/4	2/4	40.50	5.88	41.3	0	0
Twenty20	43	240	276	12	2/10	2/10	23.00	6.90	20.0	0	0

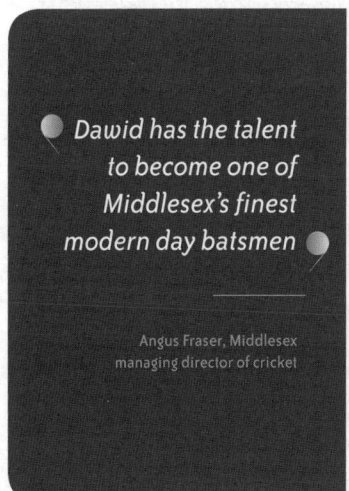

Dawid has the talent to become one of Middlesex's finest modern day batsmen

Angus Fraser, Middlesex managing director of cricket

RYAN MCLAREN

LHB RFM W1

MIDDLESEX

OVERSEAS PLAYER

NAME: Ryan McLaren
BORN: February 9, 1983, Kimberley, South Africa
SQUAD Nº: 23
OTHER TEAMS: South Africa, Eagles, Free State, Kent, Mumbai Indians
CAREER: Test debut: 2010; ODI debut: 2009; T20I debut: 2009; First-class debut: 2003; List A debut: 2003; T20 debut: 2005; County cap: 2007 (Kent)

AOC SAYS: Middlesex have recruited McLaren as their second overseas player for the duration of the FP t20. He has a proven track record in the competition having taken a hat-trick in the final against Gloucestershire in 2007 to help Kent lift the trophy. The South Africa international is a powerful lower-order hitter capable of clearing the ropes and a canny right-arm seamer with a deceptive slower ball and reliable yorker. McLaren joined Kent in 2007 as a Kolpak player but after a dispute between club and country he turned his back on county cricket to pursue an international career. He made his Test debut against England in 2010 but has since slipped out of the reckoning.

LAST WORD: "McLaren is just the kind of explosive cricketer Middlesex have lacked in T20 cricket. He is capable of scoring runs quickly and is an extremely skilful bowler at the death." *Jon Batham*

Batting & Fielding

	Mat	Inns	NO	Runs	HS	Ave	SR	100	50	Ct	St
Tests	1	1	1	33	33*	-	58.92	0	0	0	0
ODIs	10	8	2	37	12	6.16	61.66	0	0	5	0
T20Is	5	3	3	8	6*	-	88.88	0	0	1	0
First-class	85	123	20	2950	140	28.64	-	2	16	43	0
List A	115	85	33	1702	82*	32.73	87.55	0	8	38	0
Twenty20	88	60	30	623	46*	20.76	113.06	0	0	37	0

Bowling

	Mat	Balls	Runs	Wkts	BBI	BBM	Ave	Econ	SR	5w	10
Tests	1	78	43	1	1/30	1/43	43.00	3.30	78.0	0	0
ODIs	10	432	366	8	3/51	3/51	45.75	5.08	54.0	0	0
T20Is	5	119	144	9	5/19	5/19	16.00	7.26	13.2	1	0
First-class	85	13658	6822	274	8/38		24.89	2.99	49.8	11	1
List A	115	4357	3714	124	5/46	5/46	29.95	5.11	35.1	1	0
Twenty20	88	1674	2102	76	5/19	5/19	27.65	7.53	22.0	1	0

NAME: Eoin Joseph Gerard Morgan
BORN: September 10, 1986, Dublin
HEIGHT: 5ft 10in
SQUAD Nº: 7
NICKNAME: Moggie, Morgs
OTHER TEAMS: England, Ireland
CAREER: Test debut: 2010; ODI debut: 2006;
T20I debut: 2009; First-class debut: 2004;
List A debut: 2004; T20 debut: 2006; County
cap: 2008

MIDDLESEX

AOC SAYS: An innovative middle-order batsman who possesses shots that others can only dream of, Morgan has been a revelation since switching his allegiance from Ireland to England two years ago. The left-hander struck 99 on his ODI debut against Scotland as a 19-year-old and went on to represent the country of his birth at the 2007 World Cup. He showed his talent extended to the longer format by topping 1,000 Championship runs for the first time in 2008 and attracted the attention of the England selectors. Morgan made no secret of the fact that playing Test cricket for England was his ultimate ambition and he moved a step closer to that goal by representing England Lions and touring India as part of the England Performance Programme squad in 2008. He made his ODI bow for his adopted nation against West Indies the following year and went on to star in the ICC Champions Trophy with matchwinning half-centuries against Sri Lanka and South Africa. A stunning knock of 110 followed in Bangladesh and despite his middling first-class record he was rewarded with a Test debut against the same opposition at Lord's. He eased concerns that his unorthodox technique was ill-suited to Test cricket with a maiden Test ton against Pakistan at Trent Bridge and was included in the squad to tour Australia last winter. He did not feature in the Ashes but now has a chance to make a middle-order berth his own following Paul Collingwood's retirement from Test cricket.

INSIDE TRACK: "I think Eoin is in pole position to take the Test spot in England's middle-order vacated by Paul Collingwood, it's just whether he's going to be able to play enough first-class innings before the first squad is announced. He hasn't got a great first-class record so far but he has shown he's able to adapt to different conditions and play an innings according to the situation. Like all players there is obviously room for improvement, but he works very hard to improve his game. I know Andrew Strauss and Andy Flower look at the character of individuals very carefully and he's got the right temperament for international cricket. When Michael Vaughan, Marcus Trescothick and Paul Collingwood were first selected for England they didn't have great first-class statistics but proved to be inspired selections. Morgan has the ability to do the same. He's a very calm and confident guy who's very assured in what he does." *Angus Fraser*

MIDDLESEX

Batting & Fielding

	Mat	Inns	NO	Runs	HS	Ave	SR	100	50	Ct	St
Tests	6	8	0	256	130	32.00	52.56	1	0	4	0
ODIs	62	62	11	1967	115	38.56	81.38	4	11	25	0
T20Is	16	16	6	473	85*	47.30	134.75	0	3	9	0
First-class	56	92	12	2936	209*	36.70	50.40	7	13	47	1
List A	142	135	21	4218	161	37.00	83.40	7	24	46	0
Twenty20	66	62	11	1400	85*	27.45	130.35	0	6	30	0

Bowling

	Mat	Balls	Runs	Wkts	BBI	BBM	Ave	Econ	SR	5w	10
Tests	6	-	-	-	-	-	-	-	-	-	-
ODIs	62			-	-	-	-	-	-	-	-
T20Is	16	-	-	-	-	-	-	-	-	-	-
First-class	56	97	83	2	2/24	2/24	41.50	5.13	48.5	0	0
List A	142	42	49	0	-	-	-	7.00	-	0	0
Twenty20	66	-	-	-	-	-	-	-	-	-	-

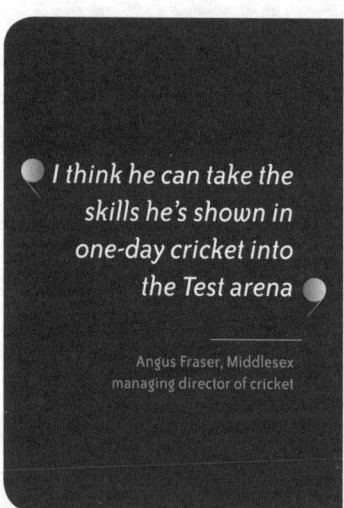

I think he can take the skills he's shown in one-day cricket into the Test arena

Angus Fraser, Middlesex managing director of cricket

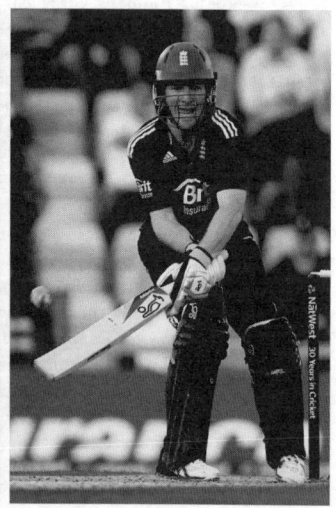

NAME: Timothy James Murtagh
BORN: August 2, 1981, Lambeth
HEIGHT: 6ft 2in
SQUAD Nº: 34
NICKNAME: Dial M
OTHER TEAMS: Surrey
CAREER: First-class debut: 2000; List A debut: 2000; T20 debut: 2003; County cap: 2008 (Middlesex)

MIDDLESEX

AOC SAYS: Murtagh is a swing bowler of lively pace who joined Middlesex from local rivals Surrey in 2007. Having spent several seasons struggling to get into the first team at Surrey he found a home at Lord's and took 64 and 60 Championship wickets in 2008 and 2009 respectively. The former England under 19 paceman is also a more than handy lower-order batsman, capable of batting at No.8 in Championship cricket. After benefitting from bowling in tandem with Dirk Nannes and Steven Finn in past seasons, he struggled as the spearhead of the attack in 2010. Murtagh – whose brother Chris also represented Surrey – now faces a battle to keep his place in the Middlesex side following the signings of Corey Collymore and Anthony Ireland and the emergence of Toby Roland-Jones.

LAST WORD: "Murtagh is still a fine cricketer but after a disappointing season in 2010 is no longer guaranteed to be the first name on the teamsheet." *Jon Batham*

Batting & Fielding

	Mat	Inns	NO	Runs	HS	Ave	SR	100	50	Ct	St
First-class	98	139	43	2168	74*	22.58	-	0	9	29	0
List A	115	76	27	595	35*	12.14	-	0	0	31	0
Twenty20	66	28	10	182	40*	10.11	110.97	0	0	14	0

Bowling

	Mat	Balls	Runs	Wkts	BBI	BBM	Ave	Econ	SR	5w	10
First-class	98	15061	8641	280	7/82	-	30.86	3.44	53.7	12	1
List A	115	5112	4418	165	4/14	4/14	26.77	5.18	30.9	0	0
Twenty20	66	1329	1857	78	6/24	6/24	23.80	8.38	17.0	1	0

SCOTT NEWMAN   LHB RM R4

MIDDLESEX

NAME: Scott Alexander Newman
BORN: November 3, 1979, Epsom
HEIGHT: 6ft 1in
SQUAD Nº: 77
NICKNAME: Ronaldo
OTHER TEAMS: Nottinghamshire, Surrey
CAREER: First-class debut: 2002; List A
debut: 2001; T20 debut: 2003; County cap:
2005 (Surrey)

AOC SAYS: An old-fashioned opening batsman of vast experience, Middlesex signed
Newman ahead of the 2010 season to complement a youthful batting unit. He produced
two centuries in a solid season but will hope to improve on a first-class average of 35
with Australian opener Chris Rogers arriving at Lord's to share the burden at the top of
the order. The left-hander started his career with Surrey and was a reliable runscorer,
surpassing 1,000 Championships runs in a season four times in the space of five years
between 2004 and 2008. After a loan spell with Nottinghamshire, Newman made a
permanent move to Trent Bridge in 2009 but endured the worst campaign of his career and
returned south after one season.

LAST WORD: "Scott is a vastly experienced county professional who adds invaluable
experience to the top of our batting line-up." *Vinny Codrington, Middlesex chief executive*

Batting & Fielding

	Mat	Inns	NO	Runs	HS	Ave	SR	100	50	Ct	St
First-class	116	199	3	7721	219	39.39	63.24	16	46	85	0
List A	94	92	4	2692	177	30.59	-		4	16	22	0
Twenty20	49	46	4	923	81*	21.97	109.61	0	4	18	0

Bowling

	Mat	Balls	Runs	Wkts	BBI	BBM	Ave	Econ	SR	5w	10
First-class	116	78	57	0	-	-	-	4.38	-	0	0
List A	94	-	-	-	-	-	-	-	-	-	-
Twenty20	49	-	-	-	-	-	-	-	-	-	-

SAM ROBSON

RHB LB

NAME: Samuel David Robson
BORN: July 1, 1989, Paddington, Australia
SQUAD Nº: 12
NICKNAME: Robbo
CAREER: First-class debut: 2009; List A debut: 2008

MIDDLESEX

AOC SAYS: Robson is a top-order batsman with a solid technique and maturity beyond his years. Born in Australia to an English mother, he is set to benefit from the departure of Owais Shah to Essex and will start the season batting at No.3 in Championship cricket. Robson struck his maiden first-class ton in just his fifth match, making 110 in a six-hour knock against Essex at Lord's, and further demonstrated his ability to play long innings last season with a double century against Oxford University. His patient, accumulative batting style is likely to see him down the pecking order in one-day cricket. Robson is a contemporary and school friend of Australia Test opener Phillip Hughes and has played grade cricket for Sydney South East.

LAST WORD: "Robson is a young batsman capable of playing long innings. He's a gritty player and difficult to get out." *Jon Batham*

Batting & Fielding

	Mat	Inns	NO	Runs	HS	Ave	SR	100	50	Ct	St
First-class	15	28	0	954	204	34.07	46.46	2	4	20	0
List A	4	2	0	69	48	34.50	74.19	0	0	0	0

Bowling

	Mat	Balls	Runs	Wkts	BBI	BBM	Ave	Econ	SR	5w	10
First-class	15	24	22	0	-	-	-	5.50	-	0	0
List A	4	-	-	-	-	-	-	-	-	-	-

CHRIS ROGERS

LHB RM/LB R4 MVP87

MIDDLESEX

OVERSEAS PLAYER

NAME: Christopher John Llewellyn Rogers
BORN: August 31, 1977, Sydney
HEIGHT: 5ft 11in
SQUAD Nº: 1
NICKNAME: Bucky
OTHER TEAMS: Australia, Derbyshire, Leicestershire, Northamptonshire, Victoria, Western Australia
CAREER: Test debut: 2008; First-class debut: 1998; List A debut: 1998; T20 debut: 2005; County cap: 2008 (Derbyshire)

AOC SAYS: Middlesex recruited Rogers from Derbyshire at the end of last season in an attempt to solve their problems at the top of the order and they could hardly have picked a batsman with a better track record in county cricket. Rogers averaged a touch under 60 over four seasons with Derbyshire and also enjoyed successful spells with Leicestershire and Northamptonshire. The aggressive redheaded opener has been no less prolific in state cricket for Western Australia and was unfortunate to have had his path into the national side blocked for so many years by Matthew Hayden and Justin Langer. He was passed over for Phil Jaques when Langer retired in 2007 and made a solitary Test appearance in 2008 against India in place of the injured Matthew Hayden.

LAST WORD: "Rogers has a proven track record and could form a very effective opening partnership with Scott Newman, who is a different kind of player." *Jon Batham*

Batting & Fielding

	Mat	Inns	NO	Runs	HS	Ave	SR	100	50	Ct	St
Tests	1	2	0	19	15	9.50	70.37	0	0	1	0
First-class	178	315	22	15028	319	51.29	-	45	69	175	0
List A	129	125	7	4175	140	35.38	-	4	28	62	0
Twenty20	23	20	1	369	58	19.42	123.41	0	3	16	0

Bowling

	Mat	Balls	Runs	Wkts	BBI	BBM	Ave	Econ	SR	5w	10
Tests	1	-	-	-	-	-	-	-	-	-	-
First-class	178	230	131	1	1/16	1/16	131.00	3.41	230.0	0	0
List A	129	24	26	2	2/22	2/22	13.00	6.50	12.0	0	0
Twenty20	23	-	-	-	-	-	-	-	-	-	-

NAME: Tobias Skelton Roland-Jones
BORN: January 29, 1988, Ashford, Middlesex
SQUAD Nº: 21
CAREER: First-class debut: 2010; List A debut: 2010

MIDDLESEX

AOC SAYS: Roland-Jones was the revelation of last season for Middlesex, finishing as joint leading wicket-taker in Championship cricket with 38 victims despite only featuring in eight matches. The medium-pacer began life as a batsman and still hopes to become known as an allrounder but it was with the ball that he made his mark last season. He made an early impression by outperforming Steven Finn and Iain O'Brien in just his second Championship outing by taking 4-100 against Sussex on a featherbed track at Uxbridge. He followed that effort up with five-wicket hauls against Surrey and Worcestershire. Roland-Jones does not possess express pace but has shown exceptional consistency for an inexperienced seamer and does just enough with the ball to create problems for batsmen.

LAST WORD: "Toby has maturity beyond his years and he understands that patience and control will earn wickets." *Jon Batham*

Batting & Fielding

	Mat	Inns	NO	Runs	HS	Ave	SR	100	50	Ct	St
First-class	9	14	2	154	30*	12.83	52.20	0	0	3	0
List A	8	6	2	56	23*	14.00	88.88	0	0	3	0

Bowling

	Mat	Balls	Runs	Wkts	BBI	BBM	Ave	Econ	SR	5w	10
First-class	9	1538	814	42	5/41	9/134	19.38	3.17	36.6	2	0
List A	8	366	362	11	3/55	3/55	32.90	5.93	33.2	0	0

TOM SCOLLAY

RHB OB

MIDDLESEX

NAME: Thomas Edward Scollay
BORN: November 28, 1987, Alice Springs, Australia
SQUAD Nº: 5
CAREER: List A debut: 2010

AOC SAYS: Scollay is an exciting middle-order batsman who has progressed through the ranks at Middlesex. He made his one-day debut last season against the touring Bangladesh side and made just three but was selected to face Yorkshire in the CB40 three weeks later and showed promise with a brisk 32 off 34 balls in an otherwise disappointing batting effort. His tidy offspin also has some potential and he had Andrew Gale stumped to pick up his first senior wicket in the same match. He featured in four more matches in the competition with limited success but he can expect to have more opportunities to prove his worth in one-day cricket this season.

LAST WORD: "Scollay is an exciting prospect. He's an aggressive young batsman who has made a lot of runs in the Middlesex County Cricket League for Eastcote." *Jon Batham*

Batting & Fielding

	Mat	Inns	NO	Runs	HS	Ave	SR	100	50	Ct	St
List A	6	6	0	78	32	13.00	86.66	0	0	2	0

Bowling

	Mat	Balls	Runs	Wkts	BBI	BBM	Ave	Econ	SR	5w	10
List A	6	24	21	1	1/21	1/21	21.00	5.25	24.0	0	0

NAME: Benjamin James Matthew Scott
BORN: August 4, 1981, Isleworth
HEIGHT: 5ft 9in
SQUAD №: 22
NICKNAME: Scotty
OTHER TEAMS: Surrey, Worcestershire
CAREER: First-class debut: 2003; List A
debut: 1999; T20 debut: 2004; County cap:
2007 (Middlesex)

MIDDLESEX

AOC SAYS: Scott is considered to be among the best glovemen in the country but finds himself second-choice at Middlesex due to the emergence of promising keeper-batsman John Simpson. He had a spell on loan at Worcestershire last season to gain first-team cricket and while he is regarded as the superior keeper, Simpson is considered to offer more with the bat. Scott played a lead role when Middlesex won the Twenty20 Cup in 2008, standing up to the stumps to the pacemen and offering useful runs with his unorthodox batting, and with Adam Gilchrist not returning to Lord's this season he will hope to displace Simpson in that format.

LAST WORD: "I'm surprised Scott decided to stay at Middlesex as second-choice keeper and I'd be equally surpised if there weren't several counties interested in signing him."
Jon Batham

Batting & Fielding

	Mat	Inns	NO	Runs	HS	Ave	SR	100	50	Ct	St
First-class	77	119	22	2710	164*	27.93	49.08	3	16	211	22
List A	100	62	21	821	73*	20.02	-	0	4	81	30
Twenty20	72	51	24	443	43*	16.40	103.99	0	0	23	27

Bowling

	Mat	Balls	Runs	Wkts	BBI	BBM	Ave	Econ	SR	5w	10
First-class	77	3	1	0	-	-	-	2.00	-	0	0
List A	100	-	-	-	-	-	-	-	-	-	-
Twenty20	72	-	-	-	-	-	-	-	-	-	-

JOHN SIMPSON

LHB WK

NAME: John Andrew Simpson
BORN: July 13, 1988, Bury
HEIGHT: 5ft 10in
SQUAD Nº: 20
NICKNAME: Simmo
CAREER: First-class debut: 2009; List A debut: 2009; T20 debut: 2009

AOC SAYS: Simpson is a wicketkeeper-batsman of huge potential who has successfully displaced Ben Scott as first-choice stumper at Lord's. He made a composed 87 on his first-class debut against Northamptonshire in 2009 and was rewarded with the gloves last season. He struck his maiden first-class ton against the same opposition, hitting an unbeaten 101 at Wantage Road last April. Encouraged by that display, Middlesex promoted Simpson to open the batting but after making 58 against Sussex the experiment proved largely unsuccessful and with the signing of Australian opener Chris Rogers he will drop down to a more familiar lower-order position this season. The former England under 19 gloveman will hope to improve his record in one-day cricket in 2011 or he will find his position under threat from Scott.

LAST WORD: "Middlesex rate Simpson very highly but I'm not sure they have settled on the right place in the order to bat him." *Jon Batham*

Batting & Fielding

	Mat	Inns	NO	Runs	HS	Ave	SR	100	50	Ct	St
First-class	19	33	2	827	101*	26.67	45.21	1	3	47	2
List A	18	14	1	327	82	25.15	75.69	0	1	11	4
Twenty20	1	1	0	13	13	13.00	92.85	0	0	0	0

Bowling

	Mat	Balls	Runs	Wkts	BBI	BBM	Ave	Econ	SR	5w	10
First-class	19	-	-	-	-	-	-	-	-	-	-
List A	18	-	-	-	-	-	-	-	-	-	-
Twenty20	1	-	-	-	-	-	-	-	-	-	-

NAME: Thomas Michael John Smith
BORN: August 29, 1987, Eastbourne
HEIGHT: 5ft 9in
SQUAD Nº: 11
NICKNAME: Smudge
OTHER TEAMS: Surrey, Sussex
CAREER: First-class debut: 2007; List A
debut: 2006; T20 debut: 2007

MIDDLESEX

AOC SAYS: Smith will be vying for the role of first-choice spinner with Ollie Rayner following the retirement of Shaun Udal at the end of last season. Rayner has been signed on a loan deal from Sussex until mid-May and is likely to start the season in pole position due to his superior batting, but Smith will hope to get his chance as the pitches dry out over the season. The left-arm spinner joined Middlesex from Sussex in 2009 and impressed in T20 cricket to finish as the club's leading wicket-taker but his opportunities were restricted in the four-day format. Smith is not afraid to give the ball a tweak and spins the ball more than his predecessor Udal. He is also a capable lower-order batsman.

LAST WORD: "Smith may well be given his head later in the season when the pitches get a bit harder and bat at No.8 or No.9." *Jon Batham*

Batting & Fielding

	Mat	Inns	NO	Runs	HS	Ave	SR	100	50	Ct	St
First-class	6	10	1	123	33	13.66	30.82	0	0	3	0
List A	18	6	0	118	65	19.66	79.19	0	1	9	0
Twenty20	16	7	5	25	9*	12.50	83.33	0	0	4	0

Bowling

	Mat	Balls	Runs	Wkts	BBI	BBM	Ave	Econ	SR	5w	10
First-class	6	586	411	3	1/30	1/75	137.00	4.20	195.3	0	0
List A	18	654	617	15	3/26	3/26	41.13	5.66	43.6	0	0
Twenty20	16	251	325	18	5/24	5/24	18.05	7.76	13.9	1	0

PAUL STIRLING

RHB OB

NAME: Paul Robert Stirling
BORN: September 3, 1990, Belfast
SQUAD Nº: 39
OTHER TEAMS: Ireland
CAREER: ODI debut: 2008; T20I debut: 2009;
First-class debut: 2008; List A debut: 2008;
T20 debut: 2008

AOC SAYS: Stirling is an aggressive opening batsman and handy offspin bowler who already has considerable international experience with Ireland. He featured in the World Twenty20 last year and struck a scintillating century against the Netherlands in the 2011 World Cup. He earned a county contract with Middlesex in 2009 on the back of some strong performances for his country. Stirling holds the record for the highest ODI score by an Ireland batsman for the 177 he made against Canada last September. International commitments have so far restricted him to one T20 appearance for Middlesex but he will be available throughout 2011 and is expected to be given an opportunity in limited-overs cricket where he can take advantage of powerplays with his dynamic hitting.

LAST WORD: "Paul's batting for Ireland has highlighted his potential and he will initially feature in one-day cricket for us this season." *Angus Fraser*

Batting & Fielding

	Mat	Inns	NO	Runs	HS	Ave	SR	100	50	Ct	St
ODIs	28	28	1	955	177	35.37	88.09	1	6	14	0
T20Is	6	6	0	77	22	12.83	81.05	0	0	1	0
First-class	9	14	0	358	100	25.57	56.91	1	1	7	0
List A	45	45	1	1268	177	28.81	80.45	1	9	20	0
Twenty20	13	13	0	222	43	17.07	99.55	0	0	5	0

Bowling

	Mat	Balls	Runs	Wkts	BBI	BBM	Ave	Econ	SR	5w	10
ODIs	28	623	463	12	4/11	4/11	38.58	4.45	51.9	0	0
T20Is	6	18	25	0	-	-	-	8.33	-	0	0
First-class	9	291	153	3	2/45	3/92	51.00	3.15	97.0	0	0
List A	45	665	502	12	4/11	4/11	41.83	4.52	55.4	0	0
Twenty20	13	84	94	1	1/13	1/13	94.00	6.71	84.0	0	0

NAME: Andrew John Strauss
BORN: March 2, 1977, Johannesburg
HEIGHT: 5ft 11in
SQUAD Nº: 6
NICKNAME: Straussy, Johann, Levi, Mareman, Muppet, Lord Brocket
OTHER TEAMS: England, Northern Districts
CAREER: Test debut: 2004; List A debut: 2003; T20I debut: 2005; First-class debut: 1998; List A debut: 1997; T20 debut: 2003; County cap: 2001

MIDDLESEX

AOC SAYS: Strauss was a relative latecomer to international cricket but he swiftly made up for lost time, scoring a century on Test debut against New Zealand at Lord's and falling 17 short of a second ton in the same match after he was run out by Nasser Hussain. A compact left-hand opener with a penchant for the cut and pull, he oozed composure at the crease and was marked down as a future captain. His stunning start continued as he racked up 10 centuries in his first 30 Tests, including two in the 2005 Ashes triumph, but after he passed over as captain for the 2006/07 Ashes he suffered a dip in form and was dropped for the 2007 tour to Sri Lanka. He bounced back with a career-saving Test-best 177 against New Zealand in Napier and was named England captain in 2009 in tumultuous circumstances following the departure of Kevin Pietersen. His tenure got off to a disastrous start when England were bowled out for 51 in Jamaica but in partnership with coach Andy Flower, he has restored England's standing as one of Test cricket's leading nations. He led with distinction to reclaim the Ashes on home soil in 2009 before guiding England to a first series win Down Under in 24 years this winter – setting the tone for what was to follow with an aggressive century in the first Test at Brisbane.

INSIDE TRACK: "I made Andrew my vice-captain when I played for Middlesex and recommended that he succeed me as captain. There were traits that made him stand out as captain. I wouldn't say he's a flair captain but he has strengths that others don't possess. He doesn't make instant high-risk gambles but he's a meticulous planner and a structured thinker. That was one of the reasons why England did so well in the Ashes – because they were so well prepared. He and Andy Flower have very similar ideals and look for the same characteristics in players. I think that's why they work so well as a team. We realised at Middlesex that we had a very good, hard-working cricketer but I would question that we knew he would go on to achieve what he has. We were pretty sure he was going to have a long county career but he's surprised us by doing quite so well. That's not meant to be a negative – he will go down as one of England's great players." *Angus Fraser*

ANDREW STRAUSS

MIDDLESEX

	Mat	Inns	NO	Runs	HS	Ave	SR	100	50	Ct	St
Batting & Fielding											
Tests	82	147	6	6084	177	43.14	50.21	19	24	94	0
ODIs	126	125	8	4200	158	35.89	81.14	6	27	57	0
T20Is	4	4	0	73	33	18.25	114.06	0	0	1	0
First-class	208	368	20	14715	177	42.28	-	38	67	186	0
List A	253	246	14	7626	163	32.87	-	10	49	90	0
Twenty20	28	28	0	519	60	18.53	117.42	0	2	12	0

	Mat	Balls	Runs	Wkts	BBI	BBM	Ave	Econ	SR	5w	10
Bowling											
Tests	82	-	-	-	-	-	-	-	-	-	-
ODIs	126	6	3	0	-	-	-	3.00	-	0	0
T20Is	4	-	-	-	-	-	-	-	-	-	-
First-class	208	126	140	3	1/16	-	46.66	6.66	42.0	0	0
List A	253	6	3	0	-	-	-	3.00	-	0	0
Twenty20	28	-	-	-	-	-	-	-	-	-	-

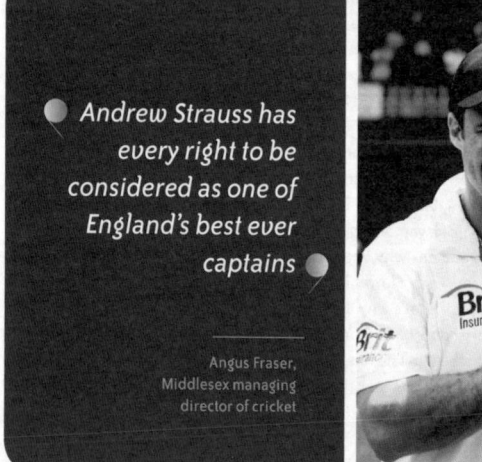

Andrew Strauss has every right to be considered as one of England's best ever captains

Angus Fraser,
Middlesex managing
director of cricket

NAME: Robert Edward Morgan Williams
BORN: January 19, 1987, Pembury
HEIGHT: 6ft
SQUAD №: 16
CAREER: First-class debut: 2007; List A
debut: 2007; T20 debut: 2010

MIDDLESEX

AOC SAYS: Williams is a pace bowler who has the ability to pin batsmen on the back foot but his career has been hampered by persistent injuries. After impressing for Durham University and the Second XI he made his Middlesex debut in 2007 and returned figures of 5-112 against Essex after ripping through the top-order. But just as his career appeared to be taking off he suffered a stress fracture that ruled him out of the entire 2008 season. He returned for Middlesex in limited-overs cricket last season but proved expensive and now faces a tough task to gain a first-team spot with a wealth of seamers at the county's disposal.

LAST WORD: "Williams is a young seamer who can be very quick when at his best but he has been plagued by stress fractures of the back." *Jon Batham*

Batting & Fielding

	Mat	Inns	NO	Runs	HS	Ave	SR	100	50	Ct	St
First-class	9	15	5	119	31	11.90	35.95	0	0	4	0
List A	6	1	1	2	2*	-	28.57	0	0	0	0
Twenty20	2	-	-	-	-	-	-	-	-	0	0

Bowling

	Mat	Balls	Runs	Wkts	BBI	BBM	Ave	Econ	SR	5w	10
First-class	9	1241	755	23	5/70	5/115	32.82	3.65	53.9	2	0
List A	6	185	248	2	2/60	2/60	124.00	8.04	92.5	0	0
Twenty20	2	24	55	0	-	-	-	13.75	-	0	0

TEAM PROFILE

FORMED: 1878
HOME GROUND: County Ground, Wantage Road
ONE-DAY NAME: Steelbacks
CAPTAIN: Andrew Hall
2010 RESULTS: CC2: 6/9; CB40: 5/7 in Group B; FP t20: Quarter-finalists

HONOURS
Gillette/NatWest/C&G/FP Trophy: (2) 1976, 1992; Benson and Hedges Cup: 1980

THE LOWDOWN
Northamptonshire will be looking to improve upon a disappointing 2010 Championship campaign that saw their promotion challenge peter out due to an underperforming batting unit and a succession of injuries to key players. Experienced opener Stephen Peters continues to get better with age but he will need more support this season from county stalwarts David Sales and Mal Loye. Northants will benefit from the services of Chaminda Vaas for the entirety of the season and the Sri Lankan will form part of a dangerous seam attack, featuring Jack Brooks, David Lucas and skipper Andrew Hall. The Steelbacks look a solid one-day unit and limited-overs cricket is perhaps their best chance of silverware. Head coach David Capel has highlighted the CB40 as a competition he believes they can do well in but promotion in the Championship remains the priority after a seven-year stint in Division Two.

HEAD COACH: DAVID CAPEL
The former England allrounder took charge of first-team affairs in 2006 having previously worked as academy director. An aggressive middle-order batsman and capable seamer, Capel spent 17 years on the playing staff at his hometown club and represented his country in 15 Tests and 23 ODIs between 1987 and 1990.

With thanks to: Andrew Radd, freelance cricket journalist; Alec Swann, former cricketer turned sports writer, Northamptonshire Evening Telegraph

	Mat	Inns	NO	Runs	HS	Ave	SR	100	50	Ct	St
SD Peters	16	30	2	1320	199	47.14	51.62	3	7	16	-
NJ O'Brien	3	6	0	216	49	36.00	83.07	0	0	7	1
N Boje	9	15	1	471	98	33.64	54.20	0	4	3	-
V Tripathi	4	7	1	196	71	32.66	54.29	0	2	3	-
RI Newton	6	11	0	357	102	32.45	70.69	1	2	1	-
D Murphy	9	15	6	276	55	30.66	41.75	0	2	26	0
AJ Hall	15	27	3	696	133	29.00	51.63	1	3	21	-
AG Wakely	13	22	0	627	108	28.50	47.89	1	4	6	-
BHN Howgego	7	13	2	292	80	26.54	42.01	0	1	3	-
JD Middlebrook	12	21	3	459	84	25.50	45.08	0	3	6	-
MB Loye	10	18	1	420	164	24.70	40.46	1	1	0	-
GC Baker	1	2	0	49	35	24.50	34.02	0	0	0	-
DJG Sales	15	28	0	680	127	24.28	52.18	1	2	20	-
DS Lucas	11	17	2	316	40*	21.06	50.47	0	0	1	-
E Chigumbura	6	10	1	189	44	21.00	46.89	0	0	0	-
DJ Willey	3	4	2	41	18*	20.50	61.19	0	0	1	-
RA White	10	19	1	363	95	20.16	60.90	0	2	3	-
PW Harrison	5	8	1	137	44	19.57	39.48	0	0	7	2
LM Daggett	12	17	8	167	48	18.55	44.65	0	0	3	-
L Evans	2	3	2	16	8*	16.00	28.07	0	0	1	-
JA Brooks	14	20	3	177	53	10.41	46.94	0	1	2	-
WPUJC Vaas	2	2	0	17	17	8.50	42.50	0	0	1	-
DA Burton	1	2	1	2	2*	2.00	25.00	0	0	1	-

Batting & Fielding

	Mat	Overs	Mdns	Runs	Wkts	BBI	BBM	Ave	Econ	SR	5w	10
DA Burton	1	20.0	4	75	5	5/75	5/75	15.00	3.75	24.0	1	0
E Chigumbura	6	114.0	17	482	20	5/92	5/109	24.10	4.22	34.2	1	0
WPUJC Vaas	2	73.2	20	161	6	4/49	4/96	26.83	2.19	73.3	0	0
AJ Hall	15	318.0	57	1047	33	4/44	5/101	31.72	3.29	57.8	0	0
DS Lucas	11	300.4	59	1038	32	5/64	7/97	32.43	3.45	56.3	1	0
JA Brooks	14	373.3	86	1260	37	4/88	5/108	34.05	3.37	60.5	0	0
LM Daggett	12	321.4	65	1058	30	4/25	6/88	35.26	3.28	64.3	0	0
DJ Willey	3	56.5	8	218	6	2/47	4/104	36.33	3.83	56.8	0	0
L Evans	2	57.0	10	201	5	3/53	4/77	40.20	3.52	68.4	0	0
JD Middlebrook	12	251.2	40	863	18	3/23	4/59	47.94	3.43	83.7	0	0
N Boje	9	230.3	42	796	15	2/47	4/159	53.06	3.45	92.2	0	0
AG Wakely	13	9.1	0	57	1	1/4	1/4	57.00	6.21	55.0	0	0
GC Baker	1	13.0	3	54	0	-	-	-	4.15	-	0	0
T Brett	1	17.0	6	38	0	-	-	-	2.23	-	0	0
BHN Howgego	7	2.0	0	16	0	-	-	-	8.00	-	0	0
RI Newton	6	2.1	0	19	0	-	-	-	8.76	-	0	0
DJG Sales	15	1.0	0	10	0	-	-	-	10.00	-	0	0
V Tripathi	4	6.0	0	28	0	-	-	-	4.66	-	0	0
RA White	10	1.0	0	7	0	-	-	-	7.00	-	0	0

Bowling

Batting & Fielding

	Mat	Inns	NO	Runs	HS	Ave	SR	100	50	Ct	St
D Murphy	8	5	4	69	31*	69.00	107.81	0	0	7	3
DJG Sales	12	12	1	408	84	37.09	86.99	0	4	5	-
RA White	7	7	0	248	69	35.42	92.53	0	3	0	-
JD Middlebrook	11	10	5	150	57*	30.00	99.33	0	1	4	-
SD Peters	10	9	1	231	56	28.87	81.05	0	2	2	-
MB Loye	8	8	0	223	66	27.87	70.34	0	2	0	-
RI Newton	7	7	0	194	66	27.71	83.62	0	1	1	-
NJ O'Brien	2	2	0	55	52	27.50	90.16	0	1	3	0
N Boje	6	6	1	132	38	26.40	103.93	0	0	1	-
AJ Hall	11	11	3	167	37	20.87	81.06	0	0	6	-
DS Lucas	5	3	2	20	11*	20.00	74.07	0	0	4	-
AG Wakely	9	9	0	153	35	17.00	73.91	0	0	2	-
DJ Willey	6	6	1	74	25	14.80	77.08	0	0	2	-
E Chigumbura	2	2	0	29	24	14.50	69.04	0	0	0	-
RI Keogh	1	1	0	11	11	11.00	42.30	0	0	1	-
LM Daggett	10	3	2	9	5	9.00	90.00	0	0	2	-
PW Harrison	2	2	0	13	13	6.50	130.00	0	0	2	0
JA Brooks	6	3	1	4	2*	2.00	80.00	0	0	0	-
GC Baker	1	1	0	0	0	0.00	0.00	0	0	0	-
V Tripathi	1	1	0	0	0	0.00	0.00	0	0	1	-
T Brett	5	1	1	2	2*	-	33.33	0	0	2	-

Bowling

	Mat	Overs	Mdns	Runs	Wkts	BBI	Ave	Econ	SR	5w
LM Daggett	10	71.0	7	330	20	4/17	16.50	4.64	21.3	0
E Chigumbura	2	11.2	0	66	3	2/22	22.00	5.82	22.6	0
N Boje	6	30.2	1	119	5	3/10	23.80	3.92	36.4	0
AJ Hall	11	67.1	1	418	15	4/39	27.86	6.22	26.8	0
DH Wigley	1	4.0	0	29	1	1/29	29.00	7.25	24.0	0
JA Brooks	6	41.0	3	203	6	3/41	33.83	4.95	41.0	0
JD Middlebrook	11	74.0	1	366	10	3/34	36.60	4.94	44.4	0
DS Lucas	5	33.0	0	201	5	1/23	40.20	6.09	39.6	0
T Brett	5	36.0	1	179	3	1/24	59.66	4.97	72.0	0
GC Baker	1	7.0	0	63	1	1/63	63.00	9.00	42.0	0
DJ Willey	6	39.5	3	212	3	2/40	70.66	5.32	79.6	0
CAL Davis	1	7.3	0	44	0	-	-	5.86	-	0
AG Wakely	9	1.0	0	6	0	-	-	6.00	-	0

	Mat	Inns	NO	Runs	HS	Ave	SR	100	50	Ct	St
SD Peters	2	2	1	79	40*	79.00	121.53	0	0	2	-
AJ Hall	17	16	10	252	40*	42.00	111.50	0	0	3	-
MB Loye	3	3	0	115	54	38.33	110.57	0	1	1	-
E Chigumbura	13	13	6	218	58*	31.14	121.78	0	1	8	-
WPUJC Vaas	17	17	1	412	73	25.75	122.98	0	4	3	-
AG Wakely	18	18	2	387	55	24.18	107.50	0	1	8	-
RA White	13	13	1	277	80	23.08	105.32	0	2	3	-
L Vincent	3	3	0	67	38	22.33	115.51	0	0	1	-
NJ O'Brien	11	10	0	215	37	21.50	115.59	0	0	9	4
N Boje	11	10	2	114	54*	14.25	134.11	0	1	4	-
DJG Sales	10	10	1	128	49	14.22	110.34	0	0	3	-
DJ Willey	17	8	3	63	19	12.60	112.50	0	0	7	-
JD Middlebrook	18	7	4	34	14*	11.33	82.92	0	0	6	-
RI Newton	1	1	0	7	7	7.00	70.00	0	0	0	-
PW Harrison	2	2	0	13	10	6.50	72.22	0	0	0	-
V Tripathi	3	1	0	6	6	6.00	120.00	0	0	2	-
LM Daggett	14	2	1	3	2*	3.00	75.00	0	0	1	-
BHN Howgego	1	1	0	1	1	1.00	100.00	0	0	0	-
D Murphy	7	1	0	0	0	0.00	0.00	0	0	4	0
JA Brooks	15	2	2	7	5*	-	175.00	0	0	4	-

Batting & Fielding

	Mat	Overs	Mdns	Runs	Wkts	BBI	Ave	Econ	SR	5w
WPUJC Vaas	17	57.3	1	364	23	3/16	15.82	6.33	15.0	0
N Boje	11	31.2	0	227	11	3/20	20.63	7.24	17.0	0
E Chigumbura	13	33.0	0	244	10	4/14	24.40	7.39	19.8	0
DJ Willey	17	23.0	0	199	8	3/33	24.87	8.65	17.2	0
JA Brooks	15	46.0	3	307	12	3/24	25.58	6.67	23.0	0
AJ Hall	17	48.5	0	423	16	2/8	26.43	8.66	18.3	0
JD Middlebrook	18	55.0	0	356	13	2/12	27.38	6.47	25.3	0
LM Daggett	14	20.0	0	190	5	1/14	38.00	9.50	24.0	0
DS Lucas	2	4.3	0	33	0	-	-	7.33	-	0
AG Wakely	18	1.0	0	11	0	-	-	11.00	-	0

Bowling

GAVIN BAKER

NORTHAMPTONSHIRE

NAME: Gavin Charles Baker
BORN: October 3, 1988, Edgware
SQUAD №: 16
CAREER: First-class debut: 2010; List A debut: 2010

AOC SAYS: Baker signed his first professional deal with Northamptonshire at the end of last season after impressing during the 2010 campaign. The Loughborough University graduate was handed a trial after a string of notable performances for Combined Universities and featured regularly for Northamptonshire's Second XI after completing his studies. He made his Championship debut against Derbyshire last August and the seam bowler showed he is also a capable lower-order batsman, making a composed 35 in the draw at Chesterfield. Baker went on to make his one-day debut in the CB40 against Gloucestershire and dismissed Chris Taylor to take his first List A wicket. He has gone through a rigorous pre-season schedule in order to prepare for his first full season in the professional game.

LAST WORD: "Baker is a medium-pacer and a more than useful lower-order batsman but I'd be surprised if he starts the season in the first team." *Alec Swann*

Batting & Fielding

	Mat	Inns	NO	Runs	HS	Ave	SR	100	50	Ct	St
First-class	5	7	1	196	66	32.66	48.87	0	2	1	0
List A	1	1	0	0	0	0.00	0.00	0	0	0	0

Bowling

	Mat	Balls	Runs	Wkts	BBI	BBM	Ave	Econ	SR	5w	10
First-class	5	543	390	5	2/35	2/112	78.00	4.30	108.6	0	0
List A	1	42	63	1	1/63	1/63	63.00	9.00	42.0	0	0

OVERSEAS PLAYER

NAME: Johan Botha
BORN: May 2, 1982, Johannesburg
SQUAD Nº: 48
OTHERS TEAMS: South Africa, Border, Eastern Province, Rajasthan Royals, Warriors
CAREER: Test debut: 2006; ODI debut: 2005; T20I debut: 2006; First-class debut: 2000; List A debut: 2001; T20 debut: 2004

AOC SAYS: Botha is Northamptonshire's second overseas signing for the FP t20 and the South African will add a wealth of experience to a depleted spin attack following the departure of his compatriot Nicky Boje at the end of last season. The offbreak bowler started life as a medium-pacer but became a spinner on the recommendation of former Proteas coach Mickey Arthur. The change initially paid dividends but after making his international bow he was suspended from bowling in 2006 after his action was deemed illegal. He is still banned from bowling his doosra due to an excessive straightening in his bowling arm but has bounced back to become a key performer in South Africa's limited-overs side. He returned to the Test side in 2010 after a two-year absence to take seven wickets against West Indies at Bridgetown.

LAST WORD: "This is the right signing for the club and Johan will be a major asset to us through his ultra-competitiveness, skill sets and experience." David Capel

Batting & Fielding

	Mat	Inns	NO	Runs	HS	Ave	SR	100	50	Ct	St
Tests	5	6	2	83	25	20.75	34.87	0	0	3	0
ODIs	74	46	15	575	46	18.54	85.31	0	0	33	0
T20Is	26	15	8	139	28*	19.85	120.86	0	0	15	0
First-class	67	111	18	3218	109	34.60	-	1	22	50	0
List A	151	105	29	1627	55*	21.40	81.02	0	4	48	0
Twenty20	68	47	20	459	44*	17.00	113.33	0	0	30	0

Bowling

	Mat	Balls	Runs	Wkts	BBI	BBM	Ave	Econ	SR	5w	10
Tests	5	1017	573	17	4/56	7/102	33.70	3.38	59.8	0	0
ODIs	74	3631	2790	69	4/19	4/19	40.43	4.61	52.6	0	0
T20Is	26	528	555	27	3/16	3/16	20.55	6.30	19.5	0	0
First-class	67	9760	4953	156	6/42		31.75	3.04	62.5	4	1
List A	151	6883	5201	138	4/19	4/19	37.68	4.53	49.8	0	0
Twenty20	68	1470	1464	63	4/19	4/19	23.23	5.97	23.3	0	0

NAME: Thomas Brett
BORN: November 13, 1989, Kettering
SQUAD Nº: 24
CAREER: First-class debut: 2010; List A
debut: 2010

AOC SAYS: Brett signed a one-year contract with his home county at the end of last season after spending six years with the Northamptonshire academy. The promising left-arm spinner made his first-class debut against Oxford University at the beginning of last season before making a handful of CB40 appearances at the end of the campaign. He is likely to get more first-team opportunities this season following the departure of Nicky Boje but faces a tough challenge on a Wantage Road track that favours the seamers and has become something of a graveyard for spinners over the past two seasons. Brett is working closely with experienced offspinner James Middlebrook to develop his game and the two may operate in tandem in the CB40.

LAST WORD: "There are high hopes for Tom at Northants and he is likely to get some games if they choose to go down the two-spinner route." *Andrew Radd*

Batting & Fielding

	Mat	Inns	NO	Runs	HS	Ave	SR	100	50	Ct	St
First-class	1	-	-	-	-	-	-	-	-	0	0
List A	5	1	1	2	2*	-	33.33	0	0	2	0

Bowling

	Mat	Balls	Runs	Wkts	BBI	BBM	Ave	Econ	SR	5w	10
First-class	1	102	38	0	-	-	-	2.23	-	0	0
List A	5	216	179	3	1/24	1/24	59.66	4.97	72.0	0	0

NAME: Jack Alexander Brooks
BORN: June 4, 1984, Oxford
HEIGHT: 6ft 2in
SQUAD Nº: 9
NICKNAME: Brooksy, Ferret
CAREER: First-class debut: 2009; List A
debut: 2009; T20 debut: 2010

NORTHAMPTONSHIRE

AOC SAYS: Brooks was the overwhelming positive in Northamptonshire's bowling attack last season with a haul of 55 wickets across all competitions in his first full season of professional cricket. The energetic seamer was something of a late developer, plying his trade with Oxfordshire in Minor Counties cricket for four years before signing for Northamptonshire in 2008. Brooks is an enthusiastic character with a great work ethic. He is hugely popular with the Northamptonshire faithful, who raised £1,000 to help fund his trip to Chennai over the winter to attend a fast bowling masterclass run by Australian legend Dennis Lillee. He is also a proficient lower-order batsman and scored his maiden first-class fifty in the victory over Gloucestershire last April.

LAST WORD: "In a team not over-burdened with extroverts, Brooks gives the side that little bit of edge. He's a super lad and brings something to the party aside from his bowling." *Andrew Radd*

Batting & Fielding											
	Mat	Inns	NO	Runs	HS	Ave	SR	100	50	Ct	St
First-class	17	23	6	197	53	11.58	49.12	0	1	3	0
List A	9	4	1	14	10	4.66	82.35	0	0	0	0
Twenty20	15	2	2	7	5*	-	175.00	0	0	4	0

Bowling											
	Mat	Balls	Runs	Wkts	BBI	BBM	Ave	Econ	SR	5w	10
First-class	17	2727	1585	46	4/76	5/108	34.45	3.48	59.2	0	0
List A	9	354	302	6	3/41	3/41	50.33	5.11	59.0	0	0
Twenty20	15	276	307	12	3/24	3/24	25.58	6.67	23.0	0	0

LEE DAGGETT   RHB RMF

NORTHAMPTONSHIRE

NAME: Lee Martin Daggett
BORN: October 1, 1982, Bury
HEIGHT: 6ft
SQUAD Nº: 10
NICKNAME: Dags, Terry, Len Dugout
OTHER TEAMS: Leicestershire, Warwickshire
CAREER: First-class debut: 2003; List A debut: 2006; T20 debut: 2007

AOC SAYS: Daggett burst onto the scene in 2004 with a haul of 8-94 for Durham University against Durham but only now is he starting to fulfil his potential. After several seasons toiling away with little reward for Warwickshire and Leicestershire, Daggett appears to have found a home at Northamptonshire. The powerful seamer was the club's standout bowler in the CB40 last season with 20 wickets at a miserly average and also a reliable performer in four-day cricket. The former Durham University sportsman of the year was rewarded with a new contract last August that will keep him at Wantage Road until at least the end of the 2012 season.

LAST WORD: "Lee has done well since he joined us. It's pleasing to see the progress he has made and more so that he's decided to sign for another two years. It's good news for player and club." *David Capel*

Batting & Fielding

	Mat	Inns	NO	Runs	HS	Ave	SR	100	50	Ct	St
First-class	39	50	21	302	48	10.41	31.13	0	0	5	0
List A	41	14	11	78	14*	26.00	70.90	0	0	6	0
Twenty20	28	5	2	7	3*	2.33	53.84	0	0	6	0

Bowling

	Mat	Balls	Runs	Wkts	BBI	BBM	Ave	Econ	SR	5w	10
First-class	39	5673	3328	91	8/94	-	36.57	3.51	62.3	2	0
List A	41	1724	1419	54	4/17	4/17	26.27	4.93	31.9	0	0
Twenty20	28	288	420	11	2/19	2/19	38.18	8.75	26.1	0	0

NAME: Luke Evans
BORN: April 26, 1987, Sunderland
HEIGHT: 6ft 7in
SQUAD Nº: 25
NICKNAME: Daisy Duke, Longshanks, Lukey, Evo, Cool Hand
OTHER TEAMS: Durham
CAREER: First-class debut: 2007; List A debut: 2009

AOC SAYS: Evans was released by his home county Durham at the end of the 2010 season and swiftly snapped up by Northamptonshire. The giant seamer impressed during a short loan spell at Wantage Road at the beginning of last season before he was recalled due to an injury crisis at Chester-le-street. Evans took four wickets against Sri Lanka A on his Durham debut in 2007 but had to wait three years for his next first-class match. He took his opportunity when it came with a second-innings haul of 3-53 in Northamptonshire's victory over Gloucestershire. He will be hoping for more regular first-team opportunities at his new county on a home track that should benefit his natural pace and bounce.

LAST WORD: "Luke knows that this is a golden opportunity for him to show what he can do in a developing, exciting side on good pitches which suit his style." *Mark Tagg, Northamptonshire chief executive*

Batting & Fielding

	Mat	Inns	NO	Runs	HS	Ave	SR	100	50	Ct	St
First-class	4	6	4	21	8*	10.50	26.25	0	0	1	0
List A	5	2	1	1	1*	1.00	9.09	0	0	1	0

Bowling

	Mat	Balls	Runs	Wkts	BBI	BBM	Ave	Econ	SR	5w	10
First-class	4	475	327	9	3/53	4/77	36.33	4.13	52.7	0	0
List A	5	144	156	5	2/53	2/53	31.20	6.50	28.8	0	0

ANDREW HALL

NORTHAMPTONSHIRE

NAME: Andrew James Hall
BORN: July 31, 1975, Johannesburg
HEIGHT: 6ft
SQUAD Nº: 1
NICKNAME: Hally
OTHER TEAMS: South Africa, Chandigarh
Lions, Dolphins, Easterns, Gauteng, Kent,
Transvaal, Worcestershire
CAREER: Test debut: 2002; ODI debut: 1999;
T20I debut: 2006; First-class debut: 1995;
List A debut: 1995; T20 debut: 2003; County
cap: 2005 (Kent), 2009 (Northamptonshire)

AOC SAYS: Hall is vastly experienced allrounder who has fulfilled a variety of roles in a first-class career stretching back 16 years. He is known predominantly for his bustling seam bowling, particularly in limited-overs cricket where he excelled bowling at the death for South Africa for a number of years, but is a capable enough batsman to have scored 163 opening the batting in a Test match against India – batting for more than six hours on a dustbowl at Kanpur in 2004. An unbeaten 99 at better than a run-a-ball against England the previous summer was a more typical innings from a belligerent batsman who likes to take the attack to the bowlers. Hall never let South Africa down in Test cricket but it was in the ODI arena that he proved most effective. He returned figures of 5-18 in a 2007 World Cup clash in Bridgetown to knock England out of the competition and on countless occasions showed nerves of steel bowling at the death to take his side to victory. He has been a consistent performer in county cricket for the best part of the decade. In 2009 he was named Northamptonshire's Player of the Year and led from the front with bat and ball last season after taking over the captaincy from Nicky Boje midway through the campaign.

INSIDE TRACK: "Andrew did a good job as skipper last season. He was the logical choice when Nicky Boje resigned. Northamptonshire sounded him out about taking over and he took on the role whole-heartedly. He can be a fiery competitor but he's quite a laidback bloke off the field – he's very friendly and affable. His pace has dropped over the years but he's still very effective at what he does. He's very canny, particularly in T20 cricket, and he's as good as anyone around at bowling at the death. There were a couple of games last year when he gave away pretty much nothing and pulled the game out of the fire for Northants. He still chips in with useful runs as well. He tends to bat at No.6 or No.7 in Championship cricket but he's capable of batting a lot higher if he wanted to. It suits the side quite well having a bit of experience further down the order. I would expect Andrew to stay in charge for the rest of his time with Northants." *Alec Swann*

Batting & Fielding

	Mat	Inns	NO	Runs	HS	Ave	SR	100	50	Ct	St
Tests	21	33	4	760	163	26.20	46.06	1	3	16	0
ODIs	88	56	13	905	81	21.04	75.04	0	3	29	0
T20Is	2	1	0	11	11	11.00	110.00	0	0	0	0
First-class	182	269	35	8140	163	34.78	-	10	49	165	0
List A	292	230	41	5489	129*	29.04	-	6	29	87	1
Twenty20	79	69	16	1270	66*	23.96	119.69	0	4	23	0

Bowling

	Mat	Balls	Runs	Wkts	BBI	BBM	Ave	Econ	SR	5w	10
Tests	21	3001	1617	45	3/1	5/20	35.93	3.23	66.6	0	0
ODIs	88	3341	2515	95	5/18	5/18	26.47	4.51	35.1	1	0
T20Is	2	48	60	3	3/22	3/22	20.00	7.50	16.0	0	0
First-class	182	27825	13321	505	6/77	-	26.37	2.87	55.0	15	1
List A	292	11710	9184	333	5/18	5/18	27.57	4.70	35.1	1	0
Twenty20	79	1573	1995	101	6/21	6/21	19.75	7.60	15.5	2	0

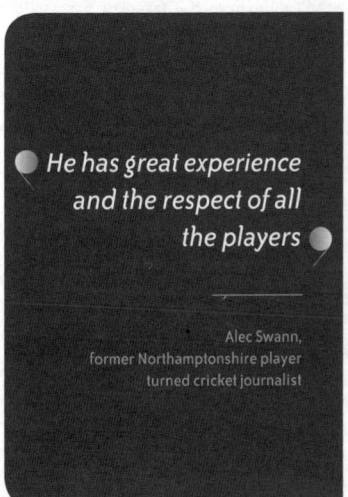

He has great experience and the respect of all the players

Alec Swann,
former Northamptonshire player
turned cricket journalist

NORTHAMPTONSHIRE

NAME: Benjamin Harry Nicholas Howgego
BORN: March 3, 1988, Kings Lynn
HEIGHT: 5ft 11in
SQUAD Nº: 27
NICKNAME: Benny
CAREER: First-class debut: 2008; List A
debut: 2009; T20 debut: 2010

AOC SAYS: There are high hopes for the compact left-handed opener at Wantage Road but Howgego is yet to back up his potential with first-class runs. He broke into the first team last season on the back of a fine run in second XI cricket after an injury to Niall O'Brien but could only muster a solitary half-century in 13 innings. However, his maiden first-class fifty – a matchsaving knock of 80 against Derbyshire at Chesterfield – showed a glimpse of his talent. Northants saw enough to give the Exeter University graduate a new two-year contract and he will be one of several candidates competing to partner Stephen Peters at the top of the order in Championship cricket.

LAST WORD: "Ben has a lot of potential but he can't afford to get overtaken. He has a solid technique and a good temperament but he needs to make big scores when given the opportunity." *Andrew Radd*

Batting & Fielding											
	Mat	Inns	NO	Runs	HS	Ave	SR	100	50	Ct	St
First-class	14	26	4	527	80	23.95	39.83	0	1	6	0
List A	1	1	0	7	7	7.00	50.00	0	0	0	0
Twenty20	1	1	0	1	1	1.00	100.00	0	0	0	0

Bowling											
	Mat	Balls	Runs	Wkts	BBI	BBM	Ave	Econ	SR	5w	10
First-class	14	12	16	0	-	-	-	8.00	-	0	0
List A	1	-	-	-	-	-	-	-	-	-	-
Twenty20	1	-	-	-	-	-	-	-	-	-	-

NAME: Malachy Bernard Loye
BORN: September 27, 1972, Northampton
HEIGHT: 6ft 3in
SQUAD №: 2
NICKNAME: Malcolm, Chairman, Jacko
OTHER TEAMS: England, Lancashire
CAREER: ODI debut: 2007; First-class debut: 1991; List A debut: 1992; T20 debut: 2003; County cap: 1994 (Northamptonshire), 2003 (Lancashire)

NORTHAMPTONSHIRE

AOC SAYS: Loye has been one of county cricket's most prolific batsmen for the best part of two decades but suffered an uncharacteristically quiet season last year as part of a struggling Northamptonshire batting unit. The veteran middle-order batsman made what at the time was a club record score of 322 not out against Glamorgan in 1998 during his first spell with Northants before signing for Lancashire in 2003. Loye featured consistently for England A for many years and eventually won an ODI call-up in 2007. He had the confidence to sweep Brett Lee for six on debut but was subsequently overlooked for the 2007 World Cup squad. Loye returned to his home county in 2009 and remains a key batsman in all formats.

LAST WORD: "Mal had a couple of innings when he looked like his old self but he struggled a bit last season and scratched around for form. I would expect him to have a better season this year." *Alec Swann*

Batting & Fielding

	Mat	Inns	NO	Runs	HS	Ave	SR	100	50	Ct	St
ODIs	7	7	0	142	45	20.28	77.17	0	0	0	0
First-class	256	410	38	14936	322*	40.15	-	42	61	119	0
List A	299	292	32	8884	127	34.16	-	10	58	64	0
Twenty20	42	41	4	1246	100	33.67	132.41	1	8	15	0

Bowling

	Mat	Balls	Runs	Wkts	BBI	BBM	Ave	Econ	SR	5w	10
ODIs	7	-	-	-	-	-	-	-	-	-	-
First-class	256	55	61	1	1/8	-	61.00	6.65	55.0	0	0
List A	299	-	-	-	-	-	-	-	-	-	-
Twenty20	42	-	-	-	-	-	-	-	-	-	-

NORTHAMPTONSHIRE

NAME: David Scott Lucas
BORN: August 19, 1978, Nottingham
HEIGHT: 6ft 3in
SQUAD Nº: 22
NICKNAME: Muke, Lukey
OTHER TEAMS: Nottinghamshire, Yorkshire
CAREER: First-class debut: 1999; List A debut: 1999; T20 debut: 2007; County cap: 2009 (Northamptonshire)

AOC SAYS: After spending much of his career on the treatment table, Lucas enjoyed a breakthrough season at the age of 31 in 2009 with a haul of 60 first-class wickets, including a career-best performance of 7-24 against Gloucestershire. The strapping left-arm seamer had been unable to hold down a first-team spot earlier in his career at Nottinghamshire or Yorkshire after suffering from a succession of injuries and had a spell playing minor counties cricket for Lincolnshire in 2006. He is now a key member of Northamptonshire's attack and continued his rejuvenation in 2010 before once again succumbing to injury and missing a large chunk of the season. Lucas appeared to be back to full fitness ahead of the 2011 season after impressing on the pre-season tour to South Africa.

LAST WORD: "The injury to Lucas was a big factor behind Northamptonshire's failure to sustain a Championship promotion challenge last season." *Andrew Radd*

Batting & Fielding

	Mat	Inns	NO	Runs	HS	Ave	SR	100	50	Ct	St
First-class	75	98	25	1391	55*	19.05	-	0	1	14	0
List A	65	29	10	205	32*	10.78	-	0	0	15	0
Twenty20	16	5	4	15	5*	15.00	93.75	0	0	2	0

Bowling

	Mat	Balls	Runs	Wkts	BBI	BBM	Ave	Econ	SR	5w	10
First-class	75	11359	6614	207	7/24	-	31.95	3.49	54.8	8	1
List A	65	2493	2342	77	4/27	4/27	30.41	5.63	32.3	0	0
Twenty20	16	219	338	8	2/37	2/37	42.25	9.26	27.3	0	0

NAME: James Daniel Middlebrook
BORN: May 13, 1977, Leeds
HEIGHT: 6ft 1in
SQUAD Nº: 7
NICKNAME: Midders, Midhouse, Midi, Dog
OTHER TEAMS: Essex, Yorkshire
CAREER: First-class debut: 1998; List A
debut: 1998; T20 debut: 2004; County cap:
2003 (Essex)

AOC SAYS: Middlebrook finds himself the frontline spinner at Northamptonshire following
the departure of Nicky Boje at the end of last season. The former Essex allrounder is a
steady offspinner and handy lower-order batsman who has benefited from greater first-
team opportunities since leaving Chelmsford at the end of the 2009 season. Middlebrook
came through the ranks at Yorkshire but never cemented a first-team place and left
Headingley in 2002. He has proven an effective limited-overs performer where his
accurate offspin is difficult to get away but he shoulders an extra burden of responsibility
in Championship cricket this season, particularly in home fixtures on a Wantage Road
track that now typically favours the seamers.

LAST WORD: "James' role last year tended to be to hold up an end. When I played at
Wantage Road the seamers were pretty much there to take the shine off the ball but the
pitches don't spin like they used to and now it's gone the other way." *Alec Swann*

Batting & Fielding

	Mat	Inns	NO	Runs	HS	Ave	SR	100	50	Ct	St
First-class	156	225	32	4884	127	25.30	-	4	19	78	0
List A	157	105	33	1406	57*	19.52	-	0	1	46	0
Twenty20	65	43	13	387	43	12.90	123.24	0	0	16	0

Bowling

	Mat	Balls	Runs	Wkts	BBI	BBM	Ave	Econ	SR	5w	10
First-class	156	25318	13313	341	6/82	-	39.04	3.15	74.2	8	1
List A	157	5497	4264	122	4/27	4/27	34.95	4.65	45.0	0	0
Twenty20	65	834	1062	28	3/13	3/13	37.92	7.64	29.7	0	0

DAVID MURPHY

RHB WK

NORTHAMPTONSHIRE

NAME: David Murphy
BORN: June 24, 1989, Welwyn Garden City
HEIGHT: 6ft 1in
SQUAD №: 21
NICKNAME: Murph, Spud
CAREER: First-class debut: 2009; List A
debut: 2010; T20 debut: 2010

AOC SAYS: A wicketkeeper of some potential and a useful lower-order batsman, Murphy enjoyed an extended run in the Northamptonshire first team last season after regular stumper Niall O'Brien underwent surgery on a finger injury. Murphy is a tall man for a keeper but attracted praise for his glovework and agility and surprised many with his batting – scoring two half-centuries at a healthy average. The Loughborough University student was rewarded with a professional contract that will keep him at Wantage Road until at least the end of the 2012 season and will now provide genuine competition for O'Brien. He is likely to start the season as second-choice but could potentially play alongside O'Brien if the Irishman is picked to play as a specialist batsman.

LAST WORD: "David came in and performed extremely well behind the stumps. He showed us something quite special with his glovework." *David Capel*

Batting & Fielding

	Mat	Inns	NO	Runs	HS	Ave	SR	100	50	Ct	St
First-class	16	24	8	522	76	32.62	42.92	0	5	41	1
List A	8	5	4	69	31*	69.00	107.81	0	0	7	3
Twenty20	7	1	0	0	0	0.00	0.00	0	0	4	0

Bowling

	Mat	Balls	Runs	Wkts	BBI	BBM	Ave	Econ	SR	5w	10
First-class	16	-	-	-	-	-	-	-	-	-	-
List A	8	-	-	-	-	-	-	-	-	-	-
Twenty20	7	-	-	-	-	-	-	-	-	-	-

ROB NEWTON

RHB LB

NAME: Robert Irving Newton
BORN: January 18, 1990, Taunton
SQUAD Nº: 19
CAREER: First-class debut: 2010; List A
debut: 2010; T20 debut: 2010

NORTHAMPTONSHIRE

AOC SAYS: After a six-year stint in Northamptonshire's academy, Newton burst onto the scene last season and finished off the campaign in style with his maiden first-class century against Leicestershire. He had already made his mark in one-day cricket with a belligerent 66 at the top of the order in the CB40 against Essex and earned the Denis Compton Award, which is given to the most promising youngster at each county, to cap a fine breakthrough season. Newton was rewarded with a new two-year deal and is set to be given an extended run in the first team across all formats this season.

LAST WORD: "Rob was fresh, vibrant and brought that youthful confidence and attitude into the games that he played. To come in and score a couple of half-centuries and cap that off with a century at the end of the season shows the ability and potential he has."
David Capel

Batting & Fielding

	Mat	Inns	NO	Runs	HS	Ave	SR	100	50	Ct	St
First-class	6	11	0	357	102	32.45	70.69	1	2	1	0
List A	8	8	0	203	66	25.37	83.19	0	1	1	0
Twenty20	1	1	0	7	7	7.00	70.00	0	0	0	0

Bowling

	Mat	Balls	Runs	Wkts	BBI	BBM	Ave	Econ	SR	5w	10
First-class	6	13	19	0	-	-	-	8.76	-	0	0
List A	8	-	-	-	-	-	-	-	-	-	-
Twenty20	1	-	-	-	-	-	-	-	-	-	-

NIALL O' BRIEN

LHB LB WK

NORTHAMPTONSHIRE

NAME: Niall John O'Brien
BORN: November 8, 1981, Dublin
HEIGHT: 5ft 7in
SQUAD Nº: 81
NICKNAME: Paddy, Nobby, Hornswoggle
OTHER TEAMS: Ireland, Kent
CAREER: ODI debut: 2006; T20I debut: 2008;
First-class debut: 2004; List A debut: 2003;
T20 debut: 2004

AOC SAYS: O'Brien is first-choice wicketkeeper at Wantage Road and a capable batsman who could potentially open the batting with Stephen Peters in Championship cricket. The former Kent stumper left Canterbury in search of first-team cricket, after Geraint Jones lost his England place, and moved to Northamptonshire in 2007. A chirpy gloveman who is never short of a word, O'Brien has impressed on the international stage for Ireland, scoring 72 in the famous 2007 World Cup win over Pakistan and making another half-century in the same competition against England. He was named Northamptonshire's Player of the Year in 2008 and appointed vice-captain midway through last season when Andrew Hall became skipper, only to be stripped of the role after an alleged breach of team disciplinary rules.

LAST WORD: "It wouldn't surprise me if O'Brien opens the batting and keeps wicket in Championship cricket like he has done in the past so Northants can play an extra bowler."
Alec Swann

Batting & Fielding

	Mat	Inns	NO	Runs	HS	Ave	SR	100	50	Ct	St
ODIs	46	46	4	1129	72	26.88	68.01	0	8	33	7
T20Is	16	15	1	260	50	18.57	97.74	0	1	10	8
First-class	84	128	14	4029	176	35.34	58.86	9	16	241	26
List A	121	100	12	2392	95	27.18	73.82	0	16	98	31
Twenty20	70	59	9	1172	84	23.44	119.34	0	5	34	25

Bowling

	Mat	Balls	Runs	Wkts	BBI	BBM	Ave	Econ	SR	5w	10
ODIs	46	-	-	-	-	-	-	-	-	-	-
T20Is	16	-	-	-	-	-	-	-	-	-	-
First-class	84	12	16	2	1/4	1/4	8.00	8.00	6.0	0	0
List A	121	-	-	-	-	-	-	-	-	-	-
Twenty20	70	-	-	-	-	-	-	-	-	-	-

NAME: Stephen David Peters
BORN: December 10, 1978, Harold Wood
HEIGHT: 5ft 11in
SQUAD Nº: 11
NICKNAME: Pedro, Geezer
OTHER TEAMS: Essex, Worcestershire
CAREER: First-class debut: 1996; List A debut: 1996; T20 debut: 2003; County cap: 2007 (Northamptonshire)

NORTHAMPTONSHIRE

AOC SAYS: The left-handed opener was earmarked as a prodigious talent at an early age and became Essex's youngest ever centurion when he scored 110 on his first-class debut against Cambridge University at 17. However, he failed to kick on and a move to Worcestershire in 2002 did little to reinvigorate his career. He moved on to pastures new in 2006 and has been a consistent scorer for Northamptonshire ever since. Peters was the bedrock of a faltering batting unit last season, top-scoring with almost twice as many Championship runs as his nearest teammate Andrew Hall. He surpassed his career-best score twice, falling one short of a maiden first-class double ton against Middlesex, and was justly rewarded with the Player of the Season award.

LAST WORD: "Stephen is now an experienced player and it's not strange territory for him to get past the 1,000 run mark. In a testing and difficult season for batsmen in Division Two, there weren't many that made that landmark." *David Capel*

Batting & Fielding

	Mat	Inns	NO	Runs	HS	Ave	SR	100	50	Ct	St
First-class	195	336	27	10746	199	34.77	-	24	54	154	0
List A	161	148	10	3063	107	22.19	-	2	18	45	0
Twenty20	17	14	3	222	61*	20.18	107.24	0	1	6	0

Bowling

	Mat	Balls	Runs	Wkts	BBI	BBM	Ave	Econ	SR	5w	10
First-class	195	35	31	1	1/19	-	31.00	5.31	35.0	0	0
List A	161	-	-	-	-	-	-	-	-	-	-
Twenty20	17	-	-	-	-	-	-	-	-	-	-

DAVID SALES

RHB RM R6

NORTHAMPTONSHIRE

NAME: David John Greenwood Sales
BORN: December 3, 1977, Carshalton
HEIGHT: 6ft
SQUAD Nº: 5
NICKNAME: Jumble, Car-boot
OTHER TEAMS: Wellington
CAREER: First-class debut: 1996; List A
debut: 1994; T20 debut: 2003; County cap:
1999

AOC SAYS: Sales is a vastly talented middle-order batsman who is unfortunate never to have represented his country. He made an unbeaten 70 on his one-day debut in 1994 and went on to become the youngest batsman to score a Championship double century at the age of 18 against Worcestershire. He continued to rewrite the record books by becoming the youngest triple centurion in Championship cricket after making 303 not out against Essex in 1999 and was named county captain in 2004. He relinquished the role abruptly in 2008 to concentrate on his batting and make a final push for international recognition but the call never came. He missed the entirety of the 2009 season due to a knee injury and struggled uncharacteristically for runs last season.

LAST WORD: "A slump can happen to anybody but it was a bit of surprise that David struggled for runs last season. I would be shocked if he has another season as poor as the last one." *Alec Swann*

Batting & Fielding

	Mat	Inns	NO	Runs	HS	Ave	SR	100	50	Ct	St
First-class	204	329	28	12145	303*	40.34	-	24	59	189	0
List A	241	229	31	6761	161	34.14	-	4	48	108	0
Twenty20	53	51	11	1202	78*	30.05	130.36	0	10	28	0

Bowling

	Mat	Balls	Runs	Wkts	BBI	BBM	Ave	Econ	SR	5w	10
First-class	204	345	184	9	4/25	-	20.44	3.20	38.3	0	0
List A	241	84	67	0	-	-	-	4.78	-	0	0
Twenty20	53	12	23	1	1/10	1/10	23.00	11.50	12.0	0	0

OVERSEAS PLAYER

NAME: Warnakulasuriya Patabendige
Ushantha Joseph Chaminda Vaas
BORN: January 27, 1974, Mattumagala, Sri Lanka
HEIGHT: 5ft 10in
SQUAD Nº: 4
OTHER TEAMS: Sri Lanka, Basnahira North,
Colts Cricket Club, Deccan Chargers,
Hampshire, Middlesex, Worcestershire
CAREER: Test debut: 1994; ODI debut: 1994;
T20I debut: 2006; First-class debut: 1990;
List A debut: 1993; T20 debut: 2005; County
cap: 2007 (Middlesex)

AOC SAYS: Vaas is the finest seam bowler ever to come out of Sri Lanka and sits fourth on the all-time list of leading wicket-takers in ODI cricket. In a distinguished international career spanning 15 years, the left-arm seamer became renowned for his skill with new ball and old and his ability to prosper in subcontinent conditions that typically favoured spin bowlers. Vaas became an excellent proponent of reverse-swing later in his career to add another weapon to his already formidable armoury. He made great strides in Test cricket in 2001 – taking 26 wickets in the 3-0 rout of West Indies to become only the second fast bowler after Imran Khan to take 14 wickets in a Test match in the subcontinent. In the same season he became the first bowler to take eight wickets in an ODI with a stunning spell of 8-19 against Zimbabwe in Colombo. He followed that effort by making history to become the first bowler to take a hat-trick with the first three balls of a match in the 2003 World Cup against Bangladesh. Vaas never quite produced the volume of runs to be described as a genuine allrounder but was nonetheless a handy No.8 who got better with age and struck his maiden Test ton against Bangladesh in 2007. He announced his Test retirement in 2009 and faded from the international scene as Sri Lanka opted for younger models in limited-overs cricket. After successful spells in county cricket with Middlesex and Worcestershire, the veteran swing bowler joined Northants for the FP t20 last season and rolled back the years to be named the PCA T20 Player of the Season after a trio of three-wicket hauls and four half-centuries. The veteran Sri Lankan will be available to Northamptonshire for the duration of the 2011 county season.

INSIDE TRACK: "Vaas will bring valuable experience to the side. He was a fantastic acquisition in T20 cricket last season and Northamptonshire will look to him to lead the attack in all competitions this season. Having Vaas at the club will benefit a young bowler like Jack Brooks who is still a relative newcomer and short of experience. Playing with and training alongside a wily old bloke like Vaas should help bring his game on and I'm sure he will be able to teach him a few tricks. Northants suffered from a succession of injuries and they will hope that Vaas can stay fit to spearhead the attack this season." *Alec Swann*

CHAMINDA VAAS

Batting & Fielding											
	Mat	Inns	NO	Runs	HS	Ave	SR	100	50	Ct	St
Tests	111	162	35	3089	100*	24.32	43.92	1	13	31	0
ODIs	322	220	72	2025	50*	13.68	72.52	0	1	60	0
T20Is	6	2	1	33	21	33.00	80.48	0	0	0	0
First-class	205	277	57	5717	134	25.98	-	4	26	57	0
List A	403	279	88	3111	76*	16.28	-	0	7	83	0
Twenty20	45	39	8	622	73	20.06	114.76	0	4	7	0

Bowling										
	Mat	Balls	Runs	Wkts	BBI	BBM	Ave	Econ	SR	5w	10
Tests	111	23438	10501	355	7/71	14/191	29.58	2.68	66.0	12	2
ODIs	322	15775	11014	400	8/19	8/19	27.53	4.18	39.4	4	0
T20Is	6	132	128	6	2/14	2/14	21.33	5.81	22.0	0	0
First-class	205	37450	17167	686	7/54	-	25.02	2.74	55.0	27	3
List A	403	19147	13257	496	8/19	8/19	26.72	4.15	38.6	4	0
Twenty20	45	927	1059	55	3/16	3/16	19.25	6.85	16.8	0	0

● *He wasn't the quickest even in his prime but he's very canny and gives very little away* ●

Alec Swann,
former Northamtonshire player
turned cricket journalist

NAME: Alex George Wakely
BORN: November 3, 1988, Hammersmith
HEIGHT: 6ft 2in
SQUAD Nº: 8
NICKNAME: Wakers, Baby Seal, Pup,
Hologram, Allan, The Hof
CAREER: First-class debut: 2007; List A
debut: 2005; T20 debut: 2009

NORTHAMPTONSHIRE

AOC SAYS: The former England under 19 captain is a top-order batsman of great potential who demonstrated his talent with a century against Sri Lanka on the 2006/07 tour of Malaysia as his teammates struggled on a spin-friendly surface. He went on to skipper his country at the 2008 World Cup but is yet to translate his form in age-group cricket into the first-class arena. A Championship century against Middlesex at Lord's season showed what he is capable of but he is yet to fire consistently and that must be Wakely's aim this season. A tall man who stands very upright at the crease, he has a classical style and is at his best hitting straight down the ground. He has the potential to develop into an opening batsman but is set to bat at No.3 this season.

LAST WORD: "Alex is a very intelligent, thoughtful lad with a good cricket brain and in the long-term could be a future county captain." *Andrew Radd*

Batting & Fielding

	Mat	Inns	NO	Runs	HS	Ave	SR	100	50	Ct	St
First-class	34	58	2	1371	113*	24.48	40.91	2	9	21	0
List A	21	20	2	256	35	14.22	67.90	0	0	4	0
Twenty20	24	23	3	473	55	23.65	110.77	0	1	9	0

Bowling

	Mat	Balls	Runs	Wkts	BBI	BBM	Ave	Econ	SR	5w	10
First-class	34	301	252	4	2/62	2/62	63.00	5.02	75.2	0	0
List A	21	24	20	2	2/14	2/14	10.00	5.00	12.0	0	0
Twenty20	24	6	11	0	-	-	-	11.00	-	0	0

ROB WHITE

NAME: Robert Allan White
BORN: October 15, 1979, Chelmsford
HEIGHT: 5ft 11in
SQUAD Nº: 18
NICKNAME: Toff, Whitey
CAREER: First-class debut: 2000; List A debut: 2002; T20 debut: 2003; County cap: 2008

AOC SAYS: White is an aggressive batsman who is at his best taking the attack to the bowling in limited-overs cricket. A faithful servant to Northamptonshire throughout his career, he made his mark in breathtaking fashion with a blistering 277 against Gloucestershire in 2002. It proved something of a false dawn as he scratched around for the next few seasons before topping 1,000 Championship runs in 2008 and coming close to matching the feat the next season. He slipped down the pecking order in four-day cricket in 2010 after a slump in form and is not guaranteed a batting spot in the Championship side but remains an integral member of the limited-overs team where he is given free rein to hit out at the top of the order.

LAST WORD: "I expect Rob to play regularly in one-day cricket where he can be very destructive but I think he'll be on the periphery of the side when it comes to the four-day format." *Alec Swann*

Batting & Fielding

	Mat	Inns	NO	Runs	HS	Ave	SR	100	50	Ct	St
First-class	97	169	16	5045	277	32.97	-	7	26	58	0
List A	83	79	3	1782	111	23.44	78.60	2	10	18	0
Twenty20	55	53	5	1122	94*	23.37	121.69	0	6	11	0

Bowling

	Mat	Balls	Runs	Wkts	BBI	BBM	Ave	Econ	SR	5w	10
First-class	97	1126	807	14	2/30	-	57.64	4.30	80.4	0	0
List A	83	54	55	2	2/18	2/18	27.50	6.11	27.0	0	0
Twenty20	55	-	-	-	-	-	-	-	-	-	-

DAVID WILLEY

NAME: David Jonathan Willey
BORN: February 28, 1990, Northampton
SQUAD Nº: 15
NICKNAME: Will
CAREER: First-class debut: 2009; List A debut: 2009; T20 debut: 2009

AOC SAYS: Willey is a promising allrounder and the son of former England player-turned-umpire Peter. He struck a half-century on his Championship debut against Leicestershire in 2009 but it is with the ball that he has shown most promise in the early stages of his career. He has impressed with his whippy left-arm seamers in T20 cricket and would have featured more in four-day cricket last season but for shin splints. Willey is a former England under 19 international and scored 65 before taking 3-45 against Bangladesh in his solitary under 19 youth Test match in 2009. He has now fully recovered from his injury problems and is expected to compete for a first-team spot in all formats this season.

LAST WORD: "David has already proven himself to be a superb T20 cricketer. Aside from his bowling he is a handy batsman and a brilliant fielder." *Andrew Radd*

Batting & Fielding

	Mat	Inns	NO	Runs	HS	Ave	SR	100	50	Ct	St
First-class	13	21	3	372	60	20.66	35.49	0	1	4	0
List A	18	15	3	149	25	12.41	67.11	0	0	5	0
Twenty20	29	14	5	120	19	13.33	103.44	0	0	10	0

Bowling

	Mat	Balls	Runs	Wkts	BBI	BBM	Ave	Econ	SR	5w	10
First-class	13	753	513	12	2/21	4/104	42.75	4.08	62.7	0	0
List A	18	347	338	6	2/40	2/40	56.33	5.84	57.8	0	0
Twenty20	29	270	312	18	3/9	3/9	17.33	6.93	15.0	0	0

329

NOTTINGHAMSHIRE
COUNTY CRICKET CLUB ®

FORMED: 1841
HOME GROUND: Trent Bridge, Nottingham
ONE-DAY NAME: Outlaws
CAPTAIN: Chris Read
2010 RESULTS: CC1: Champions; CB40: 3/7 in Group C; FP t20: Semi-finalists

HONOURS
County Championship: (6) 1907, 1929, 1981, 1987, 2005, 2010; Gillette/NatWest/C&G/FP Trophy: 1987; Benson and Hedges Cup: 1989; Sunday League: 1991

THE LOWDOWN
Nottinghamshire will hope to lift successive Championship titles for the first time in their history after clinching the title in stunning fashion on the final day of last season. Notts can lay claim to possessing the best battery of seamers in the country and benefited in 2010 from a policy of rotating their pacemen. Director of cricket Mick Newell favoured a four-man pace attack last season and that is set to continue, with Samit Patel fulfilling the spin-bowling duties. There is room for improvement in the top-order but they bat deep, with Chris Read, Steven Mullaney and Paul Franks all providing lower-order runs at crucial times in the last campaign. A clear priority this season is to win their first one-day trophy for 20 years, with captain Read admitting that leading out his team in a showpiece final at Lord's would be a highlight of his career.

DIRECTOR OF CRICKET: MICK NEWELL
Having spent eight years with Nottinghamshire as a doughty opening batsman between 1984 and 1992, Newell took control of team affairs on a temporary basis in 2002. He was given a permanent role after guiding the county to the top tier of the Championship and led them to the title three years later. Newell has also been part of the England Lions and under 19s coaching set-up.

With thanks to: Wayne Noon, Nottinghamshire assistant manager; Dave Bracegirdle, BBC Radio Nottingham cricket correspondent

	Mat	Inns	NO	Runs	HS	Ave	SR	100	50	Ct	St
HM Amla	5	7	1	463	129	77.16	64.93	1	5	1	-
DJ Hussey	5	7	1	399	251*	66.50	82.43	1	1	7	-
AC Voges	3	5	0	254	126	50.80	54.27	1	1	1	-
CMW Read	17	26	5	945	124*	45.00	57.34	2	5	60	4
MA Wagh	16	24	1	953	139	41.43	46.55	3	3	8	-
SJ Mullaney	11	17	4	512	100*	39.38	63.44	1	3	6	-
AD Brown	17	26	3	863	134	37.52	67.63	1	6	12	-
PJ Franks	16	22	1	765	114	36.42	74.05	1	6	1	-
AD Hales	12	20	1	677	136	35.63	58.71	1	4	12	-
GG White	1	1	0	29	29	29.00	37.66	0	0	1	-
SR Patel	17	28	2	750	104	28.84	60.58	1	4	9	-
BM Shafayat	7	11	0	277	159	25.18	48.93	1	0	7	-
MJ Wood	4	6	0	148	72	24.66	57.58	0	2	1	-
NJ Edwards	7	11	0	255	85	23.18	52.68	0	1	17	-
AR Adams	14	20	5	240	37	16.00	83.33	0	0	13	-
LJ Fletcher	6	9	3	96	23*	16.00	61.14	0	0	2	-
DJ Pattinson	13	14	4	101	27	10.10	34.35	0	0	0	-
SCJ Broad	2	3	0	7	6	2.33	18.42	0	0	0	-
CE Shreck	5	7	1	10	7*	1.66	27.77	0	0	4	-
GP Swann	1	1	0	1	1	1.00	20.00	0	0	0	-
RJ Sidebottom	9	7	7	66	22*	-	45.83	0	0	3	-

Batting & Fielding

	Mat	Overs	Mdn	Runs	Wkts	BBI	BBM	Ave	Econ	SR	5w	10
SCJ Broad	2	66.0	7	299	19	8/52	11/131	15.73	4.53	20.8	2	1
RJ Sidebottom	9	236.0	62	630	30	5/35	8/72	21.00	2.66	47.2	1	0
AR Adams	14	455.5	101	1508	68	6/79	8/159	22.17	3.30	40.2	4	0
PJ Franks	16	410.2	106	1129	42	3/15	6/67	26.88	2.75	58.6	0	0
CE Shreck	5	199.0	50	577	18	4/81	7/121	32.05	2.89	66.3	0	0
SJ Mullaney	11	93.4	19	321	9	4/31	4/48	35.66	3.42	62.4	0	0
DJ Pattinson	13	310.2	54	1180	33	5/95	6/158	35.75	3.80	56.4	1	0
SR Patel	17	345.3	73	1044	26	4/55	6/95	40.15	3.02	79.7	0	0
GP Swann	1	26.0	5	88	2	2/88	2/48	44.00	3.38	78.0	0	0
LJ Fletcher	6	169.2	40	563	12	3/39	4/90	46.91	3.32	84.6	0	0
GG White	1	23.0	3	104	1	1/104	1/104	104.00	4.52	138.0	0	0
AD Brown	17	9.0	0	57	0	-	-	-	6.33	-	0	0
AD Hales	12	5.5	1	26	0	-	-	-	4.45	-	0	0
DJ Hussey	5	18.0	1	82	0	-	-	-	4.55	-	0	0
AC Voges	3	1.0	0	2	0	-	-	-	2.00	-	0	0
MJ Wood	4	1.0	0	11	0	-	-	-	11.00	-	0	0

Bowling

OUTLAWS

Batting & Fielding

	Mat	Inns	NO	Runs	HS	Ave	SR	100	50	Ct	St
AC Voges	3	3	1	127	71*	63.50	79.87	0	2	1	-
DJ Hussey	3	3	1	114	80	57.00	137.34	0	1	3	-
SR Patel	12	11	1	467	108*	46.70	95.50	1	3	3	-
CMW Read	12	10	4	263	69*	43.83	109.12	0	2	8	3
HM Amla	3	2	0	86	53	43.00	116.21	0	1	0	-
AD Hales	12	11	1	370	96*	37.00	104.22	0	2	6	-
A Patel	3	3	0	81	38	27.00	84.37	0	0	0	-
MJ Wood	6	5	0	110	60	22.00	75.86	0	1	0	-
SL Elstone	4	4	1	66	30	22.00	113.79	0	0	0	-
SJ Mullaney	11	10	1	170	41	18.88	120.56	0	0	8	-
AD Brown	9	8	0	116	43	14.50	92.06	0	0	2	-
NJ Edwards	3	2	0	28	17	14.00	66.66	0	0	1	-
GG White	12	6	3	29	14	9.66	96.66	0	0	5	-
LJ Fletcher	6	3	1	16	14*	8.00	114.28	0	0	1	-
DJ Pattinson	5	1	0	8	8	8.00	133.33	0	0	3	-
PJ Franks	11	7	1	45	22	7.50	84.90	0	0	2	-
AR Adams	3	3	1	12	9	6.00	85.71	0	0	1	-
JT Ball	1	1	0	6	6	6.00	85.71	0	0	0	-
MA Wagh	2	2	0	5	3	2.50	27.77	0	0	0	-
A Carter	3	1	1	5	5*	-	50.00	0	0	1	-
RJ Sidebottom	5	2	2	2	1*	-	100.00	0	0	0	-

Bowling

	Mat	Overs	Mdns	Runs	Wkts	BBI	Ave	Econ	SR	5w
JT Ball	1	8.0	0	32	3	3/32	10.66	4.00	16.0	0
SJ Mullaney	11	53.0	1	280	13	3/24	21.53	5.28	24.4	0
SL Elstone	4	3.4	0	22	1	1/22	22.00	6.00	22.0	0
A Carter	3	10.0	0	79	3	2/42	26.33	7.90	20.0	0
RJ Sidebottom	5	31.0	0	162	6	3/45	27.00	5.22	31.0	0
GG White	12	54.3	1	306	11	5/35	27.81	5.61	29.7	1
PJ Franks	11	55.0	1	351	11	3/22	31.90	6.38	30.0	0
DJ Pattinson	5	31.0	2	200	6	3/70	33.33	6.45	31.0	0
SR Patel	12	70.2	0	368	11	2/19	33.45	5.23	38.3	0
LJ Fletcher	6	34.3	1	236	6	2/41	39.33	6.84	34.5	0
AR Adams	3	16.0	0	102	2	2/50	51.00	6.37	48.0	0
DJ Hussey	3	1.0	0	6	0	-	-	6.00	-	0
CE Shreck	2	5.1	0	37	0	-	-	7.16	-	0

OUTLAWS

	Mat	Inns	NO	Runs	HS	Ave	SR	100	50	Ct	St
DJ Hussey	17	17	5	524	81*	43.66	142.00	0	3	9	-
AD Hales	18	18	2	466	83	29.12	135.86	0	4	8	-
SR Patel	18	18	2	459	63	28.68	133.04	0	3	3	-
MJ Wood	18	17	2	328	61	21.86	111.56	0	2	1	-
CMW Read	14	12	5	145	28*	20.71	102.11	0	0	3	4
AD Brown	18	18	1	337	73*	19.82	132.15	0	2	5	-
SJ Mullaney	18	13	5	145	53	18.12	122.88	0	1	7	-
PJ Franks	9	4	2	34	23*	17.00	121.42	0	0	1	-
GG White	16	7	3	56	26*	14.00	116.66	0	0	9	-
GP Swann	1	1	0	11	11	11.00	122.22	0	0	1	-
RJ Sidebottom	11	4	2	18	11	9.00	120.00	0	0	7	-
BM Shafayat	4	2	0	10	8	5.00	142.85	0	0	2	0
DJ Pattinson	15	3	1	5	4*	2.50	41.66	0	0	6	-
SCJ Broad	3	1	0	0	0	0.00	0.00	0	0	0	-
DP Nannes	16	2	2	1	1*	-	100.00	0	0	1	-

Batting & Fielding

	Mat	Overs	Mdns	Runs	Wkts	BBI	Ave	Econ	SR	5w
GP Swann	1	4.0	0	24	2	2/24	12.00	6.00	12.0	0
LJ Fletcher	1	3.0	0	13	1	1/13	13.00	4.33	18.0	0
DJ Pattinson	15	50.0	1	353	20	4/19	17.65	7.06	15.0	0
SR Patel	18	58.0	0	377	17	3/26	22.17	6.50	20.4	0
GG White	16	36.1	0	270	12	3/22	22.50	7.46	18.0	0
SCJ Broad	3	11.5	0	90	4	2/22	22.50	7.60	17.7	0
DJ Hussey	17	3.0	1	23	1	1/0	23.00	7.66	18.0	0
DP Nannes	16	58.5	0	466	17	2/20	27.41	7.92	20.7	0
SJ Mullaney	18	54.0	0	393	14	3/12	28.07	7.27	23.1	0
RJ Sidebottom	11	41.0	0	315	7	2/19	45.00	7.68	35.1	0
PJ Franks	9	24.0	0	231	5	2/45	46.20	9.62	28.8	0
AD Hales	18	0.2	0	5	0	-	-	15.00	-	0

Bowling

ANDRE ADAMS

RHB RMF W1 MVP57

NAME: Andre Ryan Adams
BORN: July 17, 1975, Auckland
HEIGHT: 5ft 11in
SQUAD Nº: 41
NICKNAME: Dre
OTHER TEAMS: New Zealand, Auckland, Essex, Kolkata Tigers
CAREER: Test debut: 2002; ODI debut: 2001; T20I debut: 2005; First-class debut: 1998; List A debut: 1997; T20 debut: 2004; County cap: 2004 (Essex), 2007 (Nottinghamshire)

AOC SAYS: Adams is a lively seamer and capable lower-order batsman who qualifies as a Kolpak player through his West Indian heritage. For a time he was a regular in New Zealand's limited overs set-up and took six wickets on Test debut against England but was never selected again. He has become one of county cricket's most reliable performers since ending his association with the Black Caps in 2007 after falling out with then coach John Bracewell. Adams has finished as Nottinghamshire's leading wicket-taker for the last two seasons and took the wicket of Shivnarine Chanderpaul that secured the Championship title in dramatic fashion against Lancashire last season. He was subsequently named Nottinghamshire's Player of the Year.

LAST WORD: "Andre is an experienced and capable performer who knows all about the county circuit." *Mick Newell*

Batting & Fielding

	Mat	Inns	NO	Runs	HS	Ave	SR	100	50	Ct	St
Tests	1	2	0	18	11	9.00	90.00	0	0	1	0
ODIs	42	34	10	419	45	17.45	100.47	0	0	8	0
T20Is	4	2	1	13	7	13.00	108.33	0	0	1	0
First-class	118	158	16	3220	124	22.67	-	3	12	81	0
List A	159	114	29	1451	90*	17.07	-	0	1	39	0
Twenty20	44	30	7	307	54*	13.34	128.45	0	1	14	0

Bowling

	Mat	Balls	Runs	Wkts	BBI	BBM	Ave	Econ	SR	5w	10
Tests	2	190	105	6	3/44	6/105	17.50	3.31	0	0	0
ODIs	40	1885	1643	53	5/22	5/22	31.00	5.22	2	1	0
T20Is	4	77	105	3	2/20	2/20	35.00	8.18	0	0	0
First-class	119	23587	11485	479	6/25	-	23.97	2.92	-	18	2
List A	159	7307	5803	196	5/7	5/7	29.60	4.76	3	3	0
Twenty20	43	906	1173	53	5/20	5/20	22.13	7.76	0	1	0

NAME: Jacob Timothy Ball
BORN: March 14, 1991, Mansfield
SQUAD Nº: 28
CAREER: First-class debut: 2011; List A
debut: 2010

NOTTINGHAMSHIRE

AOC SAYS: Ball is a promising right-arm seamer who broke into the England under 19 side last season. He made his bow for Nottinghamshire in 2009 and was dismissed for a golden duck in front of the television cameras as part of a Dwayne Smith hat-trick against Sussex. He impressed in a solitary CB40 appearance last season, taking 3-32 in a narrow defeat to Leicestershire. Ball is the nephew of former England wicketkeeper Bruce French and his older brother Jonathan has represented Nottinghamshire Second XI. Plentiful resources in the seam department mean Ball is likely to find his opportunities in Championship cricket restricted but he can expect to feature in one-day competitions.

LAST WORD: "The 40-over competition is perhaps his best route into the first team and he has already shown he can be effective in that format." *Mick Newell*

Batting & Fielding

	Mat	Inns	NO	Runs	HS	Ave	SR	100	50	Ct	St
First-class	1	2	1	4	4	4.00	57.14	0	0	0	0
List A	2	2	0	6	6	3.00	75.00		0	0	0

Bowling

	Mat	Balls	Runs	Wkts	BBI	BBM	Ave	Econ	SR	5w	10
First-class	1	126	106	3	3/72	3/106	35.33	5.04	42.00	0	0
List A	2	84	65	4	3/32	3/32	16.25	4.64	21.00	-	-

STUART BROAD   LHB RFM

NAME: Stuart Christopher John Broad
BORN: June 24, 1986, Nottingham
HEIGHT: 6ft 6in
SQUAD Nº: 16
NICKNAME: Broady
OTHER TEAMS: England, Leicestershire
CAREER: Test debut: 2007; ODI debut: 2006;
T20I debut 2006; First-class debut: 2005;
List A debut: 2005; T20 debut: 2006; County
cap: 2007 (Leicestershire)

AOC SAYS: A tall seam bowler who troubles batsmen with his pace and bounce, Broad
has made rapid progress since bursting onto the county scene with Leicestershire
in 2005. He is now a key player for England in all forms of the game and starred in
the Ashes series win in 2009, taking 5-37 – including a spell of 4-8 in 21 balls – in the
decisive fifth Test at The Oval to scoop the Man of the Match award. His father Chris was
part of England's Ashes winning side in 1986/87 – scoring three centuries in consecutive
matches along the way – and Stuart helped England win the urn Down Under for the
first time in 24 years this winter, although his tour was cut short after he sustained an
abdominal injury in the second Test victory in Adelaide. Broad broke into the Test team
in 2007 after impressing with his pace, spirit and bowling variations in the one-day side
and quickly found his feet on the 2008 tour of New Zealand, taking 3-54 in the third Test
at Napier to help England to a series victory. Bowling remains his stronger suit but he
is also an elegant batsman and possesses the talent to become a genuine allrounder
and potentially a Test No.7. He scored his maiden Test century against Pakistan at Lord's
last summer, making 169 as part of a world-record eighth-wicket stand of 332 with
Jonathan Trott. Broad returned to his home county at the start of the 2008 season after
swapping Grace Road for Trent Bridge and returned career-best figures of 8-52 against
Warwickshire last season in a rare outing in county cricket.

INSIDE TRACK: "As backroom staff we plan for a season without Broady because of his
international commitments but if he is available the rest of the squad know he is an
automatic choice. When he plays for us it's a massive bonus, as he showed last year with
19 wickets in two Championship matches. He actually started life as an opening batsman
but after he shot up in height he decided to give the bowling a go. People tend to forget
how young Stuart is because he's played so much cricket. When you're young you tend to
do things that are a bit reckless. I think over the years he'll calm down, pick his moments
and perhaps not do it so obviously." *Wayne Noon*

Batting & Fielding

	Mat	Inns	NO	Runs	HS	Ave	SR	100	50	Ct	St
Tests	34	46	6	1096	169	27.40	59.30	1	5	9	0
ODIs	73	43	14	372	45*	12.82	72.37	0	0	17	0
T20Is	29	11	5	36	10*	6.00	124.13	0	0	13	0
First-class	77	97	19	1959	169	25.11	54.10	1	12	22	0
List A	90	49	15	418	45*	12.29	71.08	0	0	19	0
Twenty20	44	13	6	45	10*	6.42	107.14	0	0	14	0

Bowling

	Mat	Balls	Runs	Wkts	BBI	BBM	Ave	Econ	SR	5w	10
Tests	34	6693	3489	99	6/91	6/87	35.24	3.12	67.6	3	0
ODIs	74	3770	3252	126	5/23	5/23	25.80	5.17	29.9	1	0
T20Is	29	611	755	35	3/17	3/17	21.57	7.41	17.4	0	0
First-class	77	13730	7630	261	8/52	-	29.23	3.33	52.6	12	1
List A	91	4552	3940	151	5/23	5/23	26.09	5.19	30.1	1	0
Twenty20	44	958	1072	55	3/13	3/13	19.49	6.71	17.4	0	0

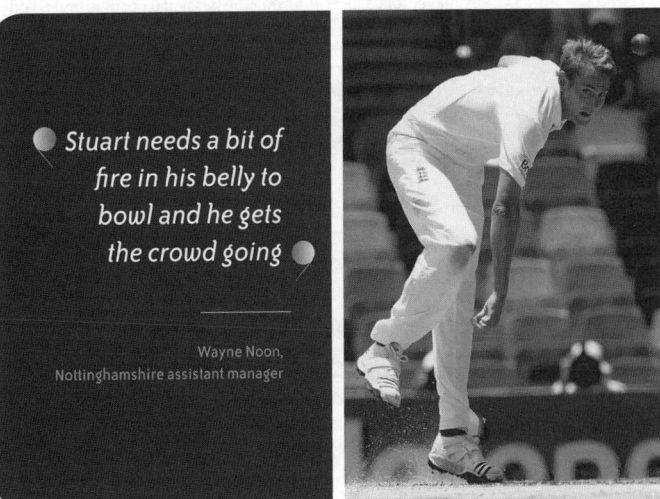

Stuart needs a bit of fire in his belly to bowl and he gets the crowd going

Wayne Noon,
Nottinghamshire assistant manager

ALI BROWN

NOTTINGHAMSHIRE

NAME: Alistair Duncan Brown
BORN: February 11, 1970, Beckenham
HEIGHT: 5ft 10in
SQUAD Nº: 3
NICKNAME: Lordy
OTHER TEAMS: England, Surrey
CAREER: ODI debut: 1996; First-class debut: 1992; List A debut: 1990; T20 debut: 2003; County cap: 1994 (Surrey), 2009 (Nottinghamshire)

AOC SAYS: Now in the twilight of his career, Brown has been one of county cricket's most destructive batsmen for more than 20 years. During a 21-year stint at Surrey he scored a first-class century against every other county and struck a world-record one-day score of 268 off 160 balls against Glamorgan in 2002. He featured intermittently for England in 16 ODIs spanning five years but struggled for consistency after scoring a ton in his third match against India. After a lean couple of seasons Brown left The Oval for Trent Bridge in 2009 and has enjoyed something of a renaissance, scoring just shy of 900 runs in each of the past two seasons.

LAST WORD: "Ali was a key player for us last season and he has had a positive impact on the field and in the dressing room." *Mick Newell*

Batting & Fielding

	Mat	Inns	NO	Runs	HS	Ave	SR	100	50	Ct	St
ODIs	16	16	0	354	118	22.12	82.90	1	1	6	0
First-class	281	440	49	16724	295*	42.77	-	46	75	276	1
List A	398	380	18	11163	268	30.83	-	19	50	130	0
Twenty20	79	79	2	1758	83	22.83	149.87	0	12	41	0

Bowling

	Mat	Balls	Runs	Wkts	BBI	BBM	Ave	Econ	SR	5w	10
ODIs	16	6	5	0	-	-	-	5.00	-	0	0
First-class	281	1417	775	6	3/25	-	129.16	3.28	236.1	0	0
List A	398	520	561	14	3/39	3/39	40.07	6.47	37.1	0	0
Twenty20	79	2	2	0	-	-	-	6.00	-	0	0

NAME: Andrew Carter
BORN: August 27, 1988, Lincoln
SQUAD Nº: 37
OTHER TEAMS: Essex
CAREER: First-class debut: 2009; List A
debut: 2009; T20 debut: 2010

AOC SAYS: Carter earned a contract at Trent Bridge in 2008 after impressing in the Lincolnshire Premier League for Bracebridge Heath. The lanky, right-arm seamer excelled for Nottinghamshire's Second XI in 2009 and gained valuable experience during a loan spell with Essex last season, where he picked up his maiden first-class five-wicket haul, against Kent at Canterbury. He was subsequently selected for England's Fast Bowling Programme and after impressing at Dennis Lillee's fast bowling academy in Chennai received a shock call-up to join England Lions in the Caribbean. After making rapid progress over the past year and developing his pace, he is now set to join Nottinghamshire's battery of first-choice seamers.

LAST WORD: "There has been a transformation with Andy. He went to Essex last season and took bundles of wickets. He bowled really well and came back with rave reports."
Dave Bracegirdle

Batting & Fielding

	Mat	Inns	NO	Runs	HS	Ave	SR	100	50	Ct	St
First-class	5	6	1	49	16*	9.80	76.56	0	0	2	0
List A	10	6	1	25	12	5.00	54.34	0	0	3	0
Twenty20	2	-	-	-	-	-	-	-	-	0	0

Bowling

	Mat	Balls	Runs	Wkts	BBI	BBM	Ave	Econ	SR	5w	10
First-class	5	923	475	16	5/40	7/121	29.68	3.08	57.6	1	0
List A	10	294	279	12	3/32	3/32	23.25	5.69	24.5	0	0
Twenty20	2	42	69	0	-	-	-	9.85	-	0	0

E

NOTTINGHAMSHIRE

NEIL EDWARDS
LHB RM R1

NAME: Neil James Edwards
BORN: October 14, 1983, Truro
HEIGHT: 6ft 3in
SQUAD Nº: 15
NICKNAME: Toastie, Shanksy
OTHER TEAMS: Somerset
CAREER: First-class debut: 2002; List A debut: 2006; T20 debut: 2003

AOC SAYS: Edwards has failed to kick on since a superb 2007 season when he scored 1,251 first-class runs for Somerset. After struggling for form and opportunities the former England under 19 batsman left Taunton for Trent Bridge in 2010 in an attempt to revive his career. The left-handed opener started promisingly with 85 on debut against Kent but suffered a dip in form and was ruled out for six weeks after breaking his hand. His bad run of luck continued when, after returning to fitness, he got hit in the face batting in the nets to bring a premature end to his season.

LAST WORD: "I saw every ball that Edwards faced for Notts last season. He got out to two or three absolutely blinding catches and I still think he will be the answer at the top of the order." *Dave Bracegirdle*

Batting & Fielding

	Mat	Inns	NO	Runs	HS	Ave	SR	100	50	Ct	St
First-class	57	95	0	3165	212	33.31	59.54	3	16	55	0
List A	8	7	0	141	65	20.14	61.30	0	1	2	0
Twenty20	1	1	0	1	1	1.00	14.28	0	0	0	0

Bowling

	Mat	Balls	Runs	Wkts	BBI	BBM	Ave	Econ	SR	5w	10
First-class	57	287	194	2	1/16	-	97.00	4.05	143.5	0	0
List A	8	-	-	-	-	-	-	-	-	-	-
Twenty20	1	-	-	-	-	-	-	-	-	-	-

NAME: Scott Liam Elstone
BORN: June 10, 1990, Burton-on-Trent
SQUAD Nº: 31
CAREER: List A debut: 2010; T20 debut: 2010

NOTTINGHAMSHIRE

AOC SAYS: Elstone signed a two-year contract with Nottinghamshire in October after impressing in Second XI cricket last season. He is primarily a top-order batsman but his promising offspin means he has the potential to develop into an allrounder. He made his full county debut last season, featuring in four CB40 matches and making a solitary Twenty20 appearance, and hit a top score of 30 in a three-run victory over Durham at Trent Bridge. He is probably a season or two away from becoming a regular in four-day cricket but can expect to feature in one-day competitions when Nottinghamshire employ a rotation policy. Elstone spent the winter continuing his cricketing education by playing club cricket in Melbourne.

LAST WORD: "Scott isn't very tall and there's not much on him but he gives the ball a mighty whack and he's an excellent fielder." *Dave Bracegirdle*

Batting & Fielding

	Mat	Inns	NO	Runs	HS	Ave	SR	100	50	Ct	St
List A	4	4	1	66	30	22.00	113.79	0	0	1	0
Twenty20	1	-	-	-	-	-	-	-	-	0	0

Bowling

	Mat	Balls	Runs	Wkts	BBI	BBM	Ave	Econ	SR	5w	10
List A	4	22	22	1	1/22	1/22	22.00	6.00	22.0	0	0
Twenty20	1	-	-	-	-	-	-	-	-	-	-

LUKE FLETCHER

NAME: Luke Jack Fletcher
BORN: September 18, 1988, Nottingham
HEIGHT: 6ft 6in
SQUAD Nº: 19
NICKNAME: Fletch, Sloff
CAREER: First-class debut: 2008; List A
debut: 2008; T20 debut: 2009

AOC SAYS: A tall, strapping paceman, Fletcher turned heads with his performances for England under 19s and enjoyed a breakthrough 2009 after taking 29 first-class wickets. The former Trent Bridge car park attendant tore through Somerset's top-order to return career-best figures of 4-38 and a blistering 92 against Hampshire gave a glimpse of his batting talent. On the back of those performances he forced his way into the England Performance squad but he found opportunities harder to come by last season and only featured in six Championship matches after struggling with his fitness. He remains a fearsome prospect with all the raw materials to reach the top and will hope to benefit from the departure of Ryan Sidebottom.

LAST WORD: "Luke is an excellent prospect and we have big hopes for him. He let himself down a bit last year in terms of fitness after bursting onto the scene." *Wayne Noon*

Batting & Fielding

	Mat	Inns	NO	Runs	HS	Ave	SR	100	50	Ct	St
First-class	16	19	6	240	92	18.46	59.11	0	1	2	0
List A	21	12	5	79	40*	11.28	87.77	0	0	2	0
Twenty20	11	2	1	2	1*	2.00	28.57	0	0	2	0

Bowling

	Mat	Balls	Runs	Wkts	BBI	BBM	Ave	Econ	SR	5w	10
First-class	16	2891	1564	50	4/38	8/131	31.28	3.24	57.8	0	0
List A	21	858	743	20	2/35	2/35	37.15	5.19	42.9	0	0
Twenty20	11	240	311	9	2/23	2/23	34.55	7.77	26.6	0	0

NAME: Paul John Franks
BORN: February 3, 1979, Sutton-in-Ashfield
HEIGHT: 6ft 2in
SQUAD Nº: 8
NICKNAME: Franksie, Pike
OTHER TEAMS: England, Midwest Rhinos
CAREER: ODI debut: 2000; First-class debut: 1996; List A debut: 1997; T20 debut: 2003; County cap: 1999

NOTTINGHAMSHIRE

AOC SAYS: Franks is part of the furniture at Trent Bridge having first represented the county at 17. An international career beckoned for the bowling allrounder after taking more than 50 wickets in consecutive seasons in 1998 and 1999 but after making his ODI debut against West Indies in 2000 he suffered a serious knee injury and slipped down the pecking order. After two seasons of relative mediocrity he bounced back in 2010 to play a lead role in Nottinghamshire's Championship triumph with canny seam bowling and hard-hitting in the lower-order. Franks spent the winter playing for Midwest Rhinos in Zimbabwe's revamped domestic T20 competition.

LAST WORD: "With Mark Ealham retiring we needed someone to step up and Franksie made that allrounder spot his own. He could easily have been Player of the Year last season." *Wayne Noon*

Batting & Fielding

	Mat	Inns	NO	Runs	HS	Ave	SR	100	50	Ct	St
ODIs	1	1	0	4	4	4.00	23.52	0	0	1	0
First-class	181	257	47	5881	123*	28.00	-	4	31	60	0
List A	170	124	37	1832	84*	21.05	-	0	5	26	0
Twenty20	50	30	13	287	29*	16.88	117.62	0	0	8	0

Bowling

	Mat	Balls	Runs	Wkts	BBI	BBM	Ave	Econ	SR	5w	10
ODIs	1	54	48	0	-	-	-	5.33	-	0	0
First-class	181	27484	15038	474	7/56	-	31.72	3.28	57.9	11	0
List A	170	6266	5227	177	6/27	6/27	29.53	5.00	35.4	2	0
Twenty20	50	479	687	20	2/12	2/12	34.35	8.60	23.9	0	0

ALEX HALES

RHB RM/OB MVP61

NAME: Alexander Daniel Hales
BORN: January 3, 1989, Hillingdon
HEIGHT: 6ft 5in
SQUAD Nº: 10
NICKNAME: Halsey, Trigg
CAREER: First-class debut: 2008; List A debut: 2008; T20 debut: 2009

AOC SAYS: A tall and powerful top-order batsman, Hales is an exciting prospect with international ambitions. He arrived at Trent Bridge on the recommendation of Jason Gallian and broke into the Nottinghamshire first team in 2009 after excelling in Second XI cricket. He immediately demonstrated his strokemaking ability with an unbeaten 150 off 102 balls in a losing cause against Worcestershire in the Pro40. Hales scored his maiden first-class century against a strong Hampshire attack at Trent Bridge last season and is set to drop down to his favoured No.3 spot across all competitions this season, with Mark Wagh elevated to open.

LAST WORD: "He can go a long way in the game and the next steps are for him to exert an influence on our results and then push for an England Lions call." *Mick Newell*

Batting & Fielding

	Mat	Inns	NO	Runs	HS	Ave	SR	100	50	Ct	St
First-class	21	34	2	1132	136	35.37	53.52	1	8	15	0
List A	26	24	2	797	150*	36.22	104.04	2	3	9	0
Twenty20	24	24	2	515	83	23.40	133.41	0	4	10	0

Bowling

	Mat	Balls	Runs	Wkts	BBI	BBM	Ave	Econ	SR	5w	10
First-class	21	275	166	3	2/63	2/63	55.33	3.62	91.6	0	0
List A	26	-	-	-	-	-	-	-	-	-	-
Twenty20	24	2	5	0	-	-	-	15.00	-	0	0

OVERSEAS PLAYER

NOTTINGHAMSHIRE

NAME: David John Hussey
BORN: July 15, 1977, Perth, Australia
HEIGHT: 5ft 11in
SQUAD Nº: 29
NICKNAME: Huss, Husscat
OTHER TEAMS: Australia, Kolkata Knight Riders, Northern Districts, Victoria
CAREER: ODI debut: 2008; T20I debut: 2008; First-class debut: 2003; List A debut 2001; T20 debut: 2004; County cap: 2004

AOC SAYS: Hussey has been one of county cricket's most prolific runscorers since joining Nottinghamshire in 2004. He amassed 1,315 first-class runs in his maiden season at Trent Bridge before helping the county to their first Championship title in 18 years in 2005. Unlike his older brother Mike, he has not been able to force his way into Australia's Test side despite stacking up the runs for Notts and Victoria but he remains a key player in their limited-overs side as a middle-order enforcer and useful offspinner. International commitments restricted Hussey to five Championship appearances last season and in 2011 he will share the overseas duties with Adam Voges in the FP t20 and play Championship cricket from the start of June.

LAST WORD: "We don't see David as an overseas player because he came here as an unknown. It was a bit of a gamble on our part, but it's a gamble that has obviously paid off." *Wayne Noon*

Batting & Fielding

	Mat	Inns	NO	Runs	HS	Ave	SR	100	50	Ct	St
ODIs	31	28	1	848	111	31.40	88.42	1	6	16	0
T20Is	28	26	3	622	88*	27.04	127.19	0	3	16	0
First-class	154	240	25	11885	275	55.27	70.96	40	52	195	0
List A	189	177	25	6029	130	39.66	-	8	40	94	0
Twenty20	137	132	26	3476	100*	32.79	136.20	1	18	74	0

Bowling

	Mat	Balls	Runs	Wkts	BBI	BBM	Ave	Econ	SR	5w	10
ODIs	31	419	378	11	4/21	4/21	34.36	5.41	38.0	0	0
T20Is	28	282	299	16	3/25	3/25	18.68	6.36	17.6	0	0
First-class	154	2644	1639	25	4/105	-	65.56	3.71	105.7	0	0
List A	189	1684	1493	38	4/21	4/21	39.28	5.31	44.3	0	0
Twenty20	137	904	1078	39	3/25	3/25	27.64	7.15	23.1	0	0

STEVEN MULLANEY

RHB RM MVP58

NOTTINGHAMSHIRE

NAME: Steven John Mullaney
BORN: November 19, 1986, Warrington
HEIGHT: 5ft 10in
SQUAD Nº: 5
NICKNAME: Mull, Cadet Mahoney
OTHER TEAMS: Lancashire
CAREER: First-class debut: 2006; List A
debut: 2006; T20 debut: 2006

AOC SAYS: Having made just a handful of appearances in five seasons with Lancashire, Mullaney moved to Nottinghamshire ahead of the 2010 season and found instant success as a like-for-like replacement for the retired Mark Ealham. The allrounder struck his maiden first-class century against Hampshire in just his second match for the county and made 97 against the same opposition two weeks later. He also proved a vital cog in the Outlaws' one-day unit with his intelligent cutters, destructive lower-order hitting and agility in the field. He was rewarded for a fine season with a contract extension that will keep him at Trent Bridge until at least 2013.

LAST WORD: "I like Steven's character and desire and I think it's fair to say that he surpassed his own expectations with what he has achieved at Trent Bridge." *Mick Newell*

Batting & Fielding

	Mat	Inns	NO	Runs	HS	Ave	SR	100	50	Ct	St
First-class	16	24	5	831	165*	43.73	72.07	2	4	11	0
List A	19	14	2	206	41	17.16	110.75	0	0	11	0
Twenty20	21	14	5	150	53	16.66	117.18	0	1	8	0

Bowling

	Mat	Balls	Runs	Wkts	BBI	BBM	Ave	Econ	SR	5w	10
First-class	16	789	446	10	4/31	4/48	44.60	3.39	78.9	0	0
List A	19	500	438	23	3/13	3/13	19.04	5.25	21.7	0	0
Twenty20	21	342	414	15	3/12	3/12	27.60	7.26	22.8	0	0

NAME: Akhil Patel
BORN: June 18, 1990, Nottingham
HEIGHT: 5ft 10in
SQUAD N°: 24
NICKNAME: Shaq, Killer, Sneaky, Slidey
OTHER TEAMS: Derbyshire
CAREER: First-class debut: 2007; List A debut: 2009

AOC SAYS: The stylish left-hand batsman made his first-class debut for Derbyshire as a 16-year-old but after struggling for first-team opportunities at the County Ground he joined his older brother Samit at Nottinghamshire in 2009. He impressed on debut with a fluent half-century against Oxford University and made his Championship bow later that summer, making a patient 37 to help Notts to victory over Sussex. Patel failed to make a Championship appearance in 2010 but showed promise as an opener in 40-over cricket and continued to excel for the Second XI. He will hope to fill the berth vacated by Mark Wagh at the top of the order when the veteran retires from the game midway through the season. Patel also offers an extra bowling option with his left-arm wrist spin and is an agile fielder.

LAST WORD: "Akhil has developed his game quicker than we anticipated and he has the potential to become an established member of our team." *Mick Newell*

Batting & Fielding

	Mat	Inns	NO	Runs	HS	Ave	SR	100	50	Ct	St
First-class	3	6	2	153	69*	38.25	53.49	0	1	2	0
List A	7	7	0	173	41	24.71	83.98	0	0	1	0

Bowling

	Mat	Balls	Runs	Wkts	BBI	BBM	Ave	Econ	SR	5w	10
First-class	3	143	76	1	1/34	1/46	76.00	3.18	143.0	0	0
List A	7	30	34	2	2/34	2/34	17.00	6.80	15.0	0	0

SAMIT PATEL

RHB SLA MVP5

NAME: Samit Rohit Patel
BORN: November 30, 1984, Leicester
HEIGHT: 5ft 8in
SQUAD Nº: 21
NICKNAME: Pilchy
OTHER TEAMS: England
CAREER: ODI debut: 2008; First-class debut: 2002; List A debut: 2002; T20 debut: 2003; County cap: 2008

AOC SAYS: Patel has been earmarked as an allrounder of considerable talent ever since excelling in the Under 15 World Cup in 2000. A hard-hitting middle-order batsman and deceptive left-arm spinner, he is ideally suited to the limited-overs format and broke into England's ODI team in 2008. He impressed with the ball, taking 5-31 against South Africa, but was soon discarded for poor fitness levels. A fine season in 2010 across all formats saw him return to the international reckoning and he was named in a 30-man preliminary squad ahead of the World Cup. Lack of fitness saw him overlooked again and he attracted the wrath of England coach Andy Flower but he remains a key man for Nottinghamshire.

LAST WORD: "A lot has been said about Samit's fitness but his ability has never been in doubt and he's a valued member of the squad." *Mick Newell*

Batting & Fielding

	Mat	Inns	NO	Runs	HS	Ave	SR	100	50	Ct	St
ODIs	11	5	0	116	31	23.20	93.54	0	0	4	0
First-class	78	120	8	4456	176	39.78	64.65	10	24	44	0
List A	114	96	15	2559	114	31.59	81.28	2	13	29	0
Twenty20	72	67	11	1462	84*	26.10	121.63	0	9	22	0

Bowling

	Mat	Balls	Runs	Wkts	BBI	BBM	Ave	Econ	SR	5w	10
ODIs	11	340	319	11	5/41	5/41	29.00	5.62	30.9	1	0
First-class	78	7740	3932	98	6/84	-	40.12	3.04	78.9	2	0
List A	114	3086	2647	97	6/13	6/13	27.28	5.14	31.8	2	0
Twenty20	72	1135	1358	54	3/11	3/11	25.14	7.17	21.0	0	0

RHB RFM MVP75

NAME: Darren John Pattinson
BORN: August 2, 1979, Grimsby
SQUAD Nº: 14
OTHER TEAMS: England, Victoria
CAREER: Test debut: 2008; First-class debut: 2007; List A debut: 2006; T20 debut: 2007; County cap: 2008

NOTTINGHAMSHIRE

AOC SAYS: The former roof tiler is best known for his surprise call-up to England's Test side to face South Africa at Headingley in 2008. It was a rapid elevation to international cricket for the swing bowler who had spent years toiling away in Melbourne club cricket for Dandenong and had just 11 first-class appearances to his name. Pattinson, who emigrated to Australia aged six, had proved a revelation after joining Nottinghamshire on the recommendation of Victoria teammate David Hussey and impressed with his ability to swing the ball away from the right-hander at reasonable pace. The horses-for-courses selection at Headingley proved unsuccessful and a slump in form followed in 2009, but he bounced back last season with 33 Championship wickets.

LAST WORD: "He has proved to be an excellent signing and is a big part of our plans in all three competitions this season." *Mick Newell*

Batting & Fielding

	Mat	Inns	NO	Runs	HS	Ave	SR	100	50	Ct	St
Tests	1	2	0	21	13	10.50	42.00	0	0	0	0
First-class	54	63	11	610	59	11.73	41.69	0	1	5	0
List A	44	16	6	69	13*	6.90	59.48	0	0	13	0
Twenty20	32	7	3	19	5	4.75	70.37	0	0	10	0

Bowling

	Mat	Balls	Runs	Wkts	BBI	BBM	Ave	Econ	SR	5w	10
Tests	1	181	96	2	2/95	2/96	48.00	3.18	90.5	0	0
First-class	54	8712	5022	148	8/35	9/97	33.93	3.45	58.8	7	0
List A	44	1737	1523	56	4/29	4/29	27.19	5.26	31.0	0	0
Twenty20	32	609	772	35	4/19	4/19	22.05	7.60	17.4	0	0

BEN PHILLIPS

NOTTINGHAMSHIRE

NAME: Ben James Phillips
BORN: September 30, 1974, Lewisham
HEIGHT: 6ft 6in
SQUAD Nº: 13
NICKNAME: Bennyphil, Bus
OTHER TEAMS: Kent, Northamptonshire, Somerset
CAREER: County debut: 1996; List A debut: 1996; T20 debut: 2003; County cap: 2005 (Northamptonshire)

AOC SAYS: Phillips signed for Nottinghamshire in November after an impressive season for Somerset in which he took 67 wickets across all formats. The veteran seamer began his career with Kent, but after taking 44 first-class wickets in his second season at St Lawrence he struggled with injury and eventually moved to Northamptonshire in 2002. After four solid but unspectacular seasons he swapped Wantage Road for Taunton and became a key member of Somerset's attack. Phillips is a direct replacement for Ryan Sidebottom, who left for Yorkshire at the end of last season, and will add a wealth of experience to Nottinghamshire's bowling unit.

LAST WORD: "In the early stages of the season, particularly at Trent Bridge, Phillips should go well. Even at 36 he's still fighting fit and has done really well in the pre-season tests. He's a proven performer it was a no-risk signing really." *Dave Bracegirdle*

Batting & Fielding

	Mat	Inns	NO	Runs	HS	Ave	SR	100	50	Ct	St
First-class	108	150	26	2581	100*	20.81	-	1	14	31	0
List A	125	76	25	946	51*	18.54	-	0	1	34	0
Twenty20	59	38	10	436	41*	15.57	134.56	0	0	19	0

Bowling

	Mat	Balls	Runs	Wkts	BBI	BBM	Ave	Econ	SR	5w	10
First-class	108	14825	7121	238	6/29	-	29.92	2.88	62.2	5	0
List A	125	5142	4166	147	4/25	4/25	28.34	4.86	34.9	0	0
Twenty20	59	1218	1645	59	4/18	4/18	27.88	8.10	20.6	0	0

NAME: Christopher Mark Wells Read
BORN: August 10, 1978, Paignton
HEIGHT: 5ft 8in
SQUAD Nº: 7
NICKNAME: Readie, Reados
OTHER TEAMS: England, Gloucestershire,
CAREER: Test debut: 1999; ODI debut 2000;
T20I debut: 2006; First-class debut: 1998;
List A debut: 1995; T20 debut: 2004; County
cap: 1999 (Nottinghamshire)

NOTTINGHAMSHIRE

AOC SAYS: Read is entering his fourth season as skipper at Trent Bridge and remains one of the most highly-regarded glovemen in the country. He was fast-tracked into the England A side before he made his first-class debut and made his Test bow against New Zealand as a 20-year-old after joining Nottinghamshire from Gloucestershire in 1998. He was dropped after just three matches and had to wait four years for a recall. While his keeping received rave reviews, Read struggled for runs at international level and was never able to cement his spot as England's first-choice stumper. His international career now appears to be over but in county cricket he remains a model of consistency with both bat and gloves.

LAST WORD: "Read should have been England's Mark Boucher. South Africa stuck with Boucher and he broke record after record. If England had done that with Readie he would have had a similar record, if not better." *Wayne Noon*

Batting & Fielding

	Mat	Inns	NO	Runs	HS	Ave	SR	100	50	Ct	St
Tests	15	23	4	360	55	18.94	39.47	0	1	48	6
ODIs	36	24	7	300	30*	17.64	73.17	0	0	41	2
T20Is	1	1	0	13	13	13.00	118.18	0	0	1	0
First-class	240	356	61	10751	240	36.44	-	18	58	711	40
List A	262	209	52	4334	135	27.60	-	2	15	256	60
Twenty20	60	53	16	944	58*	25.51	118.74	0	1	34	11

Bowling

	Mat	Balls	Runs	Wkts	BBI	BBM	Ave	Econ	SR	5w	10
Tests	15	-	-	-	-	-	-	-	-	-	-
ODIs	36	-	-	-	-	-	-	-	-	-	-
T20Is	1	-	-	-	-	-	-	-	-	-	-
First-class	240	96	90	0	-	-	-	5.62	-	0	0
List A	262	-	-	-	-	-	-	-	-	-	-
Twenty20	60	-	-	-	-	-	-	-	-	-	-

CHARLIE SHRECK

RHB RFM W2

NOTTINGHAMSHIRE

NAME: Charles Edward Shreck
BORN: January 6, 1978, Truro
HEIGHT: 6ft 7in
SQUAD Nº: 11
NICKNAME: Shrecker, Ogre, Stoat
OTHER TEAMS: Wellington
CAREER: First-class debut: 2003; List A
debut: 1999; T20 debut: 2003; County
cap: 2006

AOC SAYS: Shreck was a relative latecomer to first-class cricket, making his debut as a
25-year-old after he was spotted playing league cricket in Cornwall. The giant paceman's
burgeoning career was further put on hold after a stress fracture of his back ruled him out of
the entire 2005 season, but he returned strongly after a spell with Wellington in New Zealand
and took 61 Championship wickets in 2006, including a haul of 8-31 against Middlesex.
Shreck was rewarded with an England Lions call-up and named Nottinghamshire's Player
of the Year in 2008 after collecting 76 wickets in all competitions. He was a more peripheral
figure last season but signed a two-year extension to his contract in December.

LAST WORD: "It's important we maintain a strong group of quick bowlers and Charlie
is very much part of that. His one-day appearances will be limited to keep him fresh for
Championship matches." *Mick Newell*

NOTE: On the eve of the season it was announced that Shreck would spend a month on loan
at Kent before returning to Notts.

Batting & Fielding

	Mat	Inns	NO	Runs	HS	Ave	SR	100	50	Ct	St
First-class	85	97	54	154	19	3.58	16.79	0	0	31	0
List A	52	19	12	45	9*	6.42	-	0	0	13	0
Twenty20	22	6	5	10	6*	10.00	62.50	0	0	4	0

Bowling

	Mat	Balls	Runs	Wkts	BBI	BBM	Ave	Econ	SR	5w	10
First-class	85	17365	9390	307	8/31	-	30.58	3.24	56.5	18	2
List A	52	2309	2010	63	5/19	5/19	31.90	5.22	36.6	2	0
Twenty20	22	457	597	23	4/22	4/22	25.95	7.83	19.8	0	0

NAME: Graeme Peter Swann
BORN: March 24, 1979, Northampton
HEIGHT: 6ft
SQUAD Nº: 6
NICKNAME: Swanny, Chin
OTHER TEAMS: England,
Northamptonshire
CAREER: Test debut: 2008; ODI debut: 2000;
T20I debut: 2008; First-class debut: 1997;
List A debut: 1997; T20 debut: 2003; County
cap: 1999 (Northamptonshire)

AOC SAYS: After making his ODI debut against South Africa as a precocious 21-year-old, Swann fell out of favour with the England management and had to wait seven years for another opportunity. He made up for lost time when he returned, dismissing Gautam Gambhir and Rahul Dravid in his first over in Test cricket in Chennai, and has become England's talisman over the past three years. An offspinner who possesses great control and turns the ball appreciably, Swann played a key role in the consecutive Ashes victories, and in 2009 he collected 54 Tests wickets to become the first England spinner to pass 50 in a calendar year. He highlighted his importance across all formats by finishing as England's leading wicket-taker in their triumphant 2010 World Twenty20 campaign. He is also a flamboyant lower-order batsman and his innings of 85 against South Africa at Centurion in 2010 was the highest score by an England No.9 in 38 years. It is a remarkable turnaround for a player who admitted to falling out of love with the game at Northamptonshire after a personality clash with then coach Kepler Wessels. He swapped Wantage Road for Trent Bridge in 2005 and was immediately rejuvenated, picking up 33 Championship wickets to help Notts lift the title for the first time in 18 years. An international recall followed as Monty Panesar suffered a dip in form and Swann can now lay claim to being the world's premier spin bowler.

INSIDE TRACK: "Considering Swanny's expectations, he has probably overachieved. He is such an important player for England now in all forms of the game and there is no direct replacement for him. He's well liked by people in and outside the game – everyone wants him to do well and have a piece of him. Something clicked for him at Notts after his move from Northamptonshire. He learned to bowl on spin-friendly wickets at Wantage Road and he soon realised he had to bowl a tighter line at Trent Bridge – he couldn't toss it outside off stump and expect to rag it square. Believe it or not, he became a bit more mature with his attitude and the way he practised, and through a lot of hard work and a bit of advice here and there from various people everything came together at the right time. When Monty Panesar fell out of favour, Swanny was the automatic selection and he's just carried it on from there." *Wayne Noon*

GRAEME SWANN

Batting & Fielding											
	Mat	Inns	NO	Runs	HS	Ave	SR	100	50	Ct	St
Tests	29	36	6	741	85	24.70	82.42	0	4	25	0
ODIs	44	28	4	299	34	12.45	79.52	0	0	19	0
T20Is	22	9	6	48	15*	16.00	117.07	0	0	2	0
First-class	207	283	24	6890	183	26.60	-	4	35	155	0
List A	231	176	20	2949	83	18.90	-	0	14	78	0
Twenty20	63	47	10	735	90*	19.86	137.64	0	3	17	0

Bowling										
	Mat	Balls	Runs	Wkts	BBI	BBM	Ave	Econ	SR	5w	10
Tests	29	7431	3598	128	6/65	10/217	28.10	2.90	58.0	10	1
ODIs	45	2022	1513	62	5/28	5/28	24.40	4.48	32.6	1	0
T20Is	22	450	494	32	3/14	3/14	15.43	6.58	14.0	0	0
First-class	207	37077	18434	577	7/33	-	31.94	2.98	64.2	25	4
List A	232	9252	6797	262	5/17	5/17	25.94	4.40	35.3	3	0
Twenty20	63	1332	1486	79	3/14	3/14	18.81	6.69	16.8	0	0

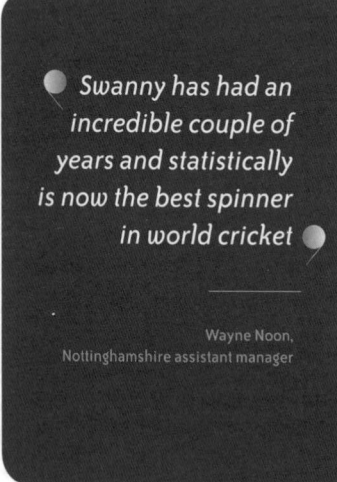

Swanny has had an incredible couple of years and statistically is now the best spinner in world cricket

Wayne Noon,
Nottinghamshire assistant manager

OVERSEAS PLAYER

NOTTINGHAMSHIRE

NAME: Adam Charles Voges
BORN: October 4, 1979, Perth, Australia
HEIGHT: 6ft 1in
SQUAD Nº: 17
NICKNAME: Kenny, Hank
OTHER TEAMS: Australia, Hampshire, Rajasthan Royals, Western Australia
CAREER: ODI debut: 2007; T20I debut: 2007; First-class debut: 2002; List A debut: 2004; T20 debut: 2006; County cap: 2008 (Nottinghamshire)

AOC SAYS: Voges wrote his name into Nottinghamshire folklore by scoring a quickfire century on the final day of the 2010 Championship season to snatch maximum batting points and help secure the title. The aggressive middle-order batsman and handy left-arm spinner also enjoyed a superb 2009 when he averaged 77.44 with the bat in Championship cricket, but despite excelling in domestic cricket for both Notts and Western Australia he has failed to hold down a regular spot in Australia's limited-overs side. Voges has shared overseas duties with David Hussey for the past three seasons and will do the same in 2011 – deputising for Hussey in Championship cricket until the end of May and featuring throughout the FP t20.

LAST WORD: "He's low maintenance and very popular in the dressing room. He did a great job on the final day of last season and his bewildering century set up the title victory."
Dave Bracegirdle

Batting & Fielding

	Mat	Inns	NO	Runs	HS	Ave	SR	100	50	Ct	St
ODIs	15	14	5	392	80*	43.55	91.16	0	2	2	0
T20Is	4	3	1	63	26	31.50	121.15	0	0	2	0
First-class	90	153	20	5278	180	39.68	50.42	10	29	110	0
List A	114	109	24	3631	104*	42.71	77.66	2	29	40	0
Twenty20	65	61	11	1597	82*	31.94	132.20	0	7	24	0

Bowling

	Mat	Balls	Runs	Wkts	BBI	BBM	Ave	Econ	SR	5w	10
ODIs	15	150	159	1	1/22	1/22	159.00	6.36	150.0	0	0
T20Is	4	12	5	2	2/5	2/5	2.50	2.50	6.0	0	0
First-class	91	2530	1375	40	4/92	-	34.37	3.26	63.2	0	0
List A	114	1262	1106	22	3/25	3/25	50.27	5.25	57.3	0	0
Twenty20	65	281	410	12	2/4	2/4	34.16	8.75	23.4	0	0

MARK WAGH

RHB OB R6

NAME: Mark Anant Wagh
BORN: October 20, 1976, Birmingham
HEIGHT: 6ft 2in
SQUAD Nº: 4
NICKNAME: Waggy
OTHER TEAMS: Warwickshire
CAREER: First-class debut: 1996;
List A debut: 1996; T20 debut: 2003;
County cap: 2000 (Warwickshire), 2007
(Nottinghamshire)

AOC SAYS: Wagh will bring a close to a successful if unfulfilled first-class career midway through the season. The elegant top-order batsman is no ordinary cricketer and having already written a book, climbed to Everest base camp and cycled from John O'Groats to Lands End, he will retire to pursue a career as a corporate lawyer. An Oxford graduate, Wagh was unfortunate not to earn an international call-up during his 10 seasons with Warwickshire. In 2001 he scored 315 against Middlesex at Lord's but succumbed to injury when an England call-up beckoned in 2005. He also proved a useful offspinner in his time at Edgbaston but since moving to Nottinghamshire he has focused on his batting and scored heavily in each of the past four seasons.

LAST WORD: "Last season Mark hardly played hardly any one-day cricket but he will open the batting in all formats until he retires halfway through the season." *Dave Bracegirdle*

Batting & Fielding

	Mat	Inns	NO	Runs	HS	Ave	SR	100	50	Ct	St
First-class	204	334	27	12204	315	39.75	-	31	58	88	0
List A	113	109	9	2720	102*	27.20	-	1	21	21	0
Twenty20	18	15	0	288	56	19.20	114.74	0	1	5	0

Bowling

	Mat	Balls	Runs	Wkts	BBI	BBM	Ave	Econ	SR	5w	10
First-class	204	8697	4611	100	7/222	-	46.11	3.18	86.9	2	0
List A	113	1096	862	25	4/35	4/35	34.48	4.71	43.8	0	0
Twenty20	18	75	106	5	2/16	2/16	21.20	8.48	15.0	0	0

NAME: Graeme Geoffrey White
BORN: April 18, 1987, Milton Keynes
HEIGHT: 5ft 11in
SQUAD №: 87
NICKNAME: Whitey, Chalky, Pony
OTHER TEAMS: Northamptonshire
CAREER: First-class debut: 2006; List A
debut: 2007; T20 debut: 2007

NOTTINGHAMSHIRE

AOC SAYS: White left Northamptonshire in 2009 in search of first-team cricket after having his route blocked by Monty Panesar and Nicky Boje at Wantage Road. The former England under 19 spinner has found opportunities hard to come by in Championship cricket at seam-friendly Trent Bridge but was a key member of the Outlaws' limited-overs side last season, particularly impressing in T20 cricket with his accuracy and subtle changes of pace. His superb fielding and useful batting make him a valuable asset in the shorter formats but he needs to develop a more threatening stock delivery if he is to feature regularly in four-day cricket.

LAST WORD: "He'll be keen to play four-day cricket and to do that he needs to show he can bat at No.8 or No.9 which he's working hard to achieve." *Mick Newell*

Batting & Fielding

	Mat	Inns	NO	Runs	HS	Ave	SR	100	50	Ct	St
First-class	9	11	2	169	65	18.77	46.17	0	1	2	0
List A	20	11	4	52	14	7.42	69.33	0	0	9	0
Twenty20	22	8	3	64	26*	12.80	114.28	0	0	10	0

Bowling

	Mat	Balls	Runs	Wkts	BBI	BBM	Ave	Econ	SR	5w	10
First-class	9	948	498	6	2/35	2/35	83.00	3.15	158.0	0	0
List A	20	632	552	21	5/35	5/35	26.28	5.24	30.0	1	0
Twenty20	22	265	361	13	3/22	3/22	27.76	8.17	20.3	0	0

TEAM PROFILE

FORMED: 1875
HOME GROUND: County Ground, Taunton
CAPTAIN: Marcus Trescothick
2010 RESULTS: CC1: 2/9; CB40: Runners-up; FP t20: Runners-up

SOMERSET
CRICKET CLUB

HONOURS

Gillette/NatWest/C&G/FP Trophy: (3) 1979, 1983, 2001; Benson and Hedges Cup: (2) 1981, 1982; Sunday League: 1979; Twenty20 Cup: 2005

THE LOWDOWN

Runners-up in all three competitions in 2010, Somerset will back themselves to shed the bridesmaid tag in 2011. The departure of Zander de Bruyn leaves a spot up for grabs in the middle-order, but the top six looks as strong as ever, while the seam bowling ranks have been considerably bolstered with the additions of Gemaal Hussain and Steve Kirby, both acquired from Gloucestershire. Form depending, Craig Kieswetter may find himself back in the England side, but with the excellent Jos Buttler on their books Somerset seem to have all bases covered. With the addition of West Indian allrounder Kieron Pollard, they will also have an embarrassment of riches for the FP t20. It will take a brave man to bet against Somerset lifting a trophy in 2011.

HEAD COACH: ANDY HURRY

A former Royal Marines fitness instructor, Hurry joined Somerset in March 2001 in a similar role, introducing yoga as a part of the side's training regime. He became Second XI coach in 2005, before leaving to coach UAE. When Mark Garaway joined England's coaching staff in 2006, Hurry returned to assume responsibility for the first team, leading the side to twin promotions – in the Championship and the Pro40 – the following season.

With thanks to: Andy Hurry; Richard Latham, Bristol and West News Agency Ltd.

Batting & Fielding

	Mat	Inns	NO	Runs	HS	Ave	SR	100	50	Ct	St
JC Hildreth	16	23	1	1440	151	65.45	67.57	7	5	7	-
ME Trescothick	16	28	4	1397	228*	58.20	65.92	4	6	26	-
Z de Bruyn	14	21	0	814	95	38.76	57.81	0	5	10	-
DA Stiff	2	4	2	71	40	35.50	79.77	0	0	0	-
DG Wright	5	7	0	236	78	33.71	74.21	0	2	4	-
AV Suppiah	16	26	3	771	125	33.52	47.82	1	4	5	-
JC Buttler	13	20	3	569	144	33.47	61.31	1	2	23	0
NRD Compton	11	17	3	465	72	33.21	49.46	0	2	5	-
PD Trego	16	23	2	693	108	33.00	72.26	1	5	12	-
M Kartik	11	12	5	199	52*	28.42	64.82	0	2	9	-
C Kieswetter	12	18	1	467	84	27.47	60.25	0	4	29	0
AC Thomas	15	20	4	328	44	20.50	44.02	0	0	1	-
BJ Phillips	11	15	3	179	55	14.91	49.31	0	1	5	-
CM Willoughby	16	18	6	85	16	7.08	86.73	0	0	1	-
MK Munday	3	3	1	0	0*	0.00	0.00	0	0	1	-

Bowling

	Mat	Overs	Mdns	Runs	Wkts	BBI	BBM	Ave	Econ	SR	5w	10
M Kartik	11	383.2	107	882	45	6/42	11/72	19.60	2.30	51.1	5	2
BJ Phillips	11	277.3	79	661	29	5/72	5/72	22.79	2.38	57.4	1	0
AC Thomas	15	377.5	85	1202	49	5/40	7/117	24.53	3.18	46.2	2	0
DG Wright	5	154.1	41	377	14	5/41	6/89	26.92	2.44	66.0	1	0
CM Willoughby	16	512.1	118	1582	58	6/101	7/97	27.27	3.08	52.9	1	0
Z de Bruyn	14	94.2	10	386	12	4/23	4/23	32.16	4.09	47.1	0	0
PD Trego	16	227.1	50	729	22	4/26	6/121	33.13	3.20	61.9	0	0
MK Munday	3	52.1	9	238	6	4/105	4/105	39.66	4.56	52.1	0	0
NRD Compton	11	14.2	0	87	2	1/1	1/1	43.50	6.06	43.0	0	0
JC Hildreth	16	13.0	0	95	1	1/95	1/95	95.00	7.30	78.0	0	0
AV Suppiah	16	99.0	18	300	3	1/21	1/21	100.00	3.03	198.0	0	0
DA Stiff	2	40.5	3	207	2	1/42	1/88	103.50	5.06	122.5	0	0

SOMERSET
CRICKET CLUB

Batting & Fielding

	Mat	Inns	NO	Runs	HS	Ave	SR	100	50	Ct	St
JC Hildreth	15	15	5	658	100*	65.80	107.51	1	5	9	-
Z de Bruyn	13	13	2	555	122*	50.45	91.88	2	3	4	-
JC Buttler	15	14	5	443	90*	49.22	152.23	0	4	10	1
C Kieswetter	10	10	0	396	107	39.60	100.50	1	2	9	2
PD Trego	15	13	2	412	147	37.45	118.73	1	1	5	-
AV Suppiah	9	7	1	173	80	28.83	94.02	0	1	4	-
NRD Compton	15	15	0	432	73	28.80	81.35	0	6	7	-
ME Trescothick	14	14	0	366	79	26.14	122.00	0	4	8	-
BJ Phillips	13	7	4	75	51*	25.00	94.93	0	1	4	-
M Kartik	10	3	1	34	26*	17.00	100.00	0	0	6	-
AC Thomas	14	6	3	43	19	14.33	110.25	0	0	6	-
MTC Waller	9	3	2	9	5	9.00	50.00	0	0	2	-
ML Turner	7	3	1	11	8	5.50	52.38	0	0	3	-
L Gregory	1	1	0	0	0	0.00	0.00	0	0	1	-
CM Willoughby	3	2	0	0	0	0.00	0.00	0	0	0	-
DG Wright	2	1	1	4	4*	-	66.66	0	0	0	-

Bowling

	Mat	Overs	Mdns	Runs	Wkts	BBI	Ave	Econ	SR	5w
L Gregory	1	10.0	1	49	4	4/49	12.25	4.90	15.0	0
AC Thomas	14	81.1	2	430	27	4/34	15.92	5.29	18.0	0
M Kartik	10	69.3	1	321	20	4/30	16.05	4.61	20.8	0
DG Wright	2	15.0	0	109	6	3/43	18.16	7.26	15.0	0
Z de Bruyn	13	53.2	0	329	16	3/27	20.56	6.16	20.0	0
ML Turner	7	40.5	0	286	12	4/36	23.83	7.00	20.4	0
BJ Phillips	13	83.5	4	466	19	4/31	24.52	5.55	26.4	0
PD Trego	15	83.0	4	460	13	2/29	35.38	5.54	38.3	0
MTC Waller	9	44.0	2	246	4	2/24	61.50	5.59	66.0	0
AV Suppiah	9	15.0	0	97	1	1/24	97.00	6.46	90.0	0
CM Willoughby	3	23.0	2	137	1	1/52	137.00	5.95	138.0	0

SOMERSET
CRICKET CLUB

	Mat	Inns	NO	Runs	HS	Ave	SR	100	50	Ct	St
JC Hildreth	19	19	5	459	77*	32.78	110.60	0	2	8	-
KA Pollard	17	16	5	354	89*	32.18	175.24	0	2	8	-
ME Trescothick	19	19	1	572	83	31.77	157.14	0	6	4	-
Z de Bruyn	19	18	8	303	95*	30.30	124.18	0	1	8	-
JC Buttler	19	14	6	240	55*	30.00	160.00	0	1	19	2
PD Trego	16	15	2	294	72*	22.61	135.48	0	1	6	-
C Kieswetter	10	10	0	220	71	22.00	102.32	0	1	9	1
NRD Compton	8	8	0	165	74	20.62	117.85	0	1	2	-
AV Suppiah	10	5	2	61	26*	20.33	108.92	0	0	6	-
M Kartik	17	3	2	18	16*	18.00	81.81	0	0	4	-
AC Thomas	19	6	3	29	14*	9.66	78.37	0	0	5	-
ML Turner	15	3	1	12	11*	6.00	50.00	0	0	3	-
BJ Phillips	18	6	1	16	5	3.20	51.61	0	0	6	-
CM Willoughby	1	1	0	2	2	2.00	50.00	0	0	0	-

	Mat	Overs	Mdns	Runs	Wkts	BBI	Ave	Econ	SR	5w
AC Thomas	19	72.5	3	460	33	3/11	13.93	6.31	13.2	0
KA Pollard	17	58.2	0	438	29	4/15	15.10	7.50	12.0	0
CM Willoughby	1	3.0	0	21	1	1/21	21.00	7.00	18.0	0
BJ Phillips	18	60.0	1	466	19	3/33	24.52	7.76	18.9	0
AV Suppiah	10	8.0	0	50	2	1/6	25.00	6.25	24.0	0
PD Trego	16	31.0	0	277	11	2/19	25.18	8.93	16.9	0
ML Turner	15	42.0	0	372	14	3/25	26.57	8.85	18.0	0
M Kartik	17	61.0	0	402	13	3/18	30.92	6.59	28.1	0
Z de Bruyn	19	28.0	0	248	7	2/21	35.42	8.85	24.0	0
MTC Waller	2	3.0	0	26	0	-	-	8.66	-	0

ALEX BARROW

RHB OB

SOMERSET

NAME: Alexander William R Barrow
BORN: May 6, 1992, Bath
SQUAD Nº: 18
CAREER: Yet to make first-team debut

AOC SAYS: Barrow is a top-order batsman who represented England under 19 last summer and registered a half-century in the first youth ODI against Sri Lanka. The right-hander will hope to make his first-team bow this season after opening the batting for Somerset's Second XI in 2010, impressing with a composed knock of 56 against Essex Second XI at Chelmsford. Barrow, who plays his club cricket for Bath, was captain of King's College in 2009 when the school was named Wisden School of the Year. He would have toured Sri Lanka this winter with England under 19 but was ruled out after undergoing surgery on his left shoulder in October and instead travelled with the first team to the Caribbean T20.

LAST WORD: "Unfortunately Alex missed out on the England under 19 tour to Sri Lanka over the winter because of injury but he's someone who has impressed us during the winter." *Andy Hurry*

EXTRAS

"You sometimes felt with Somerset last season that they could get any total they were set."
Richard Latham

NAME: James Edward Burke
BORN: January 25, 1991, Plymouth
SQUAD Nº: 58
CAREER: Yet to make first-team debut

SOMERSET

AOC SAYS: Burke is a promising allrounder who made his England under 19 debut in a youth T20I fixture against South Africa at Cape Town in 2009. He has represented Somerset's Second XI for the past three seasons, and made an unbeaten century batting at No.6 last season against a strong Hampshire attack featuring Simon Jones and Danny Briggs. A persistent back injury prevented Burke from bowling his medium-pacers for much of the 2010 campaign but Somerset have high hopes that he will develop into a genuine allrounder capable of holding down a first-team spot.

LAST WORD: "I've learned a lot up at Somerset listening and bowling at players of the quality of Marcus Trescothick and Justin Langer. I'll have to work hard, but if it works out for me, I want to play for England. That's every young cricketer's dream." *James Burke*

EXTRAS

"Every season the standard in domestic cricket rises. If we turned up and played the same standard we played last year we wouldn't win anything." Andy Hurry

SOMERSET

JOS BUTTLER

RHB WK MVP70

NAME: Joseph Charles Buttler
BORN: September 8, 1990, Taunton
SQUAD Nº: 15
NICKNAME: Jos
CAREER: First-class debut: 2009; List A
debut: 2009; T20 debut: 2009

AOC SAYS: Buttler is a batsman-wicketkeeper of vast potential who has already been earmarked as a player with an international future. The former England under 19 star made his first-class bow in 2009 as a specialist batter and featured in Somerset's Champions League Twenty20 campaign that winter. He excelled in one-day cricket last season and his stunning innings of 55 off 25 balls in the FP t20 semi-final against a formidable Nottinghamshire attack gave notice of his class. Buttler also struck his maiden first-class ton, making 144 against Hampshire, and his challenge this year is to develop his game in four-day cricket and play more innings in that vein. He will share keeping duties with Craig Kieswetter this season.

LAST WORD: "The sky is the limit for Jos. In one-day cricket he is already one of the most exciting players in the country. His range of shots and where he places the ball sets him apart." *Richard Latham*

Batting & Fielding

	Mat	Inns	NO	Runs	HS	Ave	SR	100	50	Ct	St
First-class	14	21	3	599	144	33.27	60.14	1	2	23	0
List A	16	14	5	443	90*	49.22	152.23	0	4	11	1
Twenty20	24	19	7	320	55*	26.66	146.11	0	1	22	4

Bowling

	Mat	Balls	Runs	Wkts	BBI	BBM	Ave	Econ	SR	5w	10
First-class	14	-	-	-	-	-	-	-	-	-	-
List A	16	-	-	-	-	-	-	-	-	-	-
Twenty20	24	-	-	-	-	-	-	-	-	-	-

NAME: Nicholas Richard Denis Compton
BORN: June 26, 1983, Durban
HEIGHT: 6ft 2in
SQUAD Nº: 3
NICKNAME: Compo, Compdog, Ledge,
OTHER TEAMS: Cheser
Mashonland Eagles, Middlesex
CAREER: First-class debut: 2004; List A
debut: 2001; T20 debut: 2004; County cap:
2006 (Middlesex)

SOMERSET

AOC SAYS: The grandson of England legend Denis, Compton left Middlesex for Somerset at the end of the 2009 season in an attempt to rejuvenate his career, but after a promising start to the campaign his form fell away and he lost his place in the side. The right-hand top-order batsman, who was born and raised in South Africa before moving to England study at Harrow, looked to be on the verge of international honours after scoring 1,315 first-class runs for Middlesex in 2006 but failed to kick on and swapped Lord's for Taunton in search of first-team cricket. Compton now faces a battle to reclaim a berth in Somerset's top-order if he is to fulfil his potential.

LAST WORD: "Marcus Trescothick and I share the opinion that Nick can improve rapidly in the Somerset environment and go on to higher honours." *Brian Rose, Somerset director of cricket*

Batting & Fielding

	Mat	Inns	NO	Runs	HS	Ave	SR	100	50	Ct	St
First-class	68	120	13	3663	190	34.23	49.10	9	14	35	0
List A	74	68	13	2161	131	39.29	81.05	5	13	38	0
Twenty20	47	41	1	745	74	18.62	111.36	0	5	19	0

Bowling

	Mat	Balls	Runs	Wkts	BBI	BBM	Ave	Econ	SR	5w	10
First-class	68	164	215	3	1/1	1/1	71.66	7.86	54.6	0	0
List A	74	61	53	1	1/0	1/0	53.00	5.21	61.0	0	0
Twenty20	47	-	-	-	-	-	-	-	-	-	-

ADAM DIBBLE RHB RMF

SOMERSET

NAME: Adam John Dibble
BORN: March 9, 1991, Exeter
HEIGHT: 6ft 4in
SQUAD Nº: 16
NICKNAME: Dibbs, Officer
CAREER: Yet to make first-team debut

AOC SAYS: Dibble is a tall paceman who has enjoyed considerable success playing for Somerset's Second XI over the past two seasons. He took 20 wickets in the Second XI Championship last year at an average of 20.60, including a haul of 8-21 against Sussex, and was rewarded with selection for Somerset's 15-man Caribbean T20 squad this winter. Dibble spent the previous winter furthering his cricketing education playing grade cricket in Western Australia and is working closely with new signing Steve Kirby to develop his game. With the acquisitions of Kirby and Gemaal Hussain in the close season, he has his work cut out to nail down a first-team spot but is a bright prospect for the future.

LAST WORD: "Winter training went really well. It's hard work, but it's great to be around with the other lads. I want to play in the first team. It's as simple as that, because playing first-team cricket is what it's all about for me." *Adam Dibble*

EXTRAS

"If they want to win the Championship, they need to try and make the pitches less batsman-friendly." Richard Latham

NAME: George Henry Dockrell
BORN: July 22, 1992, Dublin
SQUAD Nº: 20
OTHER TEAMS: Ireland
CAREER: ODI debut: 2010; T20I debut: 2010;
First-class debut: 2010; List A debut: 2010;
T20 debut: 2010

SOMERSET

AOC SAYS: Dockrell is a young left-arm spinner with a spindly frame and huge potential. He burst onto the scene as a 17-year-old during Ireland's 2010 World Twenty20 campaign, returning figures of 3-16 against West Indies and conceding just 19 from four overs against England. Somerset, who had been tracking the Irishman since the age of 15, swiftly snapped him up on a two-year deal last July. He is set to feature heavily in first-team cricket at Taunton this season and will benefit from working alongside world-class spin twins Murali Kartik and Ajantha Mendis. Dockrell continued to make great strides at the 2011 World Cup, taking seven wickets at a miserly economy rate.

LAST WORD: "For someone so young, he made a huge impact at the World Cup. He has to earn the right to play but it may be that we restructure the balance of the side to accommodate two spinners." *Andy Hurry*

Batting & Fielding

	Mat	Inns	NO	Runs	HS	Ave	SR	100	50	Ct	St
ODIs	22	11	5	55	19	9.16	72.36	0	0	11	0
T20Is	7	2	1	0	0*	0.00	0.00	0	0	0	0
First-class	3	4	1	34	30*	11.33	25.75	0	0	1	0
List A	24	13	6	67	19	9.57	76.13	0	0	12	0
Twenty20	14	3	2	0	0*	0.00	0.00	0	0	5	0

Bowling

	Mat	Balls	Runs	Wkts	BBI	BBM	Ave	Econ	SR	5w	10
ODIs	22	1053	739	27	4/35	4/35	27.37	4.21	39.0	0	0
T20Is	7	147	132	12	4/20	4/20	11.00	5.38	12.2	0	0
First-class	3	354	192	4	4/36	4/43	48.00	3.25	88.5	0	0
List A	24	1173	825	27	4/35	4/35	30.55	4.21	43.4	0	0
Twenty20	14	285	287	19	4/20	4/20	15.10	6.04	15.0	0	0

LEWIS GREGORY

RHB RMF

SOMERSET

NAME: Lewis Gregory
BORN: May 24, 1992, Plymouth
SQUAD Nº: 26
CAREER: List A debut: 2010

AOC SAYS: Gregory is an emerging talent who captained England under 19 on their tour of Sri Lanka this winter. The gifted allrounder made his List A debut last season against a strong Pakistan side and rose to the challenge with a haul of 4-49, including the wickets of Shahid Afridi and Abdur Razzaq. A lively right-arm seamer, Gregory took a hat-trick for Somerset's Second XI last season against Essex but he is equally adept with the bat in hand and has the makings of a genuine allrounder with international prospects. Limited-overs cricket is his best route into the first team for now.

LAST WORD: "We have had our eye on Lewis from quite an early age and he has regularly been coming up from Devon to work with us. As he gets older he will be a great asset in one-day cricket." *Brian Rose, Somerset director of cricket*

Batting & Fielding

	Mat	Inns	NO	Runs	HS	Ave	SR	100	50	Ct	St
List A	1	1	0	0	0	0.00	0.00	0	0	1	0

Bowling

	Mat	Balls	Runs	Wkts	BBI	BBM	Ave	Econ	SR	5w	10
List A	1	60	49	4	4/49	4/49	12.25	4.90	15.0	0	0

NAME: Calum John Haggett
BORN: October 30, 1990, Taunton
HEIGHT: 6ft 5in
SQUAD №: 19
CAREER: T20 debut: 2011

SOMERSET

AOC SAYS: The burly allrounder has had a dramatic start to his professional career after a routine heart scan while on duty with England under 19 revealed a faulty valve and Haggett was forced to undergo surgery. Unsurprisingly the young seamer and hard-hitting lower-order batsman missed the majority of last season as he recovered from the operation but he returned for Somerset's Second XI at the back-end of the campaign, making 87 against Essex, and thankfully is now back to full fitness. Somerset showed how highly they rate Haggett by offering him a two-year contract and he will hope to make his first-class debut this season.

LAST WORD: "It's been a difficult few months but it's great to be back in training again. I have learned a great deal from my experiences and what has happened to me has made me even more determined to succeed." *Calum Haggett*

Batting & Fielding

	Mat	Inns	NO	Runs	HS	Ave	SR	100	50	Ct	St
Twenty20	3	2	0	3	2	1.50	75.00	0	0	0	0

Bowling

	Mat	Balls	Runs	Wkts	BBI	BBM	Ave	Econ	SR	5w	10
Twenty20	3	30	32	1	1/15	1/15	32.00	6.40	30.0	0	0

JAMES HAYMAN

RHB RMF

SOMERSET

NAME: James T Hayman
BORN: November 22, 1986, Taunton
HEIGHT: 6ft 5in
SQUAD Nº: 4
NICKNAME: Blondie
CAREER: Yet to make first-team debut

AOC SAYS: Somerset signed Hayman in 2009 after the towering paceman was spotted by academy director Jason Kerr playing for a local league XI against the club's academy. He was invited to play for the Second XI and his pace and bounce persuaded Somerset's director of cricket Brian Rose to offer him a one-year deal at Taunton. Hayman, who plays his club cricket for Ashcott and Shapwick, featured in seven Second XI Championship fixtures last season and regularly took the new ball. He is well down the pecking order when it comes to first-team cricket but remains an inspiration for club cricketers across the country.

LAST WORD: "His physique is very good, he's very tall and has excellent shape and line to his bowling." *Brian Rose, Somerset director of cricket*

EXTRAS

Marcus Trescothick has been offered a £1 million incentive by Mongoose to go for his shots next summer. Trescothick, who has signed a sponsorship deal with Mongoose Bats to use their new long handle model, will win the prize from the bat makers if he clears the three-tier pavilion at Lord's in any 20- or 40-over match for Somerset.

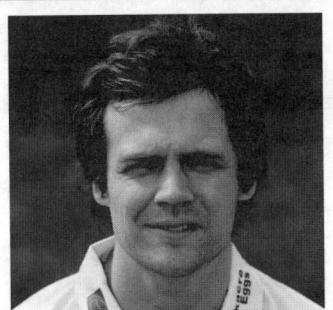

NAME: James Charles Hildreth
BORN: September 9, 1984, Milton Keynes
HEIGHT: 5ft 10in
SQUAD Nº: 25
NICKNAME: Hildy, Hildz
CAREER: First-class debut: 2003; List A debut: 2003; T20 debut: 2004; County cap: 2007

AOC SAYS: Hildreth is one of a crop of young batsmen who will hope to profit from Paul Collingwood's retirement and force his way into England's Test side this summer. He mounted a better case than most last season, scoring seven first-class centuries and amassing 1,440 Championship runs as well as averaging 65.80 in one-day cricket. The right-hand middle-order batsman has been touted as a future international ever since starring for England under 19s but threatened to let his prodigious talent go to waste after a patchy start to his first-class career. The feeling was that if he couldn't rack up the runs on a batsman's paradise at Taunton then there was little hope for him at the highest level, but an unbeaten 303 against Warwickshire in the opening fixture of the 2009 Championship season marked a turning point. The former Millfield School student blossomed under the watchful eye of Justin Langer, who described Hildreth as an "extraordinary talent". A gifted allround sportsman who played hockey for the West of England, tennis and squash for the South of England, rugby for Millfield and football for Luton Town's academy, Hildreth is an accomplished strokemaker – with a penchant for the inside-out cover drive – quick as a flash between the wickets and an adept player of spin. A potential weakness at Test level is his defensive technique against express pace but he has all the raw materials to succeed in international cricket. Hildreth's growing reputation was reflected by his appointment as England Lions captain for the winter tour of West Indies and he made an instant impact, scoring 149 against Leeward Islands before notching another ton against Windwards Islands. He will need to hit the ground running this season if he is to leapfrog Eoin Morgan and claim an England berth.

INSIDE TRACK: "Hildy played great last season. He keeps the basis of the team together. He's great against the spinners and plays an important role for us. He has still got a bit of work to do and he has to remain positive. The talent is there and you just have to get the consistency right. He can certainly go a long way. For Hildreth, being captain [of England Lions] and getting a big hundred against Leeward Islands this winter is a great achievement and he couldn't have asked for a better way to lead off his time in charge. I'm not surprised that he took the Lions captaincy on board, nor am I surprised that he has done so well." *Marcus Trescothick, Somerset captain*

SOMERSET

Batting & Fielding

	Mat	Inns	NO	Runs	HS	Ave	SR	100	50	Ct	St
First-class	117	189	15	7656	303*	44.00	-	21	37	85	0
List A	124	120	19	3332	151	32.99	-	4	14	39	0
Twenty20	77	74	11	1365	77*	21.66	118.69	0	6	30	0

Bowling

	Mat	Balls	Runs	Wkts	BBI	BBM	Ave	Econ	SR	5w	10
First-class	117	480	414	5	2/39	-	82.80	5.17	96.0	0	0
List A	124	150	185	6	2/26	2/26	30.83	7.40	25.0	0	0
Twenty20	77	169	247	10	3/24	3/24	24.70	8.76	16.9	0	0

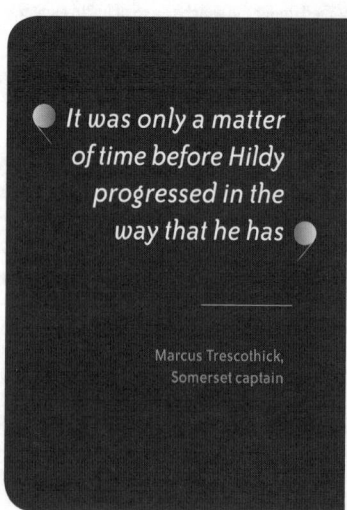

It was only a matter of time before Hildy progressed in the way that he has

Marcus Trescothick,
Somerset captain

NAME: Gemaal Maqsood Hussain
BORN: October 10, 1983, London
SQUAD Nº: 27
OTHER TEAMS: Gloucestershire
CAREER: First-class debut: 2009; List A
debut: 2009; T20 debut: 2009; County cap:
2009 (Gloucestershire)

SOMERSET

AOC SAYS: Somerset snapped up Hussain on a three-year contract in October after the
right-arm seamer took 67 first-class wickets for Gloucestershire to finish as leading
wicket-taker in Division Two in his first full season of professional cricket. A tall man who
swings the ball appreciably, Hussain turned down the offer of a new deal at Bristol stating
that a move to Taunton would improve his international prospects and he faces a new
challenge on a track that is typically less favourable to bowlers. Hussain was a latecomer
to the professional game, signing for Gloucestershire at the age of 27 after plying his trade
in club cricket in Derbyshire, and is likely to share new ball duties with former Gloucester
teammate Steve Kirby.

LAST WORD: "We feel Gemaal has the same attributes as a young, inexperienced Andy
Caddick. He is someone we firmly believe can be a matchwinner for us in the next few
seasons." *Andy Hurry*

Batting & Fielding

	Mat	Inns	NO	Runs	HS	Ave	SR	100	50	Ct	St
First-class	16	28	10	169	28*	9.38	26.00	0	0	2	0
List A	1	-	-	-	-	-	-	-	-	0	0
Twenty20	15	11	4	31	8	4.42	65.95	0	0	4	0

Bowling

	Mat	Balls	Runs	Wkts	BBI	BBM	Ave	Econ	SR	5w	10
First-class	16	2638	1604	69	5/36	9/98	23.24	3.64	38.2	2	0
List A	1	30	17	2	2/17	2/17	8.50	3.40	15.0	0	0
Twenty20	15	300	411	16	3/22	3/22	25.68	8.22	18.7	0	0

CHRIS JONES

RHB RM

SOMERSET

NAME: Christopher Robert Jones
BORN: November 5, 1990, Harold Wood
SQUAD Nº: 14
CAREER: Yet to make first-team debut

AOC SAYS: Jones is a technically correct opening batsman who got his first taste of first-team cricket last season as a substitute fielder for Craig Kieswetter against Lancashire at Taunton. It is unlikely to be his last. The right-handed batsman was handed the Second XI captaincy at the back-end of last season, replacing Robin Lett, and revelled in the role – scoring a composed 122 against Essex to lead his side to an innings victory. Jones spent the winter of 2009 in Australia, playing cricket for Sydney University and working on the campus grounds in his spare time.

LAST WORD: "I definitely want to play county cricket but I know there is a lot of hard work involved if you want to become a successful first-class player. I have a couple of hard years ahead of me, which I'm looking forward to." *Chris Jones*

Batting & Fielding

	Mat	Inns	NO	Runs	HS	Ave	SR	100	50	Ct	St
List A	1	-	-	-	-	-	-	-	-	0	0

Bowling

	Mat	Balls	Runs	Wkts	BBI	BBM	Ave	Econ	SR	5w	10
List A	1	-	-	-	-	-	-	-	-	-	-

OVERSEAS PLAYER

SOMERSET

NAME: Murali Kartik
BORN: September 11, 1976, Chennai
HEIGHT: 6ft
SQUAD Nº: 11
NICKNAME: Pirate, Gary, King, Kat, Special K
OTHER TEAMS: India, Kolkata Knight Riders, Lancashire, Middlesex, Railways
CAREER: Test debut: 2000; ODI debut: 2002; T20I debut: 2007; First-class debut: 1996; List A debut: 1996; T20 debut: 2007; County cap: 2007 (Middlesex)

AOC SAYS: Kartik is a vastly experienced slow left-arm orthodox bowler who was on the fringes of the India national side for several years but had his path blocked by Anil Kumble and Harbhajan Singh. At 34, his international career appears to be behind him but he never let his country down in his sporadic appearances and famously inspired a Test win over Australia in 2004 with match-figures of 7-76 on a Mumbai dustbowl. He remains a fearsome proposition in county cricket where he has prospered for Lancashire and Middlesex and took 45 first-class wickets in 2010, including five five-wicket hauls. A tall spinner with a classical action, he spun Somerset to victory against Warwickshire last season, getting the ball to bounce and turn sharply to bag 11 wickets in all.

LAST WORD: "I've agreed to come back because it's been fantastic to play for a side which is hungry, ambitious and wants to do well." *Murali Kartik*

Batting & Fielding

	Mat	Inns	NO	Runs	HS	Ave	SR	100	50	Ct	St
Tests	8	10	1	88	43	9.77	38.09	0	0	2	0
ODIs	37	14	5	126	32*	14.00	70.78	0	0	10	0
T20Is	1	-	-	-	-	-	-	-	-	0	0
First-class	169	211	33	3491	96	19.61	-	0	17	121	0
List A	180	86	28	676	44	11.65	-	0	0	60	0
Twenty20	78	20	9	155	28	14.09	102.64	0	0	23	0

Bowling

	Mat	Balls	Runs	Wkts	BBI	BBM	Ave	Econ	SR	5w	10
Tests	8	1932	820	24	4/44	7/76	34.16	2.54	80.5	0	0
ODIs	37	1907	1612	37	6/27	6/27	43.56	5.07	51.5	1	0
T20Is	1	24	27	0	-	-	-	6.75	-	0	0
First-class	169	36514	14485	560	9/70		25.86	2.38	65.2	32	5
List A	180	9148	6643	233	6/27	6/27	28.51	4.35	39.2	2	0
Twenty20	78	1642	1815	60	5/13	5/13	30.25	6.63	27.3	1	0

CRAIG KIESWETTER

SOMERSET

NAME: Craig Kieswetter
BORN: November 28, 1987, Johannesburg,
HEIGHT: 5ft 11in
SQUAD Nº: 22
NICKNAME: Bangle, Hobnob, Shnitz,
Kitchen Utensil
MAJOR TEAMS: England
CAREER: ODI debut: 2010; T20I debut: 2010;
First-class debut: 2007; List A debut: 2007;
T20 debut: 2007

AOC SAYS: A tidy gloveman and hard-hitting opening batsman, Kieswetter came to Somerset via Millfield School aged 18 and quickly impressed with a series of coruscating knocks in one-day cricket - including a blistering knock of 69 from 58 deliveries on his List A debut against Glamorgan. He claimed a stunning catch in the same match, and despite reservations about his wicketkeeping in some quarters he has put in several impressive displays standing up to Somerset's medium-pacers in one-day cricket. It was his batting predominantly, however, that saw him attract the interest of the England selectors. 2009 was a stellar year, as Kieswetter made 1,242 runs in the Championship at a fraction under 60 and averaged almost 50 in one-day cricket, form that earned him a call-up to the England Lions tour of UAE. Exhibiting perfect timing not only with his bat, he scored 81 against the senior side the day after he became eligible for England. That knock earned him a call-up for the tour to Bangladesh where he opened up with 143 in the first warm-up game and stroked a century in his third ODI, but received some criticism for tempering his aggressive approach. A weakness against the full straight ball raised questions about his ability against genuine pace, but he played a crucial role at the top of the innings in England's successful World Twenty20 campaign, seeing the side home alongside Kevin Pietersen in the final. The emergence of Steve Davies and the return to the fold of Matt Prior saw Kieswetter eased out of England's limited-overs plans last year, but his self-confidence and sheer power point to a return to national colours in the near future.

INSIDE TRACK: "Craig had a bit of a hard time last season. International cricket can do that to you. It can teach you some lessons and expose a few doubts. In the long run it might be a healthy thing to have happened, but it's his responsibility now to come back from Somerset a stronger package when he next plays for England. Scoring a hundred in his third ODI, being a World Twenty20 winner and getting Man of the Match in the final, a lot of English players haven't done that. He's got a good coach at Somerset in Andy Hurry and some good people to work with like Marcus Trescothick but ultimately, it's up to Craig to find his own method. I don't really use the word pinch-hitter but he's an aggressive opening batsman, much in the same mould as Sanath Jayasuriya and Adam Gilchrist." *Andy Flower, England coach*

Batting & Fielding

	Mat	Inns	NO	Runs	HS	Ave	SR	100	50	Ct	St
ODIs	12	12	0	320	107	26.66	85.79	1	1	11	2
T20Is	9	9	0	244	63	27.11	117.87	0	1	4	1
First-class	66	95	13	3161	153	38.54	-	6	17	188	2
List A	69	67	6	2359	143	38.67	91.32	6	9	67	15
Twenty20	53	52	8	1236	84	28.09	121.77	0	7	29	10

Bowling

	Mat	Balls	Runs	Wkts	BBI	BBM	Ave	Econ	SR	5w	10
ODIs	12	-	-	-	-	-	-	-	-	-	-
T20Is	9	-	-	-	-	-	-	-	-	-	-
First-class	66	-	-	-	-	-	-	-	-	-	-
List A	69	-	-	-	-	-	-	-	-	-	-
Twenty20	53	-	-	-	-	-	-	-	-	-	-

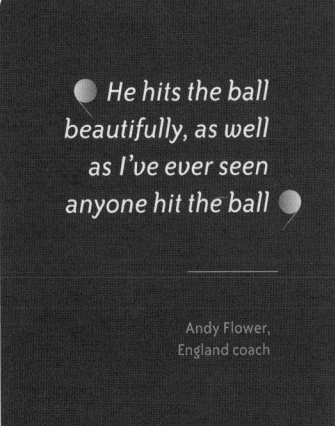

He hits the ball beautifully, as well as I've ever seen anyone hit the ball

Andy Flower,
England coach

STEVE KIRBY   RHB RFM W2

SOMERSET

NAME: Steven Paul Kirby
BORN: October 4, 1977, Bury
HEIGHT: 6ft 3in
SQUAD Nº: 9
NICKNAME: Tango
OTHER TEAMS: Gloucestershire,
Leicestershire, Yorkshire
CAREER: First-class debut: 2001; List A
debut: 2001; T20 debut: 2004; County cap:
2003 (Yorkshire), 2005 (Gloucestershire)

AOC SAYS: A fiery paceman with a decade of experience in county cricket, Kirby left
Gloucestershire at the end of last season and signed a three-year deal at Taunton. The
former Yorkshire paceman still has international ambitions and has represented England
Lions on several occasions, but time is running out to claim full honours. The right-arm
seamer left Leicestershire for Headingley before he had played a first-class match and
made an immediate impact, taking 7-50 against Kent on debut. He continued to impress
with 67 first-class wickets in 2003 and has been among the country's leading wicket-takers
more or less every season since moving to Gloucestershire in 2005.

LAST WORD: "Steve has the sort of aggression which helps a lot when you are bowling
at nine, 10 and jack. He wants to give himself every chance of playing for England and by
coming here that's what he hopes to do." *Brian Rose, Somerset director of cricket*

Batting & Fielding

	Mat	Inns	NO	Runs	HS	Ave	SR	100	50	Ct	St
First-class	131	182	58	1069	57	8.62	28.37	0	1	24	0
List A	77	33	12	88	15	4.19	43.56	0	0	14	0
Twenty20	42	19	4	58	25	3.86	68.23	0	0	8	0

Bowling

	Mat	Balls	Runs	Wkts	BBI	BBM	Ave	Econ	SR	5w	10
First-class	131	23067	13037	469	8/80	-	27.79	3.39	49.1	16	4
List A	77	3201	2971	97	5/36	5/36	30.62	5.56	33.0	1	0
Twenty20	42	864	1115	54	3/17	3/17	20.64	7.74	16.0	0	0

OVERSEAS PLAYER

SOMERSET

NAME: Balapuwaduge Ajantha Winslo Mendis
BORN: March 11, 1985, Moratuwa, Sri Lanka
SQUAD Nº: 28
OTHER TEAMS: Sri Lanka, Hampshire,
Kolkata Knight Riders, Sri Lanka Army,
Wayamba
CAREER: Test debut: 2008; ODI debut: 2008;
T20I debut: 2008; First-class debut: 2006;
List A debut: 2006; T20 debut: 2007

AOC SAYS: The Sri Lankan 'mystery' spinner has a delivery all of his own – the famous 'carrom ball'. Mendis has incredibly strong fingers which allow him to release the ball with a snap of his fingers and he combines his trademark with a mix of offbreaks, legbreaks, googlies and flippers. He exploded onto the scene in the 2008 Asia Cup, ripping through India's much-vaunted batting line-up to return figures of 6-13 and help Sri Lanka lift the trophy. He initially translated that success into the Test arena, taking 33 wickets in his first four matches, and while batsman are beginning to get to grips with his unorthodox style, he is a potentially devastating weapon in county cricket. Mendis will cover for Murali Kartik while the Indian spinner is on IPL duty.

LAST WORD: "First and foremost it came to our attention that English domestic teams struggle to play world-class spinners. Mendis will help us to bowl sides out twice." *Andy Hurry*

Batting & Fielding

	Mat	Inns	NO	Runs	HS	Ave	SR	100	50	Ct	St
Tests	15	15	4	151	78	13.72	42.29	0	1	2	0
ODIs	52	23	10	99	15*	7.61	67.80	0	0	6	0
T20Is	19	4	2	7	4*	3.50	50.00	0	0	2	0
First-class	38	49	4	578	78	12.84	54.37	0	1	11	0
List A	87	46	14	499	71*	15.59	85.88	0	2	12	0
Twenty20	50	18	9	42	15	4.66	66.66	0	0	12	0

Bowling

	Mat	Balls	Runs	Wkts	BBI	BBM	Ave	Econ	SR	5w	10
Tests	15	3867	1948	61	6/117	10/209	31.93	3.02	63.3	3	1
ODIs	52	2443	1741	89	6/13	6/13	19.56	4.27	27.4	3	0
T20Is	19	432	409	33	4/15	4/15	12.39	5.68	13.0	0	0
First-class	38	8184	3901	196	7/37	10/74	19.90	2.85	41.7	12	2
List A	87	4081	2752	157	6/12	6/12	17.52	4.04	25.9	4	0
Twenty20	50	1104	1137	69	4/9	4/9	16.47	6.17	16.0	0	0

CRAIG MESCHEDE
RHB RMF

SOMERSET

NAME: Craig Anthony Joseph Meschede
BORN: November 21, 1991, Johannesburg
SQUAD Nº: 26
CAREER: T20 debut: 2011

AOC SAYS: An allrounder who has hopes of breaking into the first team this season, Meschede is a nippy seamer and hard-hitting batsman who made his full Somerset debut over the winter in the Caribbean T20. He made an immediate impression with the bat, making 28* against Windward Islands before smashing an unbeaten 26 off 11 balls in the victory over Combined Campuses and Colleges. Meschede has a German passport through his father, making him eligible to play for England, and was awarded a county contract last June after excelling in second XI cricket, scoring a quickfire 109 against Surrey at The Oval.

LAST WORD: "Craig played a fine innings in the Caribbean T20 where he smashed it everywhere. Brian Rose has said he hits the ball like Craig Kieswetter and he will make his first-class debut this season for sure." *Richard Latham*

Batting & Fielding

	Mat	Inns	NO	Runs	HS	Ave	SR	100	50	Ct	St
Twenty20	4	4	2	55	28*	27.50	141.02	0	0	2	0

Bowling

	Mat	Balls	Runs	Wkts	BBI	BBM	Ave	Econ	SR	5w	10
Twenty20	4	-	-	-	-	-	-	-	-	-	-

OVERSEAS PLAYER

SOMERSET

NAME: Kieron Adrian Pollard
BORN: May 12, 1987, Tacarigua, Trinidad
SQUAD Nº: 55
OTHER TEAMS: West Indies, Mumbai Indians, South Australia, Trinidad
CAREER: ODI debut: 2007; T20I debut: 2008; First-class debut: 2007; List A debut: 2007; T20 debut: 2006

AOC SAYS: The West Indian masterblaster can hit the ball as hard and as far as anyone in the world game. Pollard is batting allrounder who bowls a heavy ball and regularly hits the seam but is most famous for smashing bowlers out of the park – as demonstrated on his Somerset T20 debut against Middlesex last season when he came within yards of becoming the second batsman in history to clear the Lord's pavilion. He helped Somerset reach the FP t20 Finals Day last season before suffering an eye injury in the final against Hampshire which ended his involvement in the match. Pollard is yet to convince against top-class bowlers but will nonetheless provide a huge boost to the Cidermen's T20 campaign this season.

LAST WORD: "I've seen Viv Richards and Ian Botham bat, but Pollard can hit it as far as anyone. He has the reputation to bring in the crowds and he's exceptionally exciting to watch." *Richard Latham*

Batting & Fielding

	Mat	Inns	NO	Runs	HS	Ave	SR	100	50	Ct	St
ODIs	39	35	0	726	94	20.74	103.12	0	3	16	0
T20Is	20	17	2	190	38	12.66	124.18	0	0	11	0
First-class	20	33	1	1199	174	37.46	-	3	5	32	0
List A	60	53	3	1364	94	27.28	-	0	9	30	0
Twenty20	88	77	15	1666	89*	26.87	169.82	0	9	37	0

Bowling

	Mat	Balls	Runs	Wkts	BBI	BBM	Ave	Econ	SR	5w	10
ODIs	39	1145	1008	32	3/27	3/27	31.50	5.28	35.7	0	0
T20Is	20	258	360	11	2/22	2/22	32.72	8.37	23.4	0	0
First-class	20	571	313	6	2/29	2/29	52.16	3.28	95.1	0	0
List A	60	1643	1405	61	4/32	4/32	23.03	5.13	26.9	0	0
Twenty20	88	1286	1653	87	4/15	4/15	19.00	7.71	14.7	0	0

ARUL SUPPIAH

RHB SLA R1

SOMERSET

NAME: Arul Vivasvan Suppiah
BORN: August 30, 1983, Kuala Lumpur
HEIGHT: 6ft
SQUAD Nº: 23
NICKNAME: Ruley, Ja Rule
CAREER: First-class debut: 2002; List A
debut: 2002; T20 debut: 2005; County cap:
2009

AOC SAYS: Suppiah is a gifted strokemaker and useful left-arm orthodox spinner of
Malaysian descent. Touted as a batsman of immense talent, the right-hander made his
mark in 2009 after he was given an extended run at the top of the order alongside Marcus
Trescothick. The former Millfield School student struck three Championship tons and
amassed 1,201 first-class runs in a watershed season after working closely with former
Australia Test opener Justin Langer. Suppiah found the going tougher in the last campaign
but is set to retain his opening berth in 2011. In one-day cricket he drops down the order
but his well-flighted spinners come to the fore.

LAST WORD: "If we had 11 or 15 blokes that followed his lead we would have an
outstanding cricket club. Arul has to have a chance of playing for England based on the
way he has developed." *Justin Langer, former Somerset captain*

Batting & Fielding

	Mat	Inns	NO	Runs	HS	Ave	SR	100	50	Ct	St
First-class	60	99	5	3296	151	35.06	47.49	5	18	34	0
List A	68	59	11	1347	80	28.06	-	0	7	26	0
Twenty20	52	34	9	323	32*	12.92	107.30	0	0	22	0

Bowling

	Mat	Balls	Runs	Wkts	BBI	BBM	Ave	Econ	SR	5w	10
First-class	60	3278	1932	32	3/46	-	60.37	3.53	102.4	0	0
List A	68	1235	1190	35	4/39	4/39	34.00	5.78	35.2	0	0
Twenty20	52	397	498	22	3/25	3/25	22.63	7.52	18.0	0	0

NAME: Alfonso Clive Thomas
BORN: February 9, 1977, Cape Town,
SQUAD Nº: 8
OTHER TEAMS: South Africa, Dolphins,
Northerns, Titans, Western Province
CAREER: T20I debut: 2007; First-class
debut: 1998; List A debut: 2000; T20 debut:
2004; County cap: 2008

SOMERSET

AOC SAYS: The veteran South African seamer was a revelation last season, particularly in the FP t20 where he finished as the competition's leading wicket-taker with 33 victims. Thomas is a right-arm paceman who looked set for a big future in international cricket after making his name with Northerns in his homeland but he had to wait until the age of 30 before making his Proteas bow in a T20I against Pakistan in 2007. He returned figures of 3-25 but signed a contract with Somerset in 2008 as a Kolpak player and has been one of the county's leading performers for the last three seasons. The 2010 campaign was his best yet with a haul of 109 wickets across all competitions. Thomas is also a more than capable lower-order batsman with two first-class centuries to his name.

LAST WORD: "Alfonso Thomas is probably the best medium-pacer in one-day cricket in the country." *Richard Latham*

Batting & Fielding

	Mat	Inns	NO	Runs	HS	Ave	SR	100	50	Ct	St
T20Is	1	-	-	-	-	-	-	-	-	0	0
First-class	112	158	33	3158	119*	25.26	-	2	11	32	0
List A	134	67	33	504	28*	14.82	-	0	0	30	0
Twenty20	91	31	17	172	30*	12.28	111.68	0	0	29	0

Bowling

	Mat	Balls	Runs	Wkts	BBI	BBM	Ave	Econ	SR	5w	10
T20Is	1	24	25	3	3/25	3/25	8.33	6.25	8.0	0	0
First-class	112	20188	9655	353	7/54	-	27.35	2.86	57.1	16	1
List A	134	5798	4917	178	4/18	4/18	27.62	5.08	32.5	0	0
Twenty20	91	1776	2125	112	4/27	4/27	18.97	7.17	15.8	0	0

PETER TREGO

SOMERSET

NAME: Peter David Trego
BORN: June 12, 1981, Weston-super-Mare
HEIGHT: 6ft
SQUAD Nº: 7
NICKNAME: Tregs, Darcy, Pedro Tregos
OTHER TEAMS: Kent, Middlesex
CAREER: First-class debut: 2000; List A
debut: 1999; T20 debut: 2003; County cap:
2007 (Somerset)

AOC SAYS: An aggressive allrounder who has represented England Lions, Trego is a
steady seamer and ferocious hitter of a cricket ball. The former England under 19 star
is in his second spell at Taunton, having made his first-class debut for Somerset at the
age of 19 before moving to Kent at the end of the 2002 season. After an unhappy spell at
Canterbury he began to rediscover his form at Middlesex and returned to his home county
in 2006. Trego has not looked back since, excelling in all formats but reserving his best
performances for limited-overs cricket. Innings like the 120-ball 147 against Glamorgan in
the CB40 last season can only boost his international credentials but at 29, time is running
out for the charismatic allrounder.

LAST WORD: "Peter is a very friendly lad and an immensely destructive middle-order
batsman. The reason he hasn't gone on to play for England is because he doesn't take
enough wickets." *Richard Latham*

Batting & Fielding											
	Mat	Inns	NO	Runs	HS	Ave	SR	100	50	Ct	St
First-class	99	143	20	4352	140	35.38	-	8	27	37	0
List A	108	89	18	1581	147	22.26	-	1	6	31	0
Twenty20	61	53	9	1017	79	23.11	131.73	0	3	17	0

Bowling											
	Mat	Balls	Runs	Wkts	BBI	BBM	Ave	Econ	SR	5w	10
First-class	99	9821	6256	166	6/59	-	37.68	3.82	59.1	1	0
List A	108	3800	3531	111	5/40	5/40	31.81	5.57	34.2	2	0
Twenty20	61	698	1000	34	2/17	2/17	29.41	8.59	20.5	0	0

NAME: Marcus Edward Trescothick
BORN: December 25, 1975, Keynsham
HEIGHT: 6ft 3in
SQUAD Nº: 2
NICKNAME: Banger, Tres, Tresco
OTHER TEAMS: England
CAREER: Test debut: 2000; ODI debut: 2000;
T20I debut: 2005; First-class debut: 1993;
List A debut: 2003; T20 debut: 2004; County
cap: 1999

SOMERSET

AOC SAYS: Former England coach Duncan Fletcher took a punt on Trescothick, believing he had the potential to establish himself as a Test opener despite a modest domestic record. It proved a masterstroke and the left-hander will be remembered as one of England's greatest ever openers. After making 79 on ODI debut, Trescothick was promoted to the Test side and took to the longer format like a duck to water. Compensating for minimal foot movement with a fantastic eye and a crunching cover drive, he struck a double ton against South Africa at The Oval in 2003 and set the tone for England's victorious 2005 Ashes campaign with a blistering 90 at Edgbaston. A battle with depression brought a premature end to his England career but he remains arguably the most destructive batsman on the county circuit.

LAST WORD: "My aim is to play for as long as I can, at least until I am 40 and beyond if I am fit enough." *Marcus Trescothick*

Batting & Fielding

	Mat	Inns	NO	Runs	HS	Ave	SR	100	50	Ct	St
Tests	76	143	10	5825	219	43.79	54.51	14	29	95	0
ODIs	123	122	6	4335	137	37.37	85.21	12	21	49	0
T20Is	3	3	0	166	72	55.33	126.71	0	2	2	0
First-class	271	466	27	18042	284	41.09	-	43	91	340	0
List A	334	321	25	11136	184	37.62	-	27	55	131	0
Twenty20	51	50	2	1613	107	33.60	155.69	1	14	18	0

Bowling

	Mat	Balls	Runs	Wkts	BBI	BBM	Ave	Econ	SR	5w	10
Tests	76	300	155	1	1/34	1/34	155.00	3.10	300.0	0	0
ODIs	123	232	219	4	2/7	2/7	54.75	5.66	58.0	0	0
T20Is	3	-	-	-	-	-	-	-	-	-	-
First-class	271	2704	1551	36	4/36	-	43.08	3.44	75.1	0	0
List A	334	2010	1644	57	4/50	4/50	28.84	4.90	35.2	0	0
Twenty20	51	-	-	-	-	-	-	-	-	-	-

SOMERSET

NAME: Max Thomas Charles Waller
BORN: March 3, 1988, Salisbury
HEIGHT: 6ft
SQUAD №: 10
CAREER: First-class debut: 2009; List A
debut: 2009; T20 debut: 2009

AOC SAYS: Waller is a young legspinner with a fine googly who has already impressed
in T20 cricket. Now established as Somerset's first-choice legbreak bowler following the
departure of Michael Munday, the former Millfield School student has a good temperament
and doesn't get flustered when under pressure. Unsurprisingly for a novice leggie still
learning his craft, he must work on his consistency if he is to feature more prominently in
four-day cricket, but he is progressing well and toured South Africa in 2009 as part of the
England Performance Programme. Waller has already benefited from working alongside
Murali Kartik and six weeks with 'mystery' spinner Ajantha Mendis this season should
help add more strings to his bow.

LAST WORD: "Waller bowled very well in the Caribbean T20 and having seen off the
competition of Michael Munday, he will be pushing for a place in all competitions this
season." *Richard Latham*

Batting & Fielding

	Mat	Inns	NO	Runs	HS	Ave	SR	100	50	Ct	St
First-class	4	6	1	67	28	13.40	44.96	0	0	1	0
List A	16	5	4	12	5	12.00	50.00	0	0	3	0
Twenty20	18	6	2	2	1*	0.50	15.38	0	0	6	0

Bowling

	Mat	Balls	Runs	Wkts	BBI	BBM	Ave	Econ	SR	5w	10
First-class	4	496	320	5	2/27	3/57	64.00	3.87	99.2	0	0
List A	16	504	465	11	2/24	2/24	42.27	5.53	45.8	0	0
Twenty20	18	288	347	18	3/16	3/16	19.27	7.22	16.0	0	0

CHARL WILLOUGHBY
LHB LMF W5 MVP99

NAME: Charl Myles Willoughby
BORN: December 3, 1974, Cape Town
HEIGHT: 6ft 3in
SQUAD Nº: 1
NICKNAME: Puppy, Harry
MAJOR TEAMS: South Africa, Boland, Cape Cobras, Leicestershire, Western Province
CAREER: Test debut: 2003; ODI debut: 2000; First-class debut: 1994; List A debut: 1994; T20 debut: 2004; County cap: 2005 (Leicestershire), 2007 (Somerset)

SOMERSET

AOC SAYS: Willoughby is in the twilight of his career but the left-arm seamer was as reliable as ever last season, claiming 58 first-class wickets to pass the 50-mark for the fourth consecutive county season. A tall man who now bowls no more than military medium, the South African snares his victims through metronomic accuracy and appreciable swing. Willoughby made his ODI debut against Pakistan in 2000 and played two Test matches in 2003 but suffered from a lack of variety and joined Leicestershire as a Kolpak player after fading from the international scene. He swapped Grace Road for Taunton in 2006 and was rewarded for years of hard service with a new two-year deal last July.

LAST WORD: "Charl has been a quality bowler for many years and done well for us. We would be very reluctant to lose him. His fitness is good and we look forward to him playing for the next two years." *Brian Rose, director of cricket*

Batting & Fielding

	Mat	Inns	NO	Runs	HS	Ave	SR	100	50	Ct	St
Tests	2	-	-	-	-	-	-	-	-	0	0
ODIs	3	2	0	0	0	0.00	0.00	0	0	0	0
First-class	209	233	102	801	47	6.11	-	0	0	42	0
List A	209	61	32	147	15	5.06	-	0	0	26	0
Twenty20	67	16	11	28	11	5.60	112.00	0	0	11	0

Bowling

	Mat	Balls	Runs	Wkts	BBI	BBM	Ave	Econ	SR	5w	10
Tests	2	300	125	1	1/47	1/79	125.00	2.50	300.0	0	0
ODIs	3	168	148	2	2/39	2/39	74.00	5.28	84.0	0	0
First-class	209	41933	19647	774	7/44	-	25.38	2.81	54.1	31	3
List A	209	10164	7094	255	6/16	6/16	27.81	4.18	39.8	5	0
Twenty20	67	1463	1729	71	4/9	4/9	24.35	7.09	20.6	0	0

FORMED: 1845
GROUND: The Kia Oval
ONE-DAY NAME: Lions
CAPTAIN: Rory Hamilton-Brown
2010 RESULTS: CC2: 7/9; CB40: 3/7 in
Group A; FP t20: 5/9 in South Group

HONOURS

County Championship: (19) 1890, 1891, 1892, 1894, 1895, 1899, 1914, 1950(s), 1952, 1953, 1954, 1955, 1956, 1957, 1958, 1971, 1999, 2000, 2002; Gillette/NatWest/C&G/FP Trophy: 1982; Benson and Hedges Cup: (3) 1974, 1997, 2001; Pro40/National League/CB40: 2003; Sunday League: 1996; Twenty20 Cup: 2003

THE LOWDOWN

After a disastrous 2009, Surrey showed signs of improvement in all three competitions last year but lacked the cutting edge to mount a genuine challenge for silverware. Chris Adams has always said that rebuilding the squad would be a long-term project but now, in the last year of his current contract, he will be looking for a significant improvement from his charges. A return to the top tier of the Championship remains a priority and with the likes of Chris Tremlett, Jade Dernbach, Yasir Arafat, Stuart Meaker and Chris Jordan, the Brown Caps have a battery of seamers capable of bowling their side to promotion. The batting stocks remains a worry, with Mark Ramprakash out for the first month of the season, and it remains to be seen if their array of young batsman can deliver consistent runs.

PROFESSIONAL CRICKET MANAGER: CHRIS ADAMS

A veteran of five Tests and the same number of ODIs, Adams is better known for his achievements in county cricket where he was a dependable run-scorer for Derbyshire and masterminded Sussex's maiden County Championship success. A Championship and C&G Trophy double followed in 2006, as did another Championship in 2007. After retiring at the end of 2008, Adams immediately made the move into coaching and has recruited an array of former Surrey stars as his backroom staff.

With thanks to: Chris Adams; Ian Salisbury, Surrey coach; Richard Spiller, sports editor, Surrey Advertiser

	Mat	Inns	NO	Runs	HS	Ave	SR	100	50	Ct	St
MR Ramprakash	16	28	2	1595	248	61.34	55.40	5	5	5	-
SM Davies	13	21	3	1009	137	56.05	68.59	2	8	30	0
GC Wilson	6	9	1	349	125	43.62	48.53	1	1	14	0
Younus Khan	3	5	1	155	77*	38.75	64.31	0	1	2	-
LJ Evans	2	4	0	137	98	34.25	48.23	0	1	1	-
U Afzaal	13	22	2	682	159*	34.10	56.13	1	4	4	-
JJ Roy	3	5	0	170	76	34.00	104.93	0	2	0	-
MJ Brown	1	2	0	64	47	32.00	54.23	0	0	0	-
TJ Lancefield	8	13	1	381	74	31.75	48.97	0	2	3	-
RJ Hamilton-Brown	17	29	1	844	125	30.14	84.06	2	3	11	-
MNW Spriegel	10	14	1	391	108*	30.07	47.79	2	0	10	-
CP Schofield	8	13	0	341	90	26.23	49.63	0	2	5	-
A Harinath	14	25	1	621	63	25.87	38.21	0	4	3	-
GJ Batty	15	24	2	550	67	25.00	51.35	0	2	12	-
SJ Walters	6	10	0	242	53	24.20	59.90	0	1	8	-
A Nel	7	10	0	219	96	21.90	61.00	0	1	4	-
CT Tremlett	12	17	6	230	53*	20.90	46.09	0	1	1	-
Iftikhar Anjum	3	5	1	61	29	15.25	59.80	0	0	0	-
JW Dernbach	15	20	9	154	56*	14.00	62.60	0	1	1	-
KP Pietersen	2	3	0	41	40	13.66	47.67	0	0	0	-
SC Meaker	11	14	1	175	94	13.46	41.56	0	1	3	-
TE Linley	7	10	4	55	16	9.16	37.67	0	0	4	-
TM Jewell	3	2	1	5	4*	5.00	27.77	0	0	0	-
SP Cheetham	1	1	1	0	0*	-	0.00	0	0	0	-

	Mat	Overs	Mdns	Runs	Wkts	BBI	BBM	Ave	Econ	SR	5w	10
MP Dunn	1	14.5	7	48	3	3/48	3/48	16.00	3.23	29.6	0	0
CT Tremlett	12	361.5	88	969	48	4/29	8/87	20.18	2.67	45.2	0	0
U Afzaal	13	75.3	9	217	8	2/26	3/45	27.12	2.87	56.6	0	0
JW Dernbach	15	447.0	98	1390	51	5/68	6/101	27.25	3.10	52.5	2	0
LJ Evans	2	6.0	0	30	1	1/30	1/30	30.00	5.00	36.0	0	0
TE Linley	7	170.0	46	483	16	5/105	6/136	30.18	2.84	63.7	1	0
A Nel	7	227.0	67	671	21	4/68	5/147	31.95	2.95	64.8	0	0
SC Meaker	11	269.4	48	998	29	5/48	6/81	34.41	3.70	55.7	2	0
SP Cheetham	1	16.0	1	71	2	2/71	2/71	35.50	4.43	48.0	0	0
Iftikhar Anjum	3	65.0	8	240	6	2/53	3/96	40.00	3.69	65.0	0	0
GJ Batty	15	488.5	70	1696	42	5/76	6/123	40.38	3.46	69.8	1	0
MNW Spriegel	10	65.3	3	207	5	1/5	1/5	41.40	3.16	78.6	0	0
TM Jewell	3	40.0	10	127	3	1/22	1/22	42.33	3.17	80.0	0	0
CP Schofield	8	184.0	34	606	14	4/63	4/71	43.28	3.29	78.8	0	0
SJ King	1	28.0	1	134	1	1/134	1/134	134.00	4.78	168.0	0	0
RJ Hamilton-Brown	17	47.3	1	184	1	1/17	1/17	184.00	3.87	285.0	0	0
A Harinath	14	2.0	0	12	0	-	-	-	6.00	-	0	0
TJ Lancefield	8	1.0	0	9	0	-	-	-	9.00	-	0	0
MR Ramprakash	16	1.0	0	6	0	-	-	-	6.00	-	0	0
JJ Roy	3	3.0	0	18	0	-	-	-	6.00	-	0	0
SJ Walters	6	3.0	0	15	0	-	-	-	5.00	-	0	0
GC Wilson	6	9.0	0	44	0	-	-	-	4.88	-	0	0
Younus Khan	3	18.0	0	64	0	-	-	-	3.55	-	0	0

S

Batting & Fielding

	Mat	Inns	NO	Runs	HS	Ave	SR	100	50	Ct	St
KP Pietersen	2	2	0	154	116	77.00	111.59	1	0	0	-
U Afzaal	4	4	2	124	51*	62.00	83.78	0	1	4	-
SM Davies	9	9	1	485	101	60.62	128.98	1	4	8	2
MR Ramprakash	9	9	2	326	85*	46.57	99.08	0	2	5	-
RJ Hamilton-Brown	11	11	0	478	115	43.45	150.78	1	4	2	-
SJ Walters	10	9	2	271	88	38.71	95.75	0	2	0	-
MNW Spriegel	11	10	3	268	56*	38.28	93.70	0	2	6	-
CP Schofield	8	5	1	127	64*	31.75	96.21	0	1	0	-
CT Tremlett	7	5	0	94	38	18.80	127.02	0	0	1	-
JJ Roy	6	5	0	92	60	18.40	101.09	0	1	2	-
GJ Batty	9	6	0	81	29	13.50	109.45	0	0	0	-
SP Cheetham	4	2	1	13	13*	13.00	92.85	0	0	1	-
JW Dernbach	11	5	1	36	31	9.00	112.50	0	0	3	-
ZS Ansari	1	1	0	6	6	6.00	54.54	0	0	1	-
GC Wilson	5	3	0	15	9	5.00	71.42	0	0	3	2
A Nel	3	2	1	4	3	4.00	80.00	0	0	1	-
LJ Evans	1	1	0	3	3	3.00	21.42	0	0	1	-
SC Meaker	4	2	0	2	2	1.00	22.22	0	0	0	-
TE Linley	4	3	2	0	0*	0.00	0.00	0	0	1	-
Iftikhar Anjum	2	1	1	4	4*	-	400.00	0	0	0	-

Bowling

	Mat	Overs	Mdns	Runs	Wkts	BBI	Ave	Econ	SR	5w
A Nel	3	24.0	0	140	7	3/29	20.00	5.83	20.5	0
Iftikhar Anjum	2	15.0	0	88	4	3/39	22.00	5.86	22.5	0
ZS Ansari	1	5.0	0	26	1	1/26	26.00	5.20	30.0	0
GJ Batty	9	57.0	0	339	12	3/44	28.25	5.94	28.5	0
RJ Hamilton-Brown	11	21.0	1	134	4	2/50	33.50	6.38	31.5	0
SP Cheetham	4	25.0	0	196	5	4/32	39.20	7.84	30.0	0
CP Schofield	8	56.0	1	331	8	2/40	41.37	5.91	42.0	0
CT Tremlett	7	47.5	2	351	8	2/31	43.87	7.33	35.8	0
JW Dernbach	11	76.0	0	551	12	3/29	45.91	7.25	38.0	0
MNW Spriegel	11	39.0	0	266	5	1/20	53.20	6.82	46.8	0
SC Meaker	4	24.0	0	152	2	1/34	76.00	6.33	72.0	0
TE Linley	4	22.0	0	151	1	1/51	151.00	6.86	132.0	0
U Afzaal	4	1.0	0	4	0	-	-	4.00	-	0
KP Pietersen	2	1.0	0	17	0	-	-	17.00	-	0

www.surreycricket.com / tel: 020 7820 5700

Batting & Fielding

	Mat	Inns	NO	Runs	HS	Ave	SR	100	50	Ct	St
GC Wilson	5	3	2	51	36*	51.00	175.86	0	0	5	1
SJ Walters	12	11	7	184	53*	46.00	113.58	0	1	9	-
MR Ramprakash	11	11	2	331	63*	36.77	116.54	0	3	3	-
JJ Roy	9	9	1	242	101*	30.25	148.46	1	1	2	-
SM Davies	13	13	0	389	89	29.92	162.08	0	3	14	1
RJ Hamilton-Brown	16	16	2	397	87*	28.35	125.23	0	2	5	-
MNW Spriegel	12	7	4	67	25*	22.33	79.76	0	0	7	-
JW Dernbach	5	2	1	22	12	22.00	157.14	0	0	1	-
TJ Lancefield	5	3	0	65	27	21.66	125.00	0	0	1	-
A Symonds	15	13	0	263	63	20.23	152.02	0	2	5	-
Younus Khan	11	10	0	154	59	15.40	98.08	0	1	2	-
CT Tremlett	16	3	2	14	6*	14.00	87.50	0	0	0	-
A Nel	14	8	4	30	9	7.50	136.36	0	0	1	-
U Afzaal	2	2	0	14	12	7.00	48.27	0	0	0	-
CP Schofield	16	10	1	54	15	6.00	80.59	0	0	7	-
GJ Batty	8	6	1	16	10*	3.20	72.72	0	0	2	-
TE Linley	3	1	0	1	1	1.00	33.33	0	0	0	-
SC Meaker	3	1	1	10	10*	-	142.85	0	0	1	-

Bowling

	Mat	Overs	Mdns	Runs	Wkts	BBI	Ave	Econ	SR	5w
CT Tremlett	16	60.0	1	411	24	3/17	17.12	6.85	15.0	0
TE Linley	3	9.0	0	62	3	1/17	20.66	6.88	18.0	0
GJ Batty	8	20.0	0	158	7	4/23	22.57	7.90	17.1	0
RJ Hamilton-Brown	16	18.0	0	165	7	2/23	23.57	9.16	15.4	0
A Symonds	15	32.1	0	298	12	5/18	24.83	9.26	16.0	1
CP Schofield	16	54.5	0	401	14	2/15	28.64	7.31	23.5	0
SC Meaker	3	10.0	0	88	3	2/36	29.33	8.80	20.0	0
MNW Spriegel	12	29.0	0	208	7	2/23	29.71	7.17	24.8	0
JW Dernbach	5	15.0	0	98	3	2/22	32.66	6.53	30.0	0
A Nel	14	52.0	1	381	7	2/30	54.42	7.32	44.5	0
TJ Lancefield	5	0.0	0	0	0	-	-	-	-	0

ZAFAR ANSARI

LHB SLA

SURREY

NAME: Zafar Shahaan Ansari
BORN: December 10, 1991, Ascot
HEIGHT: 5ft 10in
SQUAD Nº: 22
NICKNAME: Zaff
CAREER: List A debut: 2010

AOC SAYS: A middle-order batsman who is also a useful spinner, Ansari has been with Surrey since he was a part of their under 9 squad. He captained England under 15s and has also played for the under 17 and under 19 sides. He made his Surrey debut against Sussex in the CB40 last season and claimed his maiden professional wicket when he dismissed Joe Gatting. Ansari signed professional terms at Surrey in December 2010, putting pen to paper on a two-year summer contract, which allows him to continue studying at Cambridge University. His degree means he is unlikely to feature at The Oval for the first part of the 2011 campaign.

LAST WORD: "He's a very impressive player, a very intelligent lad and really loves his cricket." *Richard Spiller*

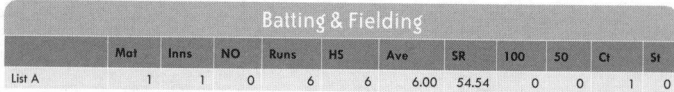

Batting & Fielding

	Mat	Inns	NO	Runs	HS	Ave	SR	100	50	Ct	St
List A	1	1	0	6	6	6.00	54.54	0	0	1	0

Bowling

	Mat	Balls	Runs	Wkts	BBI	BBM	Ave	Econ	SR	5w	10
List A	1	30	26	1	1/26	1/26	26.00	5.20	30.0	0	0

NAME: Gareth John Batty
BORN: October 13, 1977, Bradford
HEIGHT: 5ft 11in
SQUAD Nº: 13
NICKNAME: Batts, Boris, Red, Terry, Stuta
OTHER TEAMS: England, Worcestershire, Yorkshire
CAREER: Test debut: 2003; ODI debut: 2002; T20I debut: 2009; First-class debut: 1997; List A debut: 1998; T20 debut: 2003

SURREY

AOC SAYS: Batty returned to Surrey for a second spell at The Oval ahead of the 2010 season and took 42 wickets for Chris Adams' side last term. The former England international is now Surrey's chief spinner and the side will be relying heavily on his talents this summer. Batty started his career at Yorkshire before moving to Surrey and then on to Worcestershire, where he spent eight seasons before returning to The Oval. The offbreak bowler has taken over 400 first-class wickets and is likely to pass the 5,000 runs milestone in the County Championship this summer.

LAST WORD: "The spin-bowling department will be very heavily reliant on Gareth Batty, who I think bowled better than his figures suggested last summer. Without Piyush Chawla, who they thought was going to be the main man, he had to step up to do more of a number-one spinner role." *Richard Spiller*

Batting & Fielding

	Mat	Inns	NO	Runs	HS	Ave	SR	100	50	Ct	St
Tests	7	8	1	144	38	20.57	27.01	0	0	3	0
ODIs	10	8	2	30	17	5.00	41.09	0	0	4	0
T20Is	1	1	0	4	4	4.00	57.14	0	0	0	0
First-class	150	228	38	4852	133	25.53	-	2	24	103	0
List A	194	153	31	2050	83*	16.80	-	0	5	66	0
Twenty20	58	49	12	457	87	12.35	112.28	0	1	23	0

Bowling

	Mat	Balls	Runs	Wkts	BBI	BBM	Ave	Econ	SR	5w	10
Tests	7	1394	733	11	3/55	5/153	66.63	3.15	126.7	0	0
ODIs	10	440	366	5	2/40	2/40	73.20	4.99	88.0	0	0
T20Is	1	18	17	0	-	-	-	5.66	-	0	0
First-class	150	28434	14076	410	7/52	-	34.33	2.97	69.3	16	1
List A	194	7607	5791	172	5/35	5/35	33.66	4.56	44.2	1	0
Twenty20	58	1032	1331	48	4/23	4/23	27.72	7.73	21.5	0	0

MICHAEL BROWN

SURREY

NAME: Michael James Brown
BORN: February 9, 1980, Burnley
HEIGHT: 6ft
SQUAD Nº: 23
NICKNAME: Weasel, Browny
OTHER TEAMS: Hampshire, Middlesex
CAREER: First-class debut: 1999; List A debut: 2002; T20 debut: 2004; County cap: 2007 (Hampshire)

AOC SAYS: An ever-present for Surrey in the 2009 Championship, Brown didn't feature last season due to a series of injuries. The opening batsman started his career at Middlesex before moving to Hampshire in search of regular first-class cricket in 2004. His average of 40.86 in 2008 earned him a move to Surrey, where he concluded the 2009 summer just eight short of achieving 1,000 Championship runs in his first season at The Oval, while in one-day cricket he averaged 37.13 and scored 100 runs in two Twenty20 innings, not bad for a batsman supposedly better suited to four-day cricket. He underwent surgery on his left elbow at the end of last season and spent the winter working towards full fitness.

LAST WORD: "When you want to be playing and making a contribution it's very frustrating to be on the sidelines. It's worse when you come into the ground and, no matter how much the players and coaches ask about you, you don't feel a part of it. I'm looking forward to the 2011 season now." *Michael Brown*

Batting & Fielding

	Mat	Inns	NO	Runs	HS	Ave	SR	100	50	Ct	St
First-class	93	166	16	5195	133	34.63	-	9	28	71	0
List A	30	29	2	922	96*	34.14	76.32	0	7	9	0
Twenty20	12	12	1	284	77	25.81	129.68	0	1	4	0

Bowling

	Mat	Balls	Runs	Wkts	BBI	BBM	Ave	Econ	SR	5w	10
First-class	93	18	20	0	-	-	-	6.66	-	0	0
List A	30	-	-	-	-	-	-	-	-	-	-
Twenty20	12	-	-	-	-	-	-	-	-	-	-

NAME: Rory Joseph Burns
BORN: August 26, 1990, Epsom
HEIGHT: 5ft 9in
SQUAD Nº: 17
NICKNAME: Burnsy
CAREER: Yet to make first-team debut

SURREY

AOC SAYS: Burns is a graduate of Surrey's academy and signed professional terms at The Oval in December. He kept wicket for Surrey's Second XI Championship winning team in 2009 and plays club cricket for Banstead, the same side as Surrey teammates Matthew Spriegel and Tom Lancefield. Last season he averaged 66.78 in the Second XI Championship while representing the MCC Universities combined team, Hampshire and Surrey. Among his impressive displays were centuries against Sussex and Essex for the MCC Universities and an unbeaten 118 for Hampshire against Surrey. Burns, who was also a member of the Unicorns squad last season, scored an unbeaten 230 against Oxford MCCU in the MCC Championship, a competition in which he scored three centuries in five matches, averaging a Bradmanesque 99.67.

LAST WORD: "He's a quality player with both bat and gloves and with Davies and Wilson potentially away with international commitments this summer he has a chance to push his way into the side for a couple of games." *Ian Salisbury*

EXTRAS

Surrey announced a pre-tax loss of £502,000 for the 2010 financial year. However, the club's new chairman Richard Thompson remains upbeat: "The start to the 2011 year has been one of the strongest for the club ever. For the India Test and ODI, we are tracking above an Ashes series which is unheard of. We are confident that we've put in place measures that will return us to profit. 2010 was a difficult year across cricket in general, and all sports suffered a downturn in corporate hospitality. We are beginning to see the market improve."

STEVE DAVIES

LHB WK R3 MVP33

SURREY

NAME: Steven Michael Davies
BORN: June 17, 1986, Bromsgrove
HEIGHT: 5ft 11in
SQUAD Nº: 9
NICKNAME: Davo
OTHER TEAMS: England, Worcestershire
CAREER: ODI debut: 2009; T20I debut: 2009;
First-class debut: 2005; List A debut: 2003;
T20 debut: 2006

AOC SAYS: Matt Prior's understudy as England Test wicketkeeper, Davies is a regular in Andy Flower's Twenty20 side and played all five games in the one-day series against Pakistan last summer. Among his performances in that series was a knock of 87 from 67 balls, which led England to victory at Durham. The gloveman established himself as Andrew Strauss' opening partner in ODIs and finished the series with an average of 39.40. However, he only played in two of the seven ODIs during the winter's Ashes tour and missed out on a trip to the World Cup, with selector Geoff Miller believing that Prior was more suited to the low, slow wickets of the subcontinent than Davies. Nevertheless, with Prior yet to convince over 50 overs, further impressive performances for Surrey this summer will keep Davies very much in the reckoning for further international honours. Having moved from Worcestershire to Kennington at the end of the 2009 season, he was a consistent contributor in all forms of the game last year. Batting in the middle-order he notched a personal-best 1,090 first-class runs for the season at an average of 57.36, a 17-run improvement on his 2009 average, while in domestic one-day cricket he's averaged around the 50 mark in each of the last three seasons. Still only 24, Davies has already scored in excess of 5,000 first-class runs and over 3,000 runs in List A cricket.

INSIDE TRACK: "I think this is a big year for Steve, he needs to step up and take responsibility with the bat. Not just for going out and playing well and looking a million dollars, but carving scores beyond the 70s and 80s. He needs to go on and make scores that will be the difference between winning and not winning. Steve's ready for that. He's an absolutely superb batsman who has wonderful technique. We don't mind him playing at the tempo he does, but we need him to bat a session, then another session. It's his time now. He needs to kick on, that is what will take him to the next level. Steve will naturally come in around No.4 or No.5 in Championship cricket. I know he's itching to bat four, but with that he'll have to take responsibility to win games of cricket." *Chris Adams*

Batting & Fielding

	Mat	Inns	NO	Runs	HS	Ave	SR	100	50	Ct	St
ODIs	8	8	0	244	87	30.50	105.62	0	1	8	0
T20Is	5	5	0	102	33	20.40	124.39	0	0	2	1
First-class	93	155	18	5483	192	40.02	63.90	8	29	278	14
List A	109	99	12	3225	119	37.06	-	5	19	96	27
Twenty20	55	50	5	1022	89	22.71	140.00	0	5	30	6

Bowling

	Mat	Balls	Runs	Wkts	BBI	BBM	Ave	Econ	SR	5w	10
ODIs	8	-	-	-	-	-	-	-	-	-	-
T20Is	5	-	-	-	-	-	-	-	-	-	-
First-class	93	-	-	-	-	-	-	-	-	-	-
List A	109	-	-	-	-	-	-	-	-	-	-
Twenty20	55	-	-	-	-	-	-	-	-	-	-

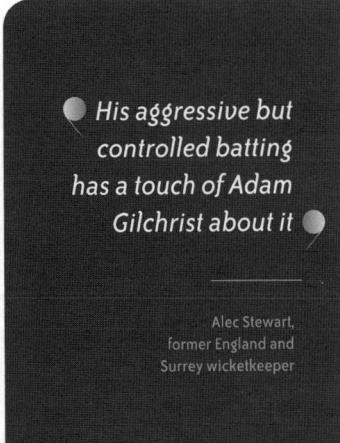

His aggressive but controlled batting has a touch of Adam Gilchrist about it

Alec Stewart,
former England and
Surrey wicketkeeper

ZANDER DE BRUYN

RHB RMF MVP29

NAME: Zander de Bruyn
BORN: July 5, 1975, Johannesburg
SQUAD Nº: 58
OTHER TEAMS: South Africa, Gauteng,
Lions, Somerset, Titans, Transvaal,
Warriors, Worcestershire
CAREER: Test debut: 2004; First-class
debut: 1995; List A debut: 1996; T20 debut:
2005; County cap: 2008 (Somerset)

AOC SAYS: De Bruyn signed a one-year deal with Surrey in December, joining Chris Adams'
side after three seasons at Somerset. He averaged 38.41 in Championship cricket and 53.41
in the one-day format for the Taunton side. He arrives at Surrey on the back of a hugely
impressive winter in South Africa with domestic side Highveld Lions. He had a brief Test
career in 2004 when he was called up for a tour of India but despite a debut knock of 83 he
was dropped after just two matches. He returned in the first Test of England's 2004 tour to
South Africa but hasn't featured for his country since.

LAST WORD: "The experience of a man like Zander de Bruyn will be utterly invaluable in
our dressing room. Although I am convinced we have some of the finest young talents in
the country in our squad, playing alongside someone with the know-how of Zander will be
hugely beneficial in all areas." *Chris Adams*

Batting & Fielding

	Mat	Inns	NO	Runs	HS	Ave	SR	100	50	Ct	St
Tests	3	5	1	155	83	38.75	37.89	0	1	0	0
First-class	175	292	31	10665	266*	40.86	-	23	57	106	0
List A	190	174	37	5174	122*	37.76	-	6	33	46	0
Twenty20	88	79	23	1690	95*	30.17	109.59	0	7	19	0

Bowling

	Mat	Balls	Runs	Wkts	BBI	BBM	Ave	Econ	SR	5w	10
Tests	3	216	92	3	2/32	2/32	30.66	2.55	72.0	0	0
First-class	175	14104	8103	207	7/67	-	39.14	3.44	68.1	3	0
List A	190	4541	4136	132	5/44	5/44	31.33	5.46	34.4	1	0
Twenty20	88	808	1198	41	4/18	4/18	29.21	8.89	19.7	0	0

NAME: Jade Winston Dernbach
BORN: March 3, 1986, Johannesburg
HEIGHT: 6ft 2in
SQUAD Nº: 16
NICKNAME: Dirtbag
CAREER: First-class debut: 2003; List A debut: 2005; T20 debut: 2005

SURREY

AOC SAYS: Surrey academy graduate Dernbach has established himself as a first-team regular at The Oval in recent seasons, and has come on in leaps and bounds in the past two years. Likely to lead Surrey's attack again this summer, Dernbach came to the fore in 2008 when he both impressed in the Pro40 and claimed figures of 6-72 against Somerset in the County Championship. The South African-born seamer spent his winter in Australia and the West Indies with England Lions and was named in Andy Flower's provisional 30-man squad ahead of the 2011 World Cup. When Ajmal Shazhad was forced to go home with a hamstring injury before England's final group game, Dernbach's exceptional form in the Caribbean was rewarded with a surprise call-up for the knockout stages.

LAST WORD: "We have been following the progress of Jade for some time and he has impressed throughout his two years on the Fast Bowling Programme and the England Performance Programme, as well as during the domestic season with Surrey." *Geoff Miller, England selector*

Batting & Fielding

	Mat	Inns	NO	Runs	HS	Ave	SR	100	50	Ct	St
First-class	54	64	23	418	56*	10.19	-	0	1	5	0
List A	60	27	10	147	31	8.64	85.96	0	0	15	0
Twenty20	34	8	2	36	12	6.00	94.73	0	0	7	0

Bowling

	Mat	Balls	Runs	Wkts	BBI	BBM	Ave	Econ	SR	5w	10
First-class	54	8073	4802	148	6/47	-	32.44	3.56	54.5	7	0
List A	60	2456	2592	95	5/31	5/31	27.28	6.33	25.8	2	0
Twenty20	34	589	894	21	3/32	3/32	42.57	9.10	28.0	0	0

MATT DUNN

LHB RFM

SURREY

NAME: Matthew Peter Dunn
BORN: May 5, 1992, Egham
HEIGHT: 6ft 1in
SQUAD Nº: 4
NICKNAME: Dunny
CAREER: First-class debut: 2010

AOC SAYS: One of the most exciting bowling prospects to have graduated from the Surrey academy in recent years, Dunn signed a two-year deal with the county in November 2010. He has represented England under 19s in Test matches and at the Under 19 World Cup, and took 3-48 in his only appearance for Surrey to date, a tour match against Bangladesh last summer. Exceptionally quick for such a young man, he is likely to get chances to impress in Surrey's first-team this summer, especially if the likes of Chris Tremlett and Jade Dernbach are called away on international duty. He plays club cricket for Egham in the Surrey Championship.

LAST WORD: "He's a fast bowler with a bright future who has played for England at youth level. He can swing the ball away from the batsman and has been clocked bowling at 90mph." *Ian Salisbury*

Batting & Fielding

	Mat	Inns	NO	Runs	HS	Ave	SR	100	50	Ct	St
First-class	1	-	-	-	-	-	-	-	-	-	-

Bowling

	Mat	Balls	Runs	Wkts	BBI	BBM	Ave	Econ	SR	5w	10
First-class	1	89	48	3	3/48	3/48	16.00	3.23	29.6	0	0

NAME: Rory James Hamilton-Brown
BORN: September 3, 1987, London
HEIGHT: 6ft
SQUAD Nº: 27
NICKNAME: Bear, Stewi, RHB, Razza, HB
OTHER TEAMS: Sussex
CAREER: First-class debut: 2005; List A debut: 2005; T20 debut: 2008

SURREY

AOC SAYS: A product of Surrey's academy, Hamilton-Brown left The Oval in 2007 to join Sussex. In his first stint at Surrey he played just a handful of one-day games and a first-class tour match against Bangladesh A. At Hove, Hamilton-Brown was part of a Pro40 and FP t20-winning side before his former captain at Sussex, Chris Adams, brought him back to London. Hamilton-Brown was instantly installed as captain at The Oval, despite being just 22 and having played only six County Championship fixtures while at Sussex. He scored two first-class centuries last summer and averaged 43.45 in the CB40 competition. In the FP t20 he scored an unbeaten 87 off 66 balls to guide the Lions to an eight-wicket victory over his former side Sussex. In addition to his undoubted talents as a batsman, Hamilton-Brown is also a very useful spin bowler, especially in limited-overs cricket. Last season he bowled 18 overs in the FP t20, taking seven wickets at an average of 23.57. A former captain of England under 19s, Hamilton's self-belief, all-round ability (including excellent fielding) and obvious leadership qualities suggest he has every chance of playing at the highest level.

INSIDE TRACK: "He has one of the toughest jobs in cricket but I thought he was fantastic last year; magnificent. He handled everything that was thrown at him and still managed to score 1,800 runs in the process. He was very impressive. He got that first year out of the way as a player and a captain. I've got no doubt that this summer will be equally as tough, it doesn't suddenly get easier. You have to apply yourself at every level on a daily basis. He's a couple of years behind Steven Davies but as soon as he starts to exhibit the qualities of batting through difficult situations and starts affecting the outcome of games, that's when the likes of Andy Flower and Geoff Miller will start to take more and more notice. He has great confidence in his own ability, which is a great attribute to have." *Chris Adams*

RORY HAMILTON-BROWN

Batting & Fielding											
	Mat	Inns	NO	Runs	HS	Ave	SR	100	50	Ct	St
First-class	25	42	3	1277	171*	32.74	78.92	4	4	17	0
List A	48	41	2	1020	115	26.15	115.38	1	4	14	0
Twenty20	41	38	3	711	87*	20.31	117.13	0	3	15	0

Bowling										
	Mat	Balls	Runs	Wkts	BBI	BBM	Ave	Econ	SR	5w	10
First-class	25	644	378	7	2/49	3/85	54.00	3.52	92.0	0	0
List A	48	996	951	28	3/28	3/28	33.96	5.72	35.5	0	0
Twenty20	41	312	415	22	4/15	4/15	18.86	7.98	14.1	0	0

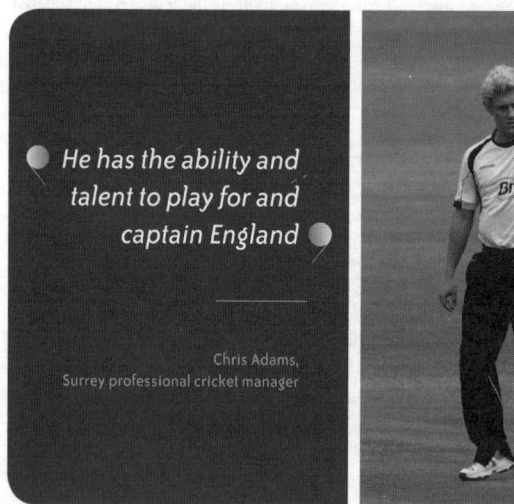

He has the ability and talent to play for and captain England

Chris Adams,
Surrey professional cricket manager

NAME: Arun Harinath
BORN: April 3, 1987, Sutton
HEIGHT: 5ft 11in
SQUAD Nº: 10
NICKNAME: The Baron
CAREER: First-class debut: 2010; List A debut: 2009

SURREY

AOC SAYS: Harinath has come through Surrey's academy and last season was the top-order batsman's first as a professional. After making three County Championship appearances in 2009 he scored 621 first-class runs for Surrey last season at an average of 25.87. He's been on Surrey's books since the age of nine and has so far made more of an inroad in the first-class game than he has in one-day cricket.

LAST WORD: "He can survive for long periods of time but the question now is can he take his game to the next level and work out how to score more runs? You couldn't wish to meet a nicer or more determined guy. He needs to add a run-scoring mentality to his game and work out his personal run-scoring options. He's proved he's got the concentration."
Ian Salisbury

Batting & Fielding

	Mat	Inns	NO	Runs	HS	Ave	SR	100	50	Ct	St
First-class	24	40	1	1001	69	25.66	40.62	0	7	7	0
List A	1	1	1	21	21*	-	80.76	0	0	0	0

Bowling

	Mat	Balls	Runs	Wkts	BBI	BBM	Ave	Econ	SR	5w	10
First-class	24	36	30	0	-	-	-	5.00	-	0	0
List A	1	-	-	-	-	-	-	-	-	-	-

TOM JEWELL

RHB RFM

SURREY

NAME: Thomas Melvin Jewell
BORN: January 13, 1991, Reading
HEIGHT: 6ft 1in
SQUAD Nº: 8
NICKNAME: Jeweller
CAREER: First-class debut: 2008; List A
debut: 2009

AOC SAYS: A bowling allrounder, Jewell signed a one-year professional contract with
Surrey in December 2010. He is a former Surrey youth player and plays club cricket for
Guildford in the Surrey Championship Premier Division, along with a number of other of
his fellow Brown Caps. His best match for Guildford came in a game against the Surrey
academy last June. He scored an impressive personal-best of 122 off 111 balls, having
already returned bowling figures of 5-48 in the match.

LAST WORD: "I was absolutely delighted to get my first professional contract, finally all the
hard work I've done at the academy has paid off! I've had a taste of first-team action and
it's let me know where I need to be to be able to get in the four-day side and stay there."
Tom Jewell

Batting & Fielding

	Mat	Inns	NO	Runs	HS	Ave	SR	100	50	Ct	St
First-class	4	2	1	5	4*	5.00	27.77	0	0	0	0
List A	2	2	1	1	1	1.00	11.11	0	0	0	0

Bowling

	Mat	Balls	Runs	Wkts	BBI	BBM	Ave	Econ	SR	5w	10
First-class	4	282	143	4	1/16	1/16	35.75	3.04	70.5	0	0
List A	2	36	56	0	-	-	-	9.33	-	0	0

NAME: Christopher James Jordan
BORN: October 4, 1988, Barbados
HEIGHT: 6ft 2in
SQUAD N°: 11
NICKNAME: CJ
CAREER: First-class debut: 2007; List A debut: 2007; T20 debut: 2008

SURREY

AOC SAYS: A hugely-promising cricketer, Jordan missed the entire 2010 campaign due to a stress fracture to his back. He returned to competitive cricket in the West Indies over the winter and has completed a gruelling rehabilitation programme. At the end of the 2009 season he was selected for the ECB Winter Performance Programme and is eligible to represent England through his grandmother. This will be a big season for Jordan, who could be a key component for Surrey if he can find his previously impressive form. First and foremost, however, the allrounder will be happy to get through the summer without any further injury problems.

LAST WORD: "He's built himself up fitness-wise over the winter and the reports I have heard say that he is bowling quickly and efficiently again. He needs to get his confidence by playing again but he's a very exciting cricketer, and at 22 he's still very young." *Ian Salisbury*

Batting & Fielding

	Mat	Inns	NO	Runs	HS	Ave	SR	100	50	Ct	St
First-class	21	25	7	433	57	24.05	48.59	0	1	7	0
List A	18	11	1	74	38	7.40	49.66	0	0	5	0
Twenty20	11	10	2	111	31	13.87	104.71	0	0	4	0

Bowling

	Mat	Balls	Runs	Wkts	BBI	BBM	Ave	Econ	SR	5w	10
First-class	21	3039	1824	45	4/84	5/73	40.53	3.60	67.5	0	0
List A	18	703	655	22	3/28	3/28	29.77	5.59	31.9	0	0
Twenty20	11	174	259	5	2/34	2/34	51.80	8.93	34.8	0	0

SIMON KING

RHB OB

NAME: Simon James King
BORN: September 4, 1987, Warlingham
HEIGHT: 6ft 1in
SQUAD Nº: 7
NICKNAME: Kingy
CAREER: First-class debut: 2009;
T20 debut: 2009

AOC SAYS: A consistent wicket-taker in the Surrey Second XI, offspinner King may get a chance to impress in the first team this season with Gareth Batty being Surrey's only other frontline spinner. He took 3-61 in the first innings of his County Championship debut against Middlesex at Lord's in 2009 and featured in Surrey's next first-class match, a draw against Derbyshire. His only first-team appearance of the 2010 campaign came against Bangladesh at The Oval, where he took the wicket of opener Jahurul Islam.

LAST WORD: "With only Gareth Batty tied in for the spinner's berth, they may be an opportunity for Simon King to come through, although he seems to have stalled a little bit. Like a lot of players he has a lot of potential, but he really needs to kick on." *Richard Spiller*

Batting & Fielding

	Mat	Inns	NO	Runs	HS	Ave	SR	100	50	Ct	St
First-class	3	2	0	8	8	4.00	25.80	0	0	0	0
Twenty20	1	1	1	5	5*	-	166.66	0	0	0	0

Bowling

	Mat	Balls	Runs	Wkts	BBI	BBM	Ave	Econ	SR	5w	10
First-class	3	405	290	5	3/61	3/95	58.00	4.29	81.0	0	0
Twenty20	1	18	28	0	-	-	-	9.33	-	0	0

TOM LANCEFIELD

LHB LM

NAME: Thomas John Lancefield
BORN: October 8, 1990, Epsom
HEIGHT: 5ft 8in
SQUAD Nº: 21
NICKNAME: Tommy, Creature, Creech
OTHER TEAMS: Tamil Union Cricket and
Athletic Club
CAREER: First-class debut: 2010; List A debut:
2009; T20 debut: 2010

SURREY

AOC SAYS: 2011 could prove to be a big summer for this exciting opening batsman. He
could have played professional rugby for Wasps but opted for a career with Surrey
instead. He's been at the county since the under 9 age group and forced his way into the
County Championship side in the second half of last season, playing seven times for Chris
Adams' side. He also made five appearances in the FP t20 before signing a professional
contract at The Oval in December. He spent time in Sri Lanka over the winter representing
the Tamil Union Cricket and Athletic Club.

LAST WORD: "Lancefield is developing quickly and is perhaps further ahead than some of
the other young lads." *Ian Salisbury*

Batting & Fielding

	Mat	Inns	NO	Runs	HS	Ave	SR	100	50	Ct	St
First-class	10	16	1	429	74	28.60	49.88	0	2	4	0
List A	1	1	0	20	20	20.00	117.64	0	0	1	0
Twenty20	5	3	0	65	27	21.66	125.00	0	0	1	0

Bowling

	Mat	Balls	Runs	Wkts	BBI	BBM	Ave	Econ	SR	5w	10
First-class	10	30	21	1	1/12	1/12	21.00	4.20	30.0	0	0
List A	1	-	-	-	-	-	-	-	-	-	-
Twenty20	5	0	0	0	-	-	-	-	-	0	0

TIM LINLEY

RHB RFM

SURREY

NAME: Timothy Edward Linley
BORN: March 23, 1982, Horseforth
HEIGHT: 6ft 2in
SQUAD Nº: 12
NICKNAME: Linners
OTHER TEAMS: Sussex
CAREER: First-class debut: 2003; List A
debut: 2009; T20 debut: 2009

AOC SAYS: A product of the MCC's university system, seamer Linley was released by Sussex in 2006 but signed for Surrey in 2009 after a number of years playing for their Second XI. 2010 proved to be a breakthrough season, with 20 first-team wickets coming his way despite the fact that he missed a large part of the summer due to a foot injury sustained after recording promising figures of 4-13 against Derbyshire. He will be looking to force his way into a regular first-team position with Surrey this season after extending his contract at The Oval by a further two years.

LAST WORD: "I can't think of many that have worked harder to get a deal and make a professional career than Tim Linley. He absolutely deserves everything he receives. Often the part you don't see as a supporter or a member is what a player brings into a dressing room and Tim is a fantastic team man, is good to have around and brings a great deal to the squad." *Chris Adams*

Batting & Fielding

	Mat	Inns	NO	Runs	HS	Ave	SR	100	50	Ct	St
First-class	20	24	5	228	42	12.00	37.74	0	0	6	0
List A	12	5	4	37	20*	37.00	78.72	0	0	1	0
Twenty20	5	2	0	9	8	4.50	112.50	0	0	1	0

Bowling

	Mat	Balls	Runs	Wkts	BBI	BBM	Ave	Econ	SR	5w	10
First-class	20	2676	1461	38	5/105	-	38.44	3.27	70.4	1	0
List A	12	420	404	5	2/38	2/38	80.80	5.77	84.0	0	0
Twenty20	5	86	104	3	1/17	1/17	34.66	7.25	28.6	0	0

NAME: Thomas Lloyd Maynard
BORN: March 25, 1989, Cardiff, Wales
HEIGHT: 6ft 2in
SQUAD Nº: 55
NICKNAME: George, Squirrel
OTHER TEAMS: Glamorgan
CAREER: First-class debut: 2007; List A
debut: 2007; T20 debut: 2007

SURREY

AOC SAYS: One of the most promising young batsmen on the county circuit, Maynard
joined Surrey on a three-year deal from Glamorgan during the close season. Tom said he
was unhappy about the treatment of his father Matthew, who resigned as Glamorgan's
director of cricket in November when he claimed his position had become untenable
amidst a major shake-up in Cardiff. Tom scored 495 first-class runs for Glamorgan last
season and smashed an unbeaten 78 off 49 balls against Surrey at The Oval in the FP t20.

LAST WORD: "We were on the receiving end of what he is capable of last season and
although this was not a signing we had planned for, it was an opportunity that was too
good not to take and I am delighted that Tom is adding further depth to what is looking like
a very strong squad." Chris Adams

Batting & Fielding

	Mat	Inns	NO	Runs	HS	Ave	SR	100	50	Ct	St
First-class	24	35	1	727	98	21.38	62.29	0	5	22	0
List A	41	39	3	1109	108	30.80	97.28	2	7	14	0
Twenty20	28	28	4	517	78*	21.54	135.69	0	3	13	0

Bowling

	Mat	Balls	Runs	Wkts	BBI	BBM	Ave	Econ	SR	5w	10
First-class	24	30	38	0	-	-	-	7.60	-	0	0
List A	41	12	32	0	-	-	-	16.00	-	0	0
Twenty20	28	-	-	-	-	-	-	-	-	-	-

STUART MEAKER

SURREY

NAME: Stuart Christopher Meaker
BORN: January 21, 1989, Durban
HEIGHT: 5ft 11in
SQUAD Nº: 18
NICKNAME: Meaksy, Herc
CAREER: First-class debut: 2008; List A debut: 2008; T20 debut: 2010

AOC SAYS: Meaker had quite a winter. He travelled to Queensland after being handed the Harold Larwood Scholarship, a new annual award that enables the young fast bowler who receives it to spend a winter in Australia receiving specialist coaching while playing grade cricket. Major flooding in the area disrupted his plans, however, so instead the South Africa-born bowler helped out with the massive clean-up operation. A genuinely exciting prospect, he took 29 first-class wickets last summer including a career-best 5-48 against Gloucestershire.

LAST WORD: "I think he could come to the fore and after Tremlett and Dernbach he could be the next seamer to come through. He's developed a ball that comes back in and now he's pretty hard work to face. I expect him to have a monster year." *Ian Salisbury*

Batting & Fielding

	Mat	Inns	NO	Runs	HS	Ave	SR	100	50	Ct	St
First-class	18	25	2	411	94	17.86	41.22	0	3	3	0
List A	15	4	2	16	10*	8.00	66.66	0	0	3	0
Twenty20	3	1	1	10	10*	-	142.85	0	0	1	0

Bowling

	Mat	Balls	Runs	Wkts	BBI	BBM	Ave	Econ	SR	5w	10
First-class	18	2493	1635	43	5/48	6/81	38.02	3.93	57.9	2	0
List A	15	492	524	11	2/21	2/21	47.63	6.39	44.7	0	0
Twenty20	3	60	88	3	2/36	2/36	29.33	8.80	20.0	0	0

NAME: Kevin Peter Pietersen
BORN: June 27, 1980, Pietermaritzburg
HEIGHT: 6ft 4in
SQUAD Nº: 24
NICKNAME: KP, Kelves, Kapes, Kev
OTHER TEAMS: England, Deccan Cargers,
Dolphins, Hampshire, KwaZulu-Natal, Natal,
Nottinghamshire, Royal Challengers Bangalore
CAREER: Test debut: 2005; ODI debut: 2004;
T20I debut: 2005; First-class debut: 1997; List A
debut: 1999; T20 debut: 2003 County cap: 2001
(Nottinghamshire), 2005 (Hampshire)

SURREY

AOC SAYS: Having spent time on loan at The Oval at the end of last season, Pietersen signed a full-time deal with Surrey over the winter, adding to the collection of England stars who ply their trade with Chris Adams' side. During his brief spell with Surrey last summer Pietersen played two Championship fixtures and scored 116 in a CB40 match against Sussex. One of 11 centrally-contracted players, Pietersen is unlikely to feature heavily for Surrey this summer, especially after returning to the England one-day side from which he was dropped for last summer's series against Pakistan. Any doubts that may have been raised about Pietersen last summer were dispelled during the winter's Ashes series in which he averaged 60 runs with a top score of 227. He played in four World Cup matches before returning to England for a hernia operation, and is now recovering in the hope he will be fit for the early season.

INSIDE TRACK: "When he first joined Surrey I was very impressed with everything: how he handled himself, his work ethic, how he spoke to the team, the effort he put in helping out in terms of what we're trying to do with the club. From that aspect he was exceptional. He got on well with players in the dressing room immediately. It's nice to know that he'll be looking for some cricket in April and May, so he will be able to give us some performances. The likelihood is that centrally-contracted players aren't going to be around a lot but when a player of that quality is available you make space for them, even if it's just for one outing. He's had a tough year but he still has the potential to be considered as England's number-one batsman. There's plenty of competition, from Alastair Cook in particular, and from Jonathan Trott. I think it would still be fair to say that Kevin has the potential to be regarded as England's premier batsman. I'm sure he'll be the first to admit that for that label to be attached to him at the moment there need to be more scores on a regular basis that affect a game. He has ability in abundance; watching him score that double hundred in Adelaide was magnificent." *Chris Adams*

KEVIN PIETERSEN

Batting & Fielding											
	Mat	Inns	NO	Runs	HS	Ave	SR	100	50	Ct	St
Tests	71	123	6	5666	227	48.42	62.37	17	21	44	0
ODIs	114	104	15	3648	116	40.98	87.00	7	22	33	0
T20Is	30	30	4	937	79	36.03	142.83	0	5	12	0
First-class	164	268	18	12253	254*	49.01	-	39	51	128	0
List A	227	208	32	7247	147	41.17	-	13	43	77	0
Twenty20	59	59	7	1662	79	31.96	139.19	0	9	21	0

Bowling										
	Mat	Balls	Runs	Wkts	BBI	BBM	Ave	Econ	SR	5w	10
Tests	71	873	584	5	1/0	1/10	116.80	4.01	174.6	0	0
ODIs	114	370	338	7	2/22	2/22	48.28	5.48	52.8	0	0
T20Is	30	30	53	1	1/27	1/27	53.00	10.60	30.0	0	0
First-class	164	5677	3295	62	4/31	-	53.14	3.48	91.5	0	0
List A	227	2360	2090	41	3/14	3/14	50.97	5.31	57.5	0	0
Twenty20	59	324	425	17	3/33	3/33	25.00	7.87	19.0	0	0

 *He scores so quickly and is so dominant when his cricket is flowing that he can be the difference between winning and drawing or losing*

Chris Adams

NAME: Mark Ravindra Ramprakash
BORN: September 5, 1969, Bushey
HEIGHT: 5ft 10in
SQUAD Nº: 77
NICKNAME: Ramps, Bloodaxe
OTHER TEAMS: England, Middlesex
CAREER: Test debut: 1991; ODI debut: 1991;
First-class debut: 1987; List A debut: 1987; T20
debut: 2003; County cap: 1990 (Middlesex),
2002 (Surrey)

AOC SAYS: Arguably the best batsman to have graced county cricket over the last two decades, Ramprakash signed a two-year contract extension with Surrey ahead of the 2011 campaign. However, he will miss at least the first month of the season due to a knee injury. Ramps has scored over 15,000 first-class runs for Surrey at an average of 74.4 and though he's just 12 months short of the 25th anniversary of his first-class debut, his batting is as dominant as ever. The Hertfordshire-born batsman has scored in excess of 1,000 first-class runs in every summer since 1998 and will almost certainly need to be a key contributor if The Oval outfit are to celebrate a return to Division One come the end of the summer.

LAST WORD: "Mark is the finest domestic batsman of his generation and still has a huge amount to offer Surrey. To have a man with his ability, experience and energy in your dressing room is simply something that cannot be bought." *Chris Adams*

Batting & Fielding

	Mat	Inns	NO	Runs	HS	Ave	SR	100	50	Ct	St
Tests	52	92	6	2350	154	27.32	36.18	2	12	39	0
ODIs	18	18	4	376	51	26.85	69.11	0	1	8	0
First-class	442	729	91	34839	301*	54.60	-	113	144	249	0
List A	407	394	64	13273	147*	40.22	-	17	85	137	0
Twenty20	63	63	10	1719	85*	32.43	125.01	0	13	21	0

Bowling

	Mat	Balls	Runs	Wkts	BBI	BBM	Ave	Econ	SR	5w	10
Tests	52	895	477	4	1/2	1/2	119.25	3.19	223.7	0	0
ODIs	18	132	108	4	3/28	3/28	27.00	4.90	33.0	0	0
First-class	442	4177	2202	34	3/32	-	64.76	3.16	122.8	0	0
List A	407	1734	1354	46	5/38	5/38	29.43	4.68	37.6	1	0
Twenty20	63	-	-	-	-	-	-	-	-	-	-

JASON ROY   RHB RM

NAME: Jason Jonathan Roy
BORN: July 21, 1990, Durban
HEIGHT: 5ft 11in
SQUAD Nº: 20
NICKNAME: JRoy
CAREER: First-class debut: 2010; List A
debut: 2008; T20 debut: 2008

AOC SAYS: Having come through the Surrey academy, Roy entered the county's record books last summer, scoring their first century in Twenty20 cricket. He did it against Kent Spitfires, smashing an unbeaten 101 off 57 balls. He also scored 76 on his first-class debut against Leicestershire and signed a two-year professional contract at The Oval in November. He ended last summer opening the batting in the County Championship and Surrey members are sure to see much more of this exciting talent during 2011.

LAST WORD: "In Jason we have one of the most destructive county batsmen playing today. He's one of the players I am certain has the ability to go all the way and I am delighted he signed a professional contract with us." *Chris Adams*

Batting & Fielding

	Mat	Inns	NO	Runs	HS	Ave	SR	100	50	Ct	St
First-class	3	5	0	170	76	34.00	104.93	0	2	0	0
List A	9	8	0	104	60	13.00	92.03	0	1	3	0
Twenty20	10	10	1	246	101*	27.33	148.19	1	1	2	0

Bowling

	Mat	Balls	Runs	Wkts	BBI	BBM	Ave	Econ	SR	5w	10
First-class	3	18	18	0	-	-	-	6.00	-	0	0
List A	9	6	12	0	-	-	-	12.00	-	0	0
Twenty20	10	-	-	-	-	-	-	-	-	-	-

NAME: Christopher Paul Schofield
BORN: October 6, 1978, Wardle, Rochdale
HEIGHT: 6ft 1in
SQUAD №: 30
NICKNAME: Schoey, Scho-boat
OTHER TEAMS: England, Lancashire
CAREER: Test debut: 2000; T20I debut: 2007;
First-class debut: 1998; T20 debut: 2003;
County cap: 2002 (Lancashire)

SURREY

AOC SAYS: Schofield's cricketing journey has been quite a remarkable one. He started his professional career at Lancashire and in 2000 was handed one of the ECB's first central contracts. However, after two Test matches against Zimbabwe in which Schofield took no wickets and scored 67 runs, the legspinning allrounder returned to county cricket and four summers later he was released by Lancashire. Schofield spent the following two years earning a living as a painter and decorator while playing Minor Counties cricket for Cheshire and Suffolk. He was picked up by Surrey in 2006 and, in a remarkable return to the top, he was named in England's squad for the 2007 World Twenty20 following an impressive Twenty20 Cup season.

LAST WORD: "How much cricket Schofield plays this summer will depend on how Surrey are looking to balance their side." *Richard Spiller*

Batting & Fielding

	Mat	Inns	NO	Runs	HS	Ave	SR	100	50	Ct	St
Tests	2	3	0	67	57	22.33	45.89	0	1	0	0
T20Is	4	4	3	24	9*	24.00	120.00	0	0	1	0
First-class	100	143	18	3644	144	29.15	-	1	26	57	0
List A	137	102	27	1794	75*	23.92	-	0	8	35	0
Twenty20	54	37	9	274	27	9.78	93.19	0	0	15	0

Bowling

	Mat	Balls	Runs	Wkts	BBI	BBM	Ave	Econ	SR	5w	10
Tests	2	108	73	0	-	-	-	4.05	-	0	0
T20Is	4	77	92	4	2/15	2/15	23.00	7.16	19.2	0	0
First-class	100	15702	8399	232	6/120	-	36.20	3.20	67.6	6	0
List A	137	4430	3857	141	5/31	5/31	27.35	5.22	31.4	2	0
Twenty20	54	939	1157	58	4/12	4/12	19.94	7.39	16.1	0	0

MATT SPRIEGEL

LHB OB

SURREY

NAME: Matthew Neil William Spriegel
BORN: March 4, 1987, Epsom
HEIGHT: 6ft 3in
SQUAD Nº: 28
NICKNAME: Spriegs
CAREER: First-class debut: 2007; List A debut: 2008; T20 debut: 2008

AOC SAYS: A regular in Surrey's CB40 and FP t20 sides last summer, Spriegel also played in 10 first-class fixtures, averaging 30.07. He scored 108 not out against Bangladesh and captained the Second XI to the Second XI Championship, taking 11 wickets at an average of 20 in his four matches. Predominantly a middle-order batsman, Spriegel will have to fight for his place in the Surrey first team this summer and a winter spent working on his already effective offspin bowling should help his cause.

LAST WORD: "We have been working on his batting consistently and he has the right attitude. He has had some good scores and he is grown up and mature enough to take it on the chin when things don't go well." *Ian Salisbury*

Batting & Fielding

	Mat	Inns	NO	Runs	HS	Ave	SR	100	50	Ct	St
First-class	31	50	3	1203	108*	25.59	41.66	3	3	23	0
List A	36	33	12	794	81*	37.80	84.82	0	6	19	0
Twenty20	31	23	11	219	25*	18.25	101.38	0	0	11	0

Bowling

	Mat	Balls	Runs	Wkts	BBI	BBM	Ave	Econ	SR	5w	10
First-class	31	1255	767	17	2/28	2/28	45.11	3.66	73.8	0	0
List A	36	1050	942	20	2/23	2/23	47.10	5.38	52.5	0	0
Twenty20	31	528	657	24	4/33	4/33	27.37	7.46	22.0	0	0

OVERSEAS PLAYER

NAME: Shaun William Tait
BORN: February 22, 1983, Bedford Park, Adelaide
HEIGHT: 6ft 4in
SQUAD Nº: 32
NICKNAME: Sloon
OTHER TEAMS: Australia. Durham, Glamorgan, Rajasthan Royals
CAREER: Test debut: 2005; ODI debut: 2007; T20I debut: 2007; First-class debut: 2002; List A debut: 2003; T20 debut: 2005

SURREY

AOC SAYS: Tait will join Surrey as an overseas player for the 2011 FP t20 and will be available for the entire tournament should the Lions make it all the way to Finals Day. The Aussie paceman has taken 81 career wickets in domestic Twenty20 at an average of 20.04, while at international level his has claimed 28 scalps at 17.78 apiece. During an ODI against England at Durham last summer, Tait bowled the second fastest recorded delivery in history. His fifth ball of the opening over of England's innings, bowled at Craig Kieswetter, clocked in at 100.1mph (161.kmph).

LAST WORD: "Games are invariably won and lost at the start and end of an innings. Having a bowler of Shaun's quality, ability and pace will make us an improved prospect for this year's FP t20." *Chris Adams*

Batting & Fielding

	Mat	Inns	NO	Runs	HS	Ave	SR	100	50	Ct	St
Tests	3	5	2	20	8	6.66	43.47	0	0	1	0
ODIs	35	7	5	25	11	12.50	86.20	0	0	8	0
T20Is	19	5	1	10	6	2.50	83.33	0	0	3	0
First-class	50	70	29	509	68	12.41	51.36	0	2	15	0
List A	98	35	19	109	22*	6.81	61.93	0	0	23	0
Twenty20	58	18	6	77	14*	6.41	74.03	0	0	12	0

Bowling

	Mat	Balls	Runs	Wkts	BBI	BBM	Ave	Econ	SR	5w	10
Tests	3	414	302	5	3/97	3/121	60.40	4.37	82.8	0	0
ODIs	35	1688	1461	62	4/39	4/39	23.56	5.19	27.2	0	0
T20Is	19	430	498	28	3/13	3/13	17.78	6.94	15.3	0	0
First-class	50	9263	5661	198	7/29	-	28.59	3.66	46.7	7	1
List A	98	4900	4171	178	8/43	8/43	23.43	5.10	27.5	3	0
Twenty20	58	1279	1624	81	4/14	4/14	20.04	7.61	15.7	0	0

SURREY

NAME: Christopher Timothy Tremlett
BORN: September 2, 1981, Southampton
HEIGHT: 6ft 7in
SQUAD Nº: 33
NICKNAME: Twiggy, Goober
OTHER TEAMS: England, Hampshire
CAREER: Test debut: 2007; ODI debut: 2005;
T20I debut: 2007; First-class debut: 2000;
List A debut: 2000; T20 debut: 2004
County cap: 2005 (Hampshire)

AOC SAYS: Tremlett's move from Hampshire to Surrey in January 2010 sparked the best 12 months of the tall paceman's career. He took a career-best 48 first-class wickets last summer at an average of 20.18 and also claimed 24 victims in Twenty20 cricket, striking at an average of 17.12. His impressive summer earned him a call to England's Ashes touring party, and when Stuart Broad's series ended prematurely Tremlett was handed a starting role in the third Test. He bowled superbly and returned figures of 5-87 in the second innings in Perth and was again in top form in the fourth Test, taking 4-26 as England reduced Australia to 98 all out. He completed the series with 3-79 in the second innings in Sydney as Andrew Strauss' side claimed their second successive innings victory over Australia. All-in-all the Surrey man played a pivotal role in England's retaining of the Ashes, taking 17 wickets across three Tests, adding to the 13 wickets he took in three appearances against India in 2007. He again replaced the injured Broad in England's squad for the World Cup and looks set to feature heavily for the Three Lions in 2011.

INSIDE TRACK: "One thing I always knew about Chris is that he has the natural ability to get the very best batsmen out. He has been able to find consistency because he has been on the park for more than three or four games in a row. Last summer he kept running in for three or four spells, leading from the front – I personally asked him to do this, to take this responsibility. It's often the case with a new county, it can get the best out of you and I think it did with Chris. The challenge for Chris now is to retain that level of performance we saw from him last year. He's gone a long way to be seriously considered for the first Test against Sri Lanka. I think he bowled quite beautifully in Australia. Immediately he looks like a Test bowler and I'm certain Andy Flower will be giving him serious consideration. I expect to see him in the first Test." *Chris Adams*

Batting & Fielding											
	Mat	Inns	NO	Runs	HS	Ave	SR	100	50	Ct	St
Tests	6	9	2	69	25*	9.85	41.56	0	0	1	0
ODIs	15	11	4	50	19*	7.14	56.17	0	0	4	0
T20Is	1	-	-	-	-	-	-	-	-	0	0
First-class	109	144	38	1903	64	17.95	-	0	7	29	0
List A	125	76	24	521	38*	10.01	-	0	0	26	0
Twenty20	41	15	6	72	13	8.00	105.88	0	0	5	0

Bowling										
	Mat	Balls	Runs	Wkts	BBI	BBM	Ave	Econ	SR	5w	10
Tests	6	1594	783	30	5/87	8/150	26.10	2.94	53.1	1	0
ODIs	15	784	705	15	4/32	4/32	47.00	5.39	52.2	0	0
T20Is	1	24	45	2	2/45	2/45	22.50	11.25	12.0	0	0
First-class	109	18678	9827	361	6/44	-	27.22	3.15	51.7	8	0
List A	125	5787	4718	170	4/25	4/25	27.75	4.89	34.0	0	0
Twenty20	41	891	1065	56	4/25	4/25	19.01	7.17	15.9	0	0

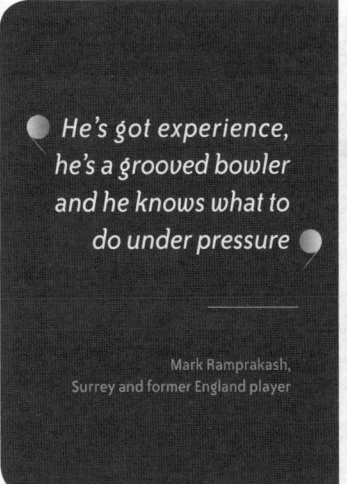

He's got experience, he's a grooved bowler and he knows what to do under pressure

Mark Ramprakash, Surrey and former England player

GARY WILSON

SURREY

NAME: Gary Craig Wilson
BORN: February 5, 1986, Dundonald, Northern Ireland
HEIGHT: 5ft 10in
SQUAD Nº: 14
NICKNAME: Gaz, Wils
OTHER TEAMS: Ireland
CAREER: ODI debut: 2007; T20I debut: 2008; First-class debut: 2005; List A debut: 2006; T20 debut: 2008

AOC SAYS: Understudy to first-choice keeper Steven Davies, Wilson's chances to impress have been few and far between, particularly because of his own international commitments with Ireland. After an impressive showing with the bat in 2010, however, he may be able to force his way into the side as a specialist batsman when Davies is available. In six first-class matches last summer, Wilson averaged 44 with the bat, including his maiden County Championship century against Leicestershire last August, a knock that attracted considerable praise from Mark Ramprakash. In March, Wilson extended his Surrey contract until 2012.

LAST WORD: "Gary is a hugely popular member of the playing staff here both in the dressing room and around the club in general. I am very pleased he extended his contract in March and look forward to him continuing to develop his game over the next two years."
Chris Adams

Batting & Fielding

	Mat	Inns	NO	Runs	HS	Ave	SR	100	50	Ct	St
ODIs	29	28	2	729	113	28.03	74.01	1	5	16	6
T20Is	15	13	1	193	29	16.08	80.75	0	0	8	0
First-class	17	25	3	665	125	30.22	-	1	2	34	1
List A	77	69	5	1497	113	23.39	68.98	1	11	51	15
Twenty20	38	31	7	372	36*	15.50	97.63	0	0	24	4

Bowling

	Mat	Balls	Runs	Wkts	BBI	BBM	Ave	Econ	SR	5w	10
ODIs	-	-	-	-	-	-	-	-	-	-	-
T20Is	-	-	-	-	-	-	-	-	-	-	-
First-class	17	66	46	0	-	-	-	4.18	-	0	0
List A	-	-	-	-	-	-	-	-	-	-	-
Twenty20	-	-	-	-	-	-	-	-	-	-	-

OVERSEAS PLAYER

NAME: Yasir Arafat Satti
BORN: March 12, 1982, Rawalpindi, Pakistan
HEIGHT: 5ft 10 in
SQUAD Nº: 26
NICKNAME: Yas
OTHER TEAMS: Pakistan, Kent, Otago, Rawalpindi, Scotland, Sussex
CAREER: Test debut: 2007; ODI debut: 2000; T20I debut: 2007; First-class debut: 1997; List A debut: 1998; T20 debut: 2006; County cap: 2006 (Sussex), 2007 (Kent)

AOC SAYS: One of the most experienced overseas players on the county scene, Arafat has joined Surrey for the entire 2011 season. A right-arm fast-medium seamer who has the ability to swing the ball both ways, the former Pakistan international is also a strong lower-order batsman, averaging 26.74 in first-class cricket. This will be Arafat's eighth season of English domestic cricket having enjoyed previous spells at Kent, Scotland and Sussex.

LAST WORD: "I'm thrilled to have signed Arafat as our overseas player. He's a wonderful player who knows county cricket inside out. He can perform in all forms of the game; he's an outstanding one-day bowler and will also be an important cog in our wheel moving forward for four-day cricket. I have a feeling we'll see some fabulous performances from him." *Chris Adams*

Batting & Fielding

	Mat	Inns	NO	Runs	HS	Ave	SR	100	50	Ct	St
Tests	3	3	1	94	50*	47.00	46.76	0	1	0	0
ODIs	11	8	3	74	27	14.80	67.27	0	0	2	0
T20Is	7	7	4	64	17	21.33	156.09	0	0	1	0
First-class	176	258	38	5884	122	26.74	-	4	31	49	0
List A	212	152	40	2371	110*	21.16	-	1	7	48	0
Twenty20	92	64	20	746	49	16.95	125.37	0	0	13	0

Bowling

	Mat	Balls	Runs	Wkts	BBI	BBM	Ave	Econ	SR	5w	10
Tests	3	627	438	9	5/161	7/210	48.66	4.19	69.6	1	0
ODIs	11	414	373	4	1/28	1/28	93.25	5.40	103.5	0	0
T20Is	7	150	195	6	3/32	3/32	32.50	7.80	25.0	0	0
First-class	176	29258	16887	713	9/35	-	23.68	3.46	41.0	42	5
List A	212	10191	8407	335	6/24	6/24	25.09	4.94	30.4	5	0
Twenty20	92	1908	2491	112	4/17	4/17	22.24	7.83	17.0	0	0

SUSSEX

FORMED: 1839
HOME GROUND: County Ground, Hove
ONE-DAY NAME: Sharks
CAPTAIN: Michael Yardy
2010 RESULTS: CC2: Champions; CB40: 2/7 in Group A; FP t20: Quarter-finalists

HONOURS

County Championship: (3) 2003, 2006, 2007; Gillette/NatWest/C&G/FP Trophy: (5) 1963, 1964, 1978, 1986, 2006; Pro40/National League/CB40: (2) 2008, 2009; Sunday League: 1982; Twenty20 Cup: 2009

THE LOWDOWN

Having suffered a shock relegation from Division One of the Championship in 2009, Sussex bounced back emphatically last year, winning exactly half of their 16 games. A consistently slick one-day side, they looked similarly unstoppable in the FP t20 until a slump in form, precipitated by the loss of several players to international duty, culminated in a last-eight defeat to Notts. It remains to be seen whether the Martlets will stutter again if they are without the likes of Matt Prior, Monty Panesar, Luke Wright and skipper Mike Yardy for large chunks of this summer, but the shrewd acquisition of bowling reinforcements in the form of Wayne Parnell, Naved Arif and the wily Rana Naved will undoubtedly bolster their first-class chances. Runs may be harder to come by than wickets for Mark Robinson's charges, and we could see plenty of chopping and changing of the top six if things don't go well in early season.

CRICKET MANAGER: MARK ROBINSON

An honest seamer with a decent county record, Robinson played with Northants, Yorkshire and finally Sussex, before calling time on a 15-year career in 2002. Taking over first-team duties at Hove after Peter Moores' elevation to ECB academy director, Robinson led the club to a magnificent double in 2006. A phlegmatic, straightforward character, Robinson has an excellent track record of nurturing youth talent.

With thanks to: Mark Robinson; Bruce Talbot, The Argus

	Mat	Inns	NO	Runs	HS	Ave	SR	100	50	Ct	St
RG Aga	2	2	1	66	66*	66.00	64.70	0	1	1	-
RSC Martin-Jenkins	9	13	3	629	130	62.90	68.51	2	5	4	-
EC Joyce	10	17	3	738	164	52.71	54.99	2	3	17	-
MW Goodwin	16	26	3	1201	142	52.21	64.56	4	5	5	-
WA Adkin	1	1	0	45	45	45.00	32.37	0	0	0	-
BC Brown	9	14	2	515	112	42.91	65.18	2	2	9	2
LJ Wright	9	12	1	465	134	42.27	80.03	1	3	3	-
CD Nash	17	29	2	1051	184	38.92	70.72	3	3	12	-
Yasir Arafat	9	9	2	255	58	36.42	49.32	0	2	1	-
LWP Wells	1	2	0	70	62	35.00	36.08	0	1	0	-
Naved-ul-Hasan	5	8	2	208	101	34.66	82.21	1	1	0	-
OP Rayner	7	10	2	256	67*	32.00	57.14	0	2	10	-
MH Yardy	9	13	2	345	100*	31.36	52.35	1	1	1	-
MJ Prior	7	11	1	296	123*	29.60	66.36	1	0	19	0
AJ Hodd	10	14	1	319	109	24.53	52.46	1	1	29	1
MA Thornely	12	21	1	467	89	23.35	44.22	0	4	8	-
JS Gatting	8	11	0	155	31	14.09	44.15	0	0	4	-
JE Anyon	11	15	0	174	34	11.60	34.93	0	0	3	-
MS Panesar	15	19	5	154	46*	11.00	29.96	0	0	1	-
CD Collymore	14	17	8	78	19*	8.66	30.70	0	0	3	-
LJ Hatchett	4	4	0	30	20	7.50	27.77	0	0	1	-
MW Machan	1	2	0	11	6	5.50	30.55	0	0	0	-
WAT Beer	2	1	1	37	37*	-	32.45	0	0	1	-

Batting & Fielding

	Mat	Overs	Mdns	Runs	Wkts	BBI	BBM	Ave	Econ	SR	5w	10
CD Nash	17	56.0	10	126	8	4/12	4/12	15.75	2.25	42.0	0	0
MA Thornely	12	21.0	2	75	4	2/14	2/14	18.75	3.57	31.5	0	0
JS Gatting	8	5.0	2	19	1	1/19	1/19	19.00	3.80	30.0	0	0
RSC Martin-Jenkins	9	201.1	35	593	30	5/45	6/77	19.76	2.94	40.2	1	0
CD Collymore	14	414.0	115	1133	57	6/48	8/90	19.87	2.73	43.5	2	0
LJ Hatchett	4	66.4	15	256	12	5/47	6/92	21.33	3.84	33.3	1	0
WAT Beer	2	32.4	7	111	5	3/31	3/61	22.20	3.39	39.2	0	0
OP Rayner	7	148.2	38	412	18	4/62	6/78	22.88	2.77	49.4	0	0
Yasir Arafat	9	256.0	43	896	36	5/74	9/117	24.88	3.50	42.6	2	0
LJ Wright	9	154.5	22	573	23	5/65	5/65	24.91	3.70	40.3	1	0
MS Panesar	15	516.2	135	1328	52	5/44	8/114	25.53	2.57	59.5	2	0
JE Anyon	11	227.2	41	767	29	3/23	5/71	26.44	3.37	47.0	0	0
Naved-ul-Hasan	5	162.4	44	532	20	4/28	7/117	26.60	3.27	48.8	0	0
WA Adkin	1	11.0	2	38	1	1/38	1/38	38.00	3.45	66.0	0	0
RG Aga	2	34.0	10	99	2	2/29	2/61	49.50	2.91	102.0	0	0
MS Chadwick	1	19.0	2	74	1	1/41	1/74	74.00	3.89	114.0	0	0
LWP Wells	1	2.0	0	16	0	-	-	-	8.00	-	0	0

Bowling

SUSSEX
SHARKS

	Mat	Inns	NO	Runs	HS	Ave	SR	100	50	Ct	St
BC Brown	2	2	1	81	58	81.00	119.11	0	1	3	0
MH Yardy	6	6	3	216	66*	72.00	127.81	0	2	3	-
OP Rayner	5	4	3	62	35*	62.00	105.08	0	0	3	-
LJ Wright	3	3	0	149	95	49.66	133.03	0	1	2	-
RSC Martin-Jenkins	6	5	3	92	35*	46.00	124.32	0	0	2	-
RG Aga	4	3	2	46	23*	46.00	69.69	0	0	0	-
EC Joyce	7	7	0	299	117	42.71	107.55	1	0	4	-
CD Nash	11	11	0	457	85	41.54	105.29	0	5	3	-
MW Goodwin	11	11	1	402	92*	40.20	113.23	0	4	1	-
AJ Hodd	10	8	2	225	91	37.50	107.65	0	1	7	6
MJ Prior	5	5	0	183	64	36.60	107.01	0	1	1	-
MA Thornely	6	6	0	186	67	31.00	76.54	0	2	2	-
WA Adkin	1	1	0	30	30	30.00	78.94	0	0	0	-
JS Gatting	10	10	2	230	71	28.75	98.29	0	2	4	-
Naved-ul-Hasan	4	3	0	50	26	16.66	125.00	0	0	0	-
CB Keegan	6	4	2	24	12	12.00	126.31	0	0	1	-
JE Anyon	1	1	0	12	12	12.00	109.09	0	0	0	-
MW Machan	1	1	0	10	10	10.00	43.47	0	0	0	-
Yasir Arafat	5	2	0	19	14	9.50	63.33	0	0	1	-
MS Panesar	12	1	0	9	9	9.00	128.57	0	0	0	-
LWP Wells	1	1	0	9	9	9.00	60.00	0	0	1	-
CJ Liddle	3	1	0	3	3	3.00	50.00	0	0	2	-
RJ Kirtley	11	2	2	7	5*	-	87.50	0	0	2	-
JA Thorpe	1	1	1	3	3*	-	60.00	0	0	0	-

	Mat	Overs	Mdns	Runs	Wkts	BBI	Ave	Econ	SR	5W
JE Anyon	1	7.0	0	29	3	3/29	9.66	4.14	14.0	0
WA Adkin	1	6.0	0	16	1	1/16	16.00	2.66	36.0	0
RJ Kirtley	11	72.4	2	476	24	4/30	19.83	6.55	18.1	0
Naved-ul-Hasan	4	29.0	1	152	7	3/37	21.71	5.24	24.8	0
LJ Wright	3	10.3	0	97	4	3/41	24.25	9.23	15.7	0
CJ Liddle	3	18.0	0	126	5	4/49	25.20	7.00	21.6	0
JA Thorpe	1	3.0	0	26	1	1/26	26.00	8.66	18.0	0
CD Nash	11	11.0	0	79	3	1/8	26.33	7.18	22.0	0
CB Keegan	6	37.5	4	246	9	2/23	27.33	6.50	25.2	0
MS Panesar	12	85.4	4	406	14	3/21	29.00	4.73	36.7	0
MH Yardy	6	38.0	1	199	5	1/10	39.80	5.23	45.6	0
OP Rayner	5	31.0	2	164	4	2/33	41.00	5.29	46.5	0
Yasir Arafat	5	33.3	0	238	5	2/37	47.60	7.10	40.2	0
RSC Martin-Jenkins	6	36.0	0	196	3	1/17	65.33	5.44	72.0	0
RG Aga	4	14.2	0	75	1	1/33	75.00	5.23	86.0	0

SUSSEX SHARKS

	Mat	Inns	NO	Runs	HS	Ave	SR	100	50	Ct	St
OP Rayner	5	3	2	69	41*	69.00	104.54	0	0	0	-
MH Yardy	8	8	4	187	76*	46.75	124.66	0	1	3	-
MJ Prior	14	14	1	443	117	34.07	169.08	1	2	6	0
BB McCullum	7	7	1	200	59*	33.33	145.98	0	1	4	-
MW Goodwin	17	17	1	405	76*	25.31	128.16	0	2	5	-
CD Nash	17	15	3	299	60*	24.91	128.32	0	1	3	-
DR Smith	13	12	1	215	49	19.54	139.61	0	0	4	-
LJ Wright	8	8	0	155	39	19.37	146.22	0	0	1	-
AJ Hodd	13	9	2	131	26	18.71	128.43	0	0	1	3
Yasir Arafat	13	10	4	104	25*	17.33	108.33	0	0	4	-
JS Gatting	17	14	4	157	30*	15.70	134.18	0	0	6	-
RSC Martin-Jenkins	7	2	1	12	11	12.00	133.33	0	0	4	-
CB Keegan	12	8	1	75	26	10.71	119.04	0	0	3	-
WAT Beer	12	5	2	32	22	10.66	96.96	0	0	4	-
EC Joyce	8	8	0	74	22	9.25	82.22	0	0	1	-
RJ Kirtley	16	5	5	21	11*	-	116.66	0	0	2	-

Batting & Fielding

	Mat	Overs	Mdns	Runs	Wkts	BBI	Ave	Econ	SR	5W
CD Nash	17	33.0	0	226	13	2/17	17.38	6.84	15.2	0
MH Yardy	8	29.0	0	159	8	2/14	19.87	5.48	21.7	0
OP Rayner	5	16.0	0	105	5	1/16	21.00	6.56	19.2	0
CB Keegan	12	40.3	0	319	12	3/11	26.58	7.87	20.2	0
WAT Beer	12	37.0	0	268	10	3/19	26.80	7.24	22.2	0
Yasir Arafat	13	47.2	0	391	13	4/34	30.07	8.26	21.8	0
RJ Kirtley	16	52.1	0	423	13	3/3	32.53	8.10	24.0	0
DR Smith	13	33.4	0	276	8	2/19	34.50	8.19	25.2	0
RSC Martin-Jenkins	7	24.0	1	200	4	1/16	50.00	8.33	36.0	0
LJ Wright	8	20.0	0	169	2	2/33	84.50	8.45	60.0	0

Bowling

WILLIAM ADKIN

LHB RM

SUSSEX

NAME: William Anthony Adkin
BORN: April 9, 1990, Redhill
HEIGHT: 6ft 10in
SQUAD Nº: 21
NICKNAME: Wadkin, Crouchy
CAREER: First-class debut: 2010; List A
debut: 2010

AOC SAYS: It's not just Adkin's height that is impressive. Having been thrown in for his Championship debut at short notice against Surrey last season, the promising allrounder compiled a watchful 45 to rescue his side from 101-7, while he claimed a wicket with his first ball in one-day cricket in a match against the touring Bangladeshis. Currently completing the last year of his degree at Southampton Solent university, Sussex expect to have Adkin's undivided attention at the end of May, with good judges suggesting he has both the talent and composure to feature much more prominently for the Martlets over the next two years.

LAST WORD: "Will has the potential to become a great allrounder. He is a good bowler, which his size helps, and although he was a bit of a late developer his batting is up to a good standard too." *Mark Robinson*

Batting & Fielding

	Mat	Inns	NO	Runs	HS	Ave	SR	100	50	Ct	St
First-class	1	1	0	45	45	45.00	32.37	0	0	0	0
List A	1	1	0	30	30	30.00	78.94	0	0	0	0

Bowling

	Mat	Balls	Runs	Wkts	BBI	BBM	Ave	Econ	SR	5w	10
First-class	1	66	38	1	1/38	1/38	38.00	3.45	66.0	0	0
List A	1	36	16	1	1/16	1/16	16.00	2.66	36.0	0	0

NAME: Naved Arif Gondal
BORN: November 2, 1981, Punjab, Pakistan
SQUAD Nº: 8
OTHER TEAMS: Gujranwala Cricket
Association, Sialkot, Sialkot Stallions
CAREER: First-class debut: 2001; List A
debut: 2001; T20 debut: 2009

SUSSEX

AOC SAYS: A late developer, particularly by Pakistani standards, Arif is a brisk left-arm seamer
with an excellent record in first class cricket. Also capable of providing some lower-order
runs, his main job will be to take the new ball alongside Amjad Khan in the Championship.
A relative unknown outside of his own country, Sussex will hope that he will also bring an X
Factor to their attack, while Monty Panesar will hope to exploit the footmarks created by Arif's
over-the-wicket approach. The 29-year-old – who has played at A team level in Pakistan –
joins the squad as a home-qualified player by virtue of his Danish wife.

LAST WORD: "Naved has had to do it the tough way. His record out there on unhelpful
wickets is outstanding and he's got the potential to change games." *Mark Robinson*

Batting & Fielding

	Mat	Inns	NO	Runs	HS	Ave	SR	100	50	Ct	St
First-class	30	38	12	410	49	15.76	-	0	0	11	0
List A	10	4	0	77	49	19.25	124.19	0	0	3	0
Twenty20	5	2	2	1	1*	-	33.33	0	0	1	0

Bowling

	Mat	Balls	Runs	Wkts	BBI	BBM	Ave	Econ	SR	5w	10
First-class	30	6167	3375	145	7/66	-	23.27	3.28	42.5	10	1
List A	10	330	361	9	3/19	3/19	40.11	6.56	36.6	0	0
Twenty20	5	108	104	6	2/13	2/13	17.33	5.77	18.0	0	0

JAMES ANYON

LHB RFM

SUSSEX

NAME: James Edward Anyon
BORN: May 5, 1983, Lancaster
HEIGHT: 6ft 2in
SQUAD №: 30
NICKNAME: Jimmy, Cheese 'n'
OTHER TEAMS: Surrey, Warwickshire
CAREER: First-class debut: 2003; List A debut: 2004; T20 debut: 2005

AOC SAYS: A product of Loughborough MCCU, Anyon made his debut for Warwickshire in 2005. Despite a reasonable record he failed, partly due to injury, to ever fully cement a spot in the first team and after playing just three games for the Bears in 2009, he was loaned out to Surrey for the final month of the season. Snapped up by Sussex over the winter, he was a valuable member of the promotion-winning squad last year, claiming 26 wickets at 27 in 10 Championship outings. The presence of Amjad Khan, Naved Arif, Wayne Parnell and Rana Naved suggests another supporting role for this reliable seamer in 2011, but Anyon has the experience and know-how to take the new ball if required. Unlikely to feature in coloured clothing barring injuries elsewhere.

LAST WORD: "He's at a great age and is hungry." *Mark Robinson*

Batting & Fielding

	Mat	Inns	NO	Runs	HS	Ave	SR	100	50	Ct	St
First-class	58	74	25	538	37*	10.97	32.39	0	0	18	0
List A	38	11	5	34	12	5.66	80.95	0	0	8	0
Twenty20	21	3	3	16	8*	-	72.72	0	0	3	0

Bowling

	Mat	Balls	Runs	Wkts	BBI	BBM	Ave	Econ	SR	5w	10
First-class	58	8727	5276	141	6/82	-	37.41	3.62	61.8	2	0
List A	38	1375	1254	41	3/6	3/6	30.58	5.47	33.5	0	0
Twenty20	21	333	481	25	3/6	3/6	19.24	8.66	13.3	0	0

NAME: William Andrew Thomas Beer
BORN: October 8, 1988, Crawley
HEIGHT: 5ft 9in
SQUAD Nº: 18
NICKNAME: Ferret, Beero
CAREER: First-class debut: 2008; List A debut: 2009; T20 debut: 2008

SUSSEX

AOC SAYS: One of a clutch of promising young leggies in county cricket, Beer announced himself in the English game in 2009, when his middle-innings bowling (including 2-29 in the final) helped Sussex to lift the Twenty20 Cup. The reward for his performances that season was a three-year deal at Hove, while the ECB also recognised his pedigree in selecting him for their Elite Spin Bowling Programme. Unlike his predecessor Mushtaq Ahmed, Beer's stock delivery is a well-flighted legbreak and he is capable of appreciable spin when conditions suit. Despite being given limited opportunities last season, he remains highly thought of on the south coast, and aged just 22 has plenty of time to the make the sort of impact his talent warrants.

LAST WORD: "I was very impressed with both of them. They have their own styles but a lot in common and they can bowl most variations." *Shane Warne on Will Beer and Somerset's Max Waller after a masterclass at The Oval in 2009*

Batting & Fielding

	Mat	Inns	NO	Runs	HS	Ave	SR	100	50	Ct	St
First-class	58	74	25	538	37*	10.97	32.39	0	0	18	0
List A	38	11	5	34	12	5.66	80.95	0	0	8	0
Twenty20	21	3	3	16	8*	-	72.72	0	0	3	0

Bowling

	Mat	Balls	Runs	Wkts	BBI	BBM	Ave	Econ	SR	5w	10
First-class	58	8727	5276	141	6/82	-	37.41	3.62	61.8	2	0
List A	38	1375	1254	41	3/6	3/6	30.58	5.47	33.5	0	0
Twenty20	21	333	481	25	3/6	3/6	19.24	8.66	13.3	0	0

BEN BROWN

RHB WK

SUSSEX

NAME: Ben Christopher Brown
BORN: November 23, 1988, Crawley
HEIGHT: 5ft 8in
SQUAD Nº: 26
CAREER: First-class debut: 2007; List A
debut: 2007; T20 debut: 2008

AOC SAYS: Another former under England 19 player, Brown made major strides last season with some assured performances at No.3 in the second half of the Championship campaign, including a second first-class ton. 400 runs at 37 earned him a new two-year contract at the club he has been with since his teenage years, and if Brown can continue to improve his already tidy glovework he has a decent chance of adding to his limited-overs appearances. Regardless of this, with Matt Prior likely to be largely unavailable because of his England commitments and spots up for grabs in Sussex's top-order, this talented local lad can expect to play a major part in Sussex's four-day side in what is potentially his breakthrough season.

LAST WORD: "He's good enough to play as a specialist batsman, but he will put pressure on Andrew Hodd for that first-team spot." *Bruce Talbot*

Batting & Fielding

	Mat	Inns	NO	Runs	HS	Ave	SR	100	50	Ct	St
First-class	10	15	2	561	112	43.15	68.83	2	2	9	2
List A	11	7	3	112	58	28.00	114.28	0	1	8	1
Twenty20	9	5	1	19	7	4.75	90.47	0	0	3	0

Bowling

	Mat	Balls	Runs	Wkts	BBI	BBM	Ave	Econ	SR	5w	10
First-class	10	-	-	-	-	-	-	-	-	-	-
List A	11	-	-	-	-	-	-	-	-	-	-
Twenty20	9	-	-	-	-	-	-	-	-	-	-

NAME: Joe Stephen Gatting
BORN: November 25, 1987, Brighton
SQUAD Nº: 25
CAREER: First-class debut: 2009; List A
debut: 2009; T20 debut: 2009

SUSSEX

AOC SAYS: The nephew of former England captain Mike and son of Brighton football legend Steve, Joe made the decision to leave football behind during the 2008/09 winter to train with the Sussex squad. Initially selected on the club's Academy Plus scheme, a brilliant century against Surrey in the pre-season Pro ARCH tournament in Abu Dhabi led to a full contract prior to the start of the 2009 season. In the two years since, Gatting has struggled for consistency, and while his excellent fielding has enabled him to tie down a regular sport in coloured clothing, a first-class average of under 30 is far from convincing. A high score of 24 in seven Championship outings in 2010 speaks for itself and he will have to show strong form in pre-season to convince his coaches he's ready to make a major contribution in 2011.

LAST WORD: "We are all excited by the prospect of watching his career develop at Hove."
Mark Robinson

Batting & Fielding

	Mat	Inns	NO	Runs	HS	Ave	SR	100	50	Ct	St
First-class	12	17	0	465	152	27.35	59.01	1	1	6	0
List A	23	22	3	555	99*	29.21	81.02	0	4	7	0
Twenty20	24	18	4	213	30*	15.21	124.56	0	0	6	0

Bowling

	Mat	Balls	Runs	Wkts	BBI	BBM	Ave	Econ	SR	5w	10
First-class	12	30	19	1	1/19	1/19	19.00	3.80	30.0	0	0
List A	23	8	5	0	-	-	-	3.75	-	0	0
Twenty20	24	-	-	-	-	-	-	-	-	-	-

1ld. lea

MURRAY GOODWIN — RHB LB R8 MVP50

SUSSEX

NAME: Murray William Goodwin
BORN: December 11, 1972, Harare, Zimbabwe
HEIGHT: 5ft 9in
SQUAD Nº: 3
NICKNAME: Snapper, Goodie, Muzz the Fuzz
OTHER TEAMS: Zimbabwe, Mashonaland, Warriors, Netherlands, Western Australia
CAREER: Test debut: 1998; ODI debut: 1998; First-class debut: 1994; List A debut: 1994; T20 debut: 2003; County cap: 2001

AOC SAYS: An all-time Sussex legend, Goodwin has failed to make 1,000 runs just three times in his 11 seasons with the Martlets. An intelligent and prolific batsman, he twice passed 1,500 as he helped the club secure their first and second Championship titles in 2003 and 2006, while another 1,200 runs in 2007 helped Sussex retain the title and secured his reputation as one of the county game's class acts. Equally effective in one-day cricket, Goodwin's finest hour as a Shark came in 2008 when a rapid 87, including a last-ball six, secured the Pro40 for Mark Robinson's side. 37 and still going strong, another 1,200 runs last season showed that the fires continue to burn brightly, while an average of 43 in 19 Tests for Zimbabwe is evidence enough of what could have been had he not walked away from the international arena more than a decade ago.

LAST WORD: "I wouldn't be surprised if he went on for another four or five years."
Bruce Talbot

Batting & Fielding

	Mat	Inns	NO	Runs	HS	Ave	SR	100	50	Ct	St
Tests	19	37	4	1414	166*	42.84	46.31	3	8	10	0
ODIs	71	70	3	1818	112*	27.13	68.50	2	8	20	0
First-class	266	461	38	20381	344*	48.18	-	63	84	144	0
List A	340	326	38	10384	167	36.05	-	13	66	103	0
Twenty20	73	68	8	1671	102*	27.85	120.47	1	9	15	0

Bowling

	Mat	Balls	Runs	Wkts	BBI	BBM	Ave	Econ	SR	5w	10
Tests	19	119	69	0	-	-	-	3.47	-	0	0
ODIs	71	248	210	4	1/12	1/12	52.50	5.08	62.0	0	0
First-class	266	713	376	7	2/23		53.71	3.16	101.8	0	0
List A	340	351	306	7	1/9	1/9	43.71	5.23	50.1	0	0
Twenty20	73	-	-	-	-	-	-	-	-	-	-

NAME: Lewis James Hatchett
BORN: January 21, 1990, Shoreham-by-Sea
SQUAD Nº: 5
NICKNAME: Hatchy, Larry, McRib, Bigfoot, The Hatchett Man
CAREER: First-class debut: 2010

SUSSEX

AOC SAYS: Like East Grinstead teammate Will Adkin, Hatchett was given the chance to impress at the end of last season and didn't disappoint. Two wickets on his Championship debut were followed by a five-fer (including four wickets in 11 balls) against Leicestershire, a match that was watched by England selector Geoff Miller. Hatchett himself put these performances down to a mixture of strength and conditioning work and a productive winter away in Australia in 2009/10 where he was able work on some technical aspects of his game and learned to bring a more relaxed attitude to his cricket. He has every chance of adding to his four first-class appearances in 2011.

LAST WORD: "Getting a contract has been my dream since I was little. Now I've really got to step up my game." *Lewis Hatchett*

Batting & Fielding

	Mat	Inns	NO	Runs	HS	Ave	SR	100	50	Ct	St
First-class	4	4	0	30	20	7.50	27.77	0	0	1	0

Bowling

	Mat	Balls	Runs	Wkts	BBI	BBM	Ave	Econ	SR	5w	10
First-class	4	400	256	12	5/47	6/92	21.33	3.84	33.3	1	0

SUSSEX

NAME: Andrew John Hodd
BORN: January 12, 1984, Chichester
HEIGHT: 5ft 10in
SQUAD Nº: 19
NICKNAME: Hoddy, Hodd-dog
OTHER TEAMS: Surrey
CAREER: First-class debut: 2003; List A
debut: 2002; T20 debut: 2005

AOC SAYS: Having left Sussex for Surrey in 2004 in search of more regular first-team cricket, Hodd returned to Hove in 2006 in the wake of Tim Ambrose's departure to Warwickshire. With Matt Prior regularly away on international duty in recent years, he has had plenty of opportunities to impress and his smart glovework and busy batting have fitted in well to the Sharks' slick one-day unit. A lack of significant contributions with the bat in four-day cricket and the emergence of Ben Brown, however, means that Hodd is no longer guaranteed the number one spot in Prior's absence and, at the age of 27, the likeable stumper knows he must get his Championship average the right side of 35 sooner rather than later.

LAST WORD: "One-day cricket worked quite well for me last year, but my Championship form fell off a little bit and I've got healthy competition from Ben Brown. I think that's good for the both of us and hopefully it will spur me on to improve my game." *Andy Hodd*

Batting & Fielding

	Mat	Inns	NO	Runs	HS	Ave	SR	100	50	Ct	St
First-class	48	68	11	1686	123	29.57	43.65	4	8	93	11
List A	37	30	8	552	91	25.09	-	0	1	29	8
Twenty20	34	17	2	199	26	13.26	117.05	0	0	11	9

Bowling

	Mat	Balls	Runs	Wkts	BBI	BBM	Ave	Econ	SR	5w	10
First-class	48	10	7	0	-	-	-	4.20	-	0	0
List A	37	-	-	-	-	-	-	-	-	-	-
Twenty20	34	-	-	-	-	-	-	-	-	-	-

NAME: Edmund Christopher Joyce
BORN: September 22, 1978, Dublin
HEIGHT: 5ft 10in
SQUAD №: 24
NICKNAME: Joycey, Spud, Piece
MAJOR TEAMS: England, Ireland, Middlesex
CAREER: ODI debut: 2006; T20I debut: 2006;
First-class debut: 1997; List A debut: 1998; T20
debut: 2003; County cap: 2002 (Middlesex)

SUSSEX

AOC SAYS: First making his name on the international stage at ICC Trophy level, Joyce boasted a staggering average of 84 in Irish green between 2001 and 2005. Returning to the side for this year's World Cup, 84 was also his highest score in the tournament, a classy knock against the West Indies, and the innings of the player who earned himself an England debut (ironically against Ireland) in 2006 following five consecutive thousand-run seasons. After a reasonable start to his full international career and a maiden ton against Australia, Joyce was one of the casualties of the post-2007 World Cup cull and, despite a stellar one-day season for Sussex in 2009 (for whom he left Middlesex after the 2008 season), was unable to force himself back in to the selectors' thoughts. Now one of handful of senior players at Hove, Joyce notched an impressive 590 runs in nine Championship appearances in 2010.

LAST WORD: "Ed's greatest strength is his ability to keep a cool head under pressure."
Andrew Strauss

Batting & Fielding

	Mat	Inns	NO	Runs	HS	Ave	SR	100	50	Ct	St
ODIs	22	22	0	619	107	28.13	65.85	1	4	6	0
T20Is	2	1	0	1	1	1.00	33.33	0	0	0	0
First-class	152	251	21	10344	211	44.97	-	24	56	126	0
List A	196	186	18	6145	146	36.57	-	8	38	65	0
Twenty20	57	53	9	709	47	16.11	95.94	0	0	15	0

Bowling

	Mat	Balls	Runs	Wkts	BBI	BBM	Ave	Econ	SR	5w	10
ODIs	22	-	-	-	-	-	-	-	-	-	-
T20Is	2	-	-	-	-	-	-	-	-	-	-
First-class	152	1287	1025	11	2/34	-	93.18	4.77	117.0	0	0
List A	196	264	309	6	2/10	2/10	51.50	7.02	44.0	0	0
Twenty20	57	6	12	0	-	-	-	12.00	-	0	0

AMJAD KHAN

RHB RFM W2

SUSSEX

NAME: Amjad Khan
BORN: October 14, 1980, Copenhagen
HEIGHT: 6ft
SQUAD Nº: 2
NICKNAME: Ammy
OTHER TEAMS: Denmark, England, Kent
CAREER: Test debut: 2009; T20I debut: 2009;
First-class debut: 2001; List A debut: 1999; T20
debut: 2004; County cap: 2005 (Kent)

AOC SAYS: Perhaps the most exciting of Sussex's winter signings, Khan has made the short journey from Canterbury to Hove as a result of Kent's increasing financial concerns. Unlikely to feature too much in coloured clothing, he will hope for a repeat of his first full season with his former county, when he claimed an impressive 63 first-class wickets. A tall bowler with a whippy action, Khan is capable of producing both conventional and reverse-swing, an attribute that earned him an England call in 2009. However, following a modest debut his international career has been stalled by a knee injury that forced him to miss most of last summer.

LAST WORD: "With his injury history, he's unlikely to play 16 Championship games. Sussex don't want Amjad Khan at 80 per cent, they need him to be explosive and taking wickets, so if it means him missing one or two games then so be it." *Bruce Talbot*

Batting & Fielding

	Mat	Inns	NO	Runs	HS	Ave	SR	100	50	Ct	St
Tests	1	-	-	-	-	-	-	-	-	0	0
T20Is	1	1	0	2	2	2.00	50.00	0	0	0	0
First-class	87	102	32	1138	78	16.25	49.65	0	4	17	0
List A	62	31	8	281	65*	12.21	-	0	1	16	0
Twenty20	26	11	4	38	15	5.42	105.55	0	0	6	0

Bowling

	Mat	Balls	Runs	Wkts	BBI	BBM	Ave	Econ	SR	5w	10
Tests	1	174	122	1	1/111	1/122	122.00	4.20	174.0	0	0
T20Is	1	24	34	2	2/34	2/34	17.00	8.50	12.0	0	0
First-class	87	14652	9151	286	6/52	-	31.99	3.74	51.2	8	0
List A	62	2447	2124	65	4/26	4/26	32.67	5.20	37.6	0	0
Twenty20	26	453	684	30	3/11	3/11	22.80	9.05	15.1	0	0

CHRIS LIDDLE   RHB LMF

NAME: Christopher John Liddle
BORN: February 1, 1989, Middlesbrough
HEIGHT: 6ft 4in
SQUAD Nº: 11
NICKNAME: Lids, Chuck, Ice Man, Dolce
OTHER TEAMS: Leicestershire
CAREER: First-class debut: 2005; List A debut: 2006; T20 debut: 2008

SUSSEX

AOC SAYS: Highly rated at Sussex, Liddle's primary aim is to make it onto the pitch this summer. Having missed the whole of the 2009 season with a stress fracture of the right ankle, he managed just three first-team appearances (all in the CB40) last year, and with plenty of bowling options at Mark Robinson's disposal he will face a tough task to break back in to the team on a permanent basis. That said, the pace and variety he offers gives him a chance of featuring in the Sharks' Twenty20 plans, a format in which he excelled in 2008. Having started his career with Leicestershire, Liddle signed a two-year contract with Sussex in October 2006; five years later and, frustratingly, they are still to find out whether he was worth the investment.

LAST WORD: "Now that he's finally fully fit, the club will definitely be looking to get a lot more cricket out of him this year." *Bruce Talbot*

Batting & Fielding

	Mat	Inns	NO	Runs	HS	Ave	SR	100	50	Ct	St
First-class	14	14	5	113	53	12.55	62.08	0	1	5	0
List A	17	4	0	16	11	4.00	48.48	0	0	8	0
Twenty20	5	2	1	10	10*	10.00	76.92	0	0	2	0

Bowling

	Mat	Balls	Runs	Wkts	BBI	BBM	Ave	Econ	SR	5w	10
First-class	14	1706	962	17	3/42	4/82	56.58	3.38	100.3	0	0
List A	17	612	658	15	4/49	4/49	43.86	6.45	40.8	0	0
Twenty20	5	116	165	10	4/15	4/15	16.50	8.53	11.6	0	0

SUSSEX

NAME: Christopher David Nash
BORN: May 19, 1983, Cuckfield
HEIGHT: 6ft
SQUAD Nº: 23
NICKNAME: Nashy, Nashdog, Hero, Beaut, Pointless
OTHER TEAMS: Otago
CAREER: First-class debut: 2002; List A debut: 2006; T20 debut: 2006; County cap: 2008 (Sussex)

AOC SAYS: A reliable, adaptable batsman, useful offspinner and sharp fielder, Nash is an integral member of Sussex's side in all forms of the game. Consistently impressive performances in limited-overs cricket since 2008 and more than 4,000 first-class runs in the past four seasons have kept the 27-year-old very much on England's radar. If the runs keep flowing in Division One and he can rediscover his very best form in 20-over cricket, there is time yet for Nash to play for his country. Particularly emphatic on the drive, Nash averaged 41 in both the Championship and CB40 in 2010.

LAST WORD: "I'm really pleased that Chris has re-signed. He is a fantastic team man and is maturing into an outstanding player. Hopefully he'll be pushing for higher honours within the game in the next couple of years." *Mike Yardy, Sussex captain*

Batting & Fielding

	Mat	Inns	NO	Runs	HS	Ave	SR	100	50	Ct	St
First-class	79	134	11	4734	184	38.48	57.13	9	24	32	0
List A	50	47	0	1292	85	27.48	83.08	0	8	11	0
Twenty20	56	50	8	866	60*	20.61	121.28	0	3	15	0

Bowling

	Mat	Balls	Runs	Wkts	BBI	BBM	Ave	Econ	SR	5w	10
First-class	79	1938	1167	27	4/12	-	43.22	3.61	71.7	0	0
List A	50	446	419	16	4/40	4/40	26.18	5.63	27.8	0	0
Twenty20	56	324	375	19	2/17	2/17	19.73	6.94	17.0	0	0

OVERSEAS PLAYER

NAME: Rana Naved-ul-Hasan
BORN: February 28, 1978, Sheikhupura
City, Pakistan
HEIGHT: 5ft 11in
SQUAD №: 16
OTHER TEAMS: Pakistan, Yorkshire
CAREER: Test debut: 2004; ODI debut: 2003;
T20I debut: 2006; First-class debut: 1995;
List A debut: 1999; T20 debut: 2005;
County cap: 2005 (Sussex)

SUSSEX

AOC SAYS: A natural entertainer, Rana Naved has given whole-hearted service to both
Yorkshire and Sussex but has never quite fulfilled his potential at international level.
A highly skilled bowler, he is best known for his ability to produce searing yorkers on
demand and his deceptive changes of pace, while his mastery of line and length make
him the ideal bowler at the start and end of an innings. A more than capable batsman, he
is sometimes deployed as a pinch-hitter in one-day cricket, while in five Championship
outings for Sussex last season he averaged 35 and struck a magnificent century. If his all-
round abilities were in doubt, he also claims to be a competent wicketkeeper.

LAST WORD: "A terrific competitor, he's particularly good at coming back for a second or
third spell and getting a couple of wickets." *Bruce Talbot*

Batting & Fielding

	Mat	Inns	NO	Runs	HS	Ave	SR	100	50	Ct	St
Tests	9	15	3	239	42*	19.91	84.15	0	0	3	0
ODIs	74	51	18	524	33	15.87	84.51	0	0	16	0
T20Is	4	2	1	18	17*	18.00	112.50	0	0	2	0
First-class	130	184	20	3689	139	22.49	-	5	10	60	0
List A	170	130	34	2094	74	21.81	-	0	10	46	0
Twenty20	56	44	17	597	95	22.11	134.45	0	1	22	0

Bowling

	Mat	Balls	Runs	Wkts	BBI	BBM	Ave	Econ	SR	5w	10
Tests	9	1565	1044	18	3/30	5/93	58.00	4.00	86.9	0	0
ODIs	74	3466	3221	110	6/27	6/27	29.28	5.57	31.5	1	0
T20Is	4	85	101	5	3/19	3/19	20.20	7.12	17.0	0	0
First-class	130	23820	13466	557	7/49	-	24.17	3.39	42.7	28	4
List A	170	8032	7024	261	6/27	6/27	26.91	5.24	30.7	3	0
Twenty20	56	1117	1290	63	4/23	4/23	20.47	6.92	17.7	0	0

MONTY PANESAR

LHB SLA W4

SUSSEX

NAME: Mudhsuden Singh Panesar
BORN: April 25, 1982, Luton
HEIGHT: 6ft 1in
SQUAD Nº: 7
NICKNAME: Monty
MAJOR TEAMS: England, Northamptonshire
CAREER: Test debut: 2006; ODI debut: 2007;
T20I debut: 2007; First-class debut: 2001; List A
debut: 2002; T20 debut: 2006; County cap: 2006
(Northamptonshire)

AOC SAYS: With hands as huge as his enthusiasm, Panesar has spun his way into English
cricket folklore. After an impressive 46 Championship wickets in 2005, he earned
himself a place on England's tour to India the following spring. A dream run in the
national side began with the prized scalp of Sachin Tendulkar, before a series of electric
performances against Pakistan in the summer of 2006 saw him leapfrog Ashley Giles as
England's premier spinner. He claimed 71 first-class wickets in total that summer and a
spot on England's Ashes tour. To the surprise of most commentators, Giles kept him out
of the side until the third Test at Perth where he claimed an impressive eight wickets,
including one of a string of five-fers that characterised his early career. Another slew of
wickets against West Indies and New Zealand seemed to have secured his spot for the
foreseeable future, but a loss of form in 2009 coupled with the emergence of Graeme
Swann has seen Panesar limited to just one Test (albeit a memorable one at Cardiff)
in the last two seasons. Having left Northants for Sussex at the end of 2009, Panesar
was back to somewhere near his attacking and economical best last season. He seems
certain to add to his 39 Test caps at some point in the near future.

INSIDE TRACK: "The longer Monty's been with us, the more he's got his confidence back.
I think he has a clear plan of what he wants to do as a bowler now. Most importantly, he
works incredibly hard at all areas of his game – we have to drag him out of the nets, he
always wants to bat and he's always asking to do extra fielding work. Off the pitch he's
quite quiet and shy, but he's comfortable in his own skin. On the pitch he's obviously
a big character and he brings a bit of fun to the game. He's very driven and keen to
succeed, which fits in to our dressing room well. It's fair to say that he's a very, very good
player so there's no reason why he can't play all forms of the game for us. As a potential
matchwinner in four-day cricket his skills do come in to play more when he is able
to bowl a long spell, but he's more than capable of doing well for us in limited-overs
cricket." *Mark Robinson*

Batting & Fielding

	Mat	Inns	NO	Runs	HS	Ave	SR	100	50	Ct	St
Tests	39	51	17	187	26	5.50	29.44	0	0	9	0
ODIs	26	8	3	26	13	5.20	28.57	0	0	3	0
T20Is	1	1	0	1	1	1.00	50.00	0	0	0	0
First-class	133	169	53	1034	46*	8.91	33.72	0	0	30	0
List A	66	23	10	135	17*	10.38	57.44	0	0	10	0
Twenty20	19	6	2	7	3*	1.75	50.00	0	0	2	0

Bowling

	Mat	Balls	Runs	Wkts	BBI	BBM	Ave	Econ	SR	5w	10
Tests	39	9042	4331	126	6/37	10/187	34.37	2.87	71.7	8	1
ODIs	26	1308	980	24	3/25	3/25	40.83	4.49	54.5	0	0
T20Is	1	24	40	2	2/40	2/40	20.00	10.00	12.0	0	0
First-class	133	29271	13809	425	7/181	-	32.49	2.83	68.8	21	3
List A	66	2951	2226	65	5/20	5/20	34.24	4.52	45.4	1	0
Twenty20	19	366	461	12	2/22	2/22	38.41	7.55	30.5	0	0

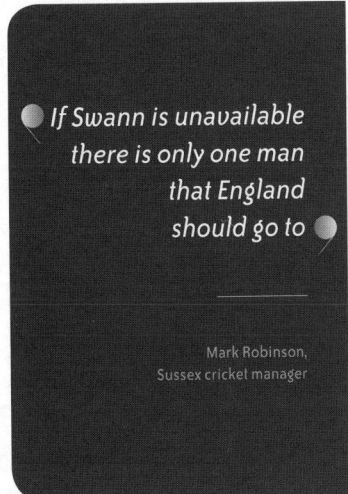

If Swann is unavailable there is only one man that England should go to

Mark Robinson,
Sussex cricket manager

SUSSEX

OVERSEAS PLAYER

NAME: Wayne Dillon Parnell
BORN: July 30, 1989, Port Elizabeth
SQUAD Nº: 72/94
NICKNAME: Pigeon, Parny
OTHER TEAMS: South Africa, Delhi
Daredevils, Eastern Province, Kent,
Warriors
CAREER: Test debut: 2010; ODI debut: 2009;
T20I debut: 2009; First-class debut: 2006;
List A debut: 2007; T20 debut: 2008

AOC SAYS: Very much on South Africa's radar even before he made his first-class debut for Eastern Province, Parnell was the skipper and standout player in South Africa's under 19s 2006 World Cup squad. Batting at No.6 in Sri Lanka, it was his rapid left-arm seamers that really caught the eye, prompting coach Ray Jennings to declare him one of the finest allrounders of his age in the world. By early 2009 he had been selected for the full South Africa side and in just his second ODI he claimed 4-25 against Australia and the Man of the Match award, a performance that showcased not only Parnell's pace but also his priceless ability to bring the ball back in to right-handers. After a successful stint with Kent in 2009 (during which Rob Key paid Parnell the ultimate compliment by comparing him to legendary Pakistani Wasim Akram, while Geraint Jones described him as the fastest bowler he'd kept to since Steve Harmison during the 2005 Ashes), he gained further international recognition in the form of his Test debut, against England in the fourth Test at The Wanderers in 2010. In the past year or so, however, his career has stalled somewhat due to injury and the emergence of Lonwabo Tsotsobe, although his presence in South Africa's recent World Cup squad shows that this talented youngster remains very much in the Proteas' plans. Lingering doubts remain about Parnell's stamina in the longer forms of the game, but if he remains fit he looks certain to be a fixture in South Africa's side sooner rather than later.

INSIDE TRACK: "The higher the level at which he is playing, the better Wayne plays. He's a huge talent, he really is. He's a left-armer with a lot of pace, he's a decent batter and he's a good fielder. He's a very good cricketer. I think he's got a big future. He knows where he wants to go as a cricketer and he knows he has a lot of work to do. He'll have to show he can come back and be effective in a second and third spell; that when he isn't picking up wickets he can keep an end tight and remain patient. It will show him the realities of Test cricket. But I expect Wayne to learn quickly." *Mickey Arthur, former South Africa coach*

Batting & Fielding

	Mat	Inns	NO	Runs	HS	Ave	SR	100	50	Ct	St
Tests	3	2	0	34	22	17.00	35.41	0	0	1	0
ODIs	19	8	2	116	49	19.33	70.73	0	0	2	0
T20Is	11	1	0	14	14	14.00	87.50	0	0	1	0
First-class	25	30	3	572	90	21.18	52.14	0	3	6	0
List A	50	29	9	373	49	18.65	76.12	0	0	9	0
Twenty20	28	8	5	46	14	15.33	97.87	0	0	3	0

Bowling

	Mat	Balls	Runs	Wkts	BBI	BBM	Ave	Econ	SR	5w	10
Tests	3	306	227	5	2/17	3/89	45.40	4.45	61.2	0	0
ODIs	19	950	945	31	5/48	5/48	30.48	5.96	30.6	2	0
T20Is	11	245	287	14	4/13	4/13	20.50	7.02	17.5	0	0
First-class	25	3797	2098	61	4/7	7/134	34.39	3.31	62.2	0	0
List A	50	2301	2150	73	5/48	5/48	29.45	5.60	31.5	2	0
Twenty20	28	575	633	28	4/13	4/13	22.60	6.60	20.5	0	0

When we find someone with genuine pace, it causes great excitement

Corrie van Zyl,
South Africa coach

SUSSEX

NAME: Matthew James Prior
BORN: February 26, 1982, Johannesburg,
HEIGHT: 5ft 11in
SQUAD Nº: 13
NICKNAME: MP, The Cheese
OTHER TEAMS: England, Victoria
CAREER: Test debut: 2007; ODI debut: 2004;
T20I debut: 2007; First-class debut: 2001;
List A debut: 2000; T20 debut: 2003; County
cap: 2003 (Sussex)

AOC SAYS: An increasingly impressive wicketkeeper and fluent batsman, Prior looks set to be England's first-choice Test gloveman for the foreseeable future. Making his ODI debut on the tour of Zimbabwe as a specialist batsman, he scored 35 in his only appearance of the series, but it was his Test debut that really turned heads. An unbeaten 126 at Lord's (full of the carving cover drives that are the standout feature of Prior's batting) was evidence enough that England had finally found a stumper with the batting ability to match Alec Stewart, and a fine 75 at Headingley seemed to have finally ended England's tiresome wicketkeeper debate. However, a poor series against India and a number of dropped catches in Sri Lanka the following winter exposed flaws with his keeping technique and Tim Ambrose replaced him for the 2008 tour of New Zealand. Prior's superior batting couldn't be ignored for long though, and he was back in the side before the end of the year. Since then, he has gone from strength to strength, and his punchy runs at No. 7 have been particularly valuable in securing back-to-back Ashes wins. Having worked with former Notts and England keeper Bruce French his glovework has improved beyond recognition and, standing back to the quicks at least, he is now as athletic and assured as any of his contemporaries. He has yet to nail down a permanent place in England's limited-overs sides, however, and with the emergence of Craig Kieswetter and Steven Davies he'll have plenty of competition this summer. One of England's most improved players, he was one of Wisden's Cricketers of the Year in 2010.

INSIDE TRACK: "I think at one point everybody was a wicketkeeping expert and wanted to comment on Matt's performances. The England wicketkeeping position was so scrutinised by the media that is was almost impossible, but because Matt's been backed more over the last year couple of years he's been consistent. He has shown his resilience by coming back from several setbacks and I think the media attention has made him a stronger character. I think he's learnt a lot about himself over the last few years and he'll be pleased that he's found out just how resilient he is. Like anybody, he'll sulk (that's normal) but he'll then turn that around and actually do something about it. You can never predict form, but the Test place should be his for the foreseeable future. He's the best keeper-batsman we've got. He's got fantastic presence and a fantastic cricket brain." *Mark Robinson*

Batting & Fielding

	Mat	Inns	NO	Runs	HS	Ave	SR	100	50	Ct	St
Tests	40	61	11	2148	131*	42.96	64.00	4	16	117	4
ODIs	68	62	9	1282	87	24.18	76.76	0	3	71	8
T20Is	10	8	2	127	32	21.16	127.00	0	0	6	3
First-class	182	282	32	10054	201*	40.21	67.08	24	56	452	28
List A	216	198	17	4935	144	27.26	-	4	27	185	31
Twenty20	66	61	5	1419	117	25.33	141.05	1	8	41	5

Bowling

	Mat	Balls	Runs	Wkts	BBI	BBM	Ave	Econ	SR	5w	10
Tests	40	-	-	-	-	-	-	-	-	-	-
ODIs	68	-	-	-	-	-	-	-	-	-	-
T20Is	10	-	-	-	-	-	-	-	-	-	-
First-class	182	-	-	-	-	-	-	-	-	-	-
List A	216	-	-	-	-	-	-	-	-	-	-
Twenty20	66	-	-	-	-	-	-	-	-	-	-

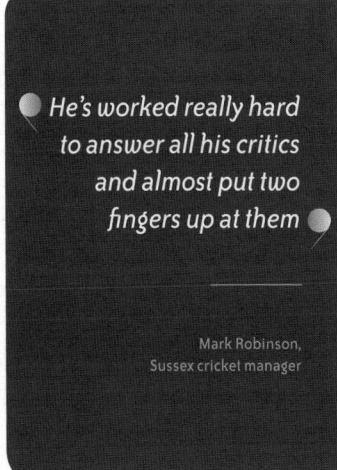

He's worked really hard to answer all his critics and almost put two fingers up at them

Mark Robinson,
Sussex cricket manager

OLLIE RAYNER   RHB OB

SUSSEX

NAME: Oliver Philip Rayner
BORN: November 1, 1985, Fallingbostel, Germany
HEIGHT: 6ft 6in
SQUAD Nº: 22
NICKNAME: Mervin, Rocket
OTHER TEAMS: Middlesex
CAREER: First-class debut: 2006; List A debut: 2006; T20 debut: 2006

AOC SAYS: A talented allrounder who earned a call-up to the England Performance Squad in 2008, Rayner signed for the Martlets in November 2005. The following summer, he became the first Sussex player to score a century on debut when he notched 101 against the touring Sri Lankans. It is the 25-year-old's offbreaks, however, that form the basis of his game, and with Monty Panesar making the move to the south coast last year his opportunities in the first team were limited to five Championship appearances and a handful of T20 and CB40 fixtures. A combination of this and the retirement of Shaun Udal led Middlesex to sign Rayner for the early weeks of this season. The deal will be reassessed in mid-May, with the outcome likely to depend on Panesar's involvement with the England squad.

LAST WORD: "He is a talented young cricketer with an excellent work ethic who is improving each season." *Angus Fraser, Middlesex managing director of cricket*

Batting & Fielding											
	Mat	Inns	NO	Runs	HS	Ave	SR	100	50	Ct	St
First-class	38	45	9	782	101	21.72	53.01	1	3	42	0
List A	20	17	9	213	61	26.62	91.41	0	1	7	0
Twenty20	17	9	2	115	41*	16.42	106.48	0	0	1	0

Bowling											
	Mat	Balls	Runs	Wkts	BBI	BBM	Ave	Econ	SR	5w	10
First-class	38	6034	3086	89	5/49	8/96	34.67	3.06	67.7	3	0
List A	20	672	670	14	2/31	2/31	47.85	5.98	48.0	0	0
Twenty20	17	235	307	9	1/16	1/16	34.11	7.83	26.1	0	0

NAME: Lou Vincent
BORN: November 11, 1978, Auckland
HEIGHT: 5ft 11in
SQUAD Nº: 78
NICKNAME: Flusher
OTHER TEAMS: New Zealand, Auckland, Lancashire, Northamptonshire, Worcestershire
CAREER: Test debut: 2001; ODI debut: 2001; T20I debut: 2006; First-class debut: 1998; List A debut: 1998; T20 debut: 2006

SUSSEX

AOC SAYS: A Test debut century against Australia in 2001 and 224 against Sri Lanka three years later marked out Vincent as a player of rare quality. Unfortunately, in between these two memorable knocks, inconsistency plagued a player who began his international career as an opener but whose free-flowing strokeplay is better suited to the middle-order. In one-day cricket, by contrast, Vincent's attacking instincts are best employed at the start of an innings – spectacularly so when he plundered 172 off just 120 balls against Zimbabwe in 2005. Having racked up plenty of runs for Auckland over the winter, the 32-year-old appears to have several seasons left in him and could prove a shrewd signing. For Sussex he will predominantly play one-day cricket but will provide cover in the Championship as and when required.

LAST WORD: "Lou is an experienced international batsman who can turn a game in his own right, and he's a brilliant fielder." *Mark Robinson*

Batting & Fielding

	Mat	Inns	NO	Runs	HS	Ave	SR	100	50	Ct	St
Tests	23	40	1	1332	224	34.15	47.11	3	9	19	0
ODIs	102	99	10	2413	172	27.11	69.88	3	11	41	0
T20Is	9	9	0	174	42	19.33	100.00	0	0	1	0
First-class	92	151	11	4922	224	35.15	-	10	29	107	0
List A	210	204	15	5761	172	30.48	-	10	29	119	3
Twenty20	63	63	4	1555	105*	26.35	123.21	2	8	25	0

Bowling

	Mat	Balls	Runs	Wkts	BBI	BBM	Ave	Econ	SR	5w	10
Tests	23	6	2	0	-	-	-	2.00	-	0	0
ODIs	102	20	25	1	1/0	1/0	25.00	7.50	20.0	0	0
T20Is	9	-	-	-	-	-	-	-	-	-	-
First-class	92	1003	527	10	2/37	-	52.70	3.15	100.3	0	0
List A	210	249	252	7	3/7	3/7	36.00	6.07	35.5	0	0
Twenty20	63	57	86	4	3/28	3/28	21.50	9.05	14.2	0	0

LUKE WELLS

LHB OB

SUSSEX

NAME: Luke William Peter Wells
BORN: December 29, 1990, Eastbourne
SQUAD №: 31
CAREER: First-class debut: 2010; List A debut: 2010

AOC SAYS: Son of former England batsman Alan, Wells signed a three-year summer contract with Sussex in October 2009 on the strength of his performances for the Second XI the preceding summer. That year he played for England's under 19 side against Bangladesh, and he also played in the inexperienced Sussex side that took on the Bangladeshis in a one-day match last summer. Last September he made his first-class debut, scoring an impressive 62 against Worcestershire and, after a productive winter in South Africa, will be pushing for further first-team honours in 2011.

LAST WORD: "If there's a young player who breaks through this season, I think it's going to be Luke. I think there will be an opportunity for him to get into the top six. He's got a good temperament and a good range of shots. He bowls a bit as well; some reasonably tidy medium pace." *Bruce Talbot*

Batting & Fielding

	Mat	Inns	NO	Runs	HS	Ave	SR	100	50	Ct	St
First-class	1	2	0	70	62	35.00	36.08	0	1	0	0
List A	1	1	0	9	9	9.00	60.00	0	0	1	0

Bowling

	Mat	Balls	Runs	Wkts	BBI	BBM	Ave	Econ	SR	5w	10
First-class	1	12	16	0	-	-	-	8.00	-	0	0
List A	1	-	-	-	-	-	-	-	-	-	-

NAME: Kirk Ogilvy Wernars
BORN: June 14, 1991, Cape Town
SQUAD Nº: 4
NICKNAME: Leupels
OTHER TEAMS: Western Province
CAREER: First-class debut: 2010; List A
debut: 2010

SUSSEX

AOC SAYS: Cricket-mad since the age of four, 19-year-old Wernars was snapped up by
Sussex after a handful of games for Western Province. Listing Brian Lara as his hero, the
allrounder clearly has his sights set high, and has made some handy contributions with
both bat and ball in his short career. In his nine matches for South Africa's under 19 side
he has had more success with the ball than the bat, but he is typically deployed a No.6 in
first-class cricket. Spotted by Sussex while playing for the Cape Cobras emerging team on
last year's pre-season trip to Dubai, Wernars qualifies for English domestic cricket under a
Dutch passport.

LAST WORD: "We've had many good reports about Kirk over the winter through our South
African connections; he's a lad with promise and a genuine allrounder. He hits the ball
hard and can open the bowling as well, which will give us more options." *Mark Robinson*

Batting & Fielding

	Mat	Inns	NO	Runs	HS	Ave	SR	100	50	Ct	St
First-class	2	4	2	77	39*	38.50	53.84	0	0	1	0
List A	11	8	4	94	37*	23.50	92.15	0	0	5	0

Bowling

	Mat	Balls	Runs	Wkts	BBI	BBM	Ave	Econ	SR	5w	10
First-class	2	70	44	3	2/11	3/30	14.66	3.77	23.3	0	0
List A	11	237	221	7	6/27	6/27	31.57	5.59	33.8	1	0

SUSSEX

NAME: Luke James Wright
BORN: March 7, 1985, Grantham
HEIGHT: 6ft
SQUAD Nº: 10
NICKNAME: Wrighty
MAJOR TEAMS: England, Leicestershire, Wellington
CAREER: ODI debut: 2007; T20I debut: 2007; First-class debut: 2003; List A debut: 2002; T20 debut: 2004; County cap: 2007 (Sussex)

AOC SAYS: An England under 19 player and three-time Denis Compton Medal winner, Wright came to real prominence in 2007 when he was the leading run-scorer in the Twenty20 Cup and smashed a round 50 on his ODI debut, against India at The Oval. This form earned him a place in England's squad for the inaugural World Twenty20 in South Africa the following autumn, but he failed to make an impact at the top of the order with just 43 runs in five innings. A superb fielder, Wright has been deployed intermittently in England's limited-overs side ever since. He is seldom given more than five or six overs with the ball, but is quicker than he looks and has a more than handy yorker. He has bowled some vital overs for England, including a superb last over to secure a tie against New Zealand in Napier in 2008 and a solitary set of six in last year's World Twenty20 final that saw Wright dismiss the dangerous Cameron White. In the one-day series that followed last winter's Ashes and the early stages of the World Cup, it appeared that Wright was slipping down the pecking order, but Paul Collingwood's loss of form and a crucial 44 against the West Indies that helped secure England's passage into the quarter-finals suggest that Wright will be in and around the team for some time.

INSIDE TRACK: "For me, Luke needs to play regularly for England or regularly for Sussex. He's not playing enough at the moment, which is stalling his development. Wright could be a genuine England allrounder in all formats of the game, but he needs to learn the role. At the moment he's spending a lot of time being 12th man around a lot of squads, which isn't helping his game. He's got a good capacity to score hundreds and take wickets in county cricket. He hasn't actually played a lot of first-class cricket, and you're not going to develop your bowling and your ability to bat for a long time if you're not playing a lot. It's a catch-22 situation really; of course he wants to be involved with the England squads, but he needs to be on the park more. It's not a criticism of England – he's a great team man and great in the field so I can understand why they want him in the squad – but from my point of view Luke could be a genuine No.7 for England. Whenever he plays regularly for Sussex he takes wickets and scores runs." *Mark Robinson*

Batting & Fielding

	Mat	Inns	NO	Runs	HS	Ave	SR	100	50	Ct	St
ODIs	46	35	4	701	52	22.61	89.29	0	2	17	0
T20Is	29	24	2	346	71	15.72	127.67	0	1	10	0
First-class	66	93	15	2867	155*	36.75	66.09	8	15	29	0
List A	144	111	18	2170	125	23.33	-	1	5	44	0
Twenty20	87	72	7	1404	103	21.60	143.70	1	4	28	0

Bowling

	Mat	Balls	Runs	Wkts	BBI	BBM	Ave	Econ	SR	5w	10
ODIs	46	1020	863	15	2/34	2/34	57.53	5.07	68.0	0	0
T20Is	29	156	219	6	1/5	1/5	36.50	8.42	26.0	0	0
First-class	66	6671	3924	101	5/65	-	38.85	3.52	66.0	3	0
List A	144	4455	3920	100	4/12	4/12	39.20	5.27	44.5	0	0
Twenty20	87	1002	1373	45	3/17	3/17	30.51	8.22	22.2	0	0

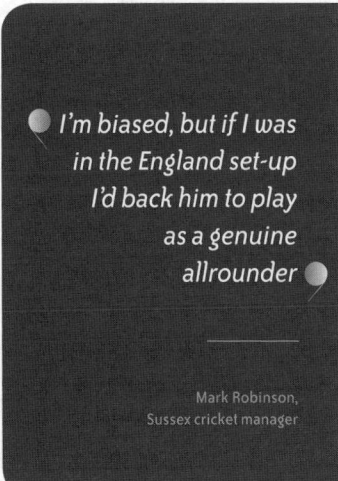

I'm biased, but if I was in the England set-up I'd back him to play as a genuine allrounder

Mark Robinson,
Sussex cricket manager

SUSSEX

NAME: Michael Howard Yardy
BORN: November 27, 1980, Pembury
HEIGHT: 6ft
SQUAD Nº: 20
NICKNAME: Yards, Paolo, Cyril
OTHER TEAMS: England, Central Districts
CAREER: ODI debut: 2006; T20I debut: 2006;
First-class debut: 2000; List A debut: 1999;
T20 debut: 2004; County Cap: 2005

AOC SAYS: A triumph of substance over style, Yardy is the original 'unfashionable cricketer', but in a career characterised by intermittent metamorphosis the Sussex stalwart has proved mighty effective for both club and country. A seamer in his early years, Yardy was a steady contributor with the bat between 2001 and 2004, but it was his 1,520 first-class runs and impressive one-day bowling in the summer of 2005 that really launched his international career. Scoring a Sussex record 257 against Bangladesh at Hove turned the selectors' heads and at the end of a stellar season he was picked for the England A tour of the Caribbean and, subsequently, the Champions Trophy squad. Making his ODI debut against Pakistan in 2006, Yardy impressed with the ball but, unfathomably, was asked to bat at No.4, a position that didn't suit his unorthodox technique. Unsurprisingly, he struggled in the unfamiliar role and was jettisoned after a handful of appearances. Taking over from the hugely successful Chris Adams at Hove in 2009, Yardy led the Sharks to T20 and Pro40 success, and when Andy Flower decided he needed a second spinner in the World Twenty20 squad Yardy got the nod. Bowling with great success alongside Graeme Swann, Yardy claimed eight wickets at 17.5 with an economy of just 6.80 as his utilitarian approach fitted in perfectly to England's carefully-scripted campaign.

INSIDE TRACK: "It's not a surprise that he's forced his way into England's one-day and T20 sides; I think the surprise is that the selectors were brave enough to give him a go again. When he first played for England I thought he did pretty well. When he was eventually left out it because he was asked to do a role that wasn't him. He's a player, like Matt Prior, who dealt with the setback of being left out of England side by just getting on with it. He's a very good situation player, which is a valuable asset. When it comes to captaincy, he's very, very solid and straightforward. He's plain speaking and leads purely by example, which makes him revered in the dressing room. In terms of his own game and how he sees himself, he's very phlegmatic and level-headed. He's very humble and he's not worried about getting dirty on the shop floor. He works so hard at his game and his fitness, so he gets the respect of the team because of the attitude he brings to his own game." *Mark Robinson*

Batting & Fielding

	Mat	Inns	NO	Runs	HS	Ave	SR	100	50	Ct	St
ODIs	28	24	8	326	60*	20.37	69.06	0	2	10	0
T20Is	14	8	5	96	35*	32.00	133.33	0	0	8	0
First-class	129	217	21	7606	257	38.80	-	15	38	99	0
List A	174	154	27	3049	98*	24.00	-	0	20	73	0
Twenty20	76	59	23	928	76*	25.77	108.79	0	2	30	0

Bowling

	Mat	Balls	Runs	Wkts	BBI	BBM	Ave	Econ	SR	5w	10
ODIs	28	1332	1075	21	3/24	3/24	51.19	4.84	63.4	0	0
T20Is	14	276	299	11	2/19	2/19	27.18	6.50	25.0	0	0
First-class	129	3441	2003	26	5/83	-	77.03	3.49	132.3	1	0
List A	174	5267	4391	109	6/27	6/27	40.28	5.00	48.3	1	0
Twenty20	76	1417	1496	61	3/21	3/21	24.52	6.33	23.2	0	0

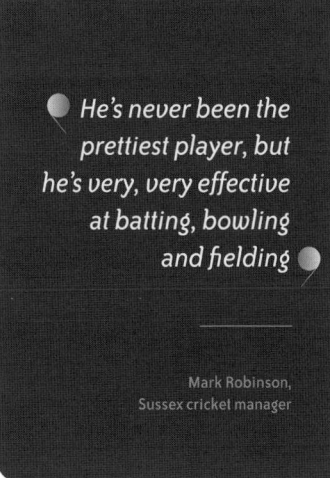

He's never been the prettiest player, but he's very, very effective at batting, bowling and fielding

Mark Robinson,
Sussex cricket manager

FORMED: 1882
HOME GROUND: County Ground, Edgbaston
ONE-DAY NAME: Bears
CAPTAIN: Jim Troughton
2010 RESULTS: CC1: 6/9; CB40: Winners; FP t20: Quarter-finalists

HONOURS

County Championship: (6) 1911, 1951, 1972, 1994, 1995, 2004; Gillette/NatWest/C&G/FP Trophy: (5) 1966, 1968, 1989, 1993, 1995; Benson and Hedges Cup: (2) 1994, 2002; CB40: 2010; Sunday League: (3) 1980, 1994, 1997

THE LOWDOWN

A topsy-turvy season in 2010 saw Warwickshire start strongly, barely score a Championship run for six weeks in the middle of the summer and end the year as CB40 winners. Going into 2011 they look a good bet to continue their excellent form in one-day cricket, but they must address their Championship batting woes if they are to avoid another relegation battle. The arrival of Will Porterfield adds solidity to the top of the order, while it is important that Darren Maddy and new skipper Jim Troughton rediscover their form. With Ian Bell and Trott in the side their top six looks formidable, but without them the likes of Ateeq Javid may be asked to step up. County cricket's MVP Neil Carter misses the start of the campaign, putting even more onus on the excellent Chris Woakes to lead the seam attack, while Imran Tahir's return to Hampshire puts a lot of pressure on Ant Botha to deliver Championship wickets.

DIRECTOR OF CRICKET: ASHLEY GILES

Ashes-winner Giles has made a seamless transition into coaching. Also an England selector, it would be no surprise to see him in charge of the national side one day, and his hands on approach to coaching has proven popular at Edgbaston. A spinner who bowled with considerable nous as well as skills during his playing days, Giles will relish the opportunity to bring on the Bears' clutch of young twirlers.

With thanks to: Jim Troughton, Warwickshire captain; Brian Halford, sports reporter, Birmingham Mail; George Dobell, cricket writer

	Mat	Inns	NO	Runs	HS	Ave	SR	100	50	Ct	St
IR Bell	6	11	1	381	104	38.10	49.28	1	2	10	-
IJL Trott	6	11	0	415	150	37.72	56.84	1	3	10	-
NM Carter	11	20	3	617	99*	36.29	73.19	0	4	0	-
R Clarke	15	28	5	673	127*	29.26	49.59	1	3	23	-
IJ Westwood	16	32	4	726	86*	25.92	42.33	0	5	6	-
V Chopra	9	18	1	409	54	24.05	42.78	0	1	9	-
CR Woakes	13	21	3	431	136*	23.94	60.36	1	1	6	-
JO Troughton	16	30	1	585	78	20.17	44.79	0	1	5	-
DL Maddy	14	27	1	499	61	19.19	41.13	0	2	16	-
AG Botha	8	14	0	248	76	17.71	46.96	0	1	7	-
RM Johnson	5	8	1	118	39	16.85	40.27	0	0	12	2
Imran Tahir	16	27	4	384	69*	16.69	79.01	0	1	4	-
KHD Barker	4	5	1	57	22	14.25	50.44	0	0	1	-
TR Ambrose	11	20	0	267	54	13.35	44.79	0	1	33	3
A Javid	4	7	0	91	48	13.00	33.70	0	0	3	-
NS Tahir	3	6	0	69	34	11.50	50.00	0	0	2	-
AS Miller	7	12	5	65	35	9.28	27.77	0	0	4	-
LJ Evans	1	2	0	18	15	9.00	31.57	0	0	1	-
WB Rankin	9	16	7	63	13	7.00	40.12	0	0	3	-
SA Piolet	1	2	0	10	6	5.00	24.39	0	0	2	-
JE Ord	1	2	0	7	6	3.50	17.07	0	0	1	-

Batting & Fielding

	Mat	Overs	Mdns	Runs	Wkts	BBI	BBM	Ave	Econ	SR	5w	10
IJL Trott	6	19.0	4	71	4	2/20	2/26	17.75	3.73	28.5	0	0
CR Woakes	13	396.2	100	1165	54	6/52	11/97	21.57	2.93	44.0	3	1
NM Carter	11	356.2	70	1129	51	5/60	9/130	22.13	3.16	41.9	4	0
R Clarke	15	212.5	31	743	32	6/63	7/91	23.21	3.49	39.9	1	0
Imran Tahir	16	430.4	58	1376	56	8/114	8/114	24.57	3.19	46.1	3	0
DL Maddy	14	206.5	62	523	21	4/37	6/53	24.90	2.52	59.0	0	0
WB Rankin	9	145.3	19	594	22	5/16	5/24	27.00	4.08	39.6	1	0
AS Miller	7	154.4	42	488	16	5/58	8/103	30.50	3.15	58.0	2	0
AG Botha	8	50.4	11	175	4	3/50	3/64	43.75	3.45	76.0	0	0
NS Tahir	3	83.0	15	238	5	2/49	3/80	47.60	2.86	99.6	0	0
KHD Barker	4	36.1	4	135	2	2/22	2/22	67.50	3.73	108.5	0	0
SA Piolet	1	17.0	3	80	1	1/67	1/80	80.00	4.70	102.0	0	0

Bowling

Batting & Fielding

	Mat	Inns	NO	Runs	HS	Ave	SR	100	50	Ct	St
IJL Trott	8	8	2	460	103	76.66	83.18	1	4	6	-
IR Bell	9	9	0	554	107	61.55	106.53	1	6	4	-
AG Botha	8	6	5	52	42	52.00	120.93	0	0	5	-
V Chopra	4	4	0	156	76	39.00	81.67	0	2	0	-
DL Maddy	14	13	5	283	74	35.37	96.58	0	1	5	-
IJ Westwood	11	9	4	166	47	33.20	93.78	0	0	2	-
JO Troughton	14	14	4	325	66*	32.50	83.54	0	2	5	-
NM Carter	13	13	0	422	101	32.46	124.11	1	2	0	-
CR Woakes	13	5	2	76	49*	25.33	205.40	0	0	2	-
R Clarke	12	8	1	169	49*	24.14	121.58	0	0	7	-
TR Ambrose	8	3	1	37	31*	18.50	100.00	0	0	7	2
KHD Barker	11	9	1	136	40	17.00	86.62	0	0	3	-
Imran Tahir	13	2	1	8	8*	8.00	266.66	0	0	4	-
WB Rankin	8	1	0	7	7	7.00	50.00	0	0	1	-
RM Johnson	6	1	1	4	4*	-	80.00	0	0	5	2

Bowling

	Mat	Overs	Mdns	Runs	Wkts	BBI	Ave	Econ	SR	5w
WB Rankin	8	41.4	0	244	15	4/34	16.26	5.85	16.6	0
Imran Tahir	13	81.0	1	431	22	5/41	19.59	5.32	22.0	1
KHD Barker	11	60.4	1	371	14	4/33	26.50	6.11	26.0	0
CR Woakes	13	87.0	7	469	15	3/16	31.26	5.39	34.8	0
DL Maddy	14	59.0	0	361	10	3/25	36.10	6.11	35.4	0
AG Botha	8	41.0	0	205	5	2/27	41.00	5.00	49.2	0
NM Carter	13	96.2	4	556	13	2/28	42.76	5.77	44.4	0
IJ Westwood	11	7.0	0	48	1	1/48	48.00	6.85	42.0	0
R Clarke	12	23.0	0	192	0	-	-	8.34	-	0
SA Piolet	1	2.0	0	19	0	-	-	9.50	-	0
NS Tahir	1	6.1	0	49	0	-	-	7.94	-	0

Batting & Fielding

	Mat	Inns	NO	Runs	HS	Ave	SR	100	50	Ct	St
IR Bell	4	4	0	166	85	41.50	137.19	0	2	0	-
DL Maddy	17	17	3	456	88	32.57	132.55	0	1	8	-
IJL Trott	12	12	2	306	72*	30.60	115.03	0	2	2	-
JO Troughton	17	16	2	365	66	26.07	119.67	0	2	7	-
R Clarke	17	14	6	200	39	25.00	121.95	0	0	9	-
CR Woakes	15	7	3	95	27*	23.75	197.91	0	0	7	-
KHD Barker	14	9	1	177	46	22.12	121.23	0	0	2	-
TR Ambrose	11	7	2	98	31*	19.60	92.45	0	0	9	4
AG Botha	17	9	4	93	26*	18.60	116.25	0	0	11	-
NM Carter	17	17	0	231	39	13.58	128.33	0	0	2	-
IJ Westwood	10	9	1	103	24*	12.87	109.57	0	0	0	-
SA Piolet	7	2	1	11	7	11.00	78.57	0	0	3	-
Imran Tahir	17	3	1	19	11	9.50	135.71	0	0	2	-
V Chopra	4	3	1	13	10*	6.50	92.85	0	0	0	-
RM Johnson	6	2	2	7	6*	-	87.50	0	0	1	2

Bowling

	Mat	Overs	Mdns	Runs	Wkts	BBI	Ave	Econ	SR	5w
KHD Barker	14	48.3	0	350	21	4/19	16.66	7.21	13.8	0
Imran Tahir	17	61.0	1	401	20	3/14	20.05	6.57	18.3	0
CR Woakes	15	42.0	1	310	15	3/21	20.66	7.38	16.8	0
AG Botha	17	37.0	0	253	12	3/16	21.08	6.83	18.5	0
SA Piolet	7	24.0	0	152	7	2/9	21.71	6.33	20.5	0
NM Carter	17	60.0	0	383	16	3/28	23.93	6.38	22.5	0
DL Maddy	17	18.0	0	164	6	1/5	27.33	9.11	18.0	0
WB Rankin	2	6.0	0	39	1	1/17	39.00	6.50	36.0	0
R Clarke	17	19.0	0	177	1	1/48	177.00	9.31	114.0	0

TOM ALLIN

RHB RMF

NAME: Thomas William Allin
BORN: November 27, 1987, Bideford
SQUAD Nº: 87
CAREER: Yet to make first-team debut

AOC SAYS: A slippery seamer who has been clocked at 85mph, Allin played for Devon before joining Warwickshire on a two-year summer deal in 2008. The then 20-year-old son of former Glamorgan and Devon spinner Tony Allin came to the Bears' attention through the MCCU programme and has now joined Warwickshire full-time after completing his studies at Cardiff. Having begun his cricketing eduction at Bideford CC, he moved to Devon League Premier Division side North Devon, taking 33 wickets in 2007 to help his side to their maiden title. Allin is highly-rated at the club and has been working hard on his batting over the winter.

LAST WORD: "He has all the attributes you look for. He hits the bat hard, will get stronger and quicker, and can hold a bat too." *Ashley Giles*

EXTRAS

"They've been very accomplished in one-day cricket for a few years now, so I expect them to challenge for the CB40 again." Brian Halford

NAME: Timothy Raymond Ambrose
BORN: December 1, 1982, Newcastle, Australia
HEIGHT: 5ft 7in
SQUAD Nº: 12
NICKNAME: Freak, Shambrose, Mole
OTHER TEAMS: England, Sussex
CAREER: Test debut: 2008; ODI debut: 2008;
T20I debut: 2008; First-class debut: 2001;
List A debut: 2001; T20 debut: 2003; County
cap: 2003 (Sussex), 2007 (Warwickshire)

WARWICKSHIRE

AOC SAYS: Matt Prior's understudy at Sussex, Ambrose moved to Warwickshire in 2006 in search of increased first-team opportunities. Injury hampered his ambitions that year, but an excellent 2007 put him in contention for international honours. When Prior's glovework was found wanting Ambrose was given his chance, and in just his second Test scored a series-turning 102 at Wellington. Unfortunately, he was unable to replicate this form when New Zealand came to England the following spring and he looked out of his depth against South Africa, losing his place to the returning Prior before the year was out. After a poor 2010 with the bat, including just 267 runs at 13 in the Championship, Ambrose now finds himself in direct competition with young stumper Richard Johnson.

LAST WORD: "Ashley Giles has gone on record to say that Richard Johnson will start in the side, so it is up to Tim to win his place back." *Brian Halford*

Batting & Fielding

	Mat	Inns	NO	Runs	HS	Ave	SR	100	50	Ct	St
Tests	11	16	1	447	102	29.80	46.41	1	3	31	0
ODIs	5	5	1	10	6	2.50	29.41	0	0	3	0
T20Is	1	-	-	-	-	-	-	-	-	1	1
First-class	120	185	15	5533	251*	32.54	51.43	9	31	279	19
List A	111	94	14	2258	135	28.22	73.76	3	8	115	20
Twenty20	42	33	8	630	77	25.20	115.38	0	2	28	14

Bowling

	Mat	Balls	Runs	Wkts	BBI	BBM	Ave	Econ	SR	5w	10
Tests	11	-	-	-	-	-	-	-	-	-	-
ODIs	5	-	-	-	-	-	-	-	-	-	-
T20Is	1	-	-	-	-	-	-	-	-	-	-
First-class	120	-	6	1	0	-	-	-	1.00	0	0
List A	111	-	-	-	-	-	-	-	-	-	-
Twenty20	42	-	-	-	-	-	-	-	-	-	-

KEITH BARKER

LHB LM

WARWICKSHIRE

NAME: Keith Hubert Douglas Barker
BORN: October 21, 1986, Manchester
SQUAD Nº: 13
CAREER: First-class debut: 2009; List A
debut: 2009; T20 debut: 2009

AOC SAYS: The godson of legendary West Indian skipper Clive Lloyd, Barker is a talented footballer who turned down a contract with Lancashire in 2005 because he had been offered terms with Blackburn the previous week. He was released by Rovers in 2008 and made his Warwickshire Second XI debut in June of the same year. Yet to establish himself in the Championship, Barker has been a consistent contributor in coloured clothing, particularly in the FP t20 where he averaged 21 with the bat and claimed 21 wickets at 15 last year. With Neil Carter certain to miss the start of the season, the 24-year-old has a great chance to establish himself as an allrounder in all forms this year if he can learn to consistently swing the new ball – an area of his game that he is currently working on.

LAST WORD: "He's got a lot going for him. He's already played some quite high-pressure knocks in the short forms of the game, he's a good athlete and he's got a good yorker."
Brian Halford

Batting & Fielding

	Mat	Inns	NO	Runs	HS	Ave	SR	100	50	Ct	St
First-class	7	9	1	85	23	10.62	52.46	0	0	1	0
List A	23	15	5	221	40	22.10	85.32	0	0	5	0
Twenty20	25	12	2	197	46	19.70	122.36	0	0	3	0

Bowling

	Mat	Balls	Runs	Wkts	BBI	BBM	Ave	Econ	SR	5w	10
First-class	7	535	310	3	2/22	2/22	103.33	3.47	178.3	0	0
List A	23	766	725	26	4/33	4/33	27.88	5.67	29.4	0	0
Twenty20	25	501	633	37	4/19	4/19	17.10	7.58	13.5	0	0

NAME: Ian Ronald Bell
BORN: April 11, 1982, Coventry
HEIGHT: 5ft 10in
SQUAD Nº: 4
NICKNAME: Belly
OTHER TEAMS: England
CAREER: Test debut: 2004; ODI debut: 2004;
T20I debut: 2006; First-class debut: 1999;
List A debut: 1999; T20 debut: 2003; County
cap: 2001

WARWICKSHIRE

AOC SAYS: The most attractive batsman in English cricket, Bell appears to be finally fulfilling the vast potential he has always shown. On the international stage, two exceptional winters – in South Africa and Australia – in the past 18 months have banished any lingering doubts about his ability to cope with the mental aspect of Test cricket, while two superb centuries for Warwickshire in the closing weeks of last season secured top-flight status and the CB40 title for a side that would love to see more of the player they always knew would reach the top. Earmarked as a future England player from his early days, Bell enjoyed a superb year in 2004, racking up an astonishing 1,714 first-class runs to earn himself a Test debut against the West Indies – during which he stroked 70 in his only innings – and a place on the winter ODI tour to Zimbabwe. Two unbeaten innings, including his maiden Test century, against Bangladesh the following summer lifted his Test average to a staggering 297 and secured him a spot in the side for the 2005 Ashes. Apart from two half-centuries at Old Trafford, however, Bell endured a tough series against Warne and McGrath, but was retained for the winter tours and top-scored against Pakistan. Three tons in successive innings against the same opposition the following summer seemed to have cemented his place for the foreseeable future, but sporadic form over the next few years led to his omission after the first Test of the 2009 tour of the West Indies. The following summer saw the start of Bell's golden run, and in the past two years he has become a more important part of England's one-day plans.

INSIDE TRACK: "I can't believe that it is Belly's Benefit Year. I am not quite sure why, as he has been a part of the England side for pretty much the same amount of time as I have. Perhaps it is because unlike myself, who is starting to be labelled as a seasoned campaigner, most people still think that Belly's best years are very much in front of him. I have to say that I agree with them. Anyone who has seen the work he has put into his game over the last couple of years will be assured that the most gifted player in our team can only get better. He is at the peak of his powers, and while plenty of us in the England side have struggled to repeat international performances for our counties, he has been remarkably consistent for Warwickshire." *Andrew Strauss, England captain*

IAN BELL

WARWICKSHIRE

Batting & Fielding											
	Mat	Inns	NO	Runs	HS	Ave	SR	100	50	Ct	St
Tests	62	106	11	4192	199	44.12	50.60	12	26	53	0
ODIs	97	94	8	3021	126*	35.12	72.76	1	18	30	0
T20Is	7	7	1	175	60*	29.16	119.86	0	1	4	0
First-class	180	302	30	12277	262*	45.13	-	33	65	130	0
List A	219	209	20	7210	158	38.14	-	7	51	76	0
Twenty20	44	43	6	926	85	25.02	114.60	0	4	16	0

Bowling										
	Mat	Balls	Runs	Wkts	BBI	BBM	Ave	Econ	SR	5w	10
Tests	62	108	76	1	1/33	1/33	76.00	4.22	108.0	0	0
ODIs	97	88	88	6	3/9	3/9	14.66	6.00	14.6	0	0
T20Is	7	-	-	-	-	-	-	-	-	-	-
First-class	180	2809	1564	47	4/4	-	33.27	3.34	59.7	0	0
List A	219	1290	1138	33	5/41	5/41	34.48	5.29	39.0	1	0
Twenty20	44	132	186	3	1/12	1/12	62.00	8.45	44.0	0	0

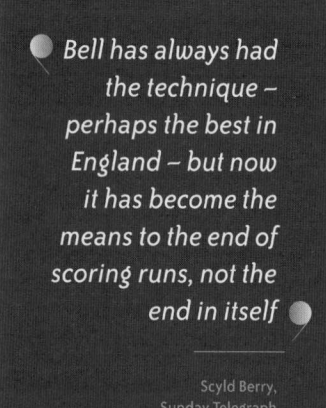

Bell has always had the technique – perhaps the best in England – but now it has become the means to the end of scoring runs, not the end in itself

Scyld Berry,
Sunday Telegraph
cricket correspondent

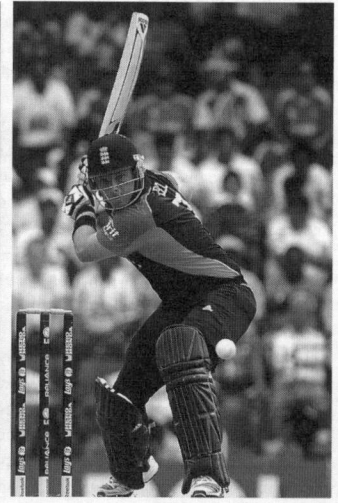

NAME: Paul Merwood Best
BORN: March 8, 1991, Nuneaton
SQUAD Nº: 34
CAREER: Yet to make first-team debut

AOC SAYS: Currently completing his studies at Oxford University, Best is set to be a fringe player this season, but is highly-rated at Edgbaston and has already captained England under 19s and Warwickshire Second XI. In two youth Tests he has impressed with the ball, claiming 10 wickets at an average of 13, while he has also played 14 limited-overs games for the national side at under 19 level. With no Imran Tahir this year, there is a chance for one of Warwickshire's young spinners to stake a claim for a spot in the first team this year, but Best will have to take plenty of Second XI wickets to convince Ashley Giles to give him a go in 2011.

LAST WORD: "He's well thought of, but they won't see a lot of him at the start of the season because he'll still be at Oxford University. He's always talked of, in a tongue-in-cheek way, as a future prime minister because of his academic credentials!" *Brian Halford*

EXTRAS

"Bell can be one of the best in the world and I've got no doubt he will be. He can do anything with a bat in his hand." Andy Flower, England coach

ANT BOTHA

LHB SLA W1

WARWICKSHIRE

NAME: Anthony Greyvensteyn Botha
BORN: November 17, 1976, Pretoria
HEIGHT: 6ft
SQUAD Nº: 44
NICKNAME: Boats
OTHER TEAMS: Derbyshire, Easterns, Natal
CAREER: First-class debut: 19996; List A debut: 1996; T20 debut: 2004; County cap: 2004 (Derbyshire), 2007 (Warwickshire)

AOC SAYS: A canny left-arm twirler and very handy batsman, Botha brings much needed experience to Warwickshire's spin bowling ranks. The club's T20 Player of the Year in both 2005 and 2006, he is predominantly a limited-overs bowler but enjoyed considerable first-class success in 2007, claiming 55 wickets at 29. Less successful in four-day cricket in the three seasons since, he remains a prized asset in all forms of the game and has opened the batting on several occasions in the Championship. A genuine allrounder at county level, he put on 118 in 25 overs with Imran Tahir against Kent last year, a partnership that played a large part in keeping Warwickshire in Division One. Tahir will not be alongside him this year, however, putting more pressure on Botha to deliver in all forms of the game.

LAST WORD: "I'm not looking for another spinner. Ant is the man in possession and I have no qualms about him heading up our spin attack next season; he has bowled matchwinning spells for us in the past. He had a frustrating time of it last year but will have a full season to show us what he has got." *Ashley Giles*

Batting & Fielding

	Mat	Inns	NO	Runs	HS	Ave	SR	100	50	Ct	St
First-class	135	209	27	4311	156*	23.68	-	4	20	102	0
List A	145	109	37	1660	60*	23.05	-	0	4	66	0
Twenty20	64	41	15	465	35*	17.88	115.67	0	0	32	0

Bowling

	Mat	Balls	Runs	Wkts	BBI	BBM	Ave	Econ	SR	5w	10
First-class	135	21596	10496	302	8/53	-	34.75	2.91	71.5	9	1
List A	145	5182	4200	142	5/43	5/43	29.57	4.86	36.4	2	0
Twenty20	64	1101	1250	60	4/14	4/14	20.83	6.81	18.3	0	0

NAME: Neil Miller Carter
BORN: January 29, 1975, Cape Town
HEIGHT: 6ft 2in
SQUAD №: 7
NICKNAME: Carts
OTHER TEAMS: Boland, Cape Cobras, Middlesex
CAREER: First-class debut: 1999; List A debut: 1999; T20 debut: 2003; County cap: 2005 (Warwickshire)

WARWICKSHIRE

AOC SAYS: Better known for his all-round abilities in limited-overs cricket, Carter enjoyed the season of his life in 2010 to be county cricket's MVP at the age of 35. Warwickshire's leading runscorer in the Championship, he also took 50 wickets in a season for the first time in his career; his efforts playing a huge part in keeping the Bears in the top flight. Carter's solid contributions with both bat and ball were also central to the club's CB40 success, while he was typically miserly in T20 cricket. A brisk swing bowler and dangerous hitter, Carter is typically deployed as an opener in one-day cricket and at No.9 in the first-class game.

LAST WORD: "It's a real blow that he's going to be out for at least the first month of the season because of a pelvic injury. I think the aim will be to get him back for the T20 because he's such a key player for them in that competition." *Brian Halford*

Batting & Fielding

	Mat	Inns	NO	Runs	HS	Ave	SR	100	50	Ct	St
First-class	107	148	24	2872	103	23.16	-	1	13	24	0
List A	167	142	15	2853	135	22.46	-	3	12	14	0
Twenty20	85	82	2	1347	58	16.83	139.44	0	2	11	0

Bowling

	Mat	Balls	Runs	Wkts	BBI	BBM	Ave	Econ	SR	5w	10
First-class	107	17725	10258	297	6/63	-	34.53	3.47	59.6	13	0
List A	167	7187	5804	220	5/31	5/31	26.38	4.84	32.6	2	0
Twenty20	85	1690	1966	84	5/19	5/19	23.40	6.97	20.1	1	0

VARUN CHOPRA RHB OB

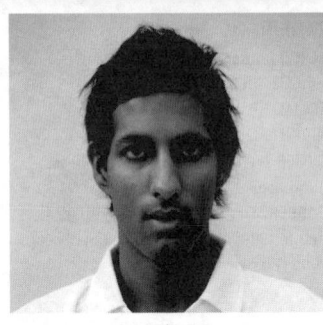

NAME: Varun Chopra
BORN: June 21, 1987, Barking
HEIGHT: 6ft 1in
SQUAD Nº: 3
NICKNAME: Chops, Chopper, Tiddles, Tidz
OTHER TEAMS: Essex
CAREER: First-class debut: 2006; List A debut: 2006; T20 debut: 2006

AOC SAYS: A talented opening batsman, Chopra impressed during his tenure as England under 19s skipper and was expected to flourish on the batsman-friendly wickets at Chelmsford. Modest returns meant that he was unable to tie down a regular first-team spot, resulting in a move to Edgbaston at the end of 2009. After a slow start to his Bears career, a broken hand (an injury that coincided with a horrendous run of form for Warwickshire's batting unit) led to a mid-season sabbatical, but he returned to make a rapid 76 in the CB40 semi-final to help see his side to Lord's. With Ashley Giles demanding more consistent contributions from his top six in 2011, this is a big year for Chopra who has the ability to push for higher honours.

LAST WORD: "When he came back after injury last season he did very well. I imagine that a first-team spot is his to lose." *Brian Halford*

Batting & Fielding

	Mat	Inns	NO	Runs	HS	Ave	SR	100	50	Ct	St
First-class	57	99	6	2661	155	28.61	46.70	2	17	49	0
List A	38	36	1	1335	102	38.14	74.24	2	12	10	0
Twenty20	16	15	4	149	51	13.54	96.12	0	1	2	0

Bowling

	Mat	Balls	Runs	Wkts	BBI	BBM	Ave	Econ	SR	5w	10
First-class	57	131	78	0	-	-	-	3.57	-	0	0
List A	38	18	18	0	-	-	-	6.00	-	0	0
Twenty20	16	-	-	-	-	-	-	-	-	-	-

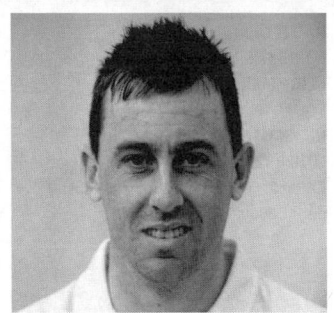

NAME: Rikki Clarke
BORN: September 29, 1981, Orsett
HEIGHT: 6ft 4in
SQUAD Nº: 81
NICKNAME: Clarkey, Crouchy
OTHER TEAMS: England, Derbyshire, Surrey
CAREER: Test match debut: 2003; ODI debut: 2003; First-class debut: 2002; List A: debut: 2001; T20 debut: 2003; County cap: 2005 (Surrey)

WARWICKSHIRE

AOC SAYS: A Second XI Championship winner in 2001, a County Championship winner in 2002 and an England player in 2003: Clarke's rise to prominence was a rapid one. After featuring against Pakistan in the summer of 2003, he replaced the injured Andrew Flintoff in the Test squad for Bangladesh the following winter, but after a solid enough showing he began to lose form with the ball. In the next three years he was only an occasional member of the ODI side, and after losing his place in the Surrey team in 2007 Clarke decided it was time for a change. A disastrous move to Derby, where he was named captain, quit and left the club all in the same year, did nothing for his reputation but he was immediately snapped up by Warwickshire, where he has rebuilt his confidence and form. Claiming 32 wickets at 23 in the Championship last year, Clarke has the potential to take centre stage for the Bears in 2011.

LAST WORD: "I have always said I wouldn't be playing cricket if I did not have the ambition to play for England." *Rikki Clarke*

Batting & Fielding

	Mat	Inns	NO	Runs	HS	Ave	SR	100	50	Ct	St
Tests	2	3	0	96	55	32.00	37.94	0	1	1	0
ODIs	20	13	0	144	39	11.07	62.06	0	0	11	0
First-class	118	188	19	6023	214	35.63	-	12	28	161	0
List A	150	124	18	2694	98*	25.41	-	0	12	70	0
Twenty20	64	59	19	926	79*	23.15	122.97	0	3	30	0

Bowling

	Mat	Balls	Runs	Wkts	BBI	BBM	Ave	Econ	SR	5w	10
Tests	2	174	60	4	2/7	3/11	15.00	2.06	43.5	0	0
ODIs	20	469	415	11	2/28	2/28	37.72	5.30	42.6	0	0
First-class	118	9852	6598	168	6/63	-	39.27	4.01	58.6	1	0
List A	150	3461	3297	80	4/49	4/49	41.21	5.71	43.2	0	0
Twenty20	64	780	1047	42	3/11	3/11	24.92	8.05	18.5	0	0

LAURIE EVANS

RHB RMF

WARWICKSHIRE

NAME: Laurie John Evans
BORN: October 12, 1987, Lambeth
HEIGHT: 6ft
SQUAD Nº: 32
NICKNAME: Lau, Evs, Augustus
OTHER TEAMS: Surrey
CAREER: First-class debut: 2007; List A debut: 2009; T20 debut: 2009

AOC SAYS: A graduate of the Surrey academy, Evans' 10-year association with the Brown Caps ended when he was released last August. Despite an excellent season in Second XI cricket, including 186 and 152 against Northants in July, he had been unable to force his way into the first team. Joining Warwickshire on a short-term loan shortly afterwards, he scored 15 and 3 in a solitary Championship appearance against Kent, and also turned out for the Seconds against his old county. Evans, who scored 133 for Durham MCCU against Lancashire in 2007, signed a one-year contract at Edgbaston in November.

LAST WORD: "I have always stayed confident because I had a lot of good people around me saying I was good enough. Thorpey [former Surrey batting coach Graham Thorpe] has been brilliant and thought I should have been playing first-team cricket somewhere. He thought I was good enough and, coming from someone like him, that was great." *Laurie Evans*

Batting & Fielding

	Mat	Inns	NO	Runs	HS	Ave	SR	100	50	Ct	St
First-class	9	18	1	543	133*	31.94	47.84	1	3	6	0
List A	2	2	1	39	36*	39.00	95.12	0	0	2	0
Twenty20	1	1	0	7	7	7.00	87.50	0	0	0	0

Bowling

	Mat	Balls	Runs	Wkts	BBI	BBM	Ave	Econ	SR	5w	10
First-class	9	36	30	1	1/30	1/30	30.00	5.00	36.0	0	0
List A	2	-	-	-	-	-	-	-	-	-	-
Twenty20	1	-	-	-	-	-	-	-	-	-	-

NAME: Maurice Holmes
BORN: May 19, 1990, Tenterden
SQUAD №: 33
CAREER: Yet to make first-team debut

WARWICKSHIRE

AOC SAYS: An offspinner with an action resembling Muttiah Muralitharan, Holmes travelled to New Zealand in 2009 with Saqlain Mushtaq to help the Black Caps prepare for their tour to Sri Lanka. Such was the impact that the gap year student made, that he was asked to travel with the squad as a net bowler. Formerly on Kent's books, Holmes was signed on a one-year contract by Warwickshire in September of the same year. Capable of bowling a genuine doosra, he has had his action verified by the ECB, and having travelled with the Bears to Barbados for their pre-season tour, he will be pushing for first-team honours in 2011.

LAST WORD: "Maurice Holmes strikes me as a bit of a gamble. But sometimes gambles pay off." *Brian Halford*

Batting & Fielding

	Mat	Inns	NO	Runs	HS	Ave	SR	100	50	Ct	St
First-class	7	13	0	146	48	11.23	29.20	0	0	6	0

Bowling

	Mat	Balls	Runs	Wkts	BBI	BBM	Ave	Econ	SR	5w	10
First-class	7	78	78	0	-	-	-	6.00	-	0	0

ATEEQ JAVID

RHB RM/OB

WARWICKSHIRE

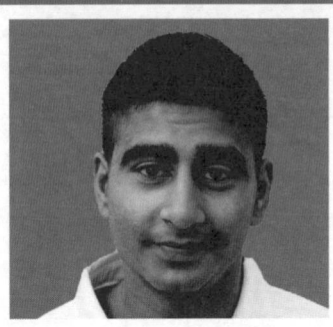

NAME: Ateeq Javid
BORN: October 15, 1989, Birmingham
SQUAD Nº: 17
CAREER: First-class debut: 2009

AOC SAYS: A naturally flamboyant batsman, Javid is one of the most exciting prospects at Edgbaston. Having made his debut against Durham MCCU in 2009, his second first-class match was the Warwickshire v England XI contest that formed part of Andrew Strauss' side's pre-Ashes preparations. He got a further taste of the big time last summer, playing four youth Tests for the under 19s against Sri Lanka, and impressed with 90 at Wantage Road and 89 at Scarborough. He also featured in four Championship matches last year, showing real grit to compile a two-hour 48 against Yorkshire at Headingley. Javid is almost certain to start in the Second XI this summer, but he has the game to push for a first-team spot sooner rather than later.

LAST WORD: "As yet he hasn't quite got the strength to get full value for his shots but he's got an excellent mentality." *Brian Halford*

Batting & Fielding											
	Mat	Inns	NO	Runs	HS	Ave	SR	100	50	Ct	St
First-class	7	13	0	146	48	11.23	29.20	0	0	6	0

Bowling											
	Mat	Balls	Runs	Wkts	BBI	BBM	Ave	Econ	SR	5w	10
First-class	7	78	78	0	-	-	-	6.00	-	0	0

RICHARD JOHNSON

RHB WK

NAME: Richard Matthew Johnson
BORN: September 1, 1988, Solihull
HEIGHT: 5ft 10in
SQUAD Nº: 16
NICKNAME: Johnno
CAREER: First-class debut: 2008; List A
debut: 2008; T20 debut: 2009

AOC SAYS: Johnson marked his Warwickshire debut with 72 against Cambridge MCCU
(still his highest first-class score), but with Tim Ambrose no longer on England's radar
he has had to wait for first-team opportunities at Edgbaston. Like a lot of Warwickshire's
batsmen, however, Ambrose struggled last year, and Johnson was given the nod for
five Championship encounters. Having played as a specialist batsman in one-day
cricket, he will be looking for consistent runs in 2011 and may play alongside Ambrose if
circumstances allow. A sharp keeper, Johnson is always very tidy behind the stumps but
must work on his power-hitting if he is to move up the order in limited-overs cricket.

LAST WORD: "I think Tim Ambrose will have to dislodge him from the wicketkeeping spot,
although he regards himself as a potential specialist batsman. I think he's got a pretty good
career ahead of him." *Brian Halford*

EXTRAS

*"In the pre-season tour of Barbados we showed we have excellent strength in depth in
our squad and we've shown our fitness remains second to none. That was a massive
factor last season and I'm sure it will be again." Jim Troughton*

DARREN MADDY

RHB RM R4 MVP23

NAME: Darren Lee Maddy
BORN: May 23, 1974, Leicester
HEIGHT: 5ft 9in
SQUAD Nº: 23
NICKNAME: Roaster, Dazza, Madds
OTHER TEAMS: England, Leicestershire
CAREER: Test debut: 1999; ODI debut: 1998; T20I debut: 2007; First-class debut: 1994; List A debut: 1993; T20 debut: 2003; County cap: 1996 (Leicestershire), 2007 (Warwickshire)

AOC SAYS: Like most of Warwickshire's batsmen, Maddy endured a dismal year with the bat in the Championship last season, but he was his consistent self in coloured clothing, averaging 35 in the CB40 and scoring 412 runs at 31 in the FP t20. Contributing 36 wickets across all formats, Maddy's all-round value to the Bears is indisputable. A veteran of three Tests and eight ODIs, all played between 1998 and 2000, Maddy's exceptional record in the early years of domestic Twenty20 helped him to resurrect his international career. The first man to reach 1,000 runs in the format, he was central to Leicestershire's 2004 and 2006 Twenty20 Cup wins and earned himself a call-up to the inaugural World Twenty20 in South Africa in 2007. Two severe injuries in recent times have threatened to end his career, but in his 37th year the desire to compete remains.

LAST WORD: "I don't think you can over-state what Madds has been through over the past couple of years. First there was the knee injury and then he had his face smashed in a horrific injury." *Ashley Giles*

Batting & Fielding

	Mat	Inns	NO	Runs	HS	Ave	SR	100	50	Ct	St
Tests	3	4	0	46	24	11.50	24.21	0	0	4	0
ODIs	8	6	0	113	53	18.83	54.85	0	1	1	0
T20Is	4	4	0	113	50	28.25	141.25	0	1	1	0
First-class	258	422	28	12807	229*	32.50	-	26	60	269	0
List A	337	311	34	8546	167*	30.85	-	11	51	131	0
Twenty20	65	65	8	1874	111	32.87	134.62	1	12	36	0

Bowling

	Mat	Balls	Runs	Wkts	BBI	BBM	Ave	Econ	SR	5w	10
Tests	3	84	40	0	-	-	-	2.85	-	0	0
ODIs	8	-	-	-	-	-	-	-	-	-	-
T20Is	4	18	26	3	2/6	2/6	8.66	8.66	6.0	0	0
First-class	258	13800	7208	227	5/37	-	31.75	3.13	60.7	5	0
List A	337	6848	5852	198	4/16	4/16	29.55	5.12	34.5	0	0
Twenty20	65	671	899	32	2/6	2/6	28.09	8.03	20.9	0	0

NAME: Christopher Liam Metters
BORN: September 12, 1990, Torquay
SQUAD Nº: 35
CAREER: Yet to make first-team debut

WARWICKSHIRE

AOC SAYS: A converted seamer, Metters was signed up at the end of last season after impressing in the Second XI. A regular for Devon between 2008 and 2010, he claimed 4-73 against Notts in the Second XI Championship and was subsequently selected for the final against Surrey. Still fairly new to spin bowling he will benefit hugely from Ashley Giles' input and spent last winter in Australia playing grade cricket in Melbourne before rejoining the squad for pre-season.

LAST WORD: "We are delighted to be offering Chris a contract as he is someone with huge scope for improvement. When we first saw him he was bowling seamers, now he is bowling spin and he really does spin it." *Dougie Brown, Warwickshire development manager*

EXTRAS

"Warwickshire like to play two spinners in Twenty20 cricket, but it will be a challenge to find someone who can bowl consistently well alongside Ant Botha this year."
Brian Halford

NAME: Andrew Stephen Miller
BORN: September 27, 1987, Preston
HEIGHT: 6ft 4in
SQUAD Nº: 11
NICKNAME: Millsy, Donk, The Hawk
CAREER: First-class debut: 2008

AOC SAYS: At Lancashire since the age of 13, Miller moved to Edgbaston during the 2006 season in search of more opportunities. After making his first-class debut for the Bears in 2008 against Bangladesh A, he was handed his Championship bow the following year and impressed everyone at Warwickshire, claiming 27 first-class wickets in 11 matches. Injury has blighted his progression over the past two seasons, but if he can remain fit he is a real prospect. A former England under 19 player, he toured India and Bangladesh and was selected for the 2006 World Cup in Sri Lanka.

LAST WORD: "He's been compared to the likes of Alan Richardson and Tim Murtagh – the sort of bowler who wears batsmen down – and he's got plenty of good batsmen out. I think he will play a lot of Championship cricket if he stays fit. In 2009 and 2010 he's looked decent but he's been injured for significant parts of both seasons." *Brian Halford*

Batting & Fielding

	Mat	Inns	NO	Runs	HS	Ave	SR	100	50	Ct	St
First-class	11	16	7	70	35	7.77	26.21	0	0	4	0

Bowling

	Mat	Balls	Runs	Wkts	BBI	BBM	Ave	Econ	SR	5w	10
First-class	11	1546	782	27	5/58	8/103	28.96	3.03	57.2	2	0

NAME: Thomas Milnes
BORN: October 6, 1992, Stourbridge
SQUAD Nº: 8
CAREER: Yet to make first-team debut

WARWICKSHIRE

AOC SAYS: A talented footballer, Milnes interrupted his season with Studley FC in 2010 to tour New Zealand with England's under 18 development squad. A product of Warwickshire's academy, he has also played a solitary youth Test for England under 19s, against Sri Lanka in Galle. A prolific wicket-taker in Second XI cricket, he will be pushing for higher honours this season, and with Neil Carter unavailable for the start of the season and Chris Woakes likely to be away on international duty at some point this summer, Milnes has a great chance to make his first-team bow.

LAST WORD: "Like Tom Allin, Milnes is in the clutch of players just under the first team." *Brian Halford*

EXTRAS

"Warwickshire cricket is in my blood and I will be working hard to uphold the great traditions of this club. I had a taste of the captaincy last season in the latter stages of the Twenty20 campaign, and I am thrilled to be taking on the position across all forms of the game." Jim Troughton

NAME: Steffan Andreas Piolet
BORN: August 8, 1988, Redhill
SQUAD Nº: 14
CAREER: First-class debut: 2009; List A
debut: 2009; T20 debut: 2009

AOC SAYS: Another product of Millfield School, Piolet joined Warwickshire from Sussex midway through the 2008 season on a trial basis. Making his first-class debut against Durham MCCU the following summer, he claimed a remarkable 10-wicket match haul, but has played just once in the Championship for the Bears, against Yorkshire last season. A steady medium-pacer, Piolet's bowling is best suited to the limited-overs game and he made a big contribution in T20 cricket in 2009. He fell out of favour somewhat last season, however, and must look to score a greater weight of runs in the Seconds to force his way back into Ashley Giles' first-team plans. Piolet signed a contract extension in 2009 that has secured his future until the end of the current season.

LAST WORD: "In one-day cricket he's a difficult bowler to face because he bowls very slow medium-pace and has good variations. Whether he's going to be a Championship cricketer, I'm not sure." *Brian Halford*

Batting & Fielding

	Mat	Inns	NO	Runs	HS	Ave	SR	100	50	Ct	St
First-class	2	4	1	41	26*	13.66	40.19	0	0	2	0
List A	12	2	0	6	4	3.00	27.27	0	0	3	0
Twenty20	18	4	1	14	7	4.66	56.00	0	0	8	0

Bowling

	Mat	Balls	Runs	Wkts	BBI	BBM	Ave	Econ	SR	5w	10
First-class	2	264	123	11	6/17	10/43	11.18	2.79	24.0	1	1
List A	12	353	317	13	3/34	3/34	24.38	5.38	27.1	0	0
Twenty20	18	354	389	17	2/9	2/9	22.88	6.59	20.8	0	0

NAME: William Thomas Stuart Porterfield
BORN: September 6, 1984, Londonderry, Northern Ireland
HEIGHT: 5ft 11in
SQUAD Nº: 10
NICKNAME: Purdy, Porty, Porters
OTHER TEAMS: Ireland, Gloucestershire
CAREER: ODI debut: 2006; T20I debut: 2008; First-class debut: 2006; List A debut: 2006; T20 debut: 2008

AOC SAYS: A veteran of 50 ODIs, Porterfield has plenty of experience at Associate level and has played at two World Cups, captaining the side to a famous win over England in the 2011 tournament. A matchwinning 85 against Bangladesh in 2007 earned him a contract with Gloucestershire, and after two modest seasons at Bristol he topped the Championship averages in a struggling side last year. Scoring 531 runs at 38 in his seven outings, the opener held together Gloucestershire's top-order for much of the season, and scored two of only three centuries that his side managed in 2010, including a brilliant 175 against his new employers. Warwickshire, who struggled themselves with the bat last year, will be hoping that Porterfield can bring similar solidity to their Championship batting, although with a first-class average of 34, he is yet to fully convince at this level. It seems likely that he will open the batting alongside Ian Westwood or Varun Chopra this season, but he is also capable of batting in the middle-order if required. A fine fielder, Porterfield produced solid if unspectacular returns in limited-overs cricket for Gloucestershire last season, and will provide another option in Warwickshire's top five for both the CB40 and FP t20. International commitments may slightly affect his Warwickshire availability as he is set to remain a key figure for Ireland for the foreseeable future. A well-respected leader and the side's most reliable runscorer alongside the recently returned Ed Joyce, he is one of his country's most important players.

LAST WORD: "I was absolutely delighted to secure the signing of William Porterfield. I see it as highly significant. Why? Well, for the last few years Warwickshire have struggled to capture these sorts of players from other counties, and the fact that we were able to convince him to come speaks volumes about the progress we've made. We're probably still not able to compete with the salaries offered elsewhere, but I believe Porterfield's arrival bears testament to the happier dressing room, the success we've had as a team and the way individual players have progressed. I'm expecting him to do really well for us. He's a very high-class batsmen who has proved his potential at international and domestic level and I believe he has a lot more to offer." *Ashley Giles*

WILLIAM PORTERFIELD

Batting & Fielding

	Mat	Inns	NO	Runs	HS	Ave	SR	100	50	Ct	St
ODIs	50	50	3	1551	112*	33.00	67.52	5	6	26	0
T20Is	17	16	1	263	46	17.53	103.95	0	0	4	0
First-class	44	77	2	2548	175	33.97	46.26	4	15	45	0
List A	105	104	4	3373	112*	33.73	70.06	5	19	46	0
Twenty20	45	44	2	897	65	21.35	124.75	0	3	18	0

Bowling

	Mat	Balls	Runs	Wkts	BBI	BBM	Ave	Econ	SR	5w	10
ODIs	50	-	-	-	-	-	-	-	-	-	-
T20Is	17	-	-	-	-	-	-	-	-	-	-
First-class	44	108	138	2	1/29	1/29	69.00	7.66	54.0	0	0
List A	105	-	-	-	-	-	-	-	-	-	-
Twenty20	45	-	-	-	-	-	-	-	-	-	-

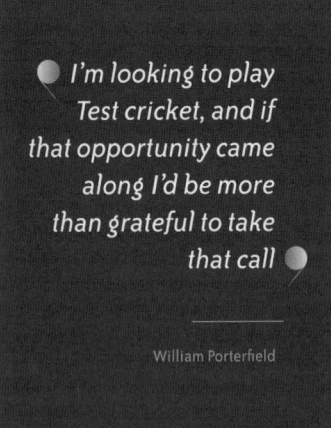

I'm looking to play Test cricket, and if that opportunity came along I'd be more than grateful to take that call

William Porterfield

NAME: William Boyd Rankin
BORN: July 5, 1984, Londonderry,
Northern Ireland
HEIGHT: 6ft 7in
SQUAD Nº: 30
NICKNAME: Boydo, Stankin
OTHER TEAMS: Ireland, Derbyshire
CAREER: ODI debut: 2007; T20I debut: 2009;
First-class debut: 2007; List A debut: 2006;
T20 debut: 2009

WARWICKSHIRE

AOC SAYS: A veritable gentle giant, Rankin made his ODI debut in 2007. Months later, he was the leading wicket-taker in Ireland's impressive World Cup campaign, and he remains the only man in Phil Simmons' side capable of troubling international-class batsmen with pace and bounce. Having spent time on the MCC staff at Lord's, he was snapped up by Derbyshire for the 2007 season, and although injuries limited his opportunities he showed enough talent to be offered an extension. However, when Warwickshire came calling he decided his future lay at Edgbaston, and he's been a key member of their side ever since. He is not always deployed in Twenty20, but he showed his wicket-taking ability in coloured clothing with 15 wickets at 16 in last year's CB40. A foot injury sustained after at Essex threatened to ruin his prospects of a second World Cup, but he recovered in time and will be looking for a big year with the Bears in 2011.

LAST WORD: "In bursts, Boyd Rankin looks like a world beater; he really can bowl some great spells. But sometimes it just doesn't happen for him." *Brian Halford*

Batting & Fielding

	Mat	Inns	NO	Runs	HS	Ave	SR	100	50	Ct	St
ODIs	29	12	9	34	7*	11.33	33.66	0	0	5	0
T20Is	6	2	1	6	5*	6.00	60.00	0	0	3	0
First-class	34	42	17	128	13	5.12	30.76	0	0	12	0
List A	58	19	12	59	9	8.42	39.07	0	0	7	0
Twenty20	9	3	2	9	5*	9.00	69.23	0	0	3	0

Bowling

	Mat	Balls	Runs	Wkts	BBI	BBM	Ave	Econ	SR	5w	10
ODIs	29	1340	1130	36	3/32	3/32	31.38	5.05	37.2	0	0
T20Is	6	144	162	7	2/25	2/25	23.14	6.75	20.5	0	0
First-class	34	4531	2867	101	5/16	8/121	28.38	3.79	44.8	3	0
List A	58	2381	2033	73	4/34	4/34	27.84	5.12	32.6	0	0
Twenty20	9	204	223	9	2/25	2/25	24.77	6.55	22.6	0	0

NAQAASH TAHIR

RHB RFM

WARWICKSHIRE

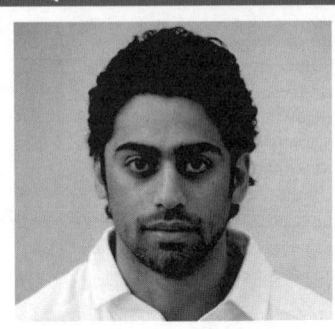

NAME: Naqaash Sarosh Tahir
BORN: November 14, 1983, Birmingham
HEIGHT: 5ft 10in
SQUAD Nº: 20
NICKNAME: Naq, Naqy
CAREER: First-class debut: 2004; List A debut: 2005

AOC SAYS: In a career blighted by injury, Warwickshire are yet to get a full season out of a bowler whom teammate Darren Maddy considers one of the most skilful he has seen. A prodigious swinger of the ball, Tahir took a wicket with just his second ball in first-class cricket in 2004 and followed this up with match-figures of 8-90 to take Warwickshire to victory over local rivals Worcestershire in the Championship. Since then, a troublesome back has seen him in and out of the side, but with a bowling average of 29 he has still managed to perform well when fit. In 2009, he showed the extent of his promise with 3-54 against an England XI, but injury struck again and he only managed three Championship matches and a solitary one-day game for the Bears in 2010. Out of contract at the end of the current campaign, this is a huge year for Tahir.

LAST WORD: "When Warwickshire played England in 2009, Andrew Strauss said that he was a superb bowler." *Brian Halford*

Batting & Fielding

	Mat	Inns	NO	Runs	HS	Ave	SR	100	50	Ct	St
First-class	52	59	16	658	49	15.30	37.13	0	0	7	0
List A	15	5	3	19	13*	9.50	73.07	0	0	1	0

Bowling

	Mat	Balls	Runs	Wkts	BBI	BBM	Ave	Econ	SR	5w	10
First-class	52	6963	3815	128	7/107	-	29.80	3.28	54.3	2	0
List A	15	523	439	5	2/47	2/47	87.80	5.03	104.6	0	0

NAME: Ian Jonathan Leonard Trott
BORN: April 22, 1981, Cape Town,
HEIGHT: 6ft 1in
SQUAD №: 9
NICKNAME: Booger
OTHER TEAMS: England, Boland, Otago
CAREER: Test debut: 2009; ODI debut: 2009;
T20I debut: 2007; First-class debut: 2000;
List A debut: 2000; T20 debut: 2003; County
cap: 2005 (Warwickshire)

WARWICKSHIRE

AOC SAYS: Since beginning his Test career with an Ashes-winning century, the good days
have far outweighed the bad for Trott, who is now one of the first names on the England
teamsheet. A minor blip in the 2009/10 series against South Africa is his only real blemish
to date, and he can currently boast a Test average of 61 and an ODI average of 56, having
amassed 445 runs at 89 in Austraia last winter and become the joint fastest player (alongside
Kevin Pietersen and Viv Richards) to reach 1,000 runs in one-day internationals. For
Warwickshire he scored 245 on his Second XI debut in 2002 and 134 on his Championship
bow the following year. Sometimes criticised for scoring too slowly, he is deemed surplus
to requirements for England's T20 side but scored a record-breaking 525 runs in the
Twenty20 Cup in 2009. Yet to hit an international six, Trott instead relies on superb timing
and impeccable placement, as demonstrated against West Indies in the World Cup – a
tournament in which he was the first batsman to reach 400 runs – when he raced to 22 off
eight balls without breaking sweat. Calm, cool and as determined as any bastman in the
game, Trott has a long international career ahead of him.

INSIDE TRACK: "His batting now is all about remaining process-focused. He used to be too
results-focused. He was always worrying about how long he had to bat, how many runs he
had to score and what the effect on his average might be. Now he just concentrates on the
little things. He makes sure he's prepared for each ball and that he concentrates on that and
nothing else. The great strength of his batting is that it is not about the situation. He stays in
the moment and simply plays each ball on its own merit. So when he came into the England
team for that huge Ashes Test, it didn't make any difference to him. He played each ball
on its merit. He loves batting. It's not his life by any means, but he does really love it. Quite
often you'll see him marking his guard just after he's hit the winning runs in a T20 match and
everyone else is celebrating. But, a couple of minutes later, he relaxes and enjoys it as much
as anyone. He's just getting to the stage where he could be rated as one of the best in the
world and, from the perspective of Andy Flower and Andrew Strauss, I'd think they are very
happy to have him in the side." *Ashley Giles*

JONATHAN TROTT

WARWICKSHIRE

Batting & Fielding

	Mat	Inns	NO	Runs	HS	Ave	SR	100	50	Ct	St
Tests	18	30	4	1600	226	61.53	48.19	5	5	9	0
ODIs	25	25	2	1280	137	55.65	78.62	3	11	5	0
T20Is	7	7	1	138	51	23.00	95.83	0	1	0	0
First-class	161	269	34	10748	226	45.73	-	25	52	151	0
List A	187	175	32	6753	137	47.22	-	14	46	59	0
Twenty20	76	71	16	2081	86*	37.83	114.90	0	13	18	0

Bowling

	Mat	Balls	Runs	Wkts	BBI	BBM	Ave	Econ	SR	5w	10
Tests	18	114	86	1	1/16	1/23	86.00	4.52	114.0	0	0
ODIs	25	171	152	2	2/31	2/31	76.00	5.33	85.5	0	0
T20Is	7	-	-	-	-	-	-	-	-	-	-
First-class	161	4358	2471	56	7/39	-	44.12	3.40	77.8	1	0
List A	187	1528	1436	54	4/55	4/55	26.59	5.63	28.2	0	0
Twenty20	76	144	234	8	2/19	2/19	29.25	9.75	18.0	0	0

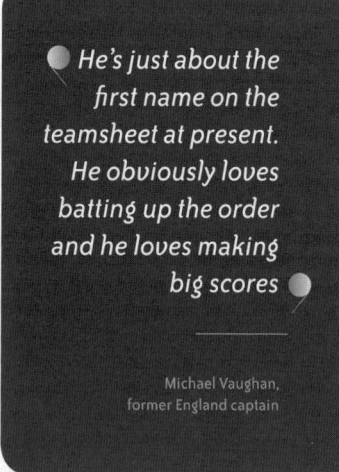

He's just about the first name on the teamsheet at present. He obviously loves batting up the order and he loves making big scores

Michael Vaughan,
former England captain

NAME: Jamie Oliver Troughton
BORN: March 2, 1979, Camden
HEIGHT: 5ft 11in
SQUAD Nº: 24
NICKNAME: Troughts
OTHER TEAMS: England
CAREER: ODI debut: 2003; First-class debut: 2001; List A debut: 1999; T20 debut: 2003; County cap: 2002

WARWICKSHIRE

AOC SAYS: Having replaced Ian Westwood as Twenty20 skipper last season, Troughton assumed full captaincy duties over the winter. While getting the best out of his charges in 2011, Troughton must also improve on a poor season with the bat that saw him average just 20 in first-class cricket. Now entering his 13th year as a Bear, Troughton peaked in 2002, scoring 1,067 runs at an average of 50.80, before appearing for England in six ODIs the following year. He was unable to make an impact at international level, however, and quickly returned to life as a county pro. An excellent fielder, Troughton is also a keen guitarist and cartoonist.

LAST WORD: "That responsibility is something that I'm craving now. I've got to that age where I'm taking that responsibility on and I think I'll benefit from it rather than it hampering me." *Jim Troughton*

Batting & Fielding

	Mat	Inns	NO	Runs	HS	Ave	SR	100	50	Ct	St
ODIs	6	5	1	36	20	9.00	47.36	0	0	1	0
First-class	126	196	15	6498	223	35.90	50.08	16	31	58	0
List A	137	121	14	3130	115*	29.25	-	2	18	48	0
Twenty20	68	62	4	1291	66	22.25	125.33	0	8	31	0

Bowling

	Mat	Balls	Runs	Wkts	BBI	BBM	Ave	Econ	SR	5w	10
ODIs	6	-	-	-	-	-	-	-	-	-	-
First-class	126	2357	1416	22	3/1	-	64.36	3.60	107.1	0	0
List A	137	736	644	25	4/23	4/23	25.76	5.25	29.4	0	0
Twenty20	68	96	127	6	2/10	2/10	21.16	7.93	16.0	0	0

IAN WESTWOOD

LHB RHB

WARWICKSHIRE

NAME: Ian James Westwood
BORN: July 13, 1982, Birmingham
HEIGHT: 5ft 8in
SQUAD Nº: 22
NICKNAME: Westy, Wezzo
CAREER: First-class debut: 2003; List A debut: 2001; T20 debut: 2005; County cap:2008

AOC SAYS: Making his Warwickshire debut in 2004, Westwood produced solid if unspectacular results in 2005 and was rewarded with a run at the top of the order in 2006, averaging 43 in first-class cricket across the season. Another solid season in 2007 cemented his place at Edgbaston, but since 2008 he has struggled for consistency, failing to average 30 in any of the last three seasons. While averaging a respectable 33 in the CB40, poor form in the Championship took its toll and he resigned the T20 captaincy to focus on his batting. A matchwinning 61 against Essex helped Warwickshire avoid relegation from the Championship but with Will Porterfield joining the club over the winter, Westwood – who has handed over the captaincy to Jim Troughton – will have to fight for an opening spot in 2010.

LAST WORD: "It's not an easy decision to step down and I know that he feels a lot better for it, which is great for him and great for Warwickshire as well." *Jim Troughton*

Batting & Fielding

	Mat	Inns	NO	Runs	HS	Ave	SR	100	50	Ct	St
First-class	82	144	16	4149	178	32.41	44.62	7	23	40	0
List A	59	49	9	928	65	23.20	-	0	3	6	0
Twenty20	38	27	12	342	49*	22.80	114.00	0	0	5	0

Bowling

	Mat	Balls	Runs	Wkts	BBI	BBM	Ave	Econ	SR	5w	10
First-class	82	371	222	6	2/39	-	37.00	3.59	61.8	0	0
List A	59	252	215	3	1/28	1/28	71.66	5.11	84.0	0	0
Twenty20	38	54	91	5	3/29	3/29	18.20	10.11	10.8	0	0

NAME: Christopher Roger Woakes
BORN: March 2, 1989, Birmingham
HEIGHT: 6ft 2in
SQUAD Nº: 19
NICKNAME: Woakesy, Jokes, Cheetah
OTHER TEAMS: England
CAREER: ODI Debut: 2011; T20I debut: 2011;
First-class debut: 2006; List A debut: 2007;
T20 debut: 2008; County cap: 2009

AOC SAYS: A consistently dangerous seamer and accomplished lower-order batsman, Woakes' stock has risen rapidly since he made his Warwickshire debut in 2006. Aged just 19, he was the county's leading wicket-taker in 2008, leading to a place in England's 30-man provisional squad for the 2009 World Twenty20. He came to further prominence that year, turning out for the MCC in the champion county fixture at Lord's, before providing a swing-bowling masterclass at Derby a month later, claiming 6-43 against the touring West Indians. Since then Woakes has continued to impress for Warwickshire in all forms of the game, and while primarily employed as a bowler he has already scored three first-class hundreds, including a century at No.8 for England Lions. More than 600 runs and 84 wickets across all competitions last year highlighted Woakes' all-round potential and it was no surprise when he was called up to replace the injured Stuart Broad for the Twenty20 and ODI series that followed the Ashes last winter. Making an immediate impact, Woakes pulled Shaun Tait for a mighty six and hit the winning run off the last ball of the game to ensure a thrilling one-wicket win in the first match of the T20 series, while in just his third ODI he claimed 6-45. With England in relatively rude health in all forms of the game at the moment, Woakes may have to bide his time before he is an international regular, but such is his talent that it seems inconceivable that he will not represent England with distinction in all forms of the game, sooner rather than later.

INSIDE TRACK: "I have long said that if I could clone one of my players it would be Chris Woakes. Everything about him is impressive. He trains hard, he works hard on his fitness, he's receptive to new ideas and he's low maintenance. He just gets on with his job. He's a great character to have around and there is a lot more to come from him. He's better known as a bowler at the moment but he has a future as a genuine allrounder. He's already got a couple of first-class centuries for us and he scored a lot of important runs in one-day cricket last season." *Ashley Giles*

CHRIS WOAKES

Batting & Fielding

	Mat	Inns	NO	Runs	HS	Ave	SR	100	50	Ct	St
ODIs	3	3	1	20	12	10.00	50.00	0	0	1	0
T20Is	2	2	2	30	19*	-	142.85	0	0	1	0
First-class	50	65	17	1423	136*	29.64	-	3	3	26	0
List A	43	22	6	211	49*	13.18	93.77	0	0	9	0
Twenty20	35	15	10	144	27*	28.80	148.45	0	0	15	0

Bowling

	Mat	Balls	Runs	Wkts	BBI	BBM	Ave	Econ	SR	5w	10
ODIs	3	158	149	7	6/45	6/45	21.28	5.65	22.5	1	0
T20Is	2	42	63	2	1/29	1/29	31.50	9.00	21.0	0	0
First-class	50	8255	4267	167	6/43	11/97	25.55	3.10	49.4	9	2
List A	43	1689	1483	44	6/45	6/45	33.70	5.26	38.3	1	0
Twenty20	35	599	830	28	4/21	4/21	29.64	8.31	21.3	0	0

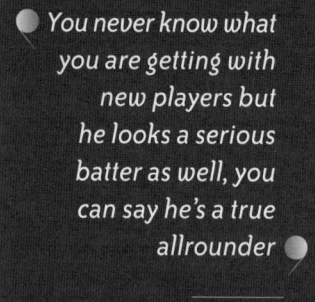

You never know what you are getting with new players but he looks a serious batter as well, you can say he's a true allrounder

Paul Collingwood,
England T20 captain

486

OVERSEAS PLAYER

WARWICKSHIRE

NAME: Mohammad Younus Khan
BORN: November 29, 1977, Mardan, Pakistan
SQUAD Nº: 75
OTHER TEAMS: Pakistan, Nottinghamshire, Peshawar Cricket Association, Rajasthan Royals, South Australia, Surrey, Yorkshire
CAREER: Test debut: 2000; ODI debut: 2000; T20I debut: 2006; First-class debut: 1999; List A debut: 1999; T20 debut: 2005; County cap: 2007 (Yorkshire)

AOC SAYS: Since scoring a century on his Test debut in 2000 there has been little doubt about Younus' class. Averaging more than 50 in 67 matches for his country, he sits alongside Mohammad Yousuf as Pakistan's most consistent contributor in the post-Inzamam era. Not a regular in the side until 2004, Younus has scored 17 Test centuries, his finest hour in whites coming in India when he scored a brilliant 267 and 84 at Bangalore. He has had two spells as skipper of the national side, leading Pakistan to World Twenty20 glory in 2009, but he has also courted controversy and was banned by the PCB in March 2010 for allegedly causing infighting within the squad. Now reinstated, he is set to miss the start of the county season for Pakistan's series against West Indies.

LAST WORD: "He is a great addition to the Bears' squad and will add tremendous depth to our batting line-up." *Ashley Giles*

Batting & Fielding

	Mat	Inns	NO	Runs	HS	Ave	SR	100	50	Ct	St
Tests	67	119	8	5617	313	50.60	53.56	17	23	74	0
ODIs	221	213	20	6213	144	32.19	74.91	6	41	113	0
T20Is	25	23	3	442	51	22.10	121.42	0	2	12	0
First-class	155	252	29	11262	313	50.50	-	35	46	165	0
List A	283	269	30	8132	144	34.02	-	10	52	153	0
Twenty20	53	50	8	1025	70	24.40	118.77	0	4	22	0

Bowling

	Mat	Balls	Runs	Wkts	BBI	BBM	Ave	Econ	SR	5w	10
Tests	67	660	407	7	2/23	4/50	58.14	3.70	94.2	0	0
ODIs	221	236	239	2	1/3	1/3	119.50	6.07	118.0	0	0
T20Is	25	22	18	3	3/18	3/18	6.00	4.90	7.3	0	0
First-class	155	2928	1705	38	4/52	-	44.86	3.49	77.0	0	0
List A	283	1097	1050	27	3/5	3/5	38.88	5.74	40.6	0	0
Twenty20	53	98	124	6	3/18	3/18	20.66	7.59	16.3	0	0

TEAM PROFILE

FORMED: 1865
HOME GROUND: New Road
ONE-DAY NAME: Royals
CAPTAIN: Daryl Mitchell
2010 RESULTS: CC2: 2/9; CB40: 5/7 in Group A; FP t20: 9/9 in North Group

HONOURS
County Championship: (5)1964, 1965, 1974, 1988, 1989; Gillette/NatWest/C&G/FP Trophy: 1994; Benson and Hedges Cup: 1991; Pro40/National League/CB40: 2007; Sunday League: (3) 1971, 1987, 1988

THE LOWDOWN
On August 12, 2010, when Vikram Solanki resigned the captaincy after his side had been demolished by Glamorgan, promotion for Worcestershire was not the thought on most people's minds. The departure of five senior players – Kabir Ali, Steve Davies, Stephen Moore, Gareth Batty and Simon Jones – and the financial strait-jacket that forced them to pare their staff down to the bare minimum had seen them cast as favourites for the wooden spoon. Having not won a single Championship game in 2009, they were sixth out of nine as Daryl Mitchell took over, but three wins from six games later they were up, pipping the side they lost to that day by five points. Their 2011 status owes much to a last day of the season run-chase; 301 in 70 overs, achieved thanks to hundreds from youngsters James Cameron and Moeen Ali, who put on 200 in the afternoon session.

DIRECTOR OF CRICKET: STEVE RHODES
Former England keeper Rhodes started out at Yorkshire before moving south to New Road to become a Worcestershire institution. Thoroughly down to earth, he's realistic about his side's goals this season: "It's important that people understand that this season is about consolidation. It will be very tough, but if we can stay up then perhaps there will be a bit more money around in a year or two."

With thanks to: Damian D'Oliveira, Worcestershire academy director and assistant coach; Mike Reeves, Worcester Evening News

www.wccc.co.uk / tel: 01905 748474

Batting & Fielding

	Mat	Inns	NO	Runs	HS	Ave	SR	100	50	Ct	St
SH Choudhry	1	1	0	63	63	63.00	40.38	0	1	1	-
MM Ali	15	28	2	1260	126	48.46	60.05	3	9	9	-
AN Kervezee	16	30	3	1190	155	44.07	72.64	3	6	14	-
DKH Mitchell	16	31	3	1180	165*	42.14	45.87	4	4	32	-
JG Cameron	10	17	1	576	105	36.00	58.29	1	3	7	-
GM Andrew	9	14	1	425	79	32.69	66.51	0	4	2	-
BJM Scott	7	12	2	313	98	31.30	46.99	0	3	30	1
PA Jaques	8	15	0	465	94	31.00	67.29	0	3	9	-
VS Solanki	15	28	1	717	114	26.55	55.84	1	4	18	-
Shakib Al Hasan	8	15	1	358	90	25.57	68.32	0	1	3	-
BF Smith	8	14	2	282	80	23.50	47.31	0	2	9	-
DA Wheeldon	7	14	1	269	65	20.69	31.42	0	2	2	-
OB Cox	9	16	4	218	59	18.16	59.72	0	1	18	1
MS Mason	8	12	2	137	51*	13.70	74.05	0	1	6	-
A Richardson	14	18	11	71	11	10.14	36.78	0	0	5	-
RA Jones	11	19	2	100	21*	5.88	26.45	0	0	7	-
JD Shantry	11	15	5	55	13*	5.50	28.94	0	0	3	-
Imran Arif	2	3	1	8	4*	4.00	32.00	0	0	1	-
CD Whelan	1	2	0	5	5	2.50	20.83	0	0	1	-

Bowling

	Mat	Overs	Mdns	Runs	Wkts	BBI	BBM	Ave	Econ	SR	5w	10
Shakib Al Hasan	8	259.0	48	783	35	7/32	8/102	22.37	3.02	44.4	3	0
A Richardson	14	524.0	153	1342	55	5/44	7/89	24.40	2.56	57.1	2	0
MS Mason	8	278.0	72	849	31	4/87	6/120	27.38	3.05	53.8	0	0
GM Andrew	9	196.4	32	656	23	4/45	5/92	28.52	3.33	51.3	0	0
SH Choudhry	1	10.0	3	32	1	1/32	1/32	32.00	3.20	60.0	0	0
RA Jones	11	298.2	48	1281	38	7/115	8/105	33.71	4.29	47.1	2	0
CD Whelan	1	9.0	1	34	1	1/21	1/34	34.00	3.77	54.0	0	0
JD Shantry	11	308.0	73	945	27	5/49	6/111	35.00	3.06	68.4	1	0
Imran Arif	2	33.0	2	141	4	2/63	3/80	35.25	4.27	49.5	0	0
MM Ali	15	179.4	29	626	17	5/36	6/39	36.82	3.48	63.4	1	0
JG Cameron	10	93.5	17	332	8	2/18	3/43	41.50	3.53	70.3	0	0
VS Solanki	15	29.0	4	96	1	1/22	1/22	96.00	3.31	174.0	0	0
AN Kervezee	16	4.3	0	63	0	-	-	-	14.00	-	0	0
DKH Mitchell	16	15.0	3	64	0	-	-	-	4.26	-	0	0

Batting & Fielding

	Mat	Inns	NO	Runs	HS	Ave	SR	100	50	Ct	St
SH Choudhry	7	6	4	115	39	57.50	98.29	0	0	3	-
PA Jaques	5	5	0	249	110	49.80	98.03	1	1	3	-
Shakib Al Hasan	5	5	0	187	91	37.40	119.10	0	2	1	-
VS Solanki	12	12	0	436	129	36.33	92.76	1	2	8	-
MM Ali	12	12	0	383	121	31.91	98.20	1	1	5	-
DKH Mitchell	12	12	3	283	70	31.44	81.55	0	1	6	-
GM Andrew	11	10	2	249	104	31.12	151.82	1	1	2	-
JG Cameron	12	11	3	236	58	29.50	89.05	0	1	1	-
AN Kervezee	12	12	0	331	111	27.58	100.00	1	0	4	-
BJM Scott	5	4	1	62	22	20.66	68.13	0	0	3	0
JK Manuel	2	2	0	26	22	13.00	118.18	0	0	2	-
JD Shantry	12	4	1	35	18	11.66	77.77	0	0	2	-
OB Cox	7	3	2	9	9*	9.00	69.23	0	0	7	2
BF Smith	5	5	0	30	19	6.00	61.22	0	0	2	-
CD Whelan	2	1	0	1	1	1.00	33.33	0	0	0	-
RA Jones	3	2	2	11	11*	-	73.33	0	0	0	-
Imran Arif	3	2	2	6	5*	-	14.28	0	0	4	-
A Richardson	2	1	1	1	1*	-	100.00	0	0	1	-

Bowling

	Mat	Overs	Mdns	Runs	Wkts	BBI	Ave	Econ	SR	5w
MS Mason	1	8.0	0	38	3	3/38	12.66	4.75	16.0	0
Shakib Al Hasan	5	29.1	1	160	9	4/32	17.77	5.48	19.4	0
A Richardson	2	15.0	0	78	4	2/22	19.50	5.20	22.5	0
CD Whelan	2	11.0	0	84	4	3/34	21.00	7.63	16.5	0
JD Shantry	12	81.4	3	487	18	3/33	27.05	5.96	27.2	0
SH Choudhry	7	33.0	0	213	6	4/54	35.50	6.45	33.0	0
VS Solanki	12	11.0	0	39	1	1/14	39.00	3.54	66.0	0
JG Cameron	12	44.1	0	292	7	4/44	41.71	6.61	37.8	0
GM Andrew	11	48.5	1	356	8	3/30	44.50	7.29	36.6	0
DKH Mitchell	12	36.0	0	187	4	2/30	46.75	5.19	54.0	0
Imran Arif	3	18.0	0	141	3	2/43	47.00	7.83	36.0	0
MM Ali	12	60.0	2	345	7	2/29	49.28	5.75	51.4	0
CJ Russell	2	9.0	0	68	1	1/23	68.00	7.55	54.0	0
RA Jones	3	21.0	0	129	1	1/47	129.00	6.14	126.0	0

www.wccc.co.uk / tel: 01905 748474

	Mat	Inns	NO	Runs	HS	Ave	SR	100	50	Ct	St
PA Jaques	14	13	3	330	78*	33.00	131.47	0	2	6	-
MM Ali	16	15	1	385	72	27.50	129.19	0	3	7	-
ST Jayasuriya	10	10	0	267	87	26.70	158.92	0	2	2	-
VS Solanki	7	6	0	121	51	20.16	114.15	0	1	2	-
DKH Mitchell	16	12	1	215	39	19.54	112.56	0	0	6	-
SPD Smith	5	4	0	67	34	16.75	117.54	0	0	3	-
JG Cameron	15	11	1	158	51*	15.80	107.48	0	1	2	-
BJM Scott	8	7	3	60	23*	15.00	85.71	0	0	2	1
AN Kervezee	16	14	2	179	35	14.91	107.18	0	0	6	-
RA Jones	6	2	1	14	9	14.00	77.77	0	0	7	-
GM Andrew	14	11	4	87	27*	12.42	145.00	0	0	2	-
Imran Arif	9	3	2	11	6*	11.00	84.61	0	0	0	-
JK Manuel	11	9	1	86	31	10.75	104.87	0	0	3	-
OB Cox	8	5	3	13	6*	6.50	108.33	0	0	2	2
JD Shantry	15	4	2	8	6*	4.00	66.66	0	0	4	-
MS Mason	1	1	0	0	0	0.00	0.00	0	0	1	-
SH Choudhry	3	3	3	15	8*	-	83.33	0	0	0	-

	Mat	Overs	Mdns	Runs	Wkts	BBI	Ave	Econ	SR	5w
JD Shantry	15	49.0	1	345	18	3/23	19.16	7.04	16.3	0
SPD Smith	5	16.0	0	116	6	2/20	19.33	7.25	16.0	0
MM Ali	16	39.1	0	285	13	3/19	21.92	7.27	18.0	0
SH Choudhry	3	7.0	0	51	2	1/24	25.50	7.28	21.0	0
JG Cameron	15	29.5	0	239	8	3/22	29.87	8.01	22.3	0
VS Solanki	7	3.0	0	31	1	1/6	31.00	10.33	18.0	0
GM Andrew	14	31.2	0	315	9	2/26	35.00	10.05	20.8	0
DKH Mitchell	16	25.2	0	210	5	1/15	42.00	8.28	30.4	0
A Richardson	2	7.0	0	45	1	1/21	45.00	6.42	42.0	0
ST Jayasuriya	10	39.0	0	278	5	1/20	55.60	7.12	46.8	0
RA Jones	6	11.0	0	119	2	1/17	59.50	10.81	33.0	0
Imran Arif	9	22.0	0	198	2	1/30	99.00	9.00	66.0	0
MS Mason	1	1.1	1	1	0	-	-	0.85	-	0

WORCESTERSHIRE

NAME: Moeen Munir Ali
BORN: June 18, 1987, Birmingham
HEIGHT: 6ft
SQUAD Nº: 8
NICKNAME: Moe
OTHER TEAMS: Warwickshire
CAREER: First-class debut: 2005; List A
debut: 2006; T20 debut 2007

AOC SAYS: Just 23, Moeen seems to have been around forever. He captained England under 19s in the Word Cup in 2006 and played for Warwickshire at a very young age but it is only in the last couple of seasons that he has started to mature as a batsman, adding substance (2,000 runs in all competitions) to the style. From a true cricketing family – brothers Kadeer and Omar and cousin Kabir are all top-notch cricketers – Moeen was Worcestershire's leading runscorer in Championship and Twenty20 cricket last season. He spent the winter playing with Tamim Iqbal and Shakib Al Hasan's side Mohammedan in Bangladesh before moving on to South Africa to gain further experience of different countries.

LAST WORD: "He is an incredibly fluid and attractive left-hander with all the shots. If you are lucky enough to see him get a big score you would be happy to pay to see him play."
Nick Knight

Batting & Fielding

	Mat	Inns	NO	Runs	HS	Ave	SR	100	50	Ct	St
First-class	49	84	7	2697	153	35.02	52.98	5	18	21	0
List A	63	59	2	1507	125	26.43	92.39	3	8	17	0
Twenty20	37	35	3	727	72	22.71	118.5	0	3	9	0

Bowling

	Mat	Balls	Runs	Wkts	BBI	BBM	Ave	Econ	SR	5w	10
First-class	49	2449	1659	27	5/36	6/39	61.44	4.06	90.7	1	0
List A	63	858	805	19	3/32	3/32	42.36	5.62	45.1	0	0
Twenty20	37	283	350	15	3/19	3/19	23.33	7.42	18.8	0	0

NAME: Gareth Mark Andrew
BORN: December 27, 1983, Yeovil
HEIGHT: 6ft
SQUAD Nº: 14
NICKNAME: Gaz, Brad, Sobers
OTHER TEAMS: Somerset
CAREER: First-class debut: 2003; List A debut: 2000; T20 debut: 2003

WORCESTERSHIRE

AOC SAYS: Yeovil Town supporting, former England under 17 and under 19 seamer Andrew signed a new one-year deal at the end of last season after rumours of an approach from Sussex. The former Somerset man has the potential to be a key part of the side and showed what he can achieve with his 60-ball 100 against Surrey in the CB40. With some further progression with the ball he has the potential to be a quality allrounder, and this season in the top flight is an excellent opportunity for him to step up and become the mainstay of the Royals' line-up.

LAST WORD: "An enigma. On his day, he's a good, solid allrounder but those days don't happen regularly enough. He needs to add consistency to his firepower. He hits it a mile with his Mongoose bat and is a more than useful bowler when he is concentrating." *Mike Reeves*

Batting & Fielding

	Mat	Inns	NO	Runs	HS	Ave	SR	100	50	Ct	St
First-class	42	59	10	1178	92*	24.04	50.64	0	7	12	0
List A	83	53	14	640	104	16.41	-	1	1	25	0
Twenty20	63	33	12	199	27*	9.47	124.37	0	7	15	0

Bowling

	Mat	Balls	Runs	Wkts	BBI	BBM	Ave	Econ	SR	5w	10
First-class	42	5495	3654	101	5/58	-	36.17	3.98	54.4	2	0
List A	83	2700	2825	83	5/31	5/31	34.03	6.27	32.5	1	0
Twenty20	63	1078	1572	52	4/22	4/22	30.23	8.74	20.7	0	0

ALEXANDER BLOFIELD

WORCESTERSHIRE

NAME: Alexander David Blofield
BORN: October 28, 1991, Shrewsbury
HEIGHT: 6ft 1in
SQUAD Nº: 12
NICKNAME: Blowers
CAREER: Yet to make first-team debut

AOC SAYS: Blofield, an offspinning allrounder, will be on a scholarship contract for 2011, enabling him to concentrate full-time on cricket and play for the Second XI. He is a product of Shrewsbury School and has been on the Worcestershire academy for four years. He has been on a gap year in Australia, teaching and playing cricket but will look to get plenty of wickets under his belt for the Seconds this year with his classical offspin. He is also an excellent fielder.

LAST WORD: "A straight A student and a very bright lad. Unfortunately he broke his thumb playing cricket out in Australia over the winter but he should be fine for the season."
Damian D'Oliveira

EXTRAS

"I feel really prepared for the new season — more so than usual. Last year was supposed to be tough and we did well, but we are not going to kid ourselves and say that it will be the same. We are going to come up against some very good players and excellent teams. It will be a big learning curve for the young guys who impressed last year and it is a chance for them to push on again." Alan Richardson

JAMES CAMERON   RHB RMF

NAME: James Gair Cameron
BORN: January 31, 1986, Harare
HEIGHT: 5ft 10in
SQUAD №: 16
NICKNAME: Jimbo, Chikange, Bushcat
CAREER: First-class debut: 2010; List A
debut: 2010; T20 debut: 2010

WORCESTERSHIRE

AOC SAYS: Signed on the nod of Royals seamer Matt Mason at the start of last summer,
Cameron impressed in 2010 and it was his swashbuckling century – his maiden ton in his
first outing as an opener – that helped secure promotion on the last day of the season. An
attacking opener, British passport-holding Cameron played for Zimbabwe age group sides
but went to university in Western Australia, where he played grade cricket for University
CC. It will be interesting to see how he copes with New Road's seaming wickets if he gets
the chance to open.

LAST WORD: "Jimbo came to us highly recommended by Tom Moody and Davie Houghton.
He is a hard working pro and proved his potential with a matchwinning hundred to help
secure promotion in 2010." *Damian D'Oliveira*

Batting & Fielding

	Mat	Inns	NO	Runs	HS	Ave	SR	100	50	Ct	St
First-class	10	17	1	576	105	36.00	58.29	1	3	7	0
List A	12	11	3	236	58	29.50	89.05	0	1	1	0
Twenty20	15	11	1	158	51*	15.80	107.48	0	1	2	0

Bowling

	Mat	Balls	Runs	Wkts	BBI	BBM	Ave	Econ	SR	5w	10
First-class	10	563	332	8	2/18	3/43	41.50	3.53	70.3	0	0
List A	12	265	292	7	4/44	4/44	41.71	6.61	37.8	0	0
Twenty20	15	179	239	8	3/22	3/22	29.87	8.01	22.3	0	0

SHAAIQ CHOUDHRY · RHB SLA

NAME: Shaaiq Hussain Choudhry
BORN: November 3, 1985, Rotherham
HEIGHT: 5ft 10in
SQUAD Nº: 17
NICKNAME: Shak
OTHER TEAMS: Warwickshire
CAREER: First-class debut: 2007; List A debut: 2010; T20 debut: 2010

AOC SAYS: A batting slow left-armer with good control and flight, Worcestershire signed Choudhry halfway through last season after a trial and he will have learned from watching Shakib Al Hasan in action at close quarters. He had previously been with Warwickshire but knee injuries slowed his progress so much that at the end of 2009 he was close to giving up on the first-class game. He was persuaded by his dad to give it one last try and dismissing Kevin Pietersen on his Surrey debut was enough on its own to vindicate his decision.

LAST WORD: "We looked at a few slow left-armers and went with Shaaiq. He learns fast and we've tried a few techncal things with him, like one-step bowling, which he's absorbed really well." *Damian D'Oliveira*

Batting & Fielding

	Mat	Inns	NO	Runs	HS	Ave	SR	100	50	Ct	St
First-class	3	4	2	199	75	99.50	43.35	0	3	1	0
List A	7	6	4	115	39	57.50	98.29	0	0	3	0
Twenty20	3	3	3	15	8*	-	83.33	0	0	0	0

Bowling

	Mat	Balls	Runs	Wkts	BBI	BBM	Ave	Econ	SR	5w	10
First-class	3	138	86	1	1/32	1/32	86.00	3.73	138.0	0	0
List A	7	198	213	6	4/54	4/54	35.50	6.45	33.0	0	0
Twenty20	3	42	51	2	1/24	1/24	25.50	7.28	21.0	0	0

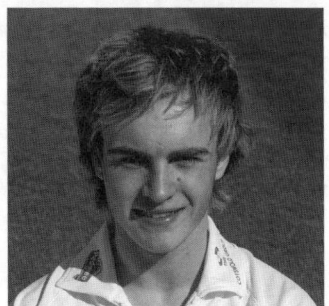

NAME: Oliver Benjamin Cox
BORN: February 2, 1992, Stourbridge
HEIGHT: 5ft 10in
SQUAD Nº: 10
NICKNAME: Coxy, Youth, Blondie
CAREER: First-class debut: 2009; List A
debut: 2010; T20 debut: 2010

WORCESTERSHIRE

AOC SAYS: A four-year contract penned at the end of 2009 shows how much
Worcestershire think of young keeper Cox, who has been fast-tracked though the county's
youth system. His first first-class match, at Taunton in 2009, saw him stump Marcus
Trescothick and stroke a sparky 61. He was not a keeper when he joined Worcestershire's
academy but Steve Rhodes suggested it might be the way forward for him. He will need to
buckle down with the bat and work further on his nifty glovework but he already looks a
promising replacement for Steve Davies.

LAST WORD: "He's got confidence in abundance, and is certainly not known for keeping
quiet behind the stumps! He loves the flashy stuff, and it's a big ask to go up to Division
One, but he has the belief." *Mike Reeves*

Batting & Fielding

	Mat	Inns	NO	Runs	HS	Ave	SR	100	50	Ct	St
First-class	10	17	4	279	61	21.46	58.00	0	2	22	2
List A	7	3	2	9	9*	9.00	69.23	0	0	7	2
Twenty20	8	5	3	13	6*	6.50	108.33	0	0	2	2

Bowling

	Mat	Balls	Runs	Wkts	BBI	BBM	Ave	Econ	SR	5w	10
First-class	10	-	-	-	-	-	-	-	-	-	-
List A	7	-	-	-	-	-	-	-	-	-	-
Twenty20	8	-	-	-	-	-	-	-	-	-	-

BRETT D'OLIVEIRA

RHB LB

WORCESTERSHIRE

NAME: Brett Louis D'Oliveira
BORN: February 28, 1992, Worcester
HEIGHT: Height 5ft 8in
SQUAD Nº: 15
NICKNAME: Dolly
CAREER: Yet to make first-team debut

AOC SAYS: D'Oliveira, son of assistant coach Damian and grandson of Worcestershire and England legend Basil, is another player on a scholarship contract. He's the youngest of Damian's three boys and has been in the academy for four years. He played Midlands under 17s, and is a hard-hitting bat at No.5 or No.6 in the order. Worcestershire reckon he is progressing nicely, and he has a good arm and good hands. He took up leggies only three years ago and was one of the stars of Worcester's Second XI Trophy side last year, as well as performing well for Bromsgrove in the Birmingham and District Premier League.

LAST WORD: "He had a shoulder op in September, having nursed the injury through last season. He dislocated it a few times but he managed to get through. He'll be better for the op and more confident." *Damian D'Oliveira*

EXTRAS

Worcestershire have been promoted three times and relegated twice in the last five years.

NICHOLAS HARRISON

RHB RM

NAME: Nicholas Luke Harrison
BORN: February 3, 1992, Bath
HEIGHT: Height 6ft 2in
SQUAD Nº: 16
NICKNAME: Harry
CAREER: Yet to make first-team debut

AOC SAYS: A tall, fast-medium bowler who swings it away from the right-hander, Harrison will be looking to become more consistent over the course of this season, for which he has earned himself a scholarship contract. He played for Wiltshire in the Minor Counties league last year with some success and says: "I moved up to Worcester in January and I've just got to take my chance. I know it's going to be really hard work but I have trained with the first team before and I just need to focus on my cricket."

LAST WORD: "He managed to break his ankle going for a walk with his family in the snow over Christmas! All being well, he'll be fit and firing this year though." *Damian D'Oliveira.*

EXTRAS

"I think the pressure will be on the other teams trying to beat us. We are the underdogs for this year, but we have a good squad and played well last year. If we can keep that momentum going this season, then hopefully we will have a good year." Moeen Ali

RICHARD JONES
RHB RFM

NAME: Richard Alan Jones
BORN: November 6, 1986, Stourbridge
HEIGHT: 6ft 2in
SQUAD Nº: 25
NICKNAME: Jonah
CAREER: First-class debut: 2007: List A
debut: 2008; Twenty20 debut: 2010

AOC SAYS: Another of Worcestershire's bright young things, Jones attended Loughborough University and played for England under 19s. A bowler and handy lower-order batter, he can be genuinely quick. He'd added some weight to his beanpole frame and in the first game of last season, with Kabir Ali and Simon Jones having left the club, he got tongues wagging with a six-fer against Middlesex at New Road (slightly overshadowed by Steve Finn's nine-wicket haul), then backed it up with a seven-fer against Sussex on the flatter track of Hove. He never quite hit the same heights but signed a two-year extension so has time to grow into his role.

LAST WORD: "He has been working hard all winter. He started really well last year and then faded. It may have been his age, or maybe the wickets just got flatter. He needs consistency, but he definitely has the class." *Mike Reeves*

Batting & Fielding

	Mat	Inns	NO	Runs	HS	Ave	SR	100	50	Ct	St
First-class	23	36	5	349	53*	11.25	39.61	0	1	11	0
List A	7	4	2	19	11*	9.50	76.00	0	0	1	0
Twenty20	6	2	1	14	9	14.00	77.77	0	0	7	0

Bowling

	Mat	Balls	Runs	Wkts	BBI	BBM	Ave	Econ	SR	5w	10
First-class	23	3430	2461	68	7/115	8/105	36.19	4.30	50.4	3	0
List A	7	228	269	1	1/47	1/47	269.00	7.07	228.0	0	0
Twenty20	6	66	119	2	1/17	1/17	59.50	10.81	33.0	0	0

NAME: Aneesh Kapil
BORN: August 3, 1993, Wolverhampton
HEIGHT: 5ft 8in
SQUAD Nº: 22
NICKNAME: Simba
CAREER: Yet to make first-team debut

WORCESTERSHIRE

AOC SAYS: Kapil has played in Worcestershire's Second XI for last three seasons, averaging 40 last year and taking a few wickets too. He opened the batting for Wolverhampton in the Birmingham League at the age of 13, reported to be the youngest since Premier Leagues were introduced in the late 1990s (and two years younger than Vikram Solanki, with whom he has been compared ever since his debut). On a bursary contract for 2010, Kapi is a flamboyant player who has a long-term deal. Apart from his batting, as a 12-year-old he registered 75mph on the ECB speed gun. John Petfield, his cricket master at Tettenhall School, sums up Kapi's talent: "I'm convinced that he will go on to play for England. I have not seen a more talented lad in 20 years of teaching."

LAST WORD: "He is a typical teenager, everything at 100 mph, and we need to calm him down mostly! He's a proper allrounder who should be aiming for the Under 19 World Cup in 2012." *Damian D'Oliveira*

EXTRAS

"The lads are best mates and many of them have grown up together – they enjoy each other's success." Damian D'Oliveira

K

WORCESTERSHIRE

ALEXEI KERVEZEE

RHB OB R1 MVP78

NAME: Alexei Nicolaas Kervezee
BORN: September 11 1989, Walvis Bay, Namibia
HEIGHT: 5ft 8in
SQUAD Nº: 5
NICKNAME: Rowdy, Cub, Bambi
OTHER TEAMS: Netherlands
CAREER: ODI debut: 2006; T20I debut: 2009; First-class debut: 2005; List A debut: 2006; T20 debut: 2009

AOC SAYS: Kervezee wants to be Worcestershire's next Graeme Hick. Like Hick, he is quiet in nature, unflappable, loves scoring runs, has all the shots and wants to play for England. One of very few 17-year-olds to play in a World Cup (for Netherlands in 2007) he did not do himself justice in the 2011 incarnation and will come back to Worcestershire eager to kick on from last year, when he scored more than 1,000 Championship runs. Kervezee debuted for the Netherlands as a 15-year-old and joined Worcestershire for the 2008 season. A steady 2009 led to a permanent berth in the batting line-up last year and he did not disappoint, scoring quickly and attractively. Kervezee said, talking to cricket writer George Dobell: "I played the whole of last season, which was really beneficial. I'd hardly played for them before last season – almost no limited-overs cricket – but I felt I learned masses last year. It took me a while to understand the pace of the game, but I worked out you actually have a bit more time. I qualify for England in November, I think. Going on a tour next winter is an achievable ambition. I've wanted to play for England since the very beginning, so if I can build on last season, hopefully I can catch the eye of the selectors. I signed a five-year contract extension at the end of last season. Why? Well, when I first came to the club as a 16- or 17-year-old, they were brilliant with me. They welcomed me with open arms and treated me like family. You remember those things. Everything is going well for me. I enjoy the dressing room, I have a flat in Worcester with my girlfriend and I'm playing regular first-team cricket. Why would I want to move? We've a talented, young squad and I'm very confident we can do well in Division One next season."

INSIDE TRACK: "He's our Mr Cricket, totally dedicated and a really hard worker. He's got great hand-eye co-ordination, fields really well at point, and when he gets going, he's a joy to watch. He's got all the shots in the world and now he needs to add consistency and to differentiate more between one-day and four-day cricket. I've challenged him to bat all day and he's almost done it. If only he could learn to drive a car he'd be the complete package!" *Damian D'Oliveira*

Batting & Fielding

	Mat	Inns	NO	Runs	HS	Ave	SR	100	50	Ct	St
ODIs	36	33	2	745	92	24.03	67.97	0	3	17	0
T20Is	6	6	0	135	39	22.50	106.29	0	0	4	0
First-class	36	62	5	2126	155	37.29	-	3	11	21	0
List A	58	55	3	1517	121*	29.17	73.14	2	6	26	0
Twenty20	23	21	2	323	39	17.00	107.30	0	0	10	0

Bowling

	Mat	Balls	Runs	Wkts	BBI	BBM	Ave	Econ	SR	5w	10
ODIs	36	24	34	0	-	-	-	8.50	-	0	0
T20Is	6	-	-	-	-	-	-	-	-	-	-
First-class	36	183	145	2	1/14	1/14	72.50	4.75	91.5	0	0
List A	58	48	73	0	-	-	-	9.12	-	0	0
Twenty20	23	-	-	-	-	-	-	-	-	-	-

People tell me there's a massive difference between the divisions, but I don't know. I'm really looking forward to the challenge

Alexei Kervezee

JOE LEACH

RHB RM

WORCESTERSHIRE

NAME: Joseph Leach
BORN: October 30, 1990, Stafford
HEIGHT: 6ft 1in
SQUAD Nº: 23
NICKNAME: Leachy, Swede
CAREER: Yet to make first-team debut

AOC SAYS: Another bright young lad from Shrewsbury School (where former Worcestershire man Paul Pridgeon is the coach), Leach has played on and off for the Second XI for the past few seasons as well as for Shropshire in the Minor Counties League and for Shrewsbury CC, helping them to the Birmingham and District Premier League title last season, scoring almost 500 runs at 40 and weighing in with some useful wickets. Leach did not get as many runs as he would have liked last year and will be looking to up the ante this season once he gets back from Bradford/Leeds MCCU duties.

LAST WORD: "Our curtain-raiser against Leeds/Bradford MCCU brings with it the chance for my former housemate to score some runs against his employer, and indeed, flatmate, in a game already being touted as 'The Battle of Flat 3B, 40 Lark Hill Road'." *Jack Shantry, Worcestershire teammate*

EXTRAS

"The club has a long history with a loyal following and it is evident that the development of younger players is of key importance to members and supporters." Chief executive David Leatherdale

NAME: Jack Kenneth Manuel
BORN: February 13, 1991, Sutton Coldfield
HEIGHT: 6ft 1in
SQUAD Nº: 26
NICKNAME: JK
CAREER: List A debut: 2010; T20 debut: 2010

WORCESTERSHIRE

AOC SAYS: Manuel has pedigree, having already played for England under 19s as recenty as last summer. He signed a two-year contract along with David Wheeldon in 2009 and will look to make a real impression this year, having played his first Pro40 and Twenty20 matches in 2010. He's a batsman who hits it as hard as anyone around and has a wide range of strokes, the best of which is probably the straight drive. Manuel also plays for Walsall in the Birmingham and District Premier League and scored over 500 runs at 44 last season. Talented from a young age, Manuel scored a double-hundred in a Twenty20 game when he was just 13.

LAST WORD: "Jack will miss the start of the year with a dislocated shoulder, which he got swimming in Australia! He's very highly rated and this could be the year that makes him." *Mike Reeves*

Batting & Fielding

	Mat	Inns	NO	Runs	HS	Ave	SR	100	50	Ct	St
List A	2	2	0	26	22	13.00	118.18	0	0	2	0
Twenty20	11	9	1	86	31	10.75	104.87	0	0	3	0

Bowling

	Mat	Balls	Runs	Wkts	BBI	BBM	Ave	Econ	SR	5w	10
List A	2	-	-	-	-	-	-	-	-	-	-
Twenty20	11	-	-	-	-	-	-	-	-	-	-

NAME: Matthew Sean Mason
BORN: March 20, 1974, Claremont, Western Australia
HEIGHT: 6ft 5in
SQUAD Nº: 24
NICKNAME: Mase, Moose
OTHER TEAMS: Western Australia
CAREER: First-class debut: 1997; List A debut: 1996; T20 debut: 2003

AOC SAYS: Testament to the value the club sees in Mason, he signed a new one-year deal at the end of last year at the age of 36, and this will be his ninth season at New Road. He doubles up as bowling coach, trying to impart his mastery of nagging line and length to the club's clutch of up-and-coming seamers. He says: "Coaching is something I am very passionate about and at Worcester I believe we have one of the strongest and most talented squads of fast bowlers in the country. The club has been very good to me and I wouldn't want to be anywhere else."

LAST WORD: "How he keeps going is astonishing. He's a wicket-to-wicket bowler, who has dropped in pace but is still very accurate. He'll put the pressure on all day long if he can stay fit." *Mike Reeves*

Batting & Fielding

	Mat	Inns	NO	Runs	HS	Ave	SR	100	50	Ct	St
First-class	98	127	31	1320	63	13.75	-	0	4	27	0
List A	81	38	15	171	25	7.43	-	0	0	16	0
Twenty20	11	5	2	18	8*	6.00	54.54	0	0	3	0

Bowling

	Mat	Balls	Runs	Wkts	BBI	BBM	Ave	Econ	SR	5w	10
First-class	98	18045	8410	311	8/45		27.04	2.79	58.0	10	1	0
List A	81	3684	2646	94	4/34	4/34	28.14	4.30	39.1	0	0
Twenty20	11	227	291	9	3/42	3/42	32.33	7.69	25.2	0	0

NAME: Daryl Keith Henry Mitchell
BORN: November 25, 1983, Badsey
HEIGHT: 5ft 10in
SQUAD Nº: 27
NICKNAME: Mitch
CAREER: First-class debut: 2005; List A debut: 2005; T20 debut: 2005

WORCESTERSHIRE

AOC SAYS: A stellar start to his captaincy career last season means the bar has been set pretty high for local lad Mitchell. He took over in early August and led Worcestershire to a hugely unlikely promotion as well as winning four CB40 matches in succession. An opening bat who debuted for the side in 2005 after working his way up through the age groups, Mitchell is an effective and gutsy rather than flamboyant player, and he bowls useful seamers as well. So impressed were the club with their man's performance that they have rewarded him with a four-year contract. It will be interesting to see how his captaincy style develops. For the moment he certainly has his young team pulling together but times will undoubtedly get tougher in Division One – Worcestershire didn't win a single game the last time they were in the top flight – and he will be looking to the experience of Vikram Solanki to guide him. Mitchell, who is the first Worcestershire captain born within the county boundary in 85 years, scored 1,180 first-class runs last year, and became only the sixth Worcestershire player to score three consecutive centuries. In 2009 he hit 298, the fifth highest score ever by a Worcestershire player (and the only ever instance of someone being out for 298 in first-class cricket). He wintered in New Zealand for the first time this year and found the Auckland wickets reminiscent of New Road, racking up nearly 1,000 runs for Cornwall CC at an average of over 70. Of this season, he says: "I'm a Worcestershire lad born and bred and come through the age groups, including the academy and I've been on the full staff for about six seasons now, so I know the ropes. This season will be tough but we're relishing the challenge."

INSIDE TRACK: "I am absolutely delighted that Daryl's services of captaincy are secured for next season. I am enjoying working with him, and look forward to seeing his progression. He's been earmarked for some time – we believe in succession planning. He's a tough cookie, a streetfighter. He may not be elegant or pretty but you can't average over 40 at New Road without being a good player." *Steve Rhodes*

DARYL MITCHELL

Batting & Fielding

	Mat	Inns	NO	Runs	HS	Ave	SR	100	50	Ct	St
First-class	64	117	16	4002	298	39.62	43.73	9	18	75	0
List A	54	43	10	1030	92	31.21	78.38	0	7	18	0
Twenty20	52	32	9	408	39	17.73	109.97	0	0	17	0

Bowling

	Mat	Balls	Runs	Wkts	BBI	BBM	Ave	Econ	SR	5w	10
First-class	64	1155	596	16	4/49	-	37.25	3.09	72.1	0	0
List A	54	1127	1102	28	4/42	4/42	39.35	5.86	40.2	0	0
Twenty20	52	791	1056	36	4/11	4/11	29.33	8.01	21.9	0	0

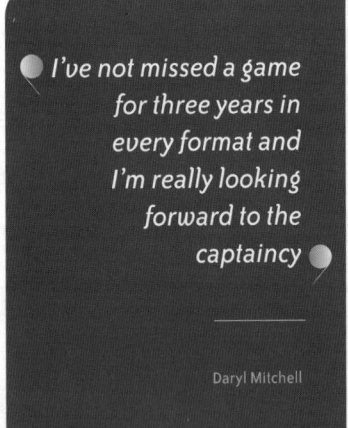

I've not missed a game for three years in every format and I'm really looking forward to the captaincy

Daryl Mitchell

NAME: Matthew Graham Pardoe
BORN: January 5, 1991, Stourbridge
HEIGHT: 6ft 1in
SQUAD Nº: 19
NICKNAME: Pards, Wedgey
CAREER: Yet to make first-team debut

AOC SAYS: Another of Worcestershire's multi-A-levelled youngsters, Pardoe is a tall and elegant, highly rated batsman who scored over 1,000 runs in Worcestershire's Second XI in all competitions (and over 900 in the Second XI Championship alone) in 2010, dominating the runscoring tables with fellow Kidderminster Victoria CC bat Neil Pinner. Pardoe has been with the academy for four years and has now graduated from a scholarship contract to a full-time two-year deal. He could well get a chance in one-day cricket for the First XI this season and he may even get a few overs.

LAST WORD: "We're currently trying to convert him from a seamer to a left-arm spinner, but he's primarily an opening batsman. Another product of our academy, Matt was one of our scholarship players last season and secured a professional contract this year."
Damian D'Oliveira

EXTRAS

Worcestershire made a profit of £103,000 for the 2010 season.

NEIL PINNER

WORCESTERSHIRE

NAME: Neil Douglas Pinner
BORN: September 28, 1990, Stourbridge
HEIGHT: 5ft 11in
SQUAD Nº: 20
NICKNAME: Pinns
CAREER: Yet to make first-team debut

AOC SAYS: He may have gone to a different school from teammate Matt Pardoe (Pinner was at RGS Worcester) but the other parallels are extraordinary. Both achieved 10 GCSEs and 3 A levels, both play for Kidderminster CC, both scored over 1,000 runs for the Second XI last year (statisticians confidently suggest this is a first), both were on the academy, and both signed two-year contracts at the end of last season). Pinner is a right-hander where Pardoe is a leftie but both are heavy scorers.

LAST WORD: "Neil, like Matt Pardoe, has come through the Academy and moved on to professional terms after a successful Second XI season in 2010 and he is working hard on developing his offspin bowling." *Damian D'Oliveira*

EXTRAS

"The club has an overwhelming history and has been home to so many legendary cricketers. As an allrounder I am thrilled and inspired to be joining the team once graced by Ian Botham, Imran Khan and Kapil Dev." *Shakib Al Hasan*

NAME: Alan Richardson
BORN: May 6, 1975, Newcastle-under-Lyme
HEIGHT: 6ft 2in
SQUAD Nº: 9
NICKNAME: Richo
OTHER TEAMS: Derbyshire, Middlesex, Warwickshire
CAREER: First-class debut: 1995; List A debut: 1995; T20 debut: 2004

WORCESTERSHIRE

AOC SAYS: You know what you are going to get with Richardson. Tireless toil, nagging accuracy, no great pace, the ability to utilise whatever the pitch has to offer. An impressive 55 wickets at 24 last season were one of the main reasons Worcestershire got promoted and he'll be looking to snare Division One batsmen using the same technique this season. If he steers clear of injury he could again be a force to be reckoned with; the thought of returning to his old job of assembling golf studs on a production line – 2,400 studs in an eight-hour shift – making him determined to extend his career as long as possible.

LAST WORD: "A great character to have in the dressing room. He was the signing of the season and told me he wished he'd come to the county earlier in his career." *Mike Reeves*

Batting & Fielding

	Mat	Inns	NO	Runs	HS	Ave	SR	100	50	Ct	St
First-class	122	127	53	832	91	11.24	-	0	1	38	0
List A	64	28	18	105	21*	10.50	-	0	0	14	0
Twenty20	11	2	1	6	6*	6.00	60.00	0	0	2	0

Bowling

	Mat	Balls	Runs	Wkts	BBI	BBM	Ave	Econ	SR	5w	10
First-class	122	22756	10699	369	8/46	-	28.99	2.82	61.6	11	1
List A	64	2806	2199	62	5/35	5/35	35.46	4.70	45.2	1	0
Twenty20	11	228	268	10	3/13	3/13	26.80	7.05	22.8	0	0

CHRIS RUSSELL

RHB RFM

WORCESTERSHIRE

NAME: Christopher James Russell
BORN: February 16, 1989, Newport, Isle of Wight
HEIGHT: 6ft 1in
SQUAD Nº: 18
NICKNAME: Goobs
CAREER: List A debut: 2010

AOC SAYS: Yet another well educated quick bowler on Worcestershire's books, Russell is from the Isle of Wight and has surprised a few batsmen in his short career with his pace. He is tall, strong and swings the new ball. He made two end-of-season appearances in the CB40 last season and also took 46 Second XI Championship wickets. Russell has played for Wolverhampton in the Birmingham and District Premier League for the last three seasons and has been their leading wicket-taker for the last two years as well as scoring some useful runs.

LAST WORD: "From what I have seen, he tends to wear the Goober bib a fair bit during training so he's obviously prone to a bit of silliness." *Mike Reeves*

Batting & Fielding

	Mat	Inns	NO	Runs	HS	Ave	SR	100	50	Ct	St
List A	2	-	-	-	-	-	-	-	-	0	0

Bowling

	Mat	Balls	Runs	Wkts	BBI	BBM	Ave	Econ	SR	5w	10
List A	2	54	68	1	1/23	1/23	68.00	7.55	54.0	0	0

OVERSEAS PLAYER

WORCESTERSHIRE

NAME: Saeed Ajmal
BORN: October 14, 1977,
Faisalabad, Punjab
HEIGHT: 5ft 4in
SQUAD Nº: 50
OTHER TEAMS: Pakistan, Faisalabad,
Islamabad Cricket Association, Khan Research
Labs, Water and Power Development Authority
CAREER: Test debut: 2009; ODI debut: 2008;
T20I debut: 2009; First-class debut: 1996; List A
debut: 1995; T20 debut: 2005

AOC SAYS: For someone of Ajmal's talent not to have made his Test debut until he was
30 seems unthinkable. Nigh on unreadable variations, a big turning doosra, and a steely
temperament are part of the package that will be on display at New Road for the FP t20
and the rest of the season thereafter, with the club hoping to replicate the success spinner
Shakib Al Hasan had in the latter half last season as the pitches got drier. Ajmal's biggest
success was in helping Pakistan to the 2009 World Twenty20 and Steve Rhodes wil be
hoping for similar performances in 2011.

LAST WORD: "Worcestershire has a special standing in Pakistan due to its association
with Imran Khan, and I am proud to be able to represent the same club as the great Imran."
Saeed Ajmal

Batting & Fielding

	Mat	Inns	NO	Runs	HS	Ave	SR	100	50	Ct	St
Tests	9	16	7	98	50	10.88	49.24	0	1	2	0
ODIs	38	26	11	116	33	7.73	58.88	0	0	6	0
T20Is	29	10	7	30	13*	10.00	103.44	0	0	4	0
First-class	92	123	42	965	53	11.91	-	0	3	30	0
List A	136	74	34	303	33	7.57	-	0	0	30	0
Twenty20	62	18	11	64	13*	9.14	104.91	0	0	9	0

Bowling

	Mat	Balls	Runs	Wkts	BBI	BBM	Ave	Econ	SR	5w	10
Tests	9	2747	1311	33	5/82	5/103	39.72	2.86	83.2	1	0
ODIs	38	1974	1436	49	4/33	4/33	29.30	4.36	40.2	0	0
T20Is	29	624	661	41	4/19	4/19	16.12	6.35	15.2	0	0
First-class	92	18475	8551	302	7/63	-	28.31	2.77	61.1	18	1
List A	136	7047	5279	191	5/18	5/18	27.63	4.49	36.8	1	0
Twenty20	62	1316	1439	86	4/19	4/19	16.73	6.56	15.3	0	0

SHAKIB AL HASAN

LHB SLA

WORCESTERSHIRE

OVERSEAS PLAYER

NAME: Shakib Al Hasan
BORN: March 24, 1987, Magura, Bangladesh
HEIGHT: 5ft 9in
SQUAD Nº: 75
NICKNAME: Shak
OTHER TEAMS: Bangladesh, Khulna Division
CAREER: Test debut: 2007; ODI debut: 2006; T20I debut: 2006; First-class debut: 2005; List A debut: 2006; T20 debut: 2006

AOC SAYS: The first Bangldeshi to play county cricket, Shakib impressed all and sundry at New Road last year with his work ethic, his quiet calm and, of course, his runs and wickets. Not to mention his fielding. One ball that spun to hit offstump and get rid of Mark Ramprakash for a duck showed people just what a classy bowler Shakib is and although he will only be around for the Twenty20, his influence is bound to be massive again this season.

LAST WORD: "I wanted him for the T20 last year and am so excited he'll be with us this time. He's ranked as the best one-day allrounder in the world and that's not a false position." *Steve Rhodes*

Batting & Fielding

	Mat	Inns	NO	Runs	HS	Ave	SR	100	50	Ct	St
Tests	21	40	2	1179	100	31.02	55.53	1	5	8	0
ODIs	108	104	17	2976	134*	34.20	77.19	5	18	30	0
T20Is	14	14	0	207	47	14.78	111.89	0	0	4	0
First-class	54	100	9	2991	129	32.86	-	4	14	28	0
List A	135	130	18	3626	134*	32.37	78.92	5	23	41	0
Twenty20	21	21	0	293	47	13.95	113.12	0	0	8	0

Bowling

	Mat	Balls	Runs	Wkts	BBI	BBM	Ave	Econ	SR	5w	10
Tests	21	5083	2410	75	7/36	9/115	32.13	2.84	67.7	7	0
ODIs	108	5518	3939	137	4/33	4/33	28.75	4.28	40.2	0	0
T20Is	14	294	328	17	4/34	4/34	19.29	6.69	17.2	0	0
First-class	54	10706	4898	164	7/32	-	29.86	2.74	65.2	12	0
List A	135	6633	4691	166	4/30	4/30	28.25	4.24	39.9	0	0
Twenty20	21	456	488	25	4/34	4/34	19.52	6.42	18.2	0	0

JACK SHANTRY

LHB LMF MVP93

NAME: Jack David Shantry
BORN: January 29, 1988, Shrewsbury
HEIGHT: 6ft 4in
SQUAD Nº: 32
NICKNAME: Shants, Mincer, Tripod
CAREER: First-class debut: 2009; List A
debut: 2009; T20 debut: 2010

WORCESTERSHIRE

AOC SAYS: When you watch Shantry on TV you find yourself wondering how he ever takes a wicket. He looks ungainly, unthreatening and not exactly in the express pace bracket. And then you see he took more wickets than any other Worcestershire bowler last year. An unorthodox action, allied to good tight lines, make him an unexpectedly tricky customer. From good cricketing stock, Shantry writes an entertaining blog on the Worcestershire website and has the potential to become one of county cricket's cult heroes. He returned home early from Australia this winter with a knee problem but should be fine for the start of the season.

LAST WORD: "He moves it away from the right-hander and I think the perception of his bowling as unthreatening actually gets him wickets." *Mike Reeves*

Batting & Fielding

	Mat	Inns	NO	Runs	HS	Ave	SR	100	50	Ct	St
First-class	15	20	6	67	13*	4.78	27.57	0	0	5	0
List A	17	5	2	42	18	14.00	73.68	0	0	2	0
Twenty20	15	4	2	8	6*	4.00	66.66	0	0	4	0

Bowling

	Mat	Balls	Runs	Wkts	BBI	BBM	Ave	Econ	SR	5w	10
First-class	15	2611	1327	35	5/49	6/111	37.91	3.04	74.6	1	0
List A	17	694	699	23	3/33	3/33	30.39	6.04	30.1	0	0
Twenty20	15	294	345	18	3/23	3/23	19.16	7.04	16.3	0	0

VIKRAM SOLANKI RHB OB R5

WORCESTERSHIRE

NAME: Vikram Singh Solanki
BORN: April 1, 1976, Udaipur, India
HEIGHT: 6ft 1in
SQUAD Nº: 3
NICKNAME: Vik
OTHER TEAMS: England, Rajasthan, Mumbai Champs
CAREER: ODI debut: 2000; T20I debut: 2005; First-class debut: 1995; List A debut: 1993; Twenty20 debut: 2004

AOC SAYS: Solanki debuted for Worcestershire as a 16-year-old and was always seen as an England prospect. His time with the national side will be remembered as much for super subs and poor management as his fluid and wristy shotmaking. The 2009 Walter Lawrence trophy for a 47-ball century shows that timing is not the only weapon in Solanki's armoury. He became captain of Worcestershire in 2005 and was in charge for five and a half topsy-turvy seasons until he stepped down in August last year, by which time he had become the longest serving county captain. Solanki also serves as a thoughtful and forthright PCA chairman.

LAST WORD: "Vik had a largely disappointing 2010 and will be looking to put things right. He is a class player but it will be interesting to see how he does without the captaincy for the first time in six years." *Mike Reeves*

Batting & Fielding

	Mat	Inns	NO	Runs	HS	Ave	SR	100	50	Ct	St
ODIs	51	46	5	1097	106	26.75	72.93	2	5	16	0
T20Is	3	3	0	76	43	25.33	124.59	0	0	3	0
First-class	267	446	26	15039	270	35.80	-	27	79	276	0
List A	362	334	28	9775	164*	31.94	-	14	55	139	0
Twenty20	48	46	0	1231	100	26.76	130.67	1	8	25	0

Bowling

	Mat	Balls	Runs	Wkts	BBI	BBM	Ave	Econ	SR	5w	10
ODIs	51	46	5	1097	106	26.75	72.93	2	5	16	0
T20Is	3	3	0	76	43	25.33	124.59	0	0	3	0
First-class	267	446	26	15039	270	35.80	-	27	79	276	0
List A	362	334	28	9775	164*	31.94	-	14	55	139	0
Twenty20	48	46	0	1231	100	26.76	130.67	1	8	25	0

NAME: David Antony Wheeldon
BORN: April 12, 1989, Stafford
HEIGHT: 5ft 8in
SQUAD Nº: 30
NICKNAME: Wheels
CAREER: First-class debut: 2009

WORCESTERSHIRE

AOC SAYS: An unflappable, determined left-handed opening batsman who is calm under pressure and capable of compiling big scores, Wheeldon had a largely disappointing 2010 in his seven Championship matches and may find James Cameron given the opportunity to open the innings ahead of him. He has always scored heavily in Second XI cricket (he made almost 1,000 runs in 2009) but the step up to first-team level has so far found him wanting. He was on the Worcestershire academy for four years and bowls an assortment of legbreaks and googlies.

LAST WORD: "He's in the Daryl Mitchell mould – he hates giving his wicket away and it doesn't bother him unduly if scoring runs is difficult." *Damian D'Oliveira*

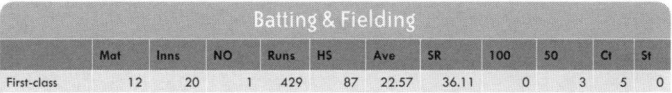

| Batting & Fielding | | | | | | | | | | | |
	Mat	Inns	NO	Runs	HS	Ave	SR	100	50	Ct	St
First-class	12	20	1	429	87	22.57	36.11	0	3	5	0

| Bowling | | | | | | | | | | |
	Mat	Balls	Runs	Wkts	BBI	BBM	Ave	Econ	SR	5w	10
First-class	12	-	-	-	-	-	-	-	-	-	-

CHRISTOPHER WHELAN

RHB RFM

WORCESTERSHIRE

NAME: Christopher David Whelan
BORN: May 8, 1986, Liverpool
HEIGHT: 6ft 2in
SQUAD Nº: 17
NICKNAME: Wheelo, Scouse
OTHER TEAMS: Middlesex
CAREER: First-class debut: 2005; List A: 2004; T20: 2008

AOC SAYS: The joker in the pack, Scouser Whelan, formerly of Middlesex, has had a bad time with injuries of late but is now fighting fit and raring to go. He had a poor 2008, a good season in 2009 and missed most of last year with a troublesome ankle, so it will be interesting to see which version of Whelan we get in 2011. He is an opening bowler with real pace and a proficient batsman. He needs to overcome his desire to get a wicket every single ball and add consistency to his undoubted talent.

LAST WORD: "The top three bowlers will be Mason, Wright and Richardson. Jones, Andrew, Shantry and Whelan will be fighting for the fourth bowling spot." *Mike Reeves*

Batting & Fielding

	Mat	Inns	NO	Runs	HS	Ave	SR	100	50	Ct	St
First-class	22	27	6	302	58	14.38	44.41	0	1	4	0
List A	24	12	2	41	11	4.10	63.07	0	0	4	0
Twenty20	16	3	2	4	2*	4.00	57.14	0	0	2	0

Bowling

	Mat	Balls	Runs	Wkts	BBI	BBM	Ave	Econ	SR	5w	10
First-class	22	2236	1715	44	5/95	-	38.97	4.60	50.8	1	0
List A	24	750	758	27	4/27	4/27	28.07	6.06	27.7	0	0
Twenty20	16	302	407	16	2/24	2/24	25.43	8.08	18.8	0	0

DAMIEN WRIGHT

RHB RFM W1

OVERSEAS PLAYER

WORCESTERSHIRE

NAME: Damien Geoffrey Wright
BORN: July 25, 1975, Casino, New South Wales
HEIGHT: 6ft 2in
SQUAD Nº: 2
NICKNAME: Moves
OTHER TEAMS: Glamorgan, Northamptonshire, Scotland. Somerset, Sussex, Tasmania, Victoria, Wellington
CAREER: First class debut: 1997; List A debut: 1997; T20 debut: 2005

AOC SAYS: Worcestershire have signed Wright for what will in effect be his last nine weeks of first-class cricket as he has now announced his retirement from Australian state cricket, although he is hoping to continue his role as Victoria's bowling coach. Like Alan Richardson and Matt Mason, the other 30 somethings in the Royals' attack, Wright will put the ball on a sixpence and build up pressure on the opposition. He will make way for Saeed Ajmal at the Twenty20 break. Wright knows plenty about success, having been instrumental in winning the Sheffield Shield with two different state sides.

LAST WORD: "Damien is an ideal bowler for early-season conditions in England. His hard-working, no-nonsense style of cricket will be terrific for our dressing room and I'm sure he'll work well with our young fast bowlers." *Steve Rhodes*

Batting & Fielding

	Mat	Inns	NO	Runs	HS	Ave	SR	100	50	Ct	St
First-class	116	175	25	3612	111	24.08	-	1	19	54	0
List A	104	79	24	929	55	16.89	-	0	4	23	0
Twenty20	24	18	5	195	38*	15.00	134.48	0	0	5	0

Bowling

	Mat	Balls	Runs	Wkts	BBI	BBM	Ave	Econ	SR	5w	10
First-class	116	23829	10796	375	8/60	-	28.78	2.71	63.5	13	0
List A	104	5311	3710	128	5/37	5/37	28.98	4.19	41.4	1	0
Twenty20	24	482	598	20	3/17	3/17	29.90	7.44	24.1	0	0

TEAM PROFILE

FORMED: 1863
HOME GROUND: Headingley Carnegie
ONE-DAY NAME: Carnegie
CAPTAIN: Andrew Gale
2010 RESULTS: CC1: 3/9; CB40: Semi-finalists; FP t20: 6/9 in North Group

THE YORKSHIRE
COUNTY CRICKET CLUB

HONOURS

County Championship: (31) 1893, 1896, 1898, 1900, 1901, 1902, 1905, 1908, 1912, 1919, 1922, 1923, 1924, 1925, 1931, 1932, 1933, 1935, 1937, 1938, 1939, 1946, 1949(s), 1959, 1960, 1962, 1963, 1966, 1967, 1968, 2001; Gillette/NatWest/C&G/FP Trophy: (3) 1965, 1969, 2002; Benson and Hedges Cup: 1987; Sunday League: 1983

THE LOWDOWN

Yorkshire-born and bred (barring Ballance, Blain, Brophy and Rafiq), this squad is full of promise but is perhaps still a work in progress. They overachieved in 2010 when, having been tipped for relegation, they finished third in County Championship Division One. Jacques Rudolph's departure may make things more difficult at Headingley this summer, but the return of Ryan Sidebottom will be welcomed in all forms of the game. With a strong academy programme bearing fruit in the first team, this side could be a force to be reckoned with for years to come. It's not all about the kids though; in the likes of Anthony McGrath, Gerard Brophy and Sidebottom, Yorkshire have some wise old heads to call upon when the going gets tough. They'll be a side no one takes lightly this season.

HEAD COACH: MARTYN MOXON

Martyn Moxon is Yorkshire through and through, having first represented the county of his birth in 1980, and his calm exterior has rubbed off on his squad. He says: "I was very pleased with the way things went last year but I think we're going to have to be a whole lot better in all areas this season if we want to recreate the same success or, ideally, win some silverware."

With thanks to: Joe Sayers, Yorkshire batsman; Graham Hardcastle, Northern Echo; James Buttler, editor, YCM

Batting & Fielding

	Mat	Inns	NO	Runs	HS	Ave	SR	100	50	Ct	St
RM Pyrah	7	7	2	304	134*	60.80	64.13	1	1	4	-
A Lyth	16	29	0	1509	142	52.03	59.38	3	9	9	-
JA Rudolph	16	29	2	1375	228*	50.92	58.23	4	6	20	-
AW Gale	13	23	4	876	151*	46.10	56.99	3	3	2	-
AU Rashid	16	24	8	732	76	45.75	56.87	0	6	14	-
A McGrath	16	29	1	1219	124*	43.53	47.74	3	9	9	-
JM Bairstow	16	29	7	918	81	41.72	62.11	0	8	29	5
AZ Lees	1	1	0	38	38	38.00	37.25	0	0	0	-
DJ Wainwright	7	6	3	108	39	36.00	63.90	0	0	1	-
LJ Hodgson	2	2	0	67	34	33.50	54.91	0	0	1	-
GL Brophy	9	17	1	472	103	29.50	52.73	1	1	20	0
JJ Sayers	9	14	0	395	63	28.21	37.65	0	5	3	-
GS Ballance	3	5	2	84	43	28.00	79.24	0	0	1	-
A Shahzad	9	12	3	238	45	26.44	35.68	0	0	1	-
TT Bresnan	6	9	1	203	70	25.37	46.99	0	2	2	-
CG Roebuck	1	1	0	23	23	23.00	32.39	0	0	0	-
JE Root	2	3	1	38	20*	19.00	52.05	0	0	1	-
CJ Geldart	1	1	0	17	17	17.00	26.15	0	0	0	-
Azeem Rafiq	3	3	1	29	13*	14.50	93.54	0	0	0	-
SA Patterson	14	17	4	184	39*	14.15	30.36	0	0	3	-
TL Best	9	9	0	86	40	9.55	49.71	0	0	4	-
JR Lowe	1	1	0	5	5	5.00	22.72	0	0	0	0
MA Ashraf	4	4	0	15	10	3.75	21.73	0	0	1	-
OJ Hannon-Dalby	17	15	7	29	11*	3.62	11.98	0	0	1	-

Bowling

	Mat	Overs	Mdns	Runs	Wkts	BBI	BBM	Ave	Econ	SR	5w	10
BW Sanderson	1	18.0	3	50	5	5/50	5/50	10.00	2.77	21.6	1	0
MA Ashraf	4	75.0	20	212	11	5/32	6/45	19.27	2.82	40.9	1	0
SA Patterson	14	392.5	96	1201	45	5/50	7/69	26.68	3.05	52.3	1	0
A Shahzad	9	292.2	47	1013	34	5/51	8/121	29.79	3.46	51.5	1	0
AU Rashid	16	504.4	67	1784	57	5/87	9/208	31.29	3.53	53.1	3	0
TT Bresnan	6	188.2	42	538	17	5/52	7/85	31.64	2.85	66.4	1	0
OJ Hannon-Dalby	17	382.4	61	1372	34	5/68	7/122	40.35	3.58	67.5	2	0
TL Best	9	198.0	20	793	18	4/86	4/85	44.05	4.00	66.0	0	0
RM Pyrah	7	84.4	16	326	7	2/8	2/29	46.57	3.85	72.5	0	0
DJ Wainwright	7	184.2	27	716	14	3/48	4/126	51.14	3.88	79.0	0	0
Azeem Rafiq	3	88.0	13	268	5	4/92	4/158	53.60	3.04		0	0
LJ Hodgson	2	30.5	6	128	2	1/42	1/42	64.00	4.15	92.5	0	0
JAR Blain	1	14.0	7	20	0	-	-	-	1.42	-	0	0
A Lyth	16	2.0	0	16	0	-	-	-	8.00	-	0	0
A McGrath	16	74.0	13	226	0	-	-	-	3.05	-	0	0
JE Root	2	7.0	0	27	0	-	-	-	3.85	-	0	0
JA Rudolph	16	11.0	2	43	0	-	-	-	3.90	-	0	0
JJ Sayers	9	24.0	3	61	0	-	-	-	2.54	-	0	0

Batting & Fielding

	Mat	Inns	NO	Runs	HS	Ave	SR	100	50	Ct	St
JA Rudolph	13	13	4	861	124*	95.66	91.79	4	5	4	-
A McGrath	12	11	3	414	77*	51.75	89.41	0	4	7	-
GL Brophy	11	10	2	315	93*	39.37	96.62	0	3	8	3
AW Gale	13	13	1	458	125*	38.16	93.27	1	1	4	-
JM Bairstow	9	8	3	153	46*	30.60	130.76	0	0	7	0
TT Bresnan	7	6	3	90	58	30.00	97.82	0	1	1	-
A Lyth	13	12	0	348	91	29.00	91.09	0	2	5	-
JJ Sayers	1	1	0	29	29	29.00	111.53	0	0	1	-
DJ Wainwright	7	3	2	16	9*	16.00	114.28	0	0	2	-
AU Rashid	13	5	2	44	22*	14.66	80.00	0	0	3	-
RM Pyrah	13	3	0	33	29	11.00	137.50	0	0	3	-
SA Patterson	13	1	0	0	0	0.00	0.00	0	0	2	-
BW Sanderson	7	1	1	12	12*	-	133.33	0	0	4	-
A Shahzad	6	2	2	12	9*	-	171.42	0	0	1	-
TL Best	5	1	1	8	8*	-	160.00	0	0	1	-

Bowling

	Mat	Overs	Mdns	Runs	Wkts	BBI	Ave	Econ	SR	5w
TL Best	5	26.2	0	166	10	4/46	16.60	6.30	15.8	0
SA Patterson	13	92.0	4	470	21	6/32	22.38	5.10	26.2	1
BW Sanderson	7	29.0	0	167	7	2/17	23.85	5.75	24.8	0
RM Pyrah	13	81.0	1	484	20	4/24	24.20	5.97	24.3	0
TT Bresnan	7	55.0	2	309	12	3/40	25.75	5.61	27.5	0
A McGrath	12	22.5	0	137	5	2/24	27.40	6.00	27.4	0
AU Rashid	13	82.0	2	396	12	3/28	33.00	4.82	41.0	0
DJ Wainwright	7	42.0	0	260	6	2/31	43.33	6.19	42.0	0
A Shahzad	6	48.0	0	277	6	4/34	46.16	5.77	48.0	0

	Mat	Inns	NO	Runs	HS	Ave	SR	100	50	Ct	St
A McGrath	12	10	4	251	73*	41.83	110.57	0	1	7	-
HH Gibbs	15	15	3	443	101*	36.91	148.16	1	2	8	-
AW Gale	14	14	2	382	65*	31.83	128.61	0	4	7	-
GS Ballance	3	3	1	60	48*	30.00	83.33	0	0	1	-
A Lyth	10	10	0	227	59	22.70	156.55	0	1	4	-
JM Bairstow	15	13	3	219	49*	21.90	125.14	0	0	4	1
JA Rudolph	12	12	0	227	53	18.91	106.57	0	1	5	-
CJ McKay	8	6	3	54	21*	18.00	180.00	0	0	1	-
AU Rashid	16	10	1	128	34	14.22	117.43	0	0	4	-
RM Pyrah	16	10	3	89	22*	12.71	127.14	0	0	8	-
GL Brophy	12	9	1	97	31*	12.12	106.59	0	0	7	2
A Shahzad	3	1	0	12	12	12.00	300.00	0	0	2	-
TL Best	8	3	2	10	10*	10.00	166.66	0	0	4	-
Azeem Rafiq	10	3	1	2	1*	1.00	50.00	0	0	3	-
DJ Wainwright	3	1	0	0	0	0.00	0.00	0	0	1	-
LJ Hodgson	2	1	1	39	39*	-	114.70	0	0	1	-
SA Patterson	14	3	3	3	3*	-	50.00	0	0	1	-

Batting & Fielding

	Mat	Overs	Mdns	Runs	Wkts	BBI	Ave	Econ	SR	5w
DJ Wainwright	3	10.0	0	78	5	3/32	15.60	7.80	12.0	0
AU Rashid	16	61.0	0	428	26	4/20	16.46	7.01	14.0	0
RM Pyrah	16	58.0	0	408	21	3/12	19.42	7.03	16.5	0
TT Bresnan	1	4.0	0	21	1	1/21	21.00	5.25	24.0	0
CJ McKay	8	31.0	0	258	10	4/33	25.80	8.32	18.6	0
BW Sanderson	2	4.4	0	26	1	1/13	26.00	5.57	28.0	0
LJ Hodgson	2	6.0	0	59	2	2/29	29.50	9.83	18.0	0
SA Patterson	14	50.4	0	450	15	4/30	30.00	8.88	20.2	0
A McGrath	12	10.0	0	92	3	2/19	30.66	9.20	20.0	0
TL Best	8	29.2	0	243	7	2/26	34.71	8.28	25.1	0
Azeem Rafiq	10	28.1	0	271	7	3/23	38.71	9.62	24.1	0
A Shahzad	3	12.0	0	93	2	1/21	46.50	7.75	36.0	0
JA Rudolph	12	1.0	0	13	0	-	-	13.00	-	0

Bowling

MOIN ASHRAF

RHB RFM

YORKSHIRE

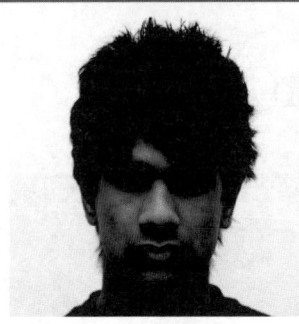

NAME: Moin Aqeeb Ashraf
BORN: January 5 1992, Bradford
HEIGHT: 6ft 2in
SQUAD Nº: 23
NICKNAME: Mo
CAREER: First-class debut: 2010

AOC SAYS: A genuinely quick bowler who is particularly effective with the new ball, Ashraf made his first-class debut against Loughborough University last May. His first County Championship appearance came in September when he took two first-innings wickets against title-chasing Nottinghamshire but it was in his next game, against Kent, that Ashraf really showed his potential with his maiden five-wicket haul and he was subsequently rewarded with a professional contract at the end of the season. With Tim Bresnan and Ajmal Shahzad likely to be on international duty, Ashraf should have ample opportunity to develop his undoubted talent in first-team cricket this season.

LAST WORD: "We were all really pleased with how Ashraf came in and hit the ground running. He's a good character who bowls with good pace – he swings it too. If he stays fit he'll feature this season." *Martyn Moxon*

Batting & Fielding

	Mat	Inns	NO	Runs	HS	Ave	SR	100	50	Ct	St
First-class	4	4	0	15	10	3.75	21.73	0	0	1	0

Bowling

	Mat	Balls	Runs	Wkts	BBI	BBM	Ave	Econ	SR	5w	10
First-class	4	450	212	11	5/32	6/45	19.27	2.82	40.9	1	0

NAME: Jonathan Marc Bairstow
BORN: September 26, 1989, Bradford
HEIGHT: 6ft
SQUAD Nº: 21
NICKNAME: Bluey
CAREER: First-class debut: 2009; List A
debut: 2009; T20 debut: 2010

YORKSHIRE

AOC SAYS: Quiet and unassuming off the pitch, Bairstow is a confident young wicketkeeper-batsman with talent in abundance. Despite still being in search of his maiden first-class century, Bairstow averages 43 in the County Championship, often playing as a specialist batsman with Gerard Brophy taking the gloves. There is room for improvement in limited-overs cricket, where he is yet to score a fifty, but he is a free-scoring strokemaker with all the raw materials to succeed in the shorter formats. The son of Yorkshire wicketkeeping legend David, the younger Bairstow is assured of good support from the Leeds faithful.

LAST WORD: "He has this real aura about him. He doesn't say much, he just gets on and does his job and often it's good enough. He's a real talent. The other thing about him is that he's exceptional under pressure; if you've seen the number of times he's finished games off for them, he's the lad they want in when things start getting tight at the end of an innings." *Graham Hardcastle*

Batting & Fielding

	Mat	Inns	NO	Runs	HS	Ave	SR	100	50	Ct	St
First-class	31	53	14	1676	85	42.97	-	0	15	51	5
List A	17	13	3	179	46*	17.90	116.23	0	0	11	0
Twenty20	15	13	3	219	49*	21.90	125.14	0	0	4	1

Bowling

	Mat	Balls	Runs	Wkts	BBI	BBM	Ave	Econ	SR	5w	10
First-class	31	-	-	-	-	-	-	-	-	-	-
List A	17	-	-	-	-	-	-	-	-	-	-
Twenty20	15	-	-	-	-	-	-	-	-	-	-

GARY BALLANCE LHB LB

YORKSHIRE

NAME: Gary Simon Ballance
BORN: November 22, 1989, Harare
HEIGHT: 6ft
SQUAD Nº: 19
NICKNAME: Gazza, GB
OTHER TEAMS: Derbyshire
CAREER: First-class debut: 2008; List A debut: 2006; T20 debut: 2010

AOC SAYS: A highly-rated left-hander, Ballance is a powerful batsman who is extremely capable in the field. His chances were limited last season but a successful winter with Midwest Rhinos in Zimbabwe will have helped his development and 2011 could prove to be his breakthrough summer. Ballance, the nephew of former Zimbabwe skipper David Houghton, joined Yorkshire's academy from Derbyshire in 2008 and signed a three-year contract at Headingley at the end of his first season. Last summer he scored one century and eight fifties in Yorkshire's Second XI and an unbeaten 31 in his only County Championship appearance, which came against Somerset.

LAST WORD: "Ballance looks a real talent. He clubs it around and has got great hand speed and real power when he strikes the ball. He's one of those natural fielders who you think won't ever drop too many." *Graham Hardcastle*

Batting & Fielding

	Mat	Inns	NO	Runs	HS	Ave	SR	100	50	Ct	St
First-class	13	21	2	808	132	42.52	51.26	4	1	15	0
List A	10	9	1	338	135*	42.25	83.45	1	1	4	0
Twenty20	9	9	1	138	48*	17.25	87.34	0	0	3	0

Bowling

	Mat	Balls	Runs	Wkts	BBI	BBM	Ave	Econ	SR	5w	10
First-class	13	6	3	0	-	-	-	3.00	-	0	0
List A	10	-	-	-	-	-	-	-	-	-	-
Twenty20	9	-	-	-	-	-	-	-	-	-	-

NAME: John Angus Rae Blain
BORN: January 4, 1979, Edinburgh
HEIGHT: 6ft 2in
SQUAD №: 44
NICKNAME: Blainy, Haggis, William, JB
OTHER TEAMS: Scotland, Northamptonshire
CAREER: ODI debut: 1999; T20I debut: 2007; First-class debut: 1996; List A debut: 1996; T20 debut: 2007

YORKSHIRE

AOC SAYS: A former footballer with Falkirk, Blain had a spell with Yorkshire between 2004 and 2006 before leaving Headingley to represent his country in the Friends Provident Trophy. The right-arm seamer returned to the White Rose county as a player/coach in October 2008 after returning career-best ODI figures of 5-22 against Netherlands earlier that year. Blain was expected to play for Scotland in the 2009 World Twenty20 but walked out after a disagreement over team tactics and his international career now appears to be over. His only first-team appearance since returning to Yorkshire was in a match against Loughborough University last summer but he plays a key role helping to bring through young talent at the club.

LAST WORD: "John's main role is to bring along the younger bowlers, but he's also a regular in the Second XI." *James Buttler*

Batting & Fielding

	Mat	Inns	NO	Runs	HS	Ave	SR	100	50	Ct	St
ODIs	33	25	6	284	41	14.94	54.93	0	0	8	0
T20Is	6	3	1	4	3*	2.00	80.00	0	0	1	0
First-class	43	47	16	495	93	15.96	-	0	2	12	0
List A	102	66	25	635	41	15.48	-	0	0	27	0
Twenty20	6	3	1	4	3*	2.00	80.00	0	0	1	0

Bowling

	Mat	Balls	Runs	Wkts	BBI	BBM	Ave	Econ	SR	5w	10
ODIs	33	1329	1173	41	5/22	5/22	28.60	5.29	32.4	1	0
T20Is	6	120	108	6	2/23	2/23	18.00	5.40	20.0	0	0
First-class	43	6029	4286	120	6/42		35.71	4.26	50.2	4	0
List A	102	4388	3679	143	5/22	5/22	25.72	5.03	30.6	4	0
Twenty20	6	120	108	6	2/23	2/23	18.00	5.40	20.0	0	0

TIM BRESNAN RHB RMF

YORKSHIRE

NAME: Timothy Thomas Bresnan
BORN: February 28, 1985, Pontefract
HEIGHT: 6ft
SQUAD №: 16
NICKNAME: Brezzy Lad, Brez, Brezza, Tikka
OTHER TEAMS: England
CAREER: Test debut: 2009; ODI debut: 2006;
T20I debut: 2006; First-class debut: 2003;
List A debut: 2001; T20 debut: 2003; County
cap: 2006

AOC SAYS: England commitments restricted Bresnan to just six Championship matches
for Yorkshire last summer and, after taking 11 wickets in two Ashes Tests over the winter,
he is unlikely to feature any more prominently for the White Rose this summer. Bresnan
has thrived on the international stage, especially in one-day cricket. He returned figures
of 5-48 in the thrilling tie with India in the 2011 World Cup and was an integral part of the
team that won the World Twenty20 last year. There has always been firm belief among
the Yorkshire faithful that Bresnan would go on to represent his country and Carnegie
wicketkeeper Gerard Brophy will tell you that he hits the gloves a couple of yards quicker
than one might think. He has been pigeonholed – perhaps by the southern press – as
an honest, broad-beamed Yorkshire workhorse but that does him a disservice as he is
in fact an intelligent, skilful cricketer revelling under Andrew Strauss and Andy Flower's
command. A criticism of Bresnan used to be that he was two-fer and three-fer bowler but
that is gradually dissipating. Bresnan himself believes his game has developed a lot over
the last few years: "I'm a lot more consistent with the ball. Not that I didn't know where it
was going back then but now I've got it on a string. We've got a young side at Yorkshire but
a side that has played quite a bit of cricket together. We've all grown up together so we
know each other inside out. There's no reason why we can't challenge for honours."

INSIDE TRACK: "I've played with Brez for many years; we played our first Yorkshire Schools
game together at the age of 12. He has always had the talent and the ability to perform. It
was only a matter of time before he made it on to the bigger stage. He's developed as
a bowler and he's a smart cricketer. He's got the ability to bowl where he wants, when he
wants and he's become a very skilful bowler. It seems like he's been around for a long time
already but he's still relatively young and I was very impressed with his performances
over the winter in Australia. He's been a reliable part of England's team – he's a go-to-man
at certain stages of important games – and his batting is not to be underestimated either."
Joe Sayers

Batting & Fielding

	Mat	Inns	NO	Runs	HS	Ave	SR	100	50	Ct	St
Tests	7	5	0	164	91	32.80	35.49	0	1	3	0
ODIs	42	34	12	496	80	22.54	94.11	0	1	9	0
T20Is	16	10	5	76	23*	15.20	115.15	0	0	5	0
First-class	100	131	22	2976	126*	27.30	47.47	3	14	41	0
List A	178	126	39	1671	80	19.20	91.26	0	4	45	0
Twenty20	63	44	17	457	42	16.92	114.53	0	0	20	0

Bowling

	Mat	Balls	Runs	Wkts	BBI	BBM	Ave	Econ	SR	5w	10
Tests	7	1482	707	25	4/50	6/75	28.28	2.86	59.2	0	0
ODIs	42	2091	1832	49	5/48	5/48	37.38	5.25	42.6	1	0
T20Is	16	310	389	11	3/10	3/10	35.36	7.52	28.1	0	0
First-class	100	16633	8559	268	5/42	-	31.93	3.08	62.0	4	0
List A	177	7679	6467	191	5/48	5/48	33.85	5.05	40.2	1	0
Twenty20	63	1245	1516	58	3/10	3/10	26.13	7.30	21.4	0	0

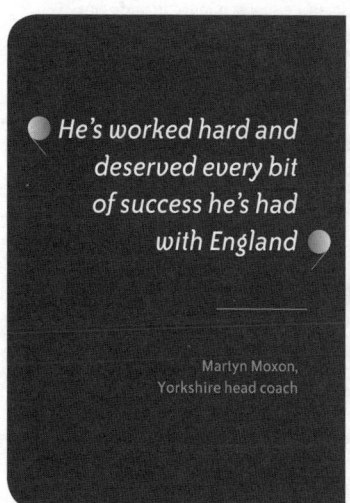

He's worked hard and deserved every bit of success he's had with England

Martyn Moxon,
Yorkshire head coach

GERARD BROPHY

RHB WK

YORKSHIRE

NAME: Gerard Louis Brophy
BORN: November 26, 1975, Welkom, South Africa
HEIGHT: 5 ft 11in
SQUAD Nº: 20
NICKNAME: Scuba
OTHER TEAMS: Free State, Gauteng, Ireland, Northamptonshire, Transvaal
CAREER: First-class debut: 1996; List A debut: 1997; T20 debut: 2003; County cap: 2008 (Yorkshire)

AOC SAYS: With the emergence of young keeper-batsman Jonny Bairstow, Brophy found himself out of Yorkshire's County Championship side at the start of last summer but returned to the four-day side for the second half of the season. Bairstow will challenge Brophy for the gloves again this year in Championship cricket, but the veteran South African remains an integral member of the limited-overs sides with his innovative batting and reliable keeping. After averaging 44 in 2009, 472 runs in 17 innings in the last campaign would have come as a disappointment to Brophy and he will need to hit the ground running this season if he is to remain first-choice stumper at Headingley.

LAST WORD: "Brophy is a proper keeper-batsman; he scores hundreds, and game-changing hundreds too." *Graham Hardcastle*

Batting & Fielding

	Mat	Inns	NO	Runs	HS	Ave	SR	100	50	Ct	St
First-class	115	184	22	5118	185	31.59	-	7	26	286	21
List A	112	92	19	1992	93*	27.28	-	0	13	110	22
Twenty20	48	41	9	678	57*	21.18	121.50	0	2	21	7

Bowling

	Mat	Balls	Runs	Wkts	BBI	BBM	Ave	Econ	SR	5w	10
First-class	115	12	1	0	-	-	-	0.50	-	0	0
List A	112	-	-	-	-	-	-	-	-	-	-
Twenty20	48	-	-	-	-	-	-	-	-	-	-

NAME: Andrew William Gale
BORN: November 28, 1983, Dewsbury
HEIGHT: 6ft 2in
SQUAD Nº: 26
NICKNAME: Galey
CAREER: First-class debut: 2004; List A
debut: 2002; T20 debut: 2004; County cap:
2008

YORKSHIRE

AOC SAYS: Gale is a fighter, more Paul Collingwood than Ian Bell, and leads by example
for Yorkshire, directing his young charges who willingly follow his aggressive brand of
captaincy. He became the club's youngest professional skipper when he took the reins at
the age of 26 years and 24 days at the end of the 2009 season and responded by averaging
47.50 in the County Championship, leading a relegation-tipped side to third place in
Division One. He has been in fine form for England Lions in the Caribbean this winter and,
having previously captained England's second-string, an international call-up is perhaps
not too far away.

LAST WORD: "Gale is a future England captain, he's that well thought of. He reminds me a
little bit of Graeme Smith when he bats, although he's far easier on the eye, and it will be
interesting to see how he develops. I don't think it will be long before he plays for England,
he'll be in that shake-up to replace Collingwood." *Graham Hardcastle*

Batting & Fielding

	Mat	Inns	NO	Runs	HS	Ave	SR	100	50	Ct	St
First-class	67	107	6	3707	151*	36.70	-	10	15	30	0
List A	92	84	10	2285	125*	30.87	-	1	12	16	0
Twenty20	56	51	9	1172	91	27.90	120.70	0	9	26	0

Bowling

	Mat	Balls	Runs	Wkts	BBI	BBM	Ave	Econ	SR	5w	10
First-class	67	24	47	1	1/33	1/33	47.00	11.75	24.0	0	0
List A	92	-	-	-	-	-	-	-	-	-	-
Twenty20	56	-	-	-	-	-	-	-	-	-	-

OLIVER HANNON-DALBY   LHB RFM

NAME: Oliver James Hannon-Dalby
BORN: June 20, 1989, Halifax
HEIGHT: 6ft 8in
SQUAD Nº: 12
NICKNAME: Bunse, Dave, OHD, Shaggy
CAREER: First-class debut: 2008

AOC SAYS: The towering seamer burst onto the scene last season with 34 Championship wickets, including a career-best 5-68 in the second fixture of the season, against Somerset at Headingley. Hannon-Dalby matches England giants Steven Finn and Chris Tremlett for height, and while he doesn't possess their pace he has shown good consistency for a young seamer still finding his way in the game. His effectiveness waned as the season neared its end, as so often happens with developing pacemen, and he will need to work on his stamina this summer. The Yorkshire academy graduate is set for an extended run in the side with Ajmal Shahzad and Tim Bresnan's availability restricted by England commitments and he will hope to make his debut in limited-overs cricket as well.

LAST WORD: "Hannon-Dalby and Patterson were both key bowlers last year; tall lads who complement the skiddier bowlers well. Oliver has a bit of experience now and I think he'll be even stronger this year." *Graham Hardcastle*

Batting & Fielding

	Mat	Inns	NO	Runs	HS	Ave	SR	100	50	Ct	St
First-class	18	16	7	30	11*	3.33	12.14	0	0	1	0

Bowling

	Mat	Balls	Runs	Wkts	BBI	BBM	Ave	Econ	SR	5w	10
First-class	18	2470	1486	35	5/68	7/122	42.45	3.60	70.5	2	0

NAME: Lee John Hodgson
BORN: June 29, 1986, Middlesbrough
HEIGHT: 5ft 11in
SQUAD Nº: 15
NICKNAME: Hodgy
OTHER TEAMS: Surrey
CAREER: Fist-class debut: 2008; List A
debut: 2008; T20 debut: 2010

YORKSHIRE

AOC SAYS: Hodgson rejoined Yorkshire from Surrey at the end of the 2008 season but
has so far found his chances limited at Headingley. A series of niggling injuries restricted
his involvement in 2009 and his only first-class appearance came in a match against
Cambridge University. Last summer he played his cricket in the Second XI, scoring 365
Second XI Championship runs at 33.18. Hodgson will be hoping to stay injury free and
capitalise on any first-team opportunities handed to him, but with Yorkshire's wealth of
seam-bowling he will have to push hard with the seconds to get a look-in.

LAST WORD: "He's a combative, plucky allrounder who bowls medium-fast and is a solid
batsman. He's Richard Pyrah's understudy in the Yorkshire set-up, to be honest. He has
struggled with the odd niggle and 2011 will be a big season for him." *James Buttler*

Batting & Fielding

	Mat	Inns	NO	Runs	HS	Ave	SR	100	50	Ct	St
First-class	4	5	0	165	63	33.00	49.40	0	1	3	0
List A	6	1	0	9	9	9.00	100.00	0	0	4	0
Twenty20	2	1	1	39	39*	-	114.70	0	0	1	0

Bowling

	Mat	Balls	Runs	Wkts	BBI	BBM	Ave	Econ	SR	5w	10
First-class	4	299	216	2	1/42	1/42	108.00	4.33	149.5	0	0
List A	6	156	160	2	2/44	2/44	80.00	6.15	78.0	0	0
Twenty20	2	36	59	2	2/29	2/29	29.50	9.83	18.0	0	0

NAME: James Edward Lee
BORN: December 23, 1988, Sheffield
HEIGHT: 6ft 1in
SQUAD Nº: 28
NICKNAME: Binga
CAREER: First-class debut: 2006; List A debut: 2009

AOC SAYS: A former England under 19 player, Lee is a genuinely sharp, thrusting bowler and hard-hitting lower-order batsman. He didn't feature in Yorkshire's first team last summer but took 12 Second XI Trophy wickets at an average of 27 and claimed a further 12 victims in the Second XI Championship. He spent the winter playing cricket in Australia and will be hoping to challenge for a first-team spot this season. In 2009 he caught the eye in the Pro40, taking seven wickets at an impressive 16.57 runs apiece, and helped the Second XI beat local rivals Lancashire in the Trophy Final later that summer.

LAST WORD: "He's a quick bowler, a bit like Darren Gough in his style. He loves a good swing at No.9 too. He has come back from Australia refreshed and raring to go. As his youth international pedigree would suggest, he's capable of producing the goods for Yorkshire as and when England calls come for the senior bowlers." *James Buttler*

Batting & Fielding

	Mat	Inns	NO	Runs	HS	Ave	SR	100	50	Ct	St
First-class	2	3	1	24	21*	12.00	48.00	0	0	1	0
List A	4	-	-	-	-	-	-	-	-	0	0

Bowling

	Mat	Balls	Runs	Wkts	BBI	BBM	Ave	Econ	SR	5w	10
First-class	2	168	149	2	2/63	2/113	74.50	5.32	84.0	0	0
List A	4	106	116	7	3/43	3/43	16.57	6.56	15.1	0	0

NAME: Adam Lyth
BORN: September 25, 1987, Whitby
HEIGHT: 5ft 9in
SQUAD Nº: 9
NICKNAME: Peanut
CAREER: First-class debut: 2007; List A debut: 2006; T20 debut: 2006; County cap: 2010

YORKSHIRE

AOC SAYS: Lyth was named the PCA Young Player of the Year award after an outstanding 2010 and was rewarded with a call-up for England Lions' tour of the Caribbean this winter. The elegant left-handed opener scored 1,509 first-class runs and was the first batsman to pass the 1,000 mark in Championship cricket – reaching the tally before the end of May. The former England under 19 star continued his good form over the winter, opening the West Indies tour with consecutive half-centuries against Leeward Islands and Barbados. His path into the England side looks blocked for now, with Andrew Strauss and Alastair Cook maintaining a firm grip on the opening spots, but Lyth has the talent to push for international honours further down the line.

LAST WORD: "He's a typical left-hander; he cuts the ball well and he's very fluent when he gets going. If it's there to hit he'll give it a crack. I think he will always open, I can't see them dropping him down the order. It will be him and Sayers or Ballance up top in the Championship." *Graham Hardcastle*

Batting & Fielding

	Mat	Inns	NO	Runs	HS	Ave	SR	100	50	Ct	St
First-class	41	66	0	2623	142	39.74	-	4	18	24	0
List A	42	36	3	883	109*	26.75	86.90	1	3	14	0
Twenty20	19	17	0	244	59	14.35	145.23	0	1	6	0

Bowling

	Mat	Balls	Runs	Wkts	BBI	BBM	Ave	Econ	SR	5w	10
First-class	41	313	171	3	1/12	1/12	57.00	3.27	104.3	0	0
List A	42	18	14	0	-	-	-	4.66	-	0	0
Twenty20	19	-	-	-	-	-	-	-	-	-	-

ANTHONY MCGRATH

YORKSHIRE

NAME: Anthony McGrath
BORN: October 6, 1975, Bradford
HEIGHT: 6ft 2in
SQUAD Nº: 10
NICKNAME: Gripper
OTHER TEAMS: England
CAREER: Test debut: 2003; ODI debut: 2003;
First-class debut: 1995; List A debut: 1995;
T20 debut: 2004; County cap: 1999

AOC SAYS: The former Yorkshire captain has been a prolific runscorer for the White Rose since making his debut in 1995 and returned to form last summer with 1,219 first-class runs and three Championship centuries after a two-season slump. McGrath had a spell in the England side in 2003 but was quickly discarded, despite starting his Test career with consecutive half-centuries against Zimbabwe and taking three wickets on debut with his gentle seamers. His gracious handing over of the captaincy in 2009 after a loss of form with the bat further boosted his already lofty standing with the Yorkshire faithful and he remains a key member of the Tykes' batting unit.

LAST WORD: "Gritty when required, dashing when the mood takes him, Anthony has been the man for most occasions in all forms of the game during his 16-year Yorkshire career."
James Buttler

Batting & Fielding

	Mat	Inns	NO	Runs	HS	Ave	SR	100	50	Ct	St
Tests	4	5	0	201	81	40.20	50.00	0	2	3	0
ODIs	14	12	2	166	52	16.60	47.02	0	1	4	0
First-class	231	389	27	13565	211	37.47	-	32	66	164	0
List A	288	266	40	7472	148	33.06	-	7	44	97	0
Twenty20	57	54	12	1311	73*	31.21	115.30	0	8	24	0

Bowling

	Mat	Balls	Runs	Wkts	BBI	BBM	Ave	Econ	SR	5w	10
Tests	4	102	56	4	3/16	3/16	14.00	3.29	25.5	0	0
ODIs	14	228	175	4	1/13	1/13	43.75	4.60	57.0	0	0
First-class	231	8436	4234	114	5/39	-	37.14	3.01	74.0	1	0
List A	288	3095	2610	80	4/41	4/41	32.62	5.05	38.6	0	0
Twenty20	57	451	656	20	3/27	3/27	32.80	8.72	22.5	0	0

NAME: Steven Andrew Patterson
BORN: October 3, 1983, Hull
HEIGHT: 6ft 4in
SQUAD Nº: 17
NICKNAME: Patto, Dead Man
CAREER: First-class debut: 2005; List A debut: 2003; T20 debut: 2009

YORKSHIRE

AOC SAYS: Patterson took advantage of Tim Bresnan and Ajmal Shahzad's international commitments to enjoy his best season to date in 2010. The man-mountain seamer took 45 first-class wickets, and also impressed in the CB40 with 21 victims at 21.95 apiece. The Tykes will again rely on Patterson and fellow paceman Oliver Hannon-Dalby to fill the void left by their England contingent. Away from cricket, Patterson is a regular fundraiser for the British Lung Foundation in memory of his two cousins who tragically died in 2009. Steven wanted to continue the efforts of his cousins, who fundraised for the charity before their untimely passing, and did so by running the New York Marathon last year.

LAST WORD: "Patterson is a tall wicket-taker and became a fundamental part of the attack last year. He has a bit of experience now and is expected to hold a place down in the side in all forms." *Graham Hardcastle*

Batting & Fielding

	Mat	Inns	NO	Runs	HS	Ave	SR	100	50	Ct	St
First-class	29	33	9	350	46	14.58	31.11	0	0	6	0
List A	39	14	12	83	25*	41.50	-	0	0	5	0
Twenty20	16	4	3	3	3*	3.00	42.85	0	0	1	0

Bowling

	Mat	Balls	Runs	Wkts	BBI	BBM	Ave	Econ	SR	5w	10
First-class	29	4163	2184	67	5/50	7/69	32.59	3.14	62.1	1	0
List A	39	1677	1413	44	6/32	6/32	32.11	5.05	38.1	1	0
Twenty20	16	340	507	16	4/30	4/30	31.68	8.94	21.2	0	0

RICHARD PYRAH

RHB RMF MVP92

YORKSHIRE

NAME: Richard Michael Pyrah
BORN: November 1, 1982, Dewsbury
HEIGHT: 6ft
SQUAD Nº: 27
NICKNAME: Pyro
CAREER: First-class debut: 2004; List A
debut: 2001; T20 debut: 2005; County cap:
2010

AOC SAYS: Pyrah has been pigeonholed as a limited-overs specialist for much of his career but the allrounder showed he is a more than capable cricketer in the longer format last season with a first-class batting average of 60.80, including a career-best 134* against Loughborough University. He couldn't replicate his form with the bat in the CB40 but more than made up for it with the ball, taking 20 wickets at an average of 24.20 and claiming a further 21 victims in the FP t20. Pyrah is sure to be one of the first names on the teamsheet in limited-overs cricket this season but the challenge is to establish himself as a first-choice Championship pick.

LAST WORD: "He continues to develop as a versatile all-round cricketer. He has played the majority of his cricket in the one-day arena and he is as good a fielder at backward point as anyone in the country." *James Buttler*

Batting & Fielding

	Mat	Inns	NO	Runs	HS	Ave	SR	100	50	Ct	St
First-class	22	28	4	801	134*	33.37	53.40	2	4	13	0
List A	82	53	13	775	67	19.37	-	0	1	28	0
Twenty20	47	31	9	250	33*	11.36	101.62	0	0	19	0

Bowling

	Mat	Balls	Runs	Wkts	BBI	BBM	Ave	Econ	SR	5w	10
First-class	22	1372	817	16	2/8	-	51.06	3.57	85.7	0	0
List A	82	2590	2459	100	5/50	5/50	24.59	5.69	25.9	1	0
Twenty20	47	696	844	43	4/20	4/20	19.62	7.27	16.1	0	0

NAME: Azeem Rafiq
BORN: February 27, 1991, Pakistan
HEIGHT: 5ft 9in
SQUAD Nº: 30
NICKNAME: Rafa, Az
CAREER: First-class debut: 2009; List A debut: 2009; T20 debut: 2008

YORKSHIRE

AOC SAYS: Rafiq is one of the brightest young talents in England but he has some ground to make up this season after an outburst on social networking site Twitter led to him being banned from all cricket for a month last season. The offspinning allrounder reacted angrily after he was dropped by England under 19 coach John Abrahams for breaking a team curfew and must show he has learnt from the experience if he is to fulfil his vast potential. Rafiq moved to England from Pakistan in 2001 and made his debut for Yorkshire's Second XI in 2007. The former England under 19 captain took five wickets on his first-class debut against Sussex and went on to register a blistering 95-ball century in his next match, batting at No.9 against Worcestershire.

LAST WORD: "The Twitter storm that saw him banned from all forms of cricket for one month of the 2010 season was a step back for Azeem, who had shown signs of rich potential in 2009." *James Buttler*

Batting & Fielding

	Mat	Inns	NO	Runs	HS	Ave	SR	100	50	Ct	St
First-class	7	8	1	146	100	20.85	74.11	1	0	1	0
List A	2	-	-	-	-	-	-	-	-	1	0
Twenty20	15	6	3	20	11*	6.66	58.82	0	0	5	0

Bowling

	Mat	Balls	Runs	Wkts	BBI	BBM	Ave	Econ	SR	5w	10
First-class	7	1275	755	15	4/92	5/89	50.33	3.55	85.0	0	0
List A	2	30	36	1	1/36	1/36	36.00	7.20	30.0	0	0
Twenty20	15	271	388	11	3/23	3/23	35.27	8.59	24.6	0	0

GURMAN RANDHAWA

YORKSHIRE

NAME: Gurman Singh Randhawa
BORN: 25 January 1992, Huddersfield
HEIGHT: 5ft 9in
SQUAD Nº: 25
NICKNAME: Gurm
CAREER: Yet to make first-team debut

AOC SAYS: Randhawa was named Yorkshire's Academy Player of the Year in both 2009 and 2010 and signed his first professional contract with the club at the end of last season. He returned impressive figures in the Second XI Championship last summer, collecting 32 wickets at 20.15 and also claimed 10 dismissals in the Second XI Trophy at an average of 23.8. The left-arm spinner was a member of the England under 19 party which toured Sri Lanka over the winter, playing in two youth Tests and two youth ODIs. A hugely exciting talent.

LAST WORD: "We pride ourselves on our academy; we've got some good systems in place here and traditionally we like to give players the opportunity to play first-class cricket. Gurman Randhawa is one who could potentially step up to the first team this season."
Martyn Moxon

EXTRAS

"There's no reason they shouldn't challenge in every competition. They've got depth in their batting and the bowlers to take wickets." Graham Hardcastle

NAME: Adil Usman Rashid
BORN: February 17, 1988, Bradford
HEIGHT: 5ft 8in
SQUAD Nº: 3
NICKNAME: Dilly
OTHER TEAMS: England, South Australia
CAREER: ODI debut: 2009; T20I debut:
20009; First-class debut: 2006; List A debut:
2006; T20 debut: 2008; County cap: 2008

YORKSHIRE

AOC SAYS: After a disappointing winter away with England in which he played the role of water-carrier, Rashid returned to county cricket in glorious form for Yorkshire last summer. The legspinning allrounder enjoyed his most productive season to date, taking 57 wickets and averaging 45.75 with the bat in first-class cricket. There is plenty of room for improvement in his batting in one-day cricket but his bowling was equally strong across all formats, with a haul of 26 wickets at 16.46 apiece in the FP t20. Rashid was snapped up by South Australia for the Big Bash Twenty20 and helped his side to the title, finishing as the tournament's third highest wicket-taker. The challenge for Rashid is to prove he can carry his prolific domestic form into the international arena but England appear reluctant to give this exciting young talent his head just yet, and with Graeme Swann firmly established as first-choice spinner they will have to upset the balance of a winning side to accommodate him. After touring South Africa in 2009, he lost his spot as England's second-choice spinner to Monty Pansear at the start of last season but if he produces another season like the last, he will prove impossible to ignore. His call-up to England's 2011 World Cup squad after Mike Yardy returned home revealed he is still very much in the selectors' thoughts but Andy Flower and Andrew Strauss are right to show patience with this tantalising prospect.

INSIDE TRACK: "Adil's had a very busy winter with England Lions and he's developing well; particularly in the limited-overs form of the game. We'll be looking to him to win matches for us in the second half of the season when the wickets dry out. I was out in Pretoria with the England Performance Programme squad last winter and it was a challenging time for him. I'm pleased to say he's bounced back and he put together a solid season for us last year. The way Twenty20 cricket is going, spinners don't often give the ball as much air as they would in a four-day match and that's something that Adil will be aware of. Twenty20 is a big part of the modern game but he won't want to lose the spin and dip that he's got in his four-day method. It's all part of his education towards becoming a Test player." *Joe Sayers*

YORKSHIRE

Batting & Fielding											
	Mat	Inns	NO	Runs	HS	Ave	SR	100	50	Ct	St
ODIs	5	4	1	60	31*	20.00	111.11	0	0	2	0
T20Is	5	2	1	10	9*	10.00	52.63	0	0	0	0
First-class	73	103	21	3024	157*	36.87	-	4	19	38	0
List A	55	34	10	343	41*	14.29	72.05	0	0	20	0
Twenty20	44	24	7	210	34	12.35	101.44	0	0	11	0

Bowling										
	Mat	Balls	Runs	Wkts	BBI	BBM	Ave	Econ	SR	5w	10
ODIs	5	204	191	3	1/16	1/16	63.66	5.61	68.0	0	0
T20Is	5	84	120	3	1/11	1/11	40.00	8.57	28.0	0	0
First-class	73	13646	7958	241	7/107	9/177	33.02	3.49	56.6	13	0
List A	55	2001	1684	43	3/28	3/28	39.16	5.04	46.5	0	0
Twenty20	44	882	1044	59	4/20	4/20	17.69	7.10	14.9	0	0

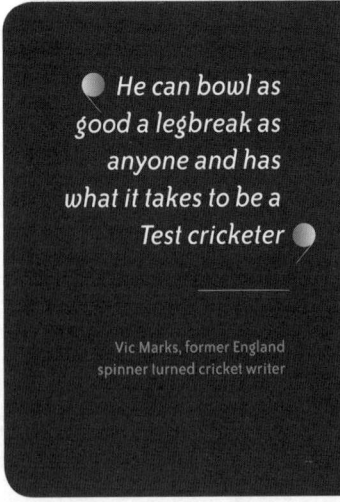

He can bowl as good a legbreak as anyone and has what it takes to be a Test cricketer

Vic Marks, former England spinner turned cricket writer

NAME: Joseph Edward Root
BORN: December 30, 1990, Sheffield
HEIGHT: 6ft
SQUAD Nº: 5
NICKNAME: Rooty
CAREER: First-class debut: 2010; List A
debut: 2009

YORKSHIRE

AOC SAYS: Root is a promising opening batsman, who made his first-class debut against Loughborough University last season. The former England under 19 right-hander had impressed on his List A debut in 2009, making 63 against Essex in the Pro40, and will have his eye on Joe Sayers' opening berth this year after an impressive Second XI Championship campaign in 2010, in which he scored 514 runs at an average of 51.40. Root is also a capable offbreak bowler and took 3-20 for England under 19s against Sri Lanka in a youth Test last season.

LAST WORD: "He was at the Darren Lehmann Academy over the winter, and has a bit of Michael Vaughan about him. He bowls a bit of offspin and is a very correct, good-looking bat. He scored mountains of runs in 2009 for the Second XI before a growth spurt meant he had to adjust his technique." *James Buttler*

Batting & Fielding											
	Mat	Inns	NO	Runs	HS	Ave	SR	100	50	Ct	St
First-class	2	3	1	38	20*	19.00	52.05	0	0	1	0
List A	1	1	0	63	63	63.00	66.31	0	1	1	0

Bowling											
	Mat	Balls	Runs	Wkts	BBI	BBM	Ave	Econ	SR	5w	10
First-class	2	42	27	0	-	-	-	3.85	-	0	0
First-class	2	42	27	0	-	-	-	3.85	-	0	0
List A	1	-	-	-	-	-	-	-	-	-	-

BEN SANDERSON

RHB RMF

NAME: Ben William Sanderson
BORN: January 3, 1989, Sheffield
HEIGHT: 6ft
SQUAD Nº: 18
NICKNAME: Sando
CAREER: First-class debut: 2008; List A debut: 2010; T20 debut: 2010

AOC SAYS: Medium-pacer Sanderson played two County Championship matches in 2008 but his only first-class cricket since saw him return a five-wicket haul against Loughborough University last summer. His opportunities have been restricted to one-day cricket and he impressed last season with seven wickets at 23.85 in the CB40 competition. Sanderson is a proven second-string performer who took 15 wickets in the Second XI Championship last summer and will look to teammate Oliver Hannon-Dalby for inspiration as he attempts to convince the Yorkshire staff that he is ready for an extended run in the first team.

LAST WORD: "Sanderson did a good job for us when he got a chance last year; he's worked hard on his skills and has a really good temperament. He's got quite a lot of experience playing for the Second XI and doesn't get flustered easily." *Martyn Moxon*

Batting & Fielding

	Mat	Inns	NO	Runs	HS	Ave	SR	100	50	Ct	St
First-class	3	2	1	6	6	6.00	54.54	0	0	0	0
List A	7	1	1	12	12*	-	133.33	0	0	4	0
Twenty20	2	-	-	-	-	-	-	-	-	0	0

Bowling

	Mat	Balls	Runs	Wkts	BBI	BBM	Ave	Econ	SR	5w	10
First-class	3	330	190	6	5/50	5/50	31.66	3.45	55.0	1	0
List A	7	174	167	7	2/17	2/17	23.85	5.75	24.8	0	0
Twenty20	2	28	26	1	1/13	1/13	26.00	5.57	28.0	0	0

NAME: Joseph John Sayers
BORN: November 5, 1983. Leeds
HEIGHT: 6ft
SQUAD Nº: 22
NICKNAME: JJ, Squirrel
CAREER: First-class debut: 2002; List A debut: 2003; T20 debut: 2005; County cap: 2007

AOC SAYS: Sayers is a gritty opener in the Geoffrey Boycott mould. His career was progressing nicely after selection for England's Performance Programme squad to tour South Africa followed 1,150 first-class runs in 2009. However, the Oxford University graduate suffered a setback last year when he was struck down by post viral fatigue disorder to bring a premature end to his season. A batsman who is most suited to four-day cricket due to his powers of concentration and rock-solid defence, Sayers returned for pre-season training and says he is ready for the challenge ahead. The former England Lion is likely to partner Adam Lyth at the top of the order in Championship cricket.

LAST WORD: "With Jacques Rudolph having left the club, Sayers will be looking to cement his place in the side in the early part of the season." *James Buttler*

Batting & Fielding

	Mat	Inns	NO	Runs	HS	Ave	SR	100	50	Ct	St
First-class	85	139	10	4360	187	33.79	37.88	10	22	51	0
List A	21	21	2	444	62	23.36	59.35	0	4	2	0
Twenty20	5	3	0	18	12	6.00	81.81	0	0	2	0

Bowling

	Mat	Balls	Runs	Wkts	BBI	BBM	Ave	Econ	SR	5w	10
First-class	85	281	147	3	3/20	3/20	49.00	3.13	93.6	0	0
List A	21	54	71	1	1/31	1/31	71.00	7.88	54.0	0	0
Twenty20	5	-	-	-	-	-	-	-	-	-	-

AJMAL SHAZHAD RFM RHB

NAME: Ajmal Shahzad
BORN: July 27, 1985, Huddersfield
HEIGHT: 6ft
SQUAD Nº: 4
NICKNAME: Ajy
OTHER TEAMS: England
CAREER: Test debut: 2010; ODI debut: 2010; T20I debut: 2010; First-class debut: 2006; List A debut: 2004; T20 debut: 2006; County cap: 2010

AOC SAYS: Shahzad has been on the fringes of the England squad since the winter of 2009/10 and played five ODIs against Australia during the Ashes tour, as well as being a member of the World Cup squad before returning home with a hamstring injury. He only featured in nine first-class matches for Yorkshire last summer due to international commitments but excelled when available, with 34 Championship wickets at 29.79. A right-arm seamer blessed with genuine pace and and a talent for swinging the ball both ways, Shahzad's ability to reverse-swing the old ball as well as find conventional movement with the new one makes him one of the most valuable commodities in English cricket. His fiery spell of 3-45 on Test debut against Bangladesh demonstrated his evident talent and he was subsequently rewarded with selection for England's historic winter tour Down Under. Shahzad, who is also a more than capable lower-order strokemaker, will be competing for a spot in the Test squad this summer with several other pacemen but already looks ready to become a regular in the ODI side. A charismatic cricketer, who is popular with his fellow professionals, Shahzad made history in 2004 when he became the first British-born Asian to represent Yorkshire and is now a cult hero at Headingley. Graham Hardcastle says: "Yorkshire will have a seriously good attack with him, Ryan Sidebottom, Tim Bresnan and the younger lads. He's clearly a very good bowler but he can bat as well, and that's a big plus for him. He's similar to his teammate Jonny Bairstow in that he's so confident; he just believes he can go out and win games. But he's slightly different in that he's more outgoing than Bairstow. He's a very cheerful lad who believes in his ability but he never comes across as arrogant."

INSIDE TRACK: "He's a great character, a confident lad but not cocky with it, and he has all the raw materials. He produces magic deliveries – he's a good bowler to chuck the ball to when a decent batsman is well set because he can conjure up something that will get people out." *Martyn Moxon*

Batting & Fielding

	Mat	Inns	NO	Runs	HS	Ave	SR	100	50	Ct	St
Tests	1	1	0	5	5	5.00	41.66	0	0	2	0
ODIs	11	8	2	39	9	6.50	65.00	0	0	4	0
T20Is	3	1	1	0	0*	-	0.00	0	0	1	0
First-class	34	41	13	814	88	29.07	41.17	0	2	8	0
List A	37	23	8	183	43*	12.20	95.81	0	0	8	0
Twenty20	16	10	3	47	17*	6.71	100.00	0	0	6	0

Bowling

	Mat	Balls	Runs	Wkts	BBI	BBM	Ave	Econ	SR	5w	10
Tests	1	102	63	4	3/45	4/63	15.75	3.70	25.5	0	0
ODIs	11	588	490	17	3/41	3/41	28.82	5.00	34.5	0	0
T20Is	3	66	97	3	2/38	2/38	32.33	8.81	22.0	0	0
First-class	34	5561	3134	94	5/51	8/121	33.34	3.38	59.1	1	0
List A	37	1806	1478	48	5/51	5/51	30.79	4.91	37.6	1	0
Twenty20	16	336	431	11	2/22	2/22	39.18	7.69	30.5	0	0

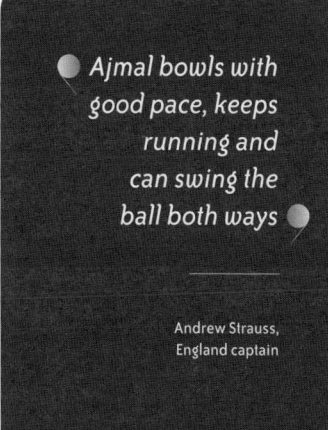

Ajmal bowls with good pace, keeps running and can swing the ball both ways

Andrew Strauss,
England captain

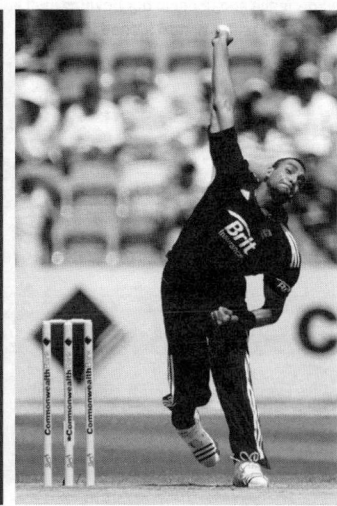

RYAN SIDEBOTTOM

LHB LFM W2

YORKSHIRE

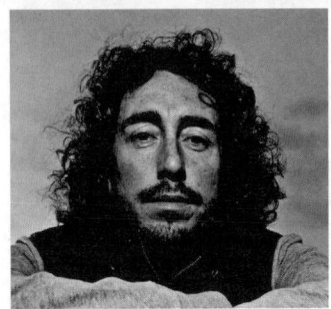

NAME: Ryan Jay Sidebottom
BORN: January 15, 1978, Huddersfield
HEIGHT: 6ft 4in
SQUAD Nº: 11
NICKNAME: Siddy
OTHER TEAMS: England, Nottinghamshire
CAREER: Test debut: 2001; ODI debut: 2001;
T20I debut: 2007; First-class debut:
1997; List A debut: 1997; T20 debut: 2003;
County cap: 2000 (Yorkshire), 2004 (Notts)

AOC SAYS: Sidebottom returns to Yorkshire having left in 2004 to join Nottinghamshire.
The left-arm seamer made his Test bow against Pakistan in 2001 and looked set to emulate
his father Arnie – who played just once for England – but returned in 2007 to scoop
England's Player of the Year award after he took 24 Test wickets at 17.08 during the tour of
New Zealand. A key performer in England's World Twenty20 success last year, he quit the
international game in September and thus will be available for Yorkshire all season.

LAST WORD: "I am delighted that Ryan has chosen Yorkshire ahead of other counties. I
think that proves his Yorkshire pride in that he wants to return to Headingley and add his
experience and talent to our bowling attack." *Martyn Moxon*

Batting & Fielding

	Mat	Inns	NO	Runs	HS	Ave	SR	100	50	Ct	St
Tests	22	31	11	313	31	15.65	34.66	0	0	5	0
ODIs	25	18	8	133	24	13.30	68.55	0	0	6	0
T20Is	18	1	1	5	5*	-	125.00	0	0	5	0
First-class	147	184	59	1592	54	12.73	-	0	1	49	0
List A	173	82	38	500	32	11.36	-	0	0	36	0
Twenty20	50	11	8	63	17*	21.00	98.43	0	0	17	0

Bowling

	Mat	Balls	Runs	Wkts	BBI	BBM	Ave	Econ	SR	5w	10
Tests	22	4812	2231	79	7/47	10/139	28.24	2.78	60.9	5	1
ODIs	25	1277	1039	29	3/19	3/19	35.82	4.88	44.0	0	0
T20Is	18	367	437	23	3/16	3/16	19.00	7.14	15.9	0	0
First-class	147	25904	12106	475	7/47		25.48	2.80	54.5	20	2
List A	173	7662	5573	178	6/40	6/40	31.30	4.36	43.0	2	0
Twenty20	50	1058	1216	58	3/16	3/16	20.96	6.89	18.2	0	0

NAME: David John Wainwright
BORN: March 21, 1985, Pontefract
HEIGHT: 5ft 9in
SQUAD №: 29
NICKNAME: Wainers
CAREER: First-class debut: 2004; List A debut: 2005; T20 debut: 2007; County cap: 2010

YORKSHIRE

AOC SAYS: After taking 26 wickets and averaging 42 with the bat in 10 first-class appearances for Yorkshire in 2009, Wainwright earned a place on the England Performance Programme to tour South Africa that winter. However, after earning his county cap at the start of the 2010 campaign, injuries and a loss of form saw the left-arm orthodox spinner take just 14 wickets in seven first-class matches. With Adil Rashid firmly established as first-choice spinner at Headingley, Wainwright has had to wait patiently for opportunities in Championship cricket but he remains an integral player in limited-overs cricket.

LAST WORD: "Wainwright will probably play a lot of one-day cricket this season but his problem is Azeem Rafiq. If Rafiq can put his Twitter rant behind him I think he's an exceptional talent, but the thing that gives Wainwright the edge at the moment is his batting. I think Rafiq has all the talent in the world though; it will be a toss up between the two when Rashid is away or when they want to play two spinners." *Graham Hardcastle*

Batting & Fielding

	Mat	Inns	NO	Runs	HS	Ave	SR	100	50	Ct	St
First-class	31	37	11	925	104*	35.57	54.37	2	2	10	0
List A	41	19	11	136	26	17.00	70.83	0	0	9	0
Twenty20	18	6	3	9	3*	3.00	47.36	0	0	6	0

Bowling

	Mat	Balls	Runs	Wkts	BBI	BBM	Ave	Econ	SR	5w	10
First-class	31	4498	2552	70	5/134		36.45	3.40	64.2	1	0
List A	41	1494	1184	33	3/26	3/26	35.87	4.75	45.2	0	0
Twenty20	18	311	366	18	3/6	3/6	20.33	7.06	17.2	0	0

Other
Teams

unicorns

FORMED: 2010
HOME GROUND: Various, several
fixtures at Wormsley
CAPTAIN: Keith Parsons
2010 RESULTS: CB40: 6/9 in Group A

THE LOWDOWN

The Unicorns were one of the success stories of 2010. Formed by the ECB and administered by the Minor Counties, the side was set up ostensibly to ensure there were three groups of seven in the CB 40, but this mix of players without first-class contracts surpassed expectations, showing the big boys what a bit of hunger, a lot of skill, and the presence of a couple of wise old heads can achieve, claiming three county scalps in Sussex, Glamorgan and Worcestershire. The highlight of their season was the highest ever successful 40-over run-chase when they scored 325 against Sussex, who boasted five bowlers with international experience. Four players from the squad went on to get county contracts – Wes Durston, Mike O'Shea, Rory Burns and Ed Young.

Last year's squad was selected by coach Phil Oliver from the Minor Counties, Mark Alleyne from the MCC and Min Patel from the Club Cricket Conference from a pool of over 200 players after the ECB invited nominations from Premier League clubs, Minor Counties, MCC Universities, MCC YCs and individuals. This year there were even more applications and the squad was whittled down to 70, and then 29 after trials at Derby, Malvern College and Whitgift School. All the players are England-qualified, most are young, and the Unicorns' only income comes from the ECB's PRFPs (performance-related fee payments), which reward clubs for playing English-qualified players under 26, with higher payments for under 22-year-olds. Ten players were retained from 2010 while there are 19 new faces. Six of the squad will be juggling studying with representing Unicorns this summer – Luke Blackaby (Durham), Tom Craddock, Luis Reece & Adam Wilson (Leeds/Bradford), Tom Friend and Dominic Reed (Cardiff).

The side plays several of its games at the Getty Estate in Wormsley. Coach Phil Oliver says: "It's great to be able to practise and play at Wormsley. Tim Munton has been great with us and the facilities are just fantastic. Obviously it helps all round – in terms of crowds and finances – for us to play home games as near our opponents as possible, but we are very happy at Wormsley." In addition, the Unicorns A team will compete in the Second XI Trophy one-day competition this year, taking over the fixtures traditionally filled by the Minor Counties XI, so players will get even more chances to shine. What will happen in 2012 when the ECB juggle the fixture make-up yet again is anyone's guess but in these cash-strapped times, Unicorns are making a geat case for retention. What price them playing Twenty20 cricket next year?

With thanks to: Phil Oliver, Unicorns team manager; Gordon Child, Unicorns team administrator; Keith Parsons, Unicorns captain; Paul Bedford, ECB head of non first-class cricket.

	Mat	Inns	NO	Runs	HS	Ave	SR	100	50	Ct	St
MP O'Shea	8	7	0	355	90	50.71	93.17	0	3	2	-
WJ Durston	4	4	0	201	117	50.25	130.51	1	1	1	-
KA Parsons	11	10	2	388	89	48.50	87.98	0	3	2	-
JPT Knappett	11	10	0	364	91	36.40	84.06	0	4	6	2
JG Thompson	11	10	0	241	54	24.10	117.56	0	1	2	-
NC Saker	7	6	2	87	40*	21.75	73.10	0	0	2	-
C Brown	3	2	1	20	19	20.00	45.45	0	0	1	-
ND Hancock	10	8	1	113	29	16.14	94.95	0	0	3	-
Atiq-ur-Rehman	2	2	0	29	29	14.50	59.18	0	0	1	-
CP Murtagh	10	9	0	121	31	13.44	62.05	0	0	2	-
RG Querl	11	8	3	64	28*	12.80	86.48	0	0	2	-
SM Park	8	7	1	62	21	10.33	74.69	0	0	2	-
Arfan Akram	1	1	0	8	8	8.00	50.00	0	0	0	-
EGC Young	2	2	0	13	12	6.50	56.52	0	0	0	-
JS Ahmed	2	2	1	5	4*	5.00	33.33	0	0	0	-
T Mees	4	2	1	2	2*	2.00	66.66	0	0	2	-
CT Peploe	4	2	1	2	2	2.00	100.00	0	0	2	-
TG Sharp	1	1	0	0	0	0.00	0.00	0	0	0	-
JS Miles	11	3	3	9	5*	-	75.00	0	0	2	-

Batting and Fielding

	Mat	Overs	Mdn	Runs	Wkts	BBI	Ave	Econ	SR	5w	10
TG Sharp	1	5.0	0	20	1	1/20	20.00	4.00	30.0	0	0
CT Peploe	4	24.0	0	105	4	2/23	26.25	4.37	36.0	0	0
C Brown	3	22.4	0	103	2	2/50	51.50	4.54	68.0	0	0
ND Hancock	10	46.1	1	241	10	5/64	24.10	5.22	27.7	1	0
WJ Durston	4	26.0	1	137	4	2/28	34.25	5.26	39.0	0	0
RG Querl	11	71.1	0	411	14	4/41	29.35	5.77	30.5	0	0
MP O'Shea	8	19.2	0	121	1	1/38	121.00	6.25	116.0	0	0
JG Thompson	11	7.0	0	45	0	-	-	6.42	-	0	0
NC Saker	7	38.0	3	250	4	2/54	62.50	6.57	57.0	0	0
JS Miles	11	66.0	2	444	10	3/49	44.40	6.72	39.6	0	0
T Mees	4	23.5	0	167	2	2/47	83.50	7.00	71.5	0	0
JS Ahmed	2	12.0	0	104	1	1/58	104.00	8.66	72.0	0	0
EGC Young	2	6.4	0	58	0	-	-	8.70	-	0	0
KA Parsons	11	2.0	0	29	0	-	-	14.50	-	0	0

Bowling

UNICORNS

JAHID AHMED

RHB RFM

NAME: Jahid Sheikh Ahmed
BORN: February 20, 1986, Chelmsford
SQUAD Nº: 1
OTHER TEAMS: Essex, Northants 2nd XI, Surrey 2nd XI, MCC YCs
CAREER: First-class debut: 2005; List A debut: 2006; T20 debut: 2006

AOC SAYS: Jahid Ahmed has been around a bit, debuting for Essex back in 2005. He has real pace, possibly more than anyone in the squad, and is a decent death bowler. He is however a bit erratic and unlikely to make the starting XI unless there are injuries or availability issues. He moved from the Essex to the Kent League in 2010, playing at Blackheath.

Batting & Fielding	Mat	Inns	NO	Runs	HS	Ave	SR	100	50	Ct	St
First-class	7	6	4	49	16*	24.50	63.63	0	0	3	0
List A	8	4	3	6	4*	6.00	35.29	0	0	2	0
Twenty20	2	-	-	-	-	-	-	-	-	0	0

Bowling	Mat	Balls	Runs	Wkts	BBI	BBM	Ave	Econ	SR	5w	10
First-class	7	733	542	13	3/42	-	41.69	4.43	56.3	0	0
List A	8	312	306	11	4/32	4/32	27.81	5.88	28.3	0	0
Twenty20	2	36	56	2	1/25	1/25	28.00	9.33	18.0	0	0

CHRIS BENHAM

RHB OB

NAME: Christopher Charles Benham
BORN: March 24, 1983, Frimley
SQUAD Nº: 2
OTHER TEAMS: Hampshire, Loughborough MCCU, MCC
CAREER: First-class debut: 2004; List A debut: 2001; T20 debut: 2006

AOC SAYS: Benham was released by Hampshire at the end of last season having represented them since he was 10. A class bat, he is one of the older members of the squad and will be looking at the Unicorns as a springboard back into county cricket à la Wes Durston. He will probably bat at No.4 and bowl a few gentle offies. He says: "I still have a huge desire to play cricket at the highest level."

Batting & Fielding	Mat	Inns	NO	Runs	HS	Ave	SR	100	50	Ct	St
First-class	48	80	3	2103	111	27.31	49.30	2	10	51	0
List A	55	50	6	1564	158	35.54	-	4	7	25	0
Twenty20	37	32	4	447	59	15.96	104.92	0	1	20	0

Bowling	Mat	Balls	Runs	Wkts	BBI	BBM	Ave	Econ	SR	5w	10
First-class	48	30	37	0	-	-	-	7.40	-	0	0
List A	55	-	-	-	-	-	-	-	-	-	-
Twenty20	37	-	-	-	-	-	-	-	-	-	-

LUKE BLACKABY

LHB LM

NAME: Luke Alexander Blackaby
BORN: February 1, 1991, Farnborough, Kent
SQUAD Nº: 3
OTHER TEAMS: Kent 2nd XI, Durham MCCU
CAREER: First-class debut: 2010

AOC SAYS: Blackaby is a little left-handed bat from Durham MCCU. He has played for Sevenoaks Vine since 2007, and had a good all-round season last year. He also averaged 40 for Durham MCCU and coach Phil Oliver says: "He has an excellent attitude, a good technique and is very strong square of the wicket. He reminds me a little bit of Ian Bell at the same age."

	Mat	Inns	NO	Runs	HS	Ave	SR	100	50	Ct	St
First-class	2	1	0	38	38	38.00	46.91	0	0	0	0

	Mat	Balls	Runs	Wkts	BBI	BBM	Ave	Econ	SR	5w	10
First-class	2	6	11	0	-	-	-	11.00	-	0	0

CHRIS BROWN

RHB OB

NAME: Christopher Brown
BORN: August 16, 1974, Oldham
OTHER TEAMS: Badureliya Sports Club, Derbyshire 2nd XI, Essex 2nd XI, Glamorgan 2nd XI, Lancashire 2nd XI, Somerset 2nd XI, Minor Counties, Cheshire, Norfolk
SQUAD Nº: 4
CAREER: First-class debut: 2006; List A debut: 2001

AOC SAYS: The second oldest member of the squad, Brown is an experienced offspinner who has done the rounds, including spending some time at Lancs. He is probably the pick of the Unicorns' spin bowlers, with excellent control and variation of pace. He captains Norfolk and the Unicorns A side and is likely to play only if the side needs an extra spinner.

	Mat	Inns	NO	Runs	HS	Ave	SR	100	50	Ct	St
First-class	4	6	1	45	21	9.00	35.15	0	0	2	0
List A	9	7	2	88	33	17.60	-	0	0	3	0

	Mat	Balls	Runs	Wkts	BBI	BBM	Ave	Econ	SR	5w	10
First-class	4	366	163	6	2/10	2/34	27.16	2.67	61.0	0	0
List A	9	412	302	7	2/39	2/39	43.14	4.39	58.8	0	0

UNICORNS

JAMES CAMPBELL — RHB RM

NAME: James Robert Alexander Campbell
BORN: November 25, 1988, Dorchester
SQUAD №: 5
OTHER TEAMS: Gloucestershire 2nd XI, Somerset 2nd XI, Leeds/
Bradford MCCU
CAREER: Yet to make first-team debut

AOC SAYS: Campbell is a right-handed, hard-hitting opener, playing good club cricket
for Bath. He is a serious candidate for a starting spot, his brilliant fielding counting in his
favour. He has been involved with the Gloucestershire academy and Second XI sides over
the past five years without managing to get a contract. In 2010 he scored almost 800 runs at
over 50 in league cricket as Bath won the West of England Premier League.

TOM CRADDOCK — RHB LB

NAME: Thomas Richard Craddock
BORN: July 13, 1989, Huddersfield
SQUAD №: 6
OTHER TEAMS: Northants 2nd XI, Leeds/Bradford MCCU, MCCU
CAREER: Yet to make first-team debut

AOC SAYS: One of six current university boys in the squad, Craddock plays up at Leeds /
Bradford MCCU. He is a big-turning legspinner who has impresssd in the pre-season nets. He
took 72 wickets for Holmfirth in 2009 and then 79 for the Huddersfield Cricket League
winners Honley last year, winning back-to-back Young Cricketer of the Year awards.
Craddock played for Northants Second XI and MCCU last year, as well as bowling against
England's Test batsmen in the nets at Loughborough.

DAN DAVIS

RHB RM

NAME: Daniel Francis Davis
BORN: January 23, 1989, Bristol
SQUAD Nº: 7
OTHER TEAMS: Somerset 2nd XI, Cornwall
CAREER: Yet to make first-team debut

AOC SAYS: Davis was playing for Cornwall at 16 and is a special talent. He bats and fields brilliantly and is technically very good; playing the spinners adeptly, sweeping hard, and bowling little medium-pacers. And he has an excellent attitude to boot. He plays for Callington in the the Cornwall League and was their top runscorer with 618 league runs last year. He played for Somerset Second XI from 2007 to 2009.

PAUL DIXEY

RHB WK

NAME: Paul Garrod Dixey
BORN: November 2, 1987, Canterbury
SQUAD Nº: 8
OTHER TEAMS: England under 19, Kent, Notts 2nd XI, Durham MCCU
CAREER: First-class debut: 2005; List A debut: 2007

AOC SAYS: Released by Kent at end of last year after five years on the staff, Dixey is one of five wicketkeepers in the squad. He played for England under 19 in 2006 and will probably be one of the stand-by stumpers. He likes the big stage and is a competent batsman – on his NatWest Pro40 debut in 2009, he hit a six and a four in the last over to win the game. Dixey also played for Durham MCCU, scoring a hundred against home county Kent. He had trials with Leicestershire during pre-season this year.

	Mat	Inns	NO	Runs	HS	Ave	SR	100	50	Ct	St
First-class	13	22	1	334	103	15.90	42.54	1	0	27	6
List A	4	3	2	32	16	32.00	106.66	0	0	4	0

	Mat	Balls	Runs	Wkts	BBI	BBM	Ave	Econ	SR	5w	10
First-class	13	-	-	-	-	-	-	-	-	-	-
List A	4	-	-	-	-	-	-	-	-	-	-

UNICORNS

NED ECKERSLEY
RHB WK

NAME: Edmund John Eckersley
BORN: August 9, 1989, Oxford
SQUAD Nº: 9
OTHER TEAMS: Middlesex 2nd XI, Northants 2nd XI, MCC, MCC YCs
CAREER: List A debut: 2008

AOC SYAS: Eckersley has been with the MCC YCs for the last four years and is recognised as one of their best players. He is a quality batsman-keeper and had an excellent 2010 for them, as well as playing a few games for Northants Second XI. MCC head coach Mark Alleyne says: "Ned is a real big match player. He's got a first class temperament." He was selected for 12th man duties during England's famous Ashes victory at Lord's in 2009, and fielded on the fourth day.

Batting & Fielding

	Mat	Inns	NO	Runs	HS	Ave	SR	100	50	Ct	St
List A	1	1	0	1	1	1.00	33.33	0	0	3	0

Bowling

	Mat	Balls	Runs	Wkts	BBI	BBM	Ave	Econ	SR	5w	10
List A	1	-	-	-	-	-	-	-	-	-	-

TOM FRIEND
RHB RMF

NAME: Tom Friend
BORN: May 3, 1991, Newport, Isle of Wight
SQUAD Nº: 10
OTHER TEAMS: Worcestershire 2nd XI, Cardiff MCCU
CAREER: Yet to make first-team debut

AOC SAYS: An Isle of Wight lad and a product of the Ventnor CC stable, Friend is the youngest player in the squad. A tall, aggressive quick bowler, currently at Cardiff Uni, he is likely to play in the early games and open the bowling. If there is a weakness, it is that he needs to work on his overall fitness. He has been playing Birmingham & District Premier League cricket with Bromsgrove for the past two seasons while studying in Cardiff and also turned out for Worcestershire Second XI.

ALAN ISON

RHB RMF

NAME: Alan Roy Ison
BORN: November 16, 1990, Barking
SQUAD Nº: 11
OTHER TEAMS: Essex 2nd XI
CAREER: Yet to make first-team debut

AOC SAYS: An unorthodox allrounder who bowls a bit off the wrong foot, and is a good exponent of the yorker. Ison gives it a mighty smack, and has a good chance of playing for Unicorns this season. A club cricketer at Upminster, he came somewhat out of the blue as a nomination from his club. He scored almost 1,000 runs for Upminster last year and took a few wickets too, as well as playing some Second XI cricket for Essex.

JOSH KNAPPETT

RHB WK

NAME: Joshua Philip Thomas Knappett
BORN: April 15, 1985, Westminster
SQUAD Nº: 12
OTHER TEAMS: Worcestershire, Middlesex 2nd XI, Worcestershire 2nd XI, British Universities, Oxford MCCU
CAREER: First class debut: 2004; List A debut: 2010

AOC SAYS: Knappett played every game last year, averaging over 35 and ending up second leading runscorer behind Keith Parsons. He is very much the gloveman in possession and after his great year in 2010, will be hard to dislodge. The Finchley-based keeper was unlucky not to get a contract somewhere and is considered one of the senior Unicorns despite his relatively young age. He made his first-class debut for Worcestershire in 2007, going on to captain their Second XI regularly but his first-team chances were limited by the presence of Steven Davies.

	Mat	Inns	NO	Runs	HS	Ave	SR	100	50	Ct	St
First-class	13	20	3	523	100*	30.76	50.67	1	3	26	3
List A	11	10	0	364	91	36.40	84.06	0	4	6	2

	Mat	Balls	Runs	Wkts	BBI	BBM	Ave	Econ	SR	5w	10
First-class	13	-	-	-	-	-	-	-	-	-	-
List A	11	-	-	-	-	-	-	-	-	-	-

UNICORNS

ROBIN LETT

RHB RM

NAME: Robin Jonathan Hugh Lett
BORN: December 23, 1986, Westminster
SQUAD Nº: 13
OTHER TEAMS: Somerset, Oxford MCCU
CAREER: First-class debut: 2006

AOC SYAS: Lett, who hit 50 on first-team debut in 2006 but never quite managed to hold down a place in the first team, was captain of Somerset Second XI in 2010, scoring plenty of runs, but was released at the end of the season. 6ft 2in, with a build like Marcus Trescothick he has a chance of starting at the top of the order. He is a teammate of fellow Unicorn James Campbell at Bath CC, who won the West of England Premier League last year.

	Mat	Inns	NO	Runs	HS	Ave	SR	100	50	Ct	St
First-class	12	17	2	401	76*	26.73	74.81	0	5	4	0

	Mat	Balls	Runs	Wkts	BBI	BBM	Ave	Econ	SR	5w	10
First-class	12	102	67	1	1/39	1/67	67.00	3.94	102.0	0	0

JONATHAN MILES

RHB LMF

NAME: Jonathan Samuel Miles
BORN: February 21, 1986, Sutton Coldfield
SQUAD Nº: 14
OTHER TEAMS: Notts 2nd XI, Surrey 2nd XI, Worcestershire 2nd XI, MCC YCs, Lincolnshire, Norfolk
CAREER: List A debut: 2008

AOC SAYS: Miles played all 11 games for Unicorns last year, took 10 wickets and generally impressed. He plays for Sleaford in the Lincs Cricket Board Premier League, taking 29 wickets at just over 20 last season. He also plays with Unicorns teammate Chris Brown for Norfolk, and wintered in Australia. He is a left-arm opening bowler, who can swing it back into the right-hander. He played three games for Surrey Second XI in 2007, played for MCC YCs in 2008 and 2009 and turned out for Notts' second-string last year.

	Mat	Inns	NO	Runs	HS	Ave	SR	100	50	Ct	St
List A	12	4	3	15	6	15.00	65.21	0	0	2	0

	Mat	Balls	Runs	Wkts	BBI	BBM	Ave	Econ	SR	5w	10
List A	12	450	488	12	3/49	3/49	40.66	6.50	37.5	0	0

JAMES ORD RHB OB

NAME: James Edward Ord
BORN: November 9, 1987, Birmingham
SQUAD Nº: 15
OTHER TEAMS: Warwickshire, Loughborough MCCU
CAREER: First class debut: 2009; List A debut: 2009

AOC SAYS: A highly rated batsman and grandson of Jimmy Ord, who was in the Warwickshire side of the 50s, Ord was on Warwickshire's books for five years. A classy, organised and technically correct opener, it's his opportunity to make a name for himself this year. In 2009, he made a 200-mile dash to play in a day/night Pro40 game which lasted just 12 balls due to rain. It rather epitomised his time with the Bears.

	Mat	Inns	NO	Runs	HS	Ave	SR	100	50	Ct	St
First-class	2	4	0	17	9	4.25	21.51	0	0	1	0
List A	2	1	0	27	27	27.00	52.94	0	0	0	0

	Mat	Balls	Runs	Wkts	BBI	BBM	Ave	Econ	SR	5w	10
First-class	2	-	-	-	-	-	-	-	-	-	-
List A	2	-	-	-	-	-	-	-	-	-	-

SEAN PARK RHB RMF WK

NAME: Sean Michael Park
BORN: April 24, 1980, Umtata, Transkei, South Africa
SQUAD Nº: 16
OTHER TEAMS: Cambridgeshire, Minor Counties
CAREER: List A debut: 2010

AOC SAYS: Park keeps wicket and is also a middle-order batsman who can bowl. His brothers Craig and Garry are from the same stock – hugely talented, great all-round sportsmen, who plays golf and tennis to a high standard. He played most of Unicorns' games last year, although with limited success. He has been an integral part of the Cambrdige Granta side for the last decade and was key to them winning the East Anglian Premier Cricket League last year.

	Mat	Inns	NO	Runs	HS	Ave	SR	100	50	Ct	St
List A	8	7	1	62	21	10.33	74.69	0	0	2	0

	Mat	Balls	Runs	Wkts	BBI	BBM	Ave	Econ	SR	5w	10
List A	8	-	-	-	-	-	-	-	-	-	-

UNICORNS

NAME: Keith Alan Parsons
BORN: May 2, 1973, Taunton
SQUAD Nº: 17
OTHER TEAMS: Somerset, Cornwall
CAREER: First-class debut: 1992; List A debut: 1993; T20 debut: 2003;
County cap: 1999 (Somerset)

AOC SAYS: Parsons was the Unicorns' leading runscorer last year, playing 11 games, and averaging almost 50. He had an excellent year as skipper and guiding hand to the youngsters. He says: "I enjoyed it and it was nice to be asked to do it. It's a great atmosphere and feels like a real team. We gelled well, we've got no hidden agenda and pretty much all of the players have something to prove. In this economic climate counties are tightening budgets and they have smaller staffs so the Unicorns works in a couple of ways – it's partly for those who have tasted first-class cricket but been released and partly for youngsters on their way up but who have not yet found a county. We had four lads last year in the set-up who got contracts and I'm really surprised a couple more did not get contracts. The Unicorns gives them a real taste of good, competitive cricket at that level." Parsons represented England at youth level, although he will always be remembered as a one-day specialist, combining muscular thumping at the death with nagging seamers which put the skids under many a run-chase. In 2001 he was named Man of the Match in the C&G final when he smashed three maximums in the closing overs and then snared a couple of wickets to help overcome Leicestershire. He was also a key man in Somerset's Twenty20 success in 2005. He'll be raring to go again this year.

Batting & Fielding

	Mat	Inns	NO	Runs	HS	Ave	SR	100	50	Ct	St
First-class	130	209	23	5324	193*	28.62	-	6	28	115	0
List A	258	226	42	5613	121	30.50	-	2	31	100	0
Twenty20	31	30	7	464	57*	20.17	117.76	0	1	9	0

Bowling

	Mat	Balls	Runs	Wkts	BBI	BBM	Ave	Econ	SR	5w	10
First-class	130	8005	4646	106	5/13	-	43.83	3.48	75.5	2	0
List A	258	6345	5319	146	5/39	5/39	36.43	5.02	43.4	1	0
Twenty20	31	338	467	18	3/12	3/12	25.94	8.28	18.7	0	0

CHRIS PEPLOE

LHB SLA

NAME: Christopher Thomas Peploe
BORN: April 26, 1981, Hammersmith
SQUAD Nº: 18
OTHER TEAMS: Middlesex, Derbyshire 2nd XI, Surrey 2nd XI, Berkshire
CAREER: First-class debut: 2003; List A debut: 2001; T20 debut: 2005

UNICORNS

AOC SAYS: He might have a bit of the slow left-armer's madness but Peploe is a fantastic spinner. He is contracted to Middlesex County Cricket League Division One champions Ealing, for whom he took 49 wickets at 17 as well as averaging 35 with the bat last year, and that means he can't play all Unicorn games. When he does play, his great control delivered from a 6ft 4in frame make him very hard to hit.

	Mat	Inns	NO	Runs	HS	Ave	SR	100	50	Ct	St
First-class	30	41	7	530	46	15.58	42.50	0	0	11	0
List A	22	12	4	38	14*	4.75	80.85	0	0	9	0
Twenty20	15	6	4	12	7	6.00	70.58	0	0	4	0

	Mat	Balls	Runs	Wkts	BBI	BBM	Ave	Econ	SR	5w	10
First-class	30	5283	2839	56	4/31	-	50.69	3.22	94.3	0	0
List A	22	960	701	30	4/38	4/38	23.36	4.38	32.0	0	0
Twenty20	15	221	378	10	3/35	3/35	37.80	10.26	22.1	0	0

JOEL POPE

RHB WK

NAME: Joel Ian Pope
BORN: October 23, 1988, Ashford, Middlesex
SQUAD Nº: 19
OTHER TEAMS: Leicestershire, Middlesex 2nd XI, MCC YCs
CAREER: List A debut: 2008

AOC SAYS: Released by Leicestershire at the end of the 2010 season, wicketkeeper-batsman Pope was previously with MCC YCs, where head coach Clive Radley said: "He has got the best pair of hands I've seen since becoming head coach here in 1991." Pope, nephew of Middlesex wicketkeeper Ben Scott, has a great record in second XI cricket, avergaing 50 for Leicestershire last year, and, according to Unicorns coach Phil Oliver was unlucky not to get a contract elsewhere.

	Mat	Inns	NO	Runs	HS	Ave	SR	100	50	Ct	St
List A	3	3	0	22	9	7.33	146.66	0	0	3	1

	Mat	Balls	Runs	Wkts	BBI	BBM	Ave	Econ	SR	5w	10
List A	3	-	-	-	-	-	-	-	-	-	-

GLEN QUERL
RHB RMF

UNICORNS

NAME: Reginald Glenn Querl
BORN: April 4, 1988, Harare
SQUAD Nº: 20
OTHER TEAMS: Zimbabwe under 19, Essex 2nd XI, Hampshire 2nd XI, MCC, MCC YCs
CAREER: List A debut: 2010

AOC SAYS: Querl played for Zimbabwe in the Under 19 World Cup in 2006, then came to England and played for Essex Second XI in 2007. He became an MCC YC in 2009 and last year scored some 500 runs and took 23 wickets. He's a right-arm bowler, with good control and an excellent yorker and possesses good variations. He also bats at No.7 or No.8 and played all 11 games last year, ending up the leading wicket-taker with 14 scalps.

	Mat	Inns	NO	Runs	HS	Ave	SR	100	50	Ct	St
List A	11	8	3	64	28*	12.80	86.48	0	0	2	0

	Mat	Balls	Runs	Wkts	BBI	BBM	Ave	Econ	SR	5w	10
List A	11	427	411	14	4/41	4/41	29.35	5.77	30.5	0	0

LUIS REECE
LHB LMF

NAME: Luis Michael Reece
BORN: August 4, 1990, Taunton
SQUAD Nº: 21
OTHER TEAMS: Lancashire 2nd XI, Leeds/Bradford MCCU
CAREER: Yet to make first-team debut

AOC SAYS: Reece is a quick left-arm seamer and top-order bat who plays for Leeds/Bradford MCCU. He's likely to play in the starting XI with his combination of skiddy pace with the ball and unorthodox batting, dotted with scoops, sweeps and reverse-sweeps. He is also the best outfielder in the side. He played for Lancashire Second XI in 2009 and played for title-winning Leyland in the Northern Premier ECB Cricket League last year, when he was leading wicket-taker with 44 at 15 and averaged over 30 with the bat.

DOMINIC REED   RHB RFM

NAME: Dominic Terrence Reed
BORN: March 27, 1990, Leicester
SQUAD Nº: 22
CAREER: Yet to make first-team debut

AOC SAYS: Reed is quick, strong, and a likely starter. He is studying at Cardiff University with Unicorns teammate Tom Friend, and has come under the influence of their director of cricket and head coach Kevin Lyons. Reed, whose older brother plays for Glamorgan, swings it away from the bat and is also a good hitter. He plays for Kegworth Town in the Leicestershire County Cricket League, and was their leading wicket-taker last season.

AMAR RASHID   RHB LB

NAME: Amar Rashid
BORN: May 16, 1986, Bradford
SQUAD Nº: 23
OTHER TEAMS: Leicestershire 2nd XI, Leeds/Bradford MCCU
CAREER: Yet to make first-team debut

AOC SAYS: Rashid, like his younger brother Adil, is a legspinner, a capable bat and a highly skilled performer. He spins it sharply and is an exciting prospect. He played for Worcestershire Second XI and then Leicestershire's second-string last year alongside Unicorns teammate Joel Pope, taking 5-9 on debut and averaging almost 30 with the bat. This year he signed for reigning champions Shepley in the Huddersfield Cricket League.

NEIL SAKER — RHB RMF

UNICORNS

NAME: Neil Clifford Saker
BORN: September 20, 1984, Tooting
SQUAD №: 24
OTHER TEAMS: Surrey, Middlesex 2nd XI, Sussex 2nd XI, Minor Counties
CAREER: First-class debut: 2003; List A debut: 2005; T20 debut: 2007

AOC SAYS: Saker, a 6ft 4in fast bowler, was the first academy player to be awarded a professional contract at Surrey. He struggled to cement a permanent spot due to injuries and was released in 2008. He played for Minor Counties in the Second XI Trophy last year and played seven games for Unicorns. He is a key part of the attack for Reigate Priory, Surrey Championship Premier Division winners last year.

	Mat	Inns	NO	Runs	HS	Ave	SR	100	50	Ct	St
First-class	18	23	4	272	58*	14.31	36.95	0	1	5	0
List A	30	17	6	161	40*	14.63	67.64	0	0	4	0
Twenty20	2	1	0	0	0	0.00	0.00	0	0	0	0

	Mat	Balls	Runs	Wkts	BBI	BBM	Ave	Econ	SR	5w	10
First-class	18	2159	1578	31	5/76	-	50.90	4.38	69.6	1	0
List A	30	1161	1192	22	4/43	4/43	54.18	6.16	52.7	0	0
Twenty20	2	30	44	1	1/28	1/28	44.00	8.80	30.0	0	0

CHRIS THOMPSON — RHB RMF

NAME: Christopher Everton Junior Thompson
BORN: June 26, 1987, Waterloo
SQUAD №: 25
OTHER TEAMS: England Under 19s, Leicestershire, Derbyshire 2nd XI, Hampshire 2nd XI, Surrey 2nd XI, Worcestershire 2nd XI, MCC YCs
CAREER: First-class debut: 2009; List A debut: 2009

AOC SAYS: Another former Surrey man, who has also been on the staff at Leicestershire, Thompson is a big hitter, a medium-pace bowler, and a very athletic fielder who has a good chance of playing several games this year. He played for England under 19 in 2005 and 2006 and has turned out in a lot of second XI cricket as well as for MCC YCs.

	Mat	Inns	NO	Runs	HS	Ave	SR	100	50	Ct	St
First-class	1	2	0	16	16	8.00	22.85	0	0	0	0
List A	3	3	2	56	39*	56.00	68.29	0	0	1	0

	Mat	Balls	Runs	Wkts	BBI	BBM	Ave	Econ	SR	5w	10
First-class	1	92	45	1	1/45	1/45	45.00	2.93	92.0	0	0
List A	3	36	51	1	1/22	1/22	51.00	8.50	36.0	0	0

JACKSON THOMPSON LHB OB

NAME: Jackson Gladwin Thompson
BORN: February 7, 1986, Nasik, India
SQUAD Nº: 26
OTHER TEAMS: Gloucestershire, Middlesex, Oxfordshire
CAREER: First-class debut: 2007; List A debut: 2002; T20 debut: 2008

UNICORNS

AOC SAYS: Thompson played all 11 Unicorns games last season and averaged in the mid-twenties, which tells a story. He has been on the books of both Middlesex and Gloucestershire and played Twenty20 for both. He was also leading runscorer for Middlesex in their 2010 Second XI Trophy campaign. He is a hugely destructive player at the top of the order and doesn't care if he is facing an international or a second XI attack.

	Mat	Inns	NO	Runs	HS	Ave	SR	100	50	Ct	St
First-class	1	2	0	32	21	16.00	37.64	0	0	0	0
List A	14	13	0	257	54	19.76	-	0	1	2	0
Twenty20	6	6	0	68	32	11.33	141.66	0	0	3	0

	Mat	Balls	Runs	Wkts	BBI	BBM	Ave	Econ	SR	5w	10
First-class	1	-	-	-	-	-	-	-	-	-	-
List A	14	60	65	0	-	-	-	6.50	-	0	0
Twenty20	6	6	8	1	1/8	1/8	8.00	8.00	6.0	0	0

MICHAEL THORNELY RHB RM

NAME: Michael Alistair Thornely
BORN: October 19, 1987, Camden
SQUAD Nº: 27
OTHER TEAMS: Sussex, Sussex 2nd XI
CAREER: First-class debut: 2007; List debut: 2007

AOC SAYS: Thornely will have been bitterly disappointed to be released by Sussex after the south coast side won Division Two of the Championship, with the right-hander playing 12 of the 16 matches. He scored 500 runs at just over 20 but he is a class batsman and the Unicorns will be looking for him to do the job Mike O'Shea and Wes Durston did last year. He has played for club side Horsham for almost 10 years.

	Mat	Inns	NO	Runs	HS	Ave	SR	100	50	Ct	St
First-class	17	30	2	522	89	18.64	39.15	0	4	15	0
List A	7	6	0	186	67	31.00	76.54	0	2	2	0

	Mat	Balls	Runs	Wkts	BBI	BBM	Ave	Econ	SR	5w	10
First-class	17	150	100	4	2/14	2/14	25.00	4.00	37.5	0	0
List A	7	-	-	-	-	-	-	-	-	-	-

UNICORNS

DAN WHEELDON   RHB RFM

NAME: Daniel Maurice Wheeldon
BORN: March 14, 1989, Nottingham
SQUAD Nº: 28
OTHER TEAMS: Yorkshire 2nd XI
CAREER: Yet to make first-team debut

AOC SAYS: Encouraged to apply by his teammates and umpire Russ Evans, big Dan Wheeldon has come out of the Derbyshire Premier League, where he took plenty of wickets for Sandiacre opening the bowling. He hits the deck hard, and has a good chance of playing. He can also bat in the middle-order, and is a real prospect. He had one game for Yorkshire Second XI last year and has also signed for Lincolnshire to play in the Minor Counties competitions in 2011.

ADAM WILSON   RHB RM

NAME: Adam David Wilson
BORN: October 10, 1988, Sheffield
SQUAD Nº: 29
OTHER TEAMS: Bradford/Leeds MCCU, MCCU
CAREER: Yet to make first-team debut

AOC SAYS: Nicknamed Willow, Wilson is a skiddy quick bowler playing up at Leeds/ Bradford MCCU while reading psychology at Leeds Met university. He is a fabulous athlete, and was far and away the fittest during the pre-season bleep tests. He played for Yorkshire throughout the age groups and last year played for MCCU in the 2nd XI Championship and for Bradford/leeds MCCU in the T20 competiition, which they lost in the final to Durham 2nd XI.

TEAM PROFILE

FORMED: 1980
HOME GROUND: Citylets Grange, Edinburgh
ONE-DAY NAME: Scottish Saltires
CAPTAIN: Gordon Drummond
2010 RESULTS: CB40: 7/7 in Group C

THE LOWDOWN

Scotland have won at least one match each season since joining the National League in 2003, and that is a record they will hope to continue in this year's CB40 campaign. The Saltires are an enthusiastic and ambitious group of players who will give their all but they face an uphill struggle against teams made up of full professionals. In past seasons their strength has been their bowling but that balance has shifted following the retirement and unavailability of several of their more experienced seamers. The signing of Australian allrounder Luke Butterworth as their overseas professional this season reflects that. Scotland have typically opted for a batting pro but the Tasmanian – arriving on the back of an outstanding season in state cricket – is primarily a bowler and will bring good balance to the side as they look to build on two CB40 victories over Leicestershire last season.

HEAD COACH: PETER STEINDL

Steindl emigrated from Australia to Scotland with his wife in 1993. The Queenslander was a limited-overs specialist medium-pacer, featuring in Scotland's 1999 World Cup squad and representing his adopted country in 10 one-day matches between 1995 and 2003. After retirement he became youth development manager for Cricket Scotland in 2006 and the following year succeeded Peter Drinnen as head coach.

With thanks to: Peter Steindl; Willie Dick, Cricket Media Scotland

Batting & Fielding

	Mat	Inns	NO	Runs	HS	Ave	SR	100	50	Ct	St
KJ Coetzer	1	1	0	51	51	51.00	80.95	0	1	1	-
GJ Bailey	12	12	1	422	123*	38.36	92.54	1	3	9	-
MM Iqbal	11	11	3	266	67	33.25	60.86	0	2	1	-
RM Haq	16	12	7	165	29*	33.00	80.09	0	0	0	-
DF Watts	14	14	1	408	98	31.38	59.13	0	4	3	-
RD Berrington	24	24	0	732	106	30.50	81.78	1	6	9	-
NFI McCallum	18	17	2	387	89*	25.80	68.37	0	1	12	-
RR Watson	4	4	0	96	48	24.00	78.68	0	0	3	-
GM Hamilton	13	13	0	285	64	21.92	60.00	0	1	2	-
PL Mommsen	12	12	0	197	80	16.41	50.25	0	1	7	-
OJ Hairs	7	7	0	110	27	15.71	76.92	0	0	0	-
GI Maiden	5	5	0	75	31	15.00	63.02	0	0	1	-
RO Hussain	6	6	0	88	42	14.66	59.06	0	0	0	-
DR Lockhart	20	18	2	233	46	14.56	57.96	0	0	12	1
GD Drummond	24	19	5	196	35*	14.00	80.65	0	0	5	-
MQ Sheikh	1	1	0	14	14	14.00	50.00	0	0	1	-
JH Davey	4	4	0	46	24	11.50	45.09	0	0	2	-
MA Parker	19	17	3	149	23	10.64	55.39	0	0	5	-
R Flannigan	5	5	0	42	22	8.40	47.19	0	0	3	-
EF Chalmers	1	1	0	8	8	8.00	72.72	0	0	0	-
G Goudie	19	14	4	78	26*	7.80	105.40	0	0	4	-
MJ Petrie	3	3	1	13	7*	6.50	56.52	0	0	0	0
RT Lyons	19	11	6	20	8	4.00	44.44	0	0	6	-
FRJ Coleman	1	1	0	0	0	0.00	0.00	0	0	0	-
JD Nel	1	1	1	11	11*	-	64.70	0	0	0	-
AC Evans	1	1	1	1	1*	-	33.33	0	0	0	-

Bowling

	Mat	Overs	Mdns	Runs	Wkts	BBI	Ave	Econ	SR	5w
JH Davey	4	20.2	3	94	6	5/9	15.66	4.62	20.3	1
G Goudie	19	132.1	8	792	30	4/46	26.40	5.99	26.4	0
MA Parker	19	128.0	9	661	25	4/33	26.44	5.16	30.7	0
RD Berrington	24	116.2	6	637	22	4/47	28.95	5.47	31.7	0
GD Drummond	24	164.0	15	706	21	2/23	33.61	4.30	46.8	0
RT Lyons	19	138.2	8	611	18	3/21	33.94	4.41	46.1	0
RR Watson	4	10.0	0	76	2	2/34	38.00	7.60	30.0	0
AC Evans	1	6.0	0	38	1	1/38	38.00	6.33	36.0	0
PL Mommsen	12	7.0	0	48	1	1/19	48.00	6.85	42.0	0
RM Haq	16	115.0	0	558	10	2/35	55.80	4.85	69.0	0
MM Iqbal	11	43.0	0	253	2	2/35	126.50	5.88	129.0	0
KJ Coetzer	1	2.0	0	23	0	-	-	11.50	-	0
NJW Laidlaw	2	9.0	0	50	0	-	-	5.55	-	0
GI Maiden	5	17.0	0	91	0	-	-	5.35	-	0
JD Nel	1	3.0	0	27	0	-	-	9.00	-	0

SCOTLAND

NAME: Richard Douglas Berrington
BORN: April 3, 1987, Pretoria
HEIGHT: 5ft 10in
SQUAD Nº: 44
NICKNAME: Berro
CAREER: ODI debut: 2008; T20I debut: 2008; First-class debut: 2007; List A debut: 2007; T20 debut: 2008

AOC SAYS: Berrington is a promising allrounder who has already attracted interest from county sides. He began the 2010 CB40 campaign with a matchwinning run-a-ball half-century as the Saltires caused an upset by defeating Leicestershire at Grace Road. Two more fifties followed in his next two innings and he finished the season with a classy 82 against a strong Warwickshire attack. The South Africa-born youngster is also a handy seamer with a happy knack of picking up wickets, as demonstrated by a career-best haul of 4-47 against Hampshire last season. On the back of those performances Berrington was offered a contract by Leicestershire but he opted to stay north of the border for the time being and signed a full-time contract with Scotland in March.

LAST WORD: "Richie had a great season for us last year. He had a couple of very good knocks against the county boys, which was good to see." *Peter Steindl*

Batting & Fielding

	Mat	Inns	NO	Runs	HS	Ave	SR	100	50	Ct	St
ODIs	16	14	1	292	84	22.46	71.74	0	2	9	0
T20Is	8	6	1	44	19*	8.80	84.61	0	0	0	0
First-class	9	15	1	317	82	22.64	38.33	0	2	11	0
List A	34	31	1	838	106	27.93	76.73	1	6	15	0
Twenty20	11	9	2	55	19*	7.85	82.08	0	0	2	0

Bowling

	Mat	Balls	Runs	Wkts	BBI	BBM	Ave	Econ	SR	5w	10
ODIs	16	470	346	10	2/14	2/14	34.60	4.41	47.0	0	0
T20Is	8	112	103	5	2/21	2/21	20.60	5.51	22.4	0	0
First-class	9	736	401	15	3/13	3/39	26.73	3.26	49.0	0	0
List A	34	872	802	24	4/47	4/47	33.41	5.51	36.3	0	0
Twenty20	11	154	149	7	2/12	2/12	21.28	5.80	22.0	0	0

OVERSEAS PLAYER

NAME: Luke Rex Butterworth
BORN: October 28, 1983, Hobart, Australia
HEIGHT: 6ft 2in
SQUAD №: 11
NICKNAME: Buttsy
OTHER TEAMS: Tasmania
CAREER: First-class debut: 2007; List A
debut: 2004; T20 debut: 2007

SCOTLAND

AOC SAYS: The allrounder made his mark in Tasmania's 2006/07 Pura Cup final victory, claiming the Man of the Match award after a superb performance with bat and ball in just his fifth first-class match. He finished his debut season with 23 wickets at 19.56 and was subsequently selected for Australia A's tour of Pakistan. The Saltires were alerted to Butterworth by his Tasmania captain George Bailey, who enjoyed a successful spell with Scotland last season. Butterworth's strength is his nippy medium-pace swing bowling but he is also a destructive middle-order batsman. The Australian will also be featuring in Scottish club cricket for Greenock.

LAST WORD: "Luke has a superb record and, being a genuine allrounder, will greatly assist with the balance and options available." *Roddy Smith, Cricket Scotland chief executive*

Batting & Fielding

	Mat	Inns	NO	Runs	HS	Ave	SR	100	50	Ct	St
First-class	40	66	7	1680	116	28.47	46.26	2	6	24	0
List A	51	43	11	710	114*	22.18	79.15	1	1	16	0
Twenty20	5	5	1	59	36	14.75	92.18	0	0	0	0

Bowling

	Mat	Balls	Runs	Wkts	BBI	BBM	Ave	Econ	SR	5w	10
First-class	40	6290	3106	127	6/51	9/77	24.45	2.96	49.5	4	0
List A	51	2139	1882	54	3/32	3/32	34.85	5.27	39.6	0	0
Twenty20	5	60	101	1	1/23	1/23	101.00	10.10	60.0	0	0

EWAN CHALMERS

RHB RM

SCOTLAND

NAME: Ewan Fraser Chalmers
BORN: October 19, 1989, Edinburgh
HEIGHT: 5ft 10in
SQUAD Nº: 7
NICKNAME: Chubby
CAREER: First-class debut: 2009; List A debut: 2010

AOC SAYS: Chalmers is a gritty top-order batsman, ideally suited to four-day cricket. A St Andrew's University graduate in Maths and Economics, he made his first-class debut in the Intercontinental Cup victory over Canada in 2009 and scored his maiden half-century in the same competition last season, making a well compiled 67 in a losing cause against Afghanistan. He made his one-day debut against India A last summer but is yet to feature for the Saltires in the CB40. Chalmers is a steady accumulator, capable of playing long innings, and is likely to again remain on the fringes of Scotland's limited-overs side, relying on injuries if he is to get his chance.

LAST WORD: "Ewan has fitted in extremely well and I'm sure he'll take any international call in his stride also." *Gordon Drummond, Scotland captain*

Batting & Fielding

	Mat	Inns	NO	Runs	HS	Ave	SR	100	50	Ct	St
First-class	4	8	1	155	67	22.14	39.94	0	1	4	0
List A	1	1	0	8	8	8.00	72.72	0	0	0	0

Bowling

	Mat	Balls	Runs	Wkts	BBI	BBM	Ave	Econ	SR	5w	10
First-class	4	-	-	-	-	-	-	-	-	-	-
List A	1	-	-	-	-	-	-	-	-	-	-

NAME: Frederick Robert John Coleman
BORN: December 15, 1991, Edinburgh
SQUAD Nº: 6
CAREER: List A debut: 2010

SCOTLAND

AOC SAYS: Coleman is a promising top-order batsman who is part of Warwickshire's academy. Earmarked from an early age as a player of huge potential, he was given his Saltires debut last season but endured a difficult start to his professional career after he dropped a catch and was dismissed for a duck against Nottinghamshire in Edinburgh. After impressing for Warwickshire under 19s he made two appearances for their Second XI in 2010 and his commitments at Edgbaston mean he is unlikely to feature regularly for the Saltires in their CB40 campaign.

LAST WORD: "Freddie is a tremendous prospect. I coached him when he was in the Scotland under 12 squad and it was obvious from way back that he would go a long way in cricket."
Neil McCallum, Scotland teammate

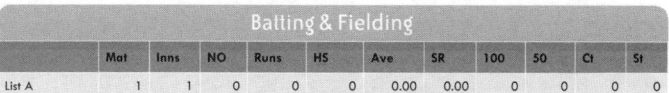

	Mat	Inns	NO	Runs	HS	Ave	SR	100	50	Ct	St
List A	1	1	0	0	0	0.00	0.00	0	0	0	0

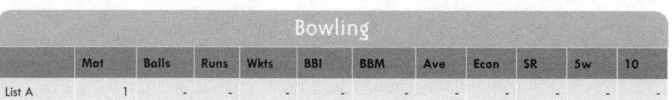

	Mat	Balls	Runs	Wkts	BBI	BBM	Ave	Econ	SR	5w	10
List A	1	-	-	-	-	-	-	-	-	-	-

SCOTLAND

GORDON DRUMMOND

RHB RMF

NAME: Gordon David Drummond
BORN: April 21, 1980, Meigle
HEIGHT: 5ft 10in
SQUAD №: 24
NICKNAME: Drummo
CAREER: ODI debut: 2007; T20I debut: 2008;
First-class debut: 2007; List A debut: 2007;
T20 debut: 2008

AOC SAYS: Drummond was the natural successor as Saltires skipper after Gavin Hamilton stepped down midway through last season. Having captained Scotland's four-day side for the last two years, he commanded respect in the dressing room and led by example with his performances on the field. A long-time servant of Scottish club side Meigle, Drummond is predominantly a nagging medium-pacer but also contributes handy runs from No.8. His coach and teammates describe him as a model professional who sets high standards for himself and the team as a whole. His career highlight to date is a haul of 4-41 against Canada in 2009 to help Scotland level a two-match ODI series.

LAST WORD: "Gordon is an excellent leader and a very good communicator with the players. He's very passionate about playing for Scotland." *Peter Steindl*

Batting & Fielding

	Mat	Inns	NO	Runs	HS	Ave	SR	100	50	Ct	St
ODIs	21	14	6	182	35*	22.75	94.79	0	0	3	0
T20Is	9	6	0	54	35	9.00	83.07	0	0	0	0
First-class	8	11	0	145	52	13.18	43.67	0	1	3	0
List A	42	33	10	289	35*	12.56	71.71	0	0	6	0
Twenty20	12	8	1	66	35	9.42	84.61	0	0	0	0

Bowling

	Mat	Balls	Runs	Wkts	BBI	BBM	Ave	Econ	SR	5w	10
ODIs	21	903	621	20	4/41	4/41	31.05	4.12	45.1	0	0
T20Is	9	179	221	7	2/14	2/14	31.57	7.40	25.5	0	0
First-class	8	1074	408	13	3/18	3/44	31.38	2.27	82.6	0	0
List A	42	1719	1284	36	4/41	4/41	35.66	4.48	47.7	0	0
Twenty20	12	233	264	10	2/14	2/14	26.40	6.79	23.3	0	0

NAME: Ryan Flannigan
BORN: June 30, 1988, Kelso
HEIGHT: 5ft 11in
SQUAD №: 88
NICKNAME: Flanners
CAREER: ODI debut: 2010; First-class debut: 2010; List A debut: 2010

SCOTLAND

AOC SAYS: The son of a Kelso baker, Flannigan is hard-hitting top-order batsman who broke into the Saltires side towards the end of last season. After featuring for Scotland against India A and Afghanistan he was handed the opportunity to open the batting in the latter stages of the CB40 campaign. He failed to make the most of his chance, registering scores of 13 in the win over Leicestershire and 1 in the defeat to Durham, but remains highly regarded. He is unlikely to begin the season in the Saltires' first-choice XI but a strong start to the summer with his club side Watsonians will see him pushing hard for a regular berth.

LAST WORD: "Ryan has turned in some great performances and spent last winter in Australia, where he learned a lot. Being involved with the Saltires has helped him to see what the next step is all about." *Peter Steindl*

Batting & Fielding

	Mat	Inns	NO	Runs	HS	Ave	SR	100	50	Ct	St
ODIs	1	1	0	0	0	0.00	0.00	0	0	0	0
First-class	1	2	0	48	32	24.00	34.53	0	0	1	0
List A	5	5	0	42	22	8.40	47.19	0	0	3	0

Bowling

	Mat	Balls	Runs	Wkts	BBI	BBM	Ave	Econ	SR	5w	10
ODIs	1	-	-	-	-	-	-	-	-	-	-
First-class	1	-	-	-	-	-	-	-	-	-	-
List A	5	-	-	-	-	-	-	-	-	-	-

GORDON GOUDIE

RHB RFM

SCOTLAND

NAME: Gordon Goudie
BORN: August 12, 1987, Aberdeen
HEIGHT: 5ft 9in
SQUAD Nº: 16
NICKNAME: G
CAREER: ODI debut: 2008; T20I debut: 2008; First-class debut: 2005; List A debut: 2004; T20 debut: 2010

AOC SAYS: Goudie is a bustling, skiddy seamer who delivers the ball at a low trajectory. He spent some time on Middlesex's books and has developed a habit of taking wickets against high-class opposition. In 2009 he returned figures of 5-73 against Australia, including the wicket of Michael Clarke, and followed that with a haul of 4-46 in the thrilling win over India A in Glasgow last summer. He was an ever-present in the Saltires' 2010 CB40 campaign, finishing as their leading wicket-taker with 17 victims, and is likely to share new ball duties with Luke Butterworth or Matthew Parker. Goudie is one of six players to hold a full-time contract with Cricket Scotland.

LAST WORD: "Gordon had a great season for us last year and took a lot of wickets. He will be one of our key frontline seamers this season." *Peter Steindl*

Batting & Fielding

	Mat	Inns	NO	Runs	HS	Ave	SR	100	50	Ct	St
ODIs	10	8	3	40	17*	8.00	66.66	0	0	3	0
T20Is	1	1	0	4	4	4.00	133.33	0	0	0	0
First-class	7	8	2	87	44*	14.50	53.04	0	0	2	0
List A	33	24	8	125	26*	7.81	83.89	0	0	7	0
Twenty20	1	1	0	4	4	4.00	133.33	0	0	0	0

Bowling

	Mat	Balls	Runs	Wkts	BBI	BBM	Ave	Econ	SR	5w	10
ODIs	10	447	374	17	5/73	5/73	22.00	5.02	26.2	1	0
T20Is	1	6	20	0	-	-	-	20.00	-	0	0
First-class	7	829	356	14	4/58	8/119	25.42	2.57	59.2	0	0
List A	33	1366	1304	46	5/73	5/73	28.34	5.72	29.6	1	0
Twenty20	1	6	20	0	-	-	-	20.00	-	0	0

NAME: Oliver James Harris
BORN: April 14, 1991, Redhill
HEIGHT: 5ft 10in
SQUAD Nº: 14
CAREER: ODI debut: 2010; List A debut: 2010

SCOTLAND

AOC SAYS: Hairs is a powerful opening batsman who made his CB40 debut for the Saltires in the last game of the 2010 campaign against Warwickshire. He is a raw talent and is yet to fire so far in his handful of appearances for Scotland but coach Peter Steindl regards him as a player of considerable potential who is capable of getting his side off to a flying start in limited-overs cricket. The left-hander demonstrated his talent with a fluent century for Scotland A against Warwickshire Second XI last season and is likely to be vying with Preston Mommsen to partner Fraser Watts at the top of the order in the CB40.

LAST WORD: "Hairs is very much like a Scottish version of Jesse Ryder. He's a hard-hitting left-hander who hammers everything out of sight. I don't think he has quite such a colourful social life though." *Willie Dick*

Batting & Fielding

	Mat	Inns	NO	Runs	HS	Ave	SR	100	50	Ct	St
ODIs	5	5	0	68	27	13.60	68.00	0	0	0	0
List A	7	7	0	110	27	15.71	76.92	0	0	0	0

Bowling

	Mat	Balls	Runs	Wkts	BBI	BBM	Ave	Econ	SR	5w	10
ODIs	5	-	-	-	-	-	-	-	-	-	-
List A	7	-	-	-	-	-	-	-	-	-	-

MAJID HAQ   LHB OB

SCOTLAND

NAME: Rana Majid Haq Khan
BORN: February 11, 1983, Paisley
HEIGHT: 5ft 10in
SQUAD Nº: 77
NICKNAME: Magic
CAREER: ODI debut: 2006; T20I debut: 2007;
First-class debut: 2004; List A debut: 2003;
T20 debut: 2007

AOC SAYS: Haq has been one of Scotland's most reliable performers for several seasons with his well-flighted offspin and lower-order batting. He was rewarded with a full-time contract last season after working hard on his fitness and mobility in the field. His economical offbreaks remain his strength but he is an effective batsman in limited-overs cricket and was used as a pinch-hitter in the 2007 World Cup after impressing in that role during Scotland's run to the World Cricket League final earlier that year. Haq is an avid Glasgow Rangers fan and his career highlight to date is a haul of 4-28 against West Indies in 2007.

LAST WORD: "We're looking to Majid to branch out and challenge himself. We're going to try and get him bowling in different areas, such as powerplays, and really look to move his game along even further." *Peter Steindl*

Batting & Fielding

	Mat	Inns	NO	Runs	HS	Ave	SR	100	50	Ct	St
ODIs	27	23	0	411	71	17.86	65.55	0	3	5	0
T20Is	8	7	3	54	21*	13.50	64.28	0	0	2	0
First-class	12	17	2	270	46	18.00	56.36	0	0	4	0
List A	81	62	11	939	71	18.41	65.75	0	4	7	0
Twenty20	11	8	4	55	21*	13.75	64.70	0	0	3	0

Bowling

	Mat	Balls	Runs	Wkts	BBI	BBM	Ave	Econ	SR	5w	10
ODIs	27	1301	1042	31	4/28	4/28	33.61	4.80	41.9	0	0
T20Is	8	150	180	6	2/16	2/16	30.00	7.20	25.0	0	0
First-class	12	2228	854	32	5/30	9/118	26.68	2.29	69.6	1	0
List A	81	3385	2873	72	4/28	4/28	39.90	5.09	47.0	0	0
Twenty20	11	222	245	10	2/15	2/15	24.50	6.62	22.2	0	0

NAME: Ross Thomas Lyons
BORN: December 8, 1984, Greenock
HEIGHT: 5ft 10in
SQUAD Nº: 8
NICKNAME: Rosco
CAREER: ODI debut: 2006; T20I debut: 2010;
First-class debut: 2006; List A debut: 2005;
T20 debut: 2010

SCOTLAND

AOC SAYS: Lyons was among the Saltires' most effective performers during the 2010 CB40
campaign with his miserly left-arm spin. He formed a useful alliance with offspinner Majid
Haq and coach Peter Steindl is likely to select two spinners more often than not again
this season. Lyons first broke into the senior Scotland set-up in 2006 and has gone on to
become a key component in recent seasons, proving particularly effective on slow Scottish
pitches that typically lack bounce. His career highlight to date is returning figures of 12.4-8-
10-4 on his first-class debut against Namibia.

LAST WORD: "Ross has improved his consistency. His left-arm spin complements Majid
Haq very well and he's developed into a very good one-day performer." *Peter Steindl*

Batting & Fielding

	Mat	Inns	NO	Runs	HS	Ave	SR	100	50	Ct	St
ODIs	25	14	10	90	28	22.50	61.22	0	0	4	0
T20Is	2	2	0	4	4	2.00	23.52	0	0	0	0
First-class	8	9	6	66	23	22.00	37.28	0	0	7	0
List A	51	31	18	152	28	11.69	61.78	0	0	13	0
Twenty20	4	2	0	4	4	2.00	23.52	0	0	1	0

Bowling

	Mat	Balls	Runs	Wkts	BBI	BBM	Ave	Econ	SR	5w	10
ODIs	25	23	901	20	3/21	3/21	45.05	4.94	54.6	0	0
T20Is	2	2	40	1	1/26	1/26	40.00	6.66	36.0	0	0
First-class	8	12	478	24	4/10	7/42	19.91	2.94	40.5	0	0
List A	51	-	1813	38	3/21	3/21	47.71	5.02	56.9	0	0
Twenty20	4	4	90	5	3/28	3/28	18.00	6.92	15.6	0	0

CALUM MACLEOD

SCOTLAND

NAME: Calum Scott MacLeod
BORN: November 15, 1988, Glasgow
HEIGHT: 6ft 2in
SQUAD Nº: 10
NICKNAME: Cloudy
OTHER TEAMS: Warwickshire
CAREER: ODI debut: 2008; T20I debut: 2009;
First-class debut: 2007; List A debut: 2008;
T20 debut: 2009

AOC SAYS: MacLeod is a fiery seamer and useful lower-order batsman in the process of resurrecting his career after undergoing remedial work on his bowling action. Having signed a two-year contract with Warwickshire in 2007, he suffered a major blow when he was reported for a suspect action during Scotland's Intercontinental Cup match against Canada in 2009. He worked closely with Warwickshire bowling coach Allan Donald to rectify the problem but left Edgbaston after he was not offered a new contract. He is the son of renowned photographer Donald MacLeod and an outstanding fielder – appearing as 12th man for England during the 2009 Ashes. Saltires coach Peter Steindl is confident MacLeod is now returning to his best form and regards him to be one of his four frontline seamers.

LAST WORD: "MacLeod's family originally hail from South Uist in the Western Isles and he's the only player in the squad who speaks Gaelic." *Willie Dick*

Batting & Fielding

	Mat	Inns	NO	Runs	HS	Ave	SR	100	50	Ct	St
ODIs	4	3	1	12	10*	6.00	63.15	0	0	0	0
T20Is	2	1	0	0	0	0.00	0.00	0	0	1	0
First-class	4	3	1	38	26	19.00	45.78	0	0	4	0
List A	11	7	2	22	10*	4.40	68.75	0	0	3	0
Twenty20	2	1	0	0	0	0.00	0.00	0	0	1	0

Bowling

	Mat	Balls	Runs	Wkts	BBI	BBM	Ave	Econ	SR	5w	10
ODIs	4	138	139	3	2/46	2/46	46.33	6.04	46.0	0	0
T20Is	2	30	56	0	-	-	-	11.20	-	0	0
First-class	4	413	214	11	4/66	6/102	19.45	3.10	37.5	0	0
List A	11	360	338	8	2/38	2/38	42.25	5.63	45.0	0	0
Twenty20	2	30	56	0	-	-	-	11.20	-	0	0

NAME: Neil Francis Ian McCallum
BORN: November 22, 1977, Edinburgh
HEIGHT: 5ft 8in
SQUAD Nº: 25
NICKNAME: Macca
CAREER: ODI debut: 2006; T20I debut: 2007;
First-class debut: 2006; List A debut: 2002;
T20 debut: 2007

AOC SAYS: McCallum has been a mainstay in Scotland's middle-order for several years and remains an integral member of the side. A busy batsman who keeps the score ticking over, he typically favours the legside and likes to sweep the spinners. McCallum was something of a late developer, making his ODI bow at 28, but he made up for lost time with 68 on debut against Pakistan. The following year he became the second Scot after Ryan Watson to score an ODI century with a stunning knock of 100 off 92 balls as Scotland fought back to defeat Ireland in the World Cricket League in Nairobi. He disappointed in last season's CB40 with a highest score of 45 against Kent at Canterbury.

LAST WORD: "It's a little known fact that McCallum once participated in the Scottish Open darts championships." *Willie Dick*

Batting & Fielding

	Mat	Inns	NO	Runs	HS	Ave	SR	100	50	Ct	St
ODIs	41	40	6	977	121*	28.73	69.68	2	4	12	0
T20Is	11	7	0	76	38	10.85	89.41	0	0	0	0
First-class	13	20	5	713	181	47.53	49.30	3	1	13	0
List A	84	80	9	1807	121*	25.45	-	4	8	28	0
Twenty20	13	9	0	80	38	8.88	84.21	0	0	1	0

Bowling

	Mat	Balls	Runs	Wkts	BBI	BBM	Ave	Econ	SR	5w	10
ODIs	41	-	-	-	-	-	-	-	-	-	-
T20Is	11	-	-	-	-	-	-	-	-	-	-
First-class	13	-	-	-	-	-	-	-	-	-	-
List A	84	-	-	-	-	-	-	-	-	-	-
Twenty20	13	-	-	-	-	-	-	-	-	-	-

GREGOR MAIDEN

RHB OB WK

NAME: Gregor Ian Maiden
BORN: July 22, 1979, Glasgow
HEIGHT: 5ft 11in
SQUAD Nº: 20
NICKNAME: Rusty
CAREER: ODI debut: 2010; T20I debut: 2008;
First-class debut: 1999; List A debut: 1999;
T20 debut: 2003

AOC SAYS: In past seasons Maiden has been a top-order batsman who offers a useful bowling option with his part-time offspin but he is now being lined up as a rival to first-choice wicketkeeper Simon Smith. Maiden is expected to be the regular stumper for his club side Grange, with his former teammate Smith vacating the role and moving to Edinburgh rivals Heriot's, and coach Peter Steindl believes he could help the balance of the Saltires side as a keeper-batsman who can bat in the top five. The Loughborough University graduate had a brief spell at Lancashire in 2003 but suffered a cruciate ligament injury soon after joining and returned to Scotland.

LAST WORD: "Gregor is working very hard towards becoming a specialist wicketkeeper. He's handy with the gloves and has the potential to offer us something a little bit different." *Peter Steindl*

Batting & Fielding

	Mat	Inns	NO	Runs	HS	Ave	SR	100	50	Ct	St
ODIs	3	3	0	66	31	22.00	63.46	0	0	0	0
T20Is	3	1	0	0	0	0.00	0.00	0	0	1	0
First-class	8	11	1	118	40	11.80	-	0	0	5	0
List A	46	32	2	437	62	14.56	-	0	1	12	0
Twenty20	4	2	1	2	2*	2.00	100.00	0	0	2	0

Bowling

	Mat	Balls	Runs	Wkts	BBI	BBM	Ave	Econ	SR	5w	10
ODIs	3	48	38	0	-	-	-	4.75	-	0	0
T20Is	3	60	58	2	1/20	1/20	29.00	5.80	30.0	0	0
First-class	8	445	239	11	3/24	-	21.72	3.22	40.4	0	0
List A	46	1338	1094	23	2/27	2/27	47.56	4.90	58.1	0	0
Twenty20	4	84	87	4	2/29	2/29	21.75	6.21	21.0	0	0

NAME: Preston Luke Mommsen
BORN: October 14, 1987, Durban
HEIGHT: 5ft 8in
SQUAD Nº: 1
CAREER: ODI debut: 2010; First-class debut: 2010; List A debut: 2010

SCOTLAND

AOC SAYS: Mommsen is an old-fashioned opening batsman who broke into the Saltires side last season. He emigrated from South Africa to Scotland as a young teenager and attended the distinguished Gordonstoun School in Moray. In 2006 he became the first schoolboy to reach 1,000 runs for the season and was rewarded with a call-up to Kent's academy. He featured twice for their Second XI but was not offered a contract and subsequently returned to Scotland. The left-hander made his CB40 debut last season after impressing in club cricket and will hope to establish himself alongside Fraser Watts at the top of the order for the Saltires this season.

LAST WORD: "While the rest of the guys sit down and celebrate a win with a jug of beer, Mommsen tends to favour a glass of rosé wine, which is rather unusual among sportsmen."
Willie Dick

Batting & Fielding

	Mat	Inns	NO	Runs	HS	Ave	SR	100	50	Ct	St
ODIs	7	7	0	142	80	20.28	48.46	0	1	2	0
First-class	2	4	0	32	18	8.00	32.65	0	0	1	0
List A	12	12	0	197	80	16.41	50.25	0	1	7	0

Bowling

	Mat	Balls	Runs	Wkts	BBI	BBM	Ave	Econ	SR	5w	10
ODIs	7	12	19	1	1/19	1/19	19.00	9.50	12.0	0	0
First-class	2	-	-	-	-	-	-	-	-	-	-
List A	12	42	48	1	1/19	1/19	48.00	6.85	42.0	0	0

MATTHEW PARKER

RHB RMF

SCOTLAND

NAME: Matthew Archibald Parker
BORN: March 2, 1989, Dundee
HEIGHT: 6ft 3in
SQUAD Nº: 23
NICKNAME: Hoggy
CAREER: ODI debut: 2010; First-class debut: 2010; List A debut: 2009

AOC SAYS: Parker is a young allrounder with a big future ahead of him. He has already attracted interest from Sussex and Durham after impressing for the Saltires with his lively pace-bowling and strokemaking in the middle-order. A member of the Timmergreens Primary School team that won the British Kwik Cricket tournament at Trent Bridge in 2002 alongside Scotland teammate Marc Petrie and Saltires hopeful Calvin Burnett, Parker impressed with 10 wickets in the CB40 last season, including a haul of 3-27 against Durham at Chester-le-Street. He also made an immediate impact on his ODI debut in 2010, taking 4-33 in the World Cricket League victory over Kenya.

LAST WORD: "Matthew has progressed really well over the past 12 months. He's grown up a lot and started to fill out a bit more as well." *Peter Steindl*

Batting & Fielding

	Mat	Inns	NO	Runs	HS	Ave	SR	100	50	Ct	St
ODIs	10	8	2	59	22	9.83	56.73	0	0	3	0
First-class	3	6	0	122	65	20.33	41.21	0	1	2	0
List A	22	20	5	161	23	10.73	54.94	0	0	5	0

Bowling

	Mat	Balls	Runs	Wkts	BBI	BBM	Ave	Econ	SR	5w	10
ODIs	10	414	327	12	4/33	4/33	27.25	4.73	34.5	0	0
First-class	3	630	333	14	4/63	7/119	23.78	3.17	45.0	0	0
List A	22	880	787	26	4/33	4/33	30.26	5.36	33.8	0	0

NAME: Simon James Stevenson Smith
BORN: December 8, 1979, Ashington
HEIGHT: 5ft 8in
SQUAD Nº: 32
NICKNAME: Smudger
CAREER: T20I debut: 2010; First-class debut: 2004; List A debut: 2004; T20 debut: 2010

SCOTLAND

AOC SAYS: Smith is acknowledged to be Scotland's best gloveman and is a busy batsman who is quick between the wickets and keeps the scoreboard ticking over. He left club side Grange at the end of last season and moved to Edinburgh rivals Heriot's after 12 seasons with the reigning Scottish champions. He will face a head-to-head challenge with his former Grange teammate Gregor Maiden for the gloves this season, following the retirement of Dougie Lockhart in January. If Smith is to win the battle he will have to improve his batting record, which has seen him fail to score a half-century for Scotland in any form of cricket.

LAST WORD: "I want my international career to kick on in all forms of the game this year and to do that I felt I needed to give myself a fresh start with Heriot's." *Simon Smith*

Batting & Fielding

	Mat	Inns	NO	Runs	HS	Ave	SR	100	50	Ct	St
T20Is	4	4	1	21	9	7.00	52.50	0	0	0	1
First-class	9	10	3	197	40	28.14	34.99	0	0	28	1
List A	12	8	2	103	41*	17.16	72.02	0	0	7	5
Twenty20	6	5	2	24	9	8.00	55.81	0	0	2	2

Bowling

	Mat	Balls	Runs	Wkts	BBI	BBM	Ave	Econ	SR	5w	10
T20Is	4	-	-	-	-	-	-	-	-	-	-
First-class	9	-	-	-	-	-	-	-	-	-	-
List A	12	-	-	-	-	-	-	-	-	-	-
Twenty20	6	-	-	-	-	-	-	-	-	-	-

RYAN WATSON

RHB RM/OB

SCOTLAND

NAME: Ryan Robert Watson
BORN: November 12, 1976, Harare
HEIGHT: 5ft 8in
SQUAD Nº: 27
NICKNAME: Rhino, Eric
CAREER: ODI debut: 2006; T20I debut: 2007;
First-class debut: 2004; List A debut: 2002;
T20 debut: 2007

AOC SAYS: Watson has been a stalwart of Scottish cricket for the best part of a decade after emigrating from South Africa at the age of 23. In 2007 he became the first Scot to score an ODI century when he smashed an unbeaten 123 against Canada. But the highlight of the big-hitting opener's career to date is a blistering 103 not out off just 44 balls in Scotland's famous National League victory over Somerset in 2003. The former Scotland captain is now in the twilight of his career and his job in recruitment means he is unlikely to feature regularly in the CB40 this season.

LAST WORD: "Ryan is finding that the time needed for preparation and being away from home is proving difficult so we're steering him more towards T20 cricket this season."
Peter Steindl

Batting & Fielding

	Mat	Inns	NO	Runs	HS	Ave	SR	100	50	Ct	St
ODIs	35	35	4	956	123*	30.83	74.33	1	6	14	0
T20Is	10	9	0	159	54	17.66	112.76	0	1	4	0
First-class	15	22	0	843	167	38.31	54.10	2	4	19	0
List A	143	138	10	3371	123*	26.33	-	3	18	56	0
Twenty20	13	12	0	197	54	16.41	103.14	0	1	5	0

Bowling

	Mat	Balls	Runs	Wkts	BBI	BBM	Ave	Econ	SR	5w	10
ODIs	35	570	528	12	3/18	3/18	44.00	5.55	47.5	0	0
T20Is	10	60	92	3	1/4	1/4	30.66	9.20	20.0	0	0
First-class	15	842	455	19	5/74		23.94	3.24	44.3	1	0
List A	143	3527	3114	81	4/24	4/24	38.44	5.29	43.5	0	0
Twenty20	13	96	112	7	2/10	2/10	16.00	7.00	13.7	0	0

NAME: David Fraser Watts
BORN: June 5, 1979, King's Lynn
HEIGHT: 5ft 11in
SQUAD Nº: 12
NICKNAME: Fraggle
CAREER: ODI debut: 2006; T20I debut: 2007;
First-class debut: 1999; List A debut: 2002;
T20 debut: 2007

SCOTLAND

AOC SAYS: Watts began life as a seam bowler before becoming an opening batsman and was a key member of Scotland's ICC Trophy winning side in 2005, scoring a half-century against Ireland in the final. While he has a good record against the Associate nations, the experienced right-hander has struggled for consistency against county sides and had a disappointing CB40 campaign in 2010. The Loughborough University graduate is still likely to start the season as the Saltires' first-choice opener, alongside either Oli Hairs or Preston Mommsen, and continues to play a key role off the field as a mentor to the up-and-coming players.

LAST WORD: "Fraser has been one of the stalwarts of the side for a while now and he adds a lot of value both on and off the pitch." *Peter Steindl*

Batting & Fielding

	Mat	Inns	NO	Runs	HS	Ave	SR	100	50	Ct	St
ODIs	32	31	1	884	101	29.46	61.68	1	8	7	0
T20Is	8	6	0	81	46	13.50	103.84	0	0	5	0
First-class	20	33	1	919	146	28.71	-	2	4	13	0
List A	121	118	10	2387	101	22.10	-	1	13	25	0
Twenty20	11	9	0	170	73	18.88	120.56	0	1	7	0

Bowling

	Mat	Balls	Runs	Wkts	BBI	BBM	Ave	Econ	SR	5w	10
ODIs	32	-	-	-	-	-	-	-	-	-	-
T20Is	8	-	-	-	-	-	-	-	-	-	-
First-class	20	-	-	-	-	-	-	-	-	-	-
List A	121	-	-	-	-	-	-	-	-	-	-
Twenty20	11	-	-	-	-	-	-	-	-	-	-

FORMED: 1883
BOARD: Koninklijke Nederlandse Cricket Bond (Royal Dutch Cricket Board)
HOMEGROUND: Various
ICC MEMBER STATUS: 1966
2010 RESULTS: CB40: 7/7 in Group B

THE LOWDOWN

Having performed admirably during the 2011 World Cup, the Netherlands will be looking to improve on their less than ideal results in the CB40 in 2010. However, they will be hampered by the fact that their most promising batsman Alexei Kervezee and their outstanding allrounder Ryan ten Doeschate – often tagged as the best player in Associate cricket – will be turning out for their counties during the competition. They are hopeful they will be able to recruit an overseas player for the summer, a role that veteran Australian batsman Michael Dighton filled for them last year, which should go some way to making up for the loss of two of their senior players, and there are definitely further reasons to be cheerful for the Dutch side; Pieter Seelar has announced himself as a spinner capable of nullifying the world's best, Peter Borren continues to develop into a hard-hitting allrounder capable of changing a game with bat and ball and Wesley Barresi looks an accomplished player at the top of the order and behind the stumps. Throw in the fact that the Jonkman twins, two of the country's best bowlers, may well complete their bowling rehabilitation in time to play some part in the competition and it looks likely that the Dutch will be running the counties a lot closer this season.

HEAD COACH: PETER DRINNEN

A wicketkeeper who played five first-class matches for Queensland between 1988-1990, Drinnen was recruited to be the technical director of Scottish cricket in 2003 and was promoted to national coach in 2006, leading the country during the 2007 World Cup, before being recruited by the Netherlands in 2008.

With thanks to Peter Drinnen; Ruud Onstein, cricket correspondent, De Telegraaf

	Mat	Inns	NO	Runs	HS	Ave	SR	100	50	Ct	St
WP Diepeveen	2	2	1	37	23	37.00	47.43	0	0	0	-
MG Dighton	11	11	1	369	110*	36.90	81.45	1	3	3	-
B Zuiderent	12	11	2	302	56	33.55	70.39	0	1	2	-
Mudassar Bukhari	11	8	2	156	69*	26.00	114.70	0	1	4	-
W Barresi	6	6	1	104	39	20.80	75.91	0	0	3	-
BP Loots	4	3	2	20	13*	20.00	133.33	0	0	1	-
Adeel Raja	2	1	0	19	19	19.00	135.71	0	0	0	-
MMA Jonkman	3	3	1	31	25*	15.50	83.78	0	0	1	-
ES Szwarczynski	12	11	0	161	75	14.63	62.89	0	1	1	-
PW Borren	12	9	1	108	21*	13.50	77.69	0	0	4	-
TLW Cooper	8	7	0	91	30	13.00	56.52	0	0	5	-
MBS Jonkman	6	3	1	24	14	12.00	61.53	0	0	1	-
TN de Grooth	5	3	0	34	17	11.33	51.51	0	0	0	-
PM Seelaar	11	7	3	33	12	8.25	47.82	0	0	4	-
AF Buurman	7	4	0	26	17	6.50	76.47	0	0	6	2
NA Statham	6	5	0	31	11	6.20	57.40	0	0	0	-
TJ Heggelman	2	1	0	3	3	3.00	50.00	0	0	0	-
BP Kruger	4	2	0	5	5	2.50	45.45	0	0	0	-
Mohammad Kashif	5	1	0	1	1	1.00	50.00	0	0	2	-
BA Westdijk	3	1	1	3	3*	-	150.00	0	0	0	-

Batting & Fielding

	Mat	Overs	Mdns	Runs	Wkts	BBI	Ave	Econ	SR	5w
BP Loots	4	23.0	1	101	4	2/26	25.25	4.39	34.5	0
Adeel Raja	2	10.0	0	47	0	-	-	4.70	-	0
PW Borren	12	66.0	3	320	5	2/18	64.00	4.84	79.2	0
MBS Jonkman	6	44.0	2	226	11	3/34	20.54	5.13	24.0	0
MMA Jonkman	3	13.0	0	67	1	1/16	67.00	5.15	78.0	0
PM Seelaar	11	68.3	0	370	13	3/31	28.46	5.40	31.6	0
MG Dighton	11	53.0	0	292	10	2/23	29.20	5.50	31.8	0
Mudassar Bukhari	11	55.3	3	325	4	2/45	81.25	5.85	83.2	0
Mohammad Kashif	5	28.0	0	177	5	2/41	35.40	6.32	33.6	0
BP Kruger	4	17.3	0	116	3	2/14	38.66	6.62	35.0	0
BA Westdijk	3	8.0	0	74	1	1/31	74.00	9.25	48.0	0

Bowling

ADEEL RAJA

RHB OB

THE NETHERLANDS

NAME: Mohammad Adeel Khalid Raja
BORN: August 15, 1980, Lahore, Punjab
CAREER: ODI debut: 2002; First-class debut:
2004; List A debut: 2001

AOC SAYS: An offspinner capable of putting big revs on the ball, Raja plays for VRA Cricket
Club and made his international debut against Sri Lanka at Colombo in the 2002 Champions
Trophy. He didn't do badly either, returning figures of 2-50 from 10 overs and dismissing
Kumar Sangakkara and Aravinda de Silva. He hit the headlines in 2007 when he failed a
random drugs test, testing positive for finasteride; a banned substance that can be found in
hair-loss treatments. It was revealed by Cricket Europe that he had previously successfully
applied for dispensation to use the drug but had omitted to renew his application. He was
handed a two-year ban, with one year suspended, but subsequently regained his place in
the side and has proven a consistent performer for the Netherlands ever since.

LAST WORD: "He did pretty well for us when he was given a go at the World Cup. He's a
bit hampered by the fact that Tom Cooper, one of our best batsmen, bowls good offies as
well, but he's been around, knows his game and will be ready to play when we need him."
Peter Drinnen

Batting & Fielding

	Mat	Inns	NO	Runs	HS	Ave	SR	100	50	Ct	St
ODIs	21	12	2	28	8*	2.80	20.14	0	0	3	0
First-class	7	9	0	62	28	6.88	25.61	0	0	0	0
List A	33	19	6	90	19	6.92	-	0	0	5	0

Bowling

	Mat	Balls	Runs	Wkts	BBI	BBM	Ave	Econ	SR	5w	10
ODIs	21	846	690	17	4/42	4/42	40.58	4.89	49.7	0	0
First-class	7	752	419	7	2/82	-	59.85	3.34	107.4	0	0
List A	33	1344	1070	24	4/42	4/42	44.58	4.77	56.0	0	0

NAME: Wesley Barresi
BORN: May 3, 1984, Johannesburg
OTHER TEAMS: Easterns
CAREER: ODI debut: 2010; First-class debut: 2004; List A debut: 2004

THE NETHERLANDS

AOC SAYS: A batsman-keeper who loves having pace on the ball, Barresi began his career with Easterns, playing four first-class games for the province in 2004/05 and notching 57 from 114 deliveries at the top of the order on debut. He followed this up with two limited-overs games in the 2005/06 season but fell from favour thereafter and switched allegiance to the Netherlands. He is one of only two players to have been awarded a full-time contract by the Dutch board, and it was his matchwinning 64* from 43 deliveries in the victory over Bangladesh at Glasgow in 2010 that propelled the Netherlands onto the main ICC Rankings table, a feat that only Ireland and Kenya among the Associate nations can match. One of the Netherlands' success stories from the 2011 World Cup, expect him to be charged with getting the Dutch innings off to a flier in the CB40 this season.

LAST WORD: "He's a fine player. He's quite a strong-willed, independent kind of guy who's pretty meticulous in his preparation and thinks a lot about his game." *Peter Drinnen*

Batting & Fielding

	Mat	Inns	NO	Runs	HS	Ave	SR	100	50	Ct	St
ODIs	15	15	2	361	64*	27.76	75.36	0	2	2	1
First-class	9	18	0	317	81	17.61	45.61	0	2	13	1
List A	25	25	3	532	64*	24.18	71.89	0	2	10	1

Bowling

	Mat	Balls	Runs	Wkts	BBI	BBM	Ave	Econ	SR	5w	10
ODIs	15	18	20	0	-	-	-	6.66	-	0	0
First-class	9	12	3	0	-	-	-	1.50	-	0	0
List A	25	18	20	0	-	-	-	6.66	-	0	0

PETER BORREN

RHB RM

NAME: Peter William Borren
BORN: August 21, 1983, Christchurch
NICKNAME: Baldrick
CAREER: ODI debut: 2006; T20I debut: 2008;
First-class debut: 2006; List A debut: 2006;
T20 debut: 2008

AOC SAYS: The Netherlands skipper is coming into the season on the back of some belligerent knocks at the World Cup, including an excellent 84 off 82 balls against Ireland at Kolkata and a 36-ball 38 against India at Delhi. Borren – alongside current Black Cap internationals Ross Taylor and Jesse Ryder – represented New Zealand at the Under 19 World Cup in 2001/02 but switched his allegiance to the Netherlands before making his international debut against Sri Lanka; although it's probably a game Borren would like to forget as he conceded 94 runs off his 10 overs with only the wicket of Lasith Malinga to show for his efforts. However, he's grown into a player of considerable stature since then – offering quick runs down the order and thrifty seamers with the ball – so much so that he was awarded the captaincy in July 2010 and is the only player other than Wesley Barresi to have a full-time contract with the Dutch board.

LAST WORD: "A good cricketer who hits the ball very hard, bowls well and is an excellent fielder. As captain, he is someone the other players look up to." *Ruud Onstein*

Batting & Fielding

	Mat	Inns	NO	Runs	HS	Ave	SR	100	50	Ct	St
ODIs	45	39	2	650	96	17.56	81.86	0	3	19	0
T20Is	10	8	2	107	37*	17.83	97.27	0	0	5	0
First-class	15	27	0	856	109	31.70	56.38	2	3	18	0
List A	66	56	4	932	96	17.92	77.92	0	3	26	0
Twenty20	11	9	3	139	37*	23.16	95.86	0	0	5	0

Bowling

	Mat	Balls	Runs	Wkts	BBI	BBM	Ave	Econ	SR	5w	10
ODIs	45	1445	1263	37	3/30	3/30	34.13	5.24	39.0	0	0
T20Is	10	210	237	7	2/19	2/19	33.85	6.77	30.0	0	0
First-class	15	2085	1095	27	3/21	4/54	40.55	3.15	77.2	0	0
List A	66	2302	1968	52	3/30	3/30	37.84	5.12	44.2	0	0
Twenty20	11	228	267	7	2/19	2/19	38.14	7.02	32.5	0	0

NAME: Mudassar Bukhari
BORN: December 26, 1983, Gujrat, Punjab
CAREER: ODI debut: 2007; T20I debut: 2008;
First-class debut: 2007; List A debut: 2007;
T20 debut: 2008

AOC SAYS: A broad, bruising allrounder who gets the ball to skid on from just back of a length and is unafraid to use the long handle, Bukhari is a vital part of the Netherlands' attack and is occasionally used as a pinch-hitter up the order. Having moved from Pakistan at the age of 14, he settled in Holland with his family and currently plays club cricket in Amsterdam. He's produced several eye-catching knocks since making his international debut against Canada in 2007 (a call-up he celebrated by taking figures of 3-24 as the Netherlands marched their way to an 117-run victory), not least his 84 against Canada in the 2009 Cricket World Cup Qualifiers or his swashbuckling 52-ball 69* against Derbyshire last season. But he remains most reliable with the ball in hand, as demonstrated when he dismissed Tamim Iqbal on his way to the impressive figures of 1-14 from six overs against Bangladesh at the World Cup.

LAST WORD: "He really showed what he was capable of during that match against Bangladesh. We think he can be a genuine matchwinner with both bat and ball." *Peter Drinnen*

Batting & Fielding

	Mat	Inns	NO	Runs	HS	Ave	SR	100	50	Ct	St
ODIs	33	25	3	351	71	15.95	67.11	0	2	5	0
T20Is	8	5	2	14	9	4.66	87.50	0	0	1	0
First-class	8	15	2	309	66*	23.76	67.61	0	2	1	0
List A	56	43	5	678	84	17.84	76.52	0	4	10	0
Twenty20	9	6	2	14	9	3.50	77.77	0	0	1	0

Bowling

	Mat	Balls	Runs	Wkts	BBI	BBM	Ave	Econ	SR	5w	10
ODIs	33	1446	1069	38	3/17	3/17	28.13	4.43	38.0	0	0
T20Is	8	154	180	6	4/33	4/33	30.00	7.01	25.6	0	0
First-class	8	1216	595	18	4/85	4/85	33.05	2.93	67.5	0	0
List A	56	2359	1878	58	3/17	3/17	32.37	4.77	40.6	0	0
Twenty20	9	177	218	7	4/33	4/33	31.14	7.38	25.2	0	0

ATSE BUURMAN

RHB WK

NAME: Atse F Buurman
BORN: March 21, 1982, Netherlands
CAREER: ODI debut: 2007; T20I debut: 2010;
First-class debut: 2007; List A debut: 2003;
T20 debut: 2010

AOC SAYS: A personal trainer by profession, Buurman is widely acknowledged to be the fittest player in the Netherlands team. A keeper who first broke into the international side against Canada in 2007, his career has been stymied by the presence of former captain Jeroen Smits and now Wesley Barresi, but he has at times been considered a good enough batsman to earn his spot on that discipline alone – and if his lively innings of 26 against Ireland at the World Cup is anything to by, that might soon become the case again. A product of the Dutch youth set-up, Buurman has represented Holland at under 15 to under 23 level, loves to use his feet and is lightning quick between the wickets.

LAST WORD: "His batting has improved out of sight over the last six months, he's been one of our biggest improvers. The make-up of the side has meant he hasn't always had as many games as he would like, but he should feature at some point this season." *Peter Drinnen*

Batting & Fielding

	Mat	Inns	NO	Runs	HS	Ave	SR	100	50	Ct	St
ODIs	17	11	2	140	34	15.55	78.21	0	0	17	3
T20Is	4	2	0	0	0	0.00	0.00	0	0	1	1
First-class	5	10	1	176	41	19.55	55.00	0	0	16	1
List A	29	20	2	262	53	14.55	-	0	1	25	5
Twenty20	5	3	0	3	3	1.00	50.00	0	0	3	1

Bowling

	Mat	Balls	Runs	Wkts	BBI	BBM	Ave	Econ	SR	5w	10
ODIs	17	-	-	-	-	-	-	-	-	-	-
T20Is	4	-	-	-	-	-	-	-	-	-	-
First-class	5	-	-	-	-	-	-	-	-	-	-
List A	29	-	-	-	-	-	-	-	-	-	-
Twenty20	5	-	-	-	-	-	-	-	-	-	-

TOM COOPER

RHB OB

NAME: Tom Lexley William Cooper
BORN: November 26, 1986, Wollongong, Australia
HEIGHT: 6ft 1in
NICKNAME: Coops
OTHER TEAMS: South Australia
CAREER: ODI debut: 2010; First-class debut: 2008; List A debut: 2008; T20 debut: 2008

AOC SAYS: A classy top-order batsman and a sparky, adaptable offspinner who gives the ball plenty of air, Cooper is one of the mainstays of the Netherlands' line-up. He began his career at New South Wales and represented Australia at under 19 level, but the Blues' superlative strength-in-depth meant he struggled for first -team opportunities and moved to South Australia in 2008 after a spell in Scotland as the overseas pro for Forfarshire CC. A former student at NSW University, he represented the Redbacks during the 2010 Champions League competition and has become a regular member of their one-day side. He's been in excellent form for the Netherlands since breaking into the team last year and did not look out of place at all during this winter's World Cup, averaging 34.80 with a top-score of 55*. With Ryan ten Doeschate away on county duty with Essex, much responsibility will rest on his shoulders during the Netherlands' CB40 campaign.

LAST WORD: "Tom's a really good, solid player. He's got a great temperament and keeps batting simple." *Peter Drinnen*

Batting & Fielding

	Mat	Inns	NO	Runs	HS	Ave	SR	100	50	Ct	St
ODIs	16	16	2	763	101	54.50	70.32	1	6	8	0
First-class	9	14	0	429	63	30.64	56.29	0	4	6	0
List A	48	47	4	1671	101	38.86	74.49	2	14	23	0
Twenty20	21	18	2	244	50	15.25	123.85	0	1	9	0

Bowling

	Mat	Balls	Runs	Wkts	BBI	BBM	Ave	Econ	SR	5w	10
ODIs	16	335	272	9	2/19	2/19	30.22	4.87	37.2	0	0
First-class	9	163	86	2	1/11	1/25	43.00	3.16	81.5	0	0
List A	48	341	274	9	2/19	2/19	30.44	4.82	37.8	0	0
Twenty20	21	-	-	-	-	-	-	-	-	-	-

TOM DE GROOTH
RHB OB

NAME: Tom Nico de Grooth
BORN: May 14, 1979, The Hague
CAREER: ODI debut: 2006; T20I debut: 2008;
First-class debut: 2004; List A debut: 2005;
T20 debut: 2008

AOC SAYS: An unorthodox middle-order batsman with all the shots, de Grooth's finest moment on the cricket pitch to date came against England in the 2009 ICC World Twenty20, where his vital, nerveless 49 propelled Netherlands to a historic victory at Lord's. He spent this winter playing club cricket in Australia with some success, but sadly he wasn't able to translate that into big scores at the recent World Cup, with his best of 28 coming in a losing cause against England at Nagpur. Talked about as an exciting, box-office talent when he first broke into the Dutch team in 2005, he's struggled for consistency at times over the course of his career but has shown that on his day he can take apart even the very best attacks.

LAST WORD: "He's an interesting player who offers you something a bit different during the middle overs. He scores both sides of the wicket, sweeps and reverse-sweeps well and is quick between the wickets." *Peter Drinnen*

Batting & Fielding

	Mat	Inns	NO	Runs	HS	Ave	SR	100	50	Ct	St
ODIs	27	26	3	437	97	19.00	62.33	0	1	6	0
T20Is	7	5	1	96	49	24.00	112.94	0	0	3	0
First-class	18	33	1	844	196	26.37	-	1	5	6	0
List A	47	43	4	651	97	16.69	60.27	0	2	8	0
Twenty20	8	6	1	96	49	19.20	110.34	0	0	3	0

Bowling

	Mat	Balls	Runs	Wkts	BBI	BBM	Ave	Econ	SR	5w	10
ODIs	27	6	2	1	1/2	1/2	2.00	2.00	6.0	0	0
T20Is	7	-	-	-	-	-	-	-	-	-	-
First-class	18	45	36	1	1/2	1/2	36.00	4.80	45.0	0	0
List A	47	42	34	3	2/32	2/32	11.33	4.85	14.0	0	0
Twenty20	8	-	-	-	-	-	-	-	-	-	-

NAME: Wilfred Peter Diepeveen
BORN: June 18, 1985, Utrecht
CAREER: First-class debut: 2010; List A debut: 2010

THE NETHERLANDS

AOC SAYS: Although the 25-year-old batsman is yet to feature for his country at international level, he has shown signs in his early career that this is likely to change. During the ICC Intercontinental Cup in 2010, Diepeveen hit an impressive 72 not out against Scotland as wickets tumbled around him, showing maturity and concentration on a wicket that was offering considerable assistance to the bowler, while he also chipped in with two handy scores during last season's CB40, notching a creditable 23 at the top of the order at Bristol against an attack that included England Lion Steve Kirby, former England spinner Richard Dawson and New Zealand international James Franklin. He'll doubtless be hoping that he can build on this performance this season and cement a regular place in the side.

LAST WORD: "A player who came on the scene last year and did well for us against Scotland. He looks a good prospect, wants to attack the ball and get on with it, so it's really just a case of getting him used to that step up in quality he'll be facing." *Peter Drinnen*

Batting & Fielding

	Mat	Inns	NO	Runs	HS	Ave	SR	100	50	Ct	St
First-class	3	6	1	171	72*	34.20	54.98	0	1	2	0
List A	2	2	1	37	23	37.00	47.43	0	0	0	0

Bowling

	Mat	Balls	Runs	Wkts	BBI	BBM	Ave	Econ	SR	5w	10
First-class	3	-	-	-	-	-	-	-	-	-	-
List A	2	-	-	-	-	-	-	-	-	-	-

TOM HEGGELMAN

RHB RM

THE NETHERLANDS

NAME: Thomas Josephus Heggelman
BORN: January 16, 1987, Schiedam
CAREER: ODI debut: 2010; First-class debut: 2010; List A debut: 2010

AOC SAYS: At the age of just 24, Heggelman is one of the Dutch's up and coming stars. The top-order batsman and useful bowler, who plays for Holland's Excelsior Cricket Club, has appeared in two ODIs to date, both of which came against Ireland in Dublin during 2010. He's already shown great potential for the Netherlands A side, most memorably when he hit 128 against Denmark back in July 2010, and with the Netherlands age group sides, whom he first represented at under 15 level against Scotland in 2001. His two appearances in the CB40 last season came against Northants and Gloucestershire, and while he didn't set the world alight with the bat he looked lively in the field and will likely receive further opportunities this year.

LAST WORD: "He's a young allrounder who bats at No.5 for his club. We tried him higher up the order last season but it didn't quite work, but he's a promising one. He's a handy bowler too, he nibbles it around, and a good character – he gives you everything he's got."
Peter Drinnen

Batting & Fielding

	Mat	Inns	NO	Runs	HS	Ave	SR	100	50	Ct	St
ODIs	2	2	0	3	2	1.50	17.64	0	0	0	0
First-class	1	2	0	46	30	23.00	52.27	0	0	0	0
List A	4	3	0	6	3	2.00	26.08	0	0	0	0

Bowling

	Mat	Balls	Runs	Wkts	BBI	BBM	Ave	Econ	SR	5w	10
ODIs	2	-	-	-	-	-	-	-	-	-	-
First-class	1	72	54	0	-	-	-	4.50	-	0	0
List A	4	-	-	-	-	-	-	-	-	-	-

NAME: Mark Benjamin Sebastiaan Jonkman
BORN: March 20, 1986, The Hague
CAREER: ODI debut: 2006; T20I debut: 2010;
First-class debut: 2006; List A debut: 2006;
T20 debut: 2010

AOC SAYS: Hailed by former Netherlands bowling coach Ian Pont as the fastest bowler in Associate cricket, Jonkman is currently undergoing remedial work on his bowling action after the ICC suspended him from bowling in international cricket after an independent test found his elbow flexed by more than 15 degrees during delivery. His absence has been a big blow to the Dutch side as he was a consistent wicket-taker for them at all levels since he made his debut against Canada at Potchefstroom in 2006 and appeared to be that rarest of things: an Associate bowler capable of troubling top-class batsmen for pace. Also a reliable lower-order batsman, Jonkman has been working hard on altering his action and it is hoped he will be available for at least part of the English season.

LAST WORD: "He's working on his action as hard as he can but no one is sure when he'll be ready; it's up to the ICC." *Ruud Onstein*

Batting & Fielding

	Mat	Inns	NO	Runs	HS	Ave	SR	100	50	Ct	St
ODIs	16	9	4	59	16	11.80	74.68	0	0	1	0
T20Is	3	1	0	1	1	1.00	12.50	0	0	2	0
First-class	6	10	3	144	43*	20.57	38.91	0	0	3	0
List A	24	14	6	95	16	11.87	74.21	0	0	3	0
Twenty20	3	1	0	1	1	1.00	12.50	0	0	2	0

Bowling

	Mat	Balls	Runs	Wkts	BBI	BBM	Ave	Econ	SR	5w	10
ODIs	16	719	565	24	3/24	3/24	23.54	4.71	29.9	0	0
T20Is	3	48	47	4	2/21	2/21	11.75	5.87	12.0	0	0
First-class	6	858	419	15	5/21	7/83	27.93	2.93	57.2	1	0
List A	24	1091	898	37	3/24	3/24	24.27	4.93	29.4	0	0
Twenty20	3	48	47	4	2/21	2/21	11.75	5.87	12.0	0	0

MAURITS JONKMAN

RHB RM

NAME: Maurits Maarten Alexander Jonkman
BORN: March 20, 1986, The Hague
CAREER: ODI debut: 2007; First-class debut: 2007; List A debut: 2007

AOC SAYS: Twin brother to Mark, Maurits doesn't quite have his brother's explosive pace but swings the ball appreciably and is still quick enough to keep the batsman honest. He too has been undergoing a programme designed to change his bowling action, although the ICC did not suspend him as they did his sibling, which will hopefully end in time for him to play some role during the English summer. A lively character who claimed three wickets on his international debut against Bermuda at the Hazelaarweg ground in Rotterdam, Jonkman has represented the Netherlands at every youth level.

LAST WORD: "We're seeing how we go with both of them, we can't say for certain how long their rehabilitation will take so we don't want to rush them. But we're looking forward to having them both back on the park – they're fantastic guys, ideal team players who give everyone a real lift." *Peter Drinnen*

Batting & Fielding

	Mat	Inns	NO	Runs	HS	Ave	SR	100	50	Ct	St
ODIs	4	2	0	20	13	10.00	39.21	0	0	1	0
First-class	4	7	1	62	18*	10.33	32.12	0	0	1	0
List A	8	6	1	55	25*	11.00	59.13	0	0	2	0

Bowling

	Mat	Balls	Runs	Wkts	BBI	BBM	Ave	Econ	SR	5w	10
ODIs	4	136	113	6	3/22	3/22	18.83	4.98	22.6	0	0
First-class	4	420	297	8	2/63	3/101	37.12	4.24	52.5	0	0
List A	8	260	198	10	3/18	3/18	19.80	4.56	26.0	0	0

MOHAMMAD KASHIF

RHB OB

NAME: Mohammad Kashif
BORN: December 3, 1984, Khanewal, Punjab
CAREER: ODI debut: 2006; T20I debut: 2010; First-class debut 2006; List A debut: 2006; T20 debut: 2010

AOC SAYS: Unlucky to have missed out on the World Cup, Kashif will provide spin bowling back up for Pieter Seelar and Adeel Raja. A more than useful fielder, he has apparently developed a fledgling doosra which has proven successful in Dutch club cricket, although it remains to be seen whether he gets a chance to employ it in the CB40 this season.
One of several players who made their international debut against Sri Lanka in 2006 at Amstelveen, Kashif enjoyed a baptism of fire on his way to returning match-figures of 2-79 from his 10 overs, although he did manage to pick up the scalps of Sanath Jayasuriya and Kumar Sangakkara. He's gone considerably better in all forms of cricket since then and has an outstanding record in T20Is, but he's hamstrung by the presence of the two senior men and it looks likely he will have to be patient this season.

LAST WORD: "He will probably feature at some stage. He's a big turner of the ball and has some useful variations." *Peter Drinnen*

Batting & Fielding

	Mat	Inns	NO	Runs	HS	Ave	SR	100	50	Ct	St
ODIs	11	3	0	1	1	0.33	5.88	0	0	2	0
T20Is	3	1	1	0	0*	-	-	0	0	1	0
First-class	6	9	4	59	24*	11.80	56.73	0	0	3	0
List A	19	7	0	16	9	2.28	42.10	0	0	5	0
Twenty20	4	1	1	0	0*	-	-	0	0	1	0

Bowling

	Mat	Balls	Runs	Wkts	BBI	BBM	Ave	Econ	SR	5w	10
ODIs	11	450	410	9	3/42	3/42	45.55	5.46	50.0	0	0
T20Is	3	42	55	4	2/28	2/28	13.75	7.85	10.5	0	0
First-class	6	919	502	16	5/53	5/53	31.37	3.27	57.4	1	0
List A	19	774	747	16	3/42	3/42	46.68	5.79	48.3	0	0
Twenty20	4	66	81	4	2/28	2/28	20.25	7.36	16.5	0	0

BRADLEY KRUGER

THE NETHERLANDS

NAME: Bradley Peter Kruger
BORN: September 17, 1988, Pretoria
CAREER: ODI debut: 2010; List A debut: 2010

AOC SAYS: A South Africa-born quick, Kruger is relatively new to the Dutch set-up, having made his ODI debut in July 2010 against Canada. The robust seamer impressed with figures of 3-21 off his eight overs, setting up a comfortable seven-wicket victory. He's turned out for Leeds/Bradford MCCU in recent seasons, as well as a number of county Second XIs, most recently Kent. The youngster didn't have the greatest of World Cups; he made just one appearance against India and was run-out for 8 and returned figures of 0-23 in three and half overs as the hosts eased to victory. However, he did produce one moment of inspiration, taking a stunning catch at long off to dismiss a certain Sachin Tendulkar. Reportedly more than useful with the bat, he has also appeared for Finedon Dolben in the Northamptonshire Premier Divison.

LAST WORD: "A good young bowler, a bit expensive at the moment but promising. He can bat as well and may move up the order as his career progresses." *Ruud Onstein*

Batting & Fielding											
	Mat	Inns	NO	Runs	HS	Ave	SR	100	50	Ct	St
ODIs	5	3	0	32	15	10.66	64.00	0	0	5	0
List A	9	5	0	37	15	7.40	60.65	0	0	5	0

Bowling										
	Mat	Balls	Runs	Wkts	BBI	BBM	Ave	Econ	SR	5w	10
ODIs	5	184	131	3	3/21	3/21	43.66	4.27	61.3	0	0
List A	9	289	247	6	3/21	3/21	41.16	5.12	48.1	0	0

NAME: Bernardus Pieters Loots
BORN: April 19, 1979, Prieska, South Africa
CAREER: ODI debut: 2010; First-class debut: 2010; List A debut: 2010

THE NETHERLANDS

AOC SAYS: An experienced medium-pacer who plays for HCC, Loots has become a permanent fixture in the Dutch side since making his international debut against Ireland at Amstelveen, where he claimed 3-16 off eight miserly overs and dismissed Paul Stirling, James Hall and the dangerous Kevin O'Brien for a duck. The 31-year-old featured regularly for Netherlands at the 2011 World Cup but struggled for penetration on the lifeless sub-continent pitches, ending the tournament with a bowling average of 103.50. He had a better time of it in the CB40 last season, where – although he didn't pick up many wickets – he operated at an impressive economy rate of 4.39 and helped build pressure at one end with his array of slower balls and steady accuracy. By all accounts a lower-order batsman in the block it or slog it vein, he's yet to translate his considerable success with the bat at club level to the national side.

LAST WORD: "A solid, accurate bowler who should suit English conditions and a dangerous batsman on his day, although he certainly hasn't shown it yet at international level." *Ruud Onstein*

Batting & Fielding											
	Mat	Inns	NO	Runs	HS	Ave	SR	100	50	Ct	St
ODIs	7	5	2	16	9*	5.33	59.25	0	0	3	0
First-class	2	4	1	11	5	3.66	16.92	0	0	0	0
List A	11	8	4	36	13*	9.00	85.71	0	0	4	0

Bowling										
	Mat	Balls	Runs	Wkts	BBI	BBM	Ave	Econ	SR	5w	10
ODIs	7	280	287	6	3/16	3/16	47.83	6.15	46.6	0	0
First-class	2	300	169	5	2/48	3/83	33.80	3.38	60.0	0	0
List A	11	418	388	10	3/16	3/16	38.80	5.56	41.8	0	0

RUUD NIJMAN

RHB RMF

THE NETHERLANDS

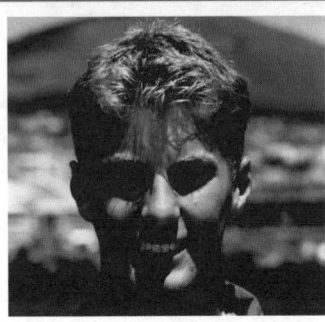

NAME: Ruud Gerard Nijman
BORN: June 15, 1982, Netherlands
CAREER: ODI debut: 2009; First-class debut: 2010; List A debut: 2009

AOC SAYS: A quicker than he looks seamer who possesses a good, accurate yorker, Nijman has been a reliable performer for the Netherlands since he first broke into the side in 2009 and was part of the side that memorably beat England at Lord's in the opening match of the ICC World Twenty20. However, he is a doubt for the coming season following a severe facial injury that he picked up while playing hockey, and it remains to be seen if he will resume his cricketing career. A qualified doctor, he has worked his way through the Netherlands' youth set-up and plays his domestic cricket for Hermes DVS.

LAST WORD: "We don't know where we are with Ruud, we'll have to see how his recovery goes, but obviously with our limited numbers, losing anyone is less than ideal." *Peter Drinnen*

Batting & Fielding											
	Mat	Inns	NO	Runs	HS	Ave	SR	100	50	Ct	St
ODIs	1	-	-	-	-	-	-	-	-	0	0
First-class	3	4	0	30	23	7.50	19.86	0	0	0	0
List A	3	2	0	25	23	12.50	75.75	0	0	1	0

Bowling										
	Mat	Balls	Runs	Wkts	BBI	BBM	Ave	Econ	SR	5w	10
ODIs	1	49	31	3	3/31	3/31	10.33	3.79	16.3	0	0
First-class	3	288	156	1	1/43	1/52	156.00	3.25	288.0	0	0
List A	3	133	113	4	3/31	3/31	28.25	5.09	33.2	0	0

NAME: Pieter Marinus Seelaar
BORN: July 2, 1987, Schiedam
CAREER: ODI debut: 2006; T20I debut: 2008;
First-class debut: 2006; List A debut: 2005;
T20 debut: 2008

AOC SAYS: One of the success stories of the Netherlands' World Cup campaign, Seelar bowled superbly throughout the tournament, claming eight wickets at 38.25 with an impressive economy rate of 5.12. Also a talented football player who plays his club cricket for Hermes DVS, he is perhaps best known for the infamous bird dance he performed when he dismissed England skipper Paul Collingwood during Netherlands' victory in the 2009 World Twenty20. Able to vary his pace well and always willing to back himself, he was able to tie down the very best batsmen in the world out in the subcontinent and will likely be skipper Paul Borren's go-to bowler during the middle overs this season.

LAST WORD: "He's a bit of an individual, but he goes about his work and he seems to thrive on stepping up a level and testing himself against the best; he likes a challenge I would guess. His batting has improved unbelievably in the last year or so; he keeps it simple now and knows his scoring areas." *Peter Drinnen*

Batting & Fielding

	Mat	Inns	NO	Runs	HS	Ave	SR	100	50	Ct	St
ODIs	27	16	9	88	34*	12.57	53.98	0	0	8	0
T20Is	9	3	0	2	1	0.66	28.57	0	0	5	0
First-class	12	21	5	264	81*	16.50	40.00	0	1	3	0
List A	51	30	14	158	34*	9.87	47.73	0	0	14	0
Twenty20	10	4	1	2	1	0.66	28.57	0	0	5	0

Bowling

	Mat	Balls	Runs	Wkts	BBI	BBM	Ave	Econ	SR	5w	10
ODIs	27	1224	995	29	3/22	3/22	34.31	4.87	42.2	0	0
T20Is	9	210	215	13	4/19	4/19	16.53	6.14	16.1	0	0
First-class	12	1791	1053	26	5/57	5/57	40.50	3.52	68.8	1	0
List A	51	2337	1872	51	3/22	3/22	36.70	4.80	45.8	0	0
Twenty20	10	234	251	13	4/19	4/19	19.30	6.43	18.0	0	0

NICK STATHAM

THE NETHERLANDS

NAME: Nick Alexander Statham
BORN: March 15, 1975, The Hague
CAREER: ODI debut: 2003; First-class debut: 2007; List A debut: 1999

AOC SAYS: A long-standing servant of Dutch cricket, Statham has entered a state of semi-retirement due to his work commitments and was forced to miss the recent World Cup. It remains to be seen whether he will be able to make himself available during the coming English domestic summer. He endured a season to forget in the CB40 last season, scoring 32 runs in five innings at an average of 6.50. Usually a top-order batsman who can offer a few steady overs of offspin, Statham made the most of his first call-up to the Dutch under 19 side by scoring a breezy 49 against Ireland, and his busy technique had him marked down as a batsman who could play a serious role in the Netherlands' development. Sadly, he's never quite made the consistent runs his talent suggested he was capable of, with his career-best of 62* coming against Kenya in the 2010 Intercontinental Cup.

LAST WORD: "Nick's got a good job and is struggling to find the time for cricket. It's a real problem for us and it won't go away until we have a fully professional outfit." *Peter Drinnen*

Batting & Fielding

	Mat	Inns	NO	Runs	HS	Ave	SR	100	50	Ct	St
ODIs	3	3	0	7	7	2.33	14.00	0	0	0	0
First-class	8	16	1	258	62*	17.20	37.28	0	2	4	0
List A	21	17	0	117	37	6.88	-	0	0	5	0

Bowling

	Mat	Balls	Runs	Wkts	BBI	BBM	Ave	Econ	SR	5w	10
ODIs	3	-	-	-	-	-	-	-	-	-	-
First-class	8	6	1	0	-	-	-	1.00	-	0	0
List A	21	60	72	1	1/60	1/60	72.00	7.20	60.0	0	0

ERIC SZWARCZYNSKI

RHB RM

NAME: Eric Stefan Szwarczynski
BORN: February 13, 1983, Vanderbijlpark, South Africa
CAREER: ODI debut: 2006; T20 debut: 2008; First-class: 2005; List A debut: 2006; T20 debut: 2008

AOC SAYS: A well-organised batsman with the discipline to occupy the crease and accumulate, Szwarczynski has been one of Netherlands' most consistent performers over the past few years following his international debut in 2006, and during the latter stages of the recent World Cup he put on some useful opening partnerships with Wesley Barresi and did enough to suggest that they could perform similar roles during this season's CB40. Another one of Holland's South Africa-born contingent, he has represented both the Netherlands A side and under 23 team. He is still looking for his maiden ton at first-class, international or limited-overs level, but has come close on a handful of occasions, most notably against Kenya in the 2010 ICC Intercontinental Cup when he put on 187 for the first wicket with Alexei Kervezee.

LAST WORD: "If there's a player you'd love to succeed, it's him. He works incredibly hard on his game, grafts away and practises every chance he gets. He's got his limitations, but he knows that and is happy to work within them." *Peter Drinnen*

Batting & Fielding

	Mat	Inns	NO	Runs	HS	Ave	SR	100	50	Ct	St
ODIs	33	32	2	805	84*	26.83	69.09	0	7	5	0
T20Is	8	7	0	185	45	26.42	100.00	0	0	2	0
First-class	13	22	0	450	93	20.45	-	0	3	5	0
List A	55	53	2	1154	84*	22.62	67.28	0	10	14	0
Twenty20	9	8	0	191	45	23.87	98.96	0	0	2	0

Bowling

	Mat	Balls	Runs	Wkts	BBI	BBM	Ave	Econ	SR	5w	10
ODIs	33	-	-	-	-	-	-	-	-	-	-
T20Is	8	-	-	-	-	-	-	-	-	-	-
First-class	13	136	98	3	2/24	2/25	32.66	4.32	45.3	0	0
List A	55	36	32	0	-	-	-	5.33	-	0	0
Twenty20	9	-	-	-	-	-	-	-	-	-	-

BEREND WESTDIJK

THE NETHERLANDS

NAME: Berend Arnold Westdijk
BORN: March 5, 1985, The Hague
CAREER: ODI debut: 2011; First-class debut: 2009; List A debut: 2010

AOC SAYS: One of the Netherlands' surprise inclusions for their squad for the 2011 World Cup, Westdijk had played only three first-class games when he was named among the 15 players travelling to the subcontinent, making his international debut in the game against England at Nagpur. He didn't have the easiest time of it during the tournament, conceding 173 runs from 23 overs with just the wicket of Ramnaresh Sarwan to show for it, but showed admirable stomach for the contest and a willingness to attack and try for wickets. A former Netherlands under 19 and under 23 international, he plays club cricket for HBS. His best performance to date for his country came during the 2010 ICC Intercontinental Cup, where he claimed three top-order wickets in the first innings against a Zimbabwe XI, including Craig Ervine, younger brother of Hampshire allrounder Sean.

LAST WORD: "He's a work in progress really, he's very new to the whole set-up and we're just learning about him really. We'll see how he develops over the season." *Peter Drinnen*

Batting & Fielding

	Mat	Inns	NO	Runs	HS	Ave	SR	100	50	Ct	St
ODIs	3	2	0	0	0	0.00	0.00	0	0	0	0
First-class	3	5	0	22	17	4.40	16.05	0	0	3	0
List A	6	3	1	3	3*	1.50	60.00	0	0	0	0

Bowling

	Mat	Balls	Runs	Wkts	BBI	BBM	Ave	Econ	SR	5w	10
ODIs	3	138	173	1	1/56	1/56	173.00	7.52	138.0	0	0
First-class	3	456	291	10	4/46	4/91	29.10	3.82	45.6	0	0
List A	6	186	247	2	1/31	1/31	123.50	7.96	93.0	0	0

NAME: Bastiaan Zuiderent
BORN: March 3, 1977, Utrecht
OTHER TEAMS: Sussex
CAREER: ODI debut: 1996; T20I debut: 2009;
First-class debut: 2001; List A debut: 1996;
T20 debut: 2003

THE NETHERLANDS

AOC SAYS: One of the Dutch's all-time stars, the evergreen Zuiderent has now appeared in four World Cups for his nation, with the undeniable highlight being the fearless 54 he made against England in 1996 when aged just 18. Stylish, composed and vastly experienced, he is one of only two Dutch players to have topped 1,000 ODI runs – the other being Essex's Ryan ten Doeschate – and has had a hand in all of the Netherlands' greatest cricketing moments in recent years. Also one of the few Dutch players to have tasted regular county cricket, Zuiderent was on the staff at Sussex between 1999 and 2004, scoring 679 first-class runs at 23.41 and 768 list A runs at 20.75. Expect him to shore up the middle-order, act as a valuable sounding board for his skipper Peter Borren and provide an excellent example to the likes of Wilfred Diepeveen and Tom Heggelman.

LAST WORD: "He's the rock of the team and brings a lot of knowledge and ability to the party. He offers good support to the captain and has been just great with the younger guys." *Peter Drinnen*

Batting & Fielding

	Mat	Inns	NO	Runs	HS	Ave	SR	100	50	Ct	St
ODIs	57	56	10	1097	77*	23.84	58.56	0	8	26	0
T20Is	6	6	1	108	43*	21.60	87.09	0	0	2	0
First-class	31	50	4	1328	149*	28.86	-	2	9	23	0
List A	138	133	19	3272	119	28.70	-	4	19	51	0
Twenty20	12	12	1	242	43*	22.00	104.31	0	0	4	0

Bowling

	Mat	Balls	Runs	Wkts	BBI	BBM	Ave	Econ	SR	5w	10
ODIs	57	-	-	-	-	-	-	-	-	-	-
T20Is	6	-	-	-	-	-	-	-	-	-	-
First-class	31	-	-	-	-	-	-	-	-	-	-
List A	138	12	15	0	-	-	-	7.50	-	0	0
Twenty20	12	-	-	-	-	-	-	-	-	-	-

YOU
SUPPORT US

WE
SUPPORT YOU

Chance to Shine
EDUCATING THROUGH CRICKET
Supported by *Brit Insurance*

1 million children educated through cricket

To support Chance to Shine buy a seat in our
online supporters' stadium **www.chancetoshine.org**

The
Tourists

CAPTAIN: Kumar Sangakkara
TEST RECORD AGAINST ENGLAND:
P21 W6 D7 L8
TEST RECORD IN ENGLAND:
P10 W2 D3 L5
2010 TEST RECORD: P6 W1 D4 L1
HONOURS: ICC World Cup: 1996;
ICC Champions Trophy: 2002(s);
Asia Cup: (3) 1986, 1997, 2004, 2008

THE LOWDOWN

Sri Lanka arrive this summer for a first tour of England since 2006. Five years ago, the hosts were held to a 1-1 draw in the Tests before the tourists dished out a 5-0 whitewash in the ODIs and England have their work cut out if they are to claim a first series win in five-day cricket over Sri Lanka since 2002. Muttiah Muralitharan was Sri Lanka's hero in 2006, taking 8-70 in the third Test at Trent Bridge to level the series, but Trevor Bayliss' side must do without his services this time around. Legendary duo Sanath Jayasuriya and Chaminda Vaas have also left the international scene, but stalwarts Kumar Sangakkara and Mahela Jayawardene remain integral members of the batting unit and allrounder Angelo Mathews is one of the brightest talents in the world game. Unorthodox paceman Lasith Malinga will spearhead the seam attack and Sri Lanka are typically well stocked in the spin department, with English cricket fans set for their first glimpse of 'mystery' spinner Ajantha Mendis. England will start as marginal favourites in the Test series due to home advantage but the tourists are currently a far more formidable outfit in limited-overs cricket.

HEAD COACH: STUART LAW

An assistant to former coach Trevor Bayliss since November 2009, Law was appointed as an interim coach for the tour of England when Bayliss stepped down following the 2011 World Cup. A prolific batsman in his playing days, Law scored more than 27,000 first-class runs at over 50 for Queensland – whom he captained to Sheffield Shield triumph – Essex, Lancashire and Derbyshire. Unlucky not to have played more for his country, Law is a veteran of 54 ODIs and scored the same number of runs in his one and only Test innings.

	Mat	Inns	NO	Runs	HS	Ave	SR	100	50	Ct	St
TM Dilshan	9	14	0	576	100	41.14	59.25	1	5	13	-
CRD Fernando	6	8	4	63	36*	15.75	31.18	0	0	2	-
DPMD Jayawardene	16	27	3	1581	213*	65.87	49.59	6	7	29	-
HAPW Jayawardene	3	4	0	150	79	37.50	48.07	0	2	6	2
CK Kapugedera	2	4	0	74	50	18.50	35.57	0	1	0	-
KMDN Kulasekara	2	4	0	96	64	24.00	49.48	0	1	0	-
MF Maharoof	3	6	0	118	59	19.66	37.94	0	1	0	-
SL Malinga	5	8	1	88	26	12.57	52.07	0	0	0	-
J Mubarak	3	5	0	24	9	4.80	29.62	0	0	3	-
TT Samaraweera	5	9	1	231	142	28.87	36.49	1	0	1	-
KC Sangakkara	15	26	1	1007	152	40.28	48.36	1	6	36	6
LPC Silva	3	4	0	89	49	22.25	47.84	0	0	4	-
WU Tharanga	5	8	0	168	52	21.00	42.00	0	1	1	-
UWMBCA Welegedara	1	-	-	-	-	-	-	-	-	1	-

Batting & Fielding

	Mat	Overs	Mdn	Runs	Wkts	BBI	BBM	Ave	Econ	SR	5w	10
TM Dilshan	9	13.0	2	59	0	-	-	-	4.53	-	0	0
CRD Fernando	6	131.2	15	508	12	3/27	4/82	42.33	3.86	65.6	0	0
DPMD Jayawardene	16	4.0	1	9	0	-	-	-	2.25	-	0	0
KMDN Kulasekara	2	38.0	5	134	0	-	-	-	3.52	-	0	0
MF Maharoof	3	39.0	7	167	1	1/125	1/125	167.00	4.28	234.0	0	0
SL Malinga	5	146.4	20	491	10	3/78	3/115	49.10	3.34	88.0	0	0
J Mubarak	3	1.0	0	8	0	-	-	-	8.00	-	0	0
TT Samaraweera	5	8.0	3	20	0	-	-	-	2.50	-	0	0
LPC Silva	3	15.0	2	60	1	1/57	1/57	60.00	4.00	90.0	0	0
UWMBCA Welegedara	1	22.0	2	76	4	2/17	4/76	19.00	3.45	33.0	0	0

Bowling

S

ODI AVERAGES AGAINST ENGLAND

Batting & Fielding

	Mat	Inns	NO	Runs	HS	Ave	SR	100	50	Ct	St
HMCM Bandara	3	1	1	28	28*	-	127.27	0	0	1	-
TM Dilshan	15	12	3	282	108*	31.33	80.55	1	1	4	-
CRD Fernando	16	9	3	64	20	10.66	64.00	0	0	3	-
DPMD Jayawardene	29	26	3	954	126*	41.47	83.46	4	4	24	-
SHT Kandamby	1	1	0	53	53	53.00	64.63	0	1	1	-
CK Kapugedera	2	1	0	1	1	1.00	16.66	0	0	1	-
KMDN Kulasekara	2	1	1	17	17*	-	70.83	0	0	1	-
MF Maharoof	8	5	1	93	58*	23.25	98.93	0	1	1	-
SL Malinga	13	8	4	10	3*	2.50	33.33	0	0	6	-
AD Mathews	2	1	0	52	52	52.00	71.23	0	1	1	-
BAW Mendis	2	1	0	5	5	5.00	71.23	0	0	0	-
J Mubarak	7	7	1	104	44*	17.33	64.59	0	0	4	-
TT Samaraweera	7	4	1	88	30	29.33	69.84	0	0	1	-
KC Sangakkara	25	22	4	524	70	29.11	68.85	0	5	24	4
LPC Silva	8	7	0	216	73	30.85	64.67	0	2	1	-
WU Tharanga	11	11	1	578	120	57.80	76.89	3	2	0	-

Bowling

	Mat	Overs	Mdns	Runs	Wkts	BBI	Ave	Econ	SR	5w
HMCM Bandara	3	25.0	1	128	3	2/43	42.66	5.12	50.0	0
TM Dilshan	15	55.0	2	248	7	2/20	35.42	4.50	47.14	0
CRD Fernando	16	137.0	2	722	36	6/27	20.05	5.27	22.8	1
DPMD Jayawardene	28	13.0	0	64	1	1/24	64.00	4.92	78.0	0
KMDN Kulasekara	2	18.0	2	61	4	2/19	15.25	3.38	27.0	0
MF Maharoof	8	64.0	5	254	13	4/31	19.53	3.96	29.5	0
SL Malinga	13	114.4	7	559	23	4/44	24.30	4.87	29.9	0
AD Mathews	2	13.0	2	46	1	1/20	46.00	3.53	78.0	0
BAW Mendis	2	19.0	0	69	1	1/34	69.00	3.63	114.0	0
TT Samaraweera	7	35.0	1	142	5	3/34	28.40	4.05	42.0	0

	Mat	Inns	NO	Runs	HS	Ave	SR	100	50	Ct	St
TM Dilshan	2	2	0	11	9	5.50	84.61	0	0	0	-
CRD Fernando	1	1	0	3	3	3.00	75.00	0	0	0	-
CU Jayasinghe	1	1	1	2	2*	-	200.00	0	0	0	-
DPMD Jayawardene	2	2	0	10	10	5.00	100.00	0	0	1	-
CK Kapugedera	2	2	0	38	22	19.00	88.37	0	0	0	-
MF Maharoof	1	1	0	8	8	8.00	100.00	0	0	0	-
SL Malinga	2	1	0	13	13	13.00	108.33	0	0	1	-
AD Mathews	1	1	0	58	58	58.00	128.88	0	1	0	-
BAW Mendis	1	-	-	-	-	-	-	-	-	0	-
NLTC Perera	1	1	1	7	7*	-	87.50	0	0	0	-
S Randiv	1	-	-	-	-	-	-	-	-	0	-
KC Sangakkara	2	2	0	37	21	18.50	112.12	0	0	2	0
WU Tharanga	1	1	0	34	34	34.00	136.00	0	0	0	-

	Mat	Overs	Mdns	Runs	Wkts	BBI	Ave	Econ	SR	5w
TM Dilshan	2	3.0	0	23	1	1/18	23.00	7.66	18.0	0
CRD Fernando	1	4.0	0	22	1	1/22	22.00	5.50	24.0	0
MF Maharoof	1	4.0	0	30	0	-	-	7.50	-	0
SL Malinga	2	7.0	0	58	1	1/33	58.00	8.28	42.0	0
A Mathews	1	1.0	0	10	0	-	-	10.00	-	0
BAW Mendis	1	4.0	0	19	0	-	-	4.75	-	0
NLTC Perera	1	2.0	0	19	2	2/19	9.50	9.50	6.0	0

TOUR SCHEDULE

May
Saturday 14 – Monday 16 — Middlesex v Sri Lankans, Uxbridge
Thursday 19 – Sunday 22 — England Lions v Sri Lankans, County Ground, Derby
Thursday 26 – Monday 30 — 1st Test v England, The SWALEC Stadium, Cardiff
June
Friday 3 – Tuesday 7 — 2nd Test v England, Lord's, London
Friday 10 – Sunday 12 — Essex v Sri Lankans, County Ground, Chelmsford
Thursday 16 – Monday 20 — 3rd Test v England, The Rose Bowl, Southampton
Wednesday 22 — Worcestershire v Sri Lankans, New Road, Worcester
Saturday 25 — Only T20I v England, County Ground, Bristol
Tuesday 28 — 1st ODI v England, The Kia Oval, London (Day/Night)
July
Friday 1 — 2nd ODI v England, Headingley Carnegie, Leeds
Sunday 3 — 3rd ODI v England, Lord's, London
Wednesday 6 — 4th ODI v England, Trent Bridge, Nottingham (Day/Night)
Saturday 9 — 5th ODI v England, Old Trafford, Manchester
Monday 11 — Only ODI v Ireland, Grange Cricket Club, Edinburgh
Wednesday 13 — Only ODI v Scotland, Grange Cricket Club, Edinburgh

B–F

SRI LANKA

MALINGA BANDARA   RHB LB

NAME: Herath Mudiyanselage Charitha Malinga Bandara
BORN: December 31, 1979, Nagoda
CAREER: Test debut: 1998; ODI debut: 2006; T20I debut: 2006; First-class debut: 1996; List A debut: 1998; T20 debut: 2005

AOC SAYS: Bandara is a legspinner and handy lower-order batsman who has enjoyed spells in county cricket with Gloucestershire and Kent. He has provided support for Muttiah Muralitharan over the years but has failed to nail down a regular spot in a sporadic international career.

	Mat	Inns	NO	Runs	HS	Ave	SR	100	50	Ct	St
Tests	8	11	3	124	43	15.50	51.66	0	0	4	0
ODIs	31	17	4	160	31	12.30	71.42	0	0	9	0
T20Is	4	3	1	12	7	6.00	80.00	0	0	1	0
First-class	156	221	46	3540	108	20.22	-	1	15	98	0
List A	137	93	29	1126	64	17.59	-	0	3	39	0
Twenty20	36	19	8	126	31*	11.45	107.69	0	0	8	0

	Mat	Balls	Runs	Wkts	BBI	BBM	Ave	Econ	SR	5w	10
Tests	8	1152	633	16	3/84	5/153	39.56	3.29	72.0	0	0
ODIs	31	1470	1232	36	4/31	4/31	34.22	5.02	40.8	0	0
T20Is	4	84	96	4	3/32	3/32	24.00	6.85	21.0	0	0
First-class	156	21565	11317	442	8/49	-	25.60	3.14	48.7	14	2
List A	137	5846	4596	189	5/22	5/22	24.31	4.71	30.9	4	0
Twenty20	36	717	903	41	3/14	3/14	22.02	7.55	17.4	0	0

DINESH CHANDIMAL   RHB OB WK

NAME: Lokuge Dinesh Chandimal
BORN: November 18, 1989, Balapitiya
CAREER: ODI debut: 2010; T20I debut: 2010; First-class debut: 2009; List A debut: 2009; T20 debut: 2008

AOC SAYS: Chandimal is an aggressive wicketkeeper-batsman in the mould of former Sri Lanka star Romesh Kaluwitharana. He was selected in Sri Lanka's 2010 World Twenty20 squad and underlined his talent with a majestic ton in his second ODI while batting at No.3 against India in Harare last year.

	Mat	Inns	NO	Runs	HS	Ave	SR	100	50	Ct	St
ODIs	4	4	2	143	111	71.50	85.11	1	0	4	1
T20Is	5	4	0	59	29	14.75	101.72	0	0	0	0
First-class	28	42	4	2161	244	56.86	73.55	7	10	54	8
List A	42	41	5	1010	111	28.05	79.77	1	8	35	2
Twenty20	23	22	1	588	75	28.00	131.83	0	3	13	2

	Mat	Balls	Runs	Wkts	BBI	BBM	Ave	Econ	SR	5w	10
ODIs	4	-	-	-	-	-	-	-	-	-	-
T20Is	5	-	-	-	-	-	-	-	-	-	-
First-class	28	12	5	0	-	-	-	2.50	-	0	0
List A	42	6	1	1	1/1	1/1	1.00	1.00	6.0	0	0
Twenty20	23	-	-	-	-	-	-	-	-	-	-

TILLAKARATNE DILSHAN   RHB OB

NAME: Tillakaratne Mudiyanselage Dilshan
BORN: October 14, 1976, Kalutara
CAREER: Test debut: 1999; ODI debut: 1999; T20I debut: 2006; First-class debut: 1994; List A debut: 1996; T20 debut: 2004

AOC SAYS: One of the game's great innovators, Dilshan's career exploded into life after he reinvented himself as an aggressive opener in 2009. The Delhi Daredevil is also a useful offspinner and outstanding fielder. Keep an eye out for the famous Dilscoop when this electrifying cricketer is batting.

	Mat	Inns	NO	Runs	HS	Ave	SR	100	50	Ct	St
Tests	66	105	11	3990	168	42.44	65.65	11	16	73	0
ODIs	202	178	30	5423	160	36.64	87.70	10	22	86	1
T20Is	32	31	5	758	96*	29.15	120.70	0	5	13	2
First-class	201	324	22	11656	200*	38.59	-	30	49	337	23
List A	297	267	43	8750	188	39.06	-	17	42	164	8
Twenty20	78	75	9	1647	96*	24.95	119.69	0	11	37	3

	Mat	Balls	Runs	Wkts	BBI	BBM	Ave	Econ	SR	5w	10
Tests	66	1304	633	19	4/10	4/10	33.31	2.91	68.6	0	0
ODIs	202	3133	2468	61	4/4	4/4	40.45	4.72	51.3	0	0
T20Is	32	120	151	4	2/4	2/4	37.75	7.55	30.0	0	0
First-class	201	3916	1884	62	5/49	-	30.38	2.88	63.1	1	0
List A	297	4493	3453	96	4/4	4/4	35.96	4.61	46.8	0	0
Twenty20	78	433	491	17	3/23	3/23	28.88	6.80	25.4	0	0

DILHARA FERNANDO   RHB RFM

NAME: Congenige Randhi Dilhara Fernando
BORN: July 19, 1979, Colombo
CAREER: Test debut: 2000; ODI debut: 2001; T20I debut: 2006; First-class debut: 1997; List A debut: 1999; T20 debut: 2004

AOC SAYS: Fernando can be a matchwinner on his day, with a bag of tricks including a well-disguised slower ball, but the right-arm paceman has suffered from a lack of consistency and has not fulfilled the potential he showed as a 21-year-old, taking six wickets against South Africa in just his second Test match.

	Mat	Inns	NO	Runs	HS	Ave	SR	100	50	Ct	St
Tests	35	40	13	198	36*	7.33	31.68	0	0	10	0
ODIs	141	57	33	239	20	9.95	61.75	0	0	27	0
T20Is	16	5	2	24	21	8.00	120.00	0	0	3	0
First-class	101	98	28	505	42	7.21	-	0	0	38	0
List A	207	85	46	332	21*	8.51	-	0	0	45	0
Twenty20	39	13	7	36	21	6.00	102.85	0	0	10	0

	Mat	Balls	Runs	Wkts	BBI	BBM	Ave	Econ	SR	5w	10
Tests	35	5404	3260	90	5/42	7/95	36.22	3.61	60.0	3	0
ODIs	141	6188	5362	180	6/27	6/27	29.78	5.19	34.3	1	0
T20Is	16	342	421	17	3/19	3/19	24.76	7.38	20.1	0	0
First-class	101	13533	8052	270	6/29	-	29.82	3.56	50.1	6	0
List A	207	9311	7779	293	6/27	6/27	26.54	5.01	31.7	2	0
Twenty20	39	858	1053	50	4/14	4/14	21.06	7.36	17.1	0	0

RANGANA HERATH — LHB SLA

SRI LANKA

NAME: Herath Mudiyanselage Rangana Keerthi Bandara Herath
BORN: March 19, 1978, Kurunegala
CAREER: Test debut: 1999; ODI debut: 2004; First-class debut: 1996; List A debut: 1998; T20 debut: 2004

AOC SAYS: The diminutive left-arm spinner burst onto the scene in 1999 with a 'mystery' ball that tied Australia in knots but he failed to kick on and had a four-year hiatus from international cricket before returning in 2004. Herath has enjoyed spells with Hampshire and Surrey and was included in Sri Lanka's 2011 World Cup squad.

	Mat	Inns	NO	Runs	HS	Ave	SR	100	50	Ct	St
Tests	24	29	6	311	80*	13.52	45.46	0	1	5	0
ODIs	15	4	2	8	4*	4.00	44.44	0	0	4	0
First-class	186	263	61	3328	80*	16.47	-	0	12	85	0
List A	127	80	33	837	88*	17.80	-	0	1	31	0
Twenty20	24	15	4	58	9	5.27	-	0	0	4	0

	Mat	Balls	Runs	Wkts	BBI	BBM	Ave	Econ	SR	5w	10
Tests	24	5665	2820	78	5/99	8/209	36.15	2.98	72.6	4	0
ODIs	15	624	426	14	3/28	3/28	30.42	4.09	44.5	0	0
First-class	186	36757	16729	675	8/43	-	24.78	2.73	54.4	38	5
List A	127	5327	3594	155	4/19	4/19	23.18	4.04	34.3	0	0
Twenty20	24	481	444	30	3/14	3/14	14.80	5.53	16.0	0	0

CHINTHAKA JAYASINGHE — RHB RM

NAME: Halwathurage Chinthaka Umesh Jayasinghe
BORN: May 19, 1978, Kalutara
CAREER: T20I debut: 2009; First-class debut: 1996; List A debut: 1998; T20 debut: 2004

AOC SAYS: An aggressive allrounder who hits the ball hard and bowls tidy medium-pacers, Jayasinghe is a useful limited-overs cricketer. He struck a quickfire 38 against India in his first T20I innings in 2009 but is yet to establish himself as a regular in Sri Lanka's one-day set-up.

	Mat	Inns	NO	Runs	HS	Ave	SR	100	50	Ct	St
T20Is	5	3	2	49	38	49.00	100.00	0	0	0	0
First-class	130	206	20	5585	142	30.02	-	9	30	107	0
List A	124	104	23	2155	94	26.60	-	0	12	48	0
Twenty20	35	31	9	644	67	29.27	133.33	0	1	10	0

	Mat	Balls	Runs	Wkts	BBI	BBM	Ave	Econ	SR	5w	10
T20Is	5	-	-	-	-	-	-	-	-	-	-
First-class	130	5246	2517	104	5/39	-	24.20	2.87	50.4	1	0
List A	124	4226	2579	110	5/44	5/44	23.44	3.66	38.4	1	0
Twenty20	35	438	535	28	4/17	4/17	19.10	7.32	15.6	0	0

MAHELA JAYAWARDENE
RHB RM

NAME: Denagamage Proboth Mahela de Silva Jayawardene
BORN: May 27, 1977, Colombo
CAREER: Test debut: 1997; ODI debut: 1998; T20I debut: 2006; First-class debut: 1995; List A debut: 1995; T20 debut: 2004

AOC SAYS: Jayawardene is Sri Lanka's record Test run-scorer and among the most classy batsmen in world cricket. His square-cut is a joy to behold and he will be the prize wicket this summer. The right-hander's career was rejuvenated after relinquishing the captaincy in 2009.

	Mat	Inns	NO	Runs	HS	Ave	SR	100	50	Ct	St
Tests	116	190	13	9527	374	53.82	52.63	28	38	165	0
ODIs	340	318	33	9320	128	32.70	77.46	13	56	178	0
T20Is	32	32	4	784	100	28.00	141.77	1	4	9	0
First-class	198	313	22	15291	374	52.54	-	45	66	257	0
List A	424	395	44	11505	163*	32.77	-	14	70	218	0
Twenty20	89	86	16	2154	110*	30.77	141.06	2	12	38	0

	Mat	Balls	Runs	Wkts	BBI	BBM	Ave	Econ	SR	5w	10
Tests	116	547	292	6	2/32	2/32	48.66	3.20	91.1	0	0
ODIs	340	582	558	7	2/56	2/56	79.71	5.75	83.1	0	0
T20Is	32	6	8	0	-	-	-	8.00	-	0	0
First-class	198	2959	1611	52	5/72	-	30.98	3.26	56.9	1	0
List A	424	1269	1141	23	3/25	3/25	49.60	5.39	55.1	0	0
Twenty20	89	69	82	3	2/22	2/22	27.33	7.13	23.0	0	0

PRASANNA JAYWARDENE
RHB WK

NAME: Hewasandatchige Asiri Prasanna Wishvanath Jayawardene
BORN: October 9, 1979, Colombo
CAREER: Test debut: 2000; ODI debut: 2003; First-class debut: 1998; List A debut: 1998; T20 debut: 2004

AOC SAYS: Jayawardene is arguably the finest keeper in the world standing up to the stumps. Kumar Sangakkara is first-choice stumper in limited-overs cricket but Jayawardene takes the gloves in Tests and showed how much his batting has improved with an unbeaten 154 against India in 2009.

	Mat	Inns	NO	Runs	HS	Ave	SR	100	50	Ct	St
Tests	36	45	6	1172	154*	30.05	49.43	2	3	67	25
ODIs	6	5	0	27	20	5.40	61.36	0	0	4	1
First-class	189	289	34	7391	229*	28.98	-	11	32	433	88
List A	121	102	9	1950	62	20.96	-	0	7	125	54
Twenty20	13	11	3	131	29*	16.37	94.92	0	0	9	4

	Mat	Balls	Runs	Wkts	BBI	BBM	Ave	Econ	SR	5w	10
Tests	36	-	-	-	-	-	-	-	-	-	-
ODIs	6	-	-	-	-	-	-	-	-	-	-
First-class	189	18	9	0	-	-	-	3.00	-	0	0
List A	121	-	-	-	-	-	-	-	-	-	-
Twenty20	13	12	8	1	1/8	1/8	8.00	4.00	12.0	0	0

THILINA KANDAMBY | LHB LB

SRI LANKA

NAME: Sahan Hewa Thilina Kandamby
BORN: June 4, 1982, Colombo
CAREER: ODI debut: 2004; T20I debut: 2008; First-class debut: 2001;
List A debut: 2001; T20 debut: 2004

AOC SAYS: Kandamby is a left-hand middle-order batsman who has failed to make the most of his ODI opportunities and slipped down the pecking order. Knocks of 93* and 91* against India in 2009 suggested he was beginning to find his feet at international level but it has thus far proved a false dawn.

	Mat	Inns	NO	Runs	HS	Ave	SR	100	50	Ct	St
ODIs	33	31	6	814	93*	32.56	71.27	0	5	5	0
T20Is	4	4	0	13	10	3.25	61.90	0	0	3	0
First-class	113	171	13	5905	202	37.37	-	13	24	64	0
List A	157	136	20	3681	128*	31.73	74.66	2	24	41	0
Twenty20	29	28	3	470	47*	18.80	115.19	0	0	13	0

	Mat	Balls	Runs	Wkts	BBI	BBM	Ave	Econ	SR	5w	10
ODIs	33	168	164	2	2/37	2/37	82.00	5.85	84.0	0	0
T20Is	4	-	-	-	-	-	-	-	-	-	-
First-class	113	1941	1437	38	4/36	-	37.81	4.44	51.0	0	0
List A	157	981	862	27	4/68	4/68	31.92	5.27	36.3	0	0
Twenty20	29	93	101	5	3/21	3/21	20.20	6.51	18.6	0	0

CHAMARA KAPUGEDERA | RHB RM

NAME: Chamara Kantha Kapugedera
BORN: February 24, 1987, Kandy
CAREER: Test debut: 2006; ODI debut: 2006; T20I debut: 2006; First-class debut: 2005; List A debut: 2005; T20 debut: 2005

AOC SAYS: An aggressive middle-order batsman who already has a wealth of ODI experience, Kapugedera made his Test debut on Sri Lanka's last tour of England in 2006. The right-hander has not progressed as hoped and is no longer part of the Test set-up but at 24, time is still on his side.

	Mat	Inns	NO	Runs	HS	Ave	SR	100	50	Ct	St
Tests	8	15	3	418	96	34.83	53.18	0	4	6	0
ODIs	86	71	7	1442	95	22.53	73.08	0	7	28	0
T20Is	20	17	3	276	47	19.71	118.45	0	0	7	0
First-class	41	65	10	2048	150*	37.23	61.07	3	15	27	1
List A	157	135	13	3179	108	26.05	76.93	2	17	55	0
Twenty20	51	44	5	769	96*	19.71	123.63	0	2	20	0

	Mat	Balls	Runs	Wkts	BBI	BBM	Ave	Econ	SR	5w	10
Tests	8	12	9	0	-	-	-	4.50	-	0	0
ODIs	86	258	218	2	1/24	1/24	109.00	5.06	129.0	0	0
T20Is	20	-	-	-	-	-	-	-	-	-	-
First-class	41	425	242	4	1/1	2/39	60.50	3.41	106.2	0	0
List A	157	469	411	7	1/19	1/19	58.71	5.25	67.0	0	0
Twenty20	51	29	74	0	-	-	-	15.31	-	0	0

NUWAN KULASEKARA

RHB RFM

NAME: Kulasekara Mudiyanselage Dinesh Nuwan Kulasekara
BORN: July 22, 1982, Nittambuwa
CAREER: Test debut: 2005; ODI debut: 2003; T20I debut: 2008; First-class debut: 2002; List A debut: 2002; T20 debut: 2004

SRI LANKA

AOC SAYS: Kulasekara is a cunning seamer and among the most reliable bowlers in ODI cricket. The right-arm paceman's ability to move the ball off the seam and find reverse-swing will make him a tricky opponent in English conditions, but he is yet to replicate his limited-overs form in the Test arena.

	Mat	Inns	NO	Runs	HS	Ave	SR	100	50	Ct	St
Tests	12	17	1	262	64	16.37	44.10	0	1	4	0
ODIs	88	54	24	507	57*	16.90	72.84	0	1	20	0
T20Is	12	9	2	52	19*	7.42	110.63	0	0	5	0
First-class	74	98	21	1434	95	18.62	-	0	4	26	0
List A	166	101	43	998	84	17.20	68.40	0	2	40	0
Twenty20	28	21	7	153	30*	10.92	125.40	0	0	12	0

	Mat	Balls	Runs	Wkts	BBI	BBM	Ave	Econ	SR	5w	10
Tests	12	1678	879	26	4/21	8/58	33.80	3.14	64.5	0	0
ODIs	88	4073	3054	105	4/40	4/40	29.08	4.49	38.7	0	0
T20Is	12	269	373	11	3/4	3/4	33.90	8.31	24.4	0	0
First-class	74	10194	5502	243	7/27	-	22.64	3.23	41.9	9	1
List A	166	7486	5330	220	5/29	5/29	24.22	4.27	34.0	1	0
Twenty20	28	632	818	30	3/4	3/4	27.26	7.76	21.0	0	0

SURANGA LAKMAL

RHB RMF

NAME: Ranasinghe Arachchige Suranga Lakmal
BORN: March 10, 1987, Matara
CAREER: Test debut: 2010; ODI debut: 2009; First-class debut: 2008; List A debut: 2007; T20 debut: 2008

AOC SAYS: A tall seamer who troubles batsmen with bounce and swing, Lakmal should prosper in English conditions. He suffered from a lack of stamina in the early stages of his career but has developed well and made his Test debut against West Indies in Colombo last year, taking the wicket of Chris Gayle.

	Mat	Inns	NO	Runs	HS	Ave	SR	100	50	Ct	St
Tests	2	-	-	-	-	-	-	-	-	0	0
ODIs	6	1	1	0	0*	-	0.00	0	0	2	0
First-class	31	33	7	215	31	8.26	52.69	0	0	8	0
List A	53	22	15	36	10*	5.14	45.56	0	0	15	0
Twenty20	13	5	4	7	3*	7.00	70.00	0	0	2	0

	Mat	Balls	Runs	Wkts	BBI	BBM	Ave	Econ	SR	5w	10
Tests	2	213	132	3	2/84	2/91	44.00	3.71	71.0	0	0
ODIs	6	270	298	4	2/55	2/55	74.50	6.62	67.5	0	0
First-class	31	3900	2701	89	5/78	7/149	30.34	4.15	43.8	1	0
List A	53	2352	2125	73	5/31	5/31	29.10	5.42	32.2	2	0
Twenty20	13	277	328	15	3/30	3/30	21.86	7.10	18.4	0	0

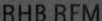

SRI LANKA

FARVEEZ MAHAROOF — RHB RFM

NAME: Mohamed Farveez Maharoof
BORN: September 7, 1984, Colombo
CAREER: Test debut: 2004; ODI debut: 2004; T20I debut: 2006; First-class debut: 2002; List A debut: 2003; T20 debut: 2004

AOC SAYS: Maharoof is a fast-bowling allrounder who delivers the ball from an open-chested action. He returned stunning ODI figures of 6-14 against West Indies in 2006 but has slipped out of the reckoning of late and signed a contract with Lancashire ahead of the 2011 season.

	Mat	Inns	NO	Runs	HS	Ave	SR	100	50	Ct	St
Tests	20	31	4	538	72	19.92	40.00	0	3	6	0
ODIs	94	64	15	984	69*	20.08	85.19	0	2	20	0
T20Is	7	4	1	23	13*	7.66	85.18	0	0	2	0
First-class	55	80	7	1758	118	24.08	49.77	3	6	33	0
List A	158	118	25	2077	70*	22.33	78.22	0	7	36	0
Twenty20	45	30	11	293	39	15.42	114.90	0	0	13	0

	Mat	Balls	Runs	Wkts	BBI	BBM	Ave	Econ	SR	5w	10
Tests	20	2628	1458	24	4/52	5/122	60.75	3.32	109.5	0	0
ODIs	94	3932	3133	121	6/14	6/14	25.89	4.78	32.4	2	0
T20Is	7	144	173	7	2/18	2/18	24.71	7.20	20.5	0	0
First-class	55	6174	3336	103	7/73	-	32.38	3.24	59.9	1	0
List A	158	6534	5239	186	6/14	6/14	28.16	4.81	35.1	2	0
Twenty20	45	912	1125	45	3/21	3/21	25.00	7.40	20.2	0	0

LASITH MALINGA — RHB RFM

NAME: Separamadu Lasith Malinga
BORN: August 28, 1983, Galle
CAREER: Test debut: 2004; ODI debut: 2004; T20I debut: 2006; First-class debut: 2001; List A debut: 2001; T20 debut: 2004

AOC SAYS: As unorthodox as they come but devastating on his day, 'Malinga the Slinger' is a whippy paceman who packs a toe-crunching yorker. He is the only bowler to have taken two World Cup hat-tricks and is arguably the world's best death bowler in limited-overs cricket.

	Mat	Inns	NO	Runs	HS	Ave	SR	100	50	Ct	St
Tests	30	37	13	275	64	11.45	44.42	0	1	7	0
ODIs	83	37	12	216	56	8.64	67.71	0	1	12	0
T20Is	29	12	7	63	27	12.60	100.00	0	0	12	0
First-class	83	100	41	584	64	9.89	40.58	0	1	23	0
List A	133	69	20	371	56	7.57	-	0	1	20	0
Twenty20	71	20	11	68	27	7.55	89.47	0	0	20	0

	Mat	Balls	Runs	Wkts	BBI	BBM	Ave	Econ	SR	5w	10
Tests	30	5209	3349	101	5/50	9/210	33.15	3.85	51.5	3	0
ODIs	83	3994	3309	125	6/38	6/38	26.47	4.97	31.9	2	0
T20Is	29	588	728	35	3/12	3/12	20.80	7.42	16.8	0	0
First-class	83	11867	7751	255	6/17	-	30.39	3.91	46.5	7	0
List A	133	6362	5289	210	6/38	6/38	25.18	4.98	30.2	3	0
Twenty20	71	1483	1721	84	4/22	4/22	20.48	6.96	17.6	0	0

ANGELO MATHEWS　　　　　　　　　　　　　　　RHB RMF

NAME: Angelo Davis Mathews
BORN: June 2, 1987, Colombo
CAREER: Test debut: 2009; ODI debut: 2008; T20I debut: 2009; First-class debut: 2006; List A debut: 2005; T20 debut: 2007

AOC SAYS: A supremely talented allrounder, Mathews is a canny seamer who has taken the new ball in Test cricket but is most destructive with the bat in hand. The right-hander is a boundary-clearer at the death in ODIs but showed his versatility by making 99 in a Test against India in 2009. He is regarded as a future Test captain.

	Mat	Inns	NO	Runs	HS	Ave	SR	100	50	Ct	St
Tests	13	17	2	527	99	35.13	57.65	0	2	4	0
ODIs	43	32	9	796	77*	34.60	85.13	0	6	13	0
T20Is	21	18	8	293	58	29.30	126.29	0	1	8	0
First-class	43	63	7	2827	270	50.48	53.96	8	11	26	0
List A	80	65	15	1485	77*	29.70	74.84	0	12	31	0
Twenty20	53	46	13	857	65*	25.96	121.04	0	3	20	0

	Mat	Balls	Runs	Wkts	BBI	BBM	Ave	Econ	SR	5w	10
Tests	13	786	421	6	1/13	2/39	70.16	3.21	131.0	0	0
ODIs	43	1320	1024	33	6/20	6/20	31.03	4.65	40.0	1	0
T20Is	21	283	346	15	3/16	3/16	23.06	7.33	18.8	0	0
First-class	43	3249	1548	36	5/47	5/62	43.00	2.85	90.2	1	0
List A	80	2013	1528	54	6/20	6/20	28.29	4.55	37.2	1	0
Twenty20	53	673	894	32	4/19	4/19	27.93	7.97	21.0	0	0

AJANTHA MENDIS　　　　　　　　　　　　　　　RHB OB/LB

NAME: Balapuwaduge Ajantha Winslo Mendis
BORN: March 11, 1985, Moratuwa
CAREER: Test debut: 2008; ODI debut: 2008; T20I debut: 2008; First-class debut: 2006; List A debut: 2006; T20 debut: 2007

AOC SAYS: Mendis exploded onto the scene by ripping through India in the 2008 Asia Cup with a mixture of googlies, legbreaks, offbreaks and his trademark 'carrom ball'. The 'mystery' spinner carried that form into Test cricket and, while opposition batsmen have started to decipher him, he remains a befuddling opponent.

	Mat	Inns	NO	Runs	HS	Ave	SR	100	50	Ct	St
Tests	15	15	4	151	78	13.72	42.29	0	1	2	0
ODIs	52	23	10	99	15*	7.61	67.80	0	0	6	0
T20Is	19	4	2	7	4*	3.50	50.00	0	0	2	0
First-class	38	49	4	578	78	12.84	54.37	0	1	11	0
List A	87	46	14	499	71*	15.59	85.88	0	2	12	0
Twenty20	50	18	9	42	15	4.66	66.66	0	0	12	0

	Mat	Balls	Runs	Wkts	BBI	BBM	Ave	Econ	SR	5w	10
Tests	15	3867	1948	61	6/117	10/209	31.93	3.02	63.3	3	1
ODIs	52	2443	1741	89	6/13	6/13	19.56	4.27	27.4	3	0
T20Is	19	432	409	33	4/15	4/15	12.39	5.68	13.0	0	0
First-class	38	8184	3901	196	7/37	10/74	19.90	2.85	41.7	12	2
List A	87	4081	2752	157	6/12	6/12	17.52	4.04	25.9	4	0
Twenty20	50	1104	1137	69	4/9	4/9	16.47	6.17	16.0	0	0

JEEVAN MENDIS LHB LB

NAME: Balapuwaduge Manukulasuriya Amith Jeevan Mendis
BORN: January 15, 1983, Colombo
CAREER: ODI debut: 2010; First-class debut: 2001; List A debut: 2001;
T20 debut: 2004

AOC SAYS: Mendis is a relative latecomer to international cricket, making his ODI debut against Zimbabwe last year at the age of 27. He demonstrated his all-round talent by taking 2-12 with his legspin before making 35* against India two days later, but was subsequently overlooked for the 2011 World Cup.

	Mat	Inns	NO	Runs	HS	Ave	SR	100	50	Ct	St
ODIs	5	3	1	47	35*	23.50	87.03	0	0	2	0
First-class	98	156	22	4208	153*	31.40	-	7	22	94	0
List A	103	90	12	1936	94	24.82	-	0	10	41	1
Twenty20	31	27	4	553	48	24.04	108.85	0	0	11	0

	Mat	Balls	Runs	Wkts	BBI	BBM	Ave	Econ	SR	5w	10
ODIs	5	168	129	4	2/12	2/12	32.25	4.60	42.0	0	0
First-class	98	5259	2920	101	5/32	-	28.91	3.33	52.0	3	0
List A	103	2030	1536	57	5/26	5/26	26.94	4.53	35.6	1	0
Twenty20	31	114	133	3	2/20	2/20	44.33	7.00	38.0	0	0

JEHAN MUBARAK LHB OB

NAME: Jehan Mubarak
BORN: January 10, 1981, Washington DC, USA
CAREER: Test debut: 2002; ODI debut: 2002; T20I debut: 2007; First-class debut: 2000; List A debut: 2000; T20 debut: 2004

AOC SAYS: An elegant left-hand middle-order batsman and restrictive offspin bowler, Mubarak has captained Sri Lanka A on several occasions but has been unable to cement his place in the senior team. He failed to grasp his opportunities in either Test or ODI cricket and is now on the fringes of the squad.

	Mat	Inns	NO	Runs	HS	Ave	SR	100	50	Ct	St
Tests	10	17	1	254	48	15.87	41.36	0	0	13	0
ODIs	38	36	6	696	72	23.20	63.27	0	4	12	0
T20Is	16	15	4	238	46*	21.63	126.59	0	0	9	0
First-class	129	223	16	6792	169	32.81	-	10	40	130	0
List A	161	154	19	4102	113	30.38	-	2	23	71	0
Twenty20	49	44	8	1015	94*	28.19	120.26	0	5	27	0

	Mat	Balls	Runs	Wkts	BBI	BBM	Ave	Econ	SR	5w	10
Tests	10	84	50	0	-	-	-	3.57	-	0	0
ODIs	38	111	76	2	1/10	1/10	38.00	4.10	55.5	0	0
T20Is	16	8	17	1	1/9	1/9	17.00	12.75	8.0	0	0
First-class	129	5705	2986	70	6/11	-	42.65	3.14	81.5	1	0
List A	161	1865	1486	47	5/50	5/50	31.61	4.78	39.6	2	0
Twenty20	49	162	230	12	4/29	4/29	19.16	8.51	13.5	0	0

THARANGA PARANAVITANA

NAME: Nishad Tharanga Paranavitana
BORN: April 15, 1982, Kegalle
CAREER: Test debut: 2009; First-class debut: 2001; List A debut: 2001; T20 debut: 2005

AOC SAYS: A tall opening batsman, Paranavitana has begun to find his feet at Test level after scoring consecutive centuries against India last year. Sri Lanka hope he will solve their long-standing problems at the top of the order and he will open with Tillakaratne Dilshan in this summer's Test series.

	Mat	Inns	NO	Runs	HS	Ave	SR	100	50	Ct	St
Tests	16	28	2	963	111	37.03	47.64	2	5	7	0
First-class	112	183	19	7160	236	43.65	52.22	19	31	110	0
List A	88	87	12	3181	166*	42.41	71.49	5	22	50	0
Twenty20	22	22	1	532	67*	25.33	136.06	0	5	10	0

	Mat	Balls	Runs	Wkts	BBI	BBM	Ave	Econ	SR	5w	10
Tests	16	90	76	1	1/26	1/26	76.00	5.06	90.0	0	0
First-class	112	1538	763	21	4/39	-	36.33	2.97	73.2	0	0
List A	88	838	646	14	4/25	4/25	46.14	4.62	59.8	0	0
Twenty20	22	96	117	4	1/3	1/3	29.25	7.31	24.0	0	0

THISARA PERERA

NAME: Narangoda Liyanaarachchilage Thisara Chirantha Perera
BORN: April 3, 1989, Colombo
CAREER: ODI debut: 2009; T20I debut: 2010; First-class debut: 2008; List A debut: 2008; T20 debut: 2008

AOC SAYS: Perera is an aggressive allrounder who earned a senior call-up in 2009 after impressing for Sri Lanka under 19s. He made an instant impact with a matchwinning 36* in an ODI against India and demonstrated his all-round ability with a haul of 5-28 against the same opposition last August.

	Mat	Inns	NO	Runs	HS	Ave	SR	100	50	Ct	St
ODIs	19	13	2	161	36*	14.63	115.00	0	0	8	0
T20Is	7	6	3	74	24	24.66	139.62	0	0	1	0
First-class	14	24	6	745	113*	41.38	91.07	1	5	10	0
List A	57	44	10	725	59	21.32	104.92	0	2	23	0
Twenty20	35	28	10	186	24	10.33	124.83	0	0	13	0

	Mat	Balls	Runs	Wkts	BBI	BBM	Ave	Econ	SR	5w	10
ODIs	19	724	637	31	5/28	5/28	20.54	5.27	23.3	2	0
T20Is	7	102	102	5	2/19	2/19	20.40	6.00	20.4	0	0
First-class	14	1373	818	24	5/69	6/139	34.08	3.57	57.2	1	0
List A	57	2071	1901	85	5/28	5/28	22.36	5.50	24.3	4	0
Twenty20	35	593	697	36	3/17	3/17	19.36	7.05	16.4	0	0

P–S

SRI LANKA

DAMMIKA PRASAD   RHB RFM

NAME: Kariyawasam Tirana Gamage Dammika Prasad
BORN: May 30, 1983, Ragama
CAREER: Test debut: 2008; ODI debut: 2006; First-class debut: 2002;
List A debut: 2002; T20 debut: 2007

AOC SAYS: The right-arm seamer announced himself on the international stage with two wickets in the first over of his ODI debut against Bangladesh before suffering a serious back injury. Prasad bounced back to take five wickets on Test debut against India and is a contender for a Test berth this summer.

	Mat	Inns	NO	Runs	HS	Ave	SR	100	50	Ct	St
Tests	6	5	0	113	47	22.60	67.66	0	0	1	0
ODIs	5	3	0	17	8	5.66	34.00	0	0	0	0
First-class	66	72	10	1305	103*	21.04	64.03	1	6	16	0
List A	60	32	7	299	31	11.96	-	0	0	11	0
Twenty20	4	4	1	14	9	4.66	63.63	0	0	1	0

	Mat	Balls	Runs	Wkts	BBI	BBM	Ave	Econ	SR	5w	10
Tests	6	1046	784	13	3/82	5/142	60.30	4.49	80.4	0	0
ODIs	5	216	217	5	2/29	2/29	43.40	6.02	43.2	0	0
First-class	66	8482	5389	190	6/25	-	28.36	3.81	44.6	5	1
List A	60	2434	1968	68	4/39	4/39	28.94	4.85	35.7	0	0
Twenty20	4	42	49	3	2/18	2/18	16.33	7.00	14.0	0	0

SURAJ RANDIV   RHB OB

NAME: Hewa Kaluhalamullage Suraj Randiv Kaluhalamulla
BORN: January 30, 1985, Matara
CAREER: Test debut: 2010; ODI debut: 2009; T20I debut: 2010; First-class debut: 2004; List A debut: 2004; T20 debut: 2005

AOC SAYS: A tall offspinner who gives it a rip and a steady lower-order batsman, Randiv is perhaps best known for infamously bowling a deliberate no-ball to prevent Virender Sehwag from reaching a century. Despite that incident, he remains a bright prospect and will benefit from the retirement of Muttiah Muralitharan.

	Mat	Inns	NO	Runs	HS	Ave	SR	100	50	Ct	St
Tests	3	3	0	26	12	8.66	29.54	0	0	0	0
ODIs	21	11	1	156	56	15.60	67.82	0	1	5	0
T20Is	6	2	0	8	6	4.00	133.33	0	0	0	0
First-class	74	101	19	1555	112	18.96	51.78	1	5	56	0
List A	85	45	7	399	56	10.50	61.95	0	1	35	0
Twenty20	19	7	1	41	20	6.83	136.66	0	0	7	0

	Mat	Balls	Runs	Wkts	BBI	BBM	Ave	Econ	SR	5w	10
Tests	3	1053	567	14	5/82	9/162	40.50	3.23	75.2	1	0
ODIs	21	950	737	22	3/23	3/23	33.50	4.65	43.1	0	0
T20Is	6	102	115	7	3/20	3/20	16.42	6.76	14.5	0	0
First-class	74	14051	7951	323	9/62	-	24.61	3.39	43.5	24	6
List A	85	3537	2705	108	5/15	5/15	25.04	4.58	32.7	2	0
Twenty20	19	322	383	19	3/20	3/20	20.15	7.13	16.9	0	0

THILAN SAMARAWEERA

NAME: Thilan Thusara Samaraweera
BORN: September 22, 1976, Colombo
CAREER: Test debut: 2001; ODI debut: 1998; First-class debut: 1995;
List A debut: 1995; T20 debut: 2004

AOC SAYS: A gritty middle-order grafter in amongst Sri Lanka's glitzy strokemakers, Samaraweera has a phenomenal Test record – particularly on slow, low subcontinent pitches. The right-hander recently returned to Sri Lanka's one-day side to add some steel to their middle-order.

	Mat	Inns	NO	Runs	HS	Ave	SR	100	50	Ct	St
Tests	63	98	17	4395	231	54.25	48.02	12	25	37	0
ODIs	52	41	11	841	105*	28.03	69.50	2	0	17	0
First-class	222	308	56	12408	231	49.23	-	33	62	177	0
List A	171	126	36	2927	105*	32.52	-	2	16	59	0
Twenty20	13	12	2	288	70	28.80	132.11	0	2	12	0

	Mat	Balls	Runs	Wkts	BBI	BBM	Ave	Econ	SR	5w	10
Tests	63	1291	679	14	4/49	6/67	48.50	3.15	92.2	0	0
ODIs	52	702	542	11	3/34	3/34	49.27	4.63	63.8	0	0
First-class	222	17458	8132	348	6/55	-	23.36	2.79	50.1	15	2
List A	171	4669	3114	109	7/30	7/30	28.56	4.00	42.8	2	0
Twenty20	13	44	37	3	3/17	3/17	12.33	5.04	14.6	0	0

KUMAR SANGAKKARA

NAME: Kumar Chokshanada Sangakkara
BORN: October 27, 1977, Matale
CAREER: Test debut: 2000; ODI debut: 2000; T20I debut: 2006; First-class debut: 1998; List A debut: 1997; T20 debut: 2004

AOC SAYS: Sri Lanka's captain is one of the game's great thinkers and a prodigiously talented batsman to boot. Sangakkara lies second behind Mahela Jayawardene in his country's list of all-time Test run-scorers and is a reliable wicketkeeper who will take the gloves in limited-overs cricket.

	Mat	Inns	NO	Runs	HS	Ave	SR	100	50	Ct	St
Tests	94	156	12	8244	287	57.25	55.95	24	34	163	20
ODIs	290	271	31	9116	138*	37.98	75.71	11	62	285	74
T20Is	29	28	3	777	78	31.08	119.19	0	6	14	9
First-class	179	285	22	12628	287	48.01	-	32	58	323	33
List A	386	363	41	12877	156*	39.99	-	19	83	387	99
Twenty20	80	76	6	2182	94	31.17	129.11	0	16	42	22

	Mat	Balls	Runs	Wkts	BBI	BBM	Ave	Econ	SR	5w	10
Tests	94	66	38	0	-	-	-	3.45	-	0	0
ODIs	288	-	-	-	-	-	-	-	-	-	-
T20Is	29	-	-	-	-	-	-	-	-	-	-
First-class	179	192	108	1	1/13	-	108.00	3.37	192.0	0	0
List A	384	-	-	-	-	-	-	-	-	-	-
Twenty20	80	-	-	-	-	-	-	-	-	-	-

SRI LANKA

CHAMARA SILVA · RHB LB

NAME: Lindamlilage Prageeth Chamara Silva
BORN: December 14, 1979, Panadura
CAREER: Test debut: 2006; ODI debut: 1999; T20I debut: 2006; First-class debut: 1997; List A debut: 1998; T20 debut: 2004

AOC SAYS: The middle-order accumulator made his ODI debut aged 19 but has never entirely convinced at international level. Silva is a silky strokemaker, particularly through the offside, but a propensity to get out when set has held him back. His Test career appears to be over but he remains a regular member of the one-day side.

	Mat	Inns	NO	Runs	HS	Ave	SR	100	50	Ct	St
Tests	11	17	1	537	152*	33.56	62.88	1	2	7	0
ODIs	71	58	7	1514	107*	29.68	70.15	1	12	20	0
T20Is	15	14	2	171	38	14.25	101.18	0	0	5	0
First-class	145	244	14	8657	152*	37.63	-	19	50	132	0
List A	208	188	29	5038	107*	31.68	-	2	35	79	0
Twenty20	35	34	6	704	56	25.14	112.10	0	1	15	0

	Mat	Balls	Runs	Wkts	BBI	BBM	Ave	Econ	SR	5w	10
Tests	11	102	65	1	1/57	1/57	65.00	3.82	102.0	0	0
ODIs	71	42	33	1	1/21	1/21	33.00	4.71	42.0	0	0
T20Is	15	18	15	1	1/4	1/4	15.00	5.00	18.0	0	0
First-class	145	2164	1506	46	4/24	-	32.73	4.17	47.0	0	0
List A	208	319	296	6	1/1	1/1	49.33	5.56	53.1	0	0
Twenty20	35	24	36	1	1/4	1/4	36.00	9.00	24.0	0	0

UPUL THARANGA · LHB WK

NAME: Warushavithana Upul Tharanga
BORN: February 2, 1985, Balapitiya
CAREER: Test debut: 2005; ODI debut: 2005; T20I debut: 2006; First-class debut: 2001; List A debut: 2003; T20 debut: 2006

AOC SAYS: A left-handed opener who failed to convince at Test level, Tharanga has carved out a career as an explosive batsman in ODIs. He smacked a spectacular century when Sri Lanka took England to the cleaners at Headingley in 2006, chasing down 324 for victory in 37.3 overs.

	Mat	Inns	NO	Runs	HS	Ave	SR	100	50	Ct	St
Tests	15	26	1	713	165	28.52	49.51	1	3	11	0
ODIs	120	115	7	3896	133	36.07	74.09	11	19	21	0
T20Is	8	8	0	114	37	14.25	116.32	0	0	1	0
First-class	82	137	4	4720	265*	35.48	-	10	19	61	1
List A	195	188	9	6197	173*	34.62	74.10	14	32	49	2
Twenty20	25	25	2	485	83*	21.08	122.78	0	3	6	0

	Mat	Balls	Runs	Wkts	BBI	BBM	Ave	Econ	SR	5w	10
Tests	15	-	-	-	-	-	-	-	-	-	-
ODIs	120	-	-	-	-	-	-	-	-	-	-
T20Is	8	-	-	-	-	-	-	-	-	-	-
First-class	82	18	4	0	-	-	1.33	-	-	0	0
List A	195	-	-	-	-	-	-	-	-	-	-
Twenty20	25	-	-	-	-	-	-	-	-	-	-

LAHIRU THIRIMANNE

LHB RMF

NAME: Hettige Don Rumesh Lahiru Thirimanne
BORN: September 8, 1989, Moratuwa
CAREER: ODI debut: 2010; First-class debut: 2008; List A debut: 2009;
T20 debut: 2009

AOC SAYS: Thirimanne is a mercurial batsman and considered to be the finest of a crop of young Sri Lankans. He showed his potential by making an assured 22 opening the batting against India on his ODI debut last year. The left-hander is still finding his feet but at the age of 21, he looks set for a big future.

	Mat	Inns	NO	Runs	HS	Ave	SR	100	50	Ct	St
ODIs	3	2	0	37	22	18.50	82.22	0	0	1	0
First-class	36	61	4	2462	148	43.19	50.96	7	14	30	0
List A	35	30	2	703	78	25.10	66.38	0	4	10	0
Twenty20	12	12	1	247	70	22.45	117.61	0	1	7	0

	Mat	Balls	Runs	Wkts	BBI	BBM	Ave	Econ	SR	5w	10
ODIs	3	-	-	-	-	-	-	-	-	-	-
First-class	36	18	19	0	-	-	-	6.33	-	0	0
List A	35	10	10	1	1/5	1/5	10.00	6.00	10.0	0	0
Twenty20	12	-	-	-	-	-	-	-	-	-	-

THILAN THUSHARA

LHB LFM

NAME: Magina Thilan Thushara Mirando
BORN: March 1, 1981, Balapitiya
CAREER: Test debut: 2003; ODI debut: 2008; T20I debut: 2008; First-class debut: 1999; List A debut: 2000; T20 debut: 2004

AOC SAYS: Thushara is an experienced left-arm seamer who was recalled to the Test side to face West Indies last year after a 15-month hiatus. He went wicketless and was subsequently dropped and was dealt a double blow when he missed out on Sri Lanka's 2011 World Cup squad.

	Mat	Inns	NO	Runs	HS	Ave	SR	100	50	Ct	St
Tests	10	14	3	94	15*	8.54	46.76	0	0	3	0
ODIs	38	27	6	392	54*	18.66	92.45	0	1	4	0
T20Is	6	2	0	4	3	2.00	50.00	0	0	2	0
First-class	101	148	17	2061	103*	15.73	-	1	6	38	0
List A	128	87	20	1159	75*	17.29	-	0	3	20	0
Twenty20	33	21	7	134	33*	9.57	95.71	0	0	12	0

	Mat	Balls	Runs	Wkts	BBI	BBM	Ave	Econ	SR	5w	10
Tests	10	1668	1040	28	5/83	6/118	37.14	3.74	59.5	1	0
ODIs	38	1676	1393	50	5/47	5/47	27.86	4.98	33.5	1	0
T20Is	6	132	179	7	2/37	2/37	25.57	8.13	18.8	0	0
First-class	101	12914	7697	256	6/50	-	30.06	3.57	50.4	8	1
List A	128	5027	4107	148	6/28	6/28	27.75	4.90	33.9	4	0
Twenty20	33	687	824	38	3/23	3/23	21.68	7.19	18.0	0	0

MALINDA WARNAPURA · LHB OB

SRI LANKA

NAME: Basnayake Shalith Malinda Warnapura
BORN: May 26, 1979, Colombo
CAREER: Test debut: 2007; ODI debut: 2007; First-class debut: 1998;
List A debut: 1998; T20 debut: 2005

AOC SAYS: Warnapura is a middle-order batsman who has found himself out of favour of late, playing his last Test in 2009. He made an immediate impact at Test level, making 82 on debut against Bangladesh before notching his maiden ton against West Indies, but was subsequently dropped after a string of low scores.

Batting & Fielding

	Mat	Inns	NO	Runs	HS	Ave	SR	100	50	Ct	St
Tests	14	24	1	821	120	35.69	58.14	2	7	14	0
ODIs	3	3	0	35	30	11.66	46.05	0	0	3	0
First-class	159	243	22	7992	242	36.16	-	19	39	106	0
List A	126	111	16	2747	111	28.91	-	4	9	52	0
Twenty20	12	12	1	139	53	12.63	101.45	0	1	4	0

Bowling

	Mat	Balls	Runs	Wkts	BBI	BBM	Ave	Econ	SR	5w	10
Tests	14	54	40	0	-	-	-	4.44	-	0	0
ODIs	3	-	-	-	-	-	-	-	-	-	-
First-class	159	7067	3329	122	6/22	-	27.28	2.82	57.9	4	0
List A	126	2390	1688	72	5/33	5/33	23.44	4.23	33.1	1	0
Twenty20	12	79	93	5	3/19	3/19	18.60	7.06	15.8	0	0

CHANAKA WELEGEDARA · RHB LFM

NAME: Uda Walawwe Mahim Bandaralage Chanaka Asanga Welegedara
BORN: March 20, 1981, Matale
CAREER: Test debut: 2007; ODI debut: 2009; T20I debut: 2010; First-class debut: 2002; List A debut: 2002; T20 debut: 2004

AOC SAYS: The left-arm paceman didn't learn to play the game until the age of 17 but he made rapid strides and took four wickets on Test debut against England. Curiously, he had to wait two years for another opportunity and his international appearances remain sporadic despite a strong action and brisk pace.

Batting & Fielding

	Mat	Inns	NO	Runs	HS	Ave	SR	100	50	Ct	St
Tests	6	6	2	27	8	6.75	54.00	0	0	2	0
ODIs	10	3	2	4	2*	4.00	44.44	0	0	2	0
T20Is	2	1	1	2	2*	-	66.66	0	0	0	0
First-class	73	90	33	576	76	10.10	41.61	0	1	15	0
List A	78	35	18	96	18*	5.64	44.65	0	0	16	0
Twenty20	26	12	8	42	12*	10.50	113.51	0	0	2	0

Bowling

	Mat	Balls	Runs	Wkts	BBI	BBM	Ave	Econ	SR	5w	10
Tests	6	993	707	12	4/87	5/163	58.91	4.27	82.7	0	0
ODIs	10	457	433	15	5/66	5/66	28.86	5.68	30.4	1	0
T20Is	2	36	61	1	1/21	1/21	61.00	10.16	36.0	0	0
First-class	73	9933	5894	200	5/34	-	29.47	3.56	49.6	6	1
List A	78	3408	2785	111	5/16	5/16	25.09	4.90	30.7	3	0
Twenty20	26	547	620	36	3/18	3/18	17.22	6.80	15.1	0	0

TEAM PROFILE

CAPTAIN: MS Dhoni
TEST RECORD AGAINST ENGLAND:
P99 W19 D46 L34
TEST RECORD IN ENGLAND:
P48 W5 D20 L23
2010 TEST RECORD: P14 W8 D3 L3
HONOURS: ICC World Cup: 1983;
ICC World Twenty20: 2007; ICC
Champions Trophy: 2002(s); Asia
Cup: (4) 1984, 1988, 1990/91, 1995,
2010

THE LOWDOWN

India arrive on British shores hoping to consolidate their position as the No.1 ranked Test nation in the world. Rahul Dravid led his side to their first Test series victory in England since 1986 when they last toured in 2007, taking the series 1-0 courtesy of a seven-wicket win in the second Test at Trent Bridge. Zaheer Khan was the hero on that occasion, returning a nine-wicket match haul in a contest best remembered for the 'confectionary controversy' after England were accused of dropping jelly beans about the crease. MS Dhoni is now the man in charge and under his stewardship India have become a formidable force across all formats. Historically, India have struggled overseas due to a lack of quality pacemen but Zaheer spearheads a pace attack that is potentially devastating on seam-friendly English tracks. They also boast a good stock of spinners but batting is their real strength, with a vastly experienced top seven that features Sachin Tendulkar – the greatest batsman of the modern era – and the game's biggest thrill-seeker in the form of Virender Sehwag. If England can build on their Ashes triumph Down Under and defeat India in a Test series for the first time since 1996 this summer, they can justifiably lay claim to being the leading nation in Test cricket.

COACH: GARY KIRSTEN

A former South Africa opening batsman who took charge of India in 2007, Kirsten is scheduled to stand down at the conclusion of the 2011 World Cup, although the BCCI have yet to announce his successor. A dogged left-hander and a model professional as a player, he has brought a strong team spirit to Indian cricket following a tumultuous period under former coach Greg Chappell.

	Mat	Inns	NO	Runs	HS	Ave	SR	100	50	Ct	St
PP Chawla	1	1	0	1	1	1.00	11.11	0	0	0	-
MS Dhoni	8	13	1	397	92	33.08	60.70	0	4	24	3
RS Dravid	17	29	3	1489	217	57.26	39.70	4	8	26	-
G Gambhir	2	4	0	361	179	90.25	47.56	1	2	5	-
Harbhajan Singh	11	15	2	219	54	16.84	77.11	0	1	2	-
KD Karthik	3	6	0	263	91	43.83	50.77	0	3	3	0
Z Khan	9	11	4	80	14*	11.42	33.89	0	0	3	-
VVS Laxman	13	20	3	584	75	34.35	44.34	0	4	16	-
A Mishra	2	2	0	35	23	17.50	71.42	0	0	1	-
A Nehra	2	3	0	19	19	6.33	29.68	0	0	2	-
MM Patel	2	3	1	19	11*	9.50	82.60	0	0	3	-
V Sehwag	11	18	1	527	106	31.00	71.79	1	4	9	-
I Sharma	2	2	2	9	8*	-	26.47	0	0	0	-
S Sreesanth	5	7	4	71	35	23.66	63.96	0	0	1	-
SR Tendulkar	24	39	4	2150	193	61.42	52.28	7	10	19	-
Yuvraj Singh	4	7	1	276	86	46.00	59.86	0	2	2	-

	Mat	Overs	Mdn	Runs	Wkts	BBI	BBM	Ave	Econ	SR	5w	10
PP Chawla	1	14.1	3	53	1	1/8	1/53	53.00	3.74	85.0	0	0
MS Dhoni	8	1.0	0	1	0	-	-	-	1.00	-	0	0
Harbhajan Singh	11	520.4	97	1393	41	5/51	7/110	33.97	2.67	76.1	3	0
Z Khan	9	355.2	92	1017	37	5/75	9/134	27.48	2.86	57.6	1	0
VVS Laxman	13	1.0	0	5	0	-	-	-	5.00	-	0	0
A Mishra	2	83.0	8	256	6	3/99	4/165	42.66	3.08	83.0	0	0
A Nehra	2	76.0	8	319	5	2/80	3/181	63.80	4.19	91.2	0	0
MM Patel	2	80.0	16	217	10	4/25	7/97	21.70	2.71	48.0	0	0
V Sehwag	11	32.0	2	117	1	1/32	1/42	117.00	3.65	192.0	0	0
I Sharma	2	59.3	6	151	6	3/57	4/89	25.16	2.53	59.5	0	0
S Sreesanth	5	186.5	45	569	18	4/70	5/100	31.61	3.04	62.2	0	0
SR Tendulkar	24	80.0	6	284	2	1/26	1/27	142.00	3.55	240.0	0	0
Yuvraj Singh	4	24.0	4	65	2	1/12	2/45	32.50	2.70	72.0	0	0

Batting & Fielding

	Mat	Inns	NO	Runs	HS	Ave	SR	100	50	Ct	St
PP Chawla	8	6	2	19	13*	4.75	55.88	0	0	2	-
M S Dhoni	19	19	3	532	96	33.25	79.16	0	3	19	7
RS Dravid	25	24	3	888	92*	42.28	77.48	0	10	20	2
G Gambhir	11	11	0	393	70	35.72	81.36	0	4	7	-
Harbhajan Singh	23	12	4	140	41*	17.50	83.33	0	0	12	-
KD Karthik	7	6	2	52	44*	13.00	60.46	0	0	6	1
Z Khan	18	11	2	73	20	8.11	70.19	0	0	4	-
V Kohli	1	1	0	8	8	8.00	160.00	0	0	1	-
VVS Laxman	8	8	0	143	33	17.87	63.83	0	0	3	-
A Nehra	7	3	1	26	24	13.00	118.18	0	0	1	-
MM Patel	10	4	3	2	1*	2.00	28.57	0	0	2	-
YK Pathan	6	5	3	82	50*	41.00	146.42	0	1	0	-
SK Raina	12	11	2	343	81*	38.11	76.90	0	4	4	-
V Sehwag	27	27	0	1008	126	37.33	102.33	1	7	15	-
I Sharma	3	0	-	-	-	-	-	-	-	-	-
RG Sharma	4	4	2	50	28	25.00	69.44	0	0	0	-
S Sreesanth	4	1	0	0	0	0.00	0.00	0	0	0	-
SR Tendulkar	37	37	4	1455	120	44.09	89.20	2	10	15	-
Yuvraj Singh	29	28	6	1187	138*	53.95	101.27	3	6	10	-

Bowling

	Mat	Overs	Mdns	Runs	Wkts	BBI	Ave	Econ	SR	5w
PP Chawla	8	420	2	385	8	3/60	48.12	5.50	52.50	0
G Gambhir	11	6	0	13	0	-	-	13.00	-	0
Harbhajan Singh	23	1302	12	912	36	5/31	25.33	4.20	36.16	2
Z Khan	18	945	10	785	25	3/26	31.40	4.98	37.80	0
A Nehra	7	326	3	236	13	6/23	18.15	4.34	25.07	1
MM Patel	10	418	4	388	14	3/18	27.71	5.56	29.85	0
YK Pathan	6	70	0	104	3	1/7	34.66	8.91	23.33	0
V Sehwag	27	354	0	329	8	3/28	41.12	5.57	44.25	0
I Sharma	3	144	0	155	5	2/41	31.00	6.45	28.80	0
S Sreesanth	4	161	1	163	10	6/55	16.30	6.07	16.10	1
SR Tendulkar	37	443	0	428	3	1/13	142.66	5.79	147.66	0
Yuvraj Singh	29	786	3	682	18	4/28	37.88	5.20	43.66	0

	Mat	Inns	NO	Runs	HS	Ave	SR	100	50	Ct	St
MS Dhoni	2	2	2	40	30*	-	142.85	0	0	0	0
G Gambhir	2	2	0	84	58	42.00	125.37	0	1	1	-
Harbhajan Singh	2	-	-	-	-	-	-	-	-	3	-
RA Jadeja	1	1	0	25	25	25.00	71.42	0	0	1	-
Z Khan	1	-	-	-	-	-	-	-	-	0	-
YK Pathan	1	1	1	33	33*	-	194.11	0	0	1	-
SK Raina	1	1	0	2	2	2.00	40.00	0	0	0	-
V Sehwag	1	1	0	68	68	68.00	130.76	0	1	0	-
I Sharma	1	-	-	-	-	-	-	-	-	0	-
RG Sharma	2	1	0	9	9	9.00	112.50	0	0	1	-
S Sreesanth	1	-	-	-	-	-	-	-	-	0	-
Yuvraj Singh	2	2	0	75	58	37.50	300.00	0	1	0	-

Batting & Fielding

	Mat	Overs	Mdns	Runs	Wkts	BBI	Ave	Econ	SR	5w
Harbhajan Singh	2	8.0	0	65	4	3/30	16.25	8.12	12.0	0
R Jadeja	1	4.0	0	26	2	2/26	13.00	6.50	12.0	0
Z Khan	1	3.0	0	26	1	1/26	26.00	8.66	18.0	0
I Sharma	1	4.0	0	36	0	-	-	9.00	-	0
S Sreesanth	1	4.0	0	38	0	-	-	9.50	-	0
Yuvraj Singh	2	2.0	0	20	0	-	-	10.00	-	0

Bowling

TOUR SCHEDULE

July

Friday 15 – Sunday 17	Somerset v Indians, County Ground, Taunton
Thursday 21 – Monday 25	1st Test v England, Lord's, London
Friday 29 – Tuesday 2	2nd Test v England, Trent Bridge, Nottingham

August

Friday 5 – Saturday 6	Northamptonshire v Indians, County Ground, Northampton
Wednesday 10 – Sunday 14	3rd Test v England, Edgbaston, Birmingham
Thursday 18 – Monday 22	4th Test v England, The Kia Oval, London
Thursday 25	Sussex v Indians, County Ground, Hove
Friday 26	Kent v Indians, St Lawrence Ground, Canterbury (Day/Night)
Monday 29	Leicestershire v Indians, Grace Road, Leicester
Wednesday 31	Only T20I v England, Old Trafford, Manchester (Day/Night)

September

Saturday 3	1st ODI v England, Emirates Durham ICG, Durham
Tuesday 6	2nd ODI v England, The Rose Bowl, Southampton (Day/Night)
Friday 9	3rd ODI v England, The Kia Oval, London (Day/Night)
Sunday 11	4th ODI v England, Lord's, London
Friday 16	5th ODI v England, SWALEC Stadium, Cardiff (Day/Night)

INDIA

R ASHWIN — RHB OB

NAME: Ravichandran Ashwin
BORN: September 17, 1986, Chennai
CAREER: ODI debut: 2010; T20I debut: 2010; First-class debut: 2006;
List A debut: 2007; T20 debut: 2007

AOC SAYS: A tall offspinner and a capable lower-order batsman, Ashwin scooped the Man of the Series award as Chennai Super Kings won the 2010 Champions League T20 in 2010. He is now established in India's limited-overs set-up and was part of their 2011 World Cup squad.

Batting & Fielding

	Mat	Inns	NO	Runs	HS	Ave	SR	100	50	Ct	St
ODIs	9	3	1	48	38	24.00	117.07	0	0	1	0
T20Is	3	-	-	-	-	-	-	-	-	0	0
First-class	34	45	12	1170	107*	35.45	56.46	2	7	15	0
List A	48	27	7	467	79	23.35	74.36	0	2	15	0
Twenty20	35	13	5	50	11*	6.25	74.62	0	0	10	0

Bowling

	Mat	Balls	Runs	Wkts	BBI	BBM	Ave	Econ	SR	5w	10
ODIs	9	516	418	18	3/24	3/24	23.22	4.86	28.6	0	0
T20Is	3	72	103	3	1/22	1/22	34.33	8.58	24.0	0	0
First-class	34	8494	3769	134	6/64	11/129	28.12	2.66	63.3	11	3
List A	48	2636	1865	65	3/24	3/24	28.69	4.24	40.5	0	0
Twenty20	35	774	814	46	4/18	4/18	17.69	6.31	16.8	0	0

PIYUSH CHAWLA — LHB LB

NAME: Piyush Pramod Chawla
BORN: December 24, 1988, Aligarh
CAREER: Test debut: 2006; ODI debut: 2007; T20I debut: 2010; First-class debut: 2005; List A debut: 2005; T20 debut: 2007

AOC SAYS: The legspinning allrounder faded from the international scene after making his Test bow aged 18 against England but received a surprise recall for the 2010 World Twenty20. He has developed a more reliable stock delivery to back-up his variations and retained his place for the 2011 World Cup.

Batting & Fielding

	Mat	Inns	NO	Runs	HS	Ave	SR	100	50	Ct	St
Tests	2	2	0	5	4	2.50	23.80	0	0	0	0
ODIs	25	12	5	38	13*	5.42	65.51	0	0	9	0
T20Is	3	-	-	-	-	-	-	-	-	2	0
First-class	69	100	9	2644	104	29.05		0	2	19	39	0
List A	80	52	14	734	93	19.31	87.06	0	4	26	0
Twenty20	60	35	11	348	33	14.50	118.36	0	0	18	0

Bowling

	Mat	Balls	Runs	Wkts	BBI	BBM	Ave	Econ	SR	5w	10
Tests	2	205	137	3	2/66	2/84	45.66	4.00	68.3	0	0
ODIs	25	1312	1117	32	4/23	4/23	34.90	5.10	41.0	0	0
T20Is	3	66	69	2	1/14	1/14	34.50	6.27	33.0	0	0
First-class	69	15476	7779	272	6/46	11/170	28.59	3.01	56.8	16	2
List A	80	3919	3287	116	6/46	6/46	28.33	5.03	33.7	1	0
Twenty20	60	1227	1502	59	3/23	3/23	25.45	7.34	20.7	0	0

SHIKHAR DHAWAN   LHB OB

NAME: Shikhar Dhawan
BORN: December 5, 1985, Delhi
CAREER: ODI debut: 2010; First-class debut: 2004; List A debut: 2005;
T20 debut: 2007

AOC SAYS: An attacking opening batsman, Dhawan was earmarked as a star of the future when he was named Player of the Tournament at the Under 19 World Cup in 2003/04. The Delhi Daredevils left-hander made his ODI debut against Australia last year but is on the fringes of the side for now.

	Mat	Inns	NO	Runs	HS	Ave	SR	100	50	Ct	St
ODIs	1	1	0	0	0	0.00	0.00	0	0	0	0
First-class	61	98	6	4110	224	44.67	-	10	19	61	0
List A	79	79	10	3024	155*	43.82	84.37	8	15	37	0
Twenty20	44	43	6	1006	75*	27.18	110.30	0	8	21	0

	Mat	Balls	Runs	Wkts	BBI	BBM	Ave	Econ	SR	5w	10
ODIs	1	-	-	-	-	-	-	-	-	-	-
First-class	61	184	107	3	2/30	2/30	35.66	3.48	61.3	0	0
List A	79	176	138	6	2/22	2/22	23.00	4.70	29.3	0	0
Twenty20	44	-	-	-	-	-	-	-	-	-	-

MS DHONI   RHB RM WK

NAME: Mahendra Singh Dhoni
BORN: July 7, 1981, Ranchi
CAREER: Test debut: 2005; ODI debut: 2004; T20I debut: 2006; First-class debut: 2000; List A debut: 2000; T20 debut: 2006

AOC SAYS: The dynamic wicketkeeper-batsman is an icon in his homeland having led with distinction since taking over the Test captaincy in 2008. He guided India to the No.1 Test ranking and is one of the most destructive batsmen in world cricket.

	Mat	Inns	NO	Runs	HS	Ave	SR	100	50	Ct	St
Tests	54	82	9	2925	148	40.06	60.32	4	20	148	25
ODIs	185	165	41	5958	183*	48.04	87.22	7	37	180	60
T20Is	26	25	8	451	46	26.52	111.63	0	0	11	3
First-class	95	148	12	5087	148	37.40	-	7	34	256	44
List A	241	217	51	7960	183*	47.95	-	13	48	247	75
Twenty20	79	72	24	1698	73*	35.37	128.53	0	7	32	19

	Mat	Balls	Runs	Wkts	BBI	BBM	Ave	Econ	SR	5w	10
Tests	54	18	19	0	-	-	-	6.33	-	0	0
ODIs	183	12	14	1	1/14	1/14	14.00	7.00	12.0	0	0
T20Is	26	-	-	-	-	-	-	-	-	-	-
First-class	95	48	39	0	-	-	-	4.87	-	0	0
List A	241	39	36	2	1/14	1/14	18.00	5.53	19.5	0	0
Twenty20	79	-	-	-	-	-	-	-	-	-	-

RAHUL DRAVID RHB OB

INDIA

NAME: Rahul Sharad Dravid
BORN: January 11, 1973, Indore
CAREER: Test debut: 1996; ODI debut: 1996; First-class debut: 1991;
List A debut: 1993; T20 debut: 2007

AOC SAYS: Dravid has been a rock in India's top-order for 15 years and is the third highest runscorer of all-time in Test cricket. The elegant and obdurate right-hander no longer players limited-overs internationals but retains the key role at No.3 in Test cricket.

	Mat	Inns	NO	Runs	HS	Ave	SR	100	50	Ct	St
Tests	150	259	29	12063	270	52.44	42.33	31	59	200	0
ODIs	339	313	40	10765	153	39.43	71.17	12	82	196	14
First-class	283	469	64	22552	270	55.68	-	63	113	342	1
List A	444	411	55	15147	153	42.54	-	21	111	233	17
Twenty20	54	47	5	1187	75*	28.26	120.02	0	6	11	0

	Mat	Balls	Runs	Wkts	BBI	BBM	Ave	Econ	SR	5w	10
Tests	150	120	39	1	1/18	1/18	39.00	1.95	120.0	0	0
ODIs	339	186	170	4	2/43	2/43	42.50	5.48	46.5	0	0
First-class	283	617	273	5	2/16	-	54.60	2.65	123.4	0	0
List A	444	477	421	4	2/43	2/43	105.25	5.29	119.2	0	0
Twenty20	54	-	-	-	-	-	-	-	-	-	-

GAUTAM GAMBHIR LHB LB

NAME: Gautam Gambhir
BORN: October 14, 1981, Delhi
CAREER: Test debut: 2004; ODI debut: 2003; T20I debut: 2007; First-class debut: 2000; List A debut: 2000; T20 debut: 2007

AOC SAYS: Gambhir is a classical and adaptable opening batsman. He was named ICC Test Player of the Year in 2009 after a stunning run of eight centuries in 13 Test matches, including a double-century in Delhi to help India to a Test series win over Australia.

	Mat	Inns	NO	Runs	HS	Ave	SR	100	50	Ct	St
Tests	38	68	5	3234	206	51.33	53.10	9	16	29	0
ODIs	113	109	10	3976	150*	40.16	86.56	9	24	32	0
T20Is	23	22	0	621	75	28.22	124.20	0	6	5	0
First-class	122	207	20	10239	233*	54.75	-	32	45	78	0
List A	215	209	16	7315	150*	37.90	-	17	42	62	0
Twenty20	72	70	5	1844	86	28.36	121.79	0	15	12	0

	Mat	Balls	Runs	Wkts	BBI	BBM	Ave	Econ	SR	5w	10
Tests	38	-	-	-	-	-	-	-	-	-	-
ODIs	113	6	13	0	-	-	-	13.00	-	0	0
T20Is	23	-	-	-	-	-	-	-	-	-	-
First-class	122	385	277	7	3/12	-	39.57	4.31	55.0	0	0
List A	215	37	36	1	1/7	1/7	36.00	5.83	37.0	0	0
Twenty20	72	-	-	-	-	-	-	-	-	-	-

HARBHAJAN SINGH   RHB OB

NAME: Harbhajan Singh
BORN: July 3, 1980, Jalandhar
CAREER: Test debut: 1998; ODI debut: 1998; T20I debut: 2006; First-class debut: 1997; List A debut: 1998; T20 debut: 2005

AOC SAYS: Harbhajan is an attacking offspinner and a fiery character. He made his name by inspiring India's remarkable Test series win over Australia in 2001 with 28 wickets in two matches and remains a dangerous proposition in all formats with his nagging line and devastating doosra.

	Mat	Inns	NO	Runs	HS	Ave	SR	100	50	Ct	St
Tests	93	129	21	2008	115	18.59	65.25	2	8	42	0
ODIs	225	121	33	1143	49	12.84	81.06	0	0	67	0
T20Is	22	9	2	84	21	12.00	112.00	0	0	6	0
First-class	157	210	38	3416	115	19.86	-	2	12	75	0
List A	275	152	41	1485	49	13.37	-	0	0	86	0
Twenty20	70	39	12	405	49*	15.00	143.61	0	0	20	0

	Mat	Balls	Runs	Wkts	BBI	BBM	Ave	Econ	SR	5w	10
Tests	93	26483	12518	393	8/84	15/217	31.85	2.83	67.3	25	5
ODIs	225	11819	8494	254	5/31	5/31	33.44	4.31	46.5	3	0
T20Is	22	480	516	16	3/30	3/30	32.25	6.45	30.0	0	0
First-class	157	40422	19039	670	8/84	-	28.41	2.82	60.3	39	7
List A	275	14311	10206	322	5/31	5/31	31.69	4.27	44.4	3	0
Twenty20	70	1446	1592	61	4/17	4/17	26.09	6.60	23.7	0	0

RAVINDRA JADEJA   LHB SLA

NAME: Ravindrasinh Anirudhsinh Jadeja
BORN: December 6, 1988, Navagam-Khed
CAREER: ODI debut: 2009; T20I debut: 2009; First-class debut: 2006; List A debut: 2006; T20 debut: 2007

AOC SAYS: The promising allrounder was selected for India's ODI side on the back of some fine performances in the IPL for Rajasthan Royals and made 61* on debut against Sri Lanka. He has since slipped down the pecking order but remains an exciting prospect.

	Mat	Inns	NO	Runs	HS	Ave	SR	100	50	Ct	St
ODIs	35	22	5	535	61*	31.47	76.97	0	4	11	0
T20Is	9	6	2	65	25	16.25	86.66	0	0	5	0
First-class	34	51	4	1939	232*	41.25	55.71	4	10	29	0
List A	72	52	15	1123	70	30.35	83.12	0	8	27	0
Twenty20	40	31	6	549	42	21.96	113.66	0	0	17	0

	Mat	Balls	Runs	Wkts	BBI	BBM	Ave	Econ	SR	5w	10
ODIs	35	1534	1245	29	4/32	4/32	42.93	4.86	52.8	0	0
T20Is	9	186	232	5	2/26	2/26	46.40	7.48	37.2	0	0
First-class	34	7232	3008	102	7/31	10/88	29.49	2.49	70.9	7	1
List A	72	3194	2369	80	4/8	4/8	29.61	4.45	39.9	0	0
Twenty20	40	393	485	13	3/15	3/15	37.30	7.40	30.2	0	0

DINESH KARTHIK

RHB WK

INDIA

NAME: Krishnakumar Dinesh Karthik
BORN: June 1, 1985, Chennai
CAREER: Test debut: 2004; ODI debut: 2004; T20I debut: 2006; First-class debut: 2003; List A debut: 2003; T20 debut: 2006

AOC SAYS: Karthik lost his place as first-choice wicketkeeper to MS Dhoni in 2006 but is a strong enough batsman to have played as a specialist opener and remains India's back-up stumper. The Tamil Nadu skipper made 91 in the third Test at The Oval on the 2007 tour of England.

Batting & Fielding

	Mat	Inns	NO	Runs	HS	Ave	SR	100	50	Ct	St
Tests	23	37	1	1000	129	27.77	50.00	1	7	51	5
ODIs	52	44	7	1008	79	27.24	74.50	0	5	31	5
T20Is	9	8	2	100	31*	16.66	113.63	0	0	5	2
First-class	89	138	9	4906	213	38.03	58.93	13	24	231	20
List A	123	105	13	2911	154*	31.64	90.45	3	14	103	22
Twenty20	72	62	13	1184	90*	24.16	126.36	0	5	46	21

Bowling

	Mat	Balls	Runs	Wkts	BBI	BBM	Ave	Econ	SR	5w	10
Tests	23	-	-	-	-	-	-	-	-	-	-
ODIs	52	-	-	-	-	-	-	-	-	-	-
T20Is	9	-	-	-	-	-	-	-	-	-	-
First-class	89	114	125	0	-	-	-	6.57	-	0	0
List A	123	-	-	-	-	-	-	-	-	-	-
Twenty20	72	12	10	1	1/10	1/10	10.00	5.00	12.0	0	0

ZAHEER KHAN

RHB LFM

NAME: Zaheer Khan
BORN: October 7, 1978, Shrirampur
CAREER: Test debut: 2000; ODI debut: 2000; T20I debut: 2006; First-class debut: 1999; List A debut: 1999; T20 debut: 2006

AOC SAYS: A canny left-arm seamer who is a great exponent of reverse-swing, Zaheer has been the spearhead of India's pace attack for the best part of a decade. He starred in India's Test series win over England in 2007 and the wily old performer will prove a formidable opponent once again this summer.

Batting & Fielding

	Mat	Inns	NO	Runs	HS	Ave	SR	100	50	Ct	St
Tests	78	103	22	1045	75	12.90	50.36	0	3	18	0
ODIs	190	99	35	781	34*	12.20	73.47	0	0	42	0
T20Is	12	4	2	13	9	6.50	130.00	0	0	2	0
First-class	142	185	37	2079	75	14.04	-	0	4	42	0
List A	243	127	43	1036	42	12.33	-	0	0	56	0
Twenty20	60	31	18	136	26	10.46	100.00	0	0	14	0

Bowling

	Mat	Balls	Runs	Wkts	BBI	BBM	Ave	Econ	SR	5w	10
Tests	78	15756	8658	271	7/87	10/149	31.94	3.29	58.1	10	1
ODIs	190	9557	7814	271	5/42	5/42	28.83	4.90	35.2	1	0
T20Is	12	250	327	13	4/19	4/19	25.15	7.84	19.2	0	0
First-class	142	29238	16180	590	9/138	-	27.42	3.32	49.5	32	8
List A	243	12205	9917	346	5/42	5/42	28.66	4.87	35.2	1	0
Twenty20	60	1314	1693	61	4/19	4/19	27.75	7.73	21.5	0	0

VIRAT KOHLI   RHB RM

NAME: Virat Kohli
BORN: November 5, 1988, Delhi
CAREER: ODI debut: 2008; T20I debut: 2010; First-class debut: 2006;
List A debut: 2006; T20 debut: 2007

AOC SAYS: Kohli is arguably world cricket's most exciting young batsman. The former India under 19 captain oozes class and confidence at the crease and after already making his mark in ODIs, it is surely just a matter of time before he makes a Test spot his own in India's middle-order.

	Mat	Inns	NO	Runs	HS	Ave	SR	100	50	Ct	St
ODIs	53	50	7	1919	118	44.62	82.36	5	13	23	0
T20Is	3	2	1	54	28	54.00	135.00	0	0	1	0
First-class	30	44	7	2131	197	57.59	57.86	7	8	27	0
List A	83	79	10	3199	124	46.36	86.67	9	19	38	0
Twenty20	62	53	8	1143	76	25.40	128.86	0	3	24	0

	Mat	Balls	Runs	Wkts	BBI	BBM	Ave	Econ	SR	5w	10
ODIs	53	64	66	0	-	-	-	6.18	-	0	0
T20Is	3	-	-	-	-	-	-	-	-	-	-
First-class	30	468	254	3	1/19	2/42	84.66	3.25	156.0	0	0
List A	83	122	118	0	-	-	-	5.80	-	0	0
Twenty20	62	150	219	2	2/25	2/25	109.50	8.76	75.0	0	0

PRAVEEN KUMAR   RHB RM

NAME: Praveenkumar Sakat Singh
BORN: October 2, 1986, Meerut
CAREER: ODI debut: 2007; T20I debut: 2008; First-class debut: 2005;
List A debut: 2005; T20 debut: 2007

AOC SAYS: A seamer who has excelled in limited-overs cricket, Praveen is a tireless workhorse capable of swinging the ball both ways and an expert on unresponsive subcontinent tracks. The Royal Challengers Bangalore paceman was ruled out of the 2011 World Cup due to an injured elbow.

	Mat	Inns	NO	Runs	HS	Ave	SR	100	50	Ct	St
ODIs	48	24	7	225	54*	13.23	85.22	0	1	11	0
T20Is	4	1	0	6	6	6.00	60.00	0	0	1	0
First-class	38	60	4	1430	98	25.53	74.47	0	8	6	0
List A	99	67	9	1225	64	21.12	100.24	0	5	19	0
Twenty20	55	31	8	315	76*	13.69	125.00	0	1	7	0

	Mat	Balls	Runs	Wkts	BBI	BBM	Ave	Econ	SR	5w	10
ODIs	48	2264	1914	57	4/31	4/31	33.57	5.07	39.7	0	0
T20Is	4	54	49	4	2/14	2/14	12.25	5.44	13.5	0	0
First-class	38	8518	3968	172	8/68	10/160	23.06	2.79	49.5	13	1
List A	99	4844	3765	143	5/32	5/32	26.32	4.66	33.8	2	0
Twenty20	55	1162	1481	50	3/18	3/18	29.62	7.64	23.2	0	0

VINAY KUMAR

RHB RFM

INDIA

NAME: Ranganath Vinay Kumar
BORN: February 12, 1984, Davanagere
CAREER: ODI debut: 2010; T20I debut: 2010; First-class debut: 2004;
List A debut: 2005; T20 debut: 2007

AOC SAYS: Vinay is a nagging seamer who relies on outswing and accuracy rather than pace to trouble batsmen. He received an ODI call-up last year on the back of some fine performances for Royal Challengers Bangalore but missed out on India's 2011 World Cup campaign, despite being named in the preliminary 30-man squad.

	Mat	Inns	NO	Runs	HS	Ave	SR	100	50	Ct	St
ODIs	2	-	-	-	-	-	-	-	-	1	0
T20Is	3	-	-	-	-	-	-	-	-	0	0
First-class	62	83	16	1047	51*	15.62	44.01	0	4	24	0
List A	53	32	9	481	82	20.91	91.61	0	2	15	0
Twenty20	51	26	8	185	25*	10.27	123.33	0	0	9	0

	Mat	Balls	Runs	Wkts	BBI	BBM	Ave	Econ	SR	5w	10
ODIs	2	102	122	2	2/51	2/51	61.00	7.17	51.0	0	0
T20Is	3	66	82	5	3/24	3/24	16.40	7.45	13.2	0	0
First-class	62	11503	5515	229	8/32	-	24.08	2.87	50.2	11	2
List A	53	2678	2120	85	4/24	4/24	24.94	4.74	31.5	0	0
Twenty20	51	986	1314	52	4/40	4/40	25.26	7.99	18.9	0	0

VVS LAXMAN

RHB OB

NAME: Vangipurappu Venkata Sai Laxman
BORN: November 1, 1974, Hyderabad
CAREER: Test debut: 1996; ODI debut: 1998; First-class debut: 1993;
List A debut: 1994; T20 debut: 2008

AOC SAYS: Laxman is a majestic middle-order batsman who lives up to his nickname – 'Very Very Special'. He has produced some of his finest Test innings when it has counted most against Australia but will look to improve upon a disappointing record against England this summer.

	Mat	Inns	NO	Runs	HS	Ave	SR	100	50	Ct	St
Tests	120	198	31	7903	281	47.32	49.35	16	49	122	0
ODIs	86	83	7	2338	131	30.76	71.23	6	10	39	0
First-class	251	406	51	18642	353	52.51	-	53	90	264	1
List A	173	166	19	5078	131	34.54	-	9	28	74	0
Twenty20	22	22	3	447	78*	23.52	115.80	0	3	4	0

	Mat	Balls	Runs	Wkts	BBI	BBM	Ave	Econ	SR	5w	10
Tests	120	324	126	2	1/2	1/2	63.00	2.33	162.0	0	0
ODIs	86	42	40	0	-	-	-	5.71	-	0	0
First-class	251	1835	754	22	3/11	-	34.27	2.46	83.4	0	0
List A	173	698	548	8	2/42	2/42	68.50	4.71	87.2	0	0
Twenty20	22	-	-	-	-	-	-	-	-	-	-

AMIT MISHRA

RHB LB

NAME: Amit Mishra
BORN: November 24, 1982, Delhi
CAREER: Test debut: 2008; ODI debut: 2003; T20I debut: 2010; First-class debut: 2000; List A debut: 2001; T20 debut: 2007

AOC SAYS: Mishra is a diminutive leggie who benefited from the retirement of Anil Kumble in 2008 to break into the Test side. The Delhi Daredevils spinner often operates in tandem with Harbhajan Singh on home soil but has found his opportunities restricted outside of the subcontinent.

	Mat	Inns	NO	Runs	HS	Ave	SR	100	50	Ct	St
Tests	10	13	2	205	50	18.63	60.11	0	1	6	0
ODIs	10	1	0	0	0	0.00	0.00	0	0	1	0
T20Is	1	-	-	-	-	-	-	-	-	0	0
First-class	101	136	20	2313	84	19.93	-	0	10	54	0
List A	84	58	19	501	45	12.84	-	0	0	25	0
Twenty20	53	30	9	334	49	15.90	107.39	0	0	14	0

	Mat	Balls	Runs	Wkts	BBI	BBM	Ave	Econ	SR	5w	10
Tests	10	2850	1429	36	5/71	7/106	39.69	3.00	79.1	1	0
ODIs	10	463	376	8	3/40	3/40	47.00	4.87	57.8	0	0
T20Is	1	24	21	1	1/21	1/21	21.00	5.25	24.0	0	0
First-class	101	21969	10668	381	6/66	-	28.00	2.91	57.6	19	1
List A	84	4355	3233	130	6/25	6/25	24.86	4.45	33.5	3	0
Twenty20	53	1175	1339	74	5/17	5/17	18.09	6.83	15.8	2	0

ASHISH NEHRA

RHB LMF

NAME: Ashish Nehra
BORN: April 29, 1979, Delhi
CAREER: Test debut: 1999; ODI debut: 2001; T20I debut: 2009; First-class debut: 1997; List A debut: 1997; T20 debut: 2008

AOC SAYS: After touring England as a 23-year-old, the left-arm seamer spent four years in the international wilderness before he was recalled to India's ODI side in 2009 on the back of creditable showings in the IPL. Nehra possesses a devastating inswinger and is now regarded as a limited-overs specialist.

	Mat	Inns	NO	Runs	HS	Ave	SR	100	50	Ct	St
Tests	17	25	11	77	19	5.50	30.07	0	0	5	0
ODIs	120	46	21	141	24	5.64	57.31	0	0	18	0
T20Is	8	3	0	22	22	7.33	137.50	0	0	3	0
First-class	78	92	30	515	43	8.30	-	0	0	24	0
List A	177	75	32	342	24	7.95	-	0	0	26	0
Twenty20	42	11	6	49	22*	9.80	98.00	0	0	15	0

	Mat	Balls	Runs	Wkts	BBI	BBM	Ave	Econ	SR	5w	10
Tests	17	3447	1866	44	4/72	6/117	42.40	3.24	78.3	0	0
ODIs	120	5751	4981	157	6/23	6/23	31.72	5.19	36.6	2	0
T20Is	8	186	274	13	3/19	3/19	21.07	8.83	14.3	0	0
First-class	78	14829	7677	257	7/14	-	29.87	3.10	57.7	12	4
List A	177	8548	7093	220	6/23	6/23	32.24	4.97	38.8	2	0
Twenty20	42	906	1130	50	3/13	3/13	22.60	7.48	18.1	0	0

PRAGYAN OJHA

LHB SLA

INDIA

NAME: Pragyan Prayash Ojha
BORN: September 5, 1986, Khurda
CAREER: Test debut: 2009; ODI debut: 2008; T20I debut: 2009; First-class debut: 2005; List A debut: 2006; T20 debut: 2007

AOC SAYS: Having broken into India's ODI side after excelling for Deccan Chargers in the IPL, the left-arm spinner made his Test bow against Sri Lanka in 2009. He showed early promise but has since fallen out of favour and was surprisingly overlooked for the 2011 World Cup.

	Mat	Inns	NO	Runs	HS	Ave	SR	100	50	Ct	St
Tests	11	13	9	67	18*	16.75	20.87	0	0	3	0
ODIs	16	9	8	41	16*	41.00	43.61	0	0	7	0
T20Is	6	1	1	10	10*	-	166.66	0	0	1	0
First-class	50	66	25	441	35	10.75	30.96	0	0	18	0
List A	59	36	19	164	20	9.64	-	0	0	19	0
Twenty20	57	19	10	32	11*	3.55	91.42	0	0	11	0

	Mat	Balls	Runs	Wkts	BBI	BBM	Ave	Econ	SR	5w	10
Tests	11	3539	1697	42	4/107	7/204	40.40	2.87	84.2	0	0
ODIs	16	835	601	20	4/38	4/38	30.05	4.31	41.7	0	0
T20Is	6	126	132	10	4/21	4/21	13.20	6.28	12.6	0	0
First-class	50	12213	5989	201	7/114	-	29.79	2.94	60.7	10	0
List A	59	3077	2257	72	5/21	5/21	31.34	4.40	42.7	1	0
Twenty20	57	1190	1371	73	4/21	4/21	18.78	6.91	16.3	0	0

MUNAF PATEL

RHB RMF

NAME: Munaf Musa Patel
BORN: July 12, 1983, Ikhar
CAREER: Test debut: 2006; ODI debut: 2006; T20I debut: 2011; First-class debut: 2003; List A debut: 2003; T20 debut: 2008

AOC SAYS: An upright paceman with shades of Glenn McGrath about him, Patel was touted as an international prospect from an early age. He does not possess devastating pace but can move the ball both ways and is likely to form part of India's pace attack in this summer's Test series.

	Mat	Inns	NO	Runs	HS	Ave	SR	100	50	Ct	St
Tests	12	13	5	56	15*	7.00	40.87	0	0	6	0
ODIs	61	27	16	74	15	6.72	66.07	0	0	11	0
T20Is	1	-	-	-	-	-	-	0	0	0	0
First-class	52	60	20	607	78	15.17	70.41	0	1	13	0
List A	107	44	22	166	28	7.54	-	0	0	27	0
Twenty20	32	9	5	37	23*	9.25	115.62	0	0	7	0

	Mat	Balls	Runs	Wkts	BBI	BBM	Ave	Econ	SR	5w	10
Tests	12	2394	1230	34	4/25	7/97	36.17	3.08	70.4	0	0
ODIs	61	2760	2242	76	4/29	4/29	29.50	4.87	36.3	0	0
T20Is	1	12	26	1	1/26	1/26	26.00	13.00	12.0	0	0
First-class	52	9400	4461	191	6/50	-	23.35	2.84	49.2	7	1
List A	107	4943	3824	134	4/21	4/21	28.53	4.64	36.8	0	0
Twenty20	32	647	826	34	3/17	3/17	24.29	7.65	19.0	0	0

YUSUF PATHAN   RHB OB

NAME: Yusuf Khan Pathan
BORN: November 17, 1982, Baroda
CAREER: ODI debut: 2008; T20I debut: 2007; First-class debut: 2001;
List A debut: 2005; T20 debut: 2007

INDIA

AOC SAYS: A muscular allrounder, Pathan is one of the most ferocious hitters of a cricket ball in the world game, as demonstrated by his 70-ball 105 against South Africa in January. The Rajasthan Royal is also a handy offspinner and a key member of India's limited-overs sides.

	Mat	Inns	NO	Runs	HS	Ave	SR	100	50	Ct	St
ODIs	51	37	11	768	123*	29.53	115.14	2	3	16	0
T20Is	19	16	4	211	37*	17.58	147.55	0	0	9	0
First-class	46	74	9	2690	210*	41.38	94.38	7	11	45	0
List A	118	99	19	2714	148	33.92	120.83	6	13	44	0
Twenty20	74	70	8	1526	100	24.61	163.20	1	9	29	0

	Mat	Balls	Runs	Wkts	BBI	BBM	Ave	Econ	SR	5w	10
ODIs	51	1328	1210	31	3/49	3/49	39.03	5.46	42.8	0	0
T20Is	19	257	373	12	2/22	2/22	31.08	8.70	21.4	0	0
First-class	46	8109	3727	120	6/47	-	31.05	2.75	67.5	10	2
List A	118	4056	3394	84	5/52	5/52	40.40	5.02	48.2	2	0
Twenty20	74	1062	1382	54	4/10	4/10	25.59	7.80	19.6	0	0

CHETESHWAR PUJARA   RHB LB

NAME: Cheteshwar Arvind Pujara
BORN: January 25, 1988, Rajkot
CAREER: Test debut: 2010; First-class debut: 2005; List A debut: 2006;
T20 debut: 2007

AOC SAYS: Earmarked as a top-order batsman with a big future, Pujara showed his talent with a swashbuckling 72 on Test debut to take India to victory over Australia in Bangalore last year. The Kolkata Knight Rider is Rahul Dravid's heir apparent as India's next Test No.3.

	Mat	Inns	NO	Runs	HS	Ave	SR	100	50	Ct	St
Tests	3	5	0	107	72	21.40	51.69	0	1	6	0
First-class	56	89	15	4130	302*	55.81	-	14	15	33	0
List A	50	50	11	2078	122*	53.28	78.38	6	13	16	0
Twenty20	18	14	3	270	45*	24.54	112.03	0	0	9	0

	Mat	Balls	Runs	Wkts	BBI	BBM	Ave	Econ	SR	5w	10
Tests	3	-	-	-	-	-	-	-	-	-	-
First-class	56	153	83	5	2/4	2/4	16.60	3.25	30.6	0	0
List A	50	-	-	-	-	-	-	-	-	-	-
Twenty20	18	-	-	-	-	-	-	-	-	-	-

SURESH RAINA   LHB OB

NAME: Suresh Kumar Raina
BORN: November 27, 1986, Muradnagar
CAREER: Test debut: 2010; ODI debut: 2005; T20I debut: 2006; First-class debut: 2003; List A debut: 2005; T20 debut: 2006

AOC SAYS: The middle-order strokemaker made his ODI debut at 19 and, after 98 matches in that format, finally made his Test bow against Sri Lanka last year. He promptly became the 12th Indian to make a ton on Test debut but has since been found out against the short ball.

Batting & Fielding

	Mat	Inns	NO	Runs	HS	Ave	SR	100	50	Ct	St
Tests	8	12	1	373	120	33.90	57.20	1	2	9	0
ODIs	114	96	20	2713	116*	35.69	89.83	3	16	49	0
T20Is	19	18	3	509	101	33.93	140.99	1	3	5	0
First-class	59	98	4	4057	203	43.15	59.74	7	27	63	0
List A	157	138	24	4228	129	37.08	91.91	4	28	64	0
Twenty20	71	68	12	2087	101	37.26	144.03	1	14	36	0

Bowling

	Mat	Balls	Runs	Wkts	BBI	BBM	Ave	Econ	SR	5w	10
Tests	8	330	214	6	2/1	2/1	35.66	3.89	55.0	0	0
ODIs	112	482	430	8	1/12	1/12	53.75	5.35	60.2	0	0
T20Is	19	24	39	1	1/6	1/6	39.00	9.75	24.0	0	0
First-class	59	1260	617	18	3/31		34.27	2.93	70.0	0	0
List A	155	1182	994	26	4/23	4/23	38.23	5.04	45.4	0	0
Twenty20	71	389	449	20	4/26	4/26	22.45	6.92	19.4	0	0

VIRENDER SEHWAG   RHB OB

NAME: Virender Sehwag
BORN: October 20, 1978, Delhi
CAREER: Test debut: 2001; ODI debut: 1999; T20I debut: 2006; First-class debut: 1998; List A debut: 1998; T20 debut: 2003

AOC SAYS: The stocky opener is the most destructive batsman of his generation. Sehwag relentlessly takes the attack to the bowlers, whatever the format, and came within seven runs of becoming the first player to register three Test triple centuries during a Test against Sri Lanka in 2009.

Batting & Fielding

	Mat	Inns	NO	Runs	HS	Ave	SR	100	50	Ct	St
Tests	87	150	6	7694	319	53.43	81.91	22	27	67	0
ODIs	235	229	9	7760	175	35.27	104.10	14	37	86	0
T20Is	14	13	0	313	68	24.07	153.43	0	2	1	0
First-class	151	251	10	12199	319	50.61	-	36	45	126	0
List A	305	294	14	9713	175	34.68	-	15	54	110	0
Twenty20	66	65	4	1609	94*	26.37	159.30	0	11	10	0

Bowling

	Mat	Balls	Runs	Wkts	BBI	BBM	Ave	Econ	SR	5w	10
Tests	87	3249	1643	39	5/104	5/118	42.12	3.03	83.3	1	0
ODIs	235	4230	3716	92	4/6	4/6	40.39	5.27	45.9	0	0
T20Is	14	6	20	0	-	-	-	20.00	-	0	0
First-class	151	7988	4143	104	5/104		39.83	3.11	76.8	1	0
List A	305	5835	5009	138	4/6	4/6	36.29	5.15	42.2	0	0
Twenty20	66	292	393	19	3/14	3/14	20.68	8.07	15.3	0	0

RHB RFM

NAME: Ishant Sharma
BORN: September 2, 1988, Delhi
CAREER: Test debut: 2007; ODI debut: 2007; T20I debut: 2008; First-class debut: 2006; List A debut: 2006; T20 debut: 2007

INDIA

AOC SAYS: Sharma is a young paceman with a fluent, classical action who burst onto the scene in 2007 after giving Ricky Ponting the run-around with his natural pace and bounce. He has found the going tough over the last year but retains all the raw ingredients to test the very best.

	Mat	Inns	NO	Runs	HS	Ave	SR	100	50	Ct	St
Tests	31	43	19	319	31*	13.29	29.56	0	0	10	0
ODIs	45	14	6	47	13	5.87	35.33	0	0	11	0
T20Is	11	2	2	8	5*	-	100.00	0	0	2	0
First-class	53	64	30	384	31*	11.29	29.56	0	0	16	0
List A	65	21	11	111	31	11.10	54.41	0	0	13	0
Twenty20	46	14	10	41	9	10.25	83.67	0	0	4	0

	Mat	Balls	Runs	Wkts	BBI	BBM	Ave	Econ	SR	5w	10
Tests	31	5644	3238	90	5/118	7/58	35.97	3.44	62.7	1	0
ODIs	45	2035	1947	63	4/38	4/38	30.90	5.74	32.3	0	0
T20Is	11	206	291	6	2/34	2/34	48.50	8.47	34.3	0	0
First-class	53	9779	5264	174	7/24	11/51	30.25	3.22	56.2	3	1
List A	65	3054	2729	97	4/25	4/25	28.13	5.36	31.4	0	0
Twenty20	46	957	1248	32	2/15	2/15	39.00	7.82	29.9	0	0

RHB OB

NAME: Rohit Gurunath Sharma
BORN: April 30, 1987, Nagpur
CAREER: ODI debut: 2007; T20I debut: 2007; First-class debut: 2006; List A debut: 2006; T20 debut: 2007

AOC SAYS: A prodigiously talented middle-order batsman, Sharma is yet to reproduce his prolific domestic form on the international stage. A majestic ODI ton against Sri Lanka last year showed a glimpse of his potential but he paid the price for his inconsistency when he was axed from India's 2011 World Cup squad.

	Mat	Inns	NO	Runs	HS	Ave	SR	100	50	Ct	St
ODIs	61	57	11	1248	114	27.13	75.72	2	5	24	0
T20Is	20	17	6	388	79*	35.27	128.90	0	4	7	0
First-class	43	64	8	3409	309*	60.87	-	10	15	29	0
List A	119	112	17	3106	142*	32.69	81.33	5	14	45	0
Twenty20	80	76	15	2019	101*	33.09	132.56	1	12	32	0

	Mat	Balls	Runs	Wkts	BBi	BBM	Ave	Econ	SR	5w	10
ODIs	61	329	265	6	2/27	2/27	44.16	4.83	54.8	0	0
T20Is	20	30	37	1	1/22	1/22	37.00	7.40	30.0	0	0
First-class	43	864	482	10	3/23	3/76	48.20	3.34	86.4	0	0
List A	119	1025	844	26	4/28	4/28	32.46	4.94	39.4	0	0
Twenty20	80	504	602	26	4/6	4/6	23.15	7.16	19.3	0	0

SREESANTH

INDIA

NAME: Shanthakumaran Sreesanth
BORN: February 6, 1983, Kothamangalam
CAREER: Test debut: 2006; ODI debut: 2005; T20I debut: 2006; First-class debut: 2002; List A debut: 2002; T20 debut: 2006

AOC SAYS: Sreesanth is a charismatic and temperamental fast bowler who revels in the rough and tumble of Test cricket. He has the ability to produce unplayable deliveries but too often lets his temper get the better of him and is never far from controversy.

Batting & Fielding

	Mat	Inns	NO	Runs	HS	Ave	SR	100	50	Ct	St
Tests	24	34	11	263	35	11.43	52.91	0	0	5	0
ODIs	52	21	10	44	10*	4.00	36.36	0	0	7	0
T20Is	10	3	2	20	19*	20.00	142.85	0	0	2	0
First-class	64	85	26	573	35	9.71	44.55	0	0	14	0
List A	81	36	15	127	33	6.04	44.56	0	0	9	0
Twenty20	44	14	9	71	19*	14.20	86.58	0	0	8	0

Bowling

	Mat	Balls	Runs	Wkts	BBI	BBM	Ave	Econ	SR	5w	10
Tests	24	4753	2778	79	5/40	8/99	35.16	3.50	60.1	3	0
ODIs	52	2428	2456	75	6/55	6/55	32.74	6.06	32.3	1	0
T20Is	10	204	288	7	2/12	2/12	41.14	8.47	29.1	0	0
First-class	64	11364	6498	191	5/40	-	34.02	3.43	59.4	6	0
List A	81	3826	3638	104	6/55	6/55	34.98	5.70	36.7	1	0
Twenty20	44	871	1270	38	3/29	3/29	33.42	8.74	22.9	0	0

SACHIN TENDULKAR

NAME: Sachin Ramesh Tendulkar
BORN: April 24, 1973, Mumbai
CAREER: Test debut: 1989; ODI debut: 1989; T20I debut: 2006; First-class debut: 1988; List A debut: 1989; T20 debut: 2006

AOC SAYS: A dream to watch. The Little Master is quite simply the finest batsman of the modern era and incredibly, he appears to have got better with age over a Test career spanning 22 years. The very definition of consistency, the middle-order maestro was named ICC Player of the Year in 2010 after a stunning season.

Batting & Fielding

	Mat	Inns	NO	Runs	HS	Ave	SR	100	50	Ct	St
Tests	177	290	32	14692	248*	56.94	-	51	59	106	0
ODIs	452	441	41	18093	200*	45.23	86.29	48	95	136	0
T20Is	1	1	0	10	10	10.00	83.33	0	0	1	0
First-class	280	442	48	23585	248*	59.86	-	78	105	174	0
List A	539	526	55	21645	200*	45.95	-	59	113	171	0
Twenty20	44	44	5	1516	89*	38.87	129.46	0	11	19	0

Bowling

	Mat	Balls	Runs	Wkts	BBI	BBM	Ave	Econ	SR	5w	10
Tests	177	4096	2388	45	3/10	3/14	53.06	3.49	91.0	0	0
ODIs	452	8032	6826	154	5/32	5/32	44.32	5.09	52.1	2	0
T20Is	1	15	12	1	1/12	1/12	12.00	4.80	15.0	0	0
First-class	280	7461	4280	70	3/10	-	61.14	3.44	106.5	0	0
List A	539	10208	8454	201	5/32	5/32	42.05	4.96	50.7	2	0
Twenty20	44	93	123	2	1/12	1/12	61.50	7.93	46.5	0	0

JAIDEV UNADKAT

RHB LFM

NAME: Jaidev Dipakbhai Unadkat
BORN: October 18, 1991, Porbandar
CAREER: Test debut: 2010; First-class debut: 2010; List A debut: 2010;
T20 debut: 2010

INDIA

AOC SAYS: Unadkat was thrust into international cricket after just a handful of first-class appearances, making his Test bow against South Africa last year. The left-arm seamer has been tipped by Wasim Akram as a player of vast talent and, if selected, will gain invaluable experience in English conditions this summer.

	Mat	Inns	NO	Runs	HS	Ave	SR	100	50	Ct	St
Tests	1	2	1	2	1*	2.00	13.33	0	0	0	0
First-class	10	12	7	55	15*	11.00	29.72	0	0	2	0
List A	16	8	3	33	14	6.60	45.83	0	0	3	0
Twenty20	7	2	1	2	2*	2.00	28.57	0	0	1	0

	Mat	Balls	Runs	Wkts	BBI	BBM	Ave	Econ	SR	5w	10
Tests	1	156	101	0	-	-	-	3.88	-	0	0
First-class	10	2148	1178	36	7/41	13/103	32.72	3.29	59.6	2	1
List A	16	798	602	22	3/14	3/14	27.36	4.52	36.2	0	0
Twenty20	7	150	170	14	3/10	3/10	12.14	6.80	10.7	0	0

MURALI VIJAY

RHB OB

NAME: Murali Vijay
BORN: April 1, 1984, Chennai
CAREER: Test debut: 2008; ODI debut: 2010; T20I debut: 2010; First-class debut: 2006; List A debut: 2006; T20 debut: 2007

AOC SAYS: A tall and stylish opening batsman, Vijay made his Test debut in trying conditions against Australia in 2008 and immediately showed his class. The Chennai Super Kings right-hander has since found his opportunities limited but remains an excellent back-up to established Test openers Gautam Gambhir and Virender Sehwag.

	Mat	Inns	NO	Runs	HS	Ave	SR	100	50	Ct	St
Tests	9	14	0	537	139	38.35	50.75	1	2	7	0
ODIs	11	11	0	196	33	17.81	61.82	0	0	6	0
T20Is	7	7	0	122	48	17.42	98.38	0	0	3	0
First-class	40	65	2	3237	243	51.38	49.47	8	14	41	0
List A	47	47	1	1841	115	40.02	78.54	6	6	25	0
Twenty20	45	43	2	1164	127	28.39	128.76	1	6	21	0

	Mat	Balls	Runs	Wkts	BBI	BBM	Ave	Econ	SR	5w	10
Tests	9	-	-	-	-	-	-	-	-	-	-
ODIs	11	-	-	-	-	-	-	-	-	-	-
T20Is	7	-	-	-	-	-	-	-	-	-	-
First-class	40	186	118	1	1/16	1/16	118.00	3.80	186.0	0	0
List A	47	209	184	7	3/13	3/13	26.28	5.28	29.8	0	0
Twenty20	45	6	4	0	-	-	-	4.00	-	0	0

UMESH YADAV RHB RFM

INDIA

NAME: Umesh Yadav
BORN: October 25, 1987, Nagpur
CAREER: ODI debut: 2010; First-class debut: 2008; List A debut: 2009;
T20 debut: 2009

AOC SAYS: Yadav has made a rapid ascent since making his first-class debut a little over two years ago. After impressing with his pace in the IPL for Delhi Daredevils, the right-arm seamer won a call-up for the 2010 World Twenty20 and was subsequently included in India's Test squad to tour South Africa over the winter.

Batting & Fielding	Mat	Inns	NO	Runs	HS	Ave	SR	100	50	Ct	St
ODIs	3	1	1	3	3*	-	100.00	0	0	1	0
First-class	19	24	15	111	24*	12.33	46.83	0	0	10	0
List A	19	13	10	65	13*	21.66	114.03	0	0	6	0
Twenty20	13	4	2	6	3*	3.00	60.00	0	0	4	0

Bowling	Mat	Balls	Runs	Wkts	BBI	BBM	Ave	Econ	SR	5w	10
ODIs	3	132	129	1	1/61	1/61	129.00	5.86	132.0	0	0
First-class	19	3184	1693	65	7/74	8/79	26.04	3.19	48.9	4	0
List A	19	859	749	18	3/40	3/40	41.61	5.23	47.7	0	0
Twenty20	13	271	357	10	2/24	2/24	35.70	7.90	27.1	0	0

YUVRAJ SINGH LHB SLA

NAME: Yuvraj Singh
BORN: December 12, 1981, Chandigarh
CAREER: Test debut: 2003; ODI debut: 2000; T20I debut: 2007; First-class debut: 1997; List A debut: 1999; T20 debut: 2003

AOC SAYS: Yuvraj is an explosive middle-order batsman and wily left-arm spinner with vast experience. The left-hander is a devastating strokemaker, as shown by his six sixes off one Stuart Broad over at the 2007 World Twenty20, but is yet to fully translate his prolific limited-overs record into the Test arena.

Batting & fielding	Mat	Inns	NO	Runs	HS	Ave	SR	100	50	Ct	St
Tests	34	52	6	1639	169	35.63	58.91	3	9	30	0
ODIs	273	251	36	8030	139	37.52	87.58	13	49	84	0
T20Is	23	22	4	567	70	31.50	151.60	0	5	6	0
First-class	95	152	18	6044	209	45.10	-	18	29	91	0
List A	343	316	47	10215	172	37.97	-	17	62	106	0
Twenty20	79	77	9	1787	71	26.27	136.10	0	10	21	0

Bowling	Mat	Balls	Runs	Wkts	BBI	BBM	Ave	Econ	SR	5w	10
Tests	34	751	431	8	2/9	2/20	53.87	3.44	93.8	0	0
ODIs	271	4652	3910	103	5/31	5/31	37.96	5.04	45.1	1	0
T20Is	23	144	194	8	3/23	3/23	24.25	8.08	18.0	0	0
First-class	95	1981	1083	20	3/25	-	54.15	3.28	99.0	0	0
List A	341	5721	4786	137	5/31	5/31	34.93	5.01	41.7	1	0
Twenty20	79	564	700	31	3/13	3/13	22.58	7.44	18.1	0	0

The
Umpires

ROB BAILEY

NAME: Robert John Bailey
BORN: October 28, 1963, Biddulph,
Stoke-on-Trent
HEIGHT: 6ft 3in
NICKNAME: Bailers
APPOINTED TO FIRST-CLASS LIST: 2006
COUNTIES AS PLAYER: Northamptonshire,
Derbyshire
ROLE: Right-hand bat, offspin bowler
COUNTY DEBUT: 1982 (Northants), 2000
(Derbyshire)
COUNTY CAP: 1985 (Northants), 2000
(Derbyshire)
TEST DEBUT: 1988
ODI DEBUT: 1985

NOTES: Officiated at Twenty20 Cup Finals Day 2008, 2009 and 2010, including the final.

Batting & Fielding

	Mat	Inns	NO	Runs	HS	Ave	SR	100	50	Ct	St
Tests	4	8	0	119	43	14.87	36.50	0	0	0	0
ODIs	4	4	2	137	43*	68.50	69.89	0	0	1	0
First-class	374	628	89	21844	224*	40.52	-	47	111	272	0
List A	396	376	65	12076	153*	38.82	-	10	79	111	0

Bowling

	Mat	Balls	Runs	Wkts	BBI	BBM	Ave	Econ	SR	5w	10
Tests	4	-	-	-	-	-	-	-	-	-	-
ODIs	4	36	25	0	-	-	-	4.16	-	0	0
First-class	374	9713	5144	121	5/54	-	42.51	3.17	80.2	2	0
List A	396	3092	-	-	-	-	-	-	-	-	-

NAME: Neil Laurence Bainton
BORN: October 2, 1970, Romford, Essex
HEIGHT: 5ft 8in
APPOINTED TO FIRST-CLASS LIST: 2006

UMPIRES

NOTES: Has been reserve umpire in two Tests, two ODIs and two T20Is, as well as umpiring in three women's ODIs.

EXTRAS

There are also ten umpires on the reserve list for 2011:

Paul Baldwin, Ismail Dawood, Mark Eggleston, Russell Evans, Andy Hicks, Graham Lloyd, Steve Malone, Martin Saggers, Billy Taylor and Alex Wharf.

MARK BENSON

NAME: Mark Richard Benson
BORN: July 6, 1958, Shoreham
HEIGHT: 5ft 10in
NICKNAME: Benny
APPOINTED TO FIRST-CLASS LIST: 2000
INTERNATIONAL PANEL: 2004-2006
ELITE PANEL: 2006-2010
TESTS UMPIRED: 27 (plus 9 as TV umpire)
ODIs UMPIRED: 72 (plus 25 as TV umpire)
T20Is UMPIRED: 19 (plus 6 as TV umpire)
COUNTY AS PLAYER: Kent
ROLE: Left-hand bat
COUNTY DEBUT: 1980
COUNTY CAP: 1981
TEST DEBUT: 1986
ODI DEBUT: 1986

NOTES: Stood in the C&G Trophy final in 2003. Umpired in the 2007 World Cup and the 2007 World Twenty20, including the final.

Batting & Fielding

	Mat	Inns	NO	Runs	HS	Ave	SR	100	50	Ct	St
Tests	1	2	0	51	30	25.50	31.48	0	0	0	0
ODIs	1	1	0	24	24	24.00	41.37	0	0	0	0
First-class	292	491	34	18387	257	40.23	-	48	99	140	0
List A	269	257	11	7838	119	31.86	-	5	53	68	0

Bowling

	Mat	Balls	Runs	Wkts	BBI	BBM	Ave	Econ	SR	5w	10
Tests	1	-	-	-	-	-	-	-	-	-	-
ODIs	1	-	-	-	-	-	-	-	-	-	-
First-class	292	467	493	5	2/55	-	98.60	6.33	93.4	0	0
List A	269	-	-	-	-	-	-	-	-	-	-

NAME: Martin John Dale Bodenham
BORN: 23 April 1950, Brighton
HEIGHT: 6ft 1in
APPOINTED TO FIRST-CLASS LIST: 2009
COUNTY AS PLAYER: 'Played for Sussex in a number of 2nd XI Championship matches'
ROLE: Batsman, wicket-keeper

UMPIRES

NOTES: He is the first man to referee in football's Premier League and umpire first-class cricket. As a ref, he was in charge of three FA Cup semis and the League Cup final in 1997, as well as being reserve referee for the European Cup final between AC Milan and Barcelona in 1994. In his career he sent off Vinnie Jones for threatening to break an opponent's legs and gave Roy Keane a yellow card while he was going off on a stretcher.

NICK COOK

NAME: Nicholas Grant Billson Cook
BORN: June17, 1956, Leicester
HEIGHT: 6ft
NICKNAME: Beast
APPOINTED TO FIRST-CLASS LIST: 2009
COUNTIES AS PLAYER: Leicestershire,
Northamptonshire
ROLE: Right-hand bat, slow left-arm bowler
COUNTY DEBUT: 1978 (Leics), 1986
(Northants)
COUNTY CAP: 1982 (Leics), 1987
(Northants)
TEST DEBUT: 1983
ODI DEBUT: 1984

Batting & Fielding

	Mat	Inns	NO	Runs	HS	Ave	SR	100	50	Ct	St
Tests	15	25	4	179	31	8.52	23.58	0	0	5	0
ODIs	3	-	-	-	-	-	-	-	-	2	0
First-class	356	365	96	3137	75	11.66	-	0	4	197	0
List A	223	89	36	491	23	9.26	-	0	0	74	0

Bowling

	Mat	Balls	Runs	Wkts	BBI	BBM	Ave	Econ	SR	5w	10
Tests	15	4174	1689	52	6/65	11/83	32.48	2.42	80.2	4	1
ODIs	3	144	95	5	2/18	2/18	19.00	3.95	28.8	0	0
First-class	356	64460	25507	879	7/34	-	29.01	2.37	73.3	31	4
List A	223	10077	6812	200	4/22	4/22	34.06	4.05	50.3	0	0

NIGEL COWLEY

NAME: Nigel Geoffrey Charles Cowley
BORN: March 1, 1953, Shaftesbury
HEIGHT: 5ft 6in
APPOINTED TO FIRST-CLASS LIST: 2000
COUNTIES AS PLAYER: Hampshire, Glamorgan
ROLE: Right-hand bat, offspin bowler
COUNTY DEBUT: 1974 (Hampshire), 1990 (Glamorgan)
COUNTY CAP: 1978 (Hampshire)

Batting & Fielding

	Mat	Inns	NO	Runs	HS	Ave	SR	100	50	Ct	St
First-class	271	375	62	7309	109*	23.35	-	2	36	105	0
List A	305	226	45	3022	74	16.69	-	0	5	69	0

Bowling

	Mat	Balls	Runs	Wkts	BBI	BBM	Ave	Econ	SR	5w	10
First-class	271	32662	14879	437	6/48		34.04	2.73	74.7	5	0
List A	305	11704	8038	248	5/24	5/24	32.41	4.12	47.1	1	0

JEFF EVANS

NAME: Jeffrey Howard Evans
BORN: August 7, 1954, Llanelli
HEIGHT: 5ft 8in
APPOINTED TO FIRST-CLASS LIST: 2001

NOTES: Played league cricket in south Wales as a right-hand bat.

UMPIRES

STEVE GALE

NAME: Stephen Clifford Gale
BORN: 3 June 1952, Shrewsbury
APPOINTED TO FIRST-CLASS LIST: 2011

NOTES: Gale has been promoted after spending three seasons on the reserve list following a playing career representing Shropshire in Minor Counties cricket between 1975 and 1987. He umpired the Second XI Knock Out final at Horsham and the Cockspur Twenty20 Cup Final at The Rose Bowl in 2010.

STEVE GARRATT

NAME: Stephen Arthur Garratt
BORN: July 5, 1953, Nottingham
HEIGHT: 6ft 2in
NICKNAME: Trigger
APPOINTED TO FIRST-CLASS LIST: 2008

NOTES: Garratt is a retired police officer.

MICHAEL GOUGH

NAME: Michael Andrew Gough
BORN: December 18, 1979, Hartlepool
HEIGHT: 6ft 5in
NICKNAME: Goughy
APPOINTED TO FIRST-CLASS LIST: 2009
COUNTIES AS PLAYER: Durham
ROLE: Right-hand bat; right-arm offspin bowler
COUNTY DEBUT: 1998

UMPIRES

NOTES: Gough started umpiring in 2005 after retirement from the first-class game; he was appointed to the ECB reserve list in 2006. He is believed to be the youngest first-class umpire in the history of the game.

Batting & Fielding

	Mat	Inns	NO	Runs	HS	Ave	SR	100	50	Ct	St
First-class	67	119	3	2952	123	25.44	-		2	15	57	0
List A	49	45	4	974	132	23.75	-		1	3	14	0

Bowling

	Mat	Balls	Runs	Wkts	BBI	BBM	Ave	Econ	SR	5w	10
First-class	67	2486	1350	30	5/66	-	45.00	3.25	82.8	1	0
List A	49	1136	947	21	3/26	3/26	45.09	5.00	54.0	0	0

IAN GOULD

NAME: Ian James Gould
BORN: August 19, 1957, Taplow
HEIGHT: 5ft 7in
NICKNAME: Gunner
APPOINTED TO FIRST-CLASS LIST: 2002
INTERNATIONAL PANEL: 2006-
ELITE PANEL: 2010-
TESTS UMPIRED: 18 (plus 9 as TV umpire and 4 as reserve umpire)
ODIs UMPIRED: 55 (plus 17 as TV umpire and 17 as reseve umpire)
T20Is UMPIRED: 15 (plus 8 as TV umpire and 4 as reserve umpire)
COUNTIES AS PLAYER: Middlesex, Sussex
ROLE: Left-hand bat, wicketkeeper
COUNTY DEBUT: 1975 (Middlesex), 1981 (Sussex)
COUNTY CAP: 1977 (Middlesex), 1981 (Sussex)
ODI DEBUT: 1983

NOTES: Officiated at the Twenty20 Finals Day at Edgbaston in 2004 and at The Oval in 2005, including standing in both finals, and again at Edgbaston in 2009. PCA Umpire of the Year 2005, 2007. Umpired in the 2007 World Cup. Stood in the Friends Provident Trophy final at Lord's in 2007.

Batting & Fielding

	Mat	Inns	NO	Runs	HS	Ave	SR	100	50	Ct	St
ODIs	18	14	2	155	42	12.91	63.78	0	0	15	3
First-class	298	399	63	8756	128	26.05	-	4	47	536	67
List A	315	270	41	4377	88	19.11	-	0	20	242	37

Bowling

	Mat	Balls	Runs	Wkts	BBI	BBM	Ave	Econ	SR	5w	10
ODIs	18	-	-	-	-	-	-	-	-	-	-
First-class	298	478	365	7	3/10	-	52.14	4.58	68.2	0	0
List A	315	20	16	1	1/0	1/0	16.00	4.80	20.0	0	0

NAME: Name: Peter John Hartley
BORN: April 18, 1960, Keighley
HEIGHT: 6ft
NICKNAME: Jack
APPOINTED TO FIRST-CLASS LIST: 2003
INTERNATIONAL PANEL: 2006-
TESTS UMPIRED: 9 as TV umpire and 4 as reserve umpire
ODIs UMPIRED: 7 (plus 10 as TV umpire and 11 as reserve umpire)
T20Is UMPIRED: 5 (plus 3 as TV umpire)
COUNTIES AS PLAYER: Warwickshire, Yorkshire, Hampshire
ROLE: Right-hand bat, right-arm fast-medium bowler
COUNTY DEBUT: 1982 (Warwickshire), 1985 (Yorkshire), 1998 (Hampshire)
COUNTY CAP: 1987 (Yorkshire), 1998 (Hampshire)

UMPIRES

NOTES: Officiated at Twenty20 Finals Day in 2006 at Trent Bridge, including standing in the final. Umpired the FP Trophy final in 2007, the Under 19 World Cup final 2008 in Malaysia and the 2010 Pro40 final.

Batting & Fielding

	Mat	Inns	NO	Runs	HS	Ave	SR	100	50	Ct	St
First-class	232	283	66	4321	127*	19.91	-	2	14	68	0
List A	269	170	62	1765	83	16.34	-	0	4	46	0

Bowling

	Mat	Balls	Runs	Wkts	BBI	BBM	Ave	Econ	SR	5w	10
First-class	232	37108	20635	683	9/41	-	30.21	3.33	54.3	23	3
List A	269	12636	-	-	-	-	-	-	-	-	-

RICHARD ILLINGWORTH

NAME: Richard Keith Illingworth
BORN: August 23, 1963, Greengates, nr Bradford
HEIGHT: 5ft 11in
NICKNAME: Harry, Lucy
APPOINTED TO FIRST-CLASS LIST: 2006
COUNTIES AS PLAYER: Worcestershire, Derbyshire
ROLE: Right-hand bat, slow left-arm bowler
COUNTY DEBUT: 1982 (Worcestershire), 2001 (Derbyshire)
COUNTY CAP: 1986 (Worcestershire)
TEST DEBUT: 1991
ODI DEBUT: 1991

NOTES: Stood at Twenty20 Finals Day in 2008, 2009 and 2010, including the final in the latter two years.

Batting & Fielding

	Mat	Inns	NO	Runs	HS	Ave	SR	100	50	Ct	St
Tests	9	14	7	128	28	18.28	32.08	0	0	5	0
ODIs	25	11	5	68	14	11.33	57.14	0	0	8	0
First-class	376	435	122	7027	120*	22.45	-	4	21	161	0
List A	381	185	87	1458	53*	14.87	-	0	1	93	0

Bowling

	Mat	Balls	Runs	Wkts	BBI	BBM	Ave	Econ	SR	5w	10
Tests	9	1485	615	19	4/96	6/150	32.36	2.48	78.1	0	0
ODIs	25	1501	1059	30	3/33	3/33	35.30	4.23	50.0	0	0
First-class	376	65868	26213	831	7/50	-	31.54	2.38	79.2	27	6
List A	381	16918	11157	412	5/24	5/24	27.08	3.95	41.0	2	0

NAME: Trevor Edward Jesty
BORN: June 2, 1948, Gosport
HEIGHT: 5ft 9in
NICKNAME: Jets
APPOINTED TO FIRST-CLASS LIST: 1994
TEST UMPIRED: 4 as reserve umpire
ODIs UMPIRED: 3 as TV umpire and 1 as reserve umpire
T20Is UMPIRED: 1 as reserve umpire
COUNTIES AS PLAYER: Hampshire, Surrey, Lancashire
ROLE: Right-hand bat, right-arm medium bowler
COUNTY DEBUT: 1966 (Hampshire), 1985 (Surrey), 1988 (Lancashire)
COUNTY CAP: 1971 (Hampshire), 1985 (Surrey), 1990 (Lancashire)
ODI DEBUT: 1983

UMPIRES

Batting & Fielding

	Mat	Inns	NO	Runs	HS	Ave	SR	100	50	Ct	St
ODIs	10	10	4	127	52*	21.16	69.78	0	1	5	0
First-class	490	777	107	21916	248	32.71	-	35	110	265	1
List A	428	394	54	9216	166*	27.10	-	7	46	106	0

Bowling

	Mat	Balls	Runs	Wkts	BBI	BBM	Ave	Econ	SR	5w	10
ODIs	10	108	93	1	1/23	1/23	93.00	5.16	108.0	0	0
First-class	490	36864	16075	585	7/75	-	27.47	2.61	63.0	19	0
List A	428	13309	9283	372	6/20	6/20	24.95	4.18	35.7	5	0

RICHARD KETTLEBOROUGH

UMPIRES

NAME: Richard Allan Kettleborough
BORN: March 15, 1973, Sheffield
HEIGHT: 5ft 10in
NICKNAME: Ketts
APPOINTED TO FIRST-CLASS LIST: 2006
INTERNATIONAL PANEL: 2008-
TESTS UMPIRED: 2 (plus 4 as TV umpire
and 2 as reserve umpire)
ODIs UMPIRED: 15 (plus 12 as TV umpire
and 8 as reserve umpire)
T20Is UMPIRED: 2 (plus 4 as TV umpire and
1 as reserve umpire)
COUNTIES AS PLAYER: Yorkshire, Middlesex
ROLE: Left-hand bat
COUNTY DEBUT: 1994 (Yorkshire), 1998
(Middlesex)

NOTES: Stood in the International 20:20 Club Championship in 2005. Stood at Twenty20
Finals Day at Edgbaston 2009, including the final, and umpired the CB40 final in 2010.

Batting & Fielding

	Mat	Inns	NO	Runs	HS	Ave	SR	100	50	Ct	St
First-class	33	56	6	1258	108	25.16	-	1	7	20	0
List A	21	16	4	290	58	24.16	-	0	1	6	0

Bowling

	Mat	Balls	Runs	Wkts	BBI	BBM	Ave	Econ	SR	5w	10
First-class	33	378	243	3	2/26	-	81.00	3.85	126.0	0	0
List A	21	270	-	-	-	-	-	-	-	-	-

NIGEL LLONG

NAME: Nigel James Llong
BORN: February 11, 1969, Ashford, Kent
HEIGHT: 6ft
NICKNAME: Nidge
APPOINTED TO FIRST-CLASS LIST: 2002
INTERNATIONAL PANEL: 2004-2006 as TV umpire; 2006-
TESTS UMPIRED: 9 (plus 12 as TV umpire and 1 as reserve umpire)
ODIs UMPIRED: 46 (plus 26 as TV umpire and 14 as reserve umpire)
T20Is UMPIRED: 15 (plus 6 as TV umpire and 3 as reserve umpire)
COUNTY AS PLAYER: Kent
ROLE: Left-hand bat, right-arm offspin bowler
COUNTY DEBUT: 1991
COUNTY CAP: 1993

UMPIRES

NOTES: Officiated at Twenty20 Finals Day at Edgbaston in 2004, including standing in the final, and again in 2007, 2009 and 2010. Umpired at 2007 World Twenty20 in South Africa.

Batting & Fielding											
	Mat	Inns	NO	Runs	HS	Ave	SR	100	50	Ct	St
First-class	68	108	11	3024	130	31.17	-	6	16	59	0
List A	136	115	24	2302	123	25.29	-	2	8	41	0

Bowling											
	Mat	Balls	Runs	Wkts	BBI	BBM	Ave	Econ	SR	5w	10
First-class	68	2273	1259	35	5/21	-	35.97	3.32	64.9	2	0
List A	136	1317	1210	40	4/24	4/24	30.25	5.51	32.9	0	0

JEREMY LLOYDS

NAME: Jeremy William Lloyds
BORN: November 17, 1954, Penang, Malaysia
HEIGHT: 5ft 11in
NICKNAME: Jerry
APPOINTED TO FIRST-CLASS LIST: 1998
INTERNATIONAL PANEL: 2002-2004 as TV umpire; 2004-2006
TESTS UMPIRED: 5 (plus 10 as TV umpire and 5 as reserve umpire)
ODIs UMPIRED: 18 (plus 22 as TV umpire and 7 as reserve umpire)
T20Is UMPIRED: 1
COUNTIES AS PLAYER: Somerset, Gloucestershire
ROLE: Left-hand bat, offspin bowler
COUNTY DEBUT: 1979 (Somerset), 1985 (Gloucestershire)
COUNTY CAP: 1982 (Somerset), 1985 (Gloucestershire)

NOTES: Stood in the C&G final in 2006. Officiated at Twenty20 Finals Day in 2007 and 2008.

Batting & Fielding

	Mat	Inns	NO	Runs	HS	Ave	SR	100	50	Ct	St
First-class	267	408	64	10679	132*	31.04	-	10	62	229	0
List A	177	150	26	1982	73*	15.98	-	0	5	58	0

Bowling

	Mat	Balls	Runs	Wkts	BBI	BBM	Ave	Econ	SR	5w	10
First-class	267	24175	12943	333	7/88	-	38.86	3.21	72.5	13	1
List A	177	1522	1129	26	3/14	3/14	43.42	4.45	58.5	0	0

NAME: Neil Alan Mallender
BORN: August 13, 1961, Kirk Sandall, Doncaster
HEIGHT: 6ft
NICKNAME: Ghostie
APPOINTED TO FIRST-CLASS LIST: 1999
INTERNATIONAL PANEL: 2002-2004
TESTS UMPIRED: 3 (plus 5 as TV umpire and 4 as reserve umpire)
ODIs UMPIRED: 22 (plus 10 as TV umpire and 2 as reserve umpire)
COUNTIES AS PLAYER: Northamptonshire, Somerset
ROLE: Right-hand bat, right-arm fast-medium bowler
COUNTY DEBUT: 1980 (Northamptonshire), 1987 (Somerset)
COUNTY CAP: 1984 (Northamptonshire), 1987 (Somerset)
TEST DEBUT: 1992

UMPIRES

NOTES: PCA Umpire of the Year 2001, 2002, 2003, 2004, 2006, 2008. Stood in the 2003 World Cup. Umpired the 2004, 2005 and 2006 C&G Trophy finals. Officiated at Twenty20 Finals Day at Edgbaston in 2007, 2008, 2009 and 2010, including standing in the final in 2008 and 2009.

Batting & Fielding

	Mat	Inns	NO	Runs	HS	Ave	SR	100	50	Ct	St
Tests	2	3	0	8	4	2.66	36.36	0	0	0	0
First-class	345	396	122	4709	100*	17.18	-	1	10	111	0
List A	325	163	75	1146	38*	13.02	-	0	0	60	0

Bowling

	Mat	Balls	Runs	Wkts	BBI	BBM	Ave	Econ	SR	5w	10
Tests	2	449	215	10	5/50	8/122	21.50	2.87	44.9	1	0
First-class	345	53215	24654	937	7/27	-	26.31	2.77	56.7	36	5
List A	325	15488	9849	387	7/37	7/37	25.44	3.81	40.0	3	0

DAVID MILLNS

NAME: David James Millns
BORN: February 27, 1965, Mansfield
HEIGHT: 6ft 3in
NICKNAME: Rocket Man
APPOINTED TO FIRST-CLASS LIST: 2009
COUNTIES AS PLAYER: Nottinghamshire,
Leicestershire
ROLE: Left-hand bat; right-arm fast-medium
bowler
COUNTY DEBUT: 1988 (Notts), 1990
(Leicestershire)
COUNTY CAP: 1991 (Leicestershire), 2000
(Notts)

Batting & Fielding

	Mat	Inns	NO	Runs	HS	Ave	SR	100	50	Ct	St
First-class	171	203	63	3082	121	22.01	-	3	8	76	0
List A	91	49	26	338	39*	14.69	-	0	0	18	0

Bowling

	Mat	Balls	Runs	Wkts	BBI	BBM	Ave	Econ	SR	5w	10
First-class	171	26571	15129	553	9/37	-	27.35	3.41	48.0	23	4
List A	91	3931	3144	83	4/26	4/26	37.87	4.79	47.3	0	0

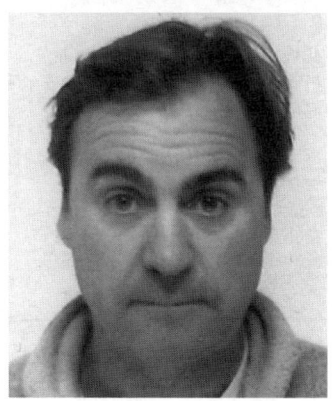

NAME: Steven Joseph O'Shaughnessy
BORN: September 9, 1961, Bury, Lancashire
APPOINTED TO FIRST-CLASS LIST: 2011

UMPIRES

NOTES: O'Shaughnessy started umpiring in 2007 and was appointed to the full list for this season.

Batting & Fielding

	Mat	Inns	NO	Runs	HS	Ave	SR	100	50	Ct	St
First-class	112	181	28	3720	159*	24.31	-	5	16	57	0
List A	176	151	23	2999	101*	23.42	-	1	15	44	0

Bowling

	Mat	Balls	Runs	Wkts	BBI	BBM	Ave	Econ	SR	5w	10
First-class	112	7179	4108	114	4/66	-	36.03	3.43	62.9	0	0
List A	176	5389	4184	115	4/17	4/17	36.38	4.65	46.8	0	0

TIM ROBINSON

NAME: Robert Timothy Robinson
BORN: November 21, 1958, Sutton-in-Ashfield
HEIGHT: 6ft
NICKNAME: Robbo
APPOINTED TO FIRST-CLASS LIST: 2007
TESTS UMPIRED: 3 as reserve umpire
ODIs UMPIRED: 1 as reserve umpire
T20Is UMPIRED: 1 as reserve umpire
COUNTY AS PLAYER: Nottinghamshire
ROLE: Right-hand opening bat
COUNTY DEBUT: 1978
COUNTY CAP: 1983
TEST DEBUT: 1984
ODI DEBUT: 1984

NOTES: TV umpire in the Pro40 final in 2010.

Batting & Fielding

	Mat	Inns	NO	Runs	HS	Ave	SR	100	50	Ct	St
Tests	29	49	5	1601	175	36.38	41.62	4	6	8	0
ODIs	26	26	0	597	83	22.96	58.18	0	3	6	0
First-class	425	739	85	27571	220*	42.15	-	63	141	257	0
List A	397	386	40	11879	139	34.33	-	9	75	120	0

Bowling

	Mat	Balls	Runs	Wkts	BBI	BBM	Ave	Econ	SR	5w	10
Tests	29	6	0	0	-	-	-	0.00	-	0	0
ODIs	26	-	-	-	-	-	-	-	-	-	-
First-class	425	259	289	4	1/22	-	72.25	6.69	64.7	0	0
List A	397	-	-	-	-	-	-	-	-	-	-

NAME: George Sharp
BORN: March12, 1950, West Hartlepool
HEIGHT: 5ft 11in
NICKNAME: Sharpy
APPOINTED TO FIRST-CLASS LIST: 1992
INTERNATIONAL PANEL: 1996-2002
TESTS UMPIRED: 15 (plus 1 as TV umpire)
ODIs UMPIRED: 31 (plus 13 as TV umpire)
COUNTY AS PLAYER: Northamptonshire
ROLE: Right-hand bat, wicketkeeper
COUNTY DEBUT: 1967
COUNTY CAP: 1973

UMPIRES

NOTES: Sharp umpired three B&H finals and one NatWest final and stood in the inaugural C&G final in 2001 and the 2002 final. He also officiated at the inaugural Twenty20 Finals Day at Trent Bridge in 2003, at Finals Day in 2005 at The Oval and in 2006 at Trent Bridge.

Batting & Fielding

	Mat	Inns	NO	Runs	HS	Ave	SR	100	50	Ct	St
First-class	306	396	81	6254	98	19.85	-	0	21	565	90
List A	285	203	52	2377	51*	15.74	-	0	1	242	50

Bowling

	Mat	Balls	Runs	Wkts	BBI	BBM	Ave	Econ	SR	5w	10
First-class	306	114	70	1	1/47	-	70.00	3.68	114.0	0	0
List A	285	-	-	-	-	-	-	-	-	-	-

JOHN STEELE

NAME: John Frederick Steele
BORN: July 23, 1946, Stafford
HEIGHT: 5ft 10in
NICKNAME: Steely
APPOINTED TO FIRST-CLASS LIST: 1997
TESTS UMPIRED: 2 as reserve umpire
COUNTIES AS PLAYER: Leicestershire, Glamorgan
ROLE: Right-hand bat, slow left-arm bowler
COUNTY DEBUT: 1970 (Leicestershire), 1984 (Glamorgan)
COUNTY CAP: 1971 (Leicestershire), 1984 (Glamorgan)

Batting & Fielding

	Mat	Inns	NO	Runs	HS	Ave	SR	100	50	Ct	St
First-class	379	605	85	15054	195	28.95	-	21	-	413	0
List A	302	219	50	3532	108*	20.89	-	1	14	146	0

Bowling

	Mat	Balls	Runs	Wkts	BBI	BBM	Ave	Econ	SR	5w	10
First-class	379	39298	15793	584	7/29	-	27.04	2.41	67.2	16	0
List A	302	12416	7485	293	5/11	5/11	25.54	3.61	42.3	4	0

NAME: Peter Willey
BORN: December 6, 1949, Sedgefield
HEIGHT: 6ft 1in
NICKNAME: Will
APPOINTED TO FIRST-CLASS LIST: 1993
INTERNATIONAL PANEL: 1996-2003
TESTS UMPIRED: 25 (plus 7 as TV umpire)
ODIs UMPIRED: 34 (plus 16 as TV umpire)
COUNTIES AS PLAYER: Northamptonshire, Leicestershire
ROLE: Right-hand bat, off-break bowler
COUNTY DEBUT: 1966 (Northamptonshire), 1984 (Leicestershire)
COUNTY CAP: 1971 (Northamptonshire), 1984 (Leicestershire)
TEST DEBUT: 1976
ODI DEBUT: 1977

UMPIRES

NOTES: Stood in the 1999 and 2003 World Cups, in the 1999 Benson and Hedges Super Cup final and in the 2004 C&G Trophy final. Officiated at Twenty20 Finals Day at The Oval in 2005 and Edgbaston in 2007, including standing in both finals. Willey is Chairman of the First-Class Umpires' Association.

Batting & Fielding

	Mat	Inns	NO	Runs	HS	Ave	SR	100	50	Ct	St
Tests	26	50	6	1184	102*	26.90	42.37	2	5	3	0
ODIs	26	24	1	538	64	23.39	62.92	0	5	4	0
First-class	559	918	121	24361	227	30.56	-	44	101	235	0
List A	458	436	43	11105	154	28.25	-	10	67	124	0

Bowling

	Mat	Balls	Runs	Wkts	BBI	BBM	Ave	Econ	SR	5w	10
Tests	26	1091	456	7	2/73	2/73	65.14	2.50	155.8	0	0
ODIs	26	1031	659	13	3/33	3/33	50.69	3.83	79.3	0	0
First-class	559	58635	23400	756	7/37	-	30.95	2.39	77.5	26	3
List A	458	18520	11143	347	4/17	4/17	32.11	3.61	53.3	0	0

Roll *of* Honour

ROLL OF HONOUR, 2010 AVERAGES AND MVPs

LV=COUNTY CHAMPIONSHIP TABLES

Division One							
Team	Mat	Won	Lost	Tied	Draw	Aban	Pts
Nottinghamshire	16	7	5	0	4	0	214
Somerset	16	6	2	0	8	0	214
Yorkshire	16	6	2	0	8	0	203
Lancashire	16	5	3	0	8	0	182
Durham	16	5	3	0	8	0	173
Warwickshire	16	6	9	0	1	0	166
Hampshire	16	3	6	0	7	0	157
Kent	16	3	7	0	6	0	151
Essex	16	2	6	0	8	0	126

Division Two							
Team	Mat	Won	Lost	Tied	Draw	Aban	Pts
Sussex	16	8	3	0	5	0	235
Worcestershire	16	7	4	0	5	0	208
Glamorgan	16	7	4	0	5	0	203
Leicestershire	16	7	5	0	4	0	199
Gloucestershire	16	6	9	0	1	0	172
Northamptonshire	16	6	7	0	3	0	167
Surrey	16	4	6	0	6	0	159
Middlesex	16	4	7	0	5	0	155
Derbyshire	16	3	7	0	6	0	138

Group A

Team	Mat	Won	Lost	Tied	N/R	Pts	Net RR
Somerset	12	10	2	0	0	20	+1.491
Sussex	12	7	3	1	1	16	+0.903
Surrey	12	6	4	1	1	14	-0.006
Lancashire	12	6	6	0	0	12	-0.315
Worcestershire	12	4	8	0	0	8	-0.196
Unicorns	12	3	7	0	2	8	-0.470
Glamorgan	12	2	8	0	2	5	-1.585

Group B

Team	Mat	Won	Lost	Tied	N/R	Pts	Net RR
Yorkshire	12	10	2	0	0	20	+0.384
Essex	12	9	2	0	1	19	+0.314
Gloucestershire	12	9	3	0	0	18	+0.659
Derbyshire	12	4	8	0	0	8	-0.037
Northamptonshire	12	4	8	0	0	8	-0.038
Middlesex	12	3	7	0	2	8	-0.445
Netherlands	12	1	10	0	1	3	-0.999

Group C

Team	Mat	Won	Lost	Tied	N/R	Pts	Net RR
Warwickshire	12	9	3	0	0	18	+0.314
Kent	12	7	3	0	2	16	+0.774
Nottinghamshire	12	7	4	0	1	15	+0.348
Hampshire	12	6	6	0	0	12	+0.006
Durham	12	5	6	0	1	11	+0.262
Leicestershire	12	4	8	0	0	8	-0.220
Scotland	12	2	10	0	0	4	-1.225

SEMI-FINALS	Taunton: Somerset 312/6 (40/40 ov); Essex 217 (29.3/40 ov)
	Somerset won by 95 runs
	Scarborough: Yorkshire 257/5 (37/37 ov); Warwickshire 260/6 (35.5/37 ov)
	Warwickshire won by 4 wickets (with 7 balls remaining, D/L method)
FINAL	Lord's: Somerset 199 (39/40 ov); Warwickshire 200/7 (39/40 ov)
	Warwickshire won by 3 wickets (with 6 balls remaining)

FRIENDS PROVIDENT t20

North Group

Team	Mat	Won	Lost	Tied	N/R	Pts	Net RR
Warwickshire	16	11	4	0	1	23	+0.403
Nottinghamshire	16	10	4	2	0	22	+0.640
Lancashire	16	9	6	0	1	19	+0.479
Northamptonshire	16	7	6	3	0	17	-0.160
Derbyshire	16	6	8	0	2	14	-0.151
Yorkshire	16	6	9	1	0	13	-0.121
Leicestershire	16	6	9	0	1	13	-0.234
Durham	16	4	8	0	4	12	-0.296
Worcestershire	16	5	10	0	1	11	-0.653

South Group

Team	Mat	Won	Lost	Tied	N/R	Pts	Net RR
Somerset	16	11	5	0	0	22	+0.418
Essex	16	10	6	0	0	20	+0.395
Sussex	16	9	7	0	0	18	+0.606
Hampshire	16	8	8	0	0	16	+0.385
Surrey	16	8	8	0	0	16	+0.183
Middlesex	16	8	8	0	0	16	+0.018
Kent	16	7	9	0	0	14	-0.163
Glamorgan	16	6	10	0	0	12	-0.979
Gloucestershire	16	5	11	0	0	10	-0.943

QUARTER-FINALS	Edgbaston: Warwickshire 153/5 (20/20 ov); Hampshire 154/5 (19.5/20 ov) *Hampshire won by 5 wickets (with 1 ball remaining)* Trent Bridge: Nottinghamshire 141/9 (20/20 ov); Sussex 128/7 (20/20 ov) *Nottinghamshire won by 13 runs* Taunton: Northamptonshire 112/6 (20/20 ov); Somerset 115/3 (17/20 ov) *Somerset won by 7 wickets (with 18 balls remaining)* Chelmsford: Lancashire 183/6 (20/20 ov); Essex 184/2 (19.1/20 ov) *Essex won by 8 wickets (with 5 balls remaining)*
SEMI-FINALS	The Rose Bowl: Essex 156/7 (20/20 ov); Hampshire 157/4 (19.2/20 ov) *Hampshire won by 6 wickets (with 4 balls remaining)* The Rose Bowl: Somerset 182/5 (20/20 ov); Nottinghamshire 117/4 (13/13 ov) *Somerset won by 3 runs (D/L method)*
FINAL	The Rose Bowl: Somerset 173/6 (20/20 ov); Hampshire 173/5 (20/20 ov) *Hampshire won (lost fewer wickets)*

Name	Mat	Inns	NO	Runs	HS	Ave	BF	SR	100	50	0	4s	6s
JC Hildreth	16	23	1	1440	151	65.45	2131	67.57	7	5	2	187	5
MR Ramprakash	16	28	2	1595	248	61.34	2879	55.40	5	5	3	221	9
ME Trescothick	16	28	4	1397	228*	58.20	2119	65.92	4	6	2	194	16
SM Davies	14	22	3	1090	137	57.36	1559	69.91	2	9	0	157	6
IJL Trott	12	21	2	1084	226	57.05	2054	52.77	3	5	2	127	0
CJL Rogers	15	27	3	1285	200	53.54	2000	64.25	4	5	1	174	3
MW Goodwin	16	26	3	1201	142	52.21	1860	64.56	4	5	3	177	9
A Lyth	16	29	0	1509	142	52.03	2541	59.38	3	9	3	208	1
MA Carberry	16	28	1	1385	164	51.29	2644	52.38	6	4	1	188	10
JA Rudolph	16	29	2	1375	228*	50.92	2361	58.23	4	6	1	202	2
MJ Cosgrove	15	26	2	1187	142	49.45	1381	85.95	5	4	4	189	8
JHK Adams	16	29	1	1351	196	48.25	3100	43.58	3	8	3	183	4
NJ Dexter	12	21	2	907	118	47.73	1502	60.38	2	5	1	138	3
AW Gale	14	24	4	950	151*	47.50	1664	57.09	3	4	2	129	2
J du Toit	13	20	1	899	154	47.31	1472	61.07	3	6	3	110	7
SD Peters	16	30	2	1320	199	47.14	2557	51.62	3	7	1	161	2
ND McKenzie	15	25	5	942	141*	47.10	1994	47.24	3	4	2	120	4
MM Ali	16	30	3	1270	126	47.03	2102	60.41	3	9	4	193	10
AU Rashid	16	24	8	732	76	45.75	1287	56.87	0	6	0	102	0
MJ Di Venuto	16	27	3	1092	129	45.50	1893	57.68	3	7	2	137	0
CMW Read	17	26	5	945	124*	45.00	1648	57.34	2	5	3	119	11
J Allenby	16	25	4	933	105	44.42	1563	59.69	1	10	2	115	8
AN Kervezee	16	30	3	1190	155	44.07	1638	72.64	3	6	2	174	14
M van Jaarsveld	17	29	2	1188	110*	44.00	2103	56.49	3	6	1	141	8
JWA Taylor	18	29	4	1095	206*	43.80	2318	47.23	3	4	4	121	2
A McGrath	16	29	1	1219	124*	43.53	2553	47.74	3	9	0	162	1
DI Stevens	15	26	3	979	197	42.56	1528	64.07	4	2	3	112	13
SM Ervine	17	27	4	976	237*	42.43	1406	69.41	1	5	2	119	15
DKH Mitchell	16	31	3	1180	165*	42.14	2572	45.87	4	4	2	159	0
JM Bairstow	16	29	7	918	81	41.72	1478	62.11	0	8	0	138	7
MA Wagh	16	24	1	953	139	41.43	2047	46.55	3	3	1	124	9
CF Hughes	12	21	2	784	156	41.26	1384	56.64	2	4	4	109	7
P Mustard	16	24	5	742	120	39.05	1330	55.78	2	4	4	85	3
CD Nash	17	29	2	1051	184	38.92	1486	70.72	3	1	4	141	8
Z de Bruyn	14	21	0	814	95	38.76	1408	57.81	0	5	1	113	5
JM Vince	16	27	4	891	180	38.73	1433	62.17	1	4	4	134	3
DJ Malan	16	29	3	1001	115	38.50	1862	53.75	3	5	2	144	1
SJ Croft	16	26	3	883	93	38.39	1694	52.12	0	8	2	118	6
MJ Walker	12	24	2	838	105	38.09	1950	42.97	1	4	1	112	5
WI Jefferson	11	20	1	722	135	38.00	1137	63.50	2	4	1	111	4
AD Brown	17	26	3	863	134	37.52	1276	67.63	1	6	1	106	9
OA Shah	13	23	1	804	156	36.54	1603	50.15	2	3	0	100	7
PJ Franks	16	22	1	765	114	36.42	1033	74.05	1	6	3	123	4
NM Carter	11	20	3	617	99*	36.29	843	73.19	0	4	1	81	10
GK Berg	15	26	5	761	125	36.23	1098	69.30	1	3	3	95	10
ID Blackwell	15	24	2	794	86	36.09	1163	68.27	0	8	1	99	6
AD Hales	12	20	1	677	136	35.63	1153	58.71	1	4	1	97	3
HJH Marshall	15	27	2	884	89*	35.36	1484	59.56	0	7	0	118	4
GP Rees	17	30	4	918	106*	35.30	1867	49.16	2	5	2	141	1
PA Nixon	16	27	1	915	106	35.19	2117	43.22	1	7	4	100	3

FIRST-CLASS BOWLING AVERAGES *Minimum of 2000 balls*

Name	Mat	Overs	Mdns	Runs	Wkts	BBI	BBM	Ave	Econ	SR	5	10
JM Anderson	10	355.2	115	884	48	6/17	11/71	18.41	2.48	44.4	3	1
M Kartik	11	383.2	107	882	45	6/42	11/72	19.60	2.30	51.1	5	2
G Chapple	14	372.4	89	1027	52	5/27	9/96	19.75	2.75	43.0	2	0
CD Collymore	14	414.0	115	1133	57	6/48	8/90	19.87	2.73	43.5	2	0
CT Tremlett	12	361.5	88	969	48	4/29	8/87	20.18	2.67	45.2	0	0
CW Henderson	16	489.3	136	1179	56	6/21	8/68	21.05	2.40	52.4	3	0
CR Wookes	14	424.2	107	1246	58	6/52	11/97	21.48	2.93	43.8	3	1
JAR Harris	14	463.4	117	1356	63	5/56	8/114	21.52	2.92	44.1	2	0
ST Finn	13	407.1	92	1410	64	9/37	14/106	22.03	3.46	38.1	4	1
DA Cosker	16	432.0	101	1128	51	5/93	7/127	22.11	2.61	50.8	1	0
NM Carter	11	356.2	70	1129	51	5/60	9/130	22.13	3.16	41.9	4	0
AR Adams	14	455.5	101	1508	68	6/79	8/159	22.17	3.30	40.2	4	0
GM Hussain	15	417.4	86	1497	67	5/36	9/98	22.34	3.58	37.4	2	0
J Lewis	16	419.3	103	1222	54	4/25	6/74	22.62	2.91	46.6	0	0
DD Masters	14	487.0	138	1223	53	5/43	8/96	23.07	2.51	55.1	1	0
DG Cork	13	407.2	102	1042	45	5/50	7/66	23.15	2.55	54.3	2	0
JEC Franklin	16	334.2	69	1083	46	7/14	8/81	23.54	3.23	43.6	1	0
A Richardson	14	524.0	153	1342	55	5/44	7/89	24.40	2.56	57.1	2	0
MJ Hoggard	15	416.4	105	1222	50	6/63	7/117	24.44	2.93	50.0	3	0
AC Thomas	15	377.5	85	1202	49	5/40	7/117	24.53	3.18	46.2	2	0
Imran Tahir	16	430.4	58	1376	56	8/114	8/114	24.57	3.19	46.1	3	0
Shakib Al Hasan	11	345.3	56	1088	43	7/32	8/102	25.30	3.14	48.2	4	0
MS Panesar	16	518.2	135	1336	52	5/44	8/114	25.69	2.57	59.8	2	0
SA Patterson	14	392.5	96	1201	45	5/50	7/69	26.68	3.05	52.3	1	0
PJ Franks	16	410.2	106	1129	42	3/15	6/67	26.88	2.75	58.6	0	0
JW Dernbach	15	447.0	98	1390	51	5/68	6/101	27.25	3.10	52.5	2	0
CM Willoughby	16	512.1	118	1582	58	6/101	7/97	27.27	3.08	52.9	1	0
NL Buck	15	381.5	88	1340	49	4/44	7/79	27.34	3.50	46.7	0	0
ID Blackwell	15	455.3	129	1205	43	5/78	9/180	28.02	2.64	63.5	2	0
JC Tredwell	12	377.0	71	1151	38	7/22	8/22	30.28	3.05	59.5	2	0
RJ Peterson	15	553.3	129	1566	51	4/10	6/104	30.70	2.82	65.1	0	0
AU Rashid	16	504.4	67	1784	57	5/87	9/208	31.29	3.53	53.1	3	0
GM Smith	16	414.3	77	1368	42	5/54	6/93	32.57	3.30	59.2	1	0
A Khan	12	372.2	82	1258	38	5/43	7/72	33.10	3.37	58.7	1	0
JA Brooks	14	373.3	86	1260	37	4/88	5/108	34.05	3.37	60.5	0	0
TD Groenewald	13	413.5	105	1295	38	5/86	8/149	34.07	3.12	65.3	1	0
JA Tomlinson	15	559.1	149	1624	46	7/85	7/85	35.30	2.90	72.9	2	0
TJ Murtagh	15	459.2	127	1405	38	5/52	8/123	36.97	3.05	72.5	2	0
LE Plunkett	15	415.4	64	1499	40	4/107	6/193	37.47	3.60	62.3	0	0
DR Briggs	13	377.2	59	1294	34	4/93	5/116	38.05	3.42	66.5	0	0
SI Mahmood	15	348.0	54	1263	33	5/55	7/76	38.27	3.62	63.2	1	0
SR Patel	17	345.3	73	1044	26	4/55	6/95	40.15	3.02	79.7	0	0
OJ Hannon-Dalby	17	382.4	61	1372	34	5/68	7/122	40.35	3.58	67.5	2	0
GJ Batty	15	488.5	70	1696	42	5/76	6/123	40.38	3.46	69.8	1	0
SM Ervine	17	362.5	77	1073	20	4/31	5/78	53.65	2.95	108.8	0	0

FIRST-CLASS WICKETKEEEPING Minimum of 20 dismissals

Name	Mat	Inns	Dis	Ct	St	Max Dis Inns	Dis/Inn
CMW Read	17	32	64	60	4	6 (6ct 0st)	2.000
JN Batty	15	28	56	53	3	5 (5ct 0st)	2.000
GO Jones	17	32	55	49	6	4 (4ct 0st)	1.718
JS Foster	16	30	53	48	5	5 (5ct 0st)	1.766
TJ New	17	30	47	46	1	4 (4ct 0st)	1.566
MA Wallace	16	31	47	43	4	4 (4ct 0st)	1.516
JA Simpson	16	31	44	42	2	5 (5ct 0st)	1.419
LD Sutton	13	22	42	37	5	5 (4ct 1st)	1.909
P Mustard	16	27	42	40	2	5 (5ct 0st)	1.555
SM Davies	14	26	38	38	0	6 (6ct 0st)	1.461
MJ Prior	13	20	36	35	1	3 (3ct 0st)	1.800
TR Ambrose	11	21	36	33	3	5 (5ct 0st)	1.714
N Pothas	9	17	33	33	0	5 (5ct 0st)	1.941
BJM Scott	7	13	31	30	1	4 (4ct 0st)	2.384
AJ Hodd	10	16	30	29	1	4 (4ct 0st)	1.875
D Murphy	11	20	30	30	0	5 (5ct 0st)	1.500
C Kieswetter	12	20	29	29	0	3 (3ct 0st)	1.450
Kamran Akmal	6	11	28	27	1	4 (4ct 0st)	2.545
AM Bates	8	14	28	28	0	4 (4ct 0st)	2.000
LJ Goddard	8	15	24	24	0	4 (4ct 0st)	1.600
JM Bairstow	16	15	23	18	5	5 (3ct 2st)	1.533
GL Brophy	9	15	20	20	0	3 (3ct 0st)	1.333

FIRST-CLASS FIELDING RECORDS *Minimum of 17 catches*

ame	Mat	Inns	Ct	Max	Ct/Inn
van Jaarsveld	17	32	36	4	1.125
KH Mitchell	16	29	32	3	1.103
J Di Venuto	16	27	29	3	1.074
E Trescothick	16	29	26	3	0.896
J Strauss	14	28	25	3	0.892
DJ Dent	16	30	24	3	0.800
Clarke	15	28	23	2	0.821
C Tredwell	12	23	21	3	0.913
J Hall	15	26	21	2	0.807
D McKenzie	15	27	21	3	0.777
JG Sales	15	26	20	4	0.769
A Rudolph	16	29	20	4	0.689
MAG Boyce	15	27	19	2	0.703
PJ Horton	16	27	19	3	0.703
WM Dalrymple	15	29	19	3	0.655
CJL Rogers	15	29	19	4	0.655
DJ Malan	16	31	19	3	0.612
VS Solanki	15	27	18	2	0.666
NJ Edwards	7	14	17	5	1.214
EC Joyce	10	18	17	2	0.944

#	Name	County	Batting	Bowling	Field	Capt.	Wins	Pld	Pts	Average
1	Carter, Neil	Warks	253.49	359.65	3	0	27.0	41	643	15.6
2	Rashid, Adil	Yorks	138.99	416.70	22	0	23.0	45	600	13.3
3	Thomas, Alfonso	Somerset	64.18	469.72	14	0	31.0	48	578	12.0
4	Trescothick, Marcus	Somerset	473.52	0.00	39	30	31.0	49	573	11.6
5	Patel, Samit	Notts	299.48	227.91	15	0	27.0	46	568	12.3
6	Woakes, Chris	Warks	116.26	399.89	16	0	26.0	41	558	13.6
7	Ervine, Sean	Hants	333.97	185.01	15	0	18.0	45	551	12.2
8	Stevens, Darren	Kent	306.91	205.26	15	0	16.0	39	543	13.9
9	Franklin, James	Gloucs	307.88	199.98	14	0	20.0	43	541	12.5
10	Adams, James	Hants	483.55	-0.15	33	0	20.0	46	536	11.6
11	Hildreth, James	Somerset	468.96	4.27	29	0	31.0	49	533	10.8
12	Smith, Tom	Lancs	251.34	235.48	27	0	17.0	39	531	13.6
13	Ali, Moeen	Worcs	354.02	133.22	21	0	15.0	42	523	12.4
14	Rudolph, Jacques	Yorks	464.38	-2.59	29	1	20.0	41	511	12.4
15	Blackwell, Ian	Durham	197.03	289.35	4	0	13.0	36	503	13.9
16	Tahir, Imran	Warks	72.28	392.15	10	0	28.0	45	502	11.1
17	Trego, Peter	Somerset	241.28	194.09	25	0	29.0	46	489	10.6
18	Cosgrove, Mark	Glamorgan	423.64	21.54	15	0	15.0	40	475	11.8
19	Masters, David	Essex	63.97	367.66	14	0	21.0	41	467	11.3
20	Cork, Dominic	Hants	84.82	329.87	17	15	20.0	43	466	10.8
21	van Jaarsveld, Martin	Kent	344.28	36.19	47	3	17.0	43	447	10.4
22	Kartik, Murali	Somerset	40.66	360.23	19	0	26.0	38	445	11.7
23	Maddy, Darren	Warks	232.30	156.96	27	0	28.0	45	444	9.87
24	Allenby, James	Glamorgan	218.39	194.33	17	0	15.0	39	444	11.3
25	Mahmood, Sajid	Lancs	132.29	271.60	13	0	16.0	36	433	12.0
26	ten Doeschate, Ryan	Essex	231.41	159.29	12	0	10.0	27	413	15.2
27	Nash, Chris	Sussex	292.91	79.98	15	0	25.0	44	412	9.35
28	Hall, Andrew	Northants	165.08	186.27	28	15	20.0	43	411	9.57
29	de Bruyn, Zander	Somerset	253.31	107.22	22	0	29.0	45	411	9.13
30	Smith, Greg	Derbyshire	158.30	209.64	18	8	12.0	42	406	9.67
31	Bopara, Ravinder	Essex	286.69	92.09	12	0	15.0	30	406	13.5
32	Phillips, Ben	Somerset	46.01	314.85	16	0	29.0	42	405	9.65
33	Davies, Steven	Surrey	319.74	0.00	70	0	14.0	34	404	11.8
34	Lyth, Adam	Yorks	363.24	-1.60	19	0	20.0	39	400	10.2
35	Chapple, Glen	Lancs	82.19	282.17	6	14	14.0	31	398	12.8
36	Henderson, Claude	Leics	51.86	323.05	9	0	15.0	37	398	10.7
37	Mustard, Philip	Durham	247.18	0.00	125	11	14.0	41	397	9.69
38	Patterson, Steven	Yorks	24.55	334.57	9	0	21.0	41	389	9.48
39	McGrath, Anthony	Yorks	315.96	28.33	23	0	21.0	40	388	9.69
40	Hamilton-Brown, Rory	Surrey	306.43	27.96	15	18	19.0	43	385	8.96
41	Gale, Andrew	Yorks	327.91	0.00	13	21	21.0	40	383	9.57
42	Read, Chris	Notts	205.86	0.00	136	16	24.0	42	381	9.08
43	Dexter, Neil	Middx	236.57	105.34	18	7	14.0	38	381	10.0
44	Carberry, Michael	Hants	327.35	17.12	20	0	15.0	39	379	9.72
45	Foster, James	Essex	185.39	0.00	154	17	22.0	46	378	8.23
46	Lewis, Jon	Gloucs	79.99	271.13	10	0	17.0	39	377	9.67
47	Peterson, Robin	Derbyshire	123.68	226.85	12	1	12.0	39	375	9.62
48	Croft, Steven	Lancs	292.16	30.01	32	0	20.0	45	374	8.31
49	Tredwell, James	Kent	84.17	245.53	30	0	14.0	29	374	12.89
50	Goodwin, Murray	Sussex	323.52	0.00	13	11	25.0	44	370	8.40

#	Name	County	Batting	Bowling	Field	Capt.	Wins	Pld	Pts	Average
51	Tremlett, Christopher	Surrey	49.85	300.43	2	0	14.0	35	366	10.47
52	Taylor, James	Leics	310.75	16.14	22	0	17.0	42	364	8.68
53	Clarke, Rikki	Warks	179.66	116.13	41	0	26.0	44	363	8.25
54	Jones, Geraint	Kent	210.38	-0.80	136	0	17.0	43	363	8.43
55	Ramprakash, Mark	Surrey	338.31	-0.48	12	0	13.0	36	362	10.06
56	Hoggard, Matthew	Leics	11.29	310.60	7	17	17.0	40	360	9.00
57	Adams, Andre	Notts	39.60	298.06	14	0	6.0	17	358	21.04
58	Mullaney, Steve	Notts	164.87	146.90	23	0	23.0	40	357	8.92
59	Cook, Simon	Kent	27.94	303.05	6	0	15.0	39	352	9.03
60	Franks, Paul	Notts	108.66	218.06	4	0	20.0	35	350	10.01
61	Hales, Alex	Notts	299.73	-2.84	27	0	23.0	42	346	8.24
62	Mitchell, Daryl	Worcs	251.59	27.86	37	10	16.0	43	341	7.94
63	Briggs, Danny	Hants	22.63	288.40	10	0	17.0	38	338	8.88
64	Berg, Gareth	Middx	189.73	108.61	22	0	15.0	40	335	8.38
65	McKenzie, Neil	Hants	278.49	6.19	32	0	17.0	42	333	7.93
66	Mahmood, Azhar	Kent	96.36	217.37	5	0	11.0	30	330	10.99
67	Murtagh, Tim	Middx	39.83	259.65	11	0	15.0	40	325	8.12
68	Shah, Owais	Middx	259.31	29.93	20	0	14.0	39	322	8.27
69	Harris, James	Glamorgan	35.89	272.36	4	0	10.0	26	322	12.37
70	Buttler, Jos	Somerset	220.07	0.00	70	0	31.0	46	321	6.97
71	Bairstow, Jonathan	Yorks	226.90	0.00	76	0	18.0	40	320	8.01
72	Cosker, Dean	Glamorgan	39.11	255.00	11	0	14.0	38	318	8.37
73	Groenewald, Timothy	Derbyshire	36.13	257.56	10	0	13.0	38	313	8.24
74	Gidman, Alex	Gloucs	201.19	45.56	22	19	19.0	40	305	7.63
75	Pattinson, Darren	Notts	17.13	260.18	9	0	19.0	32	304	9.51
76	Malan, Dawid	Middx	259.96	6.47	22	0	15.0	43	303	7.04
77	Batty, Gareth	Surrey	71.09	206.54	11	0	12.0	31	301	9.71
78	Kervezee, Alexei	Worcs	264.82	-1.16	21	0	16.0	43	300	6.98
79	Vince, James	Hants	256.82	-1.80	28	0	17.0	40	300	7.49
80	Denly, Joseph	Kent	254.50	5.37	21	0	17.0	39	298	7.64
81	Wright, Christopher	Essex	26.58	243.48	6	0	20.0	40	296	7.40
82	Taylor, Chris	Gloucs	237.97	21.72	18	0	18.0	42	295	7.04
83	Middlebrook, James	Northants	98.17	165.25	14	0	16.0	40	292	7.30
84	Marshall, Hamish	Gloucs	243.13	4.83	26	0	19.0	40	292	7.30
85	du Toit, Jacques	Leics	249.84	-1.60	30	0	14.0	38	291	7.66
86	Walker, Matthew	Essex	247.87	9.36	13	0	20.0	38	290	7.64
87	Rogers, Chris	Derbyshire	257.14	-0.40	19	4	8.0	27	287	10.63
88	Tomlinson, James	Hants	28.90	249.18	3	0	5.0	20	286	14.30
89	Horton, Paul	Lancs	231.39	0.00	29	5	20.0	45	285	6.34
90	Durston, Wesley	Derbyshire	205.32	47.17	18	0	12.0	34	283	8.31
91	Troughton, Jim	Warks	227.66	0.00	17	9	28.0	47	282	5.99
92	Pyrah, Richard	Yorks	46.41	193.58	21	0	20.0	35	281	8.01
93	Shantry, Jack	Worcs	12.93	241.56	12	0	15.0	37	280	7.58
94	Martin-Jenkins, Robin	Sussex	114.21	141.92	9	0	15.0	22	279	12.70
95	Benkenstein, Dale	Durham	190.04	53.12	22	0	11.0	35	276	7.89
96	Brooks, Jack	Northants	24.21	229.88	6	0	17.0	33	275	8.33
97	Key, Robert	Kent	231.06	6.03	8	14	14.0	37	273	7.38
98	Dalrymple, James	Glamorgan	153.98	66.40	25	15	15.0	38	273	7.18
99	Willoughby, Charl	Somerset	11.63	250.90	2	0	8.0	19	273	14.34
100	Brown, Alistair	Notts	226.83	-0.76	20	0	26.0	43	271	6.30

INDEX

696

RIKI WESSELS

RHB WK

NOTTINGHAMSHIRE

NAME: Mattheus Hendrik Wessels
BORN: November 12, 1985, Maroochydore, Australia
HEIGHT: 5ft 11in
SQUAD Nº: 9
NICKNAME: Weasel, Blood
OTHER TEAMS: Midwest Rhinos, Nondescripts Cricket Club, Northamptonshire
CAREER: First-class debut: 2004; List A debut: 2005; T20 debut: 2005

AOC SAYS: Nottinghamshire swooped to sign Wessels three days before the start of the county season and the former Northamptonshire wicketkeeper made his mark the very next day with a quickfire century on debut in a warm-up fixture against Surrey. Wessels – the son of former South Africa and Australia Test opener Kepler – was signed by his father during his time as coach at Northants and spent five seasons at Wantage Road before he was forced to leave the club last year when changes to the UK's immigration criteria meant he didn't have the necessary working visa. A middle-order strokemaker and tidy stumper, Wessels went to play with Midwest Rhinos in Zimbabwe alongside Nottinghamshire's Paul Franks in order to secure the visa that has enabled his return to county cricket.

LAST WORD: "Riki will provide back-up for Chris Read as wicketkeeper. Beyond that he's a one-day batting option and he'll be keen to break into the team on merit." *Mick Newell*

Batting & Fielding

	Mat	Inns	NO	Runs	HS	Ave	SR	100	50	Ct	St
First-class	83	136	12	4085	146	32.94	63.33	9	22	165	12
List A	82	77	9	1934	100	28.44	95.45	1	11	62	0
Twenty20	56	47	12	970	86*	27.71	141.19	0	3	20	13

Bowling

	Mat	Balls	Runs	Wkts	BBI	BBM	Ave	Econ	SR	5w	10
First-class	83	78	42	2	1/10	1/10	21.00	3.23	39.0	0	0
List A	82	49	48	1	1/0	1/0	48.00	5.87	49.0	0	0
Twenty20	56	-	-	-	-	-	-	-	-	-	-